CRIMINAL LITIGATION

CRIMINAL LITIGATION

Editor & Co-author

Maura Butler

OXFORD
UNIVERSITY PRESS

OXFORD
UNIVERSITY PRESS

Great Clarendon Street, Oxford, OX2 6DP,
United Kingdom

Oxford University Press is a department of the University of Oxford.
It furthers the University's objective of excellence in research, scholarship,
and education by publishing worldwide. Oxford is a registered trade mark of
Oxford University Press in the UK and in certain other countries

First edition 2006
Second edition 2009
Third edition 2012

Impression: 6

Published in the United States of America by Oxford University Press
198 Madison Avenue, New York, NY 10016, United States of America

British Library Cataloguing in Publication Data

Data available

Library of Congress Control Number: 2016949484

ISBN 978–0–19–967866–2

Printed in Great Britain by
Ashford Colour Press Ltd

PREFACE

This practice-orientated textbook will prove useful to those who wish to understand how the Irish Criminal Justice System works. Its contents demonstrate the practical application of the core principles of academic law, criminology and policing studies.

Whilst primarily created to enhance the training of trainee solicitors, it will be a universally useful resource to many others to include qualified practitioners who are solicitors, barristers, judges, and police officers (Gardaí).

The objective of this book is to emulate the real-time sequential manner of the journey of an accused person, from the initial investigation of crime to the determination of that case, up to and including sentencing and any judicial reviews or appeals. The generic nature of the chapter contents includes both a prosecution and a defence perspective. Separate chapters distinguish universal principles of 'ordinary' and regulatory/white-collar crime, victims' rights, juvenile justice sentencing, appeals, and judicial reviews. Rights and obligations arising during the investigation of crime and application of evidential rules are addressed, followed by an examination of the processes that characterise the commencement of prosecutions, granting of legal aid, and stages leading to trial. Particular attention is given to the Director of Public Prosecution's choice of trial venue and to the manner in which the trial process works in both the summary and indictable jurisdiction. Discreet areas of practice are selected, such as the prohibition, defences, and penalties of the most common road traffic offences, the impact of the European Convention on Human Rights in this jurisdiction, and European arrest warrant practice and procedure. The advocacy chapter focuses on the solicitor advocate but has universal applicability for all actors in that environment. The text concludes by profiling best practice in the ethical management and governance of practitioner obligations, client care and practice management in criminal litigation work.

It is hoped that the material produced herein will demystify the practicalities of compiling and presenting a case in the criminal courts at all levels, and thereby assist comprehension in this important and specialised area of practice.

Every effort has been made to ensure that the text is accurate, but the editor would be grateful to learn of any errors or omissions. Any such comments or queries should be sent to the editor at the Law Society of Ireland.

No decision or course of action should be taken on the basis of this text and competent professional legal advice should be sought before any decision or course of action is taken.

The reader is alerted to the OUP Online Resource Centre at <http://www.oxfordtextbooks.co.uk/orc/lsim_criminal/> that supports this text in the context of the ever-changing nature of legislation and case law in this dynamic practice environment. The editor's aim is to facilitate updating of this Online Resource Centre as the need arises, with the kind cooperation of the authors.

The editor tenders grateful thanks to the commitment of all co-authors for sharing their expertise, Robert Lowney for his formatting input, Declan Bannon for his support, and especially the entire OUP team for their professionalism, advice, and support.

Maura Butler, Editor
2016

ACKNOWLEDGEMENTS

Grateful acknowledgement is made to the publishers of copyright material which appears in this book. References to Irish and European Union case-law and legislation which has been made available in the public domain is acknowledged. In particular, extracts from domestic legislation have been reproduced, with the kind permission of The Houses of the Oireachtas, in compliance with its Licence to re-use Public Sector Information subject to Oireachtas Copyright pursuant to the European Communities (Re-Use of Public Sector Information) Regulations 2005 to 2015 (SI Nos 279 of 2005, 103 of 2008, and 525 of 2015). Wherever a version of the text of legislation occurs in this text, a disclaimer is hereby applied to the effect that it is not the official text of the Act or an official restatement of the official Journal of Proceedings of Dáil Éireann or Seanad Éireann, which is the version published in hard copy under statutory authority. The source of some legislation accessed for discussion in this text is acknowledged as the compilation of legislation by the Office of the Attorney General as reproduced in the electronic Irish Statute Book (eISB), the official versions of which remain the printed versions published by Government Publications. The Revised Acts, as consolidated by the Law Reform Commission in compliance with the Government's eLegislation strategy, are acknowledged as an invaluable resource in accessing and comprehending legislation in the fulfillment of its mission to bring all amendments and changes to an Act together in one document. In all other instances where material has been accessed by individual authors of this text, that material has been expressly acknowledged by referencing the source.

AUTHORS

Catherine Almond, LLB, qualified as a solicitor in London in 1990, joined Sheehan & Partners in 1999, and became a Partner in 2015. She has conducted criminal trials in the Circuit Court, the Central Criminal Court, and the Special Criminal Court, and has extensive experience in extradition and European arrest warrant cases. She has also brought cases to the European Court of Human Rights, most recently to Grand Chamber level. Catherine is currently a member of the Legal Experts Advisory Panel (LEAP) based in London and Brussels, the European Criminal Bar Association, the Law Society of Ireland, and the Dublin Solicitors Bar Association.

Caroline Butler, BA Hons, solicitor, is the principal of a Dublin-based practice established in 2000 which specialises in criminal litigation, particularly—but not exclusively—in the areas of High Court bail, extradition, judicial review, and *habeas corpus*.

Maura Butler, BA (Legal Science), LLB, MSc IT Education, Dip Applied European Law, Pg Dip Criminological Studies, and Dip Teaching Trial Advocacy Skills, qualified as a solicitor in 1985. Having worked as a criminal defence advocate and academic, since 1999 Maura has been a course manager in the Education Department, Law Society of Ireland, delivering trainee solicitor training in criminal litigation, criminal advocacy, corporate crime, and legal practice Irish, and is the editor of this textbook. Maura has been Chairperson of The Association for Criminal Justice, Research and Development (http://www.acjrd.ie) since 2007.

Rebecca Coen, BCL, LLM (Criminal Justice), BL, is the author of *Garda Powers: Law and Practice* (Clarus Press, 2014). A senior prosecutor at the Office of the Director of Public Prosecutions, she deals with cases at every level of the criminal process but is primarily focused on the prosecution of indictable offences.

Tom Conlon, LLB, Dip Fin Serv Law, solicitor, is a former defence solicitor and prosecution solicitor and has been with the Director of Public Prosecutions since 2003, specialising in drink driving cases, *habeas corpus*, and judicial review. He is also admitted as a solicitor in Northern Ireland.

Vincent Deane, BComm, LLB, is the principal of his own legal practice in County Mayo. He is the state solicitor for County Mayo. Vincent was formerly a senior prosecution solicitor with the Office of the Director of Public Prosecutions.

Áine Flynn, LLB, MLitt Criminology, is a partner in KOD Lyons Solicitors, practising human rights and criminal law. She has taught in the Law Society of Ireland, Trinity College, and UCD, and is a member of the Law Society Human Rights Committee. She has been a legal representative on the panels of the Mental Health Tribunal and the Mental Health (Criminal Law) Review Board since 2006.

Orla Keenan, BA, TCD (TSM) (Hons), LLB, qualified as a solicitor in 2010 and works in the Office of the Director of Public Prosecutions.

Aisling Kelly, LLB, MA, is a practising barrister who specialises in criminal law. She previously worked as a solicitor with the Office of the Director of Public Prosecutions, the United Nations, and in private practice as a solicitor.

Matthew Kenny, BA, is the principal of his own firm and was previously (from 2003) a partner in Sheehan & Partners Solicitors until December 2015. Matthew was awarded the Public Interest Law Association Gold Medal for his public law work in 2013 and is on their High Level Expert Working Group of The Irish Council of Civil Liberties on providing legal advice in a Garda Station.

Professor Shane Kilcommins is a graduate of UL (BA in Law and European Studies, 1994) the University of Wales, Aberystwyth (PhD 1999), and UCC (MA in Teaching and Learning, 2007). He joined the Law School, University of Limerick in 2014 after lecturing in UCC for 13 years. He lectures in evidence law, criminal law, jurisprudence, penology, and criminology. He was a Visiting Fulbright Scholar at Temple Law School in 2008/2009. He has co-authored various funded research reports on discrimination, victims of crime, and integrative learning. He is an examiner for the Law Society of Ireland in criminal law and criminal law and criminal procedure, and has acted as an external examiner for Trinity College, UCD, DCU, DIT, and the IPA.

Jenny McGeever, BA, DIP ED, qualified as a solicitor in 1994 and has since worked full time in criminal defence work. She specialises in criminal defence work and human rights law.

Brian McLaughlin, LLB (QUB), LLM International Human Rights Law (NUI), MA Criminology (DIT), BL (Inn of Court of Northern Ireland, Kings Inns), is a principal prosecutor in the Office of the Director of Prosecutions and has substantial experience of prosecuting serious and complex criminal cases. Brian practised at the Northern Ireland Bar primarily in the fields of criminal and public law. He worked as a prosecutor in the Public Prosecution Service for Northern Ireland before joining the Office of the Director of Public Prosecutions. Brian has extensive experience in training and lecturing in law and has worked as a legal adviser to the Northern Ireland Human Rights Commission and in the delivery of international humanitarian projects.

Móirín Moynihan, BEd, MSc, qualified as solicitor in 1993. She has over 20 years' experience as a criminal law practitioner with expertise in juvenile justice and human rights.

Ronan O'Brien, BCL, HDipIT, MA, has been working exclusively in the area of criminal law since 1999. He worked with the defence firm Sheehan & Partners until 2002 and, since then, has been working in the Office of the Director of Public Prosecutions where he is currently the deputy head of the District Court Section.

Dara Robinson, LLB, qualified as a solicitor in London in 1988, and joined Sheehan & Partners in 1992, becoming a partner in 1998, and his practice covers the entire spectrum of criminal defence work. He holds a Diploma in Anti-Money Laundering from the ICA/University of Manchester Business School. He is a member of the Society's Criminal Law Committee and is Vice-Chair of the Society's Regulation of Practice Committee and a member of the Money Laundering Reporting Committee. He is a member of European Criminal Bar Association and the (UK) Association of Regulatory and Disciplinary Lawyers, as well as being a member of the LEAP Advisory Board established by the London-based Fair Trials International to provide a Europe-wide network of criminal lawyers.

Dr Eimear Spain is a Senior Lecturer the School of Law, University of Limerick. She has published numerous books, book chapters, and articles in the areas of health, criminal, constitutional, and administrative law both nationally and internationally, including a monograph entitled *The Role of Emotions in Criminal Law Defences; Duress, Necessity and Lesser Evils* (2011) with Cambridge University Press. Eimear is a founding member and co-director of the Centre for the Understanding of Emotions in Society in the University of Limerick. Eimear has worked with stakeholders including Cosc, the National Office for the Prevention of Domestic, Sexual and Gender-based Violence, the Department of Justice, An Garda Síochána, the Irish Prison Service, and the Inspector of Prisons.

INTRODUCING THE ONLINE RESOURCE CENTRE

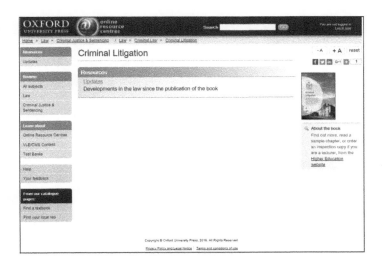

Online Resource Centres are developed to provide students and lecturers with ready-to-use learning and teaching resources. They are free-of-charge, designed to complement the textbook and offer additional materials that are suited to electronic delivery.

The Online Resource Centre to accompany *Criminal Litigation* can be found at: **www.oxford-textbooks.co.uk/orc/lsim_criminal/** and aims to feature updates written by the authors or the editor on areas where the law has changed since the book was published, or between submission of the manuscript and publication of the book.

OUTLINE CONTENTS

DETAILED CONTENTS

TABLE OF CASES

TABLE OF LEGISLATION

PART I

INTRODUCTION AND UNIVERSAL PRINCIPLES

CHAPTER 1

INTRODUCTION TO CRIMINAL LITIGATION PRACTICE AND PROCEDURE

This introductory chapter will outline the background to the process and practice of criminal litigation, briefly refer to some areas that are tangential to general practice in the Irish Criminal Process, e.g. the International Criminal Court and seizure of criminal assets, and will outline the framework and focus of this text. This manual is primarily created to enhance the training of trainee solicitors taking the Law Society of Ireland Professional Practice Course Part I, although it will prove beneficial to any stakeholder in the criminal justice process or individual who wishes to gain a greater understanding of how that process works.

1.1 Origins of Irish Criminal Law

Irish criminal law has its origins in British common law, which replaced the Celtic Brehon law system. Since the independence of the Irish state was established, legislation inherited from the British system has been developed and many other pieces of legislation since created have an identity that is distinct from such inheritance.

The regular employment of subjective rather than objective tests in assessing *mens rea* distinguishes the Irish system from its English counterpart (e.g. our law on self-defence) and aligns us more closely with the Australian or Canadian jurisprudence in criminal law. The fact of the existence of a written constitution in Ireland aligns our justice system with that of the US. It has been mooted by some practitioners that the freedoms enshrined in our Constitution are superior to those espoused in the European Convention on Human Rights. The Constitution of 1937 takes precedence over all other instruments of the criminal justice system, which includes a few remaining common law crimes, and primary and secondary legislation i.e. Acts and Statutory Instruments (SIs).

1.1.1 CRIMINAL JUSTICE POLICY AND RECENT AND CURRENT LEGISLATIVE DEVELOPMENTS

1.1.1.1 Policy

Criminal law in this jurisdiction as applied through our courts is an ever-changing and vibrant jurisprudence, which emanates from the government of the day through the policy decisions formulated in the Department of Justice and Equality, through consultation with various stakeholders.

A Draft Criminal Code prepared by the Criminal Law Codification Advisory Committee has been published by the Department's website to facilitate the obtaining of views of interested parties as to the advantages or disadvantages of implementing a code of this type. It is a partial criminal code covering the following areas of law:

- General principles.
- Non-fatal offences against the person.

- Theft and fraud offences.

- Criminal damage offences.

- Public order offences.

The Department of Justice and Equality has also developed a White Paper on Crime which aims to create a policy framework for strategies to combat and prevent crime. It examined system-wide approaches to intervention, prevention, and enforcement, with a view to reducing offending and protecting the public. The examination incorporated extensive consultation with members of the public and other interested bodies.

Under the Garda Síochána Act 2005, the Minister may set policing priorities for An Garda Síochána and, in consultation with the Garda Commissioner, priorities have been set in six key areas: gangland crime; security; policing communities; customer service; roads policing; and human trafficking.

1.1.1.2   Legislation

There is a myriad of legislation that a criminal litigation practitioner should be familiar with, as it is always necessary to go to primary sources when researching the law applicable to specific proceedings. A practitioner must be ever-alert to the introduction of new legislation which is driven either by government policy or as a result of case law decisions and must regularly assess the introduction and commencement of such legislation.

In alphabetical order here are a number of essential procedural pieces of legislation that practitioners need to be familiar with:

- Bail Act 1997 (Annotated by the Law Reform Commission)

- Children Act 2001 (Annotated by the Law Reform Commission)

- Children (Amendment) Act 2015

- Court of Appeal Act 2014

- Criminal Evidence Act 1992

- Criminal Justice Act 1984 (Annotated by the Law Reform Commission)

- Criminal Justice Act 1999

- Criminal Justice Act 2006 (Annotated by the Law Reform Commission)

- Criminal Justice Act 2007 (Annotated by the Law Reform Commission)

- Criminal Justice (Amendment) Act 2009

- Criminal Justice Act 2011 (Annotated by the Law Reform Commission)

- Criminal Justice Act 2013

- Criminal Justice (Community Service) Act 1983

- Criminal Justice (Community Service) (Amendment) Act 2011

- Criminal Justice (Drug Trafficking) Act 1996

- Criminal Justice (Forensic Evidence and DNA Database System) Act 2014

- Criminal Justice (Miscellaneous Provisions) Act 1997

- Criminal Justice (Miscellaneous Provisions) Act 2009 (Annotated by the Law Reform Commission)

- Criminal Justice (Surveillance) Act 2009

- Criminal Law Act 1997 (Annotated by the Law Reform Commission)

- Criminal Procedure Act 1967 (Annotated by the Law Reform Commission)

- Criminal Procedure Act 2010 (Annotated by the Law Reform Commission)

- Fines Act 2010 (Annotated by the Law Reform Commission)

- Fines (Payment and Recovery) Act 2014

- Garda Síochána (Amendment) Act 2015
- Sex Offenders Act 2001

In alphabetical order here are some essential substantive pieces of legislation regularly encountered in practice:

- Air Pollution Acts 1987 and 2011
- Companies Act 2014
- Competition Act 2002
- Criminal Damage Act 1991
- Criminal Justice Act 2013
- Criminal Justice (Legal Aid) Act 1962
- Criminal Justice (Money Laundering and Terrorist Financing) Act 2010 (Annotated by the Law Reform Commission)
- Criminal Justice (Psychoactive Substances) Act 2010
- Criminal Justice (Public Order) Act 1994
- Criminal Justice (Public Order) Act 2003
- Criminal Justice (Public Order) Act 2011
- Criminal Justice (Theft and Fraud Offences) Act 2001
- Criminal Law (Insanity) Act 2006 (Annotated by the Law Reform Commission)
- Criminal Law (Rape) Act 1981
- Criminal Law (Rape) (Amendment) Act 1990
- Criminal Law (Sexual Offences) Act 2006 (Annotated by the Law Reform Commission)
- Criminal Law (Sexual Offences) (Amendment) Act 2007
- Criminal Justice (Terrorists Offences) Act 2005
- Dangerous Substances Acts 1972–1979
- Environmental Protection Agency Act 1992
- Environmental (Miscellaneous Provisions) Act 2011
- Firearms Act (1925) (Annotated by the Law Reform Commission)
- Firearms Act (1964) (Annotated by the Law Reform Commission)
- Firearms Act 1971 (Annotated by the Law Reform Commission)
- Firearms and Offensive Weapons Act 1990 (Annotated by the Law Reform Commission)
- Health & Safety Legislation 1989–2005
- International Criminal Court Act 2006 (Annotated by the Law Reform Commission)
- Local Government (Water Pollution) Acts 1977–1990
- Misuse of Drugs Act 1977
- Misuse of Drugs Act 1984
- Misuse of Drugs (Amendment) Act 2015
- Non-Fatal Offences Against the Person Act 1997
- Offences Against the State Act 1939
- Offences Against the State (Amendment) Act 1998
- Protection of the Environment Act 2003
- Road Traffic Act 1961(Annotated by the Law Reform Commission)
- Road Traffic Act 1968 (Annotated by the Law Reform Commission)

- Road Traffic Act 1984 (Annotated by the Law Reform Commission)
- Road Traffic Act 1994 (Annotated by the Law Reform Commission)
- Road Traffic Act 2002 (Annotated by the Law Reform Commission)
- Road Traffic Act 2004 (Annotated by the Law Reform Commission)
- Road Traffic Act 2006 (Annotated by the Law Reform Commission)
- Road Traffic Act 2010 (Annotated by the Law Reform Commission)
- Road Traffic Act 2011
- Road Traffic (No. 2) Act 2011
- Road Traffic Act 2014
- Road Traffic (No. 2) Act 2014
- Taxes Consolidation Act (TCA) 1997 (as amended)
- Victims Rights Directive (Directive 2012/29/EU of the European Parliament and of the Council)
- Waste Management Acts 1996–2011

1.2   Regulatory Crime

Chapter 2 of this text explores regulatory crime, sometimes referred to as white collar crime or corporate crime, in great detail. It is important for the criminal litigation practitioner to recognise that there is no distinction between the practice and procedure applicable to what is referred to as 'ordinary crime' and 'regulatory crime'. If one's client is arrested on suspicion of being involved in a breach of competition legislation, health and safety legislation, environmental legislation or company law, to name a few corporate type breaches, the same general arrest detention and trial procedures will be brought to bear as would be the case for a standard (ordinary) theft or assault charge. It is therefore incumbent on a practising solicitor, who does not wish to be deemed professionally negligent, to be cognisant of the universal application of criminal litigation processes and procedures and to be in a position to advise a business client on how to avoid breaches of such legislation that could result in criminal prosecution.

As you will learn in **Chapter 2**, distinctions have traditionally been drawn between regulatory crimes and ordinary crimes on the basis that the former are *mala prohibita* (prohibited wrongs) and the latter are *mala in se* (moral wrongs). Regulatory crimes are more often thought of in terms of the end justifying the means as opposed to being value-laden in terms of justice, fairness, right, and wrong. It has also been argued that regulatory crimes are more likely to be perceived as victimless (or at least not to have a readily identifiable victim). It is further suggested that regulatory offences, for the most part, do not embody (at least traditionally) a punitive or sanctioning model of justice, preferring instead to favour compliance strategies.

Some examples that will be elaborated on later in **Chapter 2** include the following:

- Personal criminal liability can be imposed on company officers and directors and it is the duty of each company to ensure that it complies with all of the requirements of the Companies Acts where officers of the company are personally responsible for ensuring compliance.

- Under health and safety law, where a health and safety offence has been committed by a body corporate, and that offence is shown to have been committed with the consent or connivance of, or to have been attributable to any neglect on the part of any director, that person may be prosecuted in addition to the corporate body.

- Seizure and taxation of criminal assets is a means by which to lift the veil and 'get at' the controlling and guiding minds of such organised criminal organisations.

- The Director of Corporate Enforcement may share information with other prosecuting authorities, as well as tribunals of inquiry, the Revenue Commissioners, and An Garda Síochána.

- Individuals are required to become 'information reporters'. Solicitors, for example, are required to report clients' suspicious transactions to the Garda Síochána and the Revenue

Commissioners so as to prevent the use of the financial system for the purpose of money laundering.

- Where a disciplinary tribunal of a recognised body of accountants has reasonable grounds for believing that an indictable offence has been committed by a person while the person was a member of the body, the body shall inform the Director of Corporate Enforcement. There are similar provisions that auditors of companies must comply with, and a disciplinary tribunal of an accountancy body with reasonable grounds for believing that an indictable offence has been committed by one of its members must report the suspicion to the Director of Corporate Enforcement.

Many aspects of regulatory crime operate differently from the general trend of criminal law principles of *mens rea* and *actus reus* with the availability to the accused of general defences and a legal burden of proof beyond reasonable doubt placed on the prosecution. Strict liability principles and a shifting of the legal burden onto the alleged regulatory crime offender is common. A practitioner in this area of crime can therefore best serve the potential clients' needs by providing advice that prevents the possibilities of any breaches of regulatory crime.

1.3 The International Criminal Court

On 17 July 1998, 120 states adopted the Rome Statute, the legal basis for establishing the permanent International Criminal Court (ICC). It entered into force on 1 July 2002 after ratification by 60 countries; 124 countries are states parties to this Statute, 34 of whom are African states, 19 are Asia-Pacific states, 18 are from Eastern Europe, 28 are Latin American and Caribbean states, and 25 are Western European and other states. Ireland signed the Rome Statute on 7 October 1998, deposited its instrument of ratification of the Rome Statute on 11 April 2002, entering into force on 1 July of that year. It is a court of last resort and will not act if a case is investigated or prosecuted by a national judicial system unless the national proceedings were flawed.

The ICC is an independent international organisation based in The Hague in the Netherlands established to help end impunity for the perpetrators of the most serious crimes of concern to the international community, i.e. genocide, crimes against humanity and war crimes.

The structure of the ICC includes the Presidency, Judicial Divisions, the Office of the Prosecutor and the Registry. The latter serves as the administrative support for the ICC. The Presidency has an internally elected President and two Vice-Presidents, with expertise in criminal law and procedure and international law, who serve on a full-time basis for a three-year term, which is renewable. Their responsibilities focus on their judicial/legal functions, administration and external relations (promoting public awareness and understanding of the ICC). The Judicial Divisions, in exercising their functions at different stages of proceedings, comprise a Pre-Trial Division, Trial Division and an Appeals Division. Typically, the Office of the Prosecutor examines information received regarding crimes within the jurisdiction of the ICC and thereafter conducts investigations and processes prosecutions. The Prosecutor may only proceed with a case where a state is unable or unwilling to investigate or prosecute. Other structural aspects include Office of Public Counsel for victims and the Office of Public Counsel for Defence and the Assembly of States Parties, which manages a trust fund for the benefit of victims of crimes within the jurisdiction of the Court and the families of these victims.

As reported at the situations and cases page of the ICC website https://www.icc-cpi.int/Pages/Home.aspx:

> To date, four States Parties to the Rome Statute – Uganda, the Democratic Republic of the Congo, the Central African Republic and Mali – have referred situations occurring on their territories to the Court. In addition, the Security Council has referred the situation in Darfur, Sudan, and the situation in Libya – both non-States Parties. After a thorough analysis of available information, the Prosecutor has opened and is conducting investigations in all of the above-mentioned situations.

> On 31 March 2010, Pre-Trial Chamber II granted the Prosecution authorisation to open an investigation *proprio motu* in the situation of Kenya. In addition, on 3 October 2011, Pre-Trial Chamber III granted the Prosecutor's request for authorisation to open investigations *proprio motu* into the situation in Côte d'Ivoire.

On 27 January 2016, Pre-Trial Chamber I authorised the Prosecutor to proceed with an investigation for the crimes within the ICC jurisdiction, allegedly committed in and around South Ossetia, Georgia, between 1 July and 10 October 2008.

The Official Journal of the ICC was created pursuant to regulation 7 of the Regulations of the Court and contains the following texts and amendments thereto:

- The Rome Statute.
- The Rules of Procedure and Evidence.
- The Elements of Crimes.
- The Regulations of the Court.
- The Regulations of the Office of the Prosecutor.
- The Regulations of the Registry.
- The Code of Professional Conduct for Counsel.
- The Code of Judicial Ethics.
- Staff rules of the International Criminal Court.
- The Staff Regulations.
- The Financial Regulations and Rules.
- The Agreement on the Privileges and Immunities of the International Criminal Court.
- Agreement between the International Criminal Court and the United Nations.
- The Headquarters Agreement with the Host State.
- Any other material as decided by the Presidency in consultation with the Prosecutor and/or the Registrar.

Ireland's ratification of the Rome Treaty necessitated the prior amendment of the Irish Constitution as submission to the jurisdiction of the International Criminal Court meant that there was a partial transfer to the court of the sovereign power of the state to administer criminal justice. The twenty-third amendment of the Constitution inserted Article 29.9, providing that the state may ratify the Rome Statute and Ireland is therefore a member of the Assembly of States Parties.

Further information with regard to the ICC is available in William A. Schabas, *An Introduction to the International Criminal Court* (3rd edition, Cambridge University Press, 2007) and William A. Schabas, *The International Criminal Court: A Commentary on the Rome Statute* (Oxford University Press, New York, 2010).

1.4   European Union Policy

Ireland's membership of the European Union (EU) has resulted in a yielding of some sovereign power with the resultant imposition of directives that must be transposed into national legislation. However domestic criminal law matters are outside that remit.

1.4.1   EU JUSTICE AND SECURITY POLICY

The Justice and Security Brief of the EU, the Third Pillar of Maastricht (as amended by the Lisbon Treaty), concerns itself, amongst other matters, with the following: immigration, transatlantic relations, transport security, anti-terrorism policy, organised crime, biometrics and travel, economic migration and border control.

As a consequence of EU membership the Irish jurisdiction must implement EU Directives through enabling legislation. Information on current trends in policy matters at this level may be viewed online at http://ec.europa.eu/justice/index_en.htm. This website displays data on:

(a) asylum;

(b) immigration;

(c) organised crime;

(d) drug smuggling and addiction;

(e) judicial cooperation between national courts, in both civil and criminal matters;

(f) cooperation between national customs and police forces;

(g) fundamental rights;

(h) citizenship in the EU;

(i) cooperation with third countries and international organisations;

(j) the justice and home affairs '*acquis*' in the enlargement process; and

(k) the external dimension of justice and home affairs.

Matters emanating from Europe that more frequently impinge currently on the Irish criminal lawyer include extradition, the European Arrest Warrant and the European Convention on Human Rights (see **Chapter 17**).

1.4.2 EXTRADITION GENERALLY AND THE EUROPEAN ARREST WARRANT

Where a person is detained in one jurisdiction and, subject to the fulfilment of certain qualifications and procedures, is delivered to another jurisdiction in custody, s/he is referred to as 'extradited'.

The legislation in Ireland that governs extradition includes: the Extradition Act 1965; the Extradition (European Convention on the Suppression of Terrorism) Act 1987; the Extradition (Amendment) Act 1987; the Extradition (Amendment) Act 1994; the Extradition (European Union Convention) Act 2001; and the European Arrest Warrant Act 2003.

There are a number of matters that require compliance in advance of extradition, generally. They include the principle of reciprocity, under which it is presumed that the jurisdiction requesting the extradition is acting in a bona fide manner and that, as a result, the suspect will be charged for the offence for which s/he is sought. The offence must be one that is punishable by imprisonment for at least 12 months. For extradition to be applicable under the Extradition Act 1965, the suspect must be required in the requesting state to answer charges relative to conduct that would constitute a criminal offence in Ireland and the requesting state must discharge the requisite burden of proof necessary to establish that fact. This procedure establishes the dual criminality test, as discussed in *Trimbole v Governor of Mountjoy Prison* [1985] ILRM 465. It is also a requirement that the suspect must be prosecuted only for the offence for which s/he was extradited.

An offence regarded as extraditable must not be a political offence, an exclusively military offence or a revenue offence. The leading authority on what constitutes a political offence is *Finucane v McMahon* [1990] ILRM 505, and the constituents of what comprises a revenue offence were discussed in *Byrne v Conroy* [1998] 2 ILRM 113.

Reciprocal arrangements exist between Ireland and the other countries through various multilateral and unilateral treaties, whereby a suspect can be extradited from one jurisdiction for prosecution in the other. Such treaties can be given force of law through the application of Part II of the Extradition Act 1965. Part III of the Act deals with procedures specific to the UK and the Channel Islands. Applicable offences must follow the dual criminality test and must be offences that are punishable summarily with a six-month sentence or indictable offences. Offences of a political, military and revenue nature are excluded from UK extradition requests to this jurisdiction.

The European Union Conventions on Extradition of 1995 and 1996 endeavour to simplify extradition procedures between member states of the European Community. A suspect may now consent to surrender and be processed through simpler transfer and authentication procedures. Through the Extradition (European Conventions) Act 2001, these Conventions have been implemented in Ireland. Consequent upon such implementation, it has become necessary to interpret pre-existing Irish law in this area through the medium of the 2001 Act where the requesting state is a designated EU state.

Developments in this area of law are examined in detail in **Chapter 18**.

1.5   Criminal Procedure Aspects of Proceeds of Crime Legislation

The provisions of the Proceeds of Crime Act 2005 which deal with confiscation and post-conviction enforcement orders employ civil procedure methodologies exercised by the Criminal Assets Bureau. Such applications include High Court applications, and applications pursuant to s. 39 Criminal Justice Act 1994 (as amended) to forfeit seized money to the state by way of an application to the Circuit Court.

However, there are some connections between this mainly civil procedure and criminal procedure that require the criminal practitioner to engage in some applications that necessitate an acquired knowledge in this area of law. These connections exist insofar as there must be a current prosecution of the purported owner of the assets in question or a decision has been made by the Director of Public Prosecutions (DPP) to bring a prosecution against the person who has control over the property that the Criminal Assets Bureau wish to seize. An example of such a case would be a prosecution for the offence of money laundering under s. 31 of the Criminal Justice Act 1994.

Section 38 of the same Act in Part VI dealing with drug trafficking money imported or exported in cash outlines powers of search and seizure where:

(1) *A member of the Garda Síochána or an officer of customs and excise may seize and, in accordance with this section, detain any cash which is being imported into or exported from the State if its amount is not less than the prescribed sum and he has reasonable grounds for suspecting that it directly or indirectly represents any person's proceeds of, or is intended by any person for use in, drug trafficking.*

(2) *Cash seized by virtue of this section shall not be detained for more than forty-eight hours unless its detention beyond forty-eight hours is authorized by an order made by a judge of the District Court and no such order shall be made unless the judge is satisfied—*

   (a) *that there are reasonable grounds for the suspicion mentioned in subsection (1) of this section, and*

   (b) *that detention of the cash beyond forty-eight hours is justified while its origin or derivation is further investigated or consideration is given to the institution (whether in the State or elsewhere) of criminal proceedings against any person for an offence with which the cash is connected.*

The jurisdiction of the Circuit Court to make a forfeiture order regarding any cash that has been seized under s. 38 is delineated in s. 39 of the same Act on an application by or on behalf of the DPP. The judge must be 'satisfied, ... that the cash directly or indirectly represents any person's proceeds of, or is intended by any person for use in, drug trafficking'. With regard to the applicable standard of proof in such proceedings, s. 39(3) states that such a civil standard (balance of probabilities) applies 'and an order may be made under this section whether or not proceedings are brought against any person for an offence with which the cash in question is connected'. Typically, all that is required of the prosecution is to prove a link between the cash seized, which must be worth at least €6,348, and criminality, and to have evidence produced regarding how the cash was found, from whom it was seized, the explanation proffered by the purported owner of the cash and evidence of his criminal record and/or criminal associates.

In every prosecution for the supply of drugs under s. 15 of the Misuse of Drugs Act 1977 (as amended) that is prosecuted on indictment, the trial court on the application of the DPP may enquire about any financial benefit gained by the accused as a result of engagement in the offence. Section 4 of the Criminal Justice Act 1994 states at subsection (1):

(1) *Where a person has been sentenced or otherwise dealt with by a court in respect of one or more drug trafficking offences of which he has been convicted on indictment, the Director of Public Prosecutions may make, or cause to be made, an application to the court to determine whether the person convicted has benefited from drug trafficking.*

At s. 4(2) it is noted that this DPP application may occur at the conclusion of the proceedings. Section 4(6) states that:

> *The standard of proof required to determine any question arising under this Act as to—*
>
> *(a) whether a person has benefited from drug trafficking, or*
>
> *(b) the amount to be recovered in his case by virtue of this section,*
>
> *shall be that applicable in civil proceedings.*

Seizure of criminal assets in this manner is not confined to drug trafficking offences as delineated in s. 9 of the 1994 Act.

> *9.—(1) Where a person has been sentenced or otherwise dealt with in respect of an offence, other than a drug trafficking offence, of which he has been convicted on indictment, then, if an application is made, or caused to be made, to the court by the Director of Public Prosecutions the court may, subject to the provisions of this section, make a confiscation order under this section requiring the person concerned to pay such sum as the court thinks fit.*

The procedure that must be followed by a court in making forfeiture orders generally or forfeiture orders in respect of drugs offences is outlined at s. 61 and s. 62 respectively of the Criminal Justice Act 1994.

1.6 Training in Criminal Litigation Practice

Criminal justice training is engaged in by many professions. It is a core academic element of all undergraduate law degrees and is manifest in criminology studies. The Law Society of Ireland includes criminal litigation and criminal advocacy as core training for trainee solicitors and holds regular continuing professional development (CPD) criminal practice events for practitioners. Barristers (or counsel) similarly have separate training at trainee and professional level. There is a Judicial Studies Institute managed by the Courts Service where our judiciary stay abreast of current developments in criminal practice. The DPP's Office has a continuous training programme.

The Garda Training College provides a comprehensive programme for those taking initial training as a Garda. Gardaí are typically the first actors in the criminal justice process once a crime has been reported. That training includes modules on the foundations of policing, public safety, professional competence, policing with communities, crime and incident policing, traffic policing and law and procedures. Further reading that identifies, analyses and explains the many powers vested in An Garda Síochána can be studied in *Garda Powers Law and Practice* by Rebecca Coen (Clarus Press, 2014).

It is hoped that the content of this publication will prove useful to all who wish to learn the legal principles that are the foundation for the practice of criminal law in this jurisdiction.

1.6.1 LAW SOCIETY OF IRELAND PROFESSIONAL PRACTICE COURSE PART I

All trainee solicitors undertaking the Law Society of Ireland Professional Practice Course Part I (PPC I) will have successfully passed the Final Examination Part 1 (FEI) in Criminal Law. It is consequently assumed that a high level of academic expertise has been achieved, with regard to the concepts that determine the *mens rea* of crime, the *actus reus*, concepts of strict liability, levels of participation in a myriad of crimes, and the defences and exemptions applicable thereto.

The focus of training at PPC I level is to equip the trainee solicitor advocate with the procedural knowledge and skills to ensure best practice in the task of ongoing investigation, prosecution and defence of criminal allegations.

Insofar as this criminal procedure text allows, all new legislation that affects the methodology of the prosecution and defence of crime has been referred to. It is impossible to give adequate exposure to all procedures and all new legislation in a criminal litigation text aimed at the recent undergraduate embarking on a solicitor-training course.

1.6.2   THE LAW OF EVIDENCE IN CRIMINAL COURTS

Chapter 10 focuses on the implementation of the fundamental principles of evidence in a criminal litigation context. It is pre-supposed that the reader of this text is fully conversant with the rules of the law of evidence at an academic level, and is thereby competent to comprehend legal concepts such as the admissibility of evidence, burden of proof in criminal proceedings, competence and compatibility of witnesses, corroboration, opinion evidence, and illegally obtained evidence, which are some of the topics explored. Those who are unfamiliar with the law of evidence at an academic level should consult academic texts in that area of law, such as those listed at **10.7**.

1.6.3   CRIMINAL PROCESS

The reader of this text will become familiar with the powers available to the state, through the Gardaí, to investigate crime, together with the applicable rights and obligations that attach themselves to the accused and the state respectively, and the preliminary issues for an accused after the arrest, detention and charging process is complete. Such issues include regulatory crime, the position of the victim of crime, the commencement of proceedings procedures, rights to bail, and state subsidy of legal representation in the form of free legal aid. Procedural rules facilitate the remand (adjournment) of cases and the commencement of the trial process, bringing the reader through the preliminary steps of the criminal litigation process and procedure as decisions are made in relation to the method of disposal of the case.

1.6.4   TRIAL PROCEDURES

Having become familiar with relevant human rights issues, practical practice considerations, the impact of the law of evidence, the application of evidential principles as an advocate and preliminary procedural matters, as one proceeds through the sequential chapters that mirror the progress of a case being processed towards its conclusion, one becomes aware of the procedures applicable to the disposal of criminal cases. This disposal may be at either the District Court level (summary disposal) or 'on indictment' in the higher courts, which include the Circuit Criminal Court, the Special Criminal Court and the Central Criminal Court.

Required procedural steps are presented in a chronological fashion, tracing the process from the choice of venue selected by the DPP, firstly, to the disposal of crime at summary level in the District Court on either a plea of 'guilty' or 'not guilty', and secondly, at indictable level, again on either a 'guilty' plea or a 'not guilty' plea during a procedure called arraignment.

Whilst the juvenile justice system shares a lot of generally applicable criminal procedure with the adult courts, nevertheless, given the particular issues applicable to children who are accused of offending, it warrants separate and exclusive discussion.

Matters that are applicable to all forms of disposal and at various stages of the criminal process are discussed in **Chapters 14 and 16** respectively, which deal with sentencing, and appeal and judicial review procedures.

1.7   The Rules of Professional Conduct

1.7.1   INTRODUCTION

Rules that can be found in the *Guide to Professional Conduct of Solicitors in Ireland*, published by the Law Society of Ireland (The Law Society Guide), are designed to ensure the proper performance by lawyers of rules that are recognised as essential in all civilised societies.

Responsible ethical conduct by solicitors will assist public confidence in the administration of justice. This can be done through adherence to guidelines on the following issues:

    (a) the protection of the client's interests;

    (b) a consciousness of the need to redress a perceived imbalance of power between solicitor and client;

(c)   the maintenance of high professional standards between colleagues;

(d)   the administration of procedure in the courts when the solicitor is representing the client;

(e)   the maintenance of an independent profession, free of coercion from any outside forces.

The Law Society Guide incorporates the International Bar Association's Code of Ethics, the Code of Conduct for Lawyers in the European Community adopted in Strasbourg in 1988 and a Code of Conduct established by the Law Society of Ireland Criminal Law Committee. The common thread in all of these regulations is a regard for general principles, which incorporate:

(a)   the independence of lawyers;

(b)   trust and personal integrity;

(c)   confidentiality;

(d)   respect for the rules of other Bars and Law Societies within the EU.

1.7.2   SOME GUIDELINES FOR PROFESSIONAL CONDUCT FOR CRIMINAL LITIGATION PRACTITIONERS

(a)   A solicitor should not, either by him/herself or by anyone on his/her behalf, approach a person who might become a client with a view to representing that person.

(b)   Before taking instructions from any person in any criminal case, a solicitor should satisfy him/herself that the person has not already engaged the services of another solicitor in that particular case or in related proceedings.

(c)   In the event of disagreement between solicitors relating to the transfer of a solicitor's case from one solicitor to another in a criminal matter, the matter should be referred to the Guidance and Ethics Committee of the Law Society of Ireland for resolution.

(d)   Where a solicitor requires, for consultation purposes, to visit a prisoner in custody in cells within the courthouse or in the immediate vicinity of a court, the solicitor should so inform the court and seek to have the accused's case put back to enable a consultation to take place.

(e)   Where an accused is brought before a court on charges that may in normal circumstances be described as 'new charges', but such person has already retained a solicitor in related proceedings, no solicitor shall accept instructions from such person on those new charges unless s/he receives instructions in respect of all charges before the court and complies with the provision of paragraph (h) below, in discharging the retainer of the previously instructed solicitor.

(f)   A solicitor may accept an instruction to act for a client in an appeal even if that solicitor did not act for the client in the original proceedings, except where another solicitor has previously been retained and is on record in respect of the appeal.

(g)   A solicitor should not actively encourage or offer inducements to any person with a view to obtaining instructions from such a person.

(h)   A solicitor shall not accept instructions to act for a client in a case where another solicitor has already been retained in that matter without ensuring that the other solicitor's retainer is discharged. This provision will not be applicable where a solicitor is assigned by a court to act for the accused on legal aid.

A solicitor who is in breach of any of the provisions of this part of the code of conduct will be liable to disciplinary proceedings for unprofessional conduct.

1.7.3   THE PRACTICAL APPLICATION OF ETHICAL PRINCIPLES

An idealist may like to presume that every solicitor and trainee solicitor will highly prize the translation of ethical philosophy into a practical set of rules based on the wisdom of practitioners collected over many years. It would be gratifying to believe that pride in oneself, and the good name of the profession and common decency manifested through self-discipline, would be the norm for every practitioner.

In the real world, some pressures may manifest themselves, thereby impinging on such desirable characteristics. There are increasing demands on the solicitor's profession to provide a speedy and cost-effective service to the client. These pressures may create the danger of compromise of some of the basic standards referred to earlier. Such compromise should be strenuously resisted.

1.7.4   THE CONSEQUENCES OF A RELAXATION OF STANDARDS

What every practitioner must remain conscious of is that, if the high standards expected are relaxed, then such ethical transgressions may have very serious consequences. A negative effect on the reputation of a practitioner will have an automatic knock-on effect on the public's ability to trust the administration of justice. Misconduct may result in a practitioner being reported to the Law Society of Ireland Complaints Section, with the subsequent consequences of disciplinary action being taken—the ultimate sanction being that solicitor is struck off the Roll, i.e. disbarred. Professional negligence claims result where a client has suffered loss as a direct result of poor or incorrect case management by a solicitor.

1.7.5   THE DISTINCTION BETWEEN 'MISCONDUCT' AND 'NEGLIGENCE'

There is sometimes a very thin line between 'misconduct' and 'negligence'. It is therefore important to understand the importance of concepts such as:

* integrity;
* confidentiality;
* conflict of interest;
* the need to maintain professional standards;
* the unique position of the solicitor as an officer of the court.

It is necessary to learn:

* how to relate to colleagues;
* how to interact with counsel for the benefit of the client;
* how to relate to third parties in the course of transacting business on behalf of clients.

1.7.6   REGULATION

All professions have regulations that members are required to abide by. In the Law Society of Ireland Report of The Regulation 13 Review Group May 2013 it addressed what was identified as an historic phenomenon:

> not alone in Ireland, but in every legal system … the dual difficulty of lawyers engaging in improper direct unsolicited approaches to non-clients. The difficulty has been that while this practice is routinely regulated against, proof of the wrongdoing is often difficult to come by.

The review went on to say:

> In Ireland the prohibition against such conduct is, perhaps unhelpfully, cast for regulatory purposes in Regulation 13 of what are known as the 'Solicitors (Advertising) Regulations 2002' (the Regulations). Regulation 13 provides as follows:

Direct unsolicited approach to non-client:

> *(a) Without prejudice to the generality of Regulation 4(a), a solicitor shall not make or cause to be made a direct unsolicited approach to any person who is not an existing client in order that communication is made with that person with a view to being instructed to provide legal services, where such direct unsolicited approach is likely to bring the solicitors' profession into disrepute.*

(b) *Without prejudice to the generality of clause (a) of this Regulation, a solicitor shall not make or cause to be made a direct unsolicited approach to any person who is not an existing client in order that communication is made with that person with a view to being instructed to provide legal services, where such unsolicited approach is made—*

    (i)   *at an inappropriate location;*

    (ii) *at or adjacent to the scene of a calamitous event or situation affecting that person;*

    (iii) *in, at, or adjacent to, a Garda station, prison or courthouse.*

The recommendations that emanated from this Review were as follows:

SUMMARY OF RECOMMENDATIONS

The Law Society

1. Emphasis should be placed on placing barriers in the path of the intending wrongdoer, rather than relying on the prosecution of breaches.

2. The Criminal Law Committee should pursue its representations to the Department of Justice that a replaced solicitor should be paid a portion of the case fee, reflective of the work he has done to date of transfer.

3. The Society should fully support any solicitor who declines to act improperly on the instructions of an employing solicitor.

4. The Society should facilitate the establishment of an accessible register of specialists in the field of criminal law.

5. The Society should promote public awareness by communicating to persons appearing before the Criminal Courts precisely what their entitlements are.

6. As a priority, the Law Society should establish and maintain a readily accessible list of legal aid practitioners.

7. The Society should authorise evidence gathering activity in Court venues.

8. If it is the first occasion a solicitor is identified as engaging in an unsolicited approach, he/she would not necessarily be referred to the Disciplinary Tribunal but would be advised that they had been identified as part of a Society initiative and cautioned as to their future conduct.

Education

9. The existing teaching of ethics in the Law School should be augmented to include specific reference to the restrictions imposed by Regulation 13.

10. Trainee solicitors should be requested at the start of their traineeship to sign and adhere to a code of professional conduct and the declaration at the conclusion of the period of traineeship should address specifically the training provided in ethical matters.

11. The Society should run refresher courses at a reasonable fee for colleagues who wish to keep their skills current.

Practice

12. The procedures for the transfer of a legal aid file should be made more demanding.

Other bodies

13. There should be stricter supervision of access by solicitors to persons in custody.

14. The Society should avail of the introduction of Measure B (see https://www.lawsociety.ie/Documents/Regulation/Regulations/Reg13-REPORT2013.pdf) to facilitate the provision of information to detained persons as to how they can access the full range of solicitors available.

15. A centralised national system should be introduced which would facilitate the maintenance of a comprehensive and up to date list of legal aid practitioners, which information can be promulgated to the general public.

16. Persons in Garda custody should be advised of the availability on the Society's website of a list of available solicitors.

17. The Criminal Law Committee should make representations to the Irish Prison Service that persons in detention should also be advised of the list available on the Society's website.

18. The Society should engage with the translation and interpretation professionals to ensure a coincidence of expectation in relation to what is required on a professional level and in particular what is prohibited by our code of ethics.

19. The Solicitors Disciplinary Tribunal should be invited to review their rules of evidence.

The Courts

20. Information leaflets should be posted on designated notice boards in courthouses, alerting accused persons to their entitlements and pointing out the prohibition on unsolicited approaches by solicitors.

21. The information notices should be in a range of languages familiar to persons appearing before the Courts and there should be continuous review of the languages required.

22. At the Commencement of each court sitting, local practitioners should indicate to the presiding Judge by way of a list, the identities of those legal aid practitioners available in that Court room on that day in the event that an assignment is required.

1.7.7   PROFESSIONAL DUTIES OF THE CRIMINAL SOLICITOR

1.7.7.1   The defence solicitor

The defence solicitor has all of the usual professional legal duties to act in the client's best interests, but, in addition, s/he has an overriding duty not to mislead the court. Where a client admits guilt to a solicitor, s/he may continue to act, even on a 'not guilty' plea. A solicitor may permit the client to plead 'not guilty' before the court and thereafter may do everything possible during the prosecution case, e.g. cross-examine witnesses as vigorously as possible, provided that this does not involve advancing any untruthful version of events. However, a solicitor may not permit that client to go into the witness box to give false testimony or call perjured evidence. Accordingly, if a client does admit guilt to the solicitor, it is vital to point out that one can continue to act for him/her even if a 'not guilty' plea is entered, on the condition that no evidence will be called that supports what is known to be untrue.

It may be appropriate to approach the prosecution to see whether they are willing to reconsider the decision to prosecute. Under s. 6 of the Prosecution of Offences Act 1974, a solicitor is entitled to make representations to the DPP on behalf of the client. The following factors may be relevant:

(a) triviality of the offence;

(b) staleness/delay;

(c) youth or old age and infirmity of the offender (for example, one may wish to persuade the DPP to deal with a young person by way of caution rather than a prosecution);

(d) mental illness and stress.

1.7.7.2   The prosecution solicitor

The duties of the prosecuting solicitor reflect those of the defence solicitor insofar as s/he is an officer of the court and must therefore not mislead it. It is not the duty of a prosecutor to 'get a conviction at all costs'. The prosecutor must not conceal evidence from the defence or the court and must present the evidence in best practice mode in pursuit of discharging the burden of proof, which is 'beyond all reasonable doubt'. There are specific publications on the website of the DPP that have collated much detail on the required best practice expected from prosecutors (see http://www.dpp.ie).

CHAPTER 2

REGULATORY CRIME

2.1   Introduction

In examining the contours of criminal law and its application, most lawyers and criminologists are drawn to traditional 'real crime' (homicides, violent assaults, organised crime, sexual offences, requirements of *mens rea* and *actus reus*, and general defences) while ignoring white collar offences, which are often enforced by specialist agencies (J. McGrath, *Corporate and White Collar Crime in Ireland: A New Architecture of Regulatory Enforcement* (Manchester University Press, 2015)). As a society we have tended to be preoccupied with the 'punitive regulation of the poor', a project closely tied to a police–prisons way of knowing that focuses on 'crime in the streets' rather than 'crime in the suites' (see J. Braithwaite, 'What's Wrong with the Sociology of Punishment' (2003) 7(1) Theo. Crim. 5–28 at 7). The narrow exclusivity of this approach is a mistake, not least because criminalisation is now more than ever viewed as a panacea for almost any social problem. More and more Irish society is witnessing the increasing and extensive use of regulatory strategies by the Irish state. In areas such as competition law, environmental protection, health and safety law, and consumer and corporate affairs, there has been a move towards using criminalisation as the last-resort strategy when compliance through negotiation and monitoring has failed.

Distinctions have traditionally been drawn between regulatory crimes and ordinary crimes on the basis that the former are *mala prohibita* (prohibited wrongs) and the latter are *mala in se* (moral wrongs). Regulatory crimes, it was suggested, should be thought of in 'instrumental means-ends terms', as not embodying quasi-moral values such as 'justice, fairness, right, and wrong' (see N. Lacey, 'Criminalisation as Regulation: the role of the criminal law' in C. Parker et al. (eds), *Regulating Law* (Oxford University Press, 2004), p. 145). Regulatory crimes were viewed as 'quasi-administrative matters' that did not attract significant moral opprobrium or stigmatise those convicted (see F. McAuley and P. McCutcheon, *Criminal Liability* (Round Hall, 2000), p. 341). It has also been argued that regulatory crimes are more likely to be victimless (or at least not have a readily identifiable victim). Furthermore, and as noted earlier, it is suggested that regulatory offences for the most part do not embody a punitive or sanctioning model of justice, preferring instead to favour compliance strategies.

2.2   The Definition and Causes of White Collar Crime

Edwin Sutherland is reported to be the pioneer of white collar criminology. He suggested that white collar crime was 'a crime committed by a person of respectability and high social status in the course of his occupation' (see *White Collar Crime* (Dryden Press, 1949), p. 9), thus challenging the stereotypical assumptions about all crime being committed by the lower classes. He went on to note that the 'financial cost of white collar crime is probably several times as great as the financial cost of all the crimes which are customarily regarded as the "crime problem"' ('White Collar Criminality' (1940) 5(1) Am. Sociol. Rev. 1–12 at 5). More significantly, Sutherland also emphasised (*ibid.*, at 5) the impact of such crime on society:

> The financial loss from white collar crime, great as it is, is less important than the damage to social relations. White-collar crimes violate trust and therefore create distrust, which lowers social

morale and produces social disorganisation on a large scale. Other crimes produce relatively little effect on social institutions or social organisation.

A key point for Sutherland was to emphasise (*ibid.*, at 11–2) the idea that white collar criminality was real criminality. It may not feature in debates about the crime problem or on the law and order agenda, but this was a mere labelling matter: 'white collar criminality differs from lower class criminality principally in an implementation of the criminal law which segregates white-collar criminals administratively from other criminals'. The fact that it is not ordinarily called crime is facilitated by a degree of remoteness as it is far removed from one's immediate experience. If an individual overpays for goods because of price fixing, or is overcharged by banks, there is not a perception that s/he is marked out specifically as a crime victim. If, however, the same individual was robbed on the street of this money, the perception of what occurred, and the label that would attach would be different.

Defining white collar crime is problematic. As Sutherland suggested, it is 'a crime committed by a person of respectability and high social status in the course of his occupation'. There are a number of elements to this definition. It is a crime—this is an obvious element but it is often forgotten. It is *committed by persons of respectability*—that is someone with no convictions for non-white collar crime. But should it also not include corporations where they engage in criminal wrongdoing? For example, the Law Reform Commission recommended in 2005 that a corporation should be liable for manslaughter if the prosecution proves that it was grossly negligent in a way which caused death (LRC, *Report on Corporate Killing* (LRC 77-2005)). It is committed by individuals *of high social status*. Is this not problematic—are environmental offences, for example, always committed by persons of high social status? It is committed in the *course of his/her occupation*. This relates to offences such as price fixing, overcharging, false accounting, charging for unnecessary work, pilfering, bribery, money laundering, misuse of computers, telephone, photocopier, time fiddling, insider dealing, and so on. But what about tax evasion? This would not be covered by Sutherland's definition. Moreover, when false claims are made against insurance companies, this is not made in the course of employment. Can we also include another element besides Sutherland's four—*a violation of trust*? (K. Williams, *Criminology* (Oxford University Press, 2001), p. 64). Other commentators place emphasis on the organisational or economic attributes of white collar crime. It is clear therefore that considerable disagreement exists about the range of misconduct that would fall within the definition. In order to avoid the straight-jacket of overly prescriptive accounts, some commentators have accordingly attempted to develop typologies of the forms of crime that may fit under the general penumbra of white collar crime. These include: financial offences (from share dealing to bribery to tax evasion); offences against consumers (price fixing, illegal sales, unfit goods); crimes against employees; and crimes against the environment. (S. Tombs, 'Corporate Crime' in C. Hale et al. (eds), *Criminology* (Oxford University Press, 1940), pp. 267–87 at 269).

If there are tensions in relation to the definition of white collar crime, it is also the case that there is no settled agreement on causation. Whilst there is consensus that theories of crime that focus on poverty or poor socialisation cannot account for the phenomenon of white collar crime, no criminological approach has emerged to dominate the landscape. Instead, a variety of approaches can be employed, the merits of which may vary depending on ideological standpoint or the circumstances of individual cases.

To begin with, one can refer to 'classicism or rational choice theory'. This approach presupposes that crime is based on calculative reasoning, in which the actor coldly weighs up the perceived benefits and ranges them against the expected costs (likelihood and consequences of detection). As Charles Murray, for example, notes: '...offenders are extremely pragmatic. Their calculations seemed to be based on a hard headed appreciation of the facts' (see 'The Physical Environment and Community Control of Crime' in J. Wilson (ed.), *Crime and Public Policy* (ICS Press, 1983), p. 115). Similarly Richard Posner (*Economic Analysis of Law* (Little, Brown and Company, 1972), p. 365) would suggest that 'a criminal is someone who has chosen to engage in criminal activity because the expected utility of such activity to him, net of expected costs, is greater than that of any legitimate alternative activity. His calculation of advantages can be altered by changing any of a number of factors and the severity of the punishment, in the event punishment is imposed, in turn affects the expected cost of punishment.'

Weak regulation or non-enforcement therefore provides a fertile ground for white collar criminality.

Some criminologists would suggest that white collar crime can be explained by 'differential association', i.e. criminal behaviour is learnt behaviour. If an individual is in an environment where there is a surplus of favourable dispositions to law violation over unfavourable dispositions, this may contribute to his or her involvement in crime. This learning, and exposure to different definitions regarding the appropriateness or otherwise of certain behaviours, emerges out of our various associations. These associations vary by frequency, duration (a lot of time spent in the workforce), priority (loyalty to the firm), and intensity ('everyone in the trade is doing it'). As Edwin Sutherland notes: 'white collar criminality, just as other systematic criminality, is learned; that it is learned in direct or indirect association with those who already practice the behaviour; and that those who learn this criminal behaviour are segregated from frequent and intimate contacts with law-abiding behaviour. Whether a person becomes a criminal or not is determined largely by the comparative frequency and intimacy of his contacts with the two types of behaviour. This may be called the process of differential association' (see 'White Collar Criminality' (1940) 5(1) Am. Sociol. Rev. 1–12 at 10–11). Two criminologists, Gresham Sykes and David Matza, argue that criminals also learn 'techniques' that enable them to 'weaken' the hold society places over them, and to justify their wrongdoing. These techniques act as defence mechanisms that discharge the wrongdoer from the constraints associated with moral order. This is particularly true of white collar offenders who are likely to perceive themselves as conventional law-abiding citizens and not typecast as criminals. There are five such techniques: *denial of responsibility* ('I was following corporate orders'); *denial of injury* ('I did not cause any harm'); *denial of the victim* ('there is no real victim'); *condemnation of the condemners* ('they are all at it'); and, *appeal to higher loyalties* ('the company depends on me, what was I going to do?') ('Techniques of Neutralisation: a theory of delinquency' (1957) 22 Am. Sociol. Rev. 664–70).

Some also support the view that white collar crime is caused by 'strain'. Structurally induced strain in society is created through an emphasis on economic success, the pursuit of individual self-interest, competitiveness, and materialism. In the world of business, the pressure to win market share, exceed targets, and increase profits are compelling inducements. White collar crime can thus be seen as an innovative response on the part of businesses when individuals and institutions are unable to achieve their goals through legitimate channels. In these circumstances, and aware of the disjunction between institutionalised aspirations (pressures to maximise profit, growth, efficiency) and the availability of legitimate opportunities, white collar criminals will 'innovate' in order to achieve institutional goals. As Robert Merton notes, ' on the top economic levels, the pressure towards innovation not infrequently erases the distinction between business-like strivings this side of the mores and sharp practices beyond the mores ' (see 'Social Structure and Anomie' (1938) 3 Am. Sociol. Rev. 672–82 at 677). If the institution, or society, values and rewards the goal of achievement over the means by which it is attained, criminal acts may well be forgiven, understood as 'being part of the business'.

Finally, those who support 'labelling or Marxist' perspectives would draw attention to the fact that it is a mistake to see deviance simply as the infraction of some agreed rule (positivism). To do so is to ignore the fact that what constitutes crime is to some extent a product of the capacity of powerful groups to impose their definitions of crime on the behaviour of other groups. In other words, crime is not a pre-given, objective concept; rather it has an open texture, a negotiable and fluid status that allows it to be shaped to particular ends. As Howard Becker noted (*The Outsiders* (Free Press, 1963), p. 9): '[s]ocial groups create deviance by making the rules whose infraction constitutes deviance, and by applying those rules to a particular people and labelling them as outsiders'. In Ireland, Ciaran McCullagh ('Getting the Criminals We Want: the social production of the criminal population' in P Clancy (ed.), *Irish Society: sociological perspectives* (IPA, 1995), pp. 411–2) has suggested:

> The law making process is the means through which the criminal label is distributed in society. As it operates in Ireland, the process of law making distributes this level in an uneven manner. It sanctions some kinds of socially harmful behaviour and ignores others. It is aided and abetted by an enforcement system that devotes more resources to the pursuit of some kinds of law-breaking than

others... The end product of this system, is a criminal population which contains a disproportionate number of those who are poor, uneducated and unskilled.

2.3   The Failure to Treat White Collar Crime Seriously

It has long been felt that the rich and powerful are relatively immunised from the full reach of criminal law. W.G. Carson ('White Collar Crime and the Enforcement of Factory Legislation' (1970) 10(4) B. J. Crim. 383–90 at 384), for example, in examining white collar crime in factories in England in 1970 noted:

> The behaviour of persons of respectability and upper socio-economic class frequently exhibits all the essential attributes of crime but it is only very rarely dealt with as such. Systems of criminal justice favour certain economically and politically powerful groups and disfavour others, notably the poor and unskilled who comprise the bulk of the visible criminal population.

Similarly, the French philosopher Michel Foucault (*Discipline and Punish: the birth of the prison* (Penguin, 1991), p. 276) suggested:

> it would be hypocritical or naïve to believe that the law was made for all in the name of all; that it would be more prudent to recognise that it was made for the few and that it was brought to bear upon others; that in principle it applies to all citizens, but that it is addressed principally to the most numerous and least enlightened classes; that in the courts society as a whole does not judge one of its members, but that a social category with an interest in order judges another that is dedicated to disorder: 'Visit the places where people are judged, imprisoned or executed... One thing will strike you everywhere; everywhere you see two quite distinct classes of men, one of which always meets on the seats of accusers and judges, the other on the benches of the accused'... Law and justice do not hesitate to proclaim their necessary class dissymmetry.

For Foucault, then, criminality and penality were 'ways of handling illegalities, of laying down the limits of tolerance, of giving free rein to some, of putting pressure on others, of excluding a particular section' (*ibid.*, at 272). This made it possible to 'leave in the shade' certain crimes that do not follow the 'police-prosecutions-prisons' trajectory. The following vignettes are an indicator of the extent to which dissymmetry exists in Ireland in relation to perceptions of criminal wrongdoing:

- 'A Mayo farmer who pleaded guilty to seven counts of making incorrect tax returns between 1991 and 1998 and who failed to declare an investment of almost €20,000 in an offshore account received a suspended prison sentence. The offender owned land worth more than €3 million, despite having declared an annual income of just £400 over a 10-year period in the 1980s and 1990s. He held a number of bogus non-resident accounts and accounts in the names of deceased persons. The week before his case came to court he paid €316,000 to the Revenue Commissioners. According to a newspaper report about the case, the criminal was described by his parish priest as a "good, decent, honest-to-goodness" person who worked hard. The priest added that he had never seen the offender's wife without wellingtons on her when he called to the house' (S. Kilcommins et al., *Crime, Punishment and the Search for Order in Ireland* (IPA, 2004), pp. 132–3).

- 'Those who are tempted to make serious breaches of company law have little reason to fear detection and prosecution. As far as enforcement is concerned, the sound of the enforcer's footsteps on the beat is simply never heard' ('Working Group on Company Law Compliance and Enforcement' (1998), para. 2.5).

- 'The costs of crime investigated by the Revenue Commissioners far exceed the costs of street crime. The Whitaker Committee estimated that the losses incurred through white-collar crime in 1984 were more than ten times the value of all stolen property recorded by the Gardaí... The total value of property stolen in burglaries, larcenies and robberies in 2002 was €97 million. In the same year, seven times as much money was collected as a result of investigations into just three waves of illegal activity involving some of Ireland's most influential citizens... the DIRT and bogus non-resident account investigation (over €600 million); unauthorised offshore investments sold by National Irish Bank (€43 million);

and the Ansbacher deposits (€21 million)' (S. Kilcommins et al., *Crime, Punishment and the Search for Order in Ireland* (IPA, 2004), at p. 131).

- 'In a report on corruption in Ireland from 2006 to 2009 [Transparency International], concluded that there is very little of what it calls "petty" corruption such as the bribing of officials...What it did find however is that "Ireland is regarded by domestic and international observers as suffering high levels of legal corruption". It defines this as situations where political policy and political decisions are "believed" to be influenced by personal connections, patronage, political favours and donations to politicians and political parties. It sees the risks of corruption as high in relation to appointments to public bodies, a power in the control of individual ministers, in relation to the funding of political parties where "influence selling has yet to be outlawed", where political lobbying is unregulated, where political parties do not have to publish accounts and where the public contracting system is open to "significant abuse".' (See C. McCullagh, 'Two Tier Society; Two Tier Crime; Two Tier Justice' in S. Kilcommins and U. Kilkelly (eds), *Regulatory Crime in Ireland* (Firstlaw, 2010), p. 150.)

However, there has been progress in this regard in recent years including the enactment of the Electoral (Amendment) (Political Funding) Act 2012 and the Regulation of Lobbying Act 2015. The former provides for the disclosure of accounts by political parties and the maintenance of records underpinning those accounts while the 2015 Act provides for the establishment of a register of persons who carry on lobbying activities and the imposition of restrictions on involvement in lobbying by certain former designated public officials. In a recent review of Ireland's implementation of Chapter III of the United Nations Convention against Corruption (which relates to criminalisation and law enforcement), the Evaluation Team also noted a number of successes including the provision of comprehensive whistle-blower protection by the Protected Disclosures Act 2014 and the extensive nature of current anti-bribery legislation. Challenges remain, however, and the Evaluation Team recommended the swift adoption of the Criminal Justice (Corruption) Bill 2012 which will update bribery offences, provide for the liability of corporate bodies for the corrupt actions of their directors, employees, and agents, and outlaw trading in influence.

2.4   Should Criminalisation and Imprisonment be Employed at All in Relation to White Collar Crime?

Some commentators in looking at white collar crime argue that, where possible, we should not use the full force of the criminal law, the implication being that a sanctioning approach to wrongdoing is inefficient and likely to dampen the entrepreneurial spirit. Instead compliance strategies should be employed to govern white collar wrongdoing. These compliance techniques involve persuasion and dialogue, facilitate good working relationships, thereby producing more efficient outcomes. For example, the DPP, James Hamilton, argues for the increased use of administrative sanctions. The advantage of employing such measures would be that the criminal law would not be cluttered up with provisions which did not 'always carry the same moral stigma as convictions for the core criminal offences' (J. Hamilton, 'Do we need a system of administrative sanctions in Ireland?' in S. Kilcommins and U. Kilkelly (eds), Regulatory Crime in Ireland (Firstlaw, 2010), pp. 15–28, at 17). Moreover, the current levels of criminal penalties, particularly fines, do not adequately reflect the benefit to the wrongdoer, and therefore do not adequately deter. Finally, he suggests that running complex regulatory issues before lay juries is a difficult exercise (*ibid.*, at 21). Professor Irene Lynch Fannon makes a similar point ('Controlling Risk Taking: whose job is it anyway?' in S. Kilcommins and U. Kilkelly (eds), *Regulatory Crime in Ireland* (Firstlaw, 2010), pp. 113–27). She suggests that the burden of proof in criminal cases makes it difficult to obtain prosecutions. Secondly, if criminal prosecutions are pursued, it will inevitably mean more litigation given that the individuals involved 'will have the resources to test every legal argument' (*ibid.*, at 115). There would also be an increased number of constitutional challenges. Finally, she notes 'that there does not seem to be any great enthusiasm for incarceration as a means of dealing with white collar criminals' (*ibid.*, at 116). She goes on to suggest that 'the possibility of imposing a more effective civil sanction which meets and regulates the behaviour at stake, instead of worrying about a less than effective criminal sanction following an expensive criminal trial is compelling' (*ibid.*, at 127). This suggestion echoes the sentiments of the Macrory report (R. Macrory, *Regulatory Justice, Making Sanctions Effective* (Cameron May, 2008) in the UK in 2008 where it was stated:

> [c]riminal prosecution may not be, in all circumstances, the most appropriate sanction to ensure that non-compliance is addressed, any damage is remedied or behaviour is changed. The availability of other more flexible and risk based tools may result in achieving better regulatory outcomes.

Similarly, Professor Sandeep Gopalan, in a consultation session held in November 2010 on white collar crime as part of the Department of Justice and Law Reform's White Paper on Crime, warned against the over-criminalisation of conduct that was traditionally dealt with by other areas of the law. He described the effects of the criminalisation of white collar crime in the following terms:

> it undermines the coercive power of the criminal law, dilutes its expressive power, over-deters otherwise desirable business activities, conflates blameworthiness with imprisonment, creates incentives for prosecutors to abuse their powers, fuels an appetite for enhancing prison terms, increases social costs and punishes people for actions that in some instances are not even civil wrongs, let alone undertaken with the taint of moral wrongfulness.

He also alluded to the disproportionate burden of conviction on white collar offenders. In particular he suggested that that if the cost of imprisonment is the same for offenders with different earning capacities, imprisoning those with very high earning capacities is a waste of social capital, especially if the objectives of incarceration can be achieved through other means.

There is merit in these arguments. The line between poor business decision-making and criminal activity is far from clear cut. Moreover, white collar crime is hard to detect because it often occurs in private, behind closed corporate doors. It is also the case that proof is difficult in these cases, and often resource intensive. As was noted in the White Paper on Crime, Criminal Sanctions Discussion document, 'white collar offenders are more likely to have assets and to be in a position to pay fines, and to provide substantial economic restitution to their victims. From society's perspective, this may be preferable to imposing a prison sentence'.

Others like Shane Kilcommins and Barry Vaughan would suggest that whilst compliance and civil strategies should be accommodated where possible, one must also be committed to supporting criminal sanctioning strategies that send out the message to white collar criminals that their wrongdoing is treated seriously by society and will, if the circumstances warrant it, result in imprisonment like it does for street crimes (S. Kilcommins and B. Vaughan, 'The Rise of the Regulatory Irish State' in S. Kilcommins and U. Kilkelly (eds), *Regulatory Crime in Ireland* (Firstlaw, 2010), pp. 90–1). To begin with, the possibility of imprisonment for white collar crime is a mistake for a number of reasons. First, they argue that our ordinary criminal justice system is founded on the notion that public protection and security are 'essential goods' that are necessary for our self-preservation, well-being, and happiness. Most people would agree that we need a system of justice that will enable us to flourish and go about our lives free from the threat of injury or harm (such as robberies, rapes, assaults, burglaries, etc.). What is striking, however, is that the perception stills exists in Ireland that white collar crime does not threaten our security in the same way that street crime does. This is a mistake. Though it may appear more remote, more victimless, and may often be less dramatic, Kilcommins and Vaughan argue that misconduct in the banking and corporate sectors, in the workplace, in the environment, in the political arena and in the distortion of competition in the market poses as much, if not more, of a threat to our everyday lives as ordinary crime (with the potential to affect more people). Our security can be affected in a myriad of different ways by misconduct of this nature including, among other things, workplace injuries, loss of equal opportunity, loss of competition, loss of jobs, loss of reputation and the consequent devaluation of share prices and pension funds, threats to the environment, increased taxation, and increased costs for consumers. As the vignettes documented earlier reveal, Irish society has adopted a very narrow understanding of what constitutes a threat to its security, fastened to a very traditional outlook that views white collar wrongdoing as having rather benign effects. We quickly need to develop a more nuanced understanding that jettisons such traditional thinking. Jurgen Habermas, in a book entitled, *Between Facts and Norms* (Polity Press, 2008 repr.), noted that we need to move our legal system away from 'personal references and towards system relations'. These include: 'protection from environmental destruction, protection from radiation poisoning or lethal genetic damage; and, in general, protection from the uncontrolled side effects of large technological operations, pharmaceutical products, scientific experimentation, and so forth' (*ibid.*, 432–5).

Once we recognise the seriousness of white collar wrongdoing, then we must also recognise that compliance strategies alone cannot best guarantee our security. A compliance model of justice (negotiation, persuasion, and so on) speaks primarily to the 'good man' (who seeks to act in good faith and employs the law as a normative guide to conduct and action), not the 'bad man' who seeks to evade the strictures of the law. In order to encapsulate both forms of conduct, the compliance model must also be supported by a sanctioning model that includes the use of imprisonment.

To suggest otherwise would be to endorse a two-tier system of justice, something that would make a mockery of the notion of equality for all citizens before the law. If we accept the potential deterrent possibilities of imprisoning offenders for ordinary, often less serious, street crimes, then as a matter of principle we have to be prepared to accept that prison can also act as a similar deterrent for very serious white collar wrongdoing.

Finally, we should not underestimate the powerful cathartic effects that the proper use of criminal law can provide in society. Many Irish citizens have grown weary of 'wink and nod' politics, 'golden circles', 'golden handshakes', massive spends on tribunals with little or no real consequences, and the degree to which the rich and powerful appear to be immunised from the full reach of the law. In these circumstances the criminal law—and the punishments that follow it—can act as a platform for the expression of collective outrage. The criminal law is designed to uphold moral sensibilities and it permits a powerful message to be conveyed in relation to the anger felt by ordinary citizens about the commission of certain crimes. It also acts as an important safety valve, limiting the 'demoralising effects' on society of the consequences of serious misconduct. Of course, in saying this, we should be careful not to employ the criminal law to scapegoat individuals, to facilitate intolerance and repression, or to punish excessively. The courts, however, have developed a comprehensive jurisprudence (largely in the street crime field) for ensuring fairness of procedures and proportionately of punishments that should allay any concerns we have in this regard.

2.5   Regulatory Crime in Ireland

There are a number of interesting characteristics about the current use of these regulatory strategies in Ireland. Since the 1990s, we have increasingly witnessed the extensive use of regulatory strategies in areas such as competition law, environmental protection, health and safety law, and consumer and corporate affairs (see C. Scott, 'Regulatory Crime: History, Functions, Problems, Solutions' in S. Kilcommins and U. Kilkelly (eds), *Regulatory Crime in Ireland* (Firstlaw, 2010), pp. 63–86 at 69). An official report produced by the Better Regulation Unit in 2007 found that there were 213 bodies with statutory regulatory powers. These strategies are supported by a wide range of criminal sanctions available summarily and on indictment.

2.5.1   INCREASED GOVERNANCE

First, the emergence of this regulatory criminal framework is significantly different from the unified monopolies of centralised control underpinning policing and prosecution in the modern state. Arguably these new techniques and strategies can be seen as part of a pattern of more, rather than less, governance, but taking 'decentred', 'at-a-distance' forms. Prior to the nineteenth century, the institution of local policing was heavily orientated towards the 'creation of an orderly environment, especially for trade and commerce' (see J. Braithwaite, *Neoliberalism or Regulatory Capitalism* (Regulatory Institutions Network, 2005), pp. 13–14). It did not focus exclusively on offences against persons and property, but also included the regulation of 'customs, trade, highways, foodstuffs, health, labour standards, fire, forests and hunting, street life, migration and immigration communities' (see J. Braithwaite, 'The New Regulatory State and the Transformation of Criminology' (2000) 40 Brit. J. Criminol. 222–38 at 225). Throughout the nineteenth century, however, the state very gradually began to monopolise and separate the prosecutorial and policing functions, particularly for serious crimes. In terms of policing, this meant the following:

> Uniformed paramilitary police were preoccupied with the punitive regulation of the poor to the almost total exclusion of any interest in the constitution of markets and the just regulation of commerce, became one of the most universal of globalised regulatory models. So what happened to the business regulation? From the mid-19th century, factories inspectorates, mines inspectorates, liquor licensing boards, weights and measures inspectorates, health and sanitation, food inspectorates and countless others were created to begin to fill the vacuum left by constables now concentrating only on crime. Business regulation became variegated into many specialist regulatory branches (J. Braithwaite, *Neoliberalism or Regulatory Capitalism* (Regulatory Institutions Network, 2005), pp. 15–16).

In Ireland, these specialist agencies included the Bacon Marketing Board, the Irish Tourist Board, the Racing Board, the Health Authorities, CIE, Bord na gCon, and the Opticians Board.

Similarly during the course of the nineteenth century conflicts were no longer viewed as the property of the parties most directly affected. Previously strong stakeholder interests in the prosecution process, such as victims and the local community, were gradually colonised in the course of the nineteenth century by a state apparatus that acted for rather than with the public. Now, however, the Office of the DPP is, to some extent, increasingly losing its monopoly role. The number of administrative agencies that have entered the criminal justice arena, colonising the power to investigate regulatory crimes in specific areas and to prosecute summarily, has increased dramatically in Ireland in recent years. They include: the Revenue Commissioners, the Competition Authority, the Director of Consumer Affairs, the Environmental Protection Agency, the Health and Safety Authority, and the Office of the Director of Corporate Enforcement. Significantly, these agencies have both investigative and prosecution functions, with each pursuing their own agendas, policies, and practices. For example, between 2001 and 2012 the Competition Authority investigated price fixing by heating oil companies in the west of Ireland; 18 convictions were secured as a result of the investigation, including the first ever jury conviction for a price-fixing cartel in Ireland and Europe. Suspended custodial sentences were imposed by the courts ranging from six months to two years, in addition to fines ranging from €1,500 to €30,000. The National Employment Rights Authority can also initiate summary criminal prosecutions where a breach of employment rights legislation has been identified. In 2014, NERA initiated 82 prosecutions, a slight decrease from the 84 prosecutions initiated in 2013.

The Office of Environmental Enforcement within the Environmental Protection Agency (EPA) is dedicated to the implementation and enforcement of environmental legislation in Ireland. For example, on 19 February 2014 the EPA prosecuted Oxigen Environmental at Dundalk District Court. The Company pleaded guilty to a variety of offences including '[f]ailing to ensure that the activities were carried out in a manner such that emissions did not result in significant impairment of or significant interference with the environment beyond the facility boundary'. On hearing details of the offences Judge Brennan convicted the company and imposed a fine of €1,000. Costs of €9,000 were also awarded.

Similarly, the Food Safety Authority of Ireland enforces food safety legislation in Ireland. Since 2005 all enforcements are served by the Health Service Executive. In July 2014, for example, the HSE prosecuted Cameo Cinema Limited in Wexford for breach of EC (Hygiene of Foodstuffs) Regulations, 2006 (SI No. 369 of 2006). A fine of €1,000 was imposed with costs of €800 and expenses of €250.

The Health and Safety Authority can also prosecute cases summarily. On 25 March 2013, for example, Henkel Ireland Limited pleaded guilty to a charge under the Safety, Health and Welfare at Work Act 2005. The case related to an exhaust ventilation system for the company which was ineffective, badly designed, and poorly maintained, leading to chronic employee exposure to hazardous chemical agents. A fine of €3,000 was imposed in Dublin District Court.

Prosecuting a trader who has broken the law is also the ultimate sanction available to the National Consumer Agency. This power is available under the National Consumer Act 2007. In June 2014, for example, Mr Timmy Keane, a car salesman operating at VK Motors, in Harold's Cross, Dublin, was convicted at Dublin District Court of a breach of the Consumer Protection Act 2007 involving the provision of false information in relation to a vehicle's mileage. Mr Keane was fined €500 and ordered to pay compensation of €7,000. VK Motors Ltd was also convicted and fined €500.

The primary function of the Enforcement Unit of the Office of the Director of Corporate Enforcement is to gather evidence to support the possible initiation of criminal proceedings in cases of suspected breaches of company law. This work includes: determining which cases should be initiated; defining the most appropriate proceedings; instructing counsel; preparing case papers; and managing case execution and considering appeals. Principally, the above areas involve the initiation of summary prosecutions at District Court level but the enforcement unit may also involve assisting the DPP where cases have been referred there for decision as to whether prosecutions on indictment should be commenced.

In *The Director of Corporate Enforcement v Brian Scannell of Brian Scannell & Company*, 20 May 2015, the defendant was charged with five offences, including four under s. 242(1) of the Companies Act 1990, and one charge related to having acted as a Statutory Auditor when not approved to do so contrary to Regulations 21 and 23 of the European Communities (Statutory Audits) (Directive 2006/43/EC) Regulation 2010; SI No. 220 of 2010. On a plea of guilty, the court convicted the defendant of all five offences and imposed fines totalling €8,500. Similarly, in *The Director of Corporate Enforcement v Lauri Quinn*, 1 April 2014, the defendant was charged with acting as auditor of four companies when not qualified to do so contrary to s. 187(1) of the Companies Act 1990 and with completing and producing false reports as the auditors of those same companies contrary to s. 242(1) of the Companies Act 1990. The defendant pleaded guilty and was convicted of seven offences pursuant to s. 187 and a further seven charges pursuant to s. 242. A fine of €1,500 was imposed and the defendant was directed to pay prosecution costs of €1,250. Similarly, in *The Director of Corporate Enforcement v McEvoy's Self Service Drapery Limited*, 3 February 2011, the defendant was charged with five offences under s. 202 of the Companies Act 1990, which requires the keeping of proper books of account. On a plea of guilty, the court convicted the defendant of five offences under s. 202 of the Companies Act 1990, imposed fines totalling €3,000, and directed the defendant to pay prosecution costs of €1,115.

All of these administrative agencies that have entered the criminal justice arena represent more criminal regulation by the state, as well as of the state, rather than any 'hollowing out' of the state (J. Braithwaite, *Neoliberalism or Regulatory Capitalism* (Regulatory Institutions Network, 2005), p. 26). This enlargement in scope, however, is fragmented in nature, occupying diverse sites and modes of operation. Despite extensive powers to share information, there is no unifying strategy across the agencies or with other law enforcement institutions such as the DPP or Gardaí. Staffing levels, resources, workloads, and working practices vary from agency to agency. Indeed, and apart from respective annual reports, there is little in the way of an accountability structure overseeing the policy choices of the various regulatory agencies, the manner in which they invoke their considerable investigative and enforcement powers, or the way in which information is shared between them and with the Gardaí.

2.5.2   INSTRUMENTALISM

Many aspects of regulatory crime operate in opposition to the general trend of paradigmatic criminal law which permits general defences, demands both a conduct element and a fault element, and respects procedural standards such as a legal burden of proof beyond reasonable doubt. Pure doctrines of subjective culpability and the presumption of innocence are increasingly abandoned within this streamlined regulatory framework to make up for difficulties of proof in complex cases.

The increasingly instrumental nature of criminal legal regulation is evident, for example, in the introduction of 'reverse onus' provisions that require the accused to displace a presumption of guilt. Section 271(2) of the Companies Act 2014, for example, provides that where the defendant was aware of the basic facts, it 'shall be presumed that the defendant permitted the default' unless s/he can establish that s/he took all reasonable steps to prevent it or that by reason of circumstances beyond his control s/he was unable to do so. Prior to the enactment of s. 100 of the Company Law Enforcement Act 2001, which amended s. 383(2) of the 1963 Companies Act, s. 383 of the 1963 Companies Act required the prosecution in such cases to prove that the officer 'knowingly and wilfully' authorised or permitted the default refusal or contravention (see G. Bohan, 'Radical Change—Some Key Features of the Company Law Enforcement Act 2001' (2002) 15(1) Irish Tax Review 63–8).

Similarly, s. 81 of the Safety, Health and Welfare at Work Act 2005 now provides that in any proceedings for an offence under the Act consisting of a failure to comply with a duty or requirement to do something so far as is reasonably practicable, 'it shall be for the accused to prove' that it was not reasonably practicable to do more than was in fact done to satisfy the duty or requirement. Section 8(6) of the Competition Act 2002 makes the directors of an undertaking, its management or anyone acting in a similar capacity liable for criminal wrongdoing under the Act. Indeed s. 8(7) makes a presumption that such a person has consented, 'until the contrary is proved', to the doing of the acts by the undertaking which infringe s. 6 (the prevention, restriction or distortion of competition in trade in any goods or services) and s. 7 (any abuse of a dominant position in trade for any goods or services) of the Act. Section 6(2) of 2002 Act also creates a presumption that:

> an agreement between competing undertakings, a decision made by an association of competing undertakings or a concerted practice engaged in by competing undertakings the purpose of which is to
>
> a)   directly or indirectly fix prices with respect to the provision of goods or services to persons not party to the agreement, decision or concerted practice,
>
> b)   limit output or sales, or
>
> c)   share markets or customers,
>
> has as its object the prevention, restriction or distortion of competition in trade in any goods or services in the state or in any part of the state or within the common market, as the case may be, unless the defendant proves otherwise.

The system of justice that applies in the regulatory realm is thus more exculpatory in orientation than its ordinary criminal counterpart.

It is also evident in the instrumental fault element requirements of criminal regulation. The attachment of subjective mental element to wrongdoing in conventional criminal law is often severed in the regulatory criminal arena where objective standards of culpability apply. Section 223(1) of the Companies Act 2014, for example, states that it is the duty of each director of a company to ensure that the company complies with all the requirements of the Companies Acts. As such, officers are personally responsible for ensuring compliance. If it is demonstrated that a company has committed a criminal offence, and the officer was aware of the basic facts, s/he must prove that s/he has not permitted the breach and has taken all reasonable steps to prevent it under s. 271(2) of the Companies Act 2014. Similarly, s. 58 of the Criminal Justice (Theft and Fraud Offences) Act 2001 provides that any company officer or any person purporting to act in that capacity may be convicted of an offence under the Act (such as false accounting, suppression of documents) if it is proved that the offence was carried out with his/her consent, connivance, or is attributable to his/her neglect. Under s. 80 of the Health, Safety and Welfare at Work Act 2005, where a health and safety offence has been committed by a body corporate, and that offence is shown to have been committed with the consent or connivance of, or to have been attributable to any neglect on the part of any director, that person may be prosecuted in addition to the corporate body. The seizure of the proceeds of crime too is premised on the notion that criminals often put themselves beyond the reaches of the ordinary criminal code, by not becoming directly involved in the commission of offences and by strict enforcement of codes of secrecy. Seizure and taxation of criminal assets is a means by which to lift the veil and 'get at' the controlling and guiding minds of such criminal organisations.

Moreover, any defences that might exist in the regulatory area are also more specialised than might be the case in the general defences that apply in criminal law. For example, in competition law, it is a specific defence to show that the agreement, decision or concerted practice complained of, benefited from a declaration from the Competition Authority that the practice complained of contributes to improvement in the production or distribution of goods and services; or promotes technical or economic progress. Similarly, s. 78 of the Consumer Protection Act 2007 provides a defence where the accused 'exercised due diligence and took all reasonable precautions to avoid commission of the offence' and where, in a variety of ways, the matter was not wholly within the control of the accused. Finally, some of the general duties placed on employers under the Safety, Health and Welfare at Work Act 2005 are qualified by the term 'reasonably practicable'. This means that employers have exercised all due care when, having identified the hazards and assessed the risks at their workplaces, they have put into place the necessary protective and preventive measures, and where further measures would be grossly disproportionate (having regard to unusual, unforeseeable, and exceptional circumstances).

Employing instrumentalist reasoning can give rise to difficulties, particularly in relation to constitutional justice and due process safeguards. For example, in *Kavanagh v Delaney and others* [2008] IESC 1, the respondents were directors of a company at the date of the commencement of its winding up. The first respondent, D, was the managing director of the company and the sole executive director. The fourth respondent, C, was a chartered accountant and the terms of his appointment as a non-executive director were that he should receive and review financial information from the executives of the company and attend certain directors' meetings as a non-executive director. He did not play an active part in the management of the company. According to the records produced by the directors of the company, a very large deficiency in its assets occurred during the last six months of trading for which, in the view of the applicant (the official liquidator of the company), no reasonable explanation had been given. At the time of the commencement of the winding up, initiated by C, the company was unable to pay its debts. In those circumstances the applicant was obliged by s. 150 of the Companies Act 1990 (as amended by the Company Law Enforcement Act 2001) to bring restriction proceedings in relation to all of the respondents and would be guilty of a criminal offence if he did not. Believing that C had acted honestly and responsibly in relation to the affairs of the company, the applicant petitioned the Director of Corporate Enforcement to be relieved of the obligation to make a restriction application in respect of C, but the Director refused the applicant's request without giving reasons for his refusal. In the Supreme Court, it was held *inter alia* that having regard to the need to respect C's constitutional rights, not only to fair procedures, but to his good name and the associated right to earn a living by the practice of his profession, it was not appropriate to restrict C in the circumstances. As Hardiman J. noted:

> [T]he provisions may be regarded as draconian in the sense that, by reason of s. 150(2)(a) of the 1990 Act, a restriction order must be made against a respondent unless the court is satisfied that he has acted honestly and responsibly in relation to the conduct of the affairs of the Company and is also satisfied that 'there is no other reason why it would be just and equitable' to make a restriction order. The burden is placed upon the respondent to prove, not only that he has acted responsibly and honestly in relation to the Company but to prove the negative proposition '(there is no other reason . . .)' set out in the last citation from the Statute . . .

> I must confess to some doubt as to whether this blanket reversal of the onus of proof, including a requirement to prove a negative proposition, is consistent with fundamental fairness and constitutional justice.

In *PJ Carey Contractors Limited v DPP* [2012] IR 234, s. 6 of the Safety, Health and Welfare at Work Act 1989 provides, *inter alia*, that it shall be the duty of every employer to ensure, so far as is reasonably practicable, the safety, health, and welfare at work of all his or her employees and, at s. 6(2)(d), the provision of systems of work that are planned, organised, performed, and maintained so as to be, so far as is reasonably practicable, safe, and without risk to health. Section 50 of that Act provides that in any proceedings for an offence consisting of a failure to comply with a duty or requirement to do something so far as is practicable or so far as is reasonably practicable, or to use the best practicable means to do something, it shall be for the accused to prove (as the case may be) that it was not practicable or not reasonably practicable to do more than was in fact done to satisfy the duty or requirement, or that there was no better practicable means than was in fact used to satisfy the duty or requirement. The applicant was charged with certain offences contrary to the Act of 1989, in particular under s. 6, following the collapse of a trench on a building site which had resulted in the death of an employee. During the trial, uncontroverted evidence was adduced that the system of work adopted was, as far as was reasonably practicable, safe and without risk. An application was made by the applicant to withdraw the entire case from the jury on the basis that there was no case to answer given that all the evidence called from persons who were present at the time of the accident favoured the accused. Some of the charges were withdrawn. However, the applicant was convicted of offences contrary to s. 6 of the Act of 1989 regarding the alleged failure of the accused to provide a safe system of work. The prosecutor relied on the doctrine of *res ipsa loquitur* and on s. 50 of the Act of 1989, submitting that the provision reversed the legal burden of proof onto the applicant requiring it to prove that it had adopted a safe system of work. The applicant appealed against the conviction. It was held by the Court of Criminal Appeal in allowing the appeal and setting aside the conviction, that the offence under s. 6 (2)(d) of the Act of 1989 was not complete merely on proof that the trench had collapsed. It required proof of a failure to provide a safe system of work. It was also held that s. 50 of the Act of 1989 created a reversed burden of proof which cast an evidential burden only on the accused and not a substantive onus of legal proof, and that that evidential burden had been discharged by the accused.

Hardiman J. stated:

> It appears to me that, having referred to s. 50 of the Act of 1989, the trial judge then misinterpreted its purport so as to cast a substantive onus of legal proof upon the defendant ... It appears to me that the foregoing passages envisage an obligation on the defendant to explain certain things and suggests the inadequacy of such explanation. But that is a misconstruction of the effect of s. 50 which is merely to cast an evidential, and not a legal or substantive burden on the defendant. I believe that this was an error of law by the trial judge and, that if this error had not occurred, it would have been manifest that the defendant was entitled to a direction.

Aside from reverse onus provisions, the privilege against self-incrimination may also give rise to difficulties. In *Saunders v UK* (1996) 23 EHRR 313 (ECHR), the applicant was convicted for fraud in the connection of the takeover by Guinness of Distillers. Section 434 of the Companies Act 1985 compelled him, upon pain of conviction, to furnish information to inspectors that could be admitted as evidence against him in a criminal trial for participating in illegal share support schemes. The court held by 16 to 4 that the use at Saunders's trial of statements obtained from him by the Department of Trade and Industry violated Art. 6 of the European Convention on Human Rights, particularly having regard to the privilege against self-incrimination. Closer to home, in *Re National Irish Bank* [1999] 3 IR 145, inspectors were appointed under the Companies Acts 1990 to examine the affairs of National Irish Bank. Section 10 of the Act placed a duty on officers of the company to cooperate with inspectors and to produce documents and answer questions. Section 18 provided that an answer given by a person 'may be used in evidence against him'. In the Supreme Court it was held that s. 10 did not allow evidence obtained in such circumstances to be admitted in a subsequent criminal trial. Section 29 of the Company Law Enforcement Act 2001 subsequently immunised the answers given to an authorised officer from being used in any subsequent criminal proceedings. Similarly, s. 15(10) of the Criminal Justice Act 2011 provides that any statement or admission made by a person pursuant to an order under that section is not admissible as evidence in subsequent proceedings brought against the person for an offence, other than an offence under sub-ss. (15), (16), or (17) of the Act. Section 881 of the Companies Act 2014 now provides that answers given by an individual in response to a question put to him in the exercise of specified statutory powers and/or facts provided in a statement of affairs required in a winding up may be used in evidence in any civil proceedings but not in criminal proceedings, unless the prosecution in question is for perjury. Sections 392(5) and 393(3) of the Companies Act 2014 also immunises written information given by auditors pursuant to a request from the Director from being admissible without further proof in any subsequent criminal proceedings.

In *Environmental Protection Agency v Swalcliffe Limited* [2004] IEHC 190, the accused was a company which held a waste licence, subject to certain conditions, including, *inter alia*, the requirement to keep certain records. A prosecution was brought for alleged breaches of the said licence. The prosecution sought to adduce into evidence a waste licence audit report, the contents of which were based on records maintained by the accused. The accused argued that the report and the oral evidence to be adduced thereon were inadmissible on the basis that the records upon which the material part of the audit was based were not maintained voluntarily by the accused but were maintained pursuant to the requirements of the Waste Management Act 1996. The accused argued that to the extent that any of the records contained details which suggested that the accused had committed a criminal offence under the Act of 1996, it amounted to an involuntary confession and that there was no provision under the Act of 1996 permitting the admission of such involuntary confessions. In the High Court, Kearns J. held that records brought into being as part of a scheme of regulation are admissible at trial and do not violate the principle against self-incrimination.

> In my view the privilege against self-incrimination is not involved at all in this case. The rationale for the privilege is clear. It is to protect against unreliable confessions and to protect against abuses of power by the State. Quite clearly there is both a societal and individual interest in achieving both of these protections which are linked to the value placed by society upon individual privacy, personal autonomy and dignity . . . In applying for a waste licence, the accused must be taken as having freely accepted the conditions attaching to the licence, which formed part of the entire package under the regulatory scheme. It was the accused's own free choice to participate in the particular activity and at the time they chose to do so they were well aware of their record keeping obligations and of the penalties for non-compliance with the requirements of the Act of 1996.

In a recent case, *DPP v Collins* (unreported, 27 September 2007, Circuit Court), the Revenue's attempt to produce what appeared to be compelled documents in a criminal prosecution was held to infringe the accused's right to the privilege against self-incrimination. He had been sent an initial letter in relation to undeclared tax liabilities and a bogus non-resident account which stated: 'failure to comply . . . may result in . . . a referral for investigation with a view to prosecution'. If he complied, it was indicated that he would be dealt with under s. 1086(2) of the Taxes Consolidation Act 1997, and would not be subject to criminal law. The accused made a disclosure and the Revenue authorities then sought to use some of the evidence therein as part of the criminal prosecution. This was held to violate his right to the privilege against self-incrimination (Duggan, 'Disclosure to Revenue and the Privilege Against Self-Incrimination' (2008) ITR 70).

In addition, it is felt that *mens rea* 'must be presumed to be a necessary ingredient of all serious offences' (*CC v Ireland and Others* [2006] IESC 33; The Employment Equality Bill 1996 [1997] 2 IR 321). In *Brady v Environmental Protection Agency* [2007] IEHC 58, Charleton J. at para. 41 noted: 'It is difficult to see offences of absolute or strict liability being compatible with the constitutional scheme where they go beyond the regulation of society through the imposition of small penalties based upon absolute or strict liability.'

There is also, however, some Irish and ECHR support for the view that a defence of due diligence will suffice to justify a regulatory offence of strict liability. In *CC v Ireland and Others* [2006] IESC 33, for example, this was suggested by Hardiman J. in passing (though he did not rule specifically on the matter). In particular, he referred to the cases of *R v City of Sault Sainte Marine* [1978] 85 DLR 161 and the dissenting judgment of Keane J. *in Shannon Regional Fisheries Board v Cavan County Council* [1996] 3 IR 267. Moreover, the decision of Shannon Regional Fisheries Board v Cavan County Council [1996] 3 IR 267, which held that there was no requirement of a *mens rea* element for regulatory offences, has not been expressly overruled by the judgment in CC. In terms of ECHR jurisprudence, in *Salabiaku v France* (1988) 13 EHRR 379, the European Court of Human Rights held that 'the contracting states may, under certain conditions, penalize a simple or objective fact as such irrespective of whether it results from criminal intent or from negligence'. It went on to note, however, that presumptions of fact or law should be confined within 'reasonable limits'. This may provide some degree of leeway for crimes that can be classified as regulatory in nature.

Another difficulty is the emphasis that the law of evidence traditionally places on oral testimony. This may sometimes pose a dilemma in the arena of regulatory wrongdoing where documentary trails may form a central part of an investigation. Though the Criminal Evidence Act 1992 provides for an inclusionary approach to documentary evidence in criminal proceedings, this has not as of yet been extended to civil proceedings. In practice, however, lawyers in the civil context routinely agree in advance of the hearing to admit expert reports and documentary information, as a matter of procedural convenience and mutual benefit. For example, in *Shelley-Morris v Bus Átha Cliath* [2003] 1 IR 232, a personal injuries action, the Supreme Court noted that it had been agreed between the parties that medical reports from the UK would be received into evidence in substitution for oral evidence. The Bankers' Books Evidence Act 1879 as amended provides for the admissibility of copies of entries from the books and records of banks against any person as *prima facie* evidence. There is a wide definition of bankers' books in the 1879 Act, as amended, and this includes any records used in the ordinary course of the business of a bank or used in the transfer department of a bank acting as a register of securities. It should also be noted that the principles and rules of the law of evidence apply traditionally to hard copy, paper-based documents. Electronic and automated documentary evidence currently poses more difficulties. A recent Consultation Paper on *Documentary and Electronic Evidence* (LRC CP 57—2009) recommends that documentary evidence should be admissible in civil and criminal proceedings where the court is satisfied as to its relevance and necessity. It also recommends that a technology-neutral approach should be adopted so that the term 'documentary evidence' should, in general, apply to traditional paper-based documents and to electronic documents.

Finally, in defining a crime in Ireland in cases such as *Melling v O'Mathghamhna* [1962] IR 1, the Irish courts have adopted a very traditional approach, emphasising indicia such as procedural characteristics (powers of arrest, detention, bail etc.), due process safeguards (the presumption of innocence, the right to liberty, the right to a jury trial), and punitive elements. As McGrath (J. McGrath, 'The Colonisation of Real Crime in the Name of All Crime' in S. Kilcommins and B. Vaughan (eds), *Regulatory Crime in Ireland* (Firstlaw, 2010), 60–1) notes, these 'features are often associated with traditional criminal offences. This analysis has marginalised corporate criminality, often enforced by regulatory law, from the crime debate... *Melling* and the cases following it speak to real crime so attempting to make conventional crime indicia fit into regulatory contexts is inappropriate. The jurisprudence needs to be re-evaluated and a new approach must be found.'

2.5.3   INFORMATION SHARING AND MANDATORY REPORTING

What also appears to be emerging in recent years is the increasing adoption of a more variegated approach straddling both civil and criminal jurisdictions to the detection, investigation, and punishment of offences. For example, the organisational make-up of the Criminal Assets Bureau comprises Revenue Commissioners, Department of Social Community and Family Affairs officials and Gardaí, all directing their respective competencies at proceeds from criminal activities. More specifically, s. 957 of the Companies Act 2014, for example, permits authorities including the Competition Authority, An Garda Síochána, the Revenue Commissioners, the Insolvency Service of Ireland and the Irish Takeover Panel to disclose to the Director of Corporate Enforcement.

In some instances individuals are required to become 'information reporters'. Section 42 of the Criminal Justice (Money Laundering and Terrorist Financing) Act 2010 requires the financial services industry and professional service providers (including auditors, accountants, tax advisers, legal practitioners) to report suspicious transactions to the Garda Síochána and the Revenue Commissioners (S. Horan, *Corporate Crime* (Bloomsbury Professional, 2011), pp. 1529–40). Similarly, s. 931(4) of the Companies Act 2014 requires that where a disciplinary tribunal of a recognised body of accountants has reasonable grounds for believing that a category 1 or 2 offence (both of which may be prosecuted on indictment) has been committed by a person while the person was a member of the body, the body shall inform the Director of Corporate Enforcement. A similar provision exists under s. 392 of the 2014 Act as regards the auditors of a company. Statutory auditors must notify the Registrar of Companies, who will then inform the Director of Corporate Enforcement, that they have formed the opinion that the company is contravening, or has contravened, any of ss. 281 to 285 of the Act which includes an obligation to keep or cause to be kept adequate accounting records, make those records available and to preserve those accounts for a period of at least six years.

Section 447 of the Companies Act 2014 requires a receiver in the course of a receivership to report any suspected criminal activity of company officers to the DPP and the Director of Corporate Enforcement. Section 59 of the Criminal Justice (Theft and Fraud Offences) Act 2001 provides that any professional assisting in the preparation of figures or computations which might be used in the preparation of accounts, has a duty to report acts of theft, making gain or causing loss by deception, obtaining services by deception, fraud or deception through the use of a computer, false accounting, and suppression of documents. A significant broadening in the obligation to disclose information is contained in the Criminal Justice Act 2011. Section 19 of the Criminal Justice Act 2011 makes it an offence for a person to fail to disclose information to An Garda Síochána as soon as practicable and without reasonable excuse, which the individual knows or believes might be of material assistance in '(a) preventing the commission by any other person of a relevant offence, or (b) securing the apprehension, prosecution or conviction of any other person for a relevant offence'. Section three of the Act defines 'relevant offence' broadly including offences relating to banking and finance, company law, money laundering, theft, fraud, bribery, corruption, competition, consumer protection, cybercrime, and tax collection, with 30 offences specified in Schedule 1. Upon conviction on indictment a defendant may be subject to a maximum prison sentence of five years or a fine or both.

The difficulties of prosecuting regulatory crime are well documented. In addition to facilitating exchange of information and compelling certain parties to become information reporters, the authorities are increasingly also seeking to protect and encourage witnesses to come forward and provide evidence. 'Whistle-blowers' have been crucially important in Ireland in lifting the lid on various abuses such as the care of the elderly and corruption in banks (Transparency International Ireland, *An Alternative to Silence: whistle-blower protection in Ireland* (Transparency Ireland, 2010). Encouraging such witnesses to provide information ordinarily takes two forms: protection and/or immunity. In relation to protection, s. 6 of the Unfair Dismissals Act 1977, for example, provides that a dismissal will be deemed to be unfair if it was brought about as a result of the employee making a complaint to a prosecuting authority in which he or she was likely to be a witness or the employee having made a protected disclosure. Section 26 of the Employment Permits Act 2006 provides that an employer is not permitted to penalise an employee for reporting health and safety, consumer, or employment permit breaches respectively. Similarly, s. 20 of the Criminal Justice Act 2011 provides protection for employees against penalisation or threatened penalisation for making a disclosure, giving evidence in relation to a disclosure or for giving notice of an intention to disclose information in relation to a 'relevant offence' as defined in the Act. However, there is an exemption included in the act to ensure that an employer is not prevented from carrying on the business in an efficient manner or taking actions necessary for economic, technical or organisational reasons in some circumstances.

More generally, the Protected Disclosures Act 2014 requires all public sector bodies in Ireland to put in place whistle-blowing policies which meet the requirements of the Act. Where private sector businesses have policies in place, they need to review them to ensure that they are aligned to the requirements of the Act. The Act protects 'workers' in all sectors who make a 'protected disclosure'. The term 'worker' includes employees (public and private sector), contractors, trainees, agency staff, former employees, and job seekers. 'Protected disclosure' means disclosure of relevant information, which, in the reasonable belief of the worker, tends to show one or more relevant wrongdoings and came to the attention of the worker in connection with their employment. 'Relevant wrongdoings' include the commission of an offence; non-compliance with a legal obligation; health and safety threats; misuse of public monies; mismanagement by a public official; damage to the environment; or concealment or destruction of information relating to any of the foregoing. The Act protects whistle-blowers from dismissal for having made a protected disclosure. The worker can be awarded compensation of up to five years' remuneration for unfair dismissal on the grounds of having made a protected disclosure. Other protection measures provided for in the Act include: protection from penalisation by the employer; civil immunity from action for damages and a qualified privilege under defamation law; and a right of action in tort where a whistle-blower or a member of his family experiences coercion, intimidation, harassment, or discrimination at the hands of a third party; protection of his/her identity (subject to certain exceptions).

Immunity programmes are not universal. The Competition and Consumer Protection Commission, in conjunction with the Office of the Director of Public Prosecutions, however, does operates a Cartel Immunity Programme, which provides immunity from criminal prosecution for suspected individuals who are willing to cooperate and testify on behalf of the prosecution (P. Gorecki and D. McFadden, 'Criminal Cartels in Ireland: The Heating Oil Case' (2006) 11 ECLR, 631–40). A revised Cartel Immunity Programme came into effect in 2015 which enhances the provisions available to the Commission in this regard, including removing the bar on an instigator company qualifying for immunity (C. Talbot, 'The Protected Disclosures Act 2014 and the Cartel Immunity Programme 2015' (2015) 7 Commercial Law Practitioner, 178–81).

2.5.4   POWERS

Very wide powers of entry, inspection, examination, search, seizure, and analysis are given to some of these agencies. For example, under s. 64 of the Safety, Health and Welfare at Work Act 2005, health and safety inspectors are, *inter alia*, entitled to enter any place with the consent of the occupier or with a warrant and inquire into, search, examine and inspect the place and any work activity; require records to be produced; inspect and take copies of such records; remove and retain records; and require the employer or any employee to give the inspector any information that the inspector may reasonably require for the purposes of any search, examination, investigation, inspection or inquiry. In relation to company law, s. 779 of the Companies Act 2014 empowers the Director of Corporate Enforcement to require a company to produce for inspection specified books and documents in circumstances outlined in s. 780, including circumstances which suggest that fraud, illegality or prejudice may have occurred. The constitutionality of a similar provision in s. 19 of the Companies Act 1990 was upheld in *Dunnes Stores Ireland Co v Ryan* [2002] 2 IR 60. Section 787 of the Companies Act 2014 provides that a search warrant may be issued to authorise the Director of Corporate Enforcement to enter and search premises and seize and retain any material information found on the premises or in the custody or possession of any person found on the premises.

Similarly, s. 30 of the Competition Act 2002 permits the Competition Authority to summon witnesses to attend before it, examine witnesses attending, and require such witnesses to produce any document in their power or control. Section 45(4) of the same Act permits the Competition Authority to obtain a search warrant to enter by force and seize, from a premises of suspected undertakings (and the homes of individuals involved in their management) any books, records, and documents relating to the activity of an undertaking. Persons on the premises may also be required to answer certain questions relating to the activity engaged in by the undertaking. In respect of revenue offences, the Revenue authorities have very broad powers of search and seizure and can enter a business/dwelling where a trade is being carried on without a warrant (s. 905 of the Taxes Consolidation Act 1997). Section 905(2A) of the same Act provides for the issuance of search warrants to search any premises and s. 900 provides very broad powers to require the production of books, records, and other documents which may contain information relevant to liability (J. Considine and S. Kilcommins, 'The Importance of Safeguards on Revenue Powers; another perspective' (2006) 19(6) Irish Tax Review 49–54).

In *Competition Authority v The Irish Dental Association* [2005] IEHC 361 the defendant was a company limited by guarantee which had about 1,200 members being practising dentists. The plaintiff commenced proceedings against the defendant in respect of alleged breaches of the Competition Amendment Act 2012, seeking certain declarations as well as injunctive relief. In the course of those proceedings, the plaintiff obtained a search warrant authorising it to search the defendant's business premises. The warrant wrongly made reference to the defendant being involved in the business of selling, supplying or distributing motor vehicles. The plaintiff carried out the search and seized certain documents belonging to the defendant. It was common ground that the defendant had no connection whatsoever with such a business. The defendant commenced proceedings against the plaintiff on the basis that the documents so obtained had been obtained in breach of the defendant's constitutional rights and its right to privacy, with the result that they should be declared inadmissible. The court ruled:

> Where the evidence in question was obtained purely by illegal means, there was a discretion for the court to exercise which involved balancing competing interests, unless there existed also within the circumstances of that case, 'extraordinary excusing circumstances'. If on the other hand, such evidence also involved a conscious and deliberate violation of one's constitutional rights, then in the absence of extraordinary excusing circumstances, that evidence should be disallowed.

> Applying established principles, it was clear that the plaintiff had constitutional rights and that such rights of freedom and expression, most certainly and probably also those of privacy, were not too remote so as to exclude their application to the present circumstances. In the circumstances, given that the search warrant was illegal and given the existence of those rights, the activities carried out by the plaintiff on the occasion in question, had constituted a breach of the defendant's constitutional rights. Accordingly, the court had no discretion with regard to the material in question.

More recently, the Criminal Justice Act 2011 gave power to An Garda Síochána to apply to the District Court for an order compelling the provision of documents (recorded in any form) or information 'by answering questions or making a statement containing the information' (s. 15(1)) which may assist in the investigation of a 'relevant offence' in certain circumstances. As mentioned previously, 'relevant offence' is defined broadly, including offences which may not typically be considered to be white collar offences, such as the offence of theft under s. 4 of the Criminal Justice (Theft and Fraud Offences) Act 2001.

Part 2 of the same Act, the Criminal Justice Act 2011, also includes interesting provisions relating to powers of detention. Section 7(a) amends s. 4 of the Criminal Justice Act 1984 and gives investigators the opportunity to suspend a period of detention of a person detained in respect of a 'relevant offence' where there are 'reasonable grounds for believing that it is necessary for the purpose of permitting enquiries or investigations to be made for the further and proper investigation of the offence concerned'. Detention may be suspended twice; however, not more than four months may elapse from the date the detention is first suspended. Section 8 provides the Gardaí with powers to arrest and return suspects for continuation of detention where the individual has not returned for questioning as required under the Act and makes it an offence to fail to return to a Garda station for a further period of detention for questioning. The Act also contains provisions relating to rest periods between midnight and 8 a.m. (s. 7(c)) and the right of access to legal advice (s. 9); however, these provisions have yet to be commenced.

2.5.5 SANCTIONING

There is also some evidence of a possible drift towards a more punitive approach to regulation (R. Baldwin, 'The New Punitive Regulation' (2004) 67(3) MLR 351–83). Traditionally it had been said that the focus of the sanctions for many of these regulatory offences was more 'apersonal' in nature than their ordinary counterparts. The argument was that 'these were not real crimes to which stigma should attach, but were rather in the nature of administrative regulations with non-stigmatising penalties such as fines' (N. Lacey, 'Criminalisation as Regulation: The Role of Criminal Law' in C. Parker et al. (eds), *Regulating Law* (Oxford University Press, 2004), p. 161). The traditional lack of a *mens rea* requirement operated as the 'doctrinal marker of these defendants less than fully criminal status from a social point of view' (*ibid.*). But regulatory agencies have increasingly grown considerable teeth as regards prosecution. The Law Reform Commission published a report on corporate killing in 2006 and called for the introduction of two new offences: a statutory offence of corporate manslaughter for corporate entities; and, a secondary offence (grossly negligent management causing death) for corporate officers who play a role in the commission of the offence (see also D. Aherne, 'Corporate Killing in Ireland—a new paradigm' (2004) 22 ILT 235–9).

More specifically, s. 78 of the Safety, Health and Welfare at Work Act 2005 now imposes on conviction on indictment for an offence under the Act a fine not exceeding €3 million or imprisonment for a term not exceeding two years, or both. In *DPP v O'Flynn Construction Company Limited* [2007] 4 IR 500, the Circuit Court imposed a fine of €200,000 on O'Flynn Construction Company Limited which pleaded guilty to two offences contrary to the Safety, Health and Welfare at Work Act 1989, namely failing to conduct its undertaking in such a way as to ensure so far as is reasonably practicable that persons not in its employment who might be affected thereby were not exposed to risks to their safety or health, in contravention of s. 7(1) of the Safety, Health and Welfare at Work Act 1989, and failing to signpost and lay out so as to be clearly visible and identifiable the surroundings and perimeter of a construction site, in contravention of para. 18 of the fourth schedule of the Safety, Health and Welfare at Work (Construction) Regulations, 1995, in contravention of reg. 8(1)(g) of the said Regulations, contrary to s. 48(1)(c) of the Safety, Health and Welfare at Work Act 1989. The incident giving rise to the two charges occurred at what was known as Mount Oval Village in Rochestown in Cork. In September 2001 it was a very large construction development situated on over 100 acres on which it was planned that nine separate housing estates, totalling 850 houses and some apartments plus a shopping complex would be built. Boys went into the building site and a drum of wood preservative exploded after being set on fire by some of the boys. A 9-year-old boy died. O'Flynn construction appealed against the severity of the penalty. The accused submitted that the fencing of the construction site was, at the time, reasonable in all circumstances. The prosecution accepted that the breaches of the statutory and regulatory provisions governing safety at the construction site, were not a direct cause of the tragic death of the deceased, but were significant contributing factors. In dismissing the appeal, Murray C.J. noted:

> The most serious lapse on behalf of the applicant company was the delivery onto the site of a drum containing hazardous material and leaving it placed in the open without securing it against interference by persons such as children or teenagers who ventured on to it. In the circumstances the Court is satisfied that the learned Circuit Court Judge was perfectly entitled to take a serious view of the breach by the company of the relevant statutory and regulatory provisions. The breach was aggravated by the fact that it played a significant role in the combination of circumstances that led to the fatality...

> Having taken the mitigating circumstances into account the trial judge was nonetheless entitled and indeed bound to impose a penalty that reflected the seriousness of the offence so that it applied appropriate punitive and deterrent elements. Among the elements to be taken into account in assessing the severity of a fine, whether imposed on an individual or a corporate entity, is the wealth or resources of the person or company concerned. As was found by the learned trial judge the defendants in this case are a substantial company who were involved in a very substantial construction project. It could not be said to be disproportionate to their means and resources.

On conviction on indictment for competition law offences, undertakings are liable to a fine not exceeding whichever of the following amounts is the greater, namely €5 million or 10 per cent of the turnover of the undertaking in the financial year ending in the 12 months prior to conviction. Individuals are subject to the same fine limits and/or a term of imprisonment not exceeding ten years (see s. 8 of the Competition Act 2002, as amended). Following an extensive review by the Company Law Review Group and the Director of Corporate Enforcement of the several hundred criminal offences contained in the Companies Acts, s. 871 of the Companies Act 2014 creates a four-tier categorisation of company law criminal offences. This categorisation encompasses the majority of criminal offences, to the exclusion of just the most serious offences relating to market abuse, transparency, and the law of prospectuses. Both Category 1 and 2 offences may be prosecuted summarily or on indictment, and when prosecuted on indictment Category 2 offences are punishable by a fine of up to €50,000 and/or imprisonment for up to five years and Category 1 offences will be punishable by a fine of up to €500,000 and/or a sentence of imprisonment of up to ten years. Category 3 and 4 offences will be prosecutable on a summary basis only.

While, McGrath noted in 2012 that '[c]orporate crime is rarely considered to be as harmful as ordinary crime' ((2012) 3 ICLJ 71–9, 72), a series of recent cases may indicate an increasing willingness to imprison individuals convicted of serious corporate crime (*ibid.*, 75, D. Robinson, 'Collared' (2014) 180(1) GLSI 40–3). In late March of 2009, McKechnie J., in a judgment in the Central Criminal Court which considered competition law abuses by an association of Citroen car dealers (*DPP v Duffy and Duffy Motors* (unreported, 23 March 2009, Central Criminal Court) and see also *DPP v Manning* (unreported, 9 February 2007, High Court)), noted:

> These [offences] stifle competition and discourage new entrants, damaging economic and commercial liberty...[T]hey remove price choice from the consumer, deter consumer interest in product purchase and discourage variety. They reduce incentives to compete and hamper invention...If previously our society did not frown upon this type of conduct, as it did in respect of more conventional crime, that forbearance or tolerance has eroded swiftly, as the benefits of competition law become clearer...Therefore it must be realised that serious breaches of the code have to attract serious punishment [which included imprisonment].

In *DPP v Paul Murray* [2012] IECCA 60, a case concerning social welfare fraud, Finnegan J., delivering judgment for the court, emphasised the importance of deterrence in sentencing decisions in cases involving revenue fraud. It was suggested:

> for the future guidance of sentencing courts that significant and systematic frauds directed upon the public revenue—whether illegal tax evasion on the one hand or social security fraud on the other—should generally meet with an immediate and appreciable custodial sentence.

This judgment proved controversial and in *Paul Begley v DPP* [2013] IECCA 32, the CCA rejected the contention that cases involving tax evasion should be categorised separately from other offences for sentencing purposes and 'should not be read as suggesting the establishment of any parallel rules on sentencing, relative to such crimes or as contemplating any significant adjustment on how courts should value or weigh genuine factors in mitigation' [44]. Instead [43]:

> there will be some cases where an immediate sentence is justified and others where it will not be. Everything will depend on the crime, the circumstances of its commission and the personal situation of the accused. In all cases however the ultimate conclusion will be directed by general principles.

Ultimately, Mr Begley's six-year sentence for offences relating to the fraudulent evasion of customs duty was reduced to two years by the CCA as the trial judge had failed to properly consider or weigh the mitigating factors in respect of which Mr Begley was entitled to credit. In a subsequent case, *DPP v Campbell* [2014] IECA 15, the CCA applied the principles set out in the *Begley* case and sentenced the defendant to 12 months' imprisonment in respect of each of nine sample counts representing various revenue and VAT offences, each sentence to run concurrently.

There have been other notable high-profile cases in recent times in which lengthy custodial sentences have been imposed, including a case involving former solicitor, Thomas Byrne, who was convicted of 52 offences including theft, forgery, and using a false instrument, and sentenced to 16 years' imprisonment, with four years suspended (*Irish Times*, 2 December 2013). More recently, in 2015, three former Anglo Irish Bank officials were jailed for between three years and 18 months for conspiring to conceal or alter bank accounts being sought by the Revenue Commissioners (*Irish Times*, 31 July 2015). In reaching his decision, the judge noted the difficulty in dealing with defendants of previously impeccably good character and stated that the challenge to the court was to balance the interests of the accused and the public interest.

Despite this trend towards imprisonment, a custodial sentence was not imposed in the high-profile case in 2014 involving two former Anglo Irish Bank directors, Pat Whelan and Willie McAteer. Upon conviction of offences relating to the illegal purchase of Anglo Irish shares under s. 60 of the Companies Act 1963, the men were sentenced to 240 hours community service (*Irish Times*, 31 July 2014). Judge Nolan decided that '[i]t would be most unjust to jail these two men when I feel that a State agency [the financial regulator] had led the two men into error and illegality' (*Irish Times*, 30 April 2014).

Though all of this constitutes evidence of a drift towards the greater use or threatened use of criminal sanctions, it should not be pushed too far. The area of regulatory crime still, by and large, remains predominantly orientated towards a compliance model of enforcement.

(J. McGrath, *Corporate and White Collar Crime in Ireland: A New Architecture of Regulatory Enforcement* (Manchester University Press, 2015)). This is facilitated by a wide range of strategies that favour the employment of negotiation, consultation, and persuasion, rather than an exclusively sanctioning approach that would potentially polarise the various parties involved. These strategies include audits, warning letters, notices, injunctions, guidance, binding directions, and the suspension and revocation of licences. The Consumer Protection Act 2007, for example, permits the National Consumer Agency to issue prohibition orders to businesses, to take undertakings of compliance, to issue compliance notices and fixed payment penalties, in addition to prosecution functions (A. O'Neill, 'The Consumer Protection Act 2007—Enforcing the New Rules' (2008) 26 ILT 46). In 2007 the National Consumer Agency 'dealt with thousands of complaints..., had contacts with hundreds of retailers over alleged pricing offences, but issued only three fixed penalty notices and made sixteen prosecutions'.

In 2008, the Office of the Director of Corporate Enforcement (ODCE) issued 24,000 copies of their publications, closed 850 cases on an administrative basis, made a final determination on 280 initial liquidator reports, secured 20 summary convictions, secured 20 disqualifications, and one case was successfully prosecuted by the DPP following an ODCE investigation (P. Appleby, 'Compliance and Enforcement—the ODCE perspective' in S. Kilcommins and U. Kilkelly (eds), *Regulatory Crime in Ireland* (Firstlaw, 2010), p. 186). The Environmental Protection Agency (EPA) also resolves most issues of non-compliance without the need for further enforcement actions. When compliance cannot be achieved, administrative and criminal sanctions can be employed, including notifications of non-compliance. In the years 2009–2012, there were on average 900 court prosecutions brought each year and 12,000 enforcement actions (EPA, *Focus on Environmental Enforcement in Ireland: a report for the years 2009–2012* (2014), p. 2).

Similarly, the Safety, Health and Welfare at Work Act 2005 allows the Health and Safety Authority to take actions where statutory contraventions are observed or where there is a risk of serious personal injury. These actions include:

- the issuing of an improvement direction in relation to activities to which the inspector considers may involve risk to safety or health of persons. An employer is required to respond with an improvement plan;

- the issuing of an improvement notice stating the inspector's opinion that a duty holder has contravened a provision of an Act or Regulation, and requiring that the contravention be addressed within a certain time period of not less than 14 days;

- the issuing of a prohibition notice where an inspector is of the opinion that an activity is likely to involve a risk of serious personal injury to any person. This notice takes effect immediately from when the person, on whom the notice is served, receives the notice;

- the issuing of an information notice requiring a person to present to the HSA any information specified by the notice;

- the taking of summary proceedings in the District Court in relation to an offence under any of the relevant statutory provisions;

- the preparation of evidence so that the DPP can initiate proceedings on indictment for hearing in the Circuit Court.

All of these ensure that prosecutions remain relatively rare, employed as a last-resort mechanism. As Professor Colin Scott ('Regulatory Crime: History, Functions, Problems, Solutions' in S. Kilcommins and U. Kilkelly (eds), Regulatory Crime in Ireland (Firstlaw, 2010), at p. 73) has noted:

> The enforcement strategies of enforcement agencies have been arrayed in a pyramidal approach to enforcement in which the object is to maintain as much enforcement activity as possible at the base of the pyramid... This approach is said to be effective not only with businesses which are orientated to legal compliance, but also with the 'amoral calculators' for whom compliance becomes the least costly path when they know there is a credible threat of escalation to more stringent sanctions.

2.5.6   HYBRID ENFORCEMENT MECHANISMS

Finally, another striking feature of this regulatory infrastructure is the proliferation of hybrid enforcement mechanisms that can be employed by the agencies or, on occasion, by private parties. These mechanisms have also contributed to a more general 'blurring of legal forms' (A. Ashworth, 'Is the Criminal Law a Lost Cause' (2000) 116 LQR 237), conflating the functional distinctions that exist between criminal and civil law, and between regulatory wrong-doing and ordinary wrong-doing (J. McGrath, *Corporate and White Collar Crime in Ireland: A New Architecture of Regulatory Enforcement* (Manchester University Press, 2015)). For example, and apart from the possibility of a criminal prosecution by the Competition Authority, private parties can seek to initiate civil enforcement of competition law under s. 14(1) of the Competition Act 2002. Section 8(10) of the same Act provides that an action under s. 14 may be brought whether or not there has already been a criminal prosecution in relation to the matter concerned and, in addition, a s. 14 action will not prejudice the initiation of any future prosecution. Similarly, the Office of the Director of Corporate Enforcement can take civil or criminal enforcement actions. Civil enforcement actions include the use of restriction and disqualification orders.

This fragmentation in response to a breach of a regulatory offence can give rise to difficulties having regard to the principled protections generally afforded to those accused of crime. To give one instance, the Revenue may proceed against a tax defaulter through the criminal courts under s. 1078 of the Taxes Consolidation Act 1997 while also exercising its considerable civil powers to collect tax and impose civil penalties (fixed penalties and tax geared penalties) under the same Act. The latter penalties are available 'without prejudice to any other penalty to which the person may be liable'. This, as Tom O'Malley notes, can pose a 'problem for any sentencing system claiming to be guided by proportionality standards' (*Sentencing Law and Practice* (Thomson Round Hall, 1st edn, 2000), p. 128).

For example, in the *People (DPP) v Redmond* [2001] 3 IR 390, the defendant, who had previously worked as a senior official in local government in Dublin, had been charged with 10 counts of failing to make tax returns between 1989 and 1997. The prosecution case was that the defendant failed to disclose about £249,000 of income during this period. The defendant was found guilty and the trial judge imposed a total fine of £7,500 in respect of the 10 counts. The DPP appealed on the basis that this sentence was unduly lenient having regard to the gravity of the offences. In determining the proportionality of the punishment, the Court of Criminal Appeal noted that the defendant had, since his arrest, settled his civil revenue liability by paying a total sum of £782,000 to the Criminal Assets Bureau, which was acting for the Revenue Commissioners. This figure constituted the tax liability owing in relation to the criminal charges and other unspecified liabilities including interest and penalties. In order to meet this civil liability, Redmond had to sell the family home. The Court of Criminal Appeal noted that this full settlement figure was not broken down into various headings including the amount claimed in penal interest or revenue penalties. This was regrettable since information of this kind was important in determining the appropriate criminal sanction. In refusing to increase the criminal penalty, the court noted:

> Since proportionality is a key principle of sentencing, the court would endeavour to consider the cumulative sum of penalties in assessing the amount of the final one. The revenue penalties may vary, in particular with whether default in compliance is negligently or fraudulently caused. Such penalties in certain circumstances can exceed three times the difference between the tax paid and the tax actually payable. ... [T]hese are penalties which will be imposed on top of the primary obligation of every tax payer to pay the correct amount of tax. Similarly, a penal rate of interest may be applied where income tax has not been paid as a result of a fraud or neglect of the tax payer. This, too, is in the nature of a penalty. It is plainly not possible for a sentencing court in a case such as this to ignore the fact that other penalties, which may be much greater in amount than the cumulative sum of the maximum fines for these charges, have already been paid. It is therefore most unfortunate that the evidence does not extend to a statement, even approximate, to the amount of penalties so paid, or the defaults in respect of which they were imposed.

Similarly, in March 2009, a building contractor, Colm Perry, who evaded €500,000 tax over eight years, was jailed for 20 months by Judge Martin Nolan at Dublin Circuit Criminal Court. Prior to sentence he settled €499,998 of unpaid income tax and VAT returns with the Revenue Commissioners last week, but had a further €925,000 of outstanding interest and penalties accumulated on the failed returns from 1996 to 2004. Judge Nolan accepted the submission that Perry was 'a hardworking, decent man' but said he had to impose a custodial sentence to reflect the scale of his eight-year tax evasion. On appeal, Hardiman J., delivering the judgment in the Court of Criminal Appeal, allowed the appeal and noted:

> There is no doubt that the financial penalty of the same amount as the tax, in round figures half a million euros, is in the nature of a punitive consequence. We do not find evidence that the learned trial judge sufficiently considered it as such. There was a dispute in argument as to whether the interest was a punitive consequence. In our opinion in the present time, interest running at the rate of between 9% and 12% is undoubtedly punitive. This is a time when people, even with relatively substantial bank deposits, may struggle to achieve a quarter or even a smaller fraction of that. It is difficult to think of interest at the rate of 9% to 12% being imposed upon one as anything other than at least partially a punitive factor. We desire to emphasise the point that of course Mr Perry's liability to pay interest and taxes is unaffected by the Court's decision in this case.

In *DPP v Hughes* [2012] IECCA 85, the defendant, a car dealer, pleaded guilty to a number of sample counts of VAT evasion and had been sentenced to four years by the Circuit Court. On appeal to the CCA, the court noted that he had 'emptied the cupboard' to discharge his debt to the Revenue Commissioners and held that 'when considering sentence ... it would be an obvious injustice if a person were not entitled to invite a court to take into account the extent of financial reparations he has been compelled to make on the civil side'.

More recently in *Paul Begley v DPP* [2013] IECCA 32, the court held that the restitution programme entered into by the defendant, which included the payment of a lump sum of circa €219,000 to the Revenue in December 2009 with a payment schedule of between €24,000 and €33,000 per month thereafter until the outstanding balance is fully discharged, was a factor to be considered in mitigation.

The confusion that can arise between civil, administrative and criminal matters was also illustrated in *Registrar of Companies v District Judge David Anderson and System Partners Limited* [2005] 1 IR 21. System Partners Limited was late in filing its tax returns for the years 2000 and 2001. As a result, it had to pay a late filing fee of €1,200 for the year 2000 and €379 for the year 2001. Ordinarily the fee payable by a company if it filed its returns on time was €30. Subsequent to the late filing of the returns and the payment of the associated late filing fees, two prosecutions pursuant to s. 125 of the Companies Act 1963, as amended by s. 59 of the Company Law Enforcement Act 2001, were initiated in the District Court against System Partners Limited for its failure to file annual returns within the times specified for the calendar years 2000 and 2001. Section 125 of the Companies Act 1963, as amended, provided:

(1)   *Every company shall, once at least in every year, subject to section 127, make a return to the registrar of companies, being its annual return, in the prescribed form.*

(2)   *If a company fails to comply with this section, the company and every officer of the company who is in default ... shall be guilty of an offence.*

(3)   *Proceedings in relation to an offence under this section may be brought and prosecuted by the Registrar of Companies.*

At that hearing, it was drawn to the attention of the trial judge, David Anderson J., that the company had already filed the returns in question, albeit late, and had paid the associated late filing fees that were far in excess of what would have been payable if the returns had been lodged on time. Applying the principle of double jeopardy, David Anderson J. struck out the summonses because System Partners Limited had already been obliged to pay higher fees upon filing the returns late. The Registrar of Companies sought certiorari of the decision and submitted that a late filing fee was neither in form nor in substance a criminal penalty but rather a civil or administrative sanction, the object of which was to encourage the timely filing of annual returns. The late filing fees, it was argued, had no relationship with the prosecution and in so far as they were relevant it was only to issues of mitigation in respect of any fine to be imposed for the actual offence. The principle of double jeopardy was, therefore, not applicable. The High Court refused the order on the basis that the offence gave rise to a criminal sanction when there was already an administrative sanction in place (late filing return fees), and the applicant appealed to the Supreme Court. The appeal was allowed in the Supreme Court, where Geoghegan J. noted that the issue of double jeopardy did not arise, as the imposition of the initial penalty was an administrative rather than criminal matter. The payment of the substantially increased fees would, however, be a legitimate matter to take into consideration by way of mitigation of penalty if there was a conviction in the case.

The issue of double jeopardy has also been considered by the Financial Regulator's office. It is permitted to impose civil administrative sanctions for 'prescribed contraventions' of relevant legislation. These sanctions include, *inter alia*, a caution or reprimand, a monetary penalty (not exceeding €5,000,000 in the case of a corporate and unincorporated body, and not exceeding €500,000 in the case of a person), and a direction disqualifying a person from being concerned in the management of a regulated financial service provider (ss. 33AQ and 33AR of the Central Bank Act 1942). In 2008, for example, Quinn Insurance Limited was required to pay €3,250,000 and Mr Sean Quinn (senior) was also required to pay a penalty of €200,000). The Financial Regulator also has criminal powers of prosecution and enforcement. However, and in response to the problem posed by the principle of double jeopardy, no criminal prosecution will be brought if the Regulator has pursued the administrative sanctions procedure which has resulted in the imposition of a monetary penalty (N. Connery and D. Hodnett, *Regulatory Law in Ireland* (Tottel Publishing, 2009), 140–51).

The potential for blurring of the boundaries was also addressed by the Irish Supreme Court, *In the Matter of Tralee Beef and Lamb Ltd (In Liquidation) Kavanagh v Delaney & ors.* [2008] IESC 1, in which it described a restriction order, which prohibits a person from being involved in the management of a company for five years, as highly stigmatising and 'gravely damaging to the reputation of a person thus afflicted'. This would accordingly need to be taken into account in any subsequent criminal sentencing decision relating to the same misconduct. Similarly, in *People DPP v Clarkin* (10 February 2010, unreported, Court of Criminal Appeal), a trial judge, in a criminal fraudulent trading case, took into account the fact that the guilty party had also a five-year disqualification order imposed on him. Finally, in *Re Kentford Securities Ltd; DCE v McCann* [2010] IESC 59, a discretionary disqualification order was held to be 'partly penal in nature'.

CHAPTER 3

DEVELOPMENTS IN VICTIMS' RIGHTS IN IRELAND

3.1 Introduction

This chapter documents some of the legislative and policy developments relating to victims' rights in Ireland. Internationally, there has been growing recognition of the interests and needs of victims in the criminal justice system over the past few decades, where previous emphasis had been predominantly on the rights of the *offender* (Christie, 1977; O'Hara, 2005). The result, in Ireland and in other jurisdictions, has been a series of developments which seek to enhance the support provided to victims, particularly in terms of their role as witnesses in court.

3.2 Legal Developments

The Irish courts and legislature are beginning to take more account of the interests of victims of crime and there has been an expansion in service (welfare) and procedural (participatory) rights. This 'mainstreaming of victim-centred justice' (Goodey, 2005: 35) in Ireland is evident in the introduction of a series of provisions designed to accommodate victims.

3.2.1 LIVE TELEVISION LINKS

To begin with, one can refer to the introduction of live television links in the courtroom. Ordinarily, the adversarial nature of the Irish criminal process requires that witnesses are examined *viva voce* in open court. In recognition, however, of the trauma that this may impose on victims of specified sexual or violent offences (LRC 1989, 120–1) the legislature enacted s. 13 of the Criminal Evidence Act 1992 which provides that victims, among other witnesses, can give evidence in such cases *via* a live television link. In the case of victims of such offences who are under the age of 18 (s. 257(3) of the Children Act 2001) or are persons suffering from a 'mental handicap' (s. 19 of the Criminal Evidence Act 1992), there is a presumption in favour of giving evidence via television link (s. 13(1)(a)). In all other cases, leave of the court is required (s. 13(1) (b) of the Criminal Evidence Act 1992). More recently, s. 39 of the Criminal Justice Act 1999 provides that where a witness is in fear or subject to intimidation in any proceedings on indictment for an offence, that person may, with leave of the court, give evidence through a live television link. Section 29(1) of the Criminal Evidence Act 1992, as substituted by s. 24 of the Extradition (European Union Conventions) Act 2001, attempts to accommodate witnesses who are outside the state from having to attend to give evidence at trial. It provides that in any criminal proceedings, a witness other than the accused may, with leave of the court, give evidence through a live television link. Since 2001, it also applies to extradition proceedings and in particular to persons whose extradition is being sought. (See also s. 67 of the Criminal Justice (Mutual Assistance) Act 2008 which provides that a witness can give live television link evidence from another designated state.) The use of such a provision was contested in the Irish courts in the cases of both *Donnelly v Ireland* [1998] 1 IR 321 and *White v Ireland* [1995] 1 IR 268 on the grounds that it constituted an unlawful interference with an accused person's right to fairness of procedures. In neither case was the challenge successful.

More recently, in *D O'D v DPP and Judge Patricia Ryan* (unreported, 17 December 2009, High Court), the applicant had been charged with having sexual relations with two mentally impaired persons. He sought leave to quash the order of the trial judge directing the use of video link facilities pursuant to s. 13(1)(b) of the Criminal Evidence Act 1992. The applicant contended that the giving of evidence by video link by the two complainants would create a real risk that he would not get a fair trial because the giving of evidence by them by way of live video link could or would convey to the jury that they were persons with mental impairment, a matter which he disputed as part of his defence. The High Court upheld his claim, holding that evidence by video link in the circumstances carried with it a real risk of unfairness to the accused which probably could not be remedied by directions from the trial judge or statements from the prosecution. In the case, the prosecution applied for evidence to be given in this way under s. 13(1)(b) of the Act of 1992. Had the application been made under s. 13(1)(a) of the Act of 1992, it would have involved a finding that both of the complainants suffered from a 'mental handicap'. The only material put before the trial judge which expressly considered the ability of either complainant to give evidence were the statements of psychologists.

The defence objected on the grounds that it would create an inference that the complainants were vulnerable persons and persons who suffered from a mental impairment, if permitted to give evidence by way of video link. In essence, the defence argued that the issue of their mental impairment would be pre-determined and would impinge on the accused's right to a fair trial. The trial judge directed that the evidence should be given by video link under s. 13(1)(b) of the Criminal Evidence Act 1992. On appeal to the High Court, O'Neill J. overturned this decision. He stated:

> In my judgment, it is clear that evidence by video link in the circumstances of this case does carry with it a real risk of unfairness to the accused person which probably cannot be remedied by directions from the trial judge or statements from the prosecution. Manifestly, s.13 of the Act of 1992 provides for the giving evidence by video link for offences such as the ones the applicant is charged with. The discretion which the Court has under s.13(1)(b) to order evidence to be given in this way or to direct otherwise raises the difficult question as to how the Court is to achieve a correct balance between the accused's right to a fair trial and the prosecution's right in an appropriate case to have evidence given by video link. It is clear that what is required is a test that achieves the correct balance between these two competing rights.

He went on to note:

> Where the Court reaches the conclusion that the giving of evidence in this way carries with it a serious risk of unfairness to the accused which could not be corrected by an appropriate statement from the prosecution or direction from the trial judge, it should only permit the giving of evidence by video link where it was satisfied by evidence that a serious injustice would be done, in the sense of a significant impairment to the prosecution's case if evidence had to be given in the normal way, *viva voce*, thus necessitating evidence by video link in order to vindicate the right of the public to prosecute offences of this kind. The fact that the giving of evidence *viva voce* would be very unpleasant for the witness or coming to court to give evidence very inconvenient, would not be relevant factors.

Having established the test, the judge went on to hold that the trial judge did not achieve 'the correct balance in this case between the right of the applicant to a fair trial and the right of the first named respondent to prosecute the offences in question on behalf of the public'.

3.2.2   INTERMEDIARIES

Under s. 14(1) of the Criminal Evidence Act 1992, witnesses may, on application by the prosecution or the defence, also be permitted to give evidence in court through an intermediary in circumstances where they are using the live television link and are under 18 years of age or are persons with a 'mental handicap' who have reached that age in relation to a sexual offence or an offence involving violence. The trial judge can grant such an application if s/he believes that the interests of justice require that any questions for the witness be facilitated through an intermediary. Questions put to a witness in this manner shall be either in the words used by the questioner or conveyed in a manner to the witness which is appropriate to his or her age and mental condition reflecting the meaning of the questions being asked. While evidence is being given through a live television link pursuant to s. 13(1) of the Criminal Evidence Act 1992 (except through an intermediary), neither the judge, nor the barrister or solicitor concerned in the examination of the witness, shall wear a wig or gown. Moreover, if a child or a person with a mental disorder is giving evidence *via* a television link in respect of a victim impact statement, the same rule applies (s. 5 of the Criminal Procedure Act 2010).

3.2.3 PRE-TRIAL STATEMENTS

Given the emphasis placed by our adversarial system on the orality of the proceedings, pre-trial statements are not generally permitted in the Irish criminal process. The rationale underpinning the exclusion of such statements is that they constitute hearsay and ordinarily are excluded because the court is deprived of the normal methods of testing the credibility of the witness. A pre-trial statement, for example, is not given on oath; the demeanour of the witness making the statement cannot be observed by the trier of fact; and the defence has no opportunity to cross-examine the witness. The absence of this latter safeguard is of particular importance. More recently, however, it has been recognised that an overly rigid application of the hearsay rule can lead to injustice. Provision has accordingly been made for the admission of video recordings, depositions and out of court statements in certain circumstances. Under s. 16(1) of the Criminal Evidence Act 1992, for example, it provides that a video recording of any evidence given by a person under 18 years of age or a person with a mental handicap through a live television link at the preliminary examination of a sexual offence or an offence involving violence shall be admissible at trial. It also renders admissible at trial a video recording of any statement made by a person under 14 years of age or a person with a mental handicap (being a person in respect of whom such a sexual offence or an offence involving violence is alleged to have been committed) during an interview with a member of the Garda Síochána or any other person who is competent for the purpose, provided the witness is available at trial for cross examination. This provision is, as Delahunt notes, 'undoubtedly a practical step towards making the testimony of child witnesses and witnesses with an intellectual disability more easily heard within the criminal justice system' (Delahunt, 2011: 6). Section 4(b) of the Criminal Law (Human Trafficking) (Amendment) Act 2013 amended s. 16(1)(b) and extended this provision to persons under the age of 18 (other than the accused) in relation to offences related to human trafficking, committed under ss. 2, 4, or 7 of the Criminal Law (Human Trafficking) Act 2008, or child trafficking and pornography, committed under s. 3(1), (2), or (3) of the Child Trafficking and Pornography Act 1998. In these cases the video recording shall not be admitted in evidence if the court is of opinion that it is not in the interests of justice to do so. In *The People (DPP) v XY* (unreported, 15 November 2010, Central Criminal Court), for example, the accused was charged with s. 4 of the Criminal Law (Rape) (Amendment) Act 1990 after it was alleged that he forced a woman with an intellectual disability into performing the act of oral sex with him. In that case, the trial judge admitted as evidence a DVD recording of an interview with the complainant. This pre-trial recording was admitted as examination-in-chief testimony (LRC, 2011: pp. 191–2; Delahunt, 2010).

More general provision for the admission of depositions (and video recordings) at the pre-trial stage are now made under s. 4G of the Criminal Procedure Act 1967, as amended. It provides that a deposition by a witness may be admitted in evidence at the trial of the accused if it is proved that:

- the witness is dead, is unable to attend to give evidence at the trial, is prevented from so attending, or does not give evidence at the trial through fear or intimidation;

- the accused was present at the taking of the evidence; and

- an opportunity was given to cross examine and re-examine the witness.

The trial court retains a discretion to exclude such evidence if it is of the opinion that it is necessary in the interests of justice.

Moreover, under s. 255 of the Children Act 2001, a judge of the District Court, when satisfied on the evidence of a registered medical practitioner that the attendance before a court of any child would involve serious danger to the safety, health or wellbeing of the child, may take the evidence of the child concerned by way of sworn deposition or through a live television link in any case where the evidence is to be given through such a link. This section relates to certain specified offences including cruelty against children, causing or procuring a child to engage in begging, allowing a child to be in a brothel, and causing or encouraging a sexual offence on a child, the murder or manslaughter of a child, any offence involving bodily injury to a child, and most sexual offences (Walsh, 2005: 21). As will be referred to later in this text, the rules set out in s. 4F(3) of the Criminal Procedure Act 1967 apply to the taking of evidence under s. 255 of the Children Act 2001. These rules provide as follows:

(a)   when the evidence is being taken, both the accused and a judge of the District Court shall be present;

(b)   before it is taken, the judge shall inform the accused of the circumstances in which it may be admitted in evidence at the accused's trial;

(c)   the witness may be cross-examined and re-examined;

(d)   where the evidence is taken by way of sworn deposition, the deposition and any cross-examination and re-examination of the deponent shall be recorded, read to the deponent and signed by the deponent and the judge.

Part 3 of the Criminal Justice Act 2006 makes provision for the admission of a statement made by a witness in any criminal proceedings relating to an 'arrestable' offence. It can be invoked either by the prosecution or the defence. It can occur in circumstances where the witness, although available for cross-examination, refuses to give evidence, denies making the statement, or gives evidence which is materially inconsistent with it. The statement can then be admitted if it is proved that the witness made it, it is reliable, was made voluntarily, and direct oral evidence of the fact concerned would be admissible. The statement must be given on oath or affirmation or contain a declaration by the witness that the statement is true to the best of his knowledge or belief, or the court is otherwise satisfied that when the statement was made the witness understood the requirement to tell the truth. In determining whether the statement is reliable, the court will have regard to whether or not it was given on oath or affirmation or was video recorded, if there is other evidence to support its reliability, and the explanations of the witness, if any, in refusing to give evidence. The court must also be satisfied that the admission of the statement would not be contrary to the interests of justice.

3.2.4   EYE WITNESS IDENTIFICATION

In some instances eye witness identification of the perpetrators of crime will be required at the pre-trial and trial stages of criminal process. This can be very traumatic for witnesses, particularly those who are the alleged victims. There are no one-way mirror identification systems in Garda stations, and very often the victim may find himself or herself in the same room as the accused. Moreover, at a pre-trial identification parade, the witness will according to the Garda Síochána *Criminal Investigation Manual* generally be asked to 'place his/her hand on the identified person's shoulder', though fortunately it is now the case that this practice has been relaxed and the witness can, if s/he requests, make the identification by pointing to and describing the person in question (Walsh, 2002: para 6.55). Making an identification in court can also be difficult for a witness. More recently efforts have been made to alleviate this trauma. Persons giving evidence via television link under s. 13 of Criminal Evidence Act 1992 and s. 39 of the Criminal Justice Act 1999, as referred to earlier, shall not now be required to identify the accused at the trial of the offence if the accused is known to them (unless the court in the interests of justice directs otherwise). Moreover, evidence by a person other than the witness that the witness identified the accused at an identification parade as being the offender shall be admissible as evidence that the accused was so indentified.

3.2.5   VICTIM IMPACT STATEMENTS

The reduction of victim alienation has also occurred through the use of victim impact statements. Section 5 of the Criminal Justice Act 1993 made provision for the court to receive evidence or submissions concerning any effect of specified offences on the person in respect of whom an offence was committed. These offences relate to most sexual offences, offences involving violence or the threat of violence to a person, and female genital mutilation. Section 5 initially presupposed that the victims of these offences were capable themselves of giving evidence of the impact that the crime had on them (O'Malley, 2009: 885). To combat the narrowness of this presumption, the Irish courts began as a practice to admit the evidence of family members of homicide victims (see *DPP v O'Donoghue* [2007] 2 IR 336). As a result of the introduction of s. 4 of the Criminal Procedure Act 2010, a 'person in respect of whom the offence was committed' now includes a family member of that person when that person has died, is ill or is otherwise incapacitated as a result of the commission of the offence. A family member may also give evidence under s. 5(3)(b)(ii) of the Criminal Justice Act 1993, as amended, where the victim of the specified offence suffers from a mental disorder (not related to the commission of the offence). Under s. 5A of the Act, a child or a person with a mental disorder may give evidence of the impact of the crime through a live television link unless the court sees good reason to the contrary. Moreover, where a child or a person with a mental disorder is giving evidence through a live television link pursuant to s. 5A, the court may, on the application of the prosecution or the accused, direct that any questions be put to the witness through an intermediary (provided it is in the interests of justice to do so) (s. 5B Criminal Justice Act 1993, as inserted by s. 4 of the Criminal Procedure Act 2010).

The only purpose for which a victim impact statement can be received at sentencing stage is to describe the impact of the offence on the victim (or on the family members if the victim has died as a result of the offence). It cannot be used to adduce further evidence, to suggest the sentence that should be imposed or to make fresh allegations. The prosecution bears the responsibility of ensuring that the statement restricts itself in this regard. The prosecution and defence may also examine the victim on any evidence given in respect of the impact of the crime (*The People (DPP) v C(M)* (unreported, 16 June 1995, Central Criminal Court).

3.2.6   COMPETENCE

The Irish criminal process works on the assumption that all witnesses are competent to testify in court. If a dispute arises as to the competence of a particular witness, the party calling that witness bears the legal burden of proving that s/he is in fact competent. At common law, a witness demonstrates competence by showing that s/he understands the nature of an oath and is capable of giving an intelligent account. The determination as to whether a child understands the nature and consequences of an oath is one for the trial judge. See *AG v O'Sullivan* [1930] IR 553. Testimony in civil and criminal proceedings normally requires that the evidence has to be given on oath or affirmation. As was noted in *Mapp v Gilhooley* [1991] IR 253, 'the broad purpose of the rule is to ensure as far as possible that such *viva voce* evidence shall be true by the provision of a moral or religious and legal sanction against deliberate untruth'.

3.2.6.1   Children

Issues of competence primarily arise in respect of witnesses who are children or are persons with a mental disability. The law relating to both categories has become more accommodating in recent years. Traditionally, for example, a child could only give sworn evidence. If a child was capable of giving an intelligible account, but did not understand the importance of telling the truth under oath, it was still possible for him or her to give unsworn testimony under s. 30 of the 1908 Children's Act as amended by s. 28(2) of Criminal Justice Act 1914. Such testimony, however, needed to be corroborated. Such evidence could only be given if, in addition to satisfying the intelligibility criterion, the child also could demonstrate that s/he understood 'both the nature and consequences of an oath' (*R v Brasier* (1779) 1 Leach 199). A more secular common law approach, however, began to emerge in the 1970s in relation to sworn evidence; the determining factor was 'whether the child has a sufficient appreciation of the solemnity of the occasion and the added responsibility to tell the truth, which is involved in taking an oath, over and above the duty to tell the truth which is an ordinary duty of normal social conduct' (*R v Hayes* [1977] 2 All ER 288). More recently, s. 27 of the Criminal Evidence Act 1992 was enacted which provides that in any criminal proceedings the evidence of a person under 14 years of age may be received otherwise than on oath or affirmation if the court is satisfied that s/he is capable of giving an intelligible account of events which are relevant to those proceedings. Section 255 of the Children Act 2001 provides that the evidence of a child under 14 years of age may be taken or received otherwise than on oath or affirmation if the court is satisfied that the child is capable of giving an intelligible account of events which are relevant to those proceedings. It relates to certain specified offences mentioned in Part 12 and Schedule 1 of the Act. In a recent Court of Appeal decision in *The People (DPP) v PP* [2015] IECA 152, Sheehan J. held that while it is preferable that an inquiry be made into the capacity of the person under 14 to give an intelligible account of relevant proceedings prior to placing the evidence before the jury, a failure to carry out a formal inquiry in advance does not render a trial unsatisfactory. The court in this case was influenced by the fact that the absence of a formal inquiry did not result in unfairness to the appellant and that it was clear from cross-examination that the child was not only capable of giving an intelligible account but did in fact provide one. Significantly, and as we shall see later, s. 28(1) abolishes the mandatory requirement that the unsworn evidence of a child be corroborated; a trial judge now has a discretion whether a jury should be given a warning about the dangers of convicting on the unsworn evidence of a child.

3.2.6.2   Mental impairment

Persons suffering from a mental impairment were traditionally excluded from giving evidence at trial. The common law, however, then altered, and permitted such a witness to testify provided s/he was capable of understanding the nature and consequences of an oath, was capable of giving an intelligible account, and the mental disorder did not impede his or her ability to give evidence at trial (*R v Hill* (1851) 2 Den 254). If a witness has communicative difficulties, an interpreter may be provided to aid with the giving of evidence. In *The People (DPP) v Gillane* (unreported, 14 December 1998, Court of Criminal Appeal), for example, it was held that it was permissible for a witness to give identification evidence for the prosecution in a case despite the fact that he believed that staff at the Mater Hospital had inserted a microchip into his head. As the court noted, though the witness 'had very strange ideas about what was done to him when he had an operation on his head some twenty years before in the Mater Hospital, [this] does not mean that he was incapable of giving evidence'.

If, however, a mentally impaired person was not able or permitted to give sworn evidence, there was no means by which unsworn evidence could be given. In *DPP v JS* (unreported, 1983, Circuit Court), for example, a moderately mentally impaired complainant could not answer questions as to the nature of the oath or the nature of a lie at trial. She made no response when asked by the judge what the moral and legal consequences of telling a lie were. As a result, she could not be sworn and, as there was no independent evidence in the case, a *nolle prosequi* was entered (LRC, 1990: 10). Similarly, in *DPP v MW* (unreported, 1983, Circuit Court) a moderately impaired complainant alleged that she was raped in a car. The accused was charged with two counts, rape and unlawful carnal knowledge of a mentally impaired person. At the rape trial, the trial judge ruled that she was competent to take the oath. Her testimony at trial, however, was held to be contradictory and the judge directed an acquittal. Subsequently the accused was tried with the second count, unlawful carnal knowledge of a mentally impaired person. On this occasion, however, her preliminary answers on questions pertaining to the nature of an oath were less satisfactory, and the trial judge declined to have her sworn. As there was no independent evidence in the case, the prosecution was compelled to enter a *nolle prosequi* (LRC, 1990: 10).

Fortunately, s. 27(3) of the Criminal Evidence Act 1992 now provides that the evidence of a person with a 'mental handicap' may be received otherwise than on oath or affirmation if the court is satisfied that the person is capable of giving an intelligible account of events which are relevant to the proceedings. In *O'Sullivan v Hamill* [1999] 3 IR 9, O'Higgins CJ noted:

> Unsworn evidence is provided for from a person with a mental handicap 'if the court is satisfied that he is capable of giving an intelligible account of events which are relevant to those proceedings'. In my view, before that section comes into play there are two requirements on which the court has to be satisfied – (1) that the person has a mental handicap, and (2) that he is capable of giving an intelligible account of events which are relevant to the proceedings. Clearly there must be an inquiry.

Determining the answers to these questions in that inquiry at trial may require expert medical opinion evidence. A corroborative warning may need to be given to the jury in respect of the testimony of a witness suffering from a mental disability (*The People (DPP) v Molloy* (unreported, 28 July 1995, Court of Criminal Appeal)).

Determining the capacity of a witness to give an intelligible account can give rise to difficulties. In the recent *Laura Kelly* case (unreported), the complainant, who has Downs Syndrome, alleged that she was sexually assaulted at a 21st birthday party. The family claimed that shortly after Ms Kelly was put to bed, a family member entered the bedroom and saw a man in bed with her. It was alleged that Ms Kelly had most of her clothes removed and the man was naked from the waist down. However, at trial, Ms Kelly, who had 'a mental age of four', was deemed incompetent to testify and the case was dismissed. Ms Kelly's mother stated: 'She [Laura] was brought into this room in the Central Criminal Court and asked questions about numbers and colours and days of the week which had no relevance in Laura's mind. She knew that she had to go into a courtroom and tell a story so the bad man would be taken away. It was ridiculous. There is no one trained in Ireland to deal with someone similar to Laura, from the Gardaí up to the top judge in Ireland and the barristers and solicitors' (J. McEnroe, 'Family want "archaic" law overruled', Irish Examiner, 30 March 2010).

3.2.6.3 Spouse

Traditionally, too, the spouse of an accused was not competent to give evidence for the prosecution in a case, except in the case of rape or violence perpetrated on that spouse (*R v Lapworth* [1931] 1 KB 117). This was justified on the basis of marital unity (the law made no distinction between the accused and the spouse) and the importance of preserving marital harmony. The constitutionality of this rule was challenged in *The People (DPP) v JT* (1988) 3 Frewen 141. The complainant was a 20-year-old woman who had Downs Syndrome who alleged that she had been sexually abused by her father. At trial the spouse of the accused and the complainant's mother gave evidence that at the end of a television programme concerning child sexual abuse, her daughter expressed delight that the wrongdoer in the programme was eventually brought to justice. As a result of questioning her daughter on the issue, it emerged that the complainant's father had allegedly perpetrated similar abuses as those illustrated on the programme. The accused was convicted but appealed on the basis, *inter alia*, that his spouse was incompetent to testify for the prosecution. In upholding the conviction, Walsh J examined the common law rule and declared that its application on the facts of the cases would be in violation of Article 41 of the Constitution which protected family rights.

Section 21 of the Criminal Evidence Act 1992, as amended by s. 257(3) of the Children Act 2001, now provides that in any criminal proceedings a spouse of the accused is competent to give evidence for the prosecution. Such a spouse, however, is only compellable to give evidence at the instance of the prosecution in the case of an offence which involves violence or the threat of violence to the spouse, a child of the spouse or of the accused, or any person who was at the material time under the age of 18 years, or is a sexual offence alleged to have been committed in relation to a child of the spouse or the accused, or any person who was at the material time under the age of 18 years (Jackson, 1993: 202). More extensive compellability requirements for the prosecution exist for former spouses under s. 22(2) of the same Act.

3.2.7 FOCUS ON COMPLAINANT'S CIRCUMSTANCES

In more recent years the criminal justice system has also witnessed a greater awareness of the victim's perspective in the following circumstances:

• The reasons why a complainant may not have made a complaint of a sexual offence at first reasonable opportunity but still avail of the doctrine of recent complaint. This doctrine, when applied to a sexual offence, means that a voluntary complaint made at the first reasonable opportunity after the commission of the alleged offence is admissible to demonstrate consistency and credibility on the part of the complainant (see, e.g., *The People (DPP) v DR* [1998] 2 IR 106).

• A relaxation of the exclusionary rule on opinion evidence in certain circumstances, e.g. s. 3(4)(b) of the Domestic Violence Act 1996 permits an applicant for a barring order to provide opinion evidence that s/he has a legal or beneficial interest in the place of residence that is not less than that of the respondent.

• The introduction of a provision which makes it clear that the absence of resistance by a victim in a rape case does not equate with consent (s. 9 of the Criminal Law (Rape) (Amendment) Act 1990).

• Tighter restrictions that offer victims better protection against unnecessary and distressing information being raised about their sexual histories. Section 3 of the Criminal Law (Rape) Act 1981, as amended by s. 13 of the Criminal Law (Rape) (Amendment) Act 1990 now provides that, except with leave of the court, no questions shall be asked in cross-examination about the sexual experience of a complainant. Previously in a rape case where the defence was one of consent, the trial judge was obliged 'to allow unpleasant charges to be made against the complainant in connection with her past; he should not indicate to the jury that he disapproves of this being done' (*The People (DPP) v McGuinness* [1978] IR 189).

- Separate legal representation for sexual offence complainants where an application is made to admit previous sexual history (s. 34 of the Sex Offenders Act 2001).

- Greater protection of the identity of victims (see, for example, s. 7 of the Criminal Law (Rape) Act 1991, as amended; s. 11 of the Criminal Law (Human Trafficking) Act 2008; and s. 252 of the Children Act 2001) and witnesses (s. 181 of the Criminal Justice Act 2006) in criminal cases.

- The introduction of measures to restrict unjustified imputations at trial against the character of a deceased or incapacitated victim or witness (s. 33 Criminal Procedure Act 2010).

- The introduction of an exception to the rule against double jeopardy when new and compelling evidence becomes available (Part 3, Criminal Procedure Act 2010).

- The introduction of bail conditions requiring a bail applicant to refrain from going to specific locations or to meet specified persons.

- The creation of a statutory offence of intimidation of witnesses or their families (s. 41 of Criminal Justice Act 1999).

- The ability of the DPP to appeal unduly lenient sentences (s. 2 of the Criminal Justice Act 1993, as amended by s. 23 of the Criminal Justice Act 2006).

- Provisions for the payment of compensation to victims through a non-statutory scheme introduced in 1974, and a statutory scheme introduced under s. 6 of the Criminal Justice Act 1993 (Kilcommins et al., 2014: 150–3; Rogan, 2006a: 202–8; Fennell, 2010: 250–60; Vaughan and Kilcommins, 2010).

3.2.8   CORROBORATION

Over the years the common law also devised particular corroboration rules in respect of certain categories of 'suspect' witnesses such as sexual complainants, children and accomplices. Ordinarily, an accused person in a criminal trial can be convicted on the testimony of one witness alone. However, for suspect witnesses such as those cited earlier, it was required that a jury had to be given a warning of the dangers of convicting on such evidence in the absence of corroboration. The exclusionary assumptions underpinning the perception of some victims or witnesses in the Irish criminal justice system is evident, for example, in the law on the corroboration of sexual complaints. In the past the evidence of a complainant in a sexual offences case required a mandatory warning to the jury on the dangers of acting on such evidence alone. This rule was justified 'by the fear that complaints of sexual offences may sometimes be the product of spite, jealousy, psychological denial of having consented, or a reaction to having been jilted; that women with nothing to lose might seek to subject a man of high social standing to blackmail; and that the accusation of rape is easily made, but difficult to defend' (Healy, 2004: 157). More recently, however, these notions about the traits and motives of sexual complainants have largely been abandoned and the trial judge now has discretion whether or not to give such a warning to the jury (s. 7 of the Criminal Law (Rape) (Amendment) Act 1990).

In respect of the unsworn testimony of child witnesses, corroboration by some other material evidence was also required to obtain a conviction against an accused party. This could not be the unsworn evidence of another child. In *Attorney General (Kelly) v Kearns* (1946) 80 ILTR 45, for example, the defendant was charged with attempted carnal knowledge of a girl aged 9 (RB), indecent assault of the same girl, and indecent assault of two other girls also aged 9 (AH and MC respectively). Two of the girls gave evidence that they were in the defendant's house together and that each saw the unpleasant acts being perpetrated against the other (RB and AH). The other girl (MC) gave evidence that on a different date she was also in the defendant's house and that he also indecently assaulted her. Playmates of the three complainants also gave unsworn testimony that the three complainants went into the defendant's house.

Molony J held:

> Corroboration is a statutory requirement in the case of the unsworn testimony of a child of tender years. Sec. 30 of the Children Act, 1908, has the proviso '(a) A person shall not be liable to be convicted of the offence unless the testimony admitted by virtue of this section and given on behalf of the prosecution is corroborated by some other material evidence in

support thereof implicating the accused.' …[I]t is quite clear from the vast number of authorities that, to quote from the headnote in *Rex. v Coyle* [1926] N. I. 208 , 'the unsworn testimony of a child of tender years admitted by virtue of s. 30 of the Children Act, 1908, could not be corroborated within the meaning of proviso (a) to that section, by the unsworn testimony, similarly admitted, of any number of such children.'… It will be remembered that the children R. B. and A. H. both said they were together in [the defendant's] room, and each witnessed the assault upon the other. I am clear that R. B.'s story does not, in law, corroborate A. H.'s story, nor does A. H.'s story corroborate R. B.'s story—nor do any of the little girls, other than those alleged to be injured afford corroboration—simply because, in my opinion, they are incapable of giving corroboration. The same remarks apply in respect to the charge in connection with M. C.

Since there was no other evidence in the case, the prosecution failed. More recently, the legislature has moved away from the operating assumption that the evidence of children was inherently flawed or unreliable. Section 28(1) of the Criminal Evidence Act 1992 abolished the requirement that the unsworn evidence of children had to be corroborated and s. 28(2)(a) abolished the mandatory warning about the dangers of convicting on the sworn evidence of children in the absence of corroboration. Section 28(3) of the same Act also provides that the unsworn evidence of a child may corroborate unsworn evidence given by any other person, which contrasts with the decision in *Kearns* mentioned earlier. The unsworn evidence of a child could always be corroborated by sworn evidence.

There is no statutory law requiring corroboration or that a corroboration warning be given with respect to witnesses with a mental disability. However, there is some case law support for the view that in the case of such witnesses, a warning should be given of the dangers of convicting on the testimony of such witnesses in the absence of corroborative evidence (see, e.g. the Australian case of *Bromley v R* (1986) 161 CLR 315). In Ireland, in *The People (DPP) v MJM* (unreported, 28 July 1995, Court of Criminal Appeal), a trial judge invoked his discretion to give such a warning under s. 7 of the Criminal Law (Rape) (Amendment) Act 1990. The invocation was partly based on the mental status of the complainant, and in particular the fact that she had a childlike mind. It should be noted, however, that the Law Reform Commission in Ireland suggested in 1990 that there should be no corroboration requirement in respect of persons suffering from a mental disability (LRC, 1990: p. 24).

3.2.9 CIVIL REMEDY

It is also open to a victim of crime to take a civil action against the perpetrator. In *MN v SM* [2005] 4 IR 461, at 472, for example, the court considered the appropriate level of damages to order in civil proceedings for a continuum of sexual abuse over five years which culminated in the rape of a teenager. The law is also constantly evolving in this field. The Statute of Limitations Act 1957 was amended in 2000, for example, to take account of acts of sexual abuse which may result in tort actions, and in particular the capacity of some victims of this abuse to bring actions within the relevant time period. There is also a developing jurisprudence regarding civil wrongs. In a recent case of *Walsh v Byrne* [2015] IEHC 414, the plaintiff took an action for personal injuries, loss, damage, inconvenience, and expense including aggravated damages for sexual assault and battery and trespass to the person. He also sought a declaration that the entire relationship created by the defendant with the plaintiff constituted a continuum of oppression, and argued that the court should develop the law by recognising the practice of grooming for the purposes of sexual abuse as either a new tort or the development of existing tort law. White J. accepted this reasoning and recognised the 'continuum of sexual abuse' as a new tort:

> [T]he mental trauma suffered by the plaintiff, is not just confined to the acts of assault and battery, but arises also as a result of the consequences of the breach of trust of the defendant who had played such an important role in the plaintiff's life. The court's objective consideration of the purpose of the defendant's kindness, concern and considerable investment of time, to the period when the abuse stopped was for the insidious purpose of satisfying his own sexual desire. For those reasons, it is appropriate to extend the law of tort, to cover what is now a well-recognised and established pattern of wrongdoing, where a child is befriended, where trust is established and where that friendship and trust is used to perpetrate sexual abuse.

3.3   Policy Developments

3.3.1   VICTIM'S CHARTER

Irish Criminal Justice Policy has embraced victim-centred justice in recent years. The Victim's Charter marked an important policy development for crime victims (McGovern, 2002: 393; Rogan, 2006a: 153). This Charter was produced by the Department of Justice, Equality and Law Reform in September 1999, reflecting the 'commitment to giving victims of crime a central place in the criminal justice. As such it amalgamates for the first time all the elements of the criminal justice system from the victim's perspective' (Department of Justice, Equality and Law Reform, 1999: 3). In 2005, a review of the entire Charter was undertaken by the Commission for the Support of Victims of Crime. A revised *Victim's Charter and Guide to the Criminal Justice System* was produced in 2010. It attempts to increase the information available to victims of crime from the Crime Victims Helpline, the Garda Síochána, the Courts Service, the Director of Public Prosecutions (DPP), the Prison Service, the Probation Service, the Legal Aid Board, the Coroner's Service and the Criminal Injuries Compensation Tribunal. It sets out the entitlements a victim has from these various services, but it does not confer legal rights.

3.3.2   VICTIM SUPPORT ORGANISATIONS

The needs of crime victims in Ireland are also addressed by a wide variety of victims' organisations. These operate both at the national and local level. In Ireland, these groups include, *inter alia*, ADVIC, Amen, the Commission for the Support of Court Support Services, National Crime Victims' Helpline, Rape Crisis Centres, Support after Homicide, Irish Centre for Parentally Abducted Children, Irish Tourist Assistance Service, One in Four, Sexual Violence Centre Cork, Survivors of Child Abuse etc. Whilst a significant proportion are specialised in nature dealing with specific types of victim or services, some of them are key national groups.

Similarly, Victim Support at Court provides support to witnesses and victims both before and during court proceedings, including pre-trial visits and court accompaniment during proceedings. It has stated in its strategic plan for 2011–2014 that it hopes to promote its service among groups who may be 'isolated, vulnerable and/or disadvantaged' and includes people with disabilities within this cohort.

The Victims' Rights Alliance, which was launched in November 2013, is an amalgam of victims' support and human rights organisations with the purpose of ensuring that the new Victims' Rights Directive is implemented within the proposed time frame (by November 2015). SAFE Ireland is an organisation established to raise awareness about the prevalence of domestic violence and to advocate on behalf of its victims. Other associations and groups include the Irish Road Victims Association (established in 2012) and the PARC road safety group (established in 2006), which offer support to road traffic victims and their families.

In 1974, a Criminal Injuries Compensation Tribunal was established by the then Government to administer a scheme designed to alleviate some of the financial difficulties experienced by victims of violent crime and their families. The purpose of this scheme was to compensate individuals for losses arising from personal injuries as a result of violent crime or acquired while assisting another individual in preventing a crime or saving a human life. Individuals eligible to apply for compensation under this scheme include the injured person(s), the immediate family of the injured person(s) if the victim has died as a result of the crime, or those responsible for looking after the injured party.

3.3.3   THE OFFICE OF THE DIRECTOR OF PUBLIC PROSECUTIONS

The Office of the DPP has also been active in respect of victims' needs and concerns. It has, for example, published a number of documents which have implications for victims' experiences of criminal justice organisations including *The Role of the D.P.P*; *Attending Court as a Witness*; *Statement of General Guidelines for Prosecutors*; and *Prosecution Policy on the Giving of Reasons for Decisions*. A *Reasons for Decisions* pilot project commenced in Ireland in October 2008. Ordinarily the DPP is under no obligation to give reasons in respect of a decision not to prosecute, as established in cases such as *The State (McCormack) v Curran* [1987] ILRM 225 and *Eviston v DPP* (unreported, 31 July 2002). The project, however, reverses this rule with regard to homicide offences such as murder, manslaughter, infanticide, fatalities in the workplace, and vehicular manslaughter. In such cases reasons for decisions not to prosecute, or to discontinue a prosecution, were given by the Office of the DPP on request to parties closely connected with the deceased, such as members of the deceased's family or household, their legal or medical advisers, or social workers acting on their behalf. Such reasons, however, would only be given where it was possible to do so without creating an injustice.

3.3.4   THE COURTS SERVICE

The Courts Service has also issued a number of publications including *Going to Court* and *Explaining the Courts*. The Committee for Judicial Studies also recently published a guide for the Irish judiciary, entitled *The Equal Treatment of Persons in Court: guidance for the judiciary* (2011). Measures that have been taken to improve access to the courts include the use of induction loops for persons with a hearing impairment in the courtrooms of refurbished buildings, signage and contact details for court offices in Braille, wheelchair ramps in many courthouses, and wheelchair users can give evidence in many courthouses at the front of the court beside the witness box.

3.3.5   AN GARDA SÍOCHÁNA

The Gardaí have also given a number of commitments to victims of crime including an assurance regarding the provision of information on the progress of a case and on the prosecution process, as set out in its Charter for Victims of Crime. The Garda Victim Liaison Office, for example, is responsible for developing Garda Policy on victims of crime, and for ensuring the implementation of the Garda aspect of the Victims' Charter. Garda Family Liaison Officers have been introduced to provide support to victims of crime affected by traumatic crimes such as homicide, kidnap, false imprisonment, hostage siege situations, and other serious crimes where this is deemed appropriate by the local Superintendent. The role of the Family Liaison Officer is to keep the victim informed on all matters relating to the crime and to provide practical information and support. Referrals can be made by the Garda Family Liaison Office, with the consent of the victim, to ensure access to appropriate emotional and psychological support. Garda Ethnic Liaison Officers are trained to provide specific support and advice to victims of racist incidents and the Gardaí also provide a liaison scheme for the LGBT (lesbian, gay, bisexual, and transgender) community. Officers are trained to provide support to victims from this community and encourage reporting of homophobic crime where appropriate.

3.4   Administrative Developments

Along with the above policy developments in Ireland, a number of administrative developments have been implemented as part of a *Justice for Victims Initiative* to increase the level of support to victims of crime. A new executive office has been established in the Department of Justice to support crime victims (established September 2008). The core mandate of this Victims of Crime Office is to improve the continuity and quality of services to victims of crime, by state agencies and non-governmental organisations throughout the country. It works to support the development of competent, caring and efficient services to victims of crime. A reconstituted Commission for the Support of Victims of Crime occurred in September 2008. Working with an annual budget from the Department of Justice and Equality, the Commission provides funding for services and supports to victims of crime. The Commission also works to improve cohesion and consistency of service and information available to victims of crime. A Victims of Crime Consultative Forum held its first meeting in January 2009. It provides a forum for victim support organisations to put forward the views of victims with a view to shaping strategy and policy initiatives.

3.5   Legislative Developments

A Victims' Rights Bill was initiated in 2008 to make provision for the treatment of and rights of victims of criminal offences. More recently, the first commitment in the Justice and Law Reform section of the Programme for Government 2011–2016 indicated a requirement for legislation to strengthen the rights of victims of crime and their families, including greater use of victim impact statements and statutory rights to information.

Two new Bills have recently been introduced. The General Scheme of the Criminal Justice (Victims of Crime) Bill 2015 was introduced in July 2015 as part of the process of implementing the Victims' Rights Directive (*Directive 2012/29/EU establishing minimum standards on the rights, support and protection of victims of crime*), a task which must be completed by 16 November 2015. The Bill provides some important new measures to strengthen victims' rights. One of the significant developments in this proposed legislation is the increased level of information which will be provided to victims. The Bill provides that an individual contacting the Gardaí to inform them that s/he has been the victim of a criminal offence must be provided with certain information. For example, s/he should be informed about: procedures for making a complaint alleging an offence; services which provide support for victims of crime; the role of the victim in the criminal justice process; available protection measures; legal aid and entitlement to interpretation and/or translation assistance. Victims are also entitled to request certain additional information about their cases and Gardaí are obliged to provide that information 'as soon as is practicable'. For example, under this provision, a victim can request information about significant developments in the investigation of the offence or information relating to the trial of an alleged offender. Other significant developments in the Bill include the requirement that the Gardaí or the DPP provide victims with reasons for decisions not to prosecute a crime and the introduction of a process for formally reviewing a decision not to prosecute.

A notable feature of the Bill is the introduction of 'victim personal statements' which apply to offences other than those where a victim impact statement may be given. A 'victim personal statement' should 'set out how the victim has been affected by the offence including, as the case may be, physically, emotionally, financially or in any other way but shall not include any prejudicial comment on the offender or comment on the appropriate sentence be imposed on the offender'. This statement is provided to the Gardaí who will forward it to the DPP, as appropriate. These statements are submitted by the prosecutor to the trial court and served on the defence prior to sentencing and must be taken into account when determining the sentence to be imposed. Further protections for victims during investigation and whilst testifying are provided for in Part 5 of the Bill, e.g. on the application of the prosecution, special measures such as the testifying via video link or from behind a screen may be made available to a victim where the court is satisfied that this is necessary to protect him/her. This is a significant extension of the availability of the special measures which are available in the Criminal Evidence Act 1992, which were previously only available to victims of a limited number of offences.

The Criminal Law (Sexual Offences) Bill 2015 increases protection for victims of sexual offences in a number of significant ways. Perhaps most notably, the Bill introduces a procedure for regulating the disclosure of counselling records in sexual offence trials. Previously, under Irish law there was no procedure for regulation disclosure of counselling records which were held by third parties such as counsellors or social workers. Section 33 of the Bill fills this lacuna, creating a formal application process for the introduction of this evidence which is similar to the process which regulates the disclosure of sexual experience evidence. If the defence seeks disclosure of counselling records, a written application to court must be made. A hearing will then take place to determine whether disclosure should be ordered. The complainant (who is entitled to legal representation) and the record-holder are entitled to be heard at this hearing and the judge must provide reasons for the decision regarding disclosure. The section provides useful guidelines to structure judicial discretion in deciding whether to order disclosure. These guidelines, along with the possibility of imposing conditions upon disclosure orders, are designed to ensure that disclosure of records goes no further than is necessary, maximising protection of victims' privacy rights.

The Bill also amends the special measures for giving testimony as provided for in the Criminal Evidence Act 1992. The definition of 'sexual offence' in s. 2 of the 1992 Act is extended to ensure that the special measures contained in it are available for the new offences created by the 2015 Bill. This Bill repeals s. 13 of the 1992 Act which provides that wigs and gowns should not be worn by judges or legal professionals where a child is giving evidence via video link. Instead, judges and legal professionals concerned in the examination of witnesses are prohibited from wearing wigs and gowns in all circumstances where evidence is given by a child under 18 years in a sexual offence case to which the 1992 Act applies. The 2015 Bill also introduces provisions for witnesses under 18 years to give evidence from behind a screen to prevent the witness from seeing the defendant. Defendants are also prohibited from personally cross-examining witnesses who are under 14 years of age. This provision has not, however, been extended to adult complainants. The 2015 Bill amends s. 16 of the Criminal Evidence Act 1992, increasing the age limit for out-of-court video recording of complainants' evidence from 14 to 18 years of age. A final important development in the 2015 Bill is the introduction of harassment orders which may be imposed on convicted sex offenders when passing sentence or at any time before their release from prison. Such orders may prohibit the respondent from communicating with the victim and order the respondent to stay within a specified distance of the victim's home, workplace or any other place frequented by the victim. Harassment orders shall cease to have effect on the date of the respondent's release from prison or an earlier date specified by the court or the court may impose the order for a period of up to 12 months from the date of the respondent's release. Contravention of a harassment order is an offence in this Bill.

3.6   EU and ECHR Developments

3.6.1   UNITED NATIONS

A number of key developments in Europe have also promoted recognition of the needs of victims within criminal justice systems. Internationally, the General Assembly of the United Nations adopted the *Declaration of Basic Principles of Justice for Victims of Crime and Abuse of Power* in 1985. Recognising 'that the victims of crime and the victims of abuse of power, and also frequently their families, witnesses and others who aid them, are unjustly subjected to loss, damage or injury and that they may, in addition, suffer hardship when assisting in the prosecution of offenders', the Declaration set forth a number of rights which included: the right to be treated with respect and recognition; the right to be referred to adequate support services; the right to receive information about the progress of the case; the right to be present and give input to the decision-making process; the right to counsel; the right to protection of physical safety and privacy and the right of compensation, from both the offender and the state. The document is not legally binding but does set out the minimum standards for the treatment of victims of crime. Among other things, it recommends that police and the judiciary should be provided with proper training, with special emphasis given to those with special needs (Article 17). It has been described as providing 'a benchmark for victim-friendly legislation and policies' (Van Dijk, 2005: 202).

3.6.2   EUROPEAN INSTITUTIONS

The Council of Europe also recognised that it 'is essential to put victims and witnesses at the very heart of the justice system. Victims should and need to be treated with the respect and dignity they deserve when coming into contact with justice, in particular so that they are safe from secondary victimisation (http://www.coe.int/t/DGHL/StandardSetting/Victims/).

Recommendation (2006)8 provides that 'States should ensure the effective recognition of, and respect for, the rights of victims with regard to their human rights; they should, in particular, respect the security, dignity, private and family life of victims and recognise the negative effects of crime on victims' (Article 2.1). Article 3.4, in particular, points out that 'States should ensure that victims who are particularly vulnerable, either through their personal characteristics or through the circumstances of the crime, can benefit from special measures best suited to their situation'. See also Council of Europe, *Non-Criminal Remedies for Crime Victims* (Council of Europe, 2009), p. 25.

The European Union has also more recently begun to focus on the area of criminal justice, particularly following the introduction of the Maastricht Treaty in 1993, which among other things promoted greater judicial cooperation in criminal matters. Cooperation was intensified after the Tampere summit in Finland in 1999, the first European Council meeting explicitly dedicated to justice and home affairs. In 1999, the European Commission adopted a communication entitled

Crime Victims in the European Union—standards and actions. In March 2001, the Council adopted a Framework Decision on the Standing of Victims in Criminal Proceedings, which provides for minimum rights (including the right to be heard and furnish evidence, access to relevant information, the opportunity to participate and the right to compensation) to be ensured in all the territories of the EU. This was replaced in 2012 with an important directive on victims' rights, Directive 2012/29/EU establishing minimum standards on the rights, support, and protection of victims of crime (the Victims Directive).

Under the Victims Directive, victims should be 'recognised and treated in a respectful, sensitive, tailored, professional and non-discriminatory manner, in all contacts with victim support or restorative justice services or competent authorities operating within the context of criminal proceedings' (Article 1). The Directive builds on existing rights for victims and contains more tangible and comprehensive rights for victims than existed previously. The Directive also places clearer obligations on member states, including an obligation to conduct individual assessments of victims to identify vulnerability and special protection measures (Article 22). Communication with victims must now also be accessible, with an emphasis on child-sensitive communication (Article 3). Interestingly, family members of deceased victims are now defined as victims and bestowed with all the rights afforded to victims in the Directive (Article 2). Other rights include a right to access victim support services under Article 8, a right to be heard under Article 10 and a right to be informed about a decision not to prosecute the offender and a right to have such decision reviewed under Article 11. The Directive forms part of a package of measures, including measures aimed at victims of specific crimes including the Directive on Trafficking in Human Beings (Directive 2011/36/EU) and the Directive on Child Sexual Exploitation (Directive 2011/92/EU).

The European Commission also issued a proposal for a Council Directive on Compensation to Crime Victims to reduce the disparities in the compensation schemes of various member states. The Council adopted this Directive on 29 April 2004. The Directive ensures that compensation is easily accessible in practice regardless of where in the EU a person becomes the victim of a crime. Similarly, the Committee of Ministers of the Council of Europe adopted Recommendation Rec (2006)8 on assistance to victims of crime on 14 June 2006. It sets out various provisions and recommends that member states be guided by them in their domestic legislation. These provisions relate to the role of public services and victim support services, the provision of information to victims, the right to effective access to other remedies, state compensation, insurance, protection of physical and psychological integrity, confidentiality, and training.

There are also other pieces of EU law facilitating the provision of compensation to crime victims from the offender. The Regulation on Jurisdiction and the Recognition and Enforcement of Judgments in Civil and Commercial Matters (Council Regulation (EC) No 44/2001 of 22 December 2000), for example, provides that the victim may sue the offender for damages in the same court that deals with the criminal proceedings, if this is possible under national law. The same Regulation also lays down how a crime victim can enforce a judgment for damages against the offender in another member state. The Victims Directive also establishes a right to a decision on compensation from the offender in the course of criminal proceedings under Article 16.

The European Convention on Human Rights (ECHR), which Ireland incorporated at a sub-constitutional level in 2003, has also been interpreted in ways that began to afford rights to victims of crime. Though the Convention does not explicitly refer to victims of crime, the jurisprudence of the Court has placed obligations on member states to criminalise wrongdoing, 'to take preventive operational measures', to investigate and give reasons, and to adequately protect victims and witnesses at various stages in the criminal process. These obligations arise under Articles 2 (right to life), 3 (degrading treatment), 6 (fair trial), and 8 (private life) and have been analysed in cases such as *Osman v United Kingdom* [1998] EHRR 101, *X and Y v The Netherlands* (1985) 8 EHRR 235, *MC v Bulgaria* [2003] ECHR 3927/98), *A v UK* [1999] 27 EHRR 611, and *KU v Finland* [2008] 48 EHRR 1237. In 1996, for example, the court in *Doorson v The Netherlands* [1996] 22 EHRR 330 expanded its interpretation of Article 6, primarily concerned with the rights of defendants in criminal proceedings, to take account of the rights of vulnerable witnesses and defendants. It noted:

> It is true that Article 6 does not explicitly require the interests of witnesses in general, and those of victims called upon to testify in particular, to be taken into consideration. However their life, liberty or security of person may be at stake, as may interests coming generally within the ambit of Article 8 [right to a private life]. Such interests of witnesses and victims are in principle protected by other, substantive provisions of the Convention, which imply that Contracting States should organise their criminal proceedings in such a way that those

interests are not unjustifiably imperilled. Against this background, principles of fair trial also require that in appropriate cases the interests of the defence are balanced against those of witnesses or victims called upon to testify.

Recently in *Y v Slovenia* ((Application no. 41107/10) 28 August 2015, at para 106), it was held that since 'direct confrontation between the defendants charged with criminal offences of sexual violence and their alleged victims involves a risk of further traumatisation on the latter's part, in the Court's opinion personal cross-examination by the defendant should be subject to a most careful assessment by the national courts, all the more so the more intimate the questions are'. In the instant case, it was held that the manner in which the criminal proceedings were conducted failed to afford the victim the necessary protection so as to strike an appropriate balance between her rights and interests protected by Article 8 and the defence rights protected by Article 6 of the Convention. ECHR jurisprudence has been referred to in the Irish Courts. Charleton J., in examining the exclusionary rule in *The People (DPP) v Cash* [2007] IEHC 108 noted: 'the entire focus is on the accused and his rights; the rights of the community to live safely has receded out of view'. He drew attention to the ECHR, and particularly the decision of *X and Y v The Netherlands* ((1986) 8 EHRR 235), which suggests that rules which hinder a fair prosecution may be incompatible with the Convention. He then emphasised the following principle:

> Criminal trials are about the rights and obligations of the entire community; of which the accused and the victim are members ... The cases of *J.T.* [discussed at **3.2.6.3**] and ... X. and Y. make it clear that the victim, being the subject of a crime, can have interests which should be weighed in the balance as well of those of the accused.

The European Commission has also identified as a strategic priority the protection of victims of crimes and the establishment of minimum standards. In May 2011, it put forward a proposal for a Directive establishing minimum standards on the rights, support, and protection of victims of crime. It includes provisions on information rights for victims including those with disabilities, the right of access to victim support services, the right of victims to have their complaints acknowledged, the right of victims to be heard, the rights of victims in the event of a decision not to prosecute, the right to reimbursement of expenses, the identification of vulnerable victims (children and persons with disabilities are at a particular risk of harm due to their personal characteristics, and therefore are in need of special measures), the right to avoidance of contact between victim and offender, the protection of vulnerable victims during criminal proceedings, and the training of practitioners who have contact with victims. As previously mentioned, this draft Directive has been adopted and member states are given until 2015 to transpose it into law.

3.7   Challenges in Meeting Victims' Needs

Notwithstanding the increased recognition of victims in the criminal process, it remains the case, however, that many of the needs of victims continue to be unmet. It is suggested by some that a lack of knowledge among criminal justice agencies and actors about the needs of victims of crime remains a central issue. A study by A. McGrath showed that 51 per cent of members of the legal profession were unfamiliar with the provisions of the Victims Charter (2009). There are also many reported difficulties with the provision of information to victims. The European Commission suggested in 2004 that the provision of information was not secured by 'simply issuing information booklets or setting up websites, without the authorities actively providing individual victims with information' (2004: 5). The Irish Council for Civil Liberties (2008: 21) takes a similar position noting the 'lack of initiation on the part of the State actors in their role as information-providers' to victims of crime. Similarly, the SAVI (Sexual Abuse and Violence in Ireland) Report (McGee et al., 2002) identified barriers for accessing law enforcement, medical and therapeutic services for those abused and their families. Lack of information from the Gardaí and medical personnel was the main source of dissatisfaction with the services provided. Specifically, the Gardaí were seen to provide inadequate explanations of procedures being undertaken, and medical personnel were seen as needing to provide more information regarding other available services and options. In relation to counselling services, time waiting to get an appointment was the major source of dissatisfaction. The SAVI Report studied responses from 3,120 participants, finding that disclosure rates to the Gardaí were very low (McGee et al., 2002: 128–32). Regarding experiences of adult sexual assault, only 1 per cent of men and 8 per cent of women had reported their experiences to the Gardaí (6 per cent overall). Only 8 per cent of adults reported previous experiences of child sexual abuse to the Gardaí (*ibid.*: xxxvii).

There is an ongoing problem with under-reporting of crime. O'Connell and Whelan, in a study in Dublin in the early 1990s noted that 19 per cent of those surveyed did not report the crime (1994: 85). In a follow-up study a few years later, the figure was reported at 20 per cent (Kirwan and O'Connell, 2001: 10). The Quarterly National Household Survey in 2010, which asked 39,000 households about the experiences of crime among those over 18 years of age in the previous 12 months, found that 25 per cent of burglaries, 36 per cent of violent thefts, 45 per cent of assaults, and 45 per cent of acts of vandalism were not reported (Central Statistics Office, 2010).

Other issues that cause concern to victims include fear of crime (Butler and Cunningham, 2010: 429–60); intimidation by the process (Kelleher and O'Connor, 1999); attrition rates (Leane et al., 2001; Hanly et al., 2009; O'Mahony, 2009; Bartlett and Mears, 2011; Hamilton, 2011; Leahy, 2014; a lack of empathy and understanding in reporting a crime (Kilcommins et al., 2010: 57–64); the lack of private areas in courts; difficulties with procedural rules and legal definitions and directions (e.g. consent in rape cases) (Bacik et al., 1998; Cooper, 2008; Leahy, 2013); delays in the system (Hanly et al., 2009); the lack of protection and security offered by the criminal justice system (Kilcommins et al., 2010: 64–6), the lack of opportunity to participate fully in the criminal process; the lack of information on the progress of criminal prosecutions (Watson, 2000); an over-emphasis in some instances on adversarialism and its morphology of combat and contest (Kilcommins and Donnelly, 2014); under- and over-criminalisation; overcrowded courtrooms and an inability to hear the proceedings (Kilcommins et al., 2010: 168); low levels of awareness of the Crime Victims Helpline; a lack of information on claiming witness expenses (Kilcommins et al., 2010: 164–6); and inadequate support services (Mulkerrins, 2003; Bacik et al., 2007; Deane, 2007; Irish Council for Civil Liberties, 2008; Cooper, 2008; Spain et al., 2014).

The lack of recognition of vulnerable witnesses in Ireland has also been identified (Bacik et al., 2007: 10–11). Victims of crime with disabilities, for example, remain largely invisible, not least because of the difficulties they pose in relation to information gathering and fact finding for an adversarial justice system which for the most part refuses to engage with the ontological dimensions of disability (Kilcommins et al., 2014). A recent study undertaken on victims of crime with disabilities found that people with disabilities 'are not being strategically identified as a victim group, either by victim support organisations, or those engaged at a central government policy level in dealing with victims' issues' (Edwards et al., 2012: 100). The Irish court process also remains epistemically rooted in mainstream accounts of victims' needs and concerns. Such victims fit more easily within an adversarial paradigm of justice that emphasises orality, lawyer-led questioning, observation of the demeanour of a witness, the curtailment of free-flowing witness narrative, confrontation and robust cross-examination (Kilcommins and Donnelly, 2014).

3.8   Conclusion

The last few decades have clearly witnessed a shift in terms of victims' rights in Ireland, as legislative and policy measures which seek to promote and support victims in the criminal justice system have come into operation. At the same time, the emergence of a network of support organisations outside the statutory criminal justice agencies is providing assistance to victims in many different forms. The new EU Directive will aid change in this area by demanding that stakeholders re-examine the nature of their engagements with victims of crime. Though Ireland will continue to encounter difficulties in recognising the needs and concerns of victims, it is clear that over the past 40 years it has moved significantly in the direction of creating a more communicative criminal process which better embraces their experiences and voices.

3.9   Further Reading

I. Bacik, C. Maunsell and S. Gogan, *The Legal Process and Victims of Rape* (Rape Crisis Centre, 1998)

I. Bacik, L. Heffernan, P. Brazil, and M. Woods, *Report on Services and Legislation Providing Support for Victims of Crime* (Commission for the Support of Victims of Crime, 2007)

H. Bartlett and E. Mears, *Sexual Violence against People with Disabilities: data collection and barriers to disclosure* (RCNI Report: NDA Research Promotion Scheme, 2011)

R. Breen and D. Rottman, *Crime Victimisation in the Republic of Ireland* (ERSI paper no. 121) (ERSI, 1985)

M. Butler and P. Cunningham, 'Fear of Crime in Ireland: Understanding its Origins and Consequences', in P. Knepper (eds), *International Handbook of Victimology* (Taylor & Francis Ltd, 2010)

Central Statistics Office, *Quarterly National Household Survey 2010*

N. Christie, 'Conflicts as Property' (1977) 17 British Journal of Criminology 1–15

G. Coffey, 'The Victim of Crime and the Criminal Justice Process' (2006) 16 Irish Criminal Law Journal 15.

Committee for Judicial Studies, *The Equal Treatment of Persons in Court: guidance for the judiciary* (Committee for Judicial Studies, 2011)

J. Cooper, *The Emotional Effects and Subsequent Needs of Families Bereaved by Homicide: a study commissioned by Advice and Support after Homicide* (funded by the Commission for the Support of Victims of Crime, 2008)

J. Deane, 'Balancing the Scales in a Homicide Trial' (2007) 7(1) Judicial Studies Institute Journal 18

M. Delahunt, 'Improved Measures Needed for Vulnerable Witnesses in Court' Irish Times, 7 December 2010

M. Delahunt, 'Video Evidence and s. 16(1)(b) of the Criminal Evidence Act 1992' Bar Review, February 2011, pp. 2–6

C. Edwards, S. Kilcommins and G. Harold, *Access to Justice for People with Disabilities as Victims of Crime in Ireland* (National Disability Authority, 2012)

European Commission, *Report from the Commission on the basis of Article 18 of the Council Framework Decision of 15 March 2001 on the standing of victims in criminal proceedings* (SEC, 2004)

C. Fennell, *The Law of Evidence in Ireland* (3rd edn) (Bloomsbury Professional, 2010)

D. Garland, *The Culture of Control* (Oxford University Press, 2001)

J. Goodey, *Victims and Victimology: research, policy and practice* (Pearson, 2005)

C. Hanly et al., *Rape and Justice in Ireland: a national study of survivor, prosecutor and court responses to rape* (The Liffey Press, 2009)

J. Healy, *Irish Laws of Evidence* (Thomson, Round Hall, 2004)

Irish Council for Civil Liberties, *A Better Deal: The human rights of victims in the criminal justice system* (ICCL, 2008)

J. Jackson, 'Competence and Compellability of Spouses to Give Evidence' (1993) 15 Dublin University Law Journal 202–11

P. Kelleher and M. O'Connor, *Making the Links: Towards an Integrated System for the Elimination of Violence against Women in Intimate Relationships with Men* (Women's Aid, 1999)

S. Kilcommins, M. Leane, F. Donson and C. Fennell, *The Needs and Concerns of Victims of Crime in Ireland* (UCC, 2010).

S. Kilcommins, C. Edwards and T. O'Sullivan, *An International Review of Legal Provisions for Support of People with Disabilities as Victims of Crime* (ICCL, 2014)

S. Kilcommins and M. Donnelly, 'Victims of Crime with Disabilities in Ireland: hidden casualties in the "vision of victim as Everyman"' (2014) 20(3) International Review of Victimology 305–26

G. Kirwan and M. O'Connell, 'Crime Victimisation in Dublin Revisited' (2001) 11(2) Irish Criminal Law Journal 10–13

Law Reform Commission, *Consultation Paper on Child Sexual Abuse* (Law Reform Commission, 1989)

Law Reform Commission, *Report on Sexual Offences against the Mentally Handicapped* (LRC, 1990)

Law Reform Commission, *Consultation Paper on Vulnerable Adults and the Law: capacity* (LRC, 2005)

Law Reform Commission, *Report on Vulnerable Adults and the Law* (Law Reform Commission, 2006)

Law Reform Commission, *Consultation Paper on Sexual Offences and Capacity to Consent* (Law Reform Commission, 2011)

S. Leahy, 'Summing Up in Rape Trials: The Challenge of Guiding Effectively and without Prejudice' (2013) 23(4) Irish Criminal Law Journal 102.

S. Leahy, 'Bad Laws or Bad Attitudes? Assessing the Impact of Societal Attitudes upon the Conviction Rates for Rape in Ireland' (2014) 14(1) Irish Journal of Applied Social Studies 18–29

M. Leane, S. Ryan, C. Fennell and E. Egan, *Attrition in Sexual Assault Offence Cases in Ireland: A qualitative analysis* (Department of Justice, Equality and Law Reform, 2001)

H. McGee, R. Garavan, M. de Barra, J. Byrne and R. Conroy, *The SAVI Report: sexual abuse and violence in Ireland* (Liffey Press, 2002)

L. McGovern, 'The Victim and the Criminal Justice Process' in P. O'Mahony, *Criminal Justice in Ireland* (IPA, 2002) 393

A. McGrath, *The Living Victims of Homicide: analysing the needs and concerns of the co-victims of homicide within the Irish criminal justice system* (UCC, unpublished PhD thesis, 2009)

D. McGrath, *Evidence* (Thomson Round Hall, 2005)

K. Mulkerrins, 'Trial Venue and Process: the victim and the accused (2003) 3(1) Judicial Studies Institute Journal 120

M. O'Connell and A. Whelan, 'Crime Victimisation in Dublin', (1994) 4 Irish Criminal Law Journal 85

E. O'Hara, 'Victim Participation in the Criminal Process' (2005) 13 Journal of Law and Policy 229–47

P. O'Mahony, 'Ireland', in J. Lovett and L. Kelly *Different Systems, Similar Outcomes? Tracking attrition in reported rape cases across Europe* (Child and Woman Abuse Unit, 2009)

T. O'Malley, *The Irish Criminal Process* (Thomson Round Hall, 2009)

M. Rogan, 'Victims' Rights: Theory and Practice—Part 1' (2006a) 24 Irish Law Times 140

M. Rogan, 'The Role of Victims in Sentencing: The Role of Compensation Orders' (2006b) 24 Irish Law Times 202

E. Spain, S. Gibbons and S. Kilcommins, *Analysis of Text for the Final Review of the National Strategy on Domestic, Sexual and Gender Based Violence, 2010–2014* (COSC, 2014)

B. Vaughan and S. Kilcommins, *Terrorism, Rights and the Rule of Law: negotiating justice in Ireland* (Willan, 2008)

B. Vaughan and S. Kilcommins, 'The Governance of Crime and the Negotiation of Justice' (2010) 10 Criminology and Criminal Justice 59–75

J. Van Dijk, 'Benchmarking Legislation on Crime Victims: The UN Declaration of 1985' in E. Vetere and P. David, *Victims of Crime and Abuse of Power: festschrift in honour of Irene Melup* (United Nations, 2005)

D. Walsh, *Criminal Procedure* (Thomson Round Hall, 2002)

D. Walsh, *Juvenile Justice* (Thomson Round Hall, 2005)

D. Watson, *Victims of Recorded Crime in Ireland: Results of the 1996 Survey* (ERSI: Oak Tree Press, 2000)

PART II

INVESTIGATION OF CRIME— OBLIGATIONS AND RIGHTS

CHAPTER 4

THE CRIMINAL INVESTIGATION— PROSECUTION PERSPECTIVES

4.1 Introduction

The Criminal Justice Acts 2006, 2007 and more recently the Criminal Procedure Act 2010 are examples of how, in recent years, a wide range of new statutory powers have been conferred on the Gardaí as the investigators of crime in the state. The exercise of these powers, in conjunction with the pre-existing ones, necessarily encroaches upon the rights of any individual upon whom suspicion may fall. The role of the solicitor in this regard is to provide advice concerning the powers of the investigator and the rights of the suspect.

4.2 Police Powers to Stop, Inquire, Search, and Seize

4.2.1 STOP AND MAKE INQUIRIES

A member of the Gardaí has a broad range of statutory and common law powers to call upon in the prevention of crime, detection of crime, and the bringing of offenders to justice. It has been held that the Gardaí could not carry out their duties unless they had the power to make reasonable inquiries of members of the public. Accordingly, it is well established that a Garda member may approach any member of the public in order to make such inquiries. In *DPP (Stratford) v Fagan* [1994] 3 IR 265, it was held that members of An Garda Síochána had a power at common law, in the exercise of their duty to prevent and detect crime, to require motorists to stop their vehicles in order to make inquiries to ascertain whether a road traffic offence has been committed, even in the absence of a reasonable suspicion that the motorist in question has committed an offence. It was held by O'Flaherty J. that 'the power to stop must be exercised (like all powers) not in a capricious manner but in a constant fashion and with due civility and courtesy'.

4.2.2 STOP AND SEARCH

The powers to stop and search are contained within a multiple number of both general and specific statutory provisions that empower the Gardaí to stop persons for the purpose of conducting a search in order to assist in the prevention and detection of crime. An example of a limited specific power to stop and search is s. 29 of the Dublin Police Act 1842, which contains a power to search on reasonable suspicion of possession of stolen property. It appears this power is limited in its applicability to the Dublin Metropolitan Area and does not exist outside Dublin. Examples of legislation containing more general powers to stop and search are contained within various Acts of the Oireachtas. For example, s. 109(1) of the Road Traffic Act 1961, provides a power to stop motorists driving a vehicle in a public place and to keep it stationary for such period as is reasonably necessary in order for such member to discharge his duties. In other Acts the legislature has given explicit power to the Gardaí to stop persons in certain circumstances; for example s. 30(1) of the Offences Against the State Act 1939, provides the power to stop, search, interrogate and arrest any person or persons suspected of having committed or being about to commit offences scheduled within that Act. Section 23 of the Misuse of Drugs Acts 1977 and 1984 allows a Garda member to stop and search any person reasonably believed to be in possession of a controlled drug.

Vehicles and their occupants may be stopped and searched under the Criminal Law Act 1976, s. 8, under s. 22(3) of the Intoxicating Liquor Act 1960 and again via s. 23 of the Misuse of Drugs Act 1977 (as amended). The case of *DPP v Rooney* (1993) ILRM 61 established that a person stopped under any statutory power has a general right to be informed of the statutory authority under which the search is being conducted.

The implementation of s. 6 of the Criminal Justice Act 2006, in inserting a new s. 10 into the Criminal Justice (Miscellaneous Provisions) Act 1997 facilitated the lowering of the rank of Garda who can apply for or issue a search warrant. Since this Act, a Superintendent may issue a 24-hour search warrant, on the usual terms of reasonable belief and urgency. On exercise of either warrant, any persons present must give their names and addresses if asked; otherwise they will be committing an offence.

4.2.3   SEARCH AND SEIZE

The powers to search and seize are based on both statute and the common law. Following the stop and search of any person, that person may be arrested and brought to a Garda station. The suspect is usually searched under common law, primarily for the safety of the suspect and the arresting members, but also for the purpose of taking into custody any dangerous article, or other item which may be of evidentiary value found on that person. Following the commencement of the Criminal Justice Act 2006, s. 7(1) of that Act states that, where a member of the Garda Síochána who is in a public place or any other place under a power of entry authorised by law or invite finds or comes into possession of anything, and s/he has reasonable grounds for believing that it is evidence of, or relating to, the commission of an arrestable offence, s/he may seize and retain the thing for use as evidence in any criminal proceedings. In *DPP v Boyce* [2005] IECC 143, it was held that the powers to gather evidence granted by statute are in addition to, and not in extinction of, the existing lawful power of the Gardaí to gather relevant material with the consent of citizens. Section 7 of the Criminal Justice Act 2006 confers a power on a Garda to seize anything found in connection with an arrestable offence.

4.2.4   ENTRY AND SEARCH OF PREMISES

Article 40.5 of Bunreacht na hÉireann (Constitution of Ireland) states as a fundamental right: 'The dwelling of every citizen is inviolable and shall not be forcibly entered save in accordance with law.' The inviolability of the dwelling house is clearly a constitutional protection, but with qualifications in accordance with law. The common law has also been active placing limits on the state's desire to search private property ever since the decision of *Entick v Carrington* [1765] 2 Wils 275, where it was held by Camden C.J.: 'Our law holds the property of every man so sacred, that no man can set his foot upon his neighbours' close without his leave; if he does he is a trespasser, though he does no damage at all; if he tread upon a neighbour's ground he must justify it by law.'

The entry onto premises to effect an arrest or to conduct a search must take place within the parameters of a properly issued warrant or pursuant to a statutory power, as per s. 6 of the Criminal Law Act 1997, or common law power of entry without warrant, in order to be lawful.

A search warrant is a written legal authorisation to perform a specified act given to the person or persons named therein, empowering entry onto specified property to arrest a suspect or search the premises or for the seizure of specified property thereon. Warrants are usually issued on foot of statutory authority, for example, warrants may be issued under s. 26 of the Misuse of Drugs Acts 1977 to 1984; s. 48 of the Criminal Justice (Theft and Fraud Offences) Act 2001 as amended; s. 10 of the Criminal Justice (Miscellaneous Provisions) Act 1997 as amended by s. 6 Criminal Justice Act 2006; and most recently, s. 18 of the Criminal Procedure Act 2010.

A warrant may allow the search of a person only, the search of premises only or both. The length of time of a search warrant's validity depends upon the authorising statute. A warrant issued under the Child Trafficking and Pornography Act 1998 lasts for seven days, whereas by comparison a search warrant issued under s. 26 of the Misuse of Drugs Act lasts for a month.

A district judge or a peace commissioner, on consideration of sworn information (known as 'an information'), may issue most warrants. In such cases, the granting authority is obliged to act judicially and to satisfy itself that facts exist which constitute reasonable grounds, rather than simply acting on the statement of reasonable belief of the applicant. Other warrants may be issued by senior officers of the Garda Síochána, with or without the necessity for the laying of 'an information'. Section 25 of the Criminal Justice (Amendment) Act 2009 states, 'an application under any enactment to a court, or a judge of a court, for a search warrant shall be heard otherwise than in public.'

Section 9 of the Criminal Law Act 1976 refers to searches carried out under that Act or pursuant to any other power. It allows a Garda member who finds or comes into possession of anything that he believes to be evidence of an offence or suspected offence to seize and retain it for a reasonable period for use as evidence. This power is subject to an exception in respect of documents covered by legal professional privilege. Section 7(1) of the Criminal Justice Act 2006 is a similarly worded power.

Following the decision of the Supreme Court in *DPP v Kenny* [1990] 2 IR 110, it was held by a slender majority that a deliberate and conscious breach of a constitutional right occurred when the act breaching the right to professional privilege was deliberate, regardless of whether or not the actor intended to breach the constitutional right of the citizen. Accordingly, since the *Kenny* decision in the case of search warrants, errors on warrants, no matter how minor, lead to invalidity of the warrant and then to illegality of the search and thus unconstitutionality, and almost inevitable exclusion of evidence.

However, in the Court of Criminal Appeal case of *DPP v Gareth Mallon* CCA [2011] 2 IR 544, the issue raised was in what circumstances will a warrant be considered ineffective or invalid so as to give rise to the argument that evidence obtained should be excluded? The facts of *Gareth Mallon* are that on 29 November 2006, Garda Kevin Lawless swore an information on oath before a peace commissioner seeking a search warrant pursuant to s. 26 of the Misuse of Drugs Act 1977 in respect of premises described as '4 Marrowbone Close, Dublin 8'. However, the correct address of the premises searched, in which diamorphine was found, was '4 Marrowbone Lane Close, Dublin 8.' The Court of Criminal Appeal embarked on a detailed synthesis of the case law on search law to date and felt with a little perspective, a pattern does emerge from the cases. It was held that it is now clear a mere error will not invalidate a warrant, especially one which is not calculated to mislead, or perhaps just as importantly, does not mislead. Indeed, that fact that warrants perfectly regular on their face may be invalidated if it can be demonstrated by evidence that there was no jurisdiction to issue them, establishes that error alone is not the critical factor. The search warrant in the Mallon case was held to be valid. Irish law maintains an almost exclusionary rule for evidence obtained as a result of an illegal and therefore unconstitutional search of a dwelling house. Courts are therefore hesitant to invalidate warrants on the grounds of typographical or grammatical, or transcription errors, which are neither calculated to mislead, nor in truth do mislead, any reasonable reader of the words.

In the Supreme Court case of *Ali Charaf Damache and the DPP, Ireland and the Attorney General Supreme Court* [2012] IESC 11, Mr Damache had sought, by way of judicial review, a declaration that s. 29(1) of the Offences Against the State Act 1939 (as amended) was repugnant to the constitution. Mr Damache was initially investigated by the Gardaí on suspicion of conspiracy to murder but was ultimately charged with an offence contrary to s. 13 of the Post Office (Amendment) Act 1951 (as amended), namely sending a menacing message by telephone. The appellant's dwelling home had been searched on foot of a search warrant issued pursuant to s. 29(1) of the Offences Against the State Act 1939 (as amended) by Detective Superintendent Hayes, and certain property, including a mobile phone, was removed from the home. Detective Superintendent Hayes was the person responsible for commencing the investigation into the alleged conspiracy to murder and he was personally involved in that investigation. It was held by Denham C.J. (Murray J., Hardiman J., Fennelly J., Finnegan J. concurring) that the issuing of a search warrant is an administrative act but it must be exercised judicially. The literal interpretation of the words of s. 29(1) as determined by the Court of Criminal Appeal in *DPP v Birney* [2007] IR 337 did not preclude the superintendent in charge of an investigation from issuing a search warrant and a proviso cannot be inferred that the superintendent issuing the warrant should be independent of the investigation. However, the person issuing a search warrant should be an independent person. For the process of obtaining a search warrant to be meaningful, it is necessary for the person authorising the search to be in a position to assess the conflicting interests of the state or the common good and the individual in an impartial manner. There should also be reasonable grounds for establishing that an offence has been committed and that evidence may be found at the place to be searched. Any interference with the constitutional rights of individuals must be proportionate. This case was decided on its own circumstances, namely a member of the investigating team issued the warrant and the search related to the appellant's dwelling. Having regard to the foregoing, s. 29(1) of the 1939 Act was repugnant to the Constitution. Those two circumstances were at the kernel of the court's decision. The Supreme Court pointed out that it is best practice to keep a record of the basis upon which a search warrant is granted.

The exclusionary rule in the Supreme Court case of *DPP v Kenny* [1990] 2 IR 110 was subsequently overturned some 25 years later by the same Supreme Court in a judgment delivered on 15 April 2015 in the case of *DPP v JC* [2015] IESC 31.

The accused had been suspected of committing a number of burglaries. The Gardaí entered his house on foot of search warrant pursuant to s. 29 of the Offences Against the State Act 1939 issued on 10 May 2011. He was then arrested under s. 30 and admitted the offences whilst being interviewed at the Garda station. At his trial in the Circuit Court on 18 July 2012, Judge Ring directed that he be acquitted. Judge Ring held that following the decision in *Damache*, the Gardaí were trespassers in law. Following on from this the arrest was unconstitutional and, applying *Kenny*, the memoranda of interview had to be excluded. The DPP had previously argued in the Circuit Court that the arrest was lawful in circumstances where the arresting Garda had no reason to believe that the s. 29 warrant was unlawful. The DPP appealed the acquittal to the Supreme Court pursuant to the provisions of s. 23 of the Criminal Procedure Act 2010. Section 23 provides that the DPP may appeal an acquittal on a question of law where the ruling was made during the course of a trial which erroneously excluded compelling evidence. The purpose of the appeal was to invite the Supreme Court to overrule its decision in *Kenny*. Counsel for the accused at trial conceded that the last three statements contained evidence which could reasonably lead to the conviction of the accused. It had been agreed by the parties that the Circuit Court Judge was required to apply the exclusionary rule in *Kenny*. The court, however, was invited by the Director to overturn *Kenny* which provides that there is an absolute exclusion of any evidence obtained as a result of a breach of a constitutional right if the breach was deliberate and conscious. A question which arose for the Supreme Court was whether *Kenny* was correctly decided, and, if not, what was the appropriate test to be applied for the admission or exclusion of evidence obtained in circumstances where the method of taking the evidence involved a breach of constitutional rights. According to O'Donnell J:

> the issue for this Court is after all not whether the exclusionary rule in *Kenny* is inconvenient at a practical level, but rather whether as a matter of constitutional law it is right.

The Supreme Court allowed the DPP's appeal by a majority of 4 to 3, O'Donnell J., Clarke J., MacMenamin J. and Denham C.J. concurring with Hardiman J., Murray J. and McKechnie J. dissenting. The court concluded in effect that its earlier decision in *Kenny* in 1990 was wrong. In this important decision the Supreme Court therefore overturned the absolute exclusionary rule. O'Donnell J. in his conclusion remarked:

> A criminal or civil trial is the administration of justice. A central function of the administration of justice is fact finding, and truth finding. Anything that detracts from the courts' capacity to find out what occurred in fact, detracts from the truth finding function of the administration of the justice. As many courts have recognised, where cogent and compelling evidence of guilt is found but not admitted on the basis of trivial technical breach, the administration of justice far from being served, may be brought into disrepute.

O'Donnell J was satisfied that the decision in *Kenny* was wrong in principle and should be overruled.

In the judgment of Clarke J., who was satisfied that *Kenny* and *O'Brien* both fail adequately to balance the competing constitutional rights involved, he sets out a new test which should be used when a court is considering if unconstitutionally obtained evidence should be excluded or not. The new test now provides for cases where, as in this case, the person who had breached a constitutional right was not actually aware that the right had been breached. Deliberate and conscious violation of constitutional rights shall remain excluded except in exceptional circumstances.

in summary, the elements of the test are as follows:

(i)   The onus rests on the prosecution to establish the admissibility of all evidence. The test which follows is concerned with objections to the admissibility of evidence where the objection relates solely to the circumstances in which the evidence was gathered and does not concern the integrity or probative value of the evidence concerned.

(ii)   Where objection is taken to the admissibility of evidence on the grounds that it was taken in circumstances of unconstitutionality, the onus remains on the prosecution to establish either:

    (a)   that the evidence was not gathered in circumstances of unconstitutionality; or

    (b)   that, if it was, it remains appropriate for the court to nonetheless admit the evidence.

The onus in seeking to justify the admission of evidence taken in unconstitutional circumstances places an obligation on the prosecution to explain the basis on which it is said that the evidence should, nonetheless, be admitted and also to establish any facts necessary to justify such a basis.

(iii)   Any facts relied on by the prosecution to establish any of the matters referred to at (ii) must be established beyond reasonable doubt.

(iv)   Where evidence is taken in deliberate and conscious violation of constitutional rights then the evidence should be excluded save in those exceptional circumstances considered in the existing jurisprudence. In this context deliberate and conscious refers to knowledge of the unconstitutionality of the taking of the relevant evidence rather than applying to the acts concerned. The assessment as to whether evidence was taken in deliberate and conscious violation of constitutional rights requires an analysis of the conduct or state of mind not only of the individual who actually gathered the evidence concerned but also any other senior official or officials within the investigating or enforcement authority concerned who is or are involved either in that decision or in decisions of that type generally or in putting in place policies concerning evidence gathering of the type concerned.

(v)   Where evidence is taken in circumstances of unconstitutionality but where the prosecution establishes that same was not conscious and deliberate in the sense previously appearing, then a presumption against the admission for the relevant evidence arises. Such evidence should be admitted where the prosecution establishes that the evidence was obtained in circumstances where any breach of rights was due to inadvertence or derives from subsequent legal developments.

(vi)   Evidence that is obtained or gathered in circumstances where same could not have been constitutionally obtained or gathered should not be admitted even if those involved in the relevant evidence gathering were unaware due to inadvertence of the absence of authority.

In a later unanimous decision by the Supreme Court on 22 June 2015, the court declined to order a retrial pursuant to s. 23 of the Criminal Procedure Act 2010, as it would not be in the interests of justice. Denham C.J. held given the fact that:

(i)   this case has changed the law, as previously stated in *Kenny*;

(ii)   if the respondent were re-tried, he would be subject to new legal principles relating to the exclusion of evidence in search warrant cases, contrary to the situation in his earlier trial;

(iii)   three years have passed since the respondent was acquitted;

(iv)   there is no specific evidence before the court as to the impact on the victims of the crimes; and

(v)   the fact that the appellant chose this mode of appeal should not and does not give rise automatically to a re-trial on the success of the substantive issues raised;

in all the circumstances, in the interests of justice, I would affirm the acquittal of the respondent, and consequently I would order that the respondent not be re-tried for the offences.

It is best practice that following the execution of a search warrant, and the obtaining of evidence on foot of the warrant and the suspect's subsequent arrest, it is important to request disclosure from the prosecution of a copy of the warrant and any information sworn (if applicable). This is done to determine if there was jurisdiction to issue the warrant in the first place by conducting an analysis of the fulfilment of all statutory preconditions. In the absence of jurisdiction, the search warrant will be unconstitutional and any evidence obtained must be excluded in the absence of any extraordinary excusing circumstances. It should be noted in this context that s. 5 of the Criminal Justice Act 2006 permits Gardaí to designate a certain place as 'a crime scene'. This place must be a public place or another place entered into by a power of entry authorised by law or where Gardaí were expressly or impliedly invited into.

4.3   Police Powers of Arrest, Re-Arrest, Detention, and Interrogation

4.3.1   ARREST

Article 40.4.1 of the Constitution provides that: 'No citizen shall be deprived of his personal liberty save in accordance with law.' Arrest can take place with or without a warrant for the purposes of being charged, or to be brought before a court, or to be detained in a Garda station for the proper investigation of an offence. Order 16(1) of the District Court Rules 1997 provides for the issue of an arrest warrant in the first instance for the arrest of a person charging him or her with having committed an indictable offence.

It was held in the High Court in the case of *DPP v Alan Bradley* [2000] 1 IR 420 (McGuiness J.):

> In cases where proof of a valid arrest was not an essential ingredient to ground a charge, the jurisdiction of the District Court to embark on any criminal proceedings was not affected by the fact that an accused person has been brought before the court by an illegal process, and the court should consider whether there had been a deliberate and conscious violation of the accused's rights, prior to embarking on the hearing.

The most frequently used statutory provision that enables both the Gardaí and ordinary citizens to effect arrest (without warrant) is outlined in the Criminal Law Act 1997 (the 1997 Act). Section 4(1) of the 1997 Act gives any person the power to arrest without warrant anyone who is or whom he or she, with reasonable cause, suspects to be in the act of committing an arrestable offence. Section 4(2) of the 1997 Act states that where any arrestable offence has been committed any person may arrest without warrant anyone who is or whom he or she, with reasonable cause, suspects to be guilty of the offence. Section 4(3) of the 1997 Act states, where a member of the Garda Síochána, with reasonable cause, suspects that an arrestable offence has been committed, he or she may arrest without warrant anyone whom the member, with reasonable cause, suspects to be guilty of the offence. The power of citizens' arrest is limited by s. 4(4) of the 1997 Act to those situations where the person effecting the arrest with reasonable cause suspects that the person to be arrested would otherwise attempt to avoid, or is avoiding arrest by a member of the Garda Síochána. A suspect arrested by a person other than a member of the Garda Síochána shall be transferred into the custody of the Garda Síochána as soon as practicable.

An arrestable offence is defined by the 1997 Act, as amended by s. 8 of the Criminal Justice Act 2006, as one for which a person of full capacity and who has not previously been convicted may, under or by virtue of any enactment, be punished by imprisonment for a term of five years or by a more severe penalty, and includes an attempt to commit any such offence. Consequently, offences that are summary only in nature and thereby subject to a maximum of 12 months' imprisonment do not fall within the definition of 'arrestable offence'. The power to arrest without warrant is contained within a large number of statutes, some of which are purely summary matters, for example s. 49(8) of the Road Traffic Act 1994 (as amended) for drink-driving. Section 42 of the Criminal Justice Act 1999, as amended by s. 11 of the Criminal Justice Act 2006, provides that a person in prison may be arrested by the Gardaí and detained for questioning in connection with arrestable offence(s).

Persons arrested without warrant are entitled to be told the grounds upon which they are being detained, in ordinary language and general terms, unless the circumstances are such that this must be apparent to them, or unless they themselves render this impracticable, such as by running away, resisting arrest or otherwise causing a commotion. The Supreme Court has thus adopted with approval, in *The People v Walsh* [1980] IR 294, the test laid down by Viscount Simon in *Christie and Morris v Leachinsky* [1947] AC 573.

As outlined above, one can be arrested with or without warrant for the purpose of being charged with a criminal offence and to be brought before the court. One can also be arrested for the purposes of detention for questioning. Depending on the legislation under which a person is detained, they can be held for questioning in a Garda station for up to 24 hours (s. 4 Criminal Justice Act 1984), 72 hours (s. 30 Offences Against the State Act 1939, as amended), seven days (s. 2 Criminal Justice (Drug Trafficking) Act 1996) or, for certain murders and other serious offences, seven days pursuant to s. 50 of the Criminal Justice Act 2007. There is a detailed discussion in **Chapter 5** with respect to the rights of a suspect detained under any of these powers.

4.3.2   RE-ARREST

Section 10 of the Criminal Justice Act 1984 as amended by s. 23 of the Criminal Justice (Amendment) Act 2009, provides for a person's re-arrest on the authority of a warrant issued by a judge of the District Court following an application of a Garda not below the rank of Superintendent if further information has come to the knowledge of the Garda. There is a similar provision contained within s. 51 of the Criminal Justice Act 2007 relating to a person previously detained under s. 50. Furthermore, s. 30A(1) and s. 30A(3) of the Offences Against the State Act 1939, as amended by s. 187 of the Criminal Justice Act 2006, provides for re-arrest if further information has come to the knowledge of the Garda or for the purpose of charging the person forthwith or bringing the person before the Special Criminal Court as soon as practicable to be charged.

4.3.3   DETENTION

The position regarding detention for questioning was summarised by the Supreme Court in *DPP v Shaw* [1982] IR 1. In that case, Walsh J stated that 'no person may be arrested with or without a warrant for the purpose of interrogation or the securing of evidence from that person'. If there exists a practice of arresting persons for the purpose of assisting the police in their inquiries, it is unlawful. In such circumstances, the phrase is no more than a euphemism for false imprisonment.

With the exception of s. 30 of the Offences Against the State Act 1939 the concept of detention for the purposes of assisting Gardaí with their inquiries did not exist until the introduction of s. 4 of the Criminal Justice Act 1984 (as amended). More recent powers of detention include those implemented by s. 2 of the Criminal Justice (Drug Trafficking) Act 1996 (as amended) and s. 50 of the Criminal Justice Act 2007.

4.3.3.1   Section 30 of the Offences Against the State Act 1939 (as amended)

Section 30 of the Offences Against the State Act 1939 (the 1939 Act) allows a member of the Garda Síochána to stop, search, interrogate, and arrest any person suspected of involvement in the commission or attempted commission of any scheduled offence, and for that person to be detained for up to 24 hours. An amendment to the 1939 Act provisions in the Offences against the State (Amendment) Act 1998 permitted the extension of the original detention period by a further 24 hours from the time of arrest if so directed by an officer not below the rank of Chief Superintendent. This further 24-hour extension of detention is granted on application to a judge of the District Court by an officer not below the rank of Superintendent who has reasonable grounds for believing it necessary for the proper investigation of the offence. Before granting it, the District Judge concerned must be satisfied that the extension sought is necessary for the proper investigation of the offence, and that the investigation is being conducted diligently and expeditiously.

For the purposes of s. 30, a 'scheduled offence' is an offence that the government has so declared by Order. In *The People (DPP) v Quilligan* [1987] ILRM 606, the Supreme Court approved the use of s. 30 detention in the investigation of non-subversive cases involving scheduled offences. In *The People (DPP) v Howley* [1989] ILRM 629, the Supreme Court upheld the practice of questioning detainees about non-scheduled offences. Section 30 of the Offences Against the State Act 1939 detention powers continue to be used for both subversive and ordinary criminal investigations.

4.3.3.2   Section 4 of the Criminal Justice Act 1984 (as amended)

Section 4 of the Criminal Justice Act 1984, contrary to the reasoning of the Supreme Court in *DPP v Shaw* [1982] IR 1, introduced the power to detain for questioning a person reasonably suspected of having committed or having attempted to commit an 'arrestable offence', being an offence punishable by five years' imprisonment or more. A person so suspected can be arrested by a member of the Garda Síochána without warrant and conveyed to a Garda station where detention will follow if the member in charge has reasonable grounds for believing that detention is necessary for the proper investigation of the offence. Detention may be for a period of up to six hours initially, but can be extended at the direction of an officer not below the rank of Superintendent for a further period of up to six hours. Such officer must have reasonable grounds for believing that an extension is necessary for the proper investigation of the offence. Section 9 of the Criminal Justice Act 2006 permits a further extension on similar grounds for 12 hours on the direction of a Chief Superintendent. The possible interposition of an eight-hour rest period between midnight and 8 a.m. means that a person may be detained in a Garda station under s. 4 for a maximum period of 32 hours.

4.3.3.3   Section 2 of the Criminal Justice (Drug Trafficking) Act 1996 (as amended)

Section 2 of the Criminal Justice (Drug Trafficking) Act 1996 (the 1996 Act) allows for the detention of a person arrested without warrant on reasonable suspicion that the person in question has committed a drug trafficking offence as defined by the Criminal Justice Act 1994, s. 3(1). An initial six-hour detention period is allowed, subject to the Garda member in charge believing, on reasonable grounds, that the detention is necessary for the proper investigation of the offence. Thereafter an extension of up to 18 hours and a further extension of 24 hours are possible, based on the same belief of an officer not below the rank of Chief Superintendent on the same grounds, bringing the aggregate total up to two days. A further extension of up to a further three days may be granted on application to a judge of the District or Circuit Court, if the court considers such extension necessary for the proper investigation of the offence concerned, and if the court is satisfied that the investigation is being conducted diligently and expeditiously. A final possible extension of yet a further 48 hours may be granted on the basis of a similar application, bringing to seven days the total cumulative detention period permissible under the 1996 Act.

Section 10 of the Criminal Justice Act 2006 amended the detention under the Criminal Justice (Drug Trafficking) Act 1996 so that the original detention applies to a person arrested within a Garda station as well as someone brought to the station. This provision has similar application to detention under s. 4 of the Criminal Justice Act 1984.

4.3.3.4   Section 50 of the Criminal Justice Act 2007

Section 50 of the Criminal Justice Act 2007 provides for detention for up to seven days in respect of four categories of offences:

- murder involving firearms or explosives;
- murder of a Garda or prison officer;
- possession of a firearm with intent to endanger life;
- kidnapping or false imprisonment involving the use of a firearm.

4.3.3.5   Detention of a serving prisoner

Section 11 of the Criminal Justice Act 2006 amends s. 42 of the Criminal Justice Act 1999 and makes provision for applications for warrants for the arrest and detention of a serving prisoner in connection with the investigation of other offences.

4.3.4   INTERROGATION

4.3.4.1   The Judges' Rules

The Supreme Court has set out the Judges' Rules as they apply in Ireland. Walsh J in *The People (AG) v Cummins* [1972] IR 312 stated at p. 323:

> The Judges's [sic] Rules which are in force in this country are the ones mentioned in *McCarrick v Leavy* [1964] IR 225; they are sometimes called 'the Judges' Rules of 1922' though they first appeared in 1912 when the judges in England, at the request of the Home Secretary, drew up four rules as a guide for police officers in respect of communications with prisoners or persons suspected of crime. The Rules were signed by Lord Chief Justice Alverstone and were then four in number; they were printed at the end of the report of *R v Voisin* [1918] 1 KB 531. In the judgment of the Court of Criminal Appeal given in that case, the following statement appears at p. 539 of the report:
>
>> These Rules have not the force of law; they are administrative directions the observance of which the police authorities should enforce upon their subordinates as tending to the fair administration of justice. It is important that they should do so, for statements obtained from prisoners, contrary to the spirit of these rules, may be rejected as evidence by the judge presiding at the trial.

The origin of the Rules is again mentioned in *R v Cook* (1918) 34 TLR 515. By 1922 the rules mentioned in those cases had increased to a total of nine.

These nine rules (set out in the head note of that judgment) are the ones which have been followed in this state since that date. The first four of them are the ones which were originally formulated in 1912 and they are mentioned in the cases decided in 1918. The Judges' Rules that are in force in Ireland were adopted by Walsh J. as follows:

(i)   When a police officer is endeavouring to discover the author of a crime, there is no objection to his putting questions in respect thereof to any person or persons, whether suspected or not, from whom he thinks useful information may be obtained.

(ii)   When a police officer has made up his/her mind to charge a person with a crime, they should first caution the person before asking them any questions or any further questions, as the case may be.

(iii)   Persons in custody should not be questioned without the usual caution first being administered.

(iv)   If a prisoner wishes to volunteer any statement, the usual caution should first be administered. It is preferable that the last two words of such caution be omitted and that the caution end with the words 'be given in evidence'.

(v)   The caution administered to a prisoner when he is formally charged should therefore be in the following words: 'Do you wish to say anything in answer to the charge? You are not obliged to say anything unless you wish to do so, but whatever you say will be taken down in writing and may be given in evidence.' Care should be taken to avoid the suggestion that the prisoner's answers can only be used in evidence against them, as this may prevent an innocent person making a statement which might assist in clearing them of the charge.

(vi)   A statement made by a prisoner before there is time to caution them is not rendered inadmissible in evidence merely because no caution has been given, but in such a case the prisoner should be cautioned as soon as possible.

(vii)   A prisoner making a voluntary statement must not be cross-examined and no questions should be put to them about it except for the purpose of removing ambiguity in what has actually been said. For instance, if they have mentioned an hour without saying whether it was morning or evening, or have not made it clear to what individual or place they intended to refer in some part of the statement, they may be questioned sufficiently to clear up the point.

(viii)   When two or more persons are charged with the same offence and their statements are taken separately, the police should not read these statements to the other persons charged. Rather, each of such persons should be given by the police a copy of such statements and nothing should be said or done to invite a reply. If the person charged desires to make a statement in reply, the usual caution first should be administered.

(ix)   Any statement made in accordance with the above rules should, whenever possible, be taken down in writing and signed by the person making it after it has been read to them and they have been invited to make any corrections they may wish to make.

In *The People (DPP) v Farrell* [1978] IR 13, the Court of Criminal Appeal emphasised that, while they are not rules of law, the Judges' Rules have stood the test of time and will be departed from at peril. While statements obtained in breach of the rules have in very rare cases been admitted in evidence, a court will only allow this in exceptional circumstances.

To be admissible in evidence against an accused person, a statement of admission or confession must be voluntary. It must not have been made either through fear of prejudice or hope of advantage held out by a person in authority. That is to say, any person or persons associated with the investigation must not have brought about any inculpatory statement through the use of threats or inducements.

A further requirement for the introduction into evidence of an alleged admission is that it should not have been obtained by means of oppression. Lord McDermott postulated the following definition of oppression, which has since been accepted by the Court of Criminal Appeal in cases such as *The People (DPP) v McNally and Breathnach* [1981] 2 Frewen 43: 'Questioning which by its nature, duration or other attendant circumstances (including defective custody) excites hopes (such as the hope of release) or fears, or so affects the mind of the subject that his will crumbles and he speaks when otherwise he would have remained silent.'

Beyond the requirements of voluntariness and lack of oppression, in Ireland there is a further imperative that there should be a fundamental fairness of procedures in any criminal investigation. In this regard, the most frequently cited statement of the law is the following made by Griffin J. in *The People (DPP) v Shaw* [1982)] IR 1:

> The judge presiding at a criminal trial should be astute to see that, although a statement may be technically voluntary, it should nevertheless be excluded if, by reason of the manner or circumstances in which it was obtained, it falls below the standard of fairness. The reason for the exclusion is not so much the risk of an erroneous conviction as the recognition that the minimum or essential standard must be observed in the administration of justice.

4.3.5   THE CUSTODY REGULATIONS

The 'Custody Regulations' are those delineated in the Criminal Justice Act 1984 (Treatment of Persons in Garda Stations Regulations) 1987 that were implemented by SI No. 119 of 1987. They will be discussed in some considerable detail in **Chapter 5**. Rights conferred in this Statutory Instrument (SI) of necessity place concomitant obligations on the Gardaí who detain a suspect.

Access to a solicitor when a suspect is in a Garda Station for the purposes of questioning was the subject of a recent case in the Supreme Court. Following the comments of Clarke J. and Hardiman J. in the cases of *DPP v Raymond Gormley and Craig White* Supreme Court [2014] IESC 17:

> Likewise, the question as to whether a suspect is entitled to have a lawyer present does not arise on the facts of this case … however, it does need to be noted that the jurisprudence of both the ECHR and the United States Supreme Court clearly recognise that the entitlements of a suspect extend to having the relevant lawyer present.

Hardiman J. was even more specific when he said:

> Manifestly, however it will not be long before some person or other asserts a right to legal advice in custody on a broader basis. I say this in explicit terms in order that this may be considered by those whose duty it is to take into account potential developments.

On 6 May 2014, the DPP issued a direction to the Garda Síochána that where a request is made by a suspect detained in a Garda station to have his or her solicitor present during interview, that such requests should be facilitated. The Department of Justice and Equality in turn informed the Law Society of Ireland that the DPP had very recently issued a direction to the Garda Síochána about the attendance of solicitors during interviews in Garda stations. As a result of this direction, from 7 May 2014, where a request is made by a suspect who is detained in a Garda station to have his or her solicitor present during an interview, a solicitor will be allowed to attend. Accordingly, a new Garda station legal aid record claim form will be made available to practitioners.

4.3.5.1   Mandatory record keeping at the Garda station

There are record-keeping obligations placed on An Garda Síochána with respect to the detention of suspects. One such obligation is mandatory and extensive record-keeping concerning persons detained in the form of a Custody Record, which must contain the following details, in addition to details of arrest and detention:

- Any direction extending detention.

- The time and circumstances in which the suspect was informed of his/her rights.

- Any request for a solicitor and the action taken in response.

- The notification of the detention to District Headquarters.

- The suspect's waiver of an offer of suspension of questioning between midnight and 8 a.m., where made.

- The times of all interviews conducted and the persons present.

- Decisions made concerning the detention of juveniles and steps taken as a result.

- The notification of certain rights to detained foreign nationals, requests made by them and actions taken.
- Any searches of the detained person that are conducted.
- Any fingerprints, photographs and/or swabs taken.
- Any complaints made.
- Medical examinations conducted and steps taken as a consequence.
- Visits to the detainee.
- Communications by or with the detainee.
- Meals supplied.
- The time of eventual release.

4.4 Obligation to Furnish Information

The onus to provide information for the assistance of the Gardaí in their power to investigate and prevent crime can have significant implications for persons suspected of involvement in criminality. For example, s. 9(1) of the Offences against the State (Amendment) Act 1998 makes it an offence for a person to withhold information, if a person fails, without a reasonable excuse to disclose that information as soon as practicable, which information is known or believed to be of material assistance in preventing the commission or securing the apprehension, prosecution or conviction of a serious offence. The penalty on conviction on indictment is up to five years' imprisonment. Section 8 of the Criminal Law Act penalises persons who accept or agree to accept any consideration instead of providing the Gardaí with information which might be of material assistance in securing the prosecution or conviction of an offender for an arrestable offence.

4.4.1 ADVERSE INFERENCES DRAWN FROM LACK OF COOPERATION WITH QUESTIONING

Measures for coercing the provision of information have been created relative to the various powers of detention outlined at **4.3.3**. These measures are now explored in the same legislative sequence, to observe circumstances where inferences may be drawn from the failure of a detainee to answer questions permitted within the parameters of the detention powers being used. Inferences are also discussed in **Chapter 5** but from the perspective of a defence lawyer and the perspective of the detainee.

4.4.1.1 Sections 2 and 5 of the Offences Against the State (Amendment) Act 1998

Sections 2 and 5 of the Offences Against the State (Amendment) Act 1998 allow inferences to be drawn from the failure of a suspect to mention facts later relied on in his defence when being questioned by members of the Gardaí.

4.4.1.2 Sections 15 and 16 of the Criminal Justice Act 1984

The Criminal Justice Act 1984 (the 1984 Act) introduced a number of measures designed to coerce the provision of information. Section 15 of that Act obliges a person to account for the origin of any firearm in their possession, while under s. 16 a person must account for possession of certain property. Failure to furnish such an account in either case is deemed an offence.

4.4.1.3 Sections 18 and 19 of the 1984 Act

Sections 18 and 19 of the 1984 Act placed an onus on the suspect to account for any object, substance or mark on them, in their possession or at the place where they are arrested and puts an onus on a person to explain their presence at a particular location in certain circumstances.

Failure to comply with either demand, properly made, may give rise to the drawing of inferences and is capable of amounting to corroboration of any evidence in relation to which the failure or refusal is material. A person shall not be convicted of an offence solely on an inference drawn from such failure or refusal.

4.4.1.4   Sections 28 and 29 of the Criminal Justice Act 2007

Sections 18 and 19 of the 1984 Act have now been substituted by s. 28 and s. 29 of the Criminal Justice Act 2007. These new provisions impose an obligation to give an explanation in certain circumstances, similar to the circumstances in the original ss. 18 and 19. Failure to give an explanation can give rise to an adverse inference 'being allowed to be drawn'. However, the inference alone cannot ground a conviction. The person must also be cautioned as to the effect of refusing to answer a question and must be offered a reasonable opportunity to consult with a solicitor. The inference can only be drawn where the interview is electronically recorded (unless there is consent not to so record).

4.4.1.5   Section 19A Criminal Justice Act 1984

The Criminal Justice Act 2007 also introduced a new s. 19A into the Criminal Justice Act 1984. This provision allows a court to draw an inference from the failure to mention certain facts which were later relied on. Similar safeguards to those provided for in ss. 28 and 29 of the 2007 Act apply. This is potentially the widest reaching of the new provisions curbing the right to silence. This restriction will now apply to persons held under s. 4 of the Criminal Justice Act 1984 having been arrested for any arrestable offence, which can in theory include some relatively minor offences, e.g. shoplifting.

4.4.1.6   Section 7 of the Criminal Justice (Drug Trafficking) Act 1996

Section 7 of the Criminal Justice (Drug Trafficking) Act 1996 allows the drawing of similar inferences in respect of drug trafficking offences. However, the information sought to be compelled under the threat of this sanction extends to any fact relied upon in defence of any prosecution ultimately instituted. All that is necessary for an inference to be drawn is a failure to respond to questioning by disclosing such a fact, if the suspect could reasonably have been expected to mention it when questioned.

The armoury of adverse inference powers in favour of the prosecution outlined at **4.4.1** made the task of the advising defence solicitor even more difficult in the absence of any right to be present during the interview process. Now that that advising solicitor can be present during such interviews in the wake of the *Gormley and White* decision, a raft of new challenges are presented for defence solicitors, as discussed in **Chapter 5**.

4.5   Obligation to Furnish Material

The obligations placed on a detained person to furnish material to the investigating Gardaí are wide ranging and include the production of the following:

- Identity details including submission for the purposes of photography and fingerprints.

- Items in one's possession, either on the person or in one's property.

- Bodily samples.

All legislation previously outlined at **4.3.3** (as amended) makes provision for furnishing such material.

4.5.1   OFFENCES AGAINST THE STATE ACT 1939 (AS AMENDED)

Section 7 of the Criminal Law Act 1976 imposes requirements on persons detained under s. 30 of the Offences Against the State Act 1939 to furnish their identity, i.e. give correct name and address, submit to a search, allow themselves to be photographed and fingerprinted, allow skin swabs and hair samples to be taken, and to submit to the seizure for testing of anything they have in their possession.

4.5.2   CRIMINAL JUSTICE ACT 1984 (AS AMENDED)

Similar obligations to the requirements outlined at **4.5.1** on persons detained under s. 30 of the 1939 Act apply to all persons detained under s. 4 of the Criminal Justice Act 1984. It is an offence to obstruct the Gardaí acting under these powers and the failure to give a correct name and address is a criminal offence. Section 48 of the Criminal Justice Act 2007 amended s. 6 of the Criminal Justice Act 1984 by allowing reasonable force to be used where a detained person fails to cooperate with the taking of finger and palm prints.

Subsequent to 20 November 2015, the Criminal Justice (Forensic Evidence and DNA Database System) Act 2014 (the 2014 Act) introduced a new power of a member of the Garda Síochána not below the rank of Sergeant to take fingerprints and palm prints of the person arrested for the purpose of charge. In the event of a failure to cooperate with the taking of finger and palm prints there is a power to use such force as is reasonably considered necessary pursuant to s. 102 of this 2014 Act which amended s. 6A of the Criminal Justice Act 1984. The exercise of the power to use force is authorised by a Garda of the rank of an Inspector at least rather than a Superintendent previously. There appears to be no express bar in the 2014 Act on the taking of fingerprints on the basis of a voluntary common law arrangement. Under s. 8 of the Criminal Justice Act 1984, the records of fingerprints, palm prints and photographs had to be destroyed after six months unless proceedings had been instituted unless an application was made by An Garda Síochána for further retention. The Criminal Justice Act 2007 had reversed the position under s. 49, which substitutes s. 8 of the Criminal Justice Act 1984 by replacing the presumption in favour of destruction of fingerprints, palm prints and photographs with a presumption in favour of retention. Prior to 20 November 2015, An Garda Síochána could retain the records indefinitely although a person may make an application for their destruction (in the absence of the institution of proceedings relating to the taking of the prints) after 12 months, firstly to the Garda Commissioner and secondly to the District Court.

Section 102 of the 2014 Act which amended s. 8 of the Criminal Justice Act 1984, provides a new regime for the destruction of fingerprints, palm prints, and photographs on request by the suspect to the Commissioner of An Garda Síochána where they have either not been charged within 12 months of the taking of the records or where they have been charged but acquitted or proceedings were dismissed or discontinued. In the event the Garda Commissioner declines to destroy the records, an application may be made on appeal to the District Court by the suspect.

4.5.3   CRIMINAL JUSTICE (FORENSIC EVIDENCE AND DNA DATABASE SYSTEM) ACT 2014

There is extensive discussion at **10.2.6** regarding forensic evidence. In the context of this obligation on the detained person to furnish material, one's focus needs to be drawn to the now repealed s. 2 of the Criminal Justice (Forensic Evidence) Act 1990 as amended by s. 14 Criminal Justice Act 2006 which obliged persons prior to 20 November 2015 detained for questioning to submit to the taking of a number of different samples for forensic testing, when properly requested to do so, with failure amounting to obstruction under the Act. These samples typically contain a person's DNA. While the detained person's consent was required for the performance of the more invasive kinds of sampling procedures, inferences could be drawn in subsequent criminal proceedings from any failure to furnish such samples.

Further to SI No. 508 of 2015, Criminal Justice (Forensic Evidence and DNA Database System) Act 2014 (Commencement) Order 2015, 20 November 2015 was appointed as the date on which specified provisions of the Criminal Justice (Forensic Evidence and DNA Database System) Act 2014 came into operation. With regard to commencement of the 2014 Act, Part 1 is now fully operative; so too are Parts 2 to 7; Part 8 is operative, other than s. 67(2)(e); Part 9 has also commenced, other than s. 72(2)(f) in relation to Chapter 2 of Part 12; Parts 10 and 11 are operational; s. 109 is operational relating to Chapters 4 to 7 of Part 12; Chapter 4 Part 12 is operative relating to Article 7 (Council Framework Decision 2009/905/JHA, 30 November 2009) requests within the meaning of that Chapter; Chapters 5, 6, and 7 of Part 12; and Part 13 insofar as is not already in operation.

The 2014 Act (Part 2) amends the law to authorise the taking of bodily samples from persons in custody suspected of certain criminal offences for forensic testing. The 2014 Act (Part 3) provides for the taking of certain bodily samples from persons who volunteer to have such samples taken from them for the purpose of the investigation of offences or incidents that may have involved the commission of offences. The 2014 Act (Part 8) also provides for the establishment and operation by Forensic Science Ireland of the Department of Justice and Equality of a DNA Database System; to provide for the taking of certain bodily samples from persons suspected or convicted of certain criminal offences for the purpose of generating DNA profiles in respect of those persons to be entered in the investigation division of the DNA Database System; to provide for the taking of certain bodily samples from certain persons for elimination purposes and, where appropriate, the entry of their DNA profiles in the DNA Database System; to provide for the taking of bodily samples from persons, or samples from things, for the purpose of generating DNA profiles in respect of those persons or missing persons to be entered in the identification division of the DNA Database System; to provide for the purposes of that system; to provide (at Part 10), in certain circumstances, for the destruction of samples taken under this Act and the destruction, or removal from the DNA Database System, of any DNA profiles generated from those samples.

The 2014 Act has repealed the Criminal Justice (Forensic Evidence) Act 1990 and shall give effect to Council Decision 2008/615/JHA of 23 June 2008 and Council Decision 2008/616/JHA of 23 June 2008. The Criminal Justice (Forensic Evidence and DNA Database System) Act 2014 provides (at Part 12) for enhanced cooperation in relation to automated searching for or automated comparison of DNA data or automated searching for dactyloscopic data, as the case may be, and the exchange of such data and the reference data relating to them, by or between authorities that are responsible for the prevention, detection and investigation of criminal offences in the state and those other states or that other state, as the case may be. The 2014 Act also amends the criminal law relating to the taking of fingerprints and palm prints from certain persons pursuant to the Criminal Justice Act 1984 and other enactments to provide for the destruction of fingerprints, palm prints, and photographs taken from or of certain persons in certain circumstances; and to provide for related matters.

'Transitional Provisions' are provided for in s. 7 of the 2014 Act thereby preserving bodily samples that were taken either from persons prior to 20 November 2015 under the Criminal Justice (Forensic Evidence) Act 1990 or taken under a valid common law arrangement where bodily samples were provided with the consent of a suspect.

4.5.4   DRUG OFFENCE LEGISLATION

Further examples of instances of where the prosecution is enabled to obtain material from an accused include requirements outlined in s. 23 of the Misuse of Drugs Acts 1977 and 1984, to submit to a search by a member of the Gardaí who reasonably suspects the person in question to be in possession of a controlled drug. A refusal to accompany the requesting member to a Garda station for this purpose where so directed amounts to an offence under the section.

In *DPP v Garret Byrne* High Court [2014] IEHC 394, the accused was charged with refusing to provide a blood sample under s. 12 of the Road Traffic Act 2010 (as amended). Garda McDonnell, upon observing strange driving, stopped the car driven by Mr Byrne and got a smell of cannabis from the car. He searched the accused, his passenger and the car under s. 23 of the Misuse of Drugs Act 1977 (having advised the suspects of the power of search provision) but did not find anything. The Garda Dog Unit was nearby so Garda McDonnell called them and the car was again searched by the dogs but nothing found. The entire roadside detention lasted 15 minutes before the accused was arrested under s. 4(8) of the Road Traffic Act 2010. The suspect subsequently refused to give a blood sample having failed firstly to provide a urine sample. The applicant (Mr Byrne) claimed that he was unlawfully detained after he was searched as the Garda went on to search the car and the passenger without communicating anything to the accused regarding his status. It was held by Justice Hedigan that the nub of the case was a question as to whether a driver, subsequent to a search of his person and car, was unlawfully detained by the roadside while the passenger of his car was also being searched and while a Garda dog handler came on the scene to search the vehicle. The following questions were posed for the High Court:

- Was the detention at the roadside by Garda McDonnell of the accused lawful and permissible under the terms of s. 23 of the Misuse of Drugs Act?

- Was the subsequent arrest of the accused under s. 4(8) of the Road Traffic Act 2010 a lawful arrest?

- If the answer to the first two questions is 'no', is the judge required to exclude the evidence of the making of a requirement under s. 12(1)(b) of the Road Traffic Act 2010 and any evidence of a subsequent failure by the accused to comply with the requirement?

Judge Hedigan held, following *DPP v Bullman* (2009) IECCA 84 and *State (Higgins) v Farrell* (2009) 4 IR 189, that as long as a Garda acts in a reasonable manner in the exercise of the powers, he or she should not be prevented from properly investigating a crime. He stated that 'regard must be had to the fluidity of the investigation' and that the search of the car and passenger was 'part and parcel of the one investigation' and a lawful exercise of the Garda's powers under section 23.

The questions were answered:

- The detention at the roadside by Garda McDonnell of the accused was lawful and permissible under the terms of s. 23 of the Misuse of Drugs Act.

- The subsequent arrest of the accused under s. 4(8) of the Road Traffic Act 2010 was a lawful arrest.

- And as the answers to the first two questions was in the affirmative, the question as to whether or not the judge was required to exclude the evidence of the making of a requirement under s. 12(1)(b) of the Road Traffic Act 2010 and any evidence of a subsequent failure by the accused to comply with the requirement, did not arise.

4.5.5 ROAD TRAFFIC OFFENCES

Road Traffic Offences are discussed in great detail in **Chapter 15**. In the context of the current focus on a suspect's obligation to furnish material, regard should be had to further examples of Gardaí powers to obtain material from an accused to assist in the detection of crime for breaches of the Road Traffic Act, e.g. s. 9(2) of the Road Traffic Act 2010 (as amended) together with s. 10 of the Road Traffic Act 2010 (as amended), which relate to roadside and random roadside breath testing and s. 12(1)(a) and (b) of the Road Traffic Act 2010 (as amended), in relation to the provision of breath samples or blood or urine in the detection of drink-driving offences.

4.5.6 ADVERSE INFERENCE PROVISIONS

Clearly the powers of the Gardaí with regard to the collection of evidence in relation to the detection and prevention of crime have increased with the Criminal Justice Acts 2006 and 2007. Adverse inferences that may arise with regard to a detained person refusing to furnish materials requested which may be insufficient on their own to convict a person of a criminal offence, are nonetheless an important additional contribution in strengthening the prosecution case and clearly have implications for the advising defence solicitor.

4.6 Electronic Recording of Interview

Section 27 of the Criminal Justice Act 1984 stated that the Minister for Justice may by regulations provide for the recording by electronic or other similar means of the questioning of persons by members of the Garda Síochána at Garda Síochána stations or elsewhere in connection with the investigation of offences. Ten years later, in 1997 (SI No. 74 of 1997), the Criminal Justice Act 1984 (Electronic Recording of Interviews) Regulations 1997 provided for the electronic recording of interviews with suspects detained under s. 4 of the Criminal Justice Act 1984, s. 30 of the Offences against the State Act 1939, and s. 2 of the Criminal Justice (Drug Trafficking) Act in Garda stations where equipment has been provided and installed for that purpose.

Under s. 56 of the Criminal Justice Act 2007, a person charged with an offence who was interviewed electronically must apply to the court to obtain a copy of the recording. This application can be made in the District Court or the Superior Courts and is commonly known as a s. 56 Order. Following the granting of the s. 56 Order a copy of recording of questioning by Garda Síochána shall be given to the accused or their legal representative. The recording of questioning of the accused by Garda Síochána is provided for in s. 57 of the Criminal Justice Act 2007, and is admitted in evidence at the trial of a person in respect of an offence. This recording may be admitted in evidence in electronic or transcript format notwithstanding the fact it was not taken down in writing at the time it was made or the statement is not in writing and signed by the person who made it. Section 57 does not affect the admissibility of statements recorded in writing at trial and irrespective of whether the making of the statement is recorded by electronic or similar means.

CHAPTER 5

THE ARRESTED PERSON IN CUSTODY—DEFENCE PERSPECTIVES

5.1 Introduction

This chapter follows on from the various arrest and detention provisions which were outlined in detail in **Chapter 4**. It will focus on the issues which arise after your client has been arrested and detained in a Garda station under any of the four statutory provisions summarised in the charts below. It should be emphasised that these are not the only statutory provisions allowing for the arrest and detention of a person but they are the most common provisions encountered by criminal practitioners.

5.1.1 CATEGORISING DETENTION POWERS

POWER	DETENTION PERIOD	WHOSE POWER?
Arrest + s. 4: Detention CJA Act 1984	6 Hours	Member in Charge
	+ 6 Hours	Superintendent
	+ 12 Hours	Chief Superintendent

Section 7 of the Criminal Justice Act 2011 introduced a new s. 4(3)(A) into the Criminal Justice Act 1984 which allows for the suspension of s. 4 detention regarding a 'relevant offence' under that Act.

POWER	DETENTION PERIOD	WHOSE POWER?
Arrest + s. 2: Detention Criminal Justice (Drug Trafficking) Act 1996	6 Hours	Member in Charge
	+ 18 Hours	Superintendent
	+ 24 Hours	Chief Superintendent
	+ 72 Hours	Court Application by Chief Superintendent
	+ 48 Hours	Court Application by Chief Superintendent

POWER	DETENTION PERIOD	WHOSE POWER?
Arrest + s. 30 Detention Offences Against the State Act (OASA) 1939	24 Hours	Arresting Garda Detention
	+ 24 Hours	Chief Superintendent
	+ 24 Hours	Court Application by Superintendent

POWER	DETENTION PERIOD	WHOSE POWER?
Arrest + s. 50 Criminal Justice Act (CJA) 2007	6 Hours	Member in Charge
	+ 18 Hours	Superintendent
	+ 24 Hours	Chief Superintendent
	+ 72 Hours	Court Application by Chief Superintendent
	+ 48 Hours	Court Application by Chief Superintendent

Other Detentions under s. 42 of the Criminal Justice Act 1999 and under ss. 16 and 17 of the Criminal Procedure Act 2010 are dealt with in the same manner as s. 4 Detentions above.

5.1.2   RE-ARREST AFTER DETENTION

Re-arrests are possible when further information during the Garda investigation comes to light.

DETENTION POWER	AMENDING LEGISLATION
Section 4	Section 10 of the Criminal Justice Act 1984 as amended
Section 2	Section 4 of the Drug Trafficking Act 1996
Section 30	Section 11 of the Offences Against the State Act 1998
Section 50	Criminal Justice Act 2007

5.2   Legislature and Judiciary—Sources of Rights

Under the Separation of Powers doctrine established by the Irish Constitution, both the legislature and its legislative measures and the judiciary, whose judgments provide a body of case law, have been responsible, respectively, for enacting laws and for interpreting and establishing rights which relate to an arrested person in Garda custody. It must be stated at the outset that while various statutory provisions enacted by the legislature have been in place for many years for the protection and safeguarding of arrested and detained persons' rights while in Garda stations, the Higher Courts have contributed significantly to enhancing the protections afforded to arrested persons.

5.2.1   RECENT SIGNIFICANT CASE LAW

A significant development regarding the rights of an arrested person in Garda custody was a judgment delivered by the Supreme Court on 6 March 2014 that is discussed and referenced in detail in this chapter entitled, *DPP v Raymond Gormley* and *DPP v Craig White* [2014] IESC 17. This judgment has far reaching implications for the rights of detained persons in getting access to legal advice. It would not be an exaggeration to say that the consequences of this judgment for both arrested and detained persons and their legal advisers changed the legal landscape overnight and represents the most significant judgment for criminal law practitioners since *DPP v Healy* (1990) 2 IR 73.

The *Healy* judgment established that persons arrested and detained in Garda stations had a constitutional right of reasonable access to a solicitor of their choice if requested and that this was not simply a legal right. It held that a detained person was entitled to be told immediately by Gardaí once the solicitor had arrived in the Garda station and had an immediate right of access to that solicitor if requested. The court further held that there was no distinction between a request for immediate access to a solicitor by the detained person or by someone else acting *bona fide* on that detainee's behalf.

In *Gormley and White*, the Supreme Court held for the first time that where an arrested person in Garda custody positively asserts their right of access to a solicitor, certain evidence gathering (in that case, the interviewing of Mr Gormley) must not commence or, if it has commenced, must be suspended, until the requested legal consultation has taken place. It characterised that right as being integral to the right to fair procedures which was established in *The State (Healy) v Donoghue* (1976) IR 325. The court further held that this right of access to a solicitor does not apply to the prior taking of a mandatory forensic sample which was the issue that arose in *DPP v White*. Mandatory forensic samples are those that can be taken in a Garda station following arrest and detention without a person's consent being required.

The *Gormley and White* judgment is a significant legal landmark and a game changer. It is akin to those momentous events which sometimes occur in life and are marked by people knowing precisely where they were when they heard 'the news'. The more practical consequences for criminal law practitioners of this most important Supreme Court judgment will be considered later in this chapter.

While the Supreme Court judgment in *Gormley and White* represents a recent judicial intervention with regard to the rights of arrested persons in Garda custody, it should be remembered that it emerged from a litany of other previous judgments over some 30 years, spearheaded by defence solicitors on behalf of arrested persons in Garda stations. Some of these cases include:

- *The State (Healy) v Donoghue* (1976) 1 IR 325: Persons arrested and detained in Garda stations had a constitutional right of access to a solicitor.

- *Lavery v Member in Charge of Carrickmacross Garda Station* (1999) 2 IR 390: A solicitor did not have a right to attend interviews in Garda stations; this case is now overturned by *Gormley and White*.

- *People (DPP) v Finnerty* (1999) 4 IR 364: A detained person is entitled to maintain silence during a detention period, such silence shall not be admissible against the detained person as part of the prosecution case and the prosecution cannot cross-examine the accused person as to his refusal to answer questions during his detention. One needs to remember, however, that there are certain circumstances where adverse inferences may be drawn from a detainee's silence during questioning (see **4.4.1** and **5.14**).

5.2.2 RIGHTS WITH PROTECTIONS

In addition to the various legislative protections for arrested and detained persons, there are also many important rights. While the legislative protections are important, they retain the character of being something of a reluctant bulwark against the might of the state and its huge powers to deprive its citizens of their liberty. It might be said that while the existence of these legislative provisions provides protections for arrested persons, their breach occasionally results in little if any consequence. Nevertheless, defence practitioners need to be aware of their existence when representing arrested and detained persons.

5.3 Distinguishing Types of Detention

A distinction needs to be made between detention in a Garda station for the purpose of Garda investigation of a crime and detention in a Garda station for the purpose of being charged, 'bailed' or being brought to court.

5.3.1 WHAT IS MEANT BY 'AN ARRESTED PERSON'?

Regulation 2 of the Criminal Justice Act 1984 (Treatment of Persons in Custody in Garda Síochána Stations) Regulations 1987 (The Custody Regulations 1987) states that an 'arrested person' means 'a person who is taken on arrest to, or arrested in a (Garda) station'. This means that no matter what the basis is of a person's arrest, the Custody Regulations 1987 apply to their detention. It also means that the Custody Regulations 1987 do not just apply to the detention provisions outlined above at **5.1** but are applicable to all arrests.

5.3.2   TYPES OF ARREST

There are a variety of ways in which a person can be arrested by Gardaí and taken to a Garda station and the Custody Regulations apply in each case. In brief, the categories of arrests which a criminal practitioner will encounter most frequently (but not exclusively) include the following.

5.3.2.1   Serious offences

Persons arrested for serious offences are generally detained in Garda stations under s. 4 of the Criminal Justice Act 1984 (as amended) or s. 2 of the Criminal Justice (Drug Trafficking) Act 1996 or s. 30 of the Offences Against the State Act 1939 (as amended) or s. 50 of the Criminal Justice Act 2007 for the purpose of a Garda investigation of a crime as outlined at **5.1**. Detention in this context allows Gardaí to interview, fingerprint, and take forensic and other samples from the arrested person. While the Custody Regulations 1987 do not apply exclusively to arrests in this particular category, the courts will scrutinise their application with great care to ensure that statements made by arrested persons or forensic samples provided by them were obtained lawfully.

5.3.2.2   Minor offences

Persons may be arrested and taken to a Garda station for relatively minor offences such as public drunkenness, breach of the peace, and certain offences under the Road Traffic Acts. As they are minor offences, the Gardaí are not entitled to detain such persons for the purpose of investigation but only for the purpose of charge, release or court appearance. Most people arrested under this category are released on bail at the Garda station as provided for in s. 3 of the Criminal Justice (Miscellaneous Provisions) Act 1997 to appear in court at a later date. Others will be kept in custody to appear at the next available court sitting, in circumstances where Gardaí are objecting to bail or wish to attach conditions to a person's bail. Some of those arrested for minor offences may be released without charge and later summonsed to attend court. Charging and summons procedures are discussed in **Chapter 6**.

5.3.2.3   Bench warrant arrest

A further circumstance that can result in a person's arrest is where a 'bench warrant' is issued by a court directing Gardaí to arrest a named person for failing to appear in court on a previous date. If 'arrested on foot of a bench warrant', the person can be held or detained in a Garda station until they are brought to court.

5.3.2.4   Arrest warrant

Gardaí can in certain circumstances arrest a person 'on foot of an arrest warrant', following which the person will be detained in the Garda station for the purpose of charging them. This process is most common following the completion of a prior Garda investigation and a direction by the Director of Public Prosecutions (DPP) that that person is charged. The DPP Directions process is discussed at **Chapter 12**.

5.4   The Custody Regulations 1987

With regard to statutory protections for all arrested and detained persons, under any arrest category, including those outlined above, s. 7 of the Criminal Justice Act 1984 obliged the Minister for Justice to make Regulations providing for the treatment of persons in custody in Garda stations. These Custody Regulations did not come into force until 16 May 1987 (SI No. 119 of 1987) and are referred to as the Criminal Justice Act 1984 (Treatment of Persons in Garda Stations Regulations) 1987. Section 7 of the Criminal Justice Act 1984 states:

> 7(1)—*The Minister shall make regulations providing for the treatment of persons in custody in Garda Síochána stations.*

5.4.1   REGULATION 3: GENERAL PRINCIPLES

Regulation 3 of the Criminal Justice Act 1984 (Treatment of Persons in Garda Stations Regulations) 1987 is a useful starting point when considering what the Custody Regulations are all about. It expresses the general principle underpinning the Regulations, as follows:

> In carrying out their functions under these Regulations members shall act with due respect for the personal rights of persons in custody and their dignity as human persons, and shall have regard for the special needs of any of them who may be under a physical or mental disability while complying with the obligation to prevent escape from custody and continuing to act with diligence and determination in the investigation of crime and the protection and vindication of the personal rights of other persons.

The purpose of the Custody Regulations as set out in Regulation 3 is therefore effectively two-fold:

* To provide for various matters arising during an arrested and detained person's detention. This includes the notification of their arrest or detention to their family members and solicitor, provisions regarding the detention of juveniles, foreign nationals, and persons with mental disabilities, and providing for their medical treatment if required. These Regulations focus subjectively on the circumstances of the arrested and detained person.

* To provide for various matters which arise during the Garda investigation during a person's detention, including the conduct of interviews, searches of arrested persons, the taking of fingerprints and photographs. These Regulations focus on the duties of the investigating Gardaí during the detention of an arrested person.

While the aspirations contained in Regulation 3 attempt to deal with issues arising for both arrested and detained persons in Garda stations and with Gardaí whose duty it is to investigate crime, s. 7(3) of the Criminal Justice Act 1984 represents a significant dilution of such aspirations and is sometimes referred to in criminal defence litigation circles as 'the will to wound but the fear to strike' provision. This is because s. 7(3) clearly states that any breach of the Custody Regulations does not of itself render a member of An Garda Síochána liable to any criminal or civil proceedings, nor does any such breach necessarily affect the lawfulness of the custody of the detained person, nor does any such breach render inadmissible any statement obtained during the detention. The Custody Regulations therefore create rules with no penalty for their breach.

In *DPP v Spratt* (1995) 1 IR 585, O'Hanlon J held in the High Court that non-observance of the Custody Regulations would not automatically render inadmissible evidence obtained when the accused was in custody and was rather a matter to be considered by the trial judge in each case in terms of how a complained-of breach should impact on the prosecution case.

In *DPP v Diver* (2005) 3 IR 270, the Supreme Court suggested that the key issue for a trial judge was whether or not a breach of the Regulations had prejudiced the fairness of the trial of an accused person.

5.4.2   REGULATION 4: MEMBER IN CHARGE

If the aspirations contained in Regulation 3 are to have any meaning, someone in the Garda station must be responsible for ensuring the overall application of the Custody Regulations while arrested persons are detained there. Regulation 4 provides that the 'Member in Charge' in any Garda station is the responsible Garda member. He or she is 'the Garda member who is in charge of a Garda Station at a time when the Member is required to do anything pursuant to the Regulations'. It is a matter for the Superintendent of each Garda District to designate who is the Member in Charge of any Garda station at any given time. The Member in Charge is expected to ensure compliance with the Custody Regulations and should therefore remain objective and impartial and should ensure that an arrested person's rights are observed at all times.

Defence lawyers may be somewhat disappointed that Regulation 4 merely provides that 'in so far as practicable', the Member in Charge shall not be involved in the arrest of a person in custody or be involved in the investigation of the offence in respect of which the arrested person is being detained.

In *DPP (Lenihan) v McGuire* (1996) 3 IR 586, Kelly J. held that it was a factual question as to who the Member in Charge was in a Garda station at any given time, even if she or he had not been directed in writing by the Superintendent to be the Member in Charge at the particular time.

5.4.3   REGULATION 5 AND REGULATION 6: DUTIES OF MEMBER IN CHARGE

Regulation 5 states that as part of his or her the duty to ensure that the Custody Regulations are being observed, the Member in Charge shall visit persons in custody from time to time and make any necessary enquiries from the arrested person.

Regulation 6 states that a Member in Charge is responsible for maintaining a Custody Record in which an arrested person's details must be entered while being detained in the Garda station.

5.4.4   REGULATION 7: CUSTODY RECORD

Regulation 7 requires a record to be kept of the date, time, and place of arrest; the identity of the Arresting Garda (or other person effecting the arrest); the time of arrival at the Garda station; the reason for arrest; any relevant details relating to the arrested person's physical or mental condition; whether or not the arrested person is detained for the purpose of investigation under a relevant provision and, if required by the legislation in question, must enter other written details about the detention in question.

5.4.5   REGULATION 8: INFORMATION RIGHTS, INCLUDING RIGHTS TO CONSULT WITH A SOLICITOR

Regulation 8 requires the Member in Charge to inform all arrested persons, (including juveniles), without delay, or to have the detained person informed, of the reason for the arrest, the entitlement to consult with a solicitor and the right to have another person, reasonably named, to be informed of the arrest and of the detention in custody. If the person arrested is a juvenile, that detainee must be informed as above and in addition that a parent and/or guardian (or if relevant, a spouse) will be informed, as soon as practicable, of the arrest. This notification, which can be given orally, must also include information regarding the reason for the arrest and regarding the juvenile's right to consult with a solicitor. The arrested person must be told that if s/he does not wish to invoke any of these rights immediately, s/he can invoke them at a later time. This Regulation also states that the arrested person must be given a written notice of his or her rights without delay. This written notice of rights is generally referred to as a 'C 72 Form' and is available in a number of different languages.

It should be noted that the informing of the arrested person of his right to a solicitor does not of itself have to be recorded on audio or videotape. Some defence lawyers regard the absence of such technological provision as a serious omission from this regulation. Some detained persons have complained after the cessation of the custodial period that they were told by the Gardaí that if they asserted their right to access to a solicitor, it would lead to delay and thus to a longer period of detention. An arrested or detained person is entitled to nominate a solicitor of choice. If such Garda communication of the right to a solicitor was recorded, there would be clarity regarding the identity of the solicitor whom the arrested person wished to contact. It is extremely important to avoid potential conflict of interest for a solicitor and the client in circumstances where an arresting officer or the Member in Charge or other Gardaí seek to specify contacting their preferred choice of defence solicitor. The inequality of arms between Gardaí and detainees has the potential to give rise to the detainee feeling obliged to opt for calling the solicitor suggested by Gardaí. There is also the potential for the exertion of 'undue influence' on a solicitor to whom Gardaí regularly refer clients; in a worst-case scenario it might be considered more desirable that the accused person pleaded guilty as charged, rather than fight the allegation at trial.

In *DPP (Garda Padraig Lynn) v Ivan O'Kelly* (unreported, 10 February 1998, High Court): McCracken J. held that there is no obligation on the Member in Charge to ensure that the arrested person understands the notice of rights in the C72 form.

5.4.5.1   Law Society Regulation and ethical standards on right to consult with a solicitor in custody

The Law Society of Ireland Report of the Regulation 13 Review Group (May 2013) specifically references processes for access to a solicitor whilst in custody at Recommendations 13 and 19. The full report can be accessed through http://www.lawsociety.ie and is prioritised in the teaching of trainee solicitors with the report linked to the teaching materials provided. Further information can be accessed at the Solicitors (Advertising) Regulations 2002 (SI No. 518 of 2002). In December 2015 the Law Society published its first edition of its *Guidance for Solicitors Providing Legal Services in Garda Stations*. The Society has also added a *Find a Garda Station Solicitor* web search facility where solicitors can communicate their availability to attend particular Garda stations on a divisional basis by registering their contact details at http://www.lawsociety.ie/gss.

An Garda Síochana published a *Code of Practice on Access to a Solicitor by Persons in Garda Custody* in April 2015.

5.4.6   REGULATION 9: NOTIFICATION OF SOLICITOR/OTHER PERSONS

Regulation 9 deals in very specific terms initially with the arrest of juveniles who are detained in a Garda station and the obligations on the Member in Charge to notify as soon as practicable various parties of that fact. While the Custody Regulations refer to juveniles as persons 'under the age of 17 years', it is important to note that Part 6 of the Children Act 2001, commenced by SI No. 151 of 2002 deals with child suspects in a Garda station and states that a child is a 'person under 18'. The law applicable to children in the criminal justice system is dealt with specifically in **Chapter 9** of this text, but it is necessary to reference detention of children in the context of this chapter.

The custody regulation obligations in question include a requirement that the Member in Charge:

- contacts a parent and/or guardian or another person reasonably named by the juvenile if a parent or guardian are not available, or a spouse if the juvenile is married;
- informs that person of the fact of the arrest;
- informs that person about the reason for the arrest;
- confirms the fact that the juvenile is detained in Garda station custody;
- informs that the juvenile is entitled to consult with a solicitor;
- requests the parent/guardian (other person as outlined above) to attend the Garda station without delay.

While Regulation 8 requires the Member in Charge to inform or to have informed all arrested persons without delay of their right to contact a solicitor, Regulation 9(2) states that where such a request for a solicitor is made, Gardaí must contact the solicitor 'as soon as practicable'.

5.4.7   REGULATION 10: LOCATION OF GARDA STATION

Regulation 10 allows for communication of information as to what Garda station an arrested person is being detained in to be given to a solicitor or any other person if the arrested person consents.

5.4.8   REGULATION 11: SOLICITOR ACCESS/OTHER VISITS

Regulation 11 states that an arrested person has a right to have reasonable access to a solicitor of choice and a right to communicate with that solicitor privately, which consultation may take place 'in the sight but out of hearing of a member'. The interpretation of the 'reasonable access' aspect of this regulation has now been superseded by developments in the immediate aftermath of the *Gormley and White* case. It should be emphasised that while the question of whether or not an arrested person in custody was entitled to have a lawyer present during interview was not litigated in that Supreme Court case, the Supreme Court strongly hinted that this right might exist, in view of the fact that the jurisprudence of both the European Court of Human Rights [ECtHR] and the US Supreme Court recognised such an entitlement by an arrested person.

Regulation 11 also provides that an arrested person is entitled to a visit from a relative, friend or other person with an interest in the detainee's welfare provided s/he consents that the visit can be 'adequately supervised' and that it will not 'hinder or delay the investigation of crime'. Regulation 11(5) allows for an arrested person to telephone a person reasonably named by him or to send a letter, provided the Member in Charge is satisfied that neither action will 'hinder or delay the investigation of crime'. However, detainee rights of communication entitle a Garda to listen while the telephone call is being made and to read any letter which the arrested person wishes to have posted. It is also important to note that Regulation 11(6) states that before an arrested person has a supervised visit or communicates with a person other than a solicitor, the detainee shall be informed that anything said during the visit or in the communication may be given in evidence.

Shortly after *Gormley and White* in May 2014, the DPP directed that solicitors must be allowed to attend interviews in Garda stations, where the arrested person so requests. It will be recalled from the previously mentioned *DPP v Healy* (1990) Supreme Court case that an arrested person's right of access to a solicitor is a constitutional right.

In addition to that DPP direction, a Statutory Payments Scheme administered by the Legal Aid Board has been in place since 7 May 2014 to enable payments to solicitors for telephone or Garda station consultations. These payments remunerate the practitioner for time spent at a Garda station for interview and ID parade attendances and for court extension hearings in relation to any relevant detention provisions.

5.4.9   REGULATION 12: GARDA INTERVIEWS IN A GARDA STATION

Regulation 12 is a lengthy but important regulation dealing with what is usually the most pivotal and crucial part of a client's detention and of the Garda investigation itself. It is exceptionally important for defence solicitors to be fully aware of the provisions of Regulation 12 in view of the fact that they can now attend Garda interviews in a Garda station where an arrested person so requests.

The *Gormley and White* judgment impinges specifically on Regulation 12(6) in establishing the new constitutional right for an arrested person to access legal advice if requested before any questioning commences or, if it has, it must cease. For this reason, the more salient features of Regulation 12 in respect of how interviews should be conducted should be closely noted:

- Interviewing Gardaí must identify themselves by name and rank: 12(1).

- The interview must be conducted in a fair and humane manner: 12(2).

- No more than two Gardaí may question an arrested person at any one time and not more than four Gardaí may be present at any one time: 12(3).

5.4.9.1   Case law regarding Garda interviews in a Garda station

In *People (DPP) v D'Arcy* (unreported, 23 July 1997, CCA), three Gardaí participated in the interview of a juvenile who was under s. 4 detention on several occasions. The Court of Criminal Appeal said that the key issue was whether the interview was oppressive or unfair and since there was no question that it was, it had been a matter for the trial judge to decide, in exercising judicial discretion, whether to admit the statements made during questioning.

In *DPP v Smith* (unreported, 22 November 1999, CCA), the CCA held:

> Since only one person can effectively speak at any given time, the regulation should, in our view, be construed as providing that during the course of an interview while those present remain the same, only two members of the Gardaí may actually question the suspect. Breach of this regulation occurred during the question and answers session but did not affect the taking of the admitted statement, no questions having been asked at that stage.

In *DPP v Connolly* (2003) 2 IR 1 the accused person argued that an inculpatory statement made by him while in custody should be excluded as it had been taken in unfair circumstances, as only one Garda was present throughout the interview. The court found that as a matter of law there was no impropriety in questioning a suspect with only one Garda present but it did accept that it may affect the reliability of the statement.

If an interview has lasted for four hours, Regulation 12(4) requires that it must cease or be adjourned for a reasonable time. In *DPP v O'Connell* (1995) 1 IR 244, CCA, the court held that Regulation 12(4) was a mandatory provision that could not be waived by the person in custody. It held that a breach of this regulation would not automatically render an inculpatory statement inadmissible. However, that breach combined with the accused's lack of sleep and the effective denial of access to the accused's solicitor meant that the statement should be excluded.

DPP v Reddan (1995) 3 IR 560 also considered Regulation 12(4) but the statement was deemed admissible in that case.

Regulation 12(6) states that where an arrested person asks for a solicitor, he shall not be asked to make a written statement in relation to an offence until a reasonable time for the attendance of the solicitor has elapsed. This provision is now superseded by the *Gormley and White* judgment as outlined earlier.

5.4.9.2   Questioning between 12 midnight and 8 a.m.

An arrested person cannot be questioned between 12 midnight and 8 a.m. if detained under s. 4 of the Criminal Justice Act 1984, unless the Member in Charge has authorised that he can be questioned as outlined in Regulation 12(7).

The Member in Charge can only issue such an authority in three circumstances:

- Where the arrested person does not consent in writing to suspend questioning overnight. If the arrested person does consent, this consent must be recorded in writing and attached to and form part of the Custody Record.

- Where the person arrested has been taken to the Garda station 'during that period', i.e. between 12 midnight and 8 a.m.

- Where the Member in Charge believes that to delay questioning the person would involve a risk of injury to persons, serious loss of or damage to property, destruction of or interference with evidence or escape of accomplices.

5.4.9.3   Questioning a detainee with hearing disability

If an arrested person is deaf or if there are any doubts about his or her hearing ability, that arrested person cannot be questioned about an offence in the absence of an interpreter (if one is reasonably available) without written consent and the written consent of an appropriate adult if the arrested person is a juvenile (Regulation 12(8)). Where an interpreter has been requested and one is not reasonably available, any questions put to the arrested person must be in writing. It should be noted that there is no equivalent provision in respect of an interpreter for a foreign national. although it appears to be the norm that where an interpreter is requested by a foreign national or their solicitor, that service will be arranged.

5.4.9.4   Questioning a detainee who is intoxicated

Regulation 12(9) provides for circumstances where an arrested person who is under the influence of intoxicating liquor or drugs, so that s/he is unable to appreciate the significance of questions asked, or answers given cannot be questioned in relation to an offence while 'in that condition' unless the Member in Charge gives authority otherwise and has reasonable grounds for believing that to delay questioning would involve a risk of injury to persons, serious loss of or damage to property, destruction of or interference with evidence or escape of accomplices.

5.4.9.5   Detainee complaints procedure

Regulation 12(10) makes provision for an arrested person to make a complaint to a Garda in relation to his treatment while in custody. If this complaint is made during a Garda interview, that Garda must bring this complaint to the attention of the Member in Charge, if the Member in Charge is not present at the interview at that time, and a record of such complaint must be made on the Custody Record.

Regulation 12(11)(a) and (b) refers to record-keeping duties of Gardaí in respect of all relevant and important particulars which occur during interviews including the issuing of any authorities such as extending the detention time for a further allowable period of time or allowing Gardaí to question the person about a crime for which the person was not arrested. That part of Regulation 12 which requires that a handwritten note be kept by Gardaí during interview has been superseded by s. 57 of the Criminal Justice Act 2007 which commenced on 1 July 2007, although Gardaí have not yet ceased the practice of keeping handwritten notes of interviews.

Section 57 allows for the admission in evidence at trial of the videotape of the Garda interview of the detainee, whether or not a memorandum of interview was taken at the time of the interview, but that section does not apply to interviews that are not electronically recorded. While reference is made in Regulation 12(11)(b) to the procedures which must take place when an interview is not electronically recorded, this provision is largely redundant since it is now in fact the practice in almost all Garda stations that interviews are electronically recorded.

5.4.9.6   Legislation governing recording of interviews

The recording of interviews is governed by the Criminal Justice Act 1984 (Electronic Recording of Interviews) Regulations 1997. This regulation also provides for notification to the arrested person that their interview can be recorded in the Garda station. While this provision did not make the videotaping of interviews in Garda stations mandatory, judicial criticisms in a number of important cases of the failure of Gardaí to record interviews undoubtedly encouraged prosecution authorities to introduce videotaping facilities and compel their use as a rule rather than an exception. Section 56(1) of the Criminal Justice Act 2007 came into effect on 18 May 2007 and entitles an accused person, who has been charged after arrest and detention, to apply to court for a copy of the videotape of interview in the Garda station.

In *People (DPP) v Michael Murphy* (2005) 4 IR 504, the Court of Criminal Appeal held that there should be a 'marked reluctance' by the CCA to excuse failures to comply with the requirement to record interviews on video from that point forward.

In *People (DPP) v Diver* (2005) 3 IR 270, the Supreme Court quashed the appellant's conviction and held that the task of a trial judge was to assess if a breach of the regulations had prejudiced the fairness of the trial. In doing so, the court held that Gardaí were required to provide an accurate note of what transpired during an interview. In this case, the accused had been convicted of murdering his wife with the prosecution relying, *inter alia*, on what it said were inculpatory statements made during interviews. Five interviews took place and none of them were electronically recorded. The recording of interviews in handwritten form by various Gardaí was subsequently found to be grossly deficient and two of the interviews were entirely unrecorded. In deciding that the key issue was whether the failure to observe the regulations had prejudiced the fairness of the trial itself, Hardiman J. quashed the appellant's conviction and held that the task of the trial judge was to assess if a breach of the Regulations had prejudiced the fairness of the trial, Hardiman J. made the following comments:

> I wish to reiterate that the Gardaí are not entitled to exercise total editorial control in recording what has been said. Nor are they entitled to cherry pick what is to be recorded. In this case, the omission of a series of denials is utterly unacceptable. It is not that the Gardaí are required, when they are relying on written notes of an interview with the accused, to record what an interviewee has said verbatim. Regulation 12 requires that the record of the interview be 'as complete as practicable'. It must be a fair record of what was said and it is important to provide sufficient context to allow for an evaluation of what is said, especially where, as here, the accused was allegedly making ambiguous or inconclusive verbal statements and manifesting symptoms of distress. Audio visual recording is, of course, infinitely superior. It is utterly unacceptable to omit denials. It is important to provide sufficient context to allow for an evaluation of what is said, especially where, as here, the accused was allegedly making ambiguous or inconclusive verbal statements and manifesting symptoms of distress.

In *People (DPP) v Cunningham* (unreported, 27 May 2007, CCA), the Court of Criminal Appeal (CCA) held that there was no unfairness despite a failure by Gardaí to record interviews. The court accepted the prosecution argument that it would have been disruptive to move the suspect from Dundalk Garda Station which had no videotaping facilities to Carrickmacross Garda Station which was in another Garda District and which had videotaping facilities.

5.4.10   REGULATION 13: INTERVIEWING JUVENILE DETAINEES

Regulation 13 deals with the questioning of juveniles and the right of attendance at that interview of the juvenile's parent or guardian. There will be overlap with information in this text with respect to **Chapter 9** on juvenile justice which is included for necessary emphasis on the higher duty of care required with respect to litigating against children.

It should firstly be noted that a request by a parent or guardian for a solicitor to be contacted on behalf of the juvenile is regarded as if the request had been made by the juvenile detainee. A juvenile cannot be questioned in relation to an offence or asked to make a written statement unless a parent or guardian is present and unless the Member in Charge authorises that he can be questioned.

5.4.10.1   Questioning of juvenile detainees in the absence of a parent or guardian

The Member in Charge can only authorise questioning in the absence of a parent or guardian in any one of the following circumstances:

- If it has not been possible to communicate with a parent or guardian and the Gardaí have complied with Regulation 9(1)(a) in that regard.

- No parent or guardian has attended the Garda station within a reasonable time of being informed that the juvenile was in custody and a request to attend was made by Gardaí to them.

- It is not practicable for a parent or guardian to attend the Garda station within a reasonable time.

- The Member in Charge has reasonable grounds for believing that to delay questioning the person would involve a risk of injury to persons or serious loss of or damage to property, destruction of or interference with evidence or escape of accomplices.

5.4.10.2   Excluding a parent or guardian from the interview of a juvenile

A parent or guardian may be excluded from the interview of a juvenile with the authority of a Member in Charge:

- if the parent or guardian has been the victim of the offence itself or has himself been arrested for the offence;

- if the parent/guardian is suspected of complicity in the offence or if it is thought the parent/guardian, if present during questioning, would be likely to obstruct the course of justice; or

- if the conduct of the parent or guardian at the interview has been such as to amount to an obstruction of the course of justice.

If it is planned to question a juvenile in the absence of a parent or guardian, the Member in Charge must arrange for the other parent or another guardian to be present if possible and if such persons are not suitable or available, seek to have an adult relative present and if such a person is not suitable or available, seek to have a responsible adult present which person cannot be a member of An Garda Síochána.

5.4.11   REGULATION 14: INTERVIEWING FOREIGN NATIONALS

The Member in Charge must inform or cause to be informed without delay a foreign national arrested by Gardaí of a right to communicate with his or her Consul and that if desired, the Consul will be notified of his arrest. If requested, the Member in Charge must comply with the request as soon as practicable. Consular officers are entitled to visit the arrested person and arrange legal representation for the detainee.

If the foreign national is a political refugee or seeking political asylum, the Member in Charge needs the arrested person's express consent to give any information to the consular officer or to notify the consular officer of the arrest.

The necessary client care and interpretation rights applicable to foreign national clients will be discussed in **Chapter 20**.

5.4.12   REGULATION 15 CHARGING PROCEDURE

Regulation 15 delineates what has to occur if and when a person is charged following arrest and detention in a Garda station.

5.4.13   SEARCHES IN A GARDA STATION

Under Regulation 17 the Gardaí are entitled to search arrested persons in a Garda station subject to the following conditions:

* Ensuring so far as practicable that the person understands why he is being searched.

* Carrying out the search with due respect for the person being searched.

* A person in custody shall not be searched by a person of the opposite sex (other than a doctor).

* Where a search involves the removal of clothing other than outer clothing garments, no person of the opposite sex shall be present unless that person is a doctor or unless the Member in Charge considers that the presence of that person is necessary by reason of the violent conduct of the person to be searched.

* A search of a person involving removal of underclothing shall, where practicable, be carried out by a doctor.

* Where clothing or footwear is retained by Gardaí, replacements of a reasonable standard must be provided.

* A record must be made of the search of any person in custody including the names of all persons present.

* Details of any property taken from or handed over by a person in custody must be recorded and the person asked to sign the record made. If s/he refuses, this must be noted.

5.4.14   REGULATION 19: CONDITIONS OF CUSTODY

Regulation 19 covers such issues as the physical conditions of custody cells, allowing an arrested person necessary time to rest, the provision of meals, access to toilet facilities, conditions of holding cells in the Garda station, requirement placed on Gardaí to visit persons at regular intervals in cells (approximately every half hour) or, if the arrested person is drunk or under the influence of drugs, at intervals of approximately a quarter of an hour for a period of two hours or longer if his or her condition warrants it.

In *Gormley and White*, Hardiman J. gave a separate concurring judgment in which he stated that the conditions of detention must be such as to respect the suspect's rights and not to be such as would undermine the independence of a person's decision whether or not to seek legal advice.

5.4.15   REGULATION 20: NO ILL-TREATMENT

Regulation 20 prohibits the ill-treatment or threat of ill-treatment, of any kind by any person, to an arrested person, that person's family or any other person connected with him or her.

Reasonable force can only be used by a Garda if it is necessary in self-defence, to secure compliance with lawful directions, to prevent escape or to restrain the arrested person from self-injury or injury to others, damaging property or destroying or interfering with evidence.

If a Garda uses force which causes injury to an arrested person, the garda must report it to the Member in Charge, who must report it to the Superintendent of the District. If the force is used by the Member in Charge, it must be reported to the Superintendent.

Any Garda witnessing a breach of conduct, as described above, must report it to the Member in Charge or, if the breach is committed by the Member in Charge, to a Superintendent. The Superintendent must, without delay, investigate the incident or cause it to be investigated.

If an arrested person or someone (including a solicitor) makes a complaint about the conduct of a Garda, either before or after the person's arrest, this fact must be recorded in a separate document which shall be attached to and form part of the Custody Record. If the complaint alleges physical ill treatment, the Member in Charge must arrange for the person to be medically examined as soon as practicable unless he considers the complaint (against any Garda except himself) to be frivolous or vexatious.

5.4.16   REGULATION 21: MEDICAL TREATMENT IN GARDA STATION

Regulation 21 requires the Member in Charge to summon or cause to be summoned a doctor where an arrested person is injured, cannot be roused while under the influence of intoxicating liquor or drugs, fails to respond normally to questions or conversations (otherwise than owing to the influence of intoxicating liquor alone), appears to be suffering from a mental illness or appears to require medical attention.

If the Member in Charge feels the arrested person's condition is such that their immediate removal to a hospital or other suitable place is required, s/he can do that without having to first call a doctor. The Member in Charge must ensure that any instructions given by a doctor are complied with.

Medical advice must be sought also where an arrested person claims to need medication for serious conditions such as a heart condition, diabetes, epilepsy or any other serious condition. Arrested persons are entitled to see a doctor of their own choice and at their own expense. Any transfers of an arrested person to hospital or other suitable place must be notified to an immediate relative and any other relevant parties as outlined above with respect to requirements under Regulation 9. Records must be kept of all medical treatment matters.

5.4.17   REGULATION 22: MENTALLY HANDICAPPED PERSONS

Regulation 22 provides that all provisions in the Custody Regulations which relate to juveniles (arrested and detained in a Garda station) apply also to a person who is not a juvenile but whom the Member in Charge suspects or knows to be mentally handicapped. It also envisages that where practicable, the 'responsible adult' delineated in the discussion of Regulation 13(2)(c) should have experience in dealing with the mentally handicapped. This Regulation also requires that full details are kept of various relevant matters during the detention time.

5.5   The Custody Regulations and Forensic Evidence

There is extensive material available with respect to evidential issues relating to forensic evidence in **Chapter 10** which reviews changes resulting from the commencement of the majority of the sections of the Criminal Justice (Forensic Evidence and DNA Database) Act 2014. That material ought to be referenced in the context of this chapter, especially with respect to s. 13 provisions on the taking of samples from persons in custody in a Garda station. It is incumbent of all solicitors to be fully cognisant of the major changes that this 2014 Act brings to the obligations regarding the advice that must be given to the client in custody.

5.5.1   REGULATION 18: TAKING FINGERPRINTS, PHOTOGRAPHS, SWABS, AND SAMPLES

Regulation 18 states that the taking by Gardaí of fingerprints, photographs, and swabs can only occur if the appropriate legal authority is in place. If arrested for an offence for which the detainee can be detained as part of a Garda investigation under provisions, including those outlined at **5.1**, all such forensic samples can be taken. Some sample-taking requires the consent of the person being subjected to such procedures whilst others do not require such consent as outlined in the chart in **5.5.2**. The 2014 Act has made provision for the interpretation of withdrawal of consent regarding the taking of samples as a refusal, from which inferences may be drawn in specified circumstances.

In *Gormley and White* the Supreme Court held that not all evidence gathering must await an arrested person's solicitor to give evidence, where a solicitor is requested.

5.5.2   IMPLEMENTATION OF LEGISLATION IN TAKING FORENSIC SAMPLES

There are two categories of bodily fluids which can be taken during the course of a person's arrest and detention for the purpose of forensic analysis. These can only be taken following arrest for 'serious offences' as outlined at **5.3** and where that person is detained pursuant to any provisions including the four outlined in **5.1**.

The first category is mandatory non-intimate bodily fluids (discussed at **10.2.8.3**) and the other is non-mandatory intimate bodily fluids (also discussed at **10.2.8.1**). The former category was considered in the *DPP v White* aspect of the *Gormley and White* judgment and the latter category arose by default in *DPP v White*.

Legislation governing the taking of forensic samples, i.e. the Criminal Justice (Forensic Evidence and DNA Database) Act 2014 (2014 Act) has been introduced since *Gormley and White*. The application of the law of evidence generally and procedural rules in advocating in a court context are explored in **Chapter 10** where case studies at **10.5** demonstrate the application of various categories of evidence, to include forensic evidence.

THE TAKING OF FORENSIC BODILY SAMPLES DURING DETENTIONS	
MANDATORY (NON-INTIMATE)	**NON-MANDATORY (INTIMATE)**
1. No legal choice re giving of sample	1. May be legal choice re sample
2. Prior solicitor advice irrelevant	2. Prior legal advice is relevant
3. Detainee's consent irrelevant	3. Detainee's written consent required
4. Applies to adults and juveniles	4. Age of detainee relevant
5. No right to see solicitor before sample taken	5. May be a right to see solicitor first and the Garda must inform suspect of right to speak to solicitor (2014 Act)
6. Can be taken forcibly (s. 24 2014 Act)	6. Cannot be taken forcibly
7. Sample only taken on authority of Inspector	7. Sample only taken on authority of Inspector
8. Adverse inferences under s.19 Act silent re refusal to give sample	8. Refusal for good cause may be a defence but adverse inferences under s. 19 2014 Act silent re refusal to give sample

5.5.3 CONSENT IN THE TAKING OF NON-MANDATORY INTIMATE SAMPLES

It will be noted from 3 in the above chart that the detainee's consent is irrelevant with respect to mandatory non-intimate samples but must be present with respect to non-mandatory intimate samples. Obviously there must be great care taken that the consent of juvenile detainees demands a higher duty of care from the Gardaí as follows:

- Adult: Detainee consent required together with relevant accommodation where there is a hearing impediment or the detainee is a foreign national.

- 14–17 years old: Detainee plus parent/guardian consent.

- Under 14 years old: Only parent/guardian consent.

- The circumstances of dealing with those detainees with mental handicap as outlined earlier must apply standards as befit juvenile detainees.

TYPES OF SAMPLES—DESIGNATED PERSON FOR TAKING SAMPLES	
MANDATORY SAMPLES	**NON-MANDATORY SAMPLES**
Head hair/buccal (saliva) swab	Blood—Taken by doctor only
Nail/under nail: Footprint/impression from body but not part of hand or mouth	Urine—taken by person of same sex (insofar as practicable)
	Dental—Taken by dentist or doctor
	Pubic hair—Taken by doctor only
	Intimate swab—Taken by doctor only

5.6   Inferences from Failure to Provide Non-Mandatory Forensic Samples

In certain circumstances, where a person refuses to give consent for forensic samples to be taken, legal inferences may be raised at a subsequent trial in respect of that refusal. Under s. 13 of the Criminal Justice Act 2006 the penalty for non-compliance is €3,000 and/or six months' imprisonment. This Act has been amended by the adverse inferences provisions of the 2014 Act as discussed in **Chapter 10**.

No evidential 'inferences' may be drawn regarding mandatory non-intimate samples where the detainee's consent is not required, whereas such inferences may be drawn with respect to non-mandatory intimate samples, where such consent is required.

Inferences from refusal to consent, or withdrawal of consent, to taking of intimate sample arise under s. 19 of the Criminal Justice (Forensic Science and DNA Database Systems) Act 2014 are outlined at s. 19 of the Act:

19.(1)   *Subject to subsection (5), where in any proceedings against a person for an offence (other than an offence under section 160(1)) evidence is given that the accused refused without reasonable cause to give an appropriate consent required under section 12 (2)(b) or he or she without reasonable cause withdrew the appropriate consent given thereunder, then—*

    (a)   *the court, in determining—*

        (i)   *whether a charge against the accused should be dismissed under Part IA of the Criminal Procedure Act 1967 , or*

        (ii)   *whether there is a case to answer,*

and

    (b)   *the court (or, subject to the judge's directions, the jury), in determining whether the accused is guilty of the offence charged (or of any other offence of which he or she could lawfully be convicted on that charge),*

may draw such inferences from the refusal or withdrawal, as the case may be, as appear proper; and the refusal or withdrawal may, on the basis of such inferences, be treated as, or as being capable of amounting to, corroboration of any evidence in relation to which the refusal or withdrawal is material, but a person shall not be convicted of such an offence solely or mainly on an inference drawn from such refusal or withdrawal.

  (2)   *Subsection (1) shall not have effect in relation to an accused unless—*

    (a)   *he or she has been told in ordinary language by a member of the Garda Síochána when seeking his or her consent that—*

        (i)   *the sample was required for the purpose of forensic testing,*

        (ii)   *his or her consent was necessary, and*

        (iii)   *if his or her consent was not given, what the effect of a refusal or withdrawal by him or her of such consent might be,*

and

    (b)   *he or she was informed before such refusal or withdrawal of consent occurred that he or she had the right to consult a solicitor and, other than where he or she waived that right, he or she was afforded an opportunity to so consult before such refusal or withdrawal occurred.*

  (3)   *This section shall not apply to a refusal by a person to give the appropriate consent, or the withdrawal of such consent, unless the seeking of such consent by a member of the Garda Síochána is recorded by electronic or similar means or the person consents in writing to it not being so recorded.*

  (4)   *References in subsection (1) to evidence shall, in relation to the hearing of an application under Part IA of the Criminal Procedure Act 1967 for the dismissal of a charge, be taken to include a statement of the evidence to be given by a witness at the trial.*

  (5)   *This section shall not apply—*

(a) *to a protected person,*

(b) *to a person who has not attained the age of 14 years, or*

(c) *in a case where the appropriate consent has been refused, or been withdrawn, by a parent or guardian of a child unless a judge of the District Court makes an order under section 17 (6) and the child refuses to comply with the order.*

Provisions with respect to protected persons and juveniles have been amended in the 2014 Act. Application for a court order authorising the taking of an intimate sample from a child is now possible under s. 17 of the 2014 Act.

17.(1) If—

(a) *a member of the Garda Síochána is unable, having made reasonable efforts to do so, to contact a parent or guardian of a child for the purposes of ascertaining whether or not he or she consents to the taking of an intimate sample from the child under this Part,*

(b) *a parent or guardian of a child indicates to a member of the Garda Síochána that he or she cannot or will not attend at the Garda Síochána station in which the child is detained within a reasonable time for the purposes of giving consent to the taking of an intimate sample from the child under this Part,*

(c) *subject to subsection (3) of section 15 , the circumstances referred to in subsection (2) of that section exist in relation to a parent or guardian of a child,*

(d) *a parent or guardian of a child refuses to consent to the taking of an intimate sample from the child under this Part, or*

(e) *a child does not have, or the member in charge of the Garda Síochána station in which the child is detained cannot, having made reasonable efforts to do so, ascertain within a reasonable period whether he or she has, a living parent or guardian from whom consent to the taking of an intimate sample from the child may be sought under this Part, a member of the Garda Síochána not below the rank of inspector may apply to a judge of the District Court for an order authorising the taking of an intimate sample from the child.*

(2) *A member of the Garda Síochána who intends to make an application under subsection (1)shall inform the child concerned and, if it is reasonably practicable to do so, a parent or guardian of that child, other than a parent or guardian to whom section 15 (2) applies, of that intention.*

(3) *A judge of the District Court may order—*

(a) *that an application under subsection (1)shall be heard otherwise than in public, or*

(b) *that a parent or guardian of the child concerned to whom section 15 (2) applies shall be excluded from the Court during the hearing of the application,*

or both if—

(i)   *on an application in that behalf by a member of the Garda Síochána not below the rank of inspector, the judge is satisfied that it is desirable to do so in order to avoid a risk of prejudice to the investigation of the relevant offence in respect of which the child concerned is detained, or*

(ii) *the judge considers that it is otherwise desirable in the interests of justice to do so.*

(4) *A judge of the District Court shall, for the purposes of determining an application under subsection (1), have regard to the following before making an order under this section:*

(a) *the grounds on which the authorisation under section 12 (2)(a) was given for the taking of an intimate sample from the child concerned;*

(b) *if appropriate, the reasons (if any) that a parent or guardian of the child concerned (other than a parent or guardian to whom section 15 (2) applies) gave for refusing to consent to the taking of an intimate sample from that child;*

(c) *the age of the child concerned;*

(d) *the nature of the offence in respect of which the child concerned is detained; and*

(e) *whether it would be in the interests of justice in all the circumstances of the case, having due regard to the best interests of the child concerned, the interests of the victim of the offence in respect of which the child concerned is detained and the protection of society, to make an order authorising the taking of an intimate sample from the child concerned.*

(5) *If, on an application under subsection (1), a parent or guardian of the child concerned applies to be heard by the judge of the District Court, an order shall not be made under this section unless a reasonable opportunity has been given to the parent or guardian, as the case may be, of that child to be heard.*

(6) *A judge of the District Court may, if he or she considers it appropriate to do so, make an order authorising the taking of an intimate sample from the child concerned in accordance with this Part.*

(7) *If, on an application under subsection (1) in relation to a child who is detained under section 4 of the Act of 1984, a judge of the District Court makes an order under subsection (6), the judge may, on an application in that behalf by a member of the Garda Síochána not below the rank of inspector, issue a warrant authorising the detention of the child concerned for such further period as the judge may determine but not exceeding 4 hours for the purpose of having an intimate sample taken from that child.*

(8) *Subsection (7) shall not affect the operation of section 4(3) of the Act of 1984.*

(9) *When an intimate sample has been taken from a child who is detained pursuant to a warrant issued under subsection (7), the child shall be released from custody forthwith unless his or her detention is authorised apart from this section.*

5.7   'Drawing an Inference'—Ordinary Versus Legal Inferences

It is important to distinguish between ordinary inferences and legal inferences. An ordinary inference is a conclusion you can reasonably draw from facts and the conclusion reached follows logically from the facts on which it is based, e.g. before going to sleep, one looks out of a window noting that the pavement is dry. On waking and looking out of the same window, one notes that the pavement is wet. One can logically infer from this set of circumstances that it rained overnight although one did not see it rain.

A legal inference is not necessarily logical but is permitted in law simply because the legislature says so. Such inferences are created in various statutes and simply allow for the drawing of conclusions from certain facts, e.g. the fact of silence during interview by an arrested person. Such inference drawing is regarded by defence practitioners as a legislative landmine which diminishes the right of a suspect to remain silent during interrogation.

The difficulty with legal inference provisions in a forensic context is that a person may refuse to give a non-mandatory forensic sample or answer a question for any number of reasons and not simply because they are 'potentially guilty of the alleged crime' or have 'something to hide' but such conclusions are the only adverse inference that the statute envisages.

It is necessary for the defence solicitor to explain legal inferences to clients arrested and detained in Garda stations, against whom inferences may be raised during interview. This is particularly challenging as many such clients will present as vulnerable or poorly educated, or have various medical disabilities and/or have serious addictions.

It should be noted at this point that there is an onus on the state to destroy any forensic samples taken from arrested and detained persons within 12 months of their being taken if that person has not been charged with the alleged offence within that timeframe. However that time limit will not apply if the failure to prefer charges was due to the absconding of the suspect or an inability to locate him or her or because the prosecution has applied to the District Court to retain the samples. Further, if a person is charged and the case was subsequently dismissed in the District Court jurisdiction or the accused was acquitted in an indictment jurisdiction, the prosecution must destroy all forensic samples within 21 days of such dismissal or acquittal of those proceedings or the discontinuance of the proceedings unless the prosecution had applied to the District Court to retain the samples.

5.7.1   PHOTOGRAPHS

5.7.1.1   Arrest without detention

Under s. 12 of the Criminal Justice Act 2006, where a person is arrested for a minor offence (see **5.3**) which does not allow Gardaí to detain and question him or her under a provision including the four outlined at **5.1**, a Garda Sergeant can give authorisation for the taking of a photograph of the person to assist in that person's identification in relation to any proceedings which may be instituted against him in respect of the offence for which s/he was arrested. No consent from the person is required. The person can be charged with an offence of obstruction on refusing to allow the taking of the photograph for which there is a maximum sentence of 12 months and/or a fine. Part 11 of the 2014 Act reiterates this power, which also includes the taking of fingerprints and palm prints.

5.7.1.2   Arrest with detention

Section 6 of the Criminal Justice Act 1984 (as amended by the 2014 Act) determines that where a person is arrested for a serious offence and detained under a detainable provision including the four provisions outlined at **5.1**, a Garda Inspector can authorise the taking of a person's photograph. No consent from the person is required. Reasonable force can be used in the taking of the photograph provided that the arrested person is informed of the intention to use force and an Inspector has authorised the use of reasonable force and the forcible taking of the photograph is recorded electronically and the forcible taking of the photograph is carried out in the presence of a Garda Inspector.

5.7.1.3   Destruction of photograph

A detained person is entitled to apply to have forensic evidence destroyed as delineated from s. 76 to s. 80 of the 2014 Act and such destruction includes destruction of photographic evidence by way of application to the Garda Commissioner to have photographic evidence destroyed if the person has not been charged within 12 months of the taking of the photographs or where the person is charged but acquitted or where the person is charged but criminal proceedings have been withdrawn by the prosecution. Where a person so applies for the destruction of their photograph, the Garda Commissioner must acknowledge receipt of the application and make a decision on the application within four weeks. There is thereafter a right of appeal to the District Court of a refusal by the Commissioner to destroy this photographic evidence. That appeal must be made within eight weeks of the Garda Commissioner's decision and the right of appeal applies to either the applicant or to the Garda Commissioner. Such proceedings are to be heard 'otherwise than in public'.

5.7.2   FINGERPRINTS AND PALM PRINTS

5.7.2.1   Arrest with detention

Under s. 100(1) of the 2014 Act, fingerprints and palm prints can be taken from an arrested person who is arrested for the purpose of being charged with a relevant offence and before s/he is charged. A Garda Sergeant can authorise the taking of fingerprints and palm prints in these circumstances. Fingerprints can be re-taken if the first attempt fails or if the fingerprints taken are damaged or imperfect. The issue of consent from the person does not arise, due to the mandatory nature of giving such samples. Under s 100(3):

> The provisions of subsection (1A) of section 6 and section 6A of the Act of 1984 shall apply to fingerprints and palm prints taken pursuant to this section as they apply to fingerprints and palm prints taken pursuant to the said section 6.

Gardaí can use reasonable force to take fingerprints or palm prints, if authorised to do so by a Superintendent, provided that the arrested person is informed of the intention to use force, the forcible taking of this evidence is video-recorded and it occurs in the presence of a Garda Inspector. A person can be charged with the offence of obstruction if s/he frustrates this process and a maximum penalty of 12 months and/or a fine applies (s. 100(4) of the 2014 Act).

5.7.3   DESTRUCTION OF FINGERPRINTS AND PALM PRINTS

Under s. 8 of the Criminal Justice Act 1984, as amended by Part 10 of the 2014 Act a person can apply for the destruction of fingerprints and palm prints on the same basis as outlined previously at **5.7.1.3** in relation to photographs.

5.8   Suspending Section 4 Detention: Criminal Justice Act 2011, Part 2

If arrested and detained under s. 4 of the Criminal Justice Act 1984 for a 'relevant offence', a person's detention can be 'suspended' for a period of time. This suspension can occur if the Member in Charge of the Garda station in which the arrested person is detained has reasonable grounds for believing that it is necessary to allow Gardaí to conduct further investigations into the alleged offence. If the detention is suspended, the arrested person will be released from the Garda station and must be furnished with a notice setting out the date and time at which s/he is required to return to the Garda station so that their s. 4 detention can then resume.

This suspension provision arises under s. 7, Part 2 of the 2011 Act which commenced on 9 August 2011 pursuant to SI No. 411 of 2011. Section 7 of the 2011 Act introduced a new s. 4(3)(A) to the 1984 Criminal Justice Act. Whilst s. 7 is primarily aimed at serious white collar crime fraud type offences in banking, investment, company and insurance, however, more common offences under the Criminal Justice (Theft and Fraud Offences) Act 2001 are also included under the definition of 'a relevant offence' to which this section may apply, e.g. offences defined in ss. 4 and 17 of the Theft and Fraud Act. Schedule 1 of the Criminal Justice Act 2011 also includes 'relevant offences' under ss. 2 to 4 inclusive of the Criminal Damage Act 1991 where they relate to data or a storage medium in which such data is retained.

Section 4(3)(A) of the Criminal Justice Act 1984 also allows for a further second notice to be issued to the detained person by a Garda Inspector, if the date of resumption of the detention has to be changed. A person's detention under s. 4 can only be suspended for a maximum of two occasions and the total period of the suspension cannot exceed four months from the date of the first suspension.

Under s. 4A of the Criminal Justice Act 1984 as inserted by s. 8 of the Criminal Justice Act 2011, Gardaí have a power to arrest persons who do not return to the Garda station on the date in the notice. Section 4B of the 1984 Act also makes it an offence to fail to return to a Garda station in such circumstances. If a person returns to the Garda station on the resumed date given in the notice, his or her s. 4 detention resumes for the rest of the lawful period allowed under the 1984 Criminal Justice Act.

5.9   Review of *DPP v Gormley* and *DPP v White* [2014] IESC 17

The Supreme Court heard these two cases together and delivered a single judgment (Clarke J.) with which all members of the Court agreed. A separate concurring judgment was delivered by Hardiman J. The Supreme Court gave a single judgment, because a considerable portion of the background material was similar. As consistently reiterated in this chapter, these cases have far-reaching implications for the rights of detained persons in Garda stations.

Clarke J. stated that the core issues to be considered by the court were:

> whether a person arrested on foot of serious criminal charges is entitled to the benefit of legal advice prior to the commencement of any interrogation and prior to the taking of any samples for the purposes of forensic examination.

The court said that the main common question which potentially arose in both cases concerned:

> the procuring of material evidence on which an accused might be convicted at a time when the relevant accused is under arrest, has sought the attendance of a solicitor, but before the solicitor concerned has arrived.

The judgment explicitly addressed the right of a suspect in a Garda station who positively asserts a right to obtain legal advice, to have access to such legal advice before questioning or interrogation (i.e. Mr Gormley). In the case of Mr White, the court held that as he had no option in law but to give the mandatory samples required of him, Gardaí were not obliged to wait for his solicitor to advise him before taking the samples in a minimally invasive manner and without force.

The Supreme Court stated that the principal question of Irish constitutional law which was addressed in their judgment was the right to fair process, first established in the 1976 case of *State (Healy) v Donoghue* [1976] IR 325. It went on to say that this constitutional right was similar to those recognised in the European Convention on Human Rights (ECHR) as interpreted by the European Court of Human Rights (ECtHR) and in other constitutional regimes similar to our own. The impact of the ECHR in Irish jurisprudence is discussed in **Chapter 17**.

In its judgment, the Supreme Court summarised the case law of countries with legal systems similar to Ireland, including the United States, Canada, Australia, and New Zealand. It concluded that 'the overall picture is that questioning is required to cease after a request for a lawyer has been made until legal advice is available'.

The court noted that in neither case before it had it been argued that Mr Gormley or Mr White was entitled to have a solicitor present during questioning. Despite this, the court gave a strong indication that in the future such a right might be held to exist based on 'the jurisprudence of both the ECHR and the United States Supreme Court' which 'clearly recognised that the entitlements of a suspect extend to having the relevant lawyer present'.

It is noteworthy, as previously mentioned in this chapter, that in the immediate aftermath of the *Gormley and White* judgment and as a direct consequence of that judgment, the DPP announced on 7 May 2014 that the state was providing an express right of attendance by a solicitor at Garda interviews, in cases where arrested and detained persons requested it.

The Supreme Court summarised existing Irish case law in paragraph 5 of the main judgment. It considered that:

> The position to date has been that, while a constitutional right to legal advice in custody has been recognised, it has not yet been held that evidence gathering might be suspended until legal advice becomes available.

It is instructive to briefly consider the facts in both *Gormley and White* when considering the Supreme Court judgment and then consider its more practical implications for both clients and solicitors in more detail.

5.9.1   FACTS OF *DPP V GORMLEY*—STATEMENT OF CASE

Raymond Gormley was arrested in Co Donegal at 1.47 p.m. on Sunday 24 April 2005. He was informed of his rights to legal advice and at 2.15 p.m. he gave the names of two solicitors to Gardaí. The Gardaí then made efforts to contact one of the solicitors and, to that end, attended at his parents' home. The solicitor's parents directed the Gardaí to the solicitor's own home, where they left a message with his wife. All of this had happened in the period after 2.15 p.m. At 3.06 p.m., the solicitor contacted the Garda station. Unfortunately, there was a dispute as to when the solicitor said he would arrive at the Garda station but it was recorded at the time as being 'as soon as possible after 4pm'. Mr Gormley was interviewed at 3.10 p.m. and was alleged to have made a number of inculpatory statements before the solicitor's arrival at 4.48 p.m.

5.9.2   FACTS OF *DPP V WHITE*—MANDATORY SAMPLE CASE

Mr White had been arrested under s. 42 of the Criminal Justice Act 1999 (in prison) at 7.45 a.m. on 13 February 2008. He was taken to Raheny Garda Station. At 7.58 a.m., he made a request for a named solicitor. A phone call to her number shortly afterwards was answered by a recorded message, providing an emergency number, which was responded to within one minute. The solicitor arrived at the Garda station at 9.42 a.m. At 8 a.m., permission had been applied for by the appropriate Garda for the taking of various samples under the Criminal Justice (Forensic Evidence) Act 1990. This request was granted at 8.05 a.m. By 8.30 a.m., the samples (buccal swabs from his mouth and a number of hairs) had all been taken.

5.9.3   IRISH CASE LAW REFERRED TO BY THE SUPREME COURT IN
**   *GORMLEY AND WHITE***

The following case law dealing with access to legal advice by detained persons was considered in the *Gormley and White* judgment:

5.9.3.1   *The People (DPP) v Madden* (1977) IR 336 CCA

Mr Madden had not been provided with access to a lawyer prior to making a statement while under arrest and s. 30 detention. The Court of Criminal Appeal held that a person in such circumstances has a right of reasonable access to his legal advisers and that a refusal of a request to give such reasonable access would render his detention illegal. The court stated that 'reasonable' must be construed having regard to all the circumstances of each individual case and there was no obligation on Gardaí to proffer a legal adviser to a detained person 'without request'.

5.9.3.2   *The People (DPP) v Healy* (1990) 2 IR 73 SC

In this case, a family member retained a solicitor on behalf of Mr Healy who was arrested and detained under s. 30 of the Offences Against the State Act. The solicitor was denied immediate access on arrival at the Garda station until the accused completed the making of a statement. The admissions in the statement were the sole evidential basis on which Mr Healy was prosecuted. The majority of the court held that the right of reasonable access to a lawyer was constitutional in origin and not merely a legal right. The court also held that there was no distinction between the arrival of a solicitor as a result of the request of a detainee or on the request of a person acting bona fide on behalf of that detainee.

5.9.3.3   *The People (DPP) v Buck* (2002) 2 IR 268

The accused was arrested on a Sunday and Gardaí encountered difficulties in obtaining a solicitor. While he was questioned for several hours before a solicitor arrived at the Garda station, no actual written statement had been taken. After a consultation with a solicitor, Mr Buck made an inculpatory statement and later sought to have this declared inadmissible on the basis that he was subjected to interrogation prior to seeing a solicitor and prior to the statement being made.

The Supreme Court dismissed an appeal from the Court of Criminal Appeal and held that a statement was admissible where there was no causative link between the violation of the prisoner's constitutional rights and the making of the statement.

5.9.3.4   *The People (DPP) v O'Brien* (2005) 2 IR 206

The accused following arrest and detention requested the services of a solicitor but did not specify a particular solicitor. The Gardaí recommended a solicitor, consciously knowing that there would be a delay in his arrival. Gardaí continued to interrogate the accused in the meantime and the accused made certain incriminating statements. The statements were ruled inadmissible for a breach of his constitutional right to reasonable access to a lawyer.

5.9.4   EUROPEAN COURT OF HUMAN RIGHTS CASE LAW REFERRED
**   TO IN *GORMLEY AND WHITE***

The following ECtHR case law dealing with access to legal advice by detained persons was considered in the *Gormley and White* judgment:

5.9.4.1   *Salduz v Turkey* (2009) 49 EHRR 19

Seventeen-year-old Mr Salduz was arrested and interrogated by police in the absence of a lawyer. He made several admissions which he claimed were made under duress and he later denied the truth of those admissions. He alleged that his rights under Article 6(3)(c) of the ECHR had been violated. Article 6(3)(c) provides:

> *Everyone charged with a criminal offence has the following minimum rights: to defend himself in person or through legal assistance of his own choosing or, if he has not sufficient means to pay for legal assistance, to be given it free when the interests of justice so require.*

Following reference of the case to the Grand Chamber, it was held that even though Article 6 of the ECHR, in terms of criminal proceedings, was designed to ensure a fair trial, 'it does not follow that the Article has no application to pre-trial proceedings' as in the case of the police investigation and interrogation of Mr Salduz. It said further that Article 6 may be relevant before a case is sent for trial if and insofar as the fairness of the trial is likely to be seriously prejudiced by an initial failure to comply with its provisions. The Grand Chamber concluded:

> In sum, even though the applicant had the opportunity to challenge the evidence against him at the trial and subsequently on appeal, the absence of a lawyer while he was in police custody irretrievably affected his defence rights.

The Supreme Court judgment noted that in the ECtHR case of *Panovits v Cyprus* (Application No. 4268/04 (First Section) 11 December 2008), the ECtHR held that the failure to provide sufficient information about the right to legal assistance to a juvenile prior to his initial questioning by police constituted a violation of his rights under Article 6(3). The Supreme Court noted that the principles laid down in the *Salduz* case were later referred to in other cases before the ECtHR including: *Amutgan v Turkey* (Application No. 5138/04 (Fifth Section) 3 February 2009); *Cimen v Turkey* (Application No. 19582/02 (Second Section) 3 February 2009); and *Dayanan v Turkey* (Application No. 7377/03 (Second Section) 13 October 2009).

The Supreme Court further noted that in several cases before the ECtHR, an arrested person can waive their right to legal representation if this is freely and knowingly done: *Trymback v Ukraine* (Application No. 44385/02 (Fifth Section) 12 January 2012); *Tarasov v Ukraine* (Application No. 17416/03 (Fifth Section) 31 October 2013); *Bodaerenko v Ukraine* (Application No. 27892/05 (Fifth Section) 14 May 2013); and *Saunders v United Kingdom* (1997) 23 EHRR 313.

5.9.5   UK SUPREME COURT CASE REFERRED TO IN *GORMLEY AND WHITE*

The UK Supreme Court looked at the Scottish post-arrest procedure as delineated in *Cadder v Her Majesty's Advocate* (2010) UKSC 43, to ascertain if it was compatible with the ECHR. In that case, the accused had made a number of admissions in the absence of a solicitor. The court considered the *Salduz* principles mentioned earlier and held that:

> the contracting states are under a duty to organise their systems in such a way as to ensure that, unless in the particular circumstances of the case there are compelling reasons for restricting the right, a person who is detained has access to advice from a lawyer before he is subjected to police questioning.

5.9.6   INTERNATIONAL CASE LAW REFERRED TO IN *GORMLEY AND WHITE*

In *Miranda v State of Arizona* 384 US 436 (1966), by a majority, the US Supreme Court held that statements made by an accused during interview are only admissible at trial if the prosecution can show that the accused was informed of two rights, i.e.:

* the right to consult with a lawyer before and during questioning if requested; and

* the right against self-incrimination prior to being questioned by police.

5.10   Advising the Client in Custody

Significant new considerations arise for criminal practitioners in advising clients in custody following the *Gormley and White* judgment and the DPP's response to that judgment. The first consideration must be to re-state that the paramount duty of a solicitor is to act in the best interests of the client and to always have the client's interests as the primary concern. The only caveat to this obligation is that a client's concerns must not be allowed to conflict with one's professional obligations of ethical conduct.

Advising clients during detention and questioning in Garda stations has opened up a novel legal landscape. If clients' rights are to be advocated and protected at all times, competent and informed advices must be conveyed. Solicitors must inform their clients of all available options and the likely consequences of each option. In the aftermath of the judgment in *Gormley and White*, advices given by defence solicitors and decisions made during the Garda station detention and interview will impact on the conduct of a client's trial and on their lives into the future.

5.10.1   PRACTICAL STEPS PRIOR TO ATTENDING THE GARDA STATION

The first indication to a criminal defence practitioner that a client has been arrested and is in custody in a Garda station generally comes in the form of a telephone call from either Gardaí or from the family or friends of the person detained. Practitioners should keep detailed and careful notes of all such conversations and secure as much information as is possible.

Conversations with family and friends of the detained person should collate details of the name, address, age, gender, medical needs or special needs of the person arrested. If a juvenile, the practitioner must confirm whether or not a parent or guardian or appropriate adult has been contacted and if so, must obtain details of the identity and contact numbers of those persons. Any known circumstances of the arrest as provided by family/friends should be noted.

Conversations with Gardaí should assist in creating a record of the following:

- name of Notifying Garda and Arresting Garda;
- reason for and location of arrest;
- time of arrest;
- if detained, the relevant detention provisions, including the time detention was authorised and by whom;
- location of Garda station;
- name of Member in Charge;
- confirmation as to whether or not a doctor was requested by the person arrested and the time of that request;
- confirmation as to whether or not a doctor has been contacted;
- the time of the request by the person arrested to contact a solicitor;
- confirmation of whether interviewing of the suspect has taken place or whether samples have been authorised or taken.

After establishing these relevant details, solicitors should request that they speak to the client on the phone, to provide an early assurance that the practitioner is aware of the arrest and the associated details.

5.10.2   ARRESTED PERSON'S OPTIONS

Some arrested persons will inform their solicitor on the telephone that they simply require a telephone consultation and do not require the solicitor to attend at the Garda station, thereby waiving the rights to have a pre-interview consultation with the solicitor in the Garda station and to have the solicitor present during questioning. This telephone consultation selection can sometimes occur in cases where clients are arrested on very serious charges. While solicitors must respect the client's wishes in such instances and cannot foist themselves on the client in the Garda station, the single most important question for a solicitor to determine is whether or not, in any particular case, a telephone consultation alone constitutes effective legal assistance in safeguarding a person's right against self-incrimination.

In circumstances where a client insists that a telephone consultation is adequate and there is no wish to have the solicitor attend at the Garda station or the Garda interview, it is suggested that the solicitor should be alert in determining if a telephone consultation constitutes effective legal assistance in each case.

Firstly, the solicitor should be aware and make it clear to the client at the outset of their telephone consultation that they are entitled to speak on the telephone in circumstances of absolute privacy and that all matters discussed are subject to client–solicitor privilege. Even if assured by the client that this is the case, it should be emphasised that the telephone communications may be unsecured. The client may be unaware that eavesdropping can occur either deliberately or by the simple reality of the hustle and bustle of Gardaí going about their work in a Garda station as they and other personnel walk past a detained person on a telephone in the station in circumstances where the client often presents with a raised voice, in an intoxicated or distressed or angry manner. It is clear that to attempt to advise a client in such circumstances is a pointless exercise and unlikely to take place in circumstances of privacy. While any information obtained by deliberate telephonic eavesdropping would constitute a breach of legal professional privilege between client and solicitor, it may be impossible to prove that it has occurred in circumstances as just described. In addition, while covert eavesdroppers may be unable to directly make use of any information obtained, information gleaned may provide Gardaí with other lines of evidential enquiry that are not in one's client's interest.

Secondly, a solicitor should determine whether the alleged offence which has triggered the arrest a suitable one for discussion on the telephone, e.g. an arrest on suspicion of committing a sexual offence.

5.11   Client Waiver of Legal Advice

Where a client waives any rights arising from his right to legal advices, including the right to have a solicitor attend at the Garda station for a consultation and/or to attend a Garda interview, it is extremely important to endeavour to ascertain the reason for that decision by the client and to satisfy oneself, insofar as possible, that the client's decision is fully informed and made voluntarily, i.e. without undue influence from any persons who may be motivated to undermine their right not to incriminate themselves.

The client must be made aware that the absence of a solicitor attending the Garda station may have significant consequences, in particular if it is asserted by the client at a later stage of the case that admissions to offences were not made voluntarily. The solicitor should emphasise to the client that if the client wishes to waive legitimate rights, it is possible to subsequently reverse that decision and request the presence of the solicitor at the Garda station. A client should also be advised that if such a decision is taken, reversing the waiver to legal advice, the Gardaí should be asked to suspend further questioning or investigation until the solicitor–client consultation has occurred at the Garda station.

The solicitor should consider if the client is competent to make the decision to waive his rights to a face-to-face consultation and the presence of the lawyer during questioning by asking the client some appropriate questions as follows:

* Has there been any intimation that the time spent in the Garda station will be longer if there is a request for a solicitor to attend?

* Have the Gardaí promised anything to the client in return for a speeded-up interview process?

* Has the detained person been subjected to false promises of any kind including that there will be no objection to a bail application if the client 'cooperates' with a speedy investigation and make admissions?

* Have the Gardaí said that they simply wish to hold one quick interview and that the detained person won't be charged immediately as a file has to go to the DPP?

* Has the detained person been subjected to any physical or mental abuse?

* Is the detained person waiving rights simply to get to a clinic to get medication for an addiction?

Primarily, in making an assessment of the detained person's decision to waive a right to a private consultation in custody, it is important for a solicitor to remember at all times the professional obligation to provide effective legal assistance, which includes the safeguarding of the clients' rights against self-incrimination and to protect that client from being exploited or being used to bolster an otherwise weak or inadequate Garda investigation.

It is suggested that if a client discloses that any of the above circumstances exist, the solicitor must consider carefully whether a presence at the Garda station is required, to provide an equality of arms between the investigating authority and the client.

5.12   Client Vulnerabilities

A solicitor should be alert to how a client is presenting on the telephone so as to identify if the client has any particular difficulties or vulnerabilities, including a belief that the client is intoxicated, under the influence of drugs (and/or suffering from drug withdrawal symptoms), has a mental illness or other mental or psychiatric disability, has been arrested for the first time and is possibly frightened or distressed by the unfamiliarity of Garda procedures, has a low level of education and/or lacks assertiveness and is therefore easily subjected to a more aggressive Garda approach. In all such circumstances, as previously alluded to, it is questionable whether or not a telephone consultation by itself constitutes effective legal assistance to a client.

In circumstances where a client is labouring under a mental or psychiatric disability, a solicitor may have to request that an appropriate medical professional, (psychiatrist or psychologist) is contacted to assess the detained person's fitness to be questioned by Gardaí. If the request is refused, a solicitor should ask for reasons and consider whether the request should be reiterated to a more senior Garda officer in the Garda station. It is questionable whether the Garda station doctor is the most appropriate person with regard to any question of the detained person's fitness to be interviewed due to a possible conflict of interest or a lack of specific necessary qualifications.

5.13   Client Request Asking Solicitor to Attend the Garda Station

Where a solicitor receives a call from a detained client to attend at the Garda station, it is considered best practice to advise the client not to say, sign or do anything until the solicitor has attended at the Garda station for the purpose of a consultation. It is also important for the solicitor to notify Gardaí at that Garda station that the solicitor is coming to see the arrested person and to indicate an estimated time of arrival. Should the arrival time of the solicitor be delayed for any reason, the solicitor should telephone the Garda station to confirm this fact, to ensure that nothing of any significance should occur in that solicitor's absence. This is also an advisable course of action to ensure that there is a clear record regarding communication between the solicitor and Gardaí should that issue arise during the subsequent proceedings.

5.13.1   ARRIVAL AT THE GARDA STATION

A solicitor should make written record of the time of arrival at the Garda station. A three-stage approach as follows is then recommended as a useful way to proceed:

1. The solicitor should confirm with the Member in Charge that the details of arrest etc. provided earlier on the telephone are correct, whether or not a doctor was requested and, if so, whether that doctor has arrived or seen the client or is en route? If the detained person is a juvenile, the solicitor should seek confirmation as to whether or not the parent or guardian or responsible adult was contacted and details of that person's arrival or imminent arrival.

2. The solicitor should request to speak to the Arresting or Investigating Garda so as to establish the alleged circumstances of the arrest including: What is the alleged offence? Why is this client a suspect? Who made the initial complaint to Gardaí? What is the purported evidence against the suspect? While Gardaí differ in their approach to providing answers to all such requests, it should be pointed out that a solicitor cannot advise a client properly unless appraised of all relevant information of this kind and, pragmatically, any failure to provide all relevant information will only result in delays for all concerned.

3. The solicitor should then see the client for a confidential consultation and will be better placed to advise him of his options if appraised of all relevant information by the investigating Garda. If Gardaí refuse to disclose why a client is a suspect, one can only advise of a legal right to not self-incriminate and that a caution will be given by Gardaí, prior to any significant evidence gathering process in the Garda station. As already discussed the raising of inferences during interrogation by Gardaí investigating an alleged offence represents a significant inroad to the right not to self-incriminate. It is undoubtedly the case that in circumstances where full pre-interview disclosure has been provided to the solicitor, that a meaningful consultation can take place with the client and the safest initial approach during interview can be decided. In this regard, the solicitor's sole task is to defend the client actively and skilfully and protect that client's legal interests at all times.

5.13.2   SOLICITOR ATTENDANCE AT THE GARDA INTERVIEW OF THE SUSPECT

As previously stated, an arrested person has a constitutional right of immediate access to a solicitor where such a request is made of the Gardaí. On arrival at the Garda station, a solicitor also has the right of immediate access to the client. As mentioned earlier, the right of an arrested person to have a solicitor present during questioning in a Garda station was not specifically litigated in the *Gormley and White* cases but was without doubt the 'elephant in the room' during the Supreme Court's deliberations when its judgment gave a strong indication that the right to legal advice in the future may be held to extend to a right to have a lawyer present during questioning, while emphasising that it did not arise on the facts specifically outlined in *Gormley*.

5.13.3   PRACTICAL ISSUES WHICH ARISE FOR SOLICITOR AT GARDA INTERVIEW

The role of a solicitor attending at a Garda station is to provide practical, informed and effective legal assistance to the client who is arrested and detained there. The mere presence of a solicitor is not sufficient. The solicitor is not there simply to give the appearance that fairness of procedures is taking place. The solicitor may have to be proactive on many levels, in order that the client's interests are protected, provide effective informed assistance and ensure that the client's right to silence and non-self-incrimination (subject to statutory exceptions) are at all times protected. Solicitors are not present to answer questions for their clients. Suggested guidelines below are therefore general in character and further guidance has been provided in *Guidance for Solicitors Providing Legal Services in Garda Stations* (Law Society of Ireland, December 2015), while all defence solicitors adjust to the alteration of process around obligations to the client in custody, in the aftermath of *Gormley and White*.

The arrest and detention of a person for questioning by Gardaí signifies what is often the first important step in the prosecution evidence-gathering process. Much of what happens during this investigative phase of the prosecution will have a significant impact on a client's later trial, if charged with the alleged offence. Therefore the role of an attending solicitor during the interviewing of a client is crucial.

Solicitors should remember that the videotaping process can be of benefit to a client and not just Gardaí in that a permanent record is being kept of any voiced concerns the solicitor may have in relation to the client's treatment, either prior to or during interview.

5.13.3.1   Confirmation of the status quo prior to interview stage

It is suggested that some of the issues which solicitors should be alert to during the interview process would include the following:

- Is the suspect under lawful arrest and detention in the first place, entitling Gardaí to interview at all?

- Is the suspect sufficiently aware of the legal right to silence in the absence of any statutory inference exceptions to this right being invoked?

- Is the solicitor satisfied with the degree of pre-interview disclosure by Gardaí?

If the answer to the last question is in the negative, a useful approach might be to ask Gardaí to explain any deficiencies or refusals of disclosure and the reason for their existence and, having done so, to make a careful written record of that conversation. In all cases where disclosure of all relevant circumstances of the alleged Garda investigation and arrest of the client is not forthcoming, it might be prudent for the solicitor to have this fact noted on tape at the commencement of the interview. The solicitor could make a brief opening statement on tape that due to a refusal of disclosure the solicitor is unable to advise the client in a factual vacuum and has been prevented from doing so. A working example might be the following:

> My client has been arrested on suspicion of assault. I have asked for all relevant information to be furnished to me so as to advise my client further. This disclosure has been insufficient or refused and as a consequence, I cannot advise my client any further at this time.

It is suggested that in the absence of any or all relevant disclosure by Gardaí of the surrounding facts being alleged against a client, that solicitors inform their clients that they cannot advise them properly at this time and for that reason, the suspect might be best protected by relying on the right to silence.

5.13.3.2   Managing notification of alleged 'pre-interview admissions'

Gardaí may put the solicitor on notice that at an earlier time in the investigation prior to the formal videotaped interview commencing (such as at the time of arrest, during the arrested person's removal to the Garda station, on arrival at the Garda station, in a cell at the Garda station or any other place), that the arrested person made some admission. If this occurs, it might be prudent for a solicitor to raise objections to this matter at the relevant time during the videotaped interview.

The circumstances in which an earlier purported admission was made may deem it inadmissible evidence at a later trial. Should the existence of such admission arise during interview, it would be important for a solicitor not to allow the client to 'copper-fasten' repeat or agree to the fact of an earlier admission, made in questionable circumstances and prior to legal advices being obtained. In circumstances where the attending solicitor hears about purported 'earlier admissions' for the first time during the interview, it is suggested that the solicitor objects to the question, asks for the interview to be suspended, obtains full details from Gardaí of the specifics of the event and have a private consultation thereafter with the client.

5.13.3.3   Client instructions regarding alleged abuse or duress

If a client has disclosed prior to interview that s/he was subjected to either physical or mental abuse or unwarranted pressure to admit any offences, it might be prudent for a solicitor to address this disclosure on tape at the commencement of the interview. If a client is eventually charged and on trial for the alleged offence in question, a court might expect that an effective legal adviser would have any pre-interview complaints noted and recorded at the earliest possible time to corroborate the client's complaint.

5.13.3.4   Protecting the vulnerability of a client

If not satisfied that a client is either competent or fit to be interviewed but Gardaí insist on going ahead, it may be prudent to have this fact recorded and to ask Gardaí what is the basis of their decision to proceed despite the stated concerns of the solicitor. It may also be advisable to ask to speak to a more senior Garda in such circumstances or even a to higher prosecuting authority.

Solicitors should object to any atmosphere in the interview room (or indeed elsewhere during the detention) which is suggestive of an overly aggressive or oppressive approach by Gardaí. While the fact of objection may not resolve the situation at the time, it may have important consequences for the client at a later trial. In some cases, it may affect the admissibility of any admissions made by a client as a result of what can be objectively interpreted hostile, aggressive treatment by Gardaí.

A solicitor should ensure that s/he is seated beside the client during the interview. This is so that the client is reassured by the presence of the legal adviser, so that any objections made by the solicitor can be heard on tape and so that Gardaí do not seek to alienate the solicitor from the proceedings. As stated earlier, the mere presence of a solicitor in the interview room is not enough. The solicitor must be prepared to take a proactive role if required.

If Gardaí claim that they have certain types of evidence against a client (e.g. CCTV or witness statements or Garda notebook entries), the solicitor should request to view that evidence in the presence of the client. It is important that the client is advised of a right not to comment on the contents of the CCTV or other evidential matters while they are being shown or discussed and that, subject to inferences that can be raised, the right to remain silent remains throughout the interviewing process.

Where a Garda asks any question which aims to rely on a claim of anonymity, and despite a request from the solicitor, the source has not been made known to the client or the solicitor, that question should be objected to by the solicitor.

Garda questioning of the suspect should be about the alleged offence for which the arrest has occurred. While in some circumstances and with certain pre-conditions in place, Gardaí can move on to question your client about other alleged offences, solicitors should be alert to ensure that this does not occur without proper procedures being observed. It is also prudent that where a client is informed that he or she is now to be questioned about a matter other than the one for which the arrest occured, that the solicitor insists on a private consultation with the client prior to Gardaí proceeding with that proposed line of questioning. As a new alleged offence is now being investigated, the solicitor should first of all ask Gardaí for full details of any evidence to be put to a client during interview and then discuss this with the client prior to the commencement of that interview.

5.13.3.5   Objectionable questions

The following list of what defence solicitors would categorise as 'objectionable questions' from Gardaí are instructive for a solicitor attending a client in custody and/or attending at the interview of the client:

- A 'getting to know you' question, e.g. about client's background or family life, which is clearly designed to condition the client into answering questions in breach of his right to silence.

- A question that does not use clear simple language.

- A leading question which is particularly 'objectionable' in the case of a suggestible client.

- An irrelevant question, i.e. not relevant to the specific offence being investigated.

- A question asked in an aggressive, insulting or otherwise threatening way.

- A complex question containing a number of questions, which will probably confuse the client.

- A question asked repeatedly after a suspect has responded by saying 'No Comment' or 'No Answer' which can have the effect of making a client feel bullied into submission thereby undermining the right to silence.

- A question couched in hypothetical language inviting the client to speculate.

- A question touching on or offending legal professional privilege.

- A question seeking to undermine the solicitor–client relationship.

- A question suggesting previous bad character of a client.

- A question which clearly misrepresents the law and amounts to inducement or duress, i.e. the most common example of this is when Gardaí tell the client that it can only help him in court if he gives his side of the story. While certain detention provisions do in fact contain such measures, particularly in circumstances where there exists minimum mandatory sentencing, it is submitted that such provisions are distinct from the matter highlighted in this instance.

- A question which is tantamount to a speech or lecture, e.g. 'In my day, fellas like you would be tethered to lamp-post ...' etc.

- A question raised after a very lengthy period of interview, contrary to custody regulations.

- A question during a time when a client becomes unwell or distressed in any way.

- A question in which Gardaí suggest that the evidence in a case is overwhelmingly against a client. In such circumstances a suspect should not be questioned as the purpose of detention is stated in law as being for the investigation of the alleged crime. Therefore if the investigating Gardaí have already collated 'overwhelming evidence' a solicitor might invite Gardaí to release the client from detention in such circumstances and have him charged if they wish to do so.

5.13.3.6   The solicitor advises but the client decides

While the function of a solicitor is to provide full and accurate advices and assistance to a client following arrest, the ultimate decision as to how a client deals with issues arising during detention must always be made by the client as it is for the client to decide whether or not to accept any advices proffered. Some clients will say from the outset that they wish to make a statement of admission to the offence under investigation. If this arises, a solicitor should nevertheless ensure that the client understands what the Garda case against him actually is, why they are a suspect and that they have a right to silence despite the Garda case appearing 'strong on paper'. If Gardaí have very little evidence, a statement of admission can only help cure their difficulties and might even assist in providing other investigative leads where further evidence is obtained against the client. If there appears to be a significant amount of evidence against the client, it could still be the case that some essential proofs are missing. Any statement of admission will always substantially assist the prosecution and become part of the prosecution case against the client.

The client must be reassured that the ultimate decision is the client's and that it is that client's right to make such admissions if desired. It is best practice for the attending solicitor to ensure that the client is made aware of all purported evidence in Garda possession, in advance of proceeding with a desire to make a statement of admission, to ensure that a fully informed decision is being made. The client should also be told that any lawfully obtained admissions of guilt represent significant evidence against him in court and that it is a matter for the courts, and not the Gardaí, as to how s/he will be dealt with by way of sentence.

Most importantly, clients must be told that after receipt of competent legal advice, it is unlikely that the client can later challenge any decisions made by them during detention, e.g. regarding making admissions or giving consent to forensic sampling.

In circumstances where a client's instructions demonstrate the existence of a good defence, e.g. self-defence in an alleged assault charge or consent where there is an allegation of rape, solicitors should provide clear advices to that client regarding the benefits of getting an early account of this proposed defence on record.

5.14   Interview Inferences—Exceptions to the Right to Silence

Earlier in this chapter we discussed the inferences which can be raised when a person refuses to consent to the taking of certain forensic samples. Similarly, a range of legislative provisions exist that allow for inferences to be raised when an arrested and detained person remains silent during Garda interrogation. The legislation refers to the prosecution entitlement in such instances of silence 'to draw an inference' but omits to use the word 'adverse'. It is logical to deduce, however, that the only type of inference that can be drawn is an adverse one, irrespective of the reason behind an arrested person's silence.

As previously outlined, a legal inference is not necessarily logical. As well as encroaching on the right to silence of an accused person during Garda interrogation, if raised and admitted at trial it entitles the judge or jury to apply only one adverse conclusion against an accused, which is not always the most logical conclusion. A possible scenario could go as follows: Did John fail to account for a mark on his arm or a gun found in his car, under inference caution because (a) he is guilty or (b) for a range of other reasons including the fear of involving other persons if he tries to explain relevant circumstances? In Irish law, despite a lack of legal logic, if the prosecution succeed in admitting John's silence to such questions at trial, the only inference the court can accept is that at (a) and not (b).

Prior to the enactment of the Criminal Justice Act in 1984, the right to silence during Garda interviewing was absolute with a statutory exception under s. 52 of the Offences Against the State Act 1939 (as amended). Section 52 was later found to amount to a violation of the ECHR in the case of *Heaney and McGuinness v Ireland* [2000] ECHR 684. Despite this decision, various inference provisions are now in place under different criminal law statutes. All are exceptions to the right to silence and apply when arrested and detained persons are being questioned by Gardaí. Some of the more commonplace provisions encountered by practitioners are detailed below but this list is not exhaustive.

- Failure or refusal to account for objects or marks.
- Failure to account for presence at a particular place.
- Failure to mention particular facts.

5.14.1 FAILURE OR REFUSAL TO ACCOUNT FOR OBJECTS OR MARKS AND FAILURE TO ACCOUNT FOR PRESENCE AT A PARTICULAR PLACE

When the Criminal Justice Act of 1984 was enacted, s. 18 (Inferences from accused's failure or refusal to account for objects, marks etc.) and s. 19 (Inferences from accused's presence at a particular place) broke the mould in the erstwhile right to absolute silence during Garda interrogation. These provisions allow for inferences to be raised in certain circumstances, if an arrested person remains silent during Garda interview, when asked to account by the Arresting Garda in respect of the matters referred to in either section.

Sections 28 and 29 of the 2007 Act, Part 4, introduced substituted versions of ss. 18 and 19 of the Criminal Justice Act 1984 respectively, thereby substantially broadening the circumstances in which Gardaí could question suspects about marks or objects or in relation to the suspect's presence in a particular place, following the person's arrest and detention for an 'arrestable offence'. It is submitted that the substituted sections apply to 'arrested persons' and apply after arrest when a demand can be made on the suspect to give an account regarding objects, marks or presence at a location.

The power to ask a person to so give such an account includes the following statements in legislation:

- 'on being questioned' following arrest and detention by a member of the Garda Síochána in relation to the offence;
- 'at any time before the suspect is charged with the offence'; or
- 'when being charged with the offence'; or
- when being informed by a member of the Garda Síochána that s/he might be 'prosecuted for that offence'.

Section 18 allows for an arrested person to be asked by any Garda (not just the Arresting Garda) to account for any object, substance or mark, or any mark on any such object that was (i) on his person; (ii) on his clothing or footwear; (iii) otherwise in his possession; or (iv) in any place in which he was during a specified period. This power appears to entitle a Garda to question the person about objects, substances or marks sometime after the incident in question on condition the Garda believes they are attributable to a criminal offence. It is important however to emphasise that there must be independent evidence of any facts being put by Gardaí pursuant to ss. 18 and 19 of the Criminal Justice Act 1984 as amended.

When taking instructions in relation to such matters, a solicitor should remember to enquire as to whether all lawful pre-conditions have taken place, giving the Garda the power to ask for an account in the first place.

Section 19 states that any Garda (not just the Arresting Garda) can request a person to account for his or her presence at a 'particular place' at or about the time the offence is alleged to have been committed. Again this provision appears to entitle a Garda to question the person sometime after the incident in question. When taking instructions where this issue arises, it is important that the solicitor ensures that all pre-conditions have taken place, giving the Garda the power to ask for an account in the first place.

5.14.2   FAILURE TO MENTION PARTICULAR FACTS

Section 30 of the Criminal Justice Act 2007 inserted a new inference provision, s. 19A(1) into the Criminal Justice Act 1984 allowing for inferences to be raised in a completely new set of circumstances.

The generality of this provision has quite staggering consequences for an accused's right to silence when being questioned in a Garda station. It is difficult to understand how the s. 19A(1) provision could pass the 'proportionality test', a phrase referred to in *Heaney v Ireland* SC (1994) 3 IR 593. That judgment considered inference provisions and held that the right to silence was not absolute and could be restricted by certain legislative provisions provided those provisions passed a proportionality test. See also *DPP v Finnerty* (1999) 4 IR 364 and *Rock v Ireland* SC (1997) 3 IR 484. The *Rock* judgment dealt with the old ss. 18 and 19 provisions of the 1984 Criminal Justice Act prior to their later substitution.

The effect of s. 19A(1) is that serious consequences can result for a person at trial where there has been a failure by that person, following arrest, to mention particular facts which they wish to later rely on in their defence. This failure can arise 'at any time' following arrest, when being questioned, when being charged or when being informed that they may be prosecuted in the future. The section states that the fact relied on must have clearly called for an explanation at the relevant time 'being a fact which in the circumstances existing at the time clearly called for an explanation from him or her when so questioned, charged or informed, as the case may be'. It is in effect a provision demanding that an arrested person provide immediate details of any defence they may have or propose to raise, in respect of the offence under investigation.

The 2007 Act provides that a person cannot be convicted of an offence solely or mainly on such an inference being drawn. This is because the inference, if successfully admitted into evidence, amounts to 'corroboration of other evidence' against an accused. It is the case with all inference provisions discussed earlier that in the absence of any other evidence against him, a person cannot be convicted on inference provisions alone.

5.15   Safeguards for a Suspect Subject to Inference Provisions

Safeguards for a suspect who is subject to the impact of ss. 18 and 19 of the Criminal Justice Act 1984 (as amended) include the following:

- The suspect must be cautioned as to effect of failure or refusal to comply with these sections in ordinary language.

- The suspect must be afforded a reasonable opportunity to consult with a solicitor.

- The interview must be conducted electronically unless the person consents in writing to it not being so recorded.

Section 19A(2) and (3) of the 1984 Act provides certain safeguards or restrictions in respect of admissibility in court of a failure to account under s. 19A(1) which include the following:

- A request to 'give an account under s. 19' must 'clearly call' for an explanation at the time.

- The accused must be told in ordinary language what the effect of such a failure to account might be when being questioned or charged or told that he may be charged at some future date.

- A caution must be given. The accused's solicitor should ask for a copy of this caution prior to the client's interview.

- The suspect should be given a reasonable opportunity to consult a solicitor. (This provision has now been overtaken by the decision in *Gormley and White*, previously discussed in that an arrested person who proactively requests legal advice cannot be questioned until that advice is received.)

- An acccused person cannot be convicted solely or mainly on inference evidence alone in the absence of any other evidence against him.

Neither ss. 18 or 19 or 19A shall apply in relation to the questioning of a person unless it is recorded by electronic or similar means or the person consents in writing to it not being so recorded.

5.16   Disclosure to Solicitors when Inferences Raised

The issue of disclosure to solicitors attending Garda stations was not specifically litigated in *Gormley and White*. As stated earlier, the arrested person's right to have a solicitor present during interviews was authorised by the DPP in May 2014, as a direct result of the *Gormley and White* judgment. In view of the serious implications of inference provisions for arrested persons during detentions, it is difficult to see how a non-disclosure or limited disclosure policy can survive post *Gormley and White*, i.e. how can a solicitor advise a client properly in the absence of all material disclosure? This is particularly so if inferences are to be raised during interviews.

Hardiman J. addressed inference issues in *Gormley and White*, stating:

> The considerable complexity of the area of inferences, in particular, mean that proper advice would normally be given after the advisor has familiarised himself, as far as possible, with a factual content of what is alleged against his client, and what his client's general reaction to it is.

5.17   Offences Against the State (Amendment) Act 1998, Section 2

The Offences Against the State (Amendment) Act (OAS (A) Act) 1998 introduced significant encroachments on a person's right to silence in Garda custody allowing for inferences to be drawn in various circumstances including a failure to answer material questions and a failure to account for matters requiring 'an explanation'. Section 31 of the Criminal Justice Act 2007 made amendments to s. 2 of the OAS (A) Act 1998.

The new substituted provisions entitle any Garda, not just the Arresting Garda, to ask the questions contemplated in those sections, provided the Garda in question reasonably believes that the presence of objects or marks or a person's presence at a particular place is attributable to the person's participation in committing a criminal offence and the Garda informs the person of that belief.

Similarly, as with ss. 18 and 19 already discussed, the provisions of s. 2 (as amended by s. 31) shall not apply in relation to the questioning of a person by a Garda unless it is recorded by electronic or similar means or the person consents in writing to it not being so recorded.

The amendments introduced by s. 31 of the Criminal Justice Act 2007 are in similar terms to the safeguard provisions outlined above in s. 19A of the Criminal Justice Act 1984 in relation to admissibility in court of a failure to 'give account' as required by the legisation.

Case law with respect to this aspect of Criminal Procedure includes the following:

- *People (DPP) v Binead and Donohue* (unreported, 28 November 2006, CCA).

- *People (DPP) v Matthews* (unreported, 14 July 2006, CCA).

- *People (DPP) v Birney and Others* (unreported, 12 May 2006, CCA).

Other statutory provisions include s. 9 of the Criminal Justice (Amendment) Act 2009 regarding the investigation of organised crime offences under Part 7 of the Criminal Justice Act 2006.

5.18   To Be Or Not To Be … Silent

Despite the inference provisions outlined earlier and their encroachment on the right to silence, there may be some instances when it is in the client's interest to answer questions at the Garda interview and to give an account of what occurred where the detainee appears to have a good defence to the allegations being made. Alternatively, the detainee may wish to admit guilt at the earliest possible stage due to remorse or to a desire to receive a more lenient sentence. Whether or not any of these circumstances arise, it is vital that the solicitor first obtain full details of the purported Garda evidence against the client before any decision is made on how to proceed. It is also extremely important that the client is aware of his or her right to silence.

The first scenario might arise where a client is arrested on suspicion of an offence involving injuries to another person such as murder, manslaughter, assault. If the client's instructions are that his actions were simply motivated by self-defence, it might be extremely important that this account is given to Gardaí at the earliest opportunity.

Similarly, a client arrested for rape where he instructs that consent is a defence necessitates that that account is given to Gardaí at the earliest opportunity. If a client wishes to make a statement of admission, after been advised of the Garda case against him, he must be warned that he is admitting to involvement in a very serious matter in circumstances where the prosecution may have only a weak case against him. Where a client's account later proves, on other evidence, such as medical evidence or evidence from eye witnesses to the event, to have been self-serving or downright untrue or impossible, the consequences are considerably prejudicial.

The desire of an accused to make an inculpatory statement in an effort to receive a more lenient sentence is most likely to occur where the accused has been arrested on suspicion of an offence which carries a minimum mandatory sentence if there is a subsequent conviction. Offences included in this category arise following arrest on suspicion of an offence under s. 15A of the Misuse of Drugs Act 1977 (as amended) for the sale and supply of drugs with a value in excess of €13,000 or offences under the Firearms Acts. In both instances the legislation specifies that the sentencing judge may decline to impose the mandatory minimum sentence where the accused made admissions at an early stage and if 'material assistance' was given to Gardaí during questioning.

This decision is probably the most fundamental one which an arrested person has to make following detention. The solicitor can assist the client in the making of that decision by firstly explaining what the strength or weakness of the prosecution case appear to be before giving advice.

5.19   Identification (ID) Parades

Another issue which may arise for consideration during a client's detention is whether or not the client should participate in (stand on) a formal ID parade in a Garda station when so requested by Gardaí. There is no mandatory obligation on a person to take part and if the suspect does participate and is identified, this can constitute significant evidence for the prosecution case, provided that the ID parade was held in circumstances of absolute fairness. Conversely, if the suspect is not picked out, any subsequent attempt by Gardaí to have him identified informally will have little if any probative value. Solicitors are entitled, where requested by a client, to attend ID parades to assist with the absolute necessity for fairness. There is a recently established Statutory Scheme for Payment of such attendances, administered by the Legal Aid Board.

The second issue to consider is where a client does not wish to take part in the ID parade, Gardaí may seek to carry out more informal ID procedures which will have none of the safeguards attaching to formal ID parades in Garda stations, including the presence of the solicitor. Methods resorted to in the past have included an informal ID at or outside a court or other place.

There is no Statutory Code of Practice governing the holding of ID parades in Garda stations, although Gardaí do have their own guidelines governing their processes. A solicitor should bear in mind that the overall requirement of the holding of any ID parade must be one of fairness at every level and that there is no general rule of thumb which applies in every case. Some judgments from the Higher Courts on the vexatious issue of identification are dealt with in the paragraphs that follow.

5.19.1   ADVISING AND GUIDING THE CLIENT REGARDING THE ID PARADE

If the holding of an ID parade arises in the Garda station during a detention, the solicitor should consider the following approach.

5.19.1.1   Assess the case to date

The solicitor will be aware of the reason for their client's arrest, the general basis on which he has become a suspect and the extent of any evidence in the possession of Gardaí. The issue of ID parades rarely arises at an early stage of a Garda investigation unless there is little by way of other evidence in their possession. If a client is asked to stand on an ID parade, it might suggest in some cases that little if any other evidence may exist. On the other hand, Gardaí may have other evidence against the client but may wish to 'double bolt' the door so to speak, on a 'nothing to lose' type approach.

5.19.1.2   Speak to the Garda conducting the ID parade

The solicitor should have a discussion with the Garda who will be conducting the ID parade (the 'Conducting Garda') and establish that that Garda is not part of the Garda team investigating the offence in respect of which the suspect has been arrested to ensure impartiality and fairness. The solicitor should ask for a videotape of the parade if possible. In circumstances where any of the requests outlined below are refused, the solicitor must consider whether or not to advise a client not to stand on the parade, on the basis that the refusal of the information sought or request made renders the parade unfair to the client. If this should occur, ask for the reason for the refusal to give information or to accede to the request and it is most important to note this down in writing for future reference as required at trial.

Typical requests by the detainee's solicitor to the Conducting Garda include information on the following criteria:

- The physical and clothing descriptions that have been given of the alleged culprit by the eye witnesses who are attending the ID parade; a careful note should be made by the attending solicitor of these details.

- All descriptions of any eye witnesses given to Gardaí.

- If a particular item or colour of clothing is mentioned which coincides with a similar item worn by your client, request that he be allowed change his clothing.

- If one or other of the eye witness's descriptions does not coincide in any way with your client's own appearance, the solicitor could usefully consider whether or not the client should have to go through the ordeal of standing on an ID parade at all. This anomaly may also provide 'good cause' for why a client might decline to stand on the ID parade. It will most certainly assist the client at a later time, if charged, and in court of trial.

- Confirmation that the proposed eye witnesses do not have previous knowledge of the client to ensure that any purported identification it is not just a case of recognition.

- Confirmation that the eye witnesses have not already made an earlier identification of your client, for example, pointing him out to Gardaí.

- Confirmation as to how many persons (called 'volunteers') will stand on the ID parade with the detainee. While the Garda internal guidelines provide for 'at least 8 persons', the solicitor should request at least 10 to ensure that it is fair. If refused, ask that your objection is recorded by the Conducting Garda.

- Confirmation that no photographs of your client have been shown to proposed eye witnesses and that your client has not been seen by such persons in the Garda station or its environs.

- Confirmation of the wording of any caution which the Conducting Garda intends to read out at the commencement of the ID parade.

- The absence from the ID parade of all members of the investigating team or the Member in Charge of the Garda station or any Garda other than the Conducting Garda. The Garda internal guidelines, on this point, state that while the Garda in charge of the investigation may attend the ID parade, s/he should have no active part in it. There does not appear to be any necessity for the Garda heading the investigation or any of the other Gardaí mentioned above, to be present. If this request for them to absent themselves is refused, the solicitor should ask that the objection to their presence is noted by the Conducting Garda.

- Confirmation that none of the proposed eye witnesses know any persons voluntarily participating in the ID parade and confirmation that eyewitnesses have not seen any of those voluntary participants prior to the parade taking place.

- Assurance that none of the proposed eye witnesses are allowed to communicate with each other in circumstances where one has viewed the parade and others have yet to view the parade.

- Assurance that none of the proposed eye witnesses have been located in the Garda station in circumstances where they could have had an opportunity to see the client in the Garda station.

Explain to the Conducting Garda that after seeing your client for a consultation, certain requests may arise, such as the provision of washing/showering facilities and clean clothes. If the client has distinctive facial features, this will also have to be addressed prior to parade taking place. If the client has any distinctive feature, such as a facial cut, it may be advisable to ask that all persons on the parade place a sticking plaster on their faces at this place. If your client has a visible tattoo or scar or other distinctive marking, you might request that he is provided with an item of clothing to cover this feature in case of prejudice by any eye witness viewing the parade. Primarily, it is necessary to ensure that the client is placed among at least eight other persons, who are, as far as possible, similar to the client in terms of age, height, general appearance, dress, and what the Garda ID Parade Guidelines describe as 'class in life'.

5.19.1.3   Consultation with client

Armed with the above information, the client is now in a better position to decide whether or not he wishes to stand on the ID parade. Ensure that the client is in a fit condition to stand and is not in any obvious distress, whether physically or mentally. Take a careful note of the client's personal features—hair and eye colour, height, weight, or build etc. If the client does not wish to stand on the parade, check the reason for this decision and if appropriate, this reason can be communicated to the Conducting Garda later and requested to be noted down. It is important to inform the client of what will take place at the ID parade and advise that he or she must not say or do anything that would draw attention. Also the client must be advised that if picked out, s/he will be cautioned and should make no reply.

5.19.1.4   Attending the ID parade room

On arrival in the ID parade room, the client will be asked to stand in whatever position he or she chooses in the line-up. It is useful at this stage to ask the client to view the persons in the line-up and confirm satisfaction with their presence on the basis that he does not know any and that their appearance in general terms conforms to that of the client. If he raises any objections, inform the Conducting Garda of this objection and ask for replacements. If this request is refused, ask that your objection is noted down. If proceeding to participate in the parade the client should stand nearest the two people who most resemble him on the parade.

If your client's objections relate to several persons standing on the parade and a request for replacements is refused, the solicitor must consider whether or not to have a further consultation with the client, to advise him not to participate in the parade. If this occurs, the solicitor should ensure that the reason for declining is noted down by the Conducting Garda. The Conducting Garda should explain to the client what is happening and ask if he or she wishes to take part. If the client decides not to take part, no ID parade should be held.

Once the client is happy to proceed with the ID parade, the Conducting Garda will indicate if there is more than one eye witness. The client can change position in the line-up for each separate eye witness viewing. A solicitor should also ask all those on the line up to look straight ahead while the parade is underway.

5.19.1.5   ID parade

The Conducting Garda will bring or arrange for the eye witness to be brought to the ID parade room. It is important to ask that no member of the Garda investigating team perform this function as it is best practice that the Conducting Garda does so. By now, each person on the line-up will be holding a paper with a number on it in front of them, so that if the eye witness does identify anyone, that person will refer to the ID by the number.

On the arrival of the eye witness, the Conducting Garda will address the eye witness by referring to a standard form in the Crime Investigation Techniques Manual which is as follows:

> This is an identification parade. I want you to look very carefully at this line of persons and see if you can recognise the person you have come to identify (or the person who assaulted (etc.) you, or the person you saw at X place at X time on X date). Do not say anything until I ask you a question.

It is suggested that a fairer form of ID address to an eye witness would include 'see if you can recognise or not the person ...' so as to emphasise the possibility that the culprit may not be present.

The solicitor should note down how long the eye witness views the parade before that person stops viewing the parade. When asked by the Conducting Garda if the person has recognised anyone, it is very important to record the precise answer which is given and to agree this wording with the Conducting Garda as being the precise words which were said.

A variety of answers may be given by the eye witness from 'No', 'Not sure', 'Possibly No 3', 'Yes, I am almost sure', 'Yes I am absolutely certain'. Clearly the precise answer given will have consequences for the degree of certainty of identification being made. If the client is picked out on the basis of any of these replies being given, the eye witness will be asked to leave the ID parade room. The Conducting Garda will then caution the client to the effect that he has been picked and while he is not obliged to say anything, anything he does say will be noted and may be used in evidence.

It is customary practice after the ID parade is over for the Conducting Garda to enquire of the attending solicitor and the client if they have any complaints about the holding of the parade. It is most important that the solicitor requests that any concerns about the fairness of the parade are noted down at this time.

5.19.1.6   Post-parade consultation with client

The client should be made aware that while being picked out on an ID parade is not helpful, it is not conclusive and should not in any way interfere with his or her right to remain silent during any subsequent questioning.

5.20   Identification Evidence in General

The fragility and dangers of identification evidence, even when fair procedures are observed and the honesty of eye witnesses is beyond doubt, have been the frequent cause of much judicial comment and concern. The most infamous case concerning one Adolf Beck explains why this concern exists. Mr Beck was sentenced in 1896 to seven years in prison after ten eye witnesses positively identified him as a fraudster while posing as a 'Lord Willoughby'. He strongly protested his innocence. Following release, he was again convicted for similar offences in 1904 on the positive identifications of five further witnesses. While awaiting sentence in prison, the real culprit committed further similar offences, was arrested and admitted his guilt to all of the offences including those for which Mr Beck had already served seven years. The persons who had 'identified' Mr Beck as the culprit withdrew the positive identifications of him at an earlier time. Beck's release led to the setting up of a parliamentary enquiry and indirectly to the establishment of the English Court of Appeal.

The inherent dangers of identification evidence arose in the seminal Supreme Court judgment of *People (AG) v Casey No. 2*, (1963) IR 33. In that case, Kingsmill Moore J. stated:

> In our opinion it is desirable that in all cases, where the verdict depends substantially on the correctness of an identification, the jury's attention should be called in general terms to the fact that in a number of instances such identification has proved to be erroneous, to the possibilities of mistake in the case before them and to the necessity of caution.

The case of *People (DPP) v Cooney* (1998) ILRM 321 also considered the issue of identification evidence and the limited probative value which some informal ID procedures can have. In t*People (DPP) v Brazil*, (unreported, 22 March 2002, CCA), the then Chief Justice Keane held that the identification evidence of a witness who had been shown a photograph of the suspect before the ID parade would be rendered almost valueless. In *DPP v Christo* (unreported, 31 January 2005, CCA), the court held that if a witness has already independently identified a suspect, there was no need for a formal ID parade to be held and that the holding of any such ID parade in such circumstances would only serve to reinforce the identification and could be prejudicial to the accused.

In *People (DPP) v O'Reilly* (1990) 2 IR 415, the court held that where a suspect refuses to stand in an ID parade without cause, it is then open to the Gardaí to seek to rely on more informal identification procedures with considerably less safeguards for the accused.

This most important *O'Reilly* judgment outlined a non-exhaustive list of essential prerequisites for the holding of a fair ID parade:

(a)   The ID parade must contain eight or nine people of similar age, height, appearance, dress, and walk in life, as the suspect. It is extremely important that a solicitor ensures that every ID parade adheres to the criteria when considering the ID line-up, and objection should be made if not satisfied.

(b)   It is good practice for a solicitor to note the names, addresses, and ages of all persons taking part in the parade and to take a note of their general appearance and distinctive physical characteristics. Consideration should be given to requesting the Conducting Garda to take a Polaroid picture of the parade or even on a solicitor's phone.

(c)   The ID parade must be supervised by an independent Garda not involved in the case.

(d)   The eye witness must not have any opportunity to view the suspect in advance of the parade.

PART III

PROCESS, JUVENILES, AND INITIAL APPLICATIONS

CHAPTER 6

PROCESS AND PROCEDURE IN THE COMMENCEMENT OF PROCEEDINGS

6.1 The Prosecution of Criminal Behaviour

In countries with either the common law adversarial system, as exists in Ireland, or a civil law inquisitorial system as exists in countries such as France, the prosecution or prosecutor is the chief legal representative of the state in matters where an act is committed or an omission has occurred which is contrary to the prevailing criminal law. This is the legal party responsible for presenting the case, on behalf of the injured party, as investigated by the national police force, An Garda Síochána (Gardaí) in a criminal trial against an individual accused of breaking the law.

The majority of prosecutions in the Irish State are taken in the name of the Director of Public Prosecutions (DPP). The legal basis for this process was determined in the case of *People (DPP) v Roddy* [1977] IR 177. The case decided that a member of the Garda Síochána could prosecute in the DPP's name without the express consent of the DPP's Office.

Section 2(1) of the Prosecution of Offences Act 1974 (the 1974 Act) established the Office of the Director of Public Prosecutions and the holder of the office is colloquially referred to as 'the Director'. According to the 1974 Act the 'Director' shall be appointed by the Government, shall be a civil servant in the civil service of the state and independent in the performance of the functions of the office. The Director should be, on the date of appointment, either a practising barrister or solicitor for at least ten years. The Prosecution of Offences Act 1974 transferred most of the prosecutorial functions to the DPP from the Attorney General with the exception of extradition, and offences under the Official Secrets Act 1963 and the Genocide Act 1973.

6.2 Section 8 Garda Síochána Act 2005 and General Direction No. 3

The implementation of s. 8 of the Garda Síochána Act 2005, entitled 'Prosecution of offences by members of Garda Síochána' which came into force on 1 February 2007, was the first time that the relationship between the DPP and the Garda Síochána in the prosecution of offences was addressed in legislation. The relationship was examined by the Public Prosecution System Study Group (known as the Nally Group), which looked at all aspects of the prosecutorial system in Ireland, including the role of the Gardaí in relation to the prosecution of offences. Unlike in most European countries, the vast majority of prosecutions in Ireland are instituted by the Gardaí, without reference to the DPP's office.

8.—(1)   *No member of the Garda Síochána in the course of his or her official duties may institute a prosecution except as provided under this section.*

(2)   *Subject to subsection (3), any member of the Garda Síochána may institute and conduct prosecutions in a court of summary jurisdiction, but only in the name of the Director of Public Prosecutions.*

(3)   *In deciding whether to institute and in instituting or conducting a prosecution, a member of the Garda Síochána shall comply with any applicable direction (whether of a general or specific nature) given by the Director of Public Prosecutions under subsection (4).*

Section 8 (4) of the Act states:

The Director of Public Prosecutions may give, vary or rescind directions concerning the institution and conduct of prosecutions by members of the Garda Síochána.

At s. 8(5),

Directions under subsection (4) may be of a general or specific nature and may, among other things, prohibit members of the Garda Síochána from—(a) instituting or conducting prosecutions of specified types of offences or in specified circumstances, or (b) conducting prosecutions beyond a specified stage of the proceedings.

In a prosecution taken in the name of the DPP the prosecuting Garda is presumed to have complied with the section and to have complied with any relevant direction, unless the contrary is proved. However, nothing done by a member in a prosecution is invalidated solely by that member's failure to comply with the section or any relevant directions (s. 8(6)).

Section 8(7) indicates that nothing in that section:

(a)   precludes the Director of Public Prosecutions from, at any stage of the proceedings, assuming the conduct of a prosecution instituted by a member of the Garda Síochána, or

(b)   authorises a member of the Garda Síochána to institute a proceeding without the consent of the Director of Public Prosecutions if an enactment prohibits the institution of that proceeding except by or with the Director's consent.

Section 8 (8) confirms that:

(a) a direction is of a general nature if it relates to a class of prosecutions, and (b) a direction is of a specific nature if it relates to the prosecution of a person for a specific offence.

The DPP, pursuant to the powers conferred by s. 8(4) of the 2005 Act gave a Direction known as General Direction No. 3 which entered into effect on 8 November 2011. This Direction rescinded General Direction No. 2 of 3 December 2009 (see this public document on the DPP's website, http://www.dpp.ie). It states at Part 1:

Subject to the terms of this or any subsequent direction a member of the Garda Síochána may institute and conduct in the District Court any Prosecution for a criminal offence, whether the offence is a summary offence or an indictable offence. Any such prosecution shall be taken in the name of the Director of Public Prosecutions.

In paragraph 2 of the General Direction No. 3, it continued a longstanding requirement that certain categories of serious offences should not be prosecuted without the express directions of the DPP's office. The decision as to whether a prosecution should or should not be taken by the DPP were then enumerated at 2(a) to (s) of the General Direction No. 3 where specific offences were listed. These include a number of serious offences including unlawful killing including any case of murder, manslaughter, fatal road accident or other fatal accident (para 2(a)). Other offences listed include those contained in the Non Fatal Offences Against the Person Act 1997 (2.(b) and 2.(bb)) and serious offences resulting in serious injury being suffered by another road user e.g. the Road Traffic Act 1961 as amended (2.(c)). Other offences listed include an offence of a sexual nature (2.(d)) and assaulting a member of the Garda Síochána (2.(e)), allegations against members of the Garda Síochána, (2.(f)) harassment (2.(g)), endangerment (2.(h)), false imprisonment (2.(i)), terrorist offences (2.(j)), offences tried in the Special Criminal Court (2.(k)), offences involving firearms ammunition (2.(l)) and explosive offences (2.(m)), offences arising during engagement in sport (2.(n)), Official Secrets Act 1963 (2.(o)), bribery and corruption (2.(p)) and offences by elected and public officials (2.(q)). Genocide, war crimes, crimes against humanity, piracy, and hijacking also require a DPP direction as to whether a prosecution should commence (2.(r)), and finally 'those cases where it is provided by statute that proceedings may not be commenced without the consent of the DPP'.

According to s. 3(1) of the General Direction No. 3, the DPP consents to summary disposal without submission of a Garda file with a limited number of offences under the Criminal Justice (Theft and Fraud Offences) Act 2001. The remainder of this 2001 Act that are referable to theft offences require a DPP direction as to whether the case can be disposed of summarily or in the alternative on indictment in the Circuit Court. Section 4(1) of the General Direction No. 3 lists offences where the DPP elects for summary disposal without submission of a Garda file. Section 6 of the General Direction No. 3 encourages the Garda Síochána to seek directions in any case, even of a summary nature, where there is an unusual question of law involved or where the charge is without fairly recent Irish precedent.

6.3 Other Prosecutors

The Attorney General (AG) retains the power to prosecute certain offences, most notably in extradition matters. The consent of the AG is also required in relation to the commencement of proceedings relating to the Official Secrets Act 1963 and the Genocide Act 1973.

Other state and non-state entities conferred with a power to prosecute summary matters in the District Court include:

- An Post for TV licence fee evasion.

- Dublin Bus, the Luas and Iarnród Éireann for fare evasion.

- County and City Councils for offences under the Litter Pollution Act 1997 and breaches of the Planning Acts.

- The Competition Authority for offences contrary to the provisions of the Competition (Amendment) Act 1996.

- The Financial Regulator for breach of a regulatory requirement by a regulated entity, e.g. the Central Bank regarding Part III C of the Central Bank Act 1942.

- The Office of Tobacco Control for breaches of the Public Health (Tobacco) Act 2002.

The Minister for Social, Community and Family Affairs for offences under the Social Welfare Consolidation Act, 1993.

6.4 The Garda Síochána Ombudsman Commission

The Garda Síochána Ombudsman Commission (GSOC) is an independent statutory body established by s. 64 of the Garda Síochána Act 2005. GSOC is required and empowered to directly and independently investigate complaints against members of the Gardaí. The power to investigate members of the Gardaí can take place even when no complaint has been made, where it appears that a Garda may have committed an offence or behaved in a way that would justify disciplinary proceedings. If the complaint is determined admissible under s. 87 of the Garda Síochána Act 2005, a 'Designated Officer' of the GSOC is appointed pursuant to Part 4 of the Garda Síochána Act 2005. Following an investigation pursuant to s. 98 of the Garda Síochána Act 2005, a file may be submitted to the DPP, with a view to considering criminal proceedings. If the DPP, after considering the file presented by GSOC, considers criminal proceedings are appropriate then the DPP will prosecute that case summarily or on indictment, as the case circumstances dictate. Garda Síochána Ombudsman Commission prosecutions commence via Petty Sessions (Ireland) Act 1851 summonses. Section 104 of the Garda Síochána Act 2005 provides:

> Notwithstanding section 10(4) of the Petty Sessions (Ireland) Act, 1851, summary proceedings in respect of a matter relating to an offence reported to the Director of Public Prosecutions under this act may be instituted within twelve months of the offence.

In the High Court case of *Andrew Keegan and Garda Síochána Ombudsman Commission* 2012 IEHC 356 the functions of GSOC were described by Hedigan J. as follows:

> The functions of the respondent are inter alia to receive complaints from members of the public concerning the conduct the conduct of members of An Garda Síochána, to carry out the duties and exercise the powers assigned to it under part of the 2005 act and to report the results of its investigations under part 4 to the Garda Commissioner and, in appropriate cases, to the Director of Public Prosecutions and, if it reports to the Director, to send him or her a copy of each investigation file. The Respondent also has the power under s. 102 of the 2005 Act (as amended) to investigate any matter that appears to it to indicate that a garda may have committed an offence or behaved in a manner that would justify disciplinary proceedings, where it appears to the respondent desirable in the public interest to do so.

Section 102 of the Garda Síochána Act was amended by the Garda Síochána (Amendment) Act 2015 and following commencement of the Protected Disclosures Act 2014 the Garda Commissioner can also be investigated by GSOC with the consent of the Minister for Justice.

6.5   Prosecution by Common Informer or Private Prosecution

It was held in the Supreme Court in *Cumann Luthchleas Gael Teo v Judge Windle* [1994] 1 IR 525, that the right of private prosecution, both in respect of a summary offence and of an indictable offence up to the stage of an order sending the defendant forward for trial, was an important common law right that had survived the enactment of the Irish Constitution. Section 4A(2) of the Criminal Procedure Act 1967 (as amended), provides that a person shall not be sent forward for trial without the consent of the prosecutor, defined as the DPP, thus prohibiting private prosecutions progressing beyond the District Court. Private prosecutions should be initiated using the complaint system of the Petty Sessions (Ireland) Act 1851.

6.6   Health and Safety Prosecutions

The Safety, Health and Welfare at Work Act 2005 is the primary legislation for all Health and Safety Authority related prosecutions. It was commenced by Statutory Instrument (SI) No. 328 of 2005—Safety, Health and Welfare at Work Act 2005 (Commencement) Order 2005 on 1 September 2005 and replaced the Safety, Health and Welfare Act of 1989.

The Health and Safety Authority (HSA) has the right to prosecute summarily in its own name, as provided for under s. 82 of the 2005 Act and indictable matters in this area are prosecuted by the DPP. The HSA is the investigating agency and they send all files for prosecution to the DPP. They submit a comprehensive report with all files with a recommendation as to how the case should be prosecuted. Often in cases in which the HSA recommend a summary prosecution they will, however, request that the file is submitted to the DPP for a direction in circumstances where the facts outline a serious injury or a fatality. The HSA may also request a DPP direction because of the nature of the breach of health and safety legislation (e.g. asbestos sheeting left in a schoolyard) or if it is predictable that a District Judge will 'refuse jurisdiction'.

Ordinarily when summary prosecution only is recommended by the HSA, the file is sent directly to the local state solicitor who acts on behalf of the DPP. If the summary case is a based in Dublin, the HSA will brief counsel to draft summonses and prosecute the case.

6.7   Charge-Sheet Procedure and Station Bail

There are two methods of bringing a person before a District Court to answer a charge that are discussed at various points in the criminal justice process throughout this text. The first is by way of summons served on a defendant by the Gardaí, which could best be described as an invitation to attend court. It is a method devised to compel the attendance of an accused person before the District Court on a certain date to answer the complaint alleged. If the person attends court on the specified date and answers when the summons is called, it is then generally acknowledged that the summons has served its purpose and the defendant has been properly summonsed.

The second method of securing the attendance of a person before a court is by way of arrest and charge. The purpose of an arrest is to apprehend a person lawfully so that the arrested person can be brought before a court to answer the charge alleged. Once a person has been arrested, there will generally be a period of detention, at a Garda station if the offence so warrants, or the detainee will be charged 'as soon as reasonably practicable' with the offence for which the arrest was implemented.

Where a person is charged with a criminal offence at a Garda station, the District Court (Charge Sheet) Rules, 1971, provide that that person must be given a document setting out the charge and setting out the facts that are alleged. This document, which is referred to as a 'charge sheet', should also refer to the statute that it is alleged the person has contravened. The prosecuting Garda member will note on the charge sheet the remarks, if any, made by the now accused person (the accused) upon the charge being read out.

Once charged, the accused may be released on 'station bail' if the member in charge believes it prudent and providing that there are no outstanding warrants for that accused's arrest (see detailed discussion on Bail at **Chapter 7**). Section 31 of the Criminal Procedure Act 1967, as amended by s. 3 of the Criminal Justice (Miscellaneous Provisions) Act 1997, provides that the accused may be released on bail subject to entering a recognisance that the accused will attend at the District Court at the next sitting or within 30 days of the next sitting. If the accused fails to attend as outlined, the District Judge has the discretion to issue a 'bench warrant' for the arrest of the accused. Failure to answer bail is also a criminal offence under the provisions of s. 13 of the Criminal Justice Act 1984, punishable by a maximum of 12 months' imprisonment.

Certain offences are not eligible for station bail. Section 29 of the Criminal Procedure Act 1967, provides that the High Court is the only venue in which a bail application can be entertained in respect of specified serious offences such as murder, piracy, treason, genocide, and breaches of the Geneva Convention. In addition, bail applications for certain offences contrary to the Offences Against the State Act may only be made to the Special Criminal Court.

Where a person is refused station bail, the only other option is to make an application to the District Court Judge.

Once the accused is before the court, a prosecutor present on behalf of the DPP will give evidence to the District Court Judge of the arrest, charge, and caution of the accused, indicating the reply, if any, made by the accused person to the charge after caution. The charge sheet will then be lodged with the Court Registrar.

There have been major changes in bail law that impact the application of the law on bail and which are discussed in **Chapter 7**. Sections 20 and 21 of the Criminal Justice Act 2007 (CJA 2007), assert that recognisances do not now need to include monetary conditions. Section 29 of the Criminal Procedure Act 1967, has been amended by s. 78 of Criminal Justice Act 2006, to take into account new organised crime offences as defined by Part 7 of the CJA 2007.

6.8 Summons Procedure

A summons is a document served on an accused person directing the attendance of that person before a District Court to answer a complaint. The accused is not required to enter a bail bond, but, similar to the charge sheet procedure, a District Court Judge may use discretion to issue a warrant for the arrest of the accused if there is a failure to turn up in court as undertaken.

The Courts (No. 3) Act 1986 provides that District Court proceedings in respect of criminal offences may be commenced by the issuing of a summons by the relevant District Court Clerk following an application by the prosecutor in question. This procedure is referred to as 'making of a complaint'. The Civil Liability and Courts Act 2004, s. 49(9)(a) contains a rebuttable presumption that a document purporting to be a summons has been duly applied for and issued.

6.8.1 REQUIREMENTS FOR A VALID SUMMONS

A valid summons must state in ordinary language the particulars of the offence alleged, and the name and address of the accused person. It must also clearly state the time, date, and location of the proposed sitting of the District Court where the accused is requested to attend. The identity of the District Court clerk must also feature on the face of the summons.

In certain other cases, a District Court Judge has competence to hear a complaint and to issue summonses. In a case in which the defendant is a member of the Garda Síochána or a member of the judiciary, a complaint should be made by way of sworn information to a judge of the District Court who, upon being satisfied that a genuine complaint exists, may then sign and issue a summons. These summonses issue pursuant to the Petty Sessions Act 1851, s. 10, and this provision should be disclosed on the face of the summons. The procedure governing the issue of summonses by a District Court Judge is set out in the District Court Rules, 1997.

6.8.2   THE SERVICE OF A SUMMONS

Once a summons has issued, it must be served on the accused by a member of the Gardaí (other than the member who made the complaint) or by a summons server assigned to a particular court area. The service of summonses for summary offences is governed by the Courts Act 1991, s. 22, which provides that a summons may be served by either registered or recorded delivery post, or by hand. Service may be proven by way of statutory declaration. Service must be executed at least seven clear days in advance of the court hearing date, as prescribed by Order 10 Rule 20 of the District Court Rules, 1997. Once the summons has been served, the server must endorse the declaration of service on the reverse of the original summons and enter the summons with the District Court Clerk at least four clear days before the appointed date for hearing as prescribed by Order 10 Rule 21 of the District Court Rules, 1997.

6.8.3   THE RENEWAL OF A SUMMONS

The Supreme Court considered the validity of a renewed summons in *DPP v Gill* [1980] IR 263. It was held that a second or re-issued summons is valid in respect of the same offence, provided that the original complaint to the District Court Judge or the application to the District Court office for the issue of the summons was made within the applicable time limit. On occasion, a summons may lapse through not having been dealt with on the specified court date. Rule 64 of the District Court Rules 1948, provides that a fresh summons may be issued in respect of the same charge, provided that the complaint has been made within the six-month limitation period. This means that if the summons is struck out on the original date without prejudice, providing that the District Judge has heard no evidence, the prosecutor may simply reapply to the District Court Clerk for a new summons based on the original complaint. It is essential that the new summons makes reference to the same complaint as the first summons.

The above-mentioned procedure would also be relevant where a summons was applied for, but through inadvertence was never served. In the case of *DPP v McKillen* [1991] 2 IR 506, the High Court (Lavan J.) held that proceedings instituted pursuant to s. 10 of the Petty Sessions Act 1851 permitted the reissue of a summons. The first summons had not been served and it was held that the reissued summons remained grounded upon the making of the original complaint. In *Patrick Mullins v Director of Public Prosecutions* (High Court, Herbert J., unreported, 23 February 2004), it was held that the second issue of the summons could not have prejudiced the applicant in any way and it could not give rise to any form of estoppel to operate as a bar to subsequent proceedings.

6.8.4   DEFECTIVE SUMMONS AND AMENDMENT OF SUMMONS

A fundamental defect on the face of a summons, such as the omission of the location of the District Court or the identity of the District Court Clerk to whom the complaint was made, will be fatal to the success of the proceedings. A District Court Judge, who is given wide powers of amendment by Order 38 of the District Court Rules 1997, may remedy superficial defects in a summons. In *State Duggan v Evans* [1978] HC 112 ILTR 61, it was held by the High Court that the amendment of a summons is a matter for judicial discretion and, in exercising this discretion, a judge must take into account any prejudice that would accrue to the accused person arising from the implementation of the amendment sought. However, if the judge is of the opinion that the variance, defect or omission has not misled or prejudiced the defendant, the judge must amend the document or proceed as though no such defect, omission or variance, had existed.

6.9   Time Limits in Criminal Proceedings

Section 177 of the Criminal Justice Act 2006, substitutes s. 7 of the Criminal Justice Act 1951 and restricts s. 10(4) of the Petty Sessions (Ireland) Act 1851. The six-month time limit from the date of the alleged offence for the institution of summary proceedings, e.g. drink driving charges. This time limit does not apply to the following:

- scheduled offences that are listed in the Criminal Justice Act 1951 and SI No. 142 of 1972 and SI No. 282 of 1972 and the offences created by the Offences against the State (Amendment) Act 1998;

- indictable matters triable summarily at the election of the DPP;

- indictable matters prosecuted summarily with the consent of the DPP;

- hybrid offences, where the DPP can elect for trial on indictment or summary disposal, e.g. s. 3 of The Non Fatal Offences Against the Person Act 1997;

- where the DPP has consented to summary disposal to a potentially indictable matter, e.g. s. 4 of the Criminal Justice (Theft and Fraud Offences) Act 2001.

Time limits for the institution of summary proceedings end on the making of a valid complaint as opposed to the date of the charge. This complaint must be made either to the District Court Clerk or the District Court Judge, e.g. an application for the issue of a summons or an arrest warrant or the charging of a suspect by charge sheet at the moment of the tendering of 'evidence of arrest charge and caution' before the court.

The onus is on the defence solicitor to check the summons, arrest warrant or take instructions regarding the date of arrest charge and caution regarding a charge sheet. The time limits for the institution of proceedings vary depending on the statute instituting the proceedings and must be checked by the practitioner. Such statutes and time limits include the following:

- the National Monuments (Amendment) Act 1954 which has a time limit of three months from the date at which the offence came to the attention of the Commissioners for Public Works, as provided for in s. 19 of the Act;

- the Consumer Information Act 1978 with a time limit of 12 months;

- the Child Care Act 1991 with a time limit of 12 months;

- the Housing (Miscellaneous Provisions) Act 1992 with a time limit of two years;

- Excise offences with a time limit of one year, as provided for in the Finance Act 1985, s. 39;

- revenue offences with a time limit of 10 years, as provided for in the Finance Act 1983, s. 94(7);

- the Wireless Telegraphy Acts with a time limit of 12 months;

- the Garda Síochána Act 2005 with a time limit of 12 months for summary proceedings, s. 104.

6.9.1   MATTERS THAT BECOME STATUTE-BARRED

Non-compliance with statutory time limits in criminal proceedings is an absolute defence. In this context, 'month' means a calendar month (Interpretation Act 1937, s. 13) and, when computing days, the day of the alleged offence is taken to be included in the period within which the complaint ought to be made. The crucial date at which time can be said to stop running, is the date of the making of the complaint either to the District Court Clerk or the District Court Judge, and not the date of issue of the summons.

A court has no power whatever to abridge or extend a limitation period fixed by statute and, accordingly, the judicial discretion granted by Order 12 Rule 2 of the District Court Rules 1997, cannot be used to remedy such a crucial defect.

6.9.2   TIME LIMITS IN INDICTABLE OFFENCES AND DELAY

Section 177 of the Criminal Justice Act 2006, has restricted the application of s. 10(4) of the Petty Sessions (Ireland) Act 1851, stating that the six-month time limit does not apply to a scheduled offence, or an offence that is 'triable' at the election of the prosecution either on indictment or summarily, or an offence that is triable either on indictment or, subject to certain conditions including the consent of the prosecution, summarily.

In the Court of Appeal cases of *DPP v Tiarnan O'Mahoney and Bernard Daly* CA [2016] 226/15 230/15 it was decided indictable offences contrary to the Taxes Consolidation Act 1997 have a

10-year statutory time limit of initiation. In Mr Daly's case the clock was stopped by an application for an arrest warrant. However, there are generally no time limits in respect of the initiation of indictable offences. However excessive delay in initiating summary or indictable proceedings may prejudice the accused in the conduct of the defence. In the case of both summary and indictable proceedings, an order of prohibition may be sought by way of judicial review proceedings in the High Court to stop the proceedings (see **Chapter 16** for a detailed discussion of judicial review proceedings).

The courts have examined the issue of delay in several cases and a substantial body of jurisprudence on the subject has developed in recent times. In *DPP v Gill* [1980] 1 IR 263, Henchy J, in the Supreme Court held that where delay resulted in a defendant being unfairly prejudiced in making his defence, natural justice may require that the summons is dismissed. In the Supreme Court decision of *State (O'Connell) v Fawsitt and DPP* [1986] IR 362, Finlay C.J. held that where a person's trial on indictment had been delayed excessively so as to prejudice the chances of a fair trial, then the appropriate remedy by which constitutional rights could be protected and defended, is by order of prohibition to stop the trial. An equal and alternative remedy would be available in summary cases by way of application to the District Court Judge to dismiss the summons on the grounds of delay.

In the case of *Brendan McFarlane v The DPP and The Members of the Special Criminal Court* [2008] IESC 7, Kearns J. stated that the following principles appear to have been established in Irish law:

(a)   Inordinate, blameworthy or unexplained prosecutorial delay may breach an applicant's constitutional right to an expeditious trial.

(b)   Prosecutorial delay of this nature may be such that a court will presume prejudice and uphold the right to an expeditious trial by directing prohibition.

(c)   Where there is a period of significant (as distinct from minor) blameworthy prosecutorial delay less than that envisaged at (b), the court will engage in a balancing exercise between the community's right to see crimes prosecuted and the applicant's right to an expeditious trial.

(d)   Actual prejudice caused by delay, which is such as to prejudice a fair trial will always entitle an applicant to prohibition.

Kearns J. referred to the seminal US Supreme Court decision in *Barker v Wingo* 407 US 514 (1972) in which four factors were identified to determine whether a particular defendant had been deprived of his right to a speedy trial:

(i)   the length of the delay;

(ii)   the reasons for the delay;

(iii)   the role of the applicant; and

(iv)   prejudice—the right to a speedy trial was designed to protect three interests:

    (a)   the prevention of oppressive pre-trial incarceration;

    (b)   the reduction of anxiety and concern to the accused; and

    (c)   most importantly, the limitation of the possibility that the defence will be impaired.

Kearns J reiterated that prohibition must be granted only in exceptional circumstances.

In the case of *Stephen Cormack and Keith Farrell v The DPP* [2008] SC IESC 63, it was held by the Supreme Court the period of delay in the first case arising from an adjournment was not blameworthy. The applicant had failed to point to any circumstances of prejudice by reason of delay. The outcome of any balancing test was in favour of allowing the prosecution to proceed. In the second case, there was an element of unjustifiable prosecutorial delay but the applicant was in large measure responsible for the delay. The applicant needed to demonstrate more than the ordinary level of stress that could be expected.

Kearns J. refused an application for prohibition where there had been a 17-month period in which a bench warrant remained unexecuted. Although the court found that there had been culpable prosecutorial delay, there was no evidence that the defendant had suffered actual or presumptive prejudice to his ability to defend himself. Justice Kearns also noted he could see no basis for applying a separate legal regime to summary prosecutions than that which arises in the case of indictable offences. However, delay will more rapidly become blameworthy and delays of lesser magnitude will be seen as more likely to be intolerable, where summary proceedings are concerned.

In the case of *McFarlane v Ireland* (2011) 52 EHRR 20, the European Court of Human Rights, sitting as a Grand Chamber held by a majority of twelve judges to five that the remedies proposed by the state would not have provided an effective remedy and the duration of the criminal proceedings were excessive, violating Article 6, section 1 of the Convention for the Protection of Human Rights and Fundamental Freedoms, which guarantees a fair trial within a reasonable time. Mr McFarlane was awarded compensation of €15,500.

In *PB and the Director of Public Prosecutions* [2013] IEHC 401, the applicant's application for injunctive relief to prohibit 67 counts of indecent assault on the grounds of delay was refused by Judge O'Malley in the High Court. Judge O'Malley held:

> The law relating to this type of case is well settled since the decision of the Supreme Court in the case of *S.H. v Director of Public Prosecutions* [2006] 2 I.R. 575. There is no requirement for the court to inquire into the reasons for the delay or to make any assumption of the truth of the complaints. The issue is whether prejudice has arisen as a result of the delay and, if so, whether it is such as to give rise to a real or serious risk of an unfair trial. Each case falls to be considered on its own facts and in the light of the undoubted power and obligations of the trial judge to ensure a fair trial by means of appropriate rulings and directions. This includes the jurisdiction to withdraw the case from the jury where the trial considers that this is the only way to prevent injustice to the accused. There are a number of written judgments dealing with cases bringing up similar issues since S.H. and the parties in this application have both referred to them at length without any disagreement as to the applicable principles. I do not consider it necessary to discuss them further and will rely instead upon the summary set out by Charleton J. in the case of *K v His Honour Judge Carroll Moran* (unreported, 5th February, 2010) in the following nine propositions:

(1) The High Court should be slow to interfere with a decision by the Director of Public Prosecutions that a prosecution should be brought. The proper forum for the adjudication of guilt in serious criminal cases is, under the Constitution, a trial by judge and jury; *D.C. v DPP* [2005] 4 I.R. 281 at p. 284.

(2) It is to be presumed that an accused person facing a criminal trial will receive a trial in due course of law, one that is fair and abides by constitutional procedures. The trial judge is the primary party to uphold the relevant rights which are: the entitlement of the accused to a fair trial; the right of the community to have serious crime prosecuted; and the right of the victims of crime to have recourse to the forum of criminal trial where there is reasonable evidence and the trial can be fairly conducted ; *P.C. v DPP* [1999] 2 I.R. 25 at p. 77 and *The People (DPP) v J.T.* (1988) 3 Frewen 141.

(3) The onus of proof is therefore on the accused, when taking judicial review as an applicant is to stop a criminal trial. That onus is discharged only where it is proved that there is a real risk of an unfair trial occurring. In this context an unfair trial means one where any potential unfairness cannot be avoided by appropriate rulings and directions on the part of the trial judge. The unfairness of the trial must therefore be unavoidable: *Z. v DPP* [1994] 2 I.R. 476 at p. 506–507.

(4) In adjudicating on whether a real risk occurs that is unavoidable that an unfair trial will take place, the High Court on judicial review should bear in mind that a District Judge will warn himself or herself and that a trial judge will warn a jury that because of the elapse of time between the alleged occurrence of the facts giving rise to the charges, and the trial, that the accused will be handicapped by reason of the lack of precision in the presentation of the case, and the disappearance of evidence such as diaries, or potentially helpful witnesses, or by the normal failure of memory. This form of warning is now standard in all old sexual violence cases and a model form of the warning, not necessarily to be repeated in that form by all trial judges, as articulated by Haugh J. is to be found in the decision of the Court of Criminal Appeal in *The People (DPP) v E.C.* [2006] IECCA 69.

(5) The burden of a proof on an applicant in these cases is not discharged by merely making a general allegation of prejudice by reason of the years that have elapsed between the alleged events and the commencement of the criminal process. Rather, there is a burden on such an applicant to fully and actively engage with the facts of the particular case in order to demonstrate in a specific way how the risk of an unfair trial arises: *C.K. v DPP* [2007] IESC 5 and *McFarlane v DPP* [2007] 1 I.R. 134 at p.144.

(6)   Whereas previously the Supreme Court had focused upon an issue as to whether the victim could not reasonably have been expected to make a complaint of sexual violence against the accused, because of the dominion which he had exercised over her, the test now is whether the delay has resulted in prejudice to an accused so as to give rise to a real risk of an unfair trial: *H. v DPP* (2006) 3 I.R. 575 at p. 622.

(7)   Additionally, there can be circumstances, which are wholly exceptional where it would be unfair or unjust to put an accused on trial. Relevant factors include a lengthy elapse of time, old age, the sudden emergence of extreme stress in consequence of the charges, and which are beyond that associated with the normal stress that a person will feel when facing a criminal charge and, lastly, severe ill health: *P.T. v DPP* [2007] IESC 39.

(8)   Previous cases, insofar as they are referred on the basis facts that are advocated to be similar, are of limited value. The test as to whether a real risk of an unfair trial has been made out by an applicant, or that an applicant has established the wholly exceptional circumstances that had rendered unfair or unjust to put him on trial, are to be adjudicated in the light of all of the circumstances of the case: *H. v DPP* [2006] 3 I.R. 575 at p. 621.

(9)   ... it can be the case sometimes that circumstances such as extreme age or very poor health will be contributory factors to an applicant succeeding in making out that a real risk of an unavoidably fair trial is established. Old age and ill health can assist in establishing that there is prejudice by reason of a delay, since memory fails with time and the ability of an accused to instruct counsel with a view to mounting a defence can be, in extreme circumstances, undermined by those factors. Where extreme delay, old age, and serious ill health are, of themselves, pleaded as a circumstance which would make it unfair or unjust to put a specific accused on trial then, in the absence of proven prejudice, those circumstances will indeed occur rarely: *The People (DPP) v P.T.* [2007] IESC 39 and *Sparrow v Minister for Agriculture, Food and Fisheries* [2010] IESC 6.

Applying those principles to the instant case it seems to me that the applicant has not discharged the burden of showing a real or serious risk of an unfair trial.

JST and President of the Circuit Court and the Director of Public Prosecutions Supreme Court Appeal No. 66/2014 in a judgment of the Court delivered on 10 March 2015 by Denham C.J. refusing to prohibit the trial. This was on the basis of delay in the case of the appellant in the Circuit Court on 251 counts of indecent assault on a number of pupils in a school between 1979 and 1981. The appellant had brought judicial review proceedings to seek to prohibit his trial on the basis of the delay in the case, the fact that he had previously faced trial on similar charges on six occasions, his bad health and also publicity in the case. It was held by the Supreme Court in dismissing the appeal and upholding the decision of the High Court that the medical evidence before the court in relation to the appellant's health, in addition to the other factors raised by him, were insufficient to warrant prohibiting the trial. On a separate note the court dealt specifically with the issue of information in the public domain which had been pleaded by the appellant. The court held that it was not a ground on which to prohibit the trial in this case. However, the court went on to note with concern the fact that there may have been a leak of information from An Garda Síochána. In addressing this issue specifically the court stated that:

> It must be clearly understood that information about a criminal investigation in the possession of a member of An Garda Síochána, is not his personal property to be shared, or otherwise disposed of, at his or her personal discretion. It is Official information, in the possession of An Garda Síochána as a State Institution. If the Gardaí as an institution decide to publicise such information to the media, on the authority of a senior officer, that is quite a different matter. But unauthorised leaks by individual members do no credit to the force and may, in an appropriate case, lead to the prohibition of a trial.

6.9.3   TIME LIMITS IN JUVENILE CASES

In the Supreme Court judgment of *Patrick Donoghue v the Director of Public Prosecutions* [2014] IESC 56, Justice Dunne held, having regard to all the circumstances of the case and bearing in mind the fact Mr Donoghue was a child at the commission of the alleged offences contrary to the Misuse of Drugs Acts 1977 and 1984, there was 'significant, culpable prosecutorial delay'. In conclusion the Supreme Court held:

The Special duty of State authorities owed to a child or young person over and above the normal duty of expedition to ensure a speedy trial is an important factor which must be considered in deciding whether there has been blameworthy prosecutorial delay. That special duty does not of itself and without more result in the prohibition of a trial. As in any case of blameworthy prosecutorial delay, something more has to be put in the balance to outweigh the public interest in the prosecution of offences. What that may be will depend upon the facts and circumstances of any given case. In any given case, the age of the young person before the courts will be of relevance. Someone close to the age of eighteen at the time of the alleged offence is not likely to be tried as a child no matter how expeditious the State authorities may be in dealing with the matter. On the facts of this case, had the prosecution of Mr. Donoghue been conducted in a timely manner, he could and should have been prosecuted at a time when the provisions of the Children Act 2001 would have applied to him. The learned trial judge was correct in reaching his conclusion that an injunction should be granted preventing the Director of Public Prosecutions from further prosecuting the case against Mr. Donoghue.

In the Court of Appeal case of *Patrick Smith v DPP* [2015] Appeal No. 2015/37, it was held by Kelly J., in an *ex-tempore* judgment, that there was culpable delay and a substandard performance of the prosecution authorities in relation to the prosecution of an alleged robbery with firearms.

The trial judge was correct in the manner in which he applied *Donoghue*. There is no fault in the manner in which he conducted the balancing exercise. There is prejudice but this is outweighed by the right of the People of Ireland to prosecute matters of this seriousness with a potential penalty of life imprisonment.

CHAPTER 7

BAIL

7.1   Introduction

Given the inevitable and often lengthy delays between arrest and charge and the ultimate hearing of a case, the decision as to whether an accused is to be remanded in custody or released on bail is of crucial significance to an accused. Detention pending trial may cause great hardship to an accused and his or her family both economically and personally. In addition, detention pending trial may make it more difficult for an accused to prepare his defence, and may hamper his or her ability to consult with their legal advisers. The jurisdiction of the courts to grant bail is governed by the common law, the Constitution, legislative provisions—most notably the Criminal Procedure Act 1967, the Bail Act 1997 and the Criminal Justice Act 2007—and the Irish case law on the subject. As we will see, the decision on whether or not to grant an accused bail involves a careful balancing act between on the one hand an accused's constitutional right to liberty, and on the other hand the need to preserve the integrity of the trial process and the public interest in preventing crime.

7.2   The *O'Callaghan* Decision

Perhaps the most seminal exposition of the principles governing bail in Irish law can be found in the Supreme Court's judgment in *The People (Attorney General) v O'Callaghan* [1966] IR 501. In this case the defendant had been returned for trial on various criminal charges and the Attorney General opposed the granting of bail on the ground that the applicant might interfere with the witnesses for the prosecution if released. It was also contended that the Court should take into account the fact that the offences in respect of which bail was being sought were alleged to have been committed while he was already on bail in respect of other charges.

In the High Court Murnaghan J., refusing bail, stated that the fundamental consideration of the Court in deciding whether to grant bail was the likelihood of the applicant attempting to evade justice. He then enumerated the following 11 factors which should be taken into account when assessing this likelihood:

1. The nature of the accusation or in other words the seriousness of the charge. It stands to reason that the more serious the charge the greater the likelihood is that the prisoner would not appear to answer it.

2. The nature of the evidence in support of the charge. The more cogent the evidence is, the greater the likelihood of conviction and consequently the greater the likelihood of the prisoner attempting to evade justice.

3. The likely sentence to be imposed on conviction. The greater the sentence is likely to be, the greater the likelihood of the prisoner trying to avoid it. The prisoner's previous record has a bearing on the probable sentence and consequently must be before this Court.

4. The likelihood of the commission of further offences while on bail. In this connection, a prisoner facing a heavy sentence has little to lose if he commits further offences. A prisoner may consider that he has to go to prison in any event and in an effort to get money to support his family may commit further offences.

5. The possibility of the disposal of illegally acquired property. Stolen property may be stored or cached away.

6. The possibility of interference with prospective witnesses and jurors.

7. The prisoner's failure to answer to bail on a previous occasion.

8. The fact that the prisoner was caught red-handed.

9. The objection of the Attorney General or of the police authorities.

10. The substance and reliability of the bailsmen offered. (This is primarily a matter for the District Justice.)

11. The possibility of a speedy trial.

To these a twelfth was added, namely the likelihood of personal danger to the applicant.

Murnaghan J. proffered three reasons for refusing to grant bail in this case. Firstly, the Superintendent in charge of the case had given evidence that the applicant was an aggressive type and that he was of the opinion that he would interfere with witnesses if admitted to bail. Secondly, the offences were committed while the applicant was on bail in respect of earlier charges, and there was a serious risk that the applicant would commit further offences if he were granted bail. Thirdly, that due to the applicant's criminal record he would be facing a substantial sentence.

On appeal to the Supreme Court the court emphasised that an applicant for bail is entitled to the presumption of innocence and, as such, is *prima facie* entitled to their liberty.

Both O'Dalaigh C.J. and Walsh J. referred with approval to the earlier Supreme Court judgment of *The People v Crosbie and Others*, and reiterated that the fundamental test in deciding whether to allow bail or not to allow bail is the probability of the applicant evading justice if granted bail. Primarily this will be done by the applicant not surrendering at his or her trial, but included in this fundamental test is the likelihood of an accused interfering with witnesses or jurors, or the likelihood of destruction of evidence by the accused.

The Court approved the relevance and validity of the majority of Murnaghan's criteria. In relation to grounds 1, 2, 3, and 8 Walsh J. agreed that they constituted to some degree an inducement for the accused to flee justice.

On the issue of the relevance of the previous convictions of the accused, although O'Dalaigh J. stated that these should never emerge in court until they became relevant to the matter of sentencing after conviction, Walsh J. (with whom Budd J. agreed) held that it may indeed be proper to introduce such evidence in a bail hearing as the individual's past record has a bearing on the probable sentence he will receive on conviction, and thus may act as an inducement to flee justice and avoid the likelihood of a severe sentence. Walsh J. stressed, however, that it would be most undesirable if an accused's previous convictions were referred to in a way that would prejudice the pending trial. He accordingly held that the tribunal who hears such evidence should not be the tribunal of trial and, if the question of bail arises in the course of the trial itself, such evidence should not be adduced. He further opined that such evidence should only be adduced in respect of such previous convictions as would probably cause the trial judge to add substantially to the sentence he might otherwise impose in the event of conviction, in other words there must be some similarity between the class of previous convictions and the current charge. Walsh J. also specified that any such previous convictions would have to be properly proved, and open to the same examination and comment on the part of the accused as it would have been if produced after conviction. Finally Walsh J. held that, if the previous criminal record of an accused is put in evidence, it would only be just that it would also be put in the balance that on previous occasions an accused appeared for his trial.

Belatedly Walsh J. further agreed that number 7 may be indicative of a propensity on the part of the accused to evade justice. Grounds 5 and 6 again were characterised by Walsh J. as falling under the rubric of evasion of justice. With regard to number 9 of Murnaghan's criteria Walsh J., referring to the earlier decision of Hanna J. in *The State v Purcell* [1926] IR 207, held that, while any such objections are relevant to a court's decision on whether to grant bail or not, the fact of such objections is not in itself a ground for refusing bail and indeed to refuse bail on those grounds alone would be to violate the constitutional guarantees of personal liberty. Walsh J. stated that any such objections must be supported by evidence:

Where, however, there are objections they must be related to the grounds upon which bail may validly be refused. Furthermore they cannot be simply made *in vacuo* but when made must be supported by sufficient evidence to enable the Court to arrive at a conclusion of probability and the objections made must be open to questioning on the part of the accused or his counsel. It is not sufficient for the objecting authority or witness to have a belief nor can the Court act simply upon the belief of someone else. It must itself be satisfied that the objection made is sufficient to enable the Court to arrive at the necessary conclusion of probability.

Indeed the decision of Murnaghan J. to refuse bail to the applicant was reversed by the Supreme Court on the basis, *inter alia*, that there was not sufficient evidence before the Court for it to come to the conclusion that the applicant would endeavour to interfere with witnesses as a matter of probability, despite the testimony of a Superintendent as to his objection on this basis.

In relation to ground 10, Walsh highlighted that there was no requirement in law that a bails person be a homeowner, however, this would be a relevant consideration in assessing their financial ability to meet the demands of the bail. He also referred to the common law principle that the amount of bail must not be so high as to be effectively unattainable for the particular defendant.

In relation to ground 11, Walsh J. accepted that if there was no prospect of a speedy trial a court may legitimately grant bail in a case where it might not otherwise have allowed it; however, he held that the prospect of a speedy trial can never be a ground for refusing bail where it should otherwise be granted.

Walsh J. rejected the notion of protection of the accused, on the basis that, if an accused wanted protection he need not ask for bail or accept it, and that a bail motion 'cannot be used as a vehicle to import into the law the concept of protective custody for an unwilling participant'. He further held that an accused person on bail is entitled to as much protection from the law as may be required.

The Supreme Court, however, emphatically dismissed ground number 4, with O'Dalaigh C.J. opining that such reasoning was 'a denial of the whole basis of our system of law' and 'transcends respect for the requirement that a man shall be considered innocent until he is found guilty and seeks to punish him in respect of offences neither completed nor attempted'. In his judgment Walsh J. held that such a consideration represented 'a form of preventative justice which has no place in our legal system and is quite alien to the true purposes of bail'. Indeed Walsh J. considered that to apply such a criterion would raise an issue of constitutionality:

> In this country it would be quite contrary to the concept of personal liberty enshrined in the Constitution that any person should be punished in respect of any matter upon which he has not been convicted or that in any circumstances he should be deprived of his liberty upon only the belief that he will commit offences if left at liberty, save in the most extraordinary circumstances carefully spelled out by the Oireachtas and then only to secure the preservation of public peace and order or the public safety and the preservation of the State in a time of national emergency or in some situation akin to that.

The issue of the likelihood of further offences as a ground for refusing bail was revisited by the Irish courts in the case of *Ryan v DPP* [1989] IR 399, where the Director of Public Prosecutions (DPP) brought an appeal to the Irish Supreme Court in an attempt to effectively have the *O'Callaghan* decision overturned. The Supreme Court again resoundingly dismissed the possibility of refusing bail on the ground that the accused may commit further offences if released, with Finlay C.J. holding that 'an intention to commit a crime, even of the most serious type, is not in our criminal law a crime itself' and noting that 'the criminalising of mere intention has been usually a badge of an oppressive or unjust legal system'.

Further attempts to overrule *O'Callaghan* were similarly rebuffed in *The People (DPP) v Doherty* (Unreported, 26 February 1993) and *DPP v Brophy* (unreported, 2 April 1993). Since these rulings, however, the Constitution has been amended following the bail referendum in November 1996 and a new subsection 7 was inserted into Art. 40.4 of the Constitution to read:

> Provision may be made by law for the refusal of bail to a person charged with a serious offence where it is reasonably considered necessary to prevent the commission of a serious offence by that person.

Thus the landscape for bail applicants under Irish law was radically altered.

7.3 Section 2 of the Bail Act 1997 – Refusal of Bail

The Bail Act 1997 was introduced on foot of the constitutional amendment and came into operation fully on 15 May 2000. Section 2(1) of the Bail Act 1997 provides as follows:

2(1) Where an application for bail is made by a person charged with a serious offence, a court may refuse the application if the court is satisfied that such refusal is reasonably considered necessary to prevent the commission of a serious offence by that person.

In accordance with s. 2(1), before there can be discretion to refuse bail under this section, three basic criteria must be met:

- the applicant must be charged with a serious offence;
- the court must be satisfied that the refusal of bail is 'reasonably considered necessary';
- the apprehended offence must be serious.

7.3.1 A SERIOUS OFFENCE

The applicant must be charged with a serious offence.

A serious offence is defined in s. 1 of the Act as an offence specified in the Schedule to the Act which, if committed by a person of full age and capacity and not previously convicted, may be punished by a term of five years' imprisonment or by a more severe penalty. The schedule (as amended) includes offences such as murder, manslaughter, sexual offences, offences under the Non-Fatal Offences Against the Person Act 1997, offences under the Criminal Justice (Theft & Fraud Offences) Act 2001, drug trafficking, firearms offences, and organised crime offences.

7.3.2 A REFUSAL THAT IS REASONABLY CONSIDERED NECESSARY

The court must be satisfied that the refusal of bail is 'reasonably considered necessary' to prevent the commission of an offence, in other words detention must be necessary and the process by which it is determined that it is necessary must be reasonable.

7.3.3 APPREHENDED OFFENCE THAT IS SERIOUS

A court using discretion under s. 2(1) of the Bail Act must also be satisfied that the apprehended offence is serious; however, as per s. 2(3), it shall not be necessary for a court to be satisfied that the commission of a specific offence is apprehended.

7.3.4 COURT CONSIDERATIONS IN EXERCISING DISCRETION

When exercising its discretion under s. 2, the court is obliged to take the following considerations into account, and may if necessary receive evidence or submissions regarding them:

- (a) the nature and degree of seriousness of the offence with which the accused person is charged and the sentence likely to be imposed on conviction;
- (b) the nature and degree of seriousness of the offence apprehended and the sentence likely to be imposed on conviction;
- (c) the nature and strength of the evidence in support of the charge;
- (d) any conviction of the accused person for an offence committed while he or she was on bail;
- (e) any previous convictions of the accused person including any conviction the subject of an appeal (which has neither been determined nor withdrawn) to a court;
- (f) any other offence in respect of which the accused person is charged and is awaiting trial.

Where a court has taken account of one or more of these factors, it may also take into account the fact that an accused is addicted to a controlled drug, however, the fact of addiction alone is not sufficient to justify the refusal of bail. Unhelpfully, the Act does not specify how the fact of addiction is to be determined, or where the standard of proof or burden of proof lies in this regard.

While the court must take account of the factors listed in s. 2, the Supreme Court in *Maguire v DPP* [2004] 3 IR 241 emphatically stated that s. 2 did not create a discrete or isolated jurisdiction which confined the court to a consideration of these factors alone. In this case the Supreme Court held that those factors, such as the length of pre-trial incarceration and the projected date of trial, that had long been established as relevant to any consideration of bail, remained highly relevant and could naturally still be taken into consideration by the court in deciding on whether to grant bail or not.

In *McDonagh v Governor of Cloverhill Prison* [2005] 1 IR 394, the Supreme Court, in a judgment by McGuinness J., held that, as a matter of natural and constitutional justice, applicants should be made aware in advance of any matter listed in s. 2 which will be raised by the prosecution by way of objection. Furthermore, and also as a matter of natural and constitutional justice, it was stated that the accused should be given a proper opportunity either by means of evidence or submissions to challenge such an objection.

The *McDonagh* case is also authority for the principle, as noted in the earlier *O'Callaghan* decision, that any ground on which a judge purports to refuse bail must be supported by relevant evidence. It should also be noted that the earlier *O'Callaghan dicta*, that any objection to the grant of bail must relate specifically to grounds on which bail may lawfully be denied, is also equally applicable to objections under s. 2.

7.4   Section 3 of the Bail Act 1997—Renewed Application

Section 3 of the 1997 Act provides that, if a bail application is refused under s. 2 and the trial does not begin within four months of the date of refusal, the application may be renewed on the ground of delay by the prosecutor in proceeding with the trial and the court must, if satisfied that the interests of justice so require, release the person on bail. In *Maguire v DPP* [2004] 3 IR 241, it was argued that the right to re-apply for bail under s. 3 was only triggered when there was delay on the part of the prosecutor, as opposed to other sources of delay such as court congestion.

Hardiman J. in the Supreme Court preferred an interpretation of s. 3 which gave primacy to the interests of justice, rather than one which permitted that essential matter to be considered only if there was delay on the part of the prosecutor, and held that the interests of justice required a consideration of the actual time to be spent in custody no matter who was culpable or indeed whether or not anyone was culpable.

7.5   Section 4 of the Bail Act 1997—Criminal Record

Section 4 of the 1997 Act provides that an applicant's previous criminal record shall not be referred to in a manner that may prejudice his right to a fair trial. Section 2 applications can be heard otherwise than in public, or following the exclusion from the court of all persons except officers of the court, persons directly concerned, bona fide representatives of the press and such other persons as the court may permit to remain. Under s. 4(3) no information relating to the criminal record of an applicant shall be published, and the publication of information in contravention of this section constitutes an offence triable summarily or in indictment, and carrying a maximum sentence of three years or a fine of €10,000 or both.

7.6   The Criminal Justice Act 2007 and the Bail Act 1997

There have been some major changes to the Irish law on bail affected by Part 2 of the Criminal Justice Act 2007, particularly in how it amends the 1997 Act.

Section 6 of the Criminal Justice Act 2007 inserts s. 1A into the Bail Act 1997, which introduces a requirement for a signed written statement to be included in a bail application in the case of a person charged with a serious offence, as defined by the Schedule to the Bail Act 1997 (as amended). The statement must contain the following information relating to the applicant:

(a) his or her name and any other name or names previously used;

(b) his or her current occupation and any previous occupation or occupations within the immediately preceding three years;

(c) his or her source or sources of income within the immediately preceding three years;

(d) his or her property, whether wholly or partially owned by, or under the control of, the applicant and whether within or outside the state;

(e) any previous application or applications by the person for bail, indicating whether or not it was granted and, if granted, the conditions to which the recognisance was subject;

(f) any previous conviction or convictions of the applicant for a serious offence;

(g) any previous conviction or convictions of the applicant for an offence or offences committed while on bail.

Section 1A(3) provides that the statement is to be furnished as soon as is reasonably practicable before the application is made, and where written notice of the application for bail is required, e.g. in the High Court, on service of that notice. Under s. 1A(4) the requirement to furnish such a statement may be dispensed with where the prosecutor states an intention to consent to the grant of bail, or the applicant and the prosecutor consent to the dispensing of the requirement. The court may also dispense with the need for such a statement if satisfied that there is a good and sufficient reason for doing so pursuant to s. 1A(5)(c), and failure to furnish a statement does not preclude a court from considering an application for bail under 1A(13). Section 1A(12) provides the safeguard that any information contained in the statement is not admissible in any other proceedings, except for the offence of providing false or misleading information in the statement itself, which is an offence punishable with a maximum sentence of 12 months or a fine of €5,000 or both under s. 1A(11).

This latter provision in the 2007 Act proved to be a controversial one, with commentators such as the Irish Human Rights Commission arguing that the requirement to submit such a statement imposes an unfairly onerous burden on the applicant who is presumed innocent before the law. It has also been asserted that the difficulty in ascertaining such detailed information must be heightened by the fact that an accused is in custody. It should be noted that it is no longer common practice for the State to require such statements, however, its provisions remain on the statute books and the prosecution could theoretically insist on compliance with this section and require a statement to be filed.

Section 7 of the 2007 Act inserts Section 2A into the Bail Act 1997 and this provides that:

(1) Where a member of the Garda Síochána not below the rank of chief superintendent, in giving evidence in proceedings under section 2, states that he or she believes that refusal of the application is reasonably necessary to prevent the commission of a serious offence by that person, the statement is admissible as evidence that refusal of the application is reasonably necessary for that purpose.

Such evidence is not admissible in any other criminal proceedings under s. 2A(2). Furthermore, the court may direct that no information relating to the Garda officer's evidence or some part of it or any examination of the member be published, if it considers that such publication may prejudice the accused person's right to a fair trial (s. 2A(3)). Under s. 2A(4) the court may specify the duration of the publication ban, and it may at any time vary or set aside the order as it sees fit and subject to such conditions as it wishes to impose. Section 2A(6) dictates that the provision does not prejudice the admission of other belief or opinion evidence which may be tendered by any member of An Garda Síochána or other person in proceedings under s. 2 of the Act. This section, it is arguable, represents a further diminution of the rights of the accused and an erosion of the presumption of innocence, as the Garda Chief Superintendent will almost inevitably be relying on privileged or confidential information which by its nature cannot be tested by the rigours of cross-examination, thus placing the accused at a distinct disadvantage.

In the case of *DPP v Keith Wilson* (Judgment of the Supreme Court, 25 February 2011) the appellant was charged with murder. Bail was refused in the High Court on grounds arising out of s. 2A of the Bail Act 1997 as amended by s. 7 of the Criminal Justice Act 2007. Belief evidence was given by the Chief Superintendent that the appellant would commit further serious offences up to and including murder and that he was a 'hitman'. The appellant gave evidence in the High Court denying this. The appellant appealed this refusal to the Supreme Court on the basis that where such belief evidence is contradicted then the Court should afford greater weight to the appellant's evidence.

The Supreme Court, in dismissing the appeal, held that in this case the learned trial judge had evidence which he was 'entitled to have regard to' from the DPP. He also had evidence from the appellant. It was stated that the weight to be attached to the evidence on both sides is essentially and exclusively a matter for the judge who will make his decision based on that evidence in its entirety. It was held that an appellate court should be very slow to interfere with the manner in which a judge arrives at his decision where there is evidence before him which he has to evaluate in order to arrive at a decision.

In all the circumstances the Supreme Court was satisfied that there was evidence before the learned trial judge upon which he could reach the decision which he in fact reached and the weight to be attributed to such evidence was a matter for the learned trial judge.

7.7   Jurisdiction to Grant Bail

7.7.1   AN GARDA SÍOCHÁNA—STATION BAIL

Section 31 of the Criminal Procedure Act 1967 (as amended by s. 3 of the Criminal Justice (Miscellaneous Provisions) Act 1997 and s. 20 of the Criminal Justice Act 2007) provides that whenever a person is brought in custody to a Garda station by a member of An Garda Síochána, the sergeant or other Member in Charge may, if s/he considers it prudent to do so, and no warrant directing the detention of that person is in force, release that person on bail, known as 'station bail'. The member granting bail may for that purpose take from the arrested person a recognisance with or without sureties for the person's due appearance before the District Court at the appropriate time and place. A recognisance is essentially the bail contract. In return for his release the accused must sign the contract and agree to be bound by its condition, namely to surrender to the court at the appointed time and place. The recognisance in this context may include a requirement to pay a fixed sum, which will be forfeited if the accused fails to appear before the court when requested to do so ('own bond' bail). There may also be the requirement of a surety. A surety is a person who undertakes to pay a specified sum of money to the court in the event of an accused failing to surrender to the appropriate court at the appointed time and place 'independent bail'. There may be a requirement for either the bailee or surety to lodge all or a proportion of the money 'up front', but it is common practice for station bail to be simply 'own bond' bail with no lodgement of monies.

The appearance before the District Court may be before the next sittings, or at any sitting of the court in that area during a period of 30 days immediately following the next sitting. If the recognisance is conditioned for the payment of a sum of money, that sum may be accepted in lieu of a surety or sureties, and any recognisance taken or sum of money accepted under this section shall be deposited by the member of an Garda Síochána with the District Court Clerk.

Section 31 should be read in the light of s. 29 of the 1967 Act that provides that a person charged with one of a specified list of offences cannot be admitted to bail except by order of the High Court. Further, it does not apply to persons arrested, under s. 251 of the Defence Act 1954, on suspicion of being a deserter or an absentee without leave from the defence forces. Where a person fails to comply with the terms of his station bail, his recognisance may be estreated or forfeited, in the same way as a recognisance entered into before the District Court would be estreated or forfeited. Where a person is released on station bail the normal practice is for him to get a copy of the charge sheet or charge sheets, along with a copy of the recognisance he has signed with the next court date written on it. The originals are sent to the relevant District Court Clerk and copies are retained in the Garda station.

7.7.2   THE DISTRICT COURT

Bail applications are most common in the District Court because, unless directed to the Special Criminal Court, all cases begin there. The District Court's jurisdiction to grant bail is governed by s. 28 of the Criminal Procedure Act 1967 which provides:

> (1)   A [judge] of the District Court shall admit to bail a person charged before him with an offence, other than an offence to which section 29 applies, if it appears to him to be a case in which bail ought to be allowed ...

> (4)   When a [judge] grants bail to an accused person who is in custody that person shall, on completion of the recognisance be released if he is in custody for no other cause than the offence in respect of which bail was granted.

The offences in respect of which the District Court has no jurisdiction under s. 29 of the 1967 Act include murder, attempt to murder, conspiracy to murder, piracy, treason, an offence under s. 66 of the Offences Against the State Act, genocide and, as inserted under s. 78 of the Criminal Justice Act 2006, certain organised crime offences. Furthermore, where a District Judge returns an accused to the Special Criminal Court for trial, he may not be admitted to bail by the District Judge without the consent of the DPP.

7.7.2.1   Conditions of bail

The principal and fundamental bail condition has always been that the accused will appear before the court when required to do so. Section 6 of the Bail Act 1997 (as amended by s. 9 of the Criminal Justice Act 2007) prescribes another mandatory condition that the accused shall not commit an offence while on bail, and suggests a number of other possible conditions as set out below:

> (i)   that the accused person resides or remains in a particular district or place in the State,

> (ii)   that the accused person reports to a specified Garda Síochána Station at specified intervals,

> (iii)   that the accused person surrenders any passport or travel document in his or her possession or, if he or she is not in possession of a passport or travel document, that he or she refrains from applying for a passport or travel document,

> (iv)   that the accused person refrains from attending at such premises or other place as the court may specify,

> (v)   that the accused person refrains from having any contact with such person or persons as the court may specify.

It is clear that this is not an exhaustive list and the court may generally impose such other conditions, as it considers appropriate, given the particular circumstances of the case. However, any conditions imposed must not be unduly onerous or restrictive of the right to liberty, having regard to all the circumstances of the case, and should be supported by evidence adduced before the court. This was made clear in the High Court decision of Quirke J. in *Ronan v District Judge John Coughlan* [2005] 4 IR 274, where the applicant was arrested and charged with an offence contrary to the Criminal Justice (Public Order) Act 1994, and was brought before the first respondent in the District Court. Without hearing any evidence in relation to the applicant, the first respondent granted the applicant bail subject to two conditions, namely that he observe a curfew in his own home between 3 p.m. and 7 a.m. every day, and that he remain at all times in the Ballyfermot area. The District Court order was quashed by the High Court.

As in station bail as discussed above the conditions imposed in any particular case are set out in a recognisance. Section 6(2) provides that a copy of the recognisance containing the conditions of the recognisance be given to the accused and surety or sureties if any. Section 6(3) allows for an application to be made by an accused to vary the condition of bail referred to under s. 6(1)(b) whether by alteration, addition or revocation of a condition. A prosecutor is entitled under s. 6(4) to be given notice of any such application and is entitled to be heard in any such proceedings. It is often the case that a particularly onerous condition of signing on at a local station, once or even twice daily, may be relaxed as proceedings progress and an accused is regularly answering his bail by appearing in court at each and every remand. Indeed, if some special reason can be advanced as to why the reporting condition is particularly onerous on an accused, such as work commitments, the condition may often be revoked altogether.

7.7.2.2   Negotiating bail in the District Court

Typically, when an accused is first brought before the District Court, after the Garda's evidence of arrest, charge and caution in respect of an accused, the District Judge will ask whether there are objections to bail.

Ideally, the issue of bail should be canvassed with the relevant member of An Garda Síochána before the matter is called, to enable a defence solicitor to discover what, if any, the objections to bail are, and whether they are valid objections relating directly to grounds on which bail may legitimately be denied. It is also important to ascertain whether there are any terms on which bail may be agreed and, in particular, if there are any conditions of bail that will allay the member's fears that an accused will not surrender to bail if granted. If it is determined that specific conditions are being sought, the solicitor should consult with the client to see if same are agreeable to him. If a solicitor has not been given notice of objections to bail, a second calling of the case should be requested to facilitate such discussions.

The mere fact that there are no objections to bail will not ensure that an accused will be granted bail but it will certainly make this outcome more likely. A District Judge will almost inevitably seek to ascertain how many times an accused has failed to answer his bail in the past, in other words he will inquire as to the accused's past history of 'bench warrants'. This past history is often at the heart of the objections of the relevant Garda, and will often be central to the decision on whether or not bail will be granted. It is thus of vital importance to find out an accused's history of bench warrants in advance of the bail application, and the dates on which each bench warrant was 'taken'. It is essential to ascertain from the accused the circumstances in which he failed to appear in the past, whether he had any legitimate reasons for not attending, or whether his personal circumstances have changed so as to make him more likely to answer bail at the present time.

A Garda may give evidence of not being satisfied as to the identity or address of the accused and may seek time to verify information in relation to the accused. If agreeing to a remand in custody on this basis, it must always be remembered that the liberty of the accused is at stake and that the relevant inquiries should be made as a matter of priority, so that such a remand should be for as short as possible. Of course it should also be remembered that homelessness in and of itself is not a ground for refusing bail, nor is the fact that an accused is a non-national or ordinarily resident outside the jurisdiction.

If objections are to be made under s. 2 of the Bail Act 1997, the Supreme Court decision of *McDonagh v The Governor of Cloverhill Prison*, as mentioned earlier at **7.3.4**, should be noted. In the wake of that decision it is common practice for a solicitor to be furnished with written objections under s. 2.

If there are objections to bail, the relevant member of An Garda Síochána will be subject to cross-examination by the defence solicitor, followed by a defence submission emphasising the factors in favour of granting bail. The judge will then give his or her decision. The applicant may appeal to the High Court if dissatisfied with a refusal of grant for the application for bail, as per s. 28(3) of the 1967 Act.

7.7.2.3   The amount of bail

As stated earlier, recognisance is fixed with a specific debt due in the event of failure to comply with bail. Recognisance may be fixed in an applicant's 'own bond' with or without a requirement to lodge money, or the court may require one or more sureties (independent bail) with or without money lodgement. The court may also make provision for the lodgement of cash in lieu of sureties. If independent bail is fixed it is often worth asking the court if it would make provision for a cash lodgement in lieu of the surety, as it will generally be easier for an accused to lodge cash with the court than to find a suitable bails person and have them approved by the court.

Section 18 of the Criminal Justice Act 2007 amends s. 22 of the 1967 Act to provide that the court may admit a person to bail without imposing a condition in the recognisance as to payment of moneys into court by the person, if it considers it appropriate to do so having regard to the circumstances of the case, including the means of the person and the nature of the offence in relation to which the person is in custody.

Section 5(1) of the 1997 Act as amended by s. 33 of the Courts and Court Officers Act 2002 provides as follows:

(1)   Where a court admits a person who is in custody to bail [, the court may, having regard to the circumstances of the case, including the means of the person and the nature of the offence in relation to which the person is in custody, order that] the person shall not be released until—

(a)   an amount equal to one third, or

(b)   such greater amount as the court may determine,

of [any moneys to be paid into court under a recognisance] entered into by a person in connection therewith has been paid into court by the person.

It should be noted that as amended the requirement to pay in an amount equal to a third is no longer a mandatory condition. As a result, it is not at all uncommon for a court to fix bail in someone's own bond with no requirement for any cash lodgement.

As we have seen, the amount at which bail should be set was considered in the case of *The People (AG) v O'Callaghan* where Walsh J. held that: 'bail must not be fixed at a figure so large as would in effect amount to a denial of bail and in consequence lead to inevitable imprisonment'.

This ruling was upheld in the Supreme Court case of *Broderick v DPP* [2006] 1 IR 629. In this case the applicant was charged with possession, for the purpose of sale and supply, of a large quantity of drugs with an estimated value of €1.3 million and was granted bail in the District Court in terms that included, *inter alia*, that he enter his own bond in the amount of €50,000 and that he provide an independent surety in the amount of €50,000. The applicant applied to the High Court for a reduction of bail. That application was opposed on the grounds of the value of the drugs seized and of the risk of the applicant not attending his trial because of the seriousness of the charge. There was no objection to the proposed independent surety; however the surety was only prepared to put up €5,000 by way of cash lodgement. In his application to the High Court, the applicant stated that his means were limited and that he had no prospect of meeting the sum fixed for his own bail. Evidence was given of the respondent's belief that the applicant was a member of a criminal gang that would have access to cash in the amount of the bail sought and that he drove an expensive car. The applicant's assertions as to his means or those of his surety were not rebutted.

The High Court (per Butler J.) held that the value of the drugs seized suggested that the applicant would have no real difficulty in putting up the bail fixed by the District Court. The principle that bail should not be fixed at a level the applicant could not meet was accepted but it was held that the gravity of the offence justified the terms as they had been fixed.

In a judgment by Kearns J., the Supreme Court held that the High Court's ruling was in contradiction of the principle of the presumption of innocence, which must, it held, be borne in mind at all times by a judge dealing with a bail application. Kearns J. further held that there was an insufficient inquiry as to the means of the applicant but did find that:

It is not sufficient in my view for an applicant simply to rely on assertions of lack of means or to place the entire burden of the prosecution to negative assertions made in the context of the hearing of a bail application. To adopt the latter course would be to impose an impossible burden on the Gardaí, except in cases where the means of the applicant are already known to them.

The Court said that, if necessary, there could be a short adjournment to enable the Gardaí to verify the assertions of the accused. It should also be noted that the court held, *obiter dicta*, that where an applicant wished to challenge only the quantum of bail and, on that challenge the state intended to oppose the granting of bail per se, the state should give notice of that intention to the applicant in advance, so that he can consider if he wishes to retain the terms already set rather than risk losing bail altogether.

7.7.2.4   Address approved

In the case of *DPP v Kastriot Boza* (Judgment of the Supreme Court, 15 April 2011), the appellant was charged with an offence contrary to s. 7(2) and (4) of the Criminal Law Act 1997 that he did knowing or believing another to be guilty of the offence of murder, did without reasonable excuse and with intent impede his or her apprehension or prosecution. Despite objections bail was fixed in the High Court with conditions that the appellant provide an independent surety of €12,500 and that he also reside at an address to be agreed by the prosecuting Sergeant.

The only issue in this case was the address provided. As it was a provision in the High Court Order that an address was to be approved by the Gardaí, the appellant would remain in custody until such address was approved. The appellant through his solicitor provided an address with a friend in the Sandymount Area. Sergeant O'Donovan called to this address and he was told by the occupant that the appellant was welcome to sleep on the couch for a few weeks until he found somewhere else. This address was not approved by the Sergeant. Subsequently the occupant of the address in Sandymount was approved as a surety for the appellant and his solicitors made an application to the High Court for the address to be approved by the Court. Evidence was given by the Sergeant and the surety in the High Court. Mr Justice DeValera held that he preferred the evidence of the Sergeant and as the address was only temporary he was not approving same.

On appeal to the Supreme Court the appellant was successful. The Court held that it was not unreasonable that a foreign national would have difficulty in securing an address and that the appellant had no property of his own. He was welcome at the address and the occupant of that address was a surety in the case. In those circumstances the Supreme Court approved the address and released the appellant on bail.

7.7.2.5   Sureties

If a court fixes bail to include an independent surety, then for the accused to secure release on bail, he will have to arrange for the surety to be approved by the court. Section 7 of the Bail Act 1997 states that in every case the court must examine the circumstances of the proposed surety to determine his or her suitability:

(1)   A court shall in every case satisfy itself as to the sufficiency and suitability of any person proposed to be accepted as a surety for the purpose of bail.

(2)   In determining the sufficiency and suitability of a person proposed to be accepted as a surety, a court shall have regard to and may, where necessary, receive evidence or submissions concerning:

    (a)   the financial resources of the person,

    (b)   the character and antecedents of the person,

    (c)   any previous convictions of the person, and

    (d)   the relationship of the person to the accused.

The Act does not tie the court's hands in any way and only asks that the court have regard to the above factors. Indeed, Professor Dermot Walsh in his work *Criminal Procedure* (Thompson Round Hall, 2002) argues that it would be objectionable if a court was to declare a proposed surety unsuitable solely because he had previous convictions, or because of some aspect of his character or antecedents unrelated to his capacity to discharge his obligations as surety.

The usual practice is for the surety to be approved in the District Court. The defence solicitor will call the proposed surety to give evidence of the matters listed in s. 7(2) and to confirm that they are aware of the nature of an independent surety. It is always a good idea to have at least one suitable potential surety in court in cases where it can be expected that independent bail may be required, so that that person can be approved there and then. A potential bails person must bring proof of identity to court, along with up-to-date proof of their financial resources. It should be explained to the potential surety that the particular sum of money specified in the recognisance will be frozen in their particular financial account and that if the accused breaches any of his conditions of bail the surety is liable to lose or forfeit the amount of money specified. It is advisable to present the proposed surety, along with the necessary documentation, to the Garda member dealing with the application in advance of any bail application, so that they may make their own inquiries into the person's suitability.

If it is not possible to have a surety approved at the time bail is fixed, an application may be made in the absence of the accused at a later date. It is common practice for the duty Court Sergeant to deal with and facilitate such applications and to make the requisite inquiries as to the person's suitability.

If there is an objection on the part of the prosecution to the proposed surety, the court will consider submissions and, if necessary, receive evidence from both the prosecution and the defence before ruling on the matter. In the 2013 Judicial Review case of *Jingguo Li v Governor of Wheatfield Prison* [2011] IEHC 353, the applicant was charged with an offence of working without a work permit. He pleaded guilty to the charge and was sentenced by Judge Coughlan, who set an independent surety, as part of fixing recognisances. The first surety proposed was a friend and former employer of the applicant, who was rejected by the Judge, because he was deemed to have known that the applicant was working illegally and therefore 'illegal'. A second surety was also refused approval, on the same grounds. In his useful ruling President Kearns comments that 'the fact that a proposed surety knows the accused is a factor that tends in favour, not against approving the surety'.

Recognisances are normally taken from the accused and his surety or sureties by the District Judge, but if money is not available to be paid into court it may be lodged at whichever prison the accused is in custody, as prison governors also have the power to acknowledge the terms of a recognisance. A surety should be present on any occasion when an accused seeks to vary bail conditions and where an accused is sent forward for trial, because a fresh recognisance is fixed and application must again be made to the court for the approval of surety.

7.7.2.6 The renewal of bail applications

Section 28(2) of the Criminal Procedure Act 1967 (as amended) provides as follows: 'Refusal of bail at a particular appearance before the District Court shall not prevent a renewal of the application for bail at a subsequent appearance or while the accused is in custody awaiting trial'. Therefore, in theory at least, an accused may apply for bail to be granted on each appearance before the court. Also, as we have seen earlier, as per s. 6(3) of the 1997 Act, an application to vary a condition of bail can be made at any time. In reality, however, in order for an applicant to defeat a plea of *res judicata* he must show that there has been sufficient change of circumstances which warrants the court re-opening the question of bail. In his article in the *Bar Review*, 'Hearsay Evidence in Bail Cases' (1998) 4(3) *Bar Review* 129–32, Michael P. O'Higgins offers a sample of the changes in circumstances which have been presented on occasion with greater or lesser degrees of success:

- The fact that an applicant will not get a trial for an appreciable length of time.

- The fact that there has been a delay in serving the Book of Evidence.

- The fact that an anticipated trial date has been lost.

- The fact that new and relevant evidence has emerged.

- The fact that an applicant has been unable, despite efforts, to raise or find independent sureties to meet bail conditions previously set.

- The fact that an appreciable length of time has elapsed since the previous bail application.

- The fact that a previously relied upon ground of opposition to bail may have been removed or rendered less significant. For example, where in a previous application bail was refused on the basis of a fear of intimidation of a state witness who lived near the applicant and that witness has since moved to a new address or out of the country.

- The fact of the deterioration of the health of an applicant in custody or the deterioration of the health of a family member who has no one else to look after him or her.

There is also the possibility that, after the accused has been remanded in custody, there is the opportunity to take full instructions from him in custody, so that the solicitor can convey certain relevant information to the court that could not be conveyed on the first occasion that bolsters the accused candidacy for bail.

The provisions of s. 3 of the Bail Act 1997 have previously been discussed. It has been noted that this procedure applies only where a person has originally been refused bail in order to prevent the commission of a serious offence. The provision would presumably not preclude a renewed application for bail on some other ground when bail has been refused under s. 2 of the 1997 Act.

When an accused is returned for trial he is entitled to make a fresh bail application even if he had bail set or even refused in the High Court. There must generally be a change in circumstances if the District Court is to overrule the High Court on this issue.

7.7.3 COURT OF TRIAL

A court of trial has jurisdiction to grant bail to persons being tried before it after the accused has been arraigned or during the course of the trial. In this context end of trial means commencement of sentence. The Special Criminal Court has jurisdiction to admit an accused to bail where that person has been charged before it, or sent for trial before it by a District Judge, or transferred to it for trial from an ordinary court, pending trial or during trial or prior to sentencing.

7.7.4   THE HIGH COURT

The High Court has inherent jurisdiction to grant bail for any offence, even if the District Court or any other court has already dealt with the question of bail. As a result, if a person is refused bail, or if bail is fixed but cannot be taken up, in another court, they will commonly appeal that refusal or seek a variation in the High Court. The Criminal Procedure Act 1967 provides for appeals against bail decisions under s. 28(3) as substituted by s. 19 of the Criminal Justice Act 2007:

(a) *An applicant for bail or the prosecutor may appeal to the High Court if dissatisfied with a refusal or grant of the application for bail or, where bail is granted, with any matter relating to the bail.*

(b) *Where the applicant has been remanded in custody by the District Court and the offence with which the applicant is charged is triable by the Circuit Court, the High Court may transfer the appeal to the judge of the Circuit Court for the circuit in which the prison or place of detention to which the applicant has been remanded is situated.*

(c) *The judge of the Circuit Court referred to in paragraph (b) shall exercise jurisdiction in respect of the appeal.*

(d) *An appeal against a decision by the Circuit Court under this section lies to the High Court at the instance of the applicant or prosecutor.*

Accordingly, an appeal now lies to the High Court at the behest of both the prosecutor and the accused. The appeal operates as a *de novo* hearing of the matter rather than a review of the original court's exercise of discretion. The possibility of the decision on appeals being delegated to the Circuit Court (with the possibility of further appeal to the High Court), has been welcomed by some practitioners, mindful of the enormous numbers of applicants in the weekly High Court bail list.

As already noted, the High Court has exclusive jurisdiction over the grant of bail to persons charged with certain serious offences listed in s. 29 of the Criminal Procedure Act 1967 (as amended).

Appeals against refusals of bail, as well as applications for the reduction of bail or variation of conditions, must be made to the High Court by way of 'notice of motion to the prosecution solicitor' grounded on the affidavit of the applicant (Order 84 Rule 15(1), Rules of the Superior Court). The High Court bail list is usually taken on Mondays at Cloverhill Court House in Dublin. The notice of motion and affidavit should be filed with the Court and served in the Prosecution Solicitors Office by the preceding Wednesday, although orders allowing short services can be obtained from the court in special circumstances, such as an accused being before the District Court for the first time on a Thursday and being remanded in custody. It should be noted, however, that unless the matter is dealt with by consent, due to the considerable length of the court list each Monday, it is usual for short service applications to be adjourned to the following week. Orders for the production of prisoners at Cloverhill Courthouse for the following Monday should generally be sought before a High Court Judge on the preceding Thursday.

The affidavit grounding the notice of motion, with the title of the affidavit stating in which court the proceedings are then pending applying Order 84 Rule 15(1), Rules of the Superior Court, was amended by SI No. 811 of 2004 and came into operation on 29 December 2004.

It was common practice for the solicitor for the applicant to swear the affidavit grounding the notice of motion. However, on 28 January 2016 the President of the High Court issued a practice direction which provided for (a) an application for bail to the High Court, (b) an appeal from an order made on such an application, and (c) an application for bail directly to the Court of Appeal in criminal proceedings and military proceedings to be conducted by video link.

This practice direction reminded practitioners of procedures for bail hearings under SI No. 470 of 2015 (Rules of the Superior Courts (Bail Hearings) 2015) and also made a number of changes regarding changes to bail hearing dates. Under this SI, the affidavit grounding an application must be sworn by the applicant and must follow the particular format set out in the statutory instrument. The Rules of the Superior Courts are amended by the substitution for Rule 15 of Order 84 of the following rule:

15(1) An application for bail by a person in custody or an appeal by an accused person under section 28(3) of the Criminal Procedure Act 1967 shall be by motion on notice to the Chief State Solicitor grounded on the affidavit of the applicant or (as the case may be) the appellant, in this rule hereinafter referred to as the 'applicant'.

(2) Proceedings shall be entitled:

THE HIGH COURT

BAIL

THE PEOPLE (AT THE SUIT OF THE DIRECTOR OF PUBLIC PROSECUTIONS)

.V.

AT PRESENT PENDING IN THE ... COURT

AT ...

or to the appropriate effect.

(3) The affidavit of the applicant shall set forth fully the basis upon which the application is made to the High Court and in particular:

(a) shall give particulars of whether and, if so, in what other Court bail has been refused to the applicant;

(b) shall specify where the applicant is being detained;

(c) shall specify the usual place of abode or address where the applicant normally resides;

(d) shall specify the address at which it is proposed the applicant would reside, if granted bail;

(e) shall provide full particulars of the offence or offences with which the applicant is charged;

(f) shall include the identity, address and occupation of any proposed independent surety and of the amount that such surety may offer;

(g) the terms of bail which were previously fixed in relation to the offences (if any);

(h) whether there had been any previous High Court applications for bail in respect of the offences;

(i) whether any warrants for failure to appear have been issued in relation to the applicant;

(j) what surety and/or other conditions relating to bail (if any) the applicant is proposing;

(k) the personal circumstances of the applicant and in particular whether the applicant was legally aided in relation to the charges in any other Court;

(l) any other relevant circumstances.

(4) Where such an application is made to the Court sitting as the Central Criminal Court or on an appeal under section 28(3) of the Criminal Procedure Act 1967 and the applicant, being legally represented or having obtained legal advice or been given the opportunity of obtaining or being provided with such advice, is agreeable to the application being heard by live television link, averments to the following effect should be incorporated in the affidavit:

'I understand that the Court may give a direction that I may participate in the hearing of my application for bail from [insert name of prison] by means of a live television link, in which event I shall be deemed to be present at the hearing.

I further understand that the Court may not give such a direction unless—

(a) to do so would not be prejudicial to me,

(b) the interests of justice do not require my presence at the hearing,

(c) the facilities provided by a live television link between the court and the prison concerned are such as to enable—

> (i)   me to participate in and to view and hear the court proceedings,
>
> (ii)   those present in the court to see and hear me, and
>
> (iii)   myself and my legal representative to communicate in confidence during the hearing,
>
> (d)   to do so is otherwise appropriate having regard to—
>
> (i)   the nature of the application,
>
> (ii)   the complexity of the hearing,
>
> (iii)   my age, and
>
> (iv)   my mental and physical capacity, and
>
> (e)   no other circumstances exist that warrant my presence in court.
>
> Having had the opportunity to take legal advice, I confirm that I consent to the Court directing that I participate in the hearing of my application and any appeal in the manner aforementioned.'

(5)   Where such an application is made to the Court otherwise than in accordance with sub-rule (4), and the applicant being legally represented or having obtained legal advice or been given the opportunity of obtaining or being provided with such advice, is agreeable to the application being heard by live television link, averments to the following effect should be incorporated in the affidavit:

> 'I understand that the Court may give a direction that I may participate in the hearing of my application for bail from [insert name of prison] by means of a live television link, in which event I shall be deemed to be present at the hearing.
>
> I further understand that the Court:
>
> (a)   shall not give such a direction unless facilities are available which enable me to see and hear the proceedings at the hearing and to be seen and heard by those present in the courtroom in which the hearing is taking place, and
>
> (b)   shall in any event not give such a direction if:
>
> (i)   it would be unfair to me to do so, or
>
> (ii)   it would be otherwise contrary to the interests of justice to do so.
>
> Having had the opportunity to take legal advice, I confirm that I consent to the Court directing that I participate in the hearing of my application and any appeal in the manner aforementioned.'

(6)   Where an applicant has no solicitor, the Court may dispense with the necessity for a notice of motion and affidavit, and in lieu thereof shall give all appropriate directions including a direction that the applicant be brought before the Court, in person or by means of a live television link, on a date and at a time to be specified, of which the Chief State Solicitor shall be notified. The Court may on that date or at any time to which the hearing is adjourned hear the applicant and the Chief State Solicitor for the purpose of giving such directions.

(7)   Where an applicant for bail who has participated in the hearing before the High Court by means of a live television link appeals to the Court of Appeal against a refusal of an application for bail, the Court of Appeal may, on the production to it of an affidavit containing the averments mentioned in sub-rule (4) or (5) when the appeal is listed before the Court of Appeal, and confirmation by or on behalf of the appellant that the appellant has not withdrawn his or her consent to participating in the hearing by live television link, give a direction under section 33 (2) of the Prisons Act 2007 or, as the case may be, section 26 (1) of the Civil Law (Miscellaneous Provisions) Act 2008 , and dispense with the necessity for a notice of motion and further affidavit.

(8)   The Court of Appeal may in any case hear the appellant (including by live television link) and the Chief State Solicitor for the purpose of considering the giving of such a direction.

(9)   References in this rule to the Director of Public Prosecutions shall, where appropriate, be deemed to include references to the Attorney General.

(ii) by the insertion in rule 13 of Order 86C, immediately following sub-rule (19), of the following sub-rule:

'(20) The provisions of sub-rules (4), (5) and (6) of Order 84, rule 15 shall apply, with the necessary modifications, to applications under this rule to the Court of Appeal for bail.'

and

(iii) by the insertion in rule 17 of Order 86D, immediately following sub-rule (18), of the following sub-rule:

'(19) The provisions of sub-rules (4), (5) and (6) of Order 84, rule 15 shall apply, with the necessary modifications, to applications under this rule to the Court of Appeal for bail.'

From 8 February 2016 onwards, the Central Office of the High Court will not issue a return date for a notice of motion seeking bail, unless the affidavit of the applicant grounding it complies with the rules as set out in SI 470/2015 (Rules of the Superior Courts (Bail Hearings) 2015).

There is a non-statutory scheme in place to cover the legal fees, for the applicant for bail in the High Court who does not have the means to pay for representation. Generally at the conclusion of the application the applicant's counsel will seek recommendation from the High Court Judge for payment under the scheme and this recommendation will generally be made if the applicant is legally aided in the court from which they appealed. The scheme is administered by the Department of Justice and covers the cost of a solicitor and one counsel.

7.7.4.1 Bail in *Habeas Corpus* and judicial review proceedings

An applicant under Art. 40.4 of the Constitution (generally described as a Habeas Corpus application) may apply to the High Court for bail pending the resolution of the application. The principles applied by the High Court, in determining whether to grant bail in such circumstances, depend on whether the detention is preventative (as in extradition, deportation or mental-health related detention), or whether the detention is punitive in character (as in imprisonment following conviction or committal for civil contempt). The standard in the context of pre-extradition remand has been stated by the Supreme Court in *The People (AG) v Gilliland* [1985] IR 643 to be no different from the case in any other criminal case with the person awaiting extradition enjoying a presumptive right to bail. In the case of immigration or mental-health related detention, however, as noted by Kevin Costello in his work *The Law of Habeas Corpus* (Four Courts Press, 2006), the proceedings are non-criminal and there is no presumptive right to liberty. While the High Court has not yet determined the issue of the standard of proof required for the grant of bail pending a *Habeas Corpus* challenge to deportation or removal, the English High Court has consistently held that bail in such circumstances should only be granted where the applicant establishes special grounds as to why intermediate release should be granted, such as it being apparent that an error in principle has occurred, or the fact that the decision has been marred by gross unreasonableness. In the case of prisoners seeking post-conviction Habeas Corpus, the jurisdiction to grant bail is also highly circumscribed. There would seem to be two conditions which would predicate the exercise of such exceptional jurisdiction, namely that the applicant has a strong *prima facie* case and the existence of special circumstances, such as the fact that there would be a considerable delay in dealing with the application due to difficult questions of law, or the fact that the period of imprisonment is about to expire.

An applicant for judicial review may also apply to the High Court for bail pending the resolution of the application. The fact that leave has been granted to apply by way of judicial review is not in itself a ground for granting bail. Bail may be granted either at leave stage or at some point before the full hearing of the case, if the High Court is satisfied that there are good grounds for doing so. In this context, the strength of an applicant's case will be a relevant factor, and in this regard it is likely that the Court will apply similar principles as those laid down by the Court of Criminal Appeal when dealing with the availability of bail pending appeal to the Court of Criminal Appeal in *The People (DPP) v Corbally* [2001] IR 180, discussed further at **7.7.5**.

7.7.4.2 Bail pending District Court appeal to the Circuit Court

The High Court also deals with appeals relating to the variation of recognisances fixed for appeal to the Circuit Court. It should be noted that in *Burke v DPP* [2007] 2 ILRM 371, the High Court, per Charleton J., held, *obiter*, that as the entry of an appeal in the District Court entitles the accused to have the entire case reheard on appeal, that entry required the application of similar criteria for admission to bail as when the accusation was first made, unlike applications for bail following conviction in other courts. In particular, Charleton J. stated, again *obiter*, that: 'If the accused were on bail prior to conviction, this should ordinarily be the foundation on which a recognisance is determined for the purpose of an appeal'.

Section 10 of the Criminal Justice Act 2007 inserts s. 6A into the Bail Act 1997 in respect of persons appealing sentences imposed by the District Court, which stipulates that the recognisance in such case shall be subject to the following conditions, namely, that the appellant shall:

  (i)   prosecute the appeal;

  (ii) attend the sittings of the Circuit Court until the appeal has been determined; and

  (iii) not commit an offence while on bail.

7.7.5   THE COURT OF CRIMINAL APPEAL

Section 32 of the Courts of Justice Act 1924 (as amended) provides as follows:

> Leave to appeal shall be granted by the Court of Criminal Appeal in cases where the court is of the opinion that a question of law is involved, or where the trial appears to the court to have been unsatisfactory, or there appears to the court to be any other sufficient ground of appeal, and the court shall have power to make all consequential orders it may think fit, including an order admitting the appellant to bail pending the determination of his appeal or application for leave to appeal.

In the case of *DPP v Corbally* [2001] 1 IR 180, the Supreme Court was asked to rule upon the appropriate principles upon which the Court of Criminal Appeal should grant bail to a convicted person who has sought leave to appeal, or has been granted leave to appeal. The court, per Geoghegan J., held that bail should be granted where the interests of justice required it, either because of the apparent strength of the applicant's grounds of appeal, or the impending expiry of the sentence or some other special reason. In this regard Geoghegan J. stated:

> I do not think it desirable that the Court of Criminal Appeal should have to go so far as to make a definite determination as to whether 'the appeal is likely to be successful' but I think that there should be enough materials before the Court to enable it to hold that there was at least a strong chance of success before it grants bail.

The court emphasised that the applicant for bail in this situation had lost the presumption of innocence and held accordingly that the Court of Criminal Appeal should exercise its discretion sparingly. The court further held that bail could only be granted where it was not necessary to consider the entire transcript to isolate a ground of appeal of such a nature that there was a strong chance of success on appeal.

7.7.5.1   Bail pending further appeal to the Supreme Court

The question of bail pending appeal from the Court of Criminal Appeal to the Supreme Court was dealt with in *The People (DPP) v Dwyer* [2007] 2 IR 825. In this case the respondent was given two two-year suspended sentences to run concurrently in the Circuit Court. The DPP applied to the Court of Criminal Appeal for an order reviewing the sentences on the grounds that they were unduly lenient. The Court of Criminal Appeal imposed a two-year backdated sentence but did grant a certificate under s. 3 of the Criminal Justice Act 1993 allowing further appeal to the Supreme Court on a point of law. The applicant sought bail pending the outcome of the Supreme Court hearing, which was likely to take in excess of 18 months to be heard, by which time the applicant could ordinarily have expected to be released. The court, per Denham J., held that the principles to be applied when considering such an application were different from the situation where there was an appeal from a trial court to the Court of Criminal Appeal, by reason of the fact that the case has been fully opened up before the Court of Criminal Appeal and the issues had been determined by the court. Denham J. forwarded the following principles to be applied in deciding whether to grant bail in such circumstances:

1.   bail should be granted where, notwithstanding that the applicant came before the court as a convicted person, the interests of justice so required;

2.   as the applicant was a convicted person the court should exercise its discretion sparingly;

3.   the general principles of law as to the granting or withholding of bail apply and should be addressed, by oral evidence if necessary;

4.   the particular circumstances of each case should be considered:-

(a)   a factor may be that the trial court did not impose a custodial sentence, but that the Court of Criminal Appeal had;

(b)   a factor may be that the sentence would be served by the time that the appeal was heard by the Supreme Court. This may be a factor—but on its own it may not be a ground upon which to grant bail;

(c)   the particular circumstances of an applicant should be considered including: (i) family issues, (ii) work issues, (iii) educational issues, (iv) health issues, and (v) his previous conduct while on bail, if any;

(d)   the attitude of the Director of Public Prosecutions, and/or the Gardaí, to the application for bail.

7.7.6   THE SUPREME COURT

Article 34 of the Constitution confers the Supreme Court with appellate jurisdiction from all decisions of the High Court with such exceptions and subject to such regulations as may be prescribed by law. A decision on bail is not excluded by any statute, regulation or judicial decision, and accordingly a decision on bail made in the High Court or the Central Criminal Court can be appealed to the Supreme Court. As in all other matters the appellate jurisdiction of the Supreme Court in bail matters is concerned with points of law only.

7.8   Hearsay Evidence in Bail Applications

The central objections to hearsay evidence and the basis of the exclusionary approach of the law to such evidence are, firstly that such evidence is not given on oath, and secondly and most crucially, it is not capable of being tested through cross-examination. The issue of hearsay in bail applications was authoritatively addressed in the Supreme Court judgment of Keane J. (as he then was) in *DPP v McGinley* [1998] 2 IR 408. In this case the applicant was charged with having had unlawful carnal knowledge of a girl under the age of 15. During the course of the bail hearing in the High Court, a Detective Sergeant gave evidence of a threat to the complainant made by the accused, and threats to the complainant's family made by the family of the accused. Keane J. in his ruling held that there was a *prima facie* right for a bail applicant to have evidence deployed against his application given viva voce, but that a court is entitled to admit hearsay evidence in certain circumstances:

> The constitutional right of the applicant for bail to liberty must, in every case where there is an objection to the granting of bail, be balanced against the public interest in ensuring that the integrity of the trial process is protected. Where there is evidence which indicates as a matter of probability that the applicant, if granted bail, will not stand his trial or will interfere with witnesses, the right to liberty must yield to the public interest in the administration of justice. It is in that context that hearsay evidence may become admissible, where the court hearing the application is satisfied that there are sufficient grounds for not requiring the witness to give *viva voce* evidence.

Keane J. further held that if hearsay evidence is admitted:

> it would be for the court to consider what weight should be given to the evidence, having regard to the fact that the author of the statement had not been produced and to any other relevant circumstances which arose in the particular case.

In the *McGinley* case, as no reason was given as to why the relevant witnesses in the case could not give viva voce evidence, Keane J. held that the High Court Judge had erred in admitting the hearsay evidence. The *McGinley* case was expressly distinguished from the earlier Supreme Court case of *McKeon v DPP* (unreported, Supreme Court, 12 October 1995). In this case the matter came before the Supreme Court by way of an appeal brought by the appellant against an order made by the President of the High Court, Costello P., revoking bail which had previously been granted to the appellant. The application to revoke bail was based on the evidence of a Garda witness as to confidential information indicating that the appellant had obtained a false passport and had financial assistance from an illegal organisation to assist him in leaving the country. The Supreme Court held, per Hardiman J., that in this particular case such hearsay evidence was admissible but it was stressed that it is for the trial judge to decide upon the weight to be attributed to it. In *McGinley*, Keane J. noted that in *McKeon* a specific reason for not producing the author of the statement was given, i.e. the fact that the information had been communicated in confidence to the Gardaí.

The issue of hearsay in bail applications has been revisited by the Supreme Court in two more recent cases, namely *DPP v Vickers* [2009] IESC 58 [2010] 1 IR 58 and *DPP v McLoughlin* [2009] IESC 65 [2010] 1 IR 590. In *DPP v Vickers* the applicant was charged with the murder of his wife. Bail was opposed on a variety of grounds, but the principal objection to bail related to a fear that further serious offences might be committed, arising from evidence given in the High Court bail application by a close female friend of the deceased that some months before the wife's death she had told her that, in the course of an argument at home, the applicant had threatened to kill her, the children, and himself if she did not engage in a sexual act with him. In a judgment of Kearns J., the Court held that the case met all the requirements for the admission of hearsay evidence, in particular because the person who could give *viva voce* evidence was dead. In the Supreme Court case of *DPP v McLoughlin*, the applicant was charged with assault causing harm and at the application for bail in the High Court, evidence was given of witness intimidation by a Detective Inspector. On cross-examination the detective inspector agreed that there was no witness in court to say that he or she was intimidated and that this was because they were afraid to come to court. In her judgment in the case Denham J. approved *McGinley*, and found that it was appropriate in the above circumstances that hearsay evidence be adduced given the reason forwarded by the Gardaí to explain the absence of the witnesses, but specified that the judge should be careful on the weight placed on such evidence. Although in his judgment in the case Hardiman J. stated expressly that his comments on the admissibility of hearsay evidence were *obiter*, it is worth noting his view that, where it is proposed to adduce hearsay evidence, and where that proposal is objected to, there must be a full and proper hearing of the objection, and of the evidence relied on in support of the admission of hearsay evidence, and a proper ruling on this question. He further held, in a judgment expressly approving *McGinley*:

> the evidence relied upon to ground the admission of hearsay must establish something more than it is convenient to the prosecution, or to the witnesses, to have the evidence given in that form. It must establish that all reasonable steps have been taken to procure evidence in the usual form.

In the more recent case of *Damien Galvin v Governor of Cloverhill Prison and the DPP* [2013] IEHC 11, the applicant had been charged in the District Court with assault causing harm. He was denied bail by the District Judge. He alleged that his bail application was so lacking in fundamental fairness as to render his detention unlawful. During the bail application the District Judge had accepted hearsay evidence from the Prosecuting Inspector that the applicant was likely to intimidate the complainant if he was granted bail. The Garda Inspector addressed the District Judge, from outside the witness box and whilst not under oath, indicating that he possessed a statement from the complainant who believed that he would be intimidated by the applicant if he were released on bail. The applicant objected on the basis that he had not been placed on notice of the allegation being made and, thus, not given an opportunity to cross-examine the complainant in relation to this allegation. The District Judge refused bail based on this hearsay evidence.

The High Court ordered the applicant's release from custody ruling that his detention was unlawful. The High Court held that there was a breach of fair procedures as the applicant should have received advance notice that the Gardai were objecting to bail on grounds of intimidation of a witness. The court held that in certain exceptional circumstances hearsay evidence may be admitted during a bail hearing. To admit hearsay evidence, however, a court must be satisfied that there is good reason why *viva voce* evidence may not be adduced. There must be some evidence provided as to why the person alleging intimidation is not able to be present in court to give relevant evidence on which he or she might be cross-examined.

The case of *DPP v David Mulvey* (Supreme Court, 25 February 2014, [2014] IESC 18) involved an appeal by the applicant from a High Court order of 14 October 2013 refusing to admit him to bail. The applicant was charged with offences involving violent behaviour, demanding money with menaces, trespass, intimidation etc. It was held by the Supreme Court that while the trial judge was entitled to be concerned that the alleged injured parties had been intimidated, in the absence of evidence to demonstrate that the applicant was involved in or connected with the intimidation, the decision of the High Court was to be set aside.

As we have seen in its decision in *O'Callaghan*, the Supreme Court held that the fundamental test in deciding whether to allow bail or not, was the probability of the applicant evading justice. The reference to 'probability' also appears in *McKeon* and *McGinley*. In the Supreme Court case of *DPP v Vickers* [2009] IESC 58, however, Kearns J. held that s. 2 of the Bail Act 1997 effected a significant alteration to the onus of proof requirement in relation to matters addressed by the section. Kearns noted that if a test of probability had been intended by the legislature, it could easily have been specified in the Act. The Court proceeded in its ruling to introduce a test of proportionality:

> Thus while the judge dealing with an application will have to consider issues of 'likelihood' of further offending, I think it is clear that the legislation was designed to confer a wide discretion on the court. In this regard, a test of proportionality may also assist the court when evaluating belief evidence, particularly where the risk, as in this case, is of the commission of an extremely serious further offence. The decision to grant or refuse bail must take account of the degree of likelihood of the commission of further serious offences. It must assess the credibility of the deponent and must take account of the nature of the actual risk demonstrated to exist by the evidence. If of the view that a real risk of the commission of a further serious offence has been demonstrated, the decision of the court must be proportionate to the nature and gravity of the apprehended further offence. There is the world of difference between a risk of an applicant committing, say, a further burglary (albeit that this is a serious offence) and a stated threat of recent origin made by an applicant that, for example, he intended to poison a city's water supply or to carry out death threats against certain individuals. In the first example a greater degree of likelihood might require to be demonstrated before bail is refused. In the second example, the concept of proportionality might suggest that, once some degree of likelihood has been established, bail should be refused because of the extreme gravity of the apprehended offence, provided of course the fear is not merely fanciful or vague. The critical consideration in the latter circumstance is that the court be satisfied, from all the evidence adduced, that the risk is a real one. This is not to disturb in any way the requirement on the judge dealing with the matter to bear in mind the presumption of innocence, the prima facie entitlement to bail and the obligation to weigh carefully the hearsay evidence with the other evidence in the case, including the sworn evidence of the applicant.

It is worth noting in this regard, that in the case of *DPP v McLoughlin* [2009] IESC 65 [2010] 1 IR 590, also decided in 2009, a differently constituted Supreme Court appeared to endorse the well-established probability standard in its discussion of bail.

7.9   Failing to Appear On Bail

Section 9 of the Bail Act 1997 as substituted by s. 15 of the Criminal Justice Act 2007, provides that a court may 'estreat' or forfeit all or part of monies paid into court, or conditioned to be paid under the relevant recognisance, where an accused person or person who is appealing against a sentence of imprisonment imposed by the District Court fails to appear before a specified court on a specified date and time in accordance with the recognisance, or where the accused contravenes any other condition of his recognisance, and is arrested on warrant for such contravention. Under s. 9(5) of the Bail Act 1997 (as amended), the District Court may issue a warrant for the arrest of the accused person on application of a member of An Garda Síochána, on information being made in writing, and on oath by or on behalf of the member, that the person has contravened a condition of their recognisance. The warrant may be executed by any member of An Garda Síochána, even if he does not have the warrant on his person at the time of his arrest; however, the member must, as soon as practicable, produce the warrant and serve it on the arrested person. Following a failure to appear by the accused or appellant, an arrest warrant or 'bench warrant' may be issued by the court and, in accordance with s. 13 of the Criminal Justice Act 1984, the warrant may be executed by any member of An Garda Síochána, even if he does not have the warrant on his person at the time of his arrest. However, the member must, as soon as practicable, produce the warrant and serve it on the arrested person. Failure to surrender to bail without a reasonable excuse is a summary offence under s. 13 of the Criminal Justice Act 1984 (as amended by s. 23 of the Criminal Justice Act 2007). The offence is punishable by a maximum term of 12 months' imprisonment and a fine of up to €5,000 or both. Under s. 13(6) as inserted by s. 23 of the 2007 Act notwithstanding s. 10(4) of the Petty Sessions (Ireland) Act 1851, summary proceedings under this section may be instituted within 12 months from the date on which the offence was completed. The offence is treated as an offence committed while on bail for the purpose of s. 11 of the Criminal Justice Act 1984 (as amended) (see **7.10**).

7.10   Sentencing of Offences Committed While On Bail

Section 11(1) of the Criminal Justice Act 1984 as substituted by s. 22 of the Criminal Justice Act 2007 provides:

> Any sentence of imprisonment passed on person for an offence—(a) committed while on bail, whether committed before or after the commencement of section 22 of the Criminal Justice Act 2007, or (b) committed after such commencement while the person is unlawfully at large after the issue of a warrant for his or her arrest for non-compliance with a condition of the recognisance concerned, shall be consecutive on any sentence passed on him or her for a previous offence or, if he or she is sentenced in respect of two or more previous offences, on the sentence last due to expire, so however that, where two or more consecutive sentences as required by this section are passed by the District Court, the aggregate term of imprisonment in respect of those consecutive sentences shall not exceed 2 years.

Section 11 of the 1984 Act was amended by s. 10 of the Bail Act 1997 which added sub-s. (4) to s. 11 which provides that in determining the sentence to be imposed on a person for an offence committed while on bail, in circumstances where consecutive sentences must be imposed, the fact that the offence was committed while on bail shall be treated as an aggravating factor and the court must impose a sentence that is greater than would otherwise be imposed. This does not apply where the sentence for the previous offence is a life sentence or where the court considers that there are exceptional circumstances.

The Criminal Justice (Burglary of Dwellings) Act 2015, commenced on 17 January 2016, amended s. 2 of the Bail Act by inserting four new sub-ss. (2A), (2B), (2C), and (2D).

The new provisions will apply where a court is considering a bail application from an adult charged with a burglary or aggravated burglary offence. If the circumstances specified in sub-s. (2B) exist in respect of the person, namely, that the accused person was convicted of a domestic burglary committed in the five years before the bail application and that: (i) the person has been convicted of at least two domestic burglaries committed in the period starting six months before and ending six months after the alleged commission of the offence for which he or she is seeking bail, or (ii) the person has been charged with at least two domestic burglaries allegedly committed in the same period, or (iii) the person has been convicted of at least one domestic burglary committed, and charged with at least one other domestic burglary allegedly committed, in the same period 'the court must consider the existence of those circumstances as evidence that the person is likely to commit a relevant offence in a dwelling'.

CHAPTER 8

LEGAL AID, ADJOURNMENTS, AND REMANDS

8.1   The Law

The obligation on the state to ensure that a person charged with a criminal offence is in a position to fully participate in proceedings against him, and where the interests of justice so require to provide for payment for legal aid for the preparation and conduct of proceedings, is grounded in Bunreacht na hÉireann Art. 38 s. 1: 'No person shall be tried on any criminal charge save in due course of law'.

The European Convention on Human Rights (ECHR) Art. 6(3) states: 'Everyone charged with a criminal offence has the minimum rights to defend himself in person or through legal assistance of his own choosing or, if he has not sufficient means to pay for legal assistance, to be given it free when the interests of justice so require.'

The legislation governing the provision for, and administration of, a free legal aid scheme is contained in the Criminal Justice (Legal Aid) Act 1962 as amended. The long title of the Act states that it is 'An Act to make provision for the grant by the state of free legal aid to poor persons in certain criminal cases'.

8.2   The Criminal Justice (Legal Aid) Act

The Criminal Justice (Legal Aid) Act 1962 (the 1962 Act) is a relatively concise piece of legislation containing just 14 sections. It sets out the criteria for granting free legal aid in criminal cases.

Section 2, as amended:

(1)   If it appears to the District Court before which a person is charged with an offence ...

    (a)   That the means of the person before it are insufficient to enable him to obtain legal aid, and

    (b)   That by reason of the gravity of the offence with which he is charged or of exceptional circumstances it is essential in the interests of justice that he should have legal aid in the preparation and conduct of his defence before it, the said District Court... shall, on application being made to it in that behalf, grant a certificate, in respect of him for free legal aid . . .

(2)   A decision of the District Court in relation to an application under this section shall be final and shall not be appealable.

Sections 3, 4, 5, and 6 contain similarly worded provisions for the granting of free legal aid in criminal proceedings which are to be dealt with other than in the District Court i.e. trial on indictment (s. 3), appeal of conviction or penalty (s. 4), case stated on point of law to the High Court (s. 5), and an appeal to the Supreme Court in relation to a High Court decision on a question of law arising from criminal proceedings (s. 6).

Section 9:

> Before a person is granted a legal aid certificate he may be required by the court or judge, as the case may be, granting the certificate to furnish a written statement in such form as may be prescribed by the Minister by regulation ... about matters relevant for determining whether his means are insufficient to enable him to obtain legal aid.

A Statement of Means form is available on the Department of Justice website http://www. justice.ie.

8.3 Judicial Interpretation of Constitutional and Statutory Provisions

The Supreme Court in *State (Healy) v Donoghue* [1976] IR 335 held as follows:

- That the provisions of Article 38 of the constitution, in requiring a criminal trial be conducted in due course of law, import the requirement of fair procedures which furnish an accused with an adequate opportunity to defend himself against the charge made.

- That where an accused faces a serious charge and, by reason of lack of education, requires the assistance of a qualified lawyer in the preparation and conduct of a defence to the charge, then, if the accused is unable to pay for that assistance, the administration of justice requires (a) that the accused should be afforded the opportunity of obtaining such assistance at the expense of the state in accordance with the Act of 1962 even though the accused has not applied for it and (b) that the trial of the accused should not proceed against his will without such assistance if an appropriate certificate under s. 2 of the Act of 1962 has been granted in relation to the trial of the accused.

The Act of 1962 refers to the granting of legal aid 'on application being made' to the Court. This judgment, *inter alia*, imposed a duty on the state to afford the accused an opportunity to obtain legal aid even where he may not know of his right to make such an application.

The Supreme Court in a series of cases consistently held that there was no blanket requirement on the state to provide for legal aid assistance, even where an accused is charged with an offence which carries a possible sentence of imprisonment. In *Cahill v Reilly* [1994] 3 IR 547] Denham J. stated:

> I am not deciding that in all cases where there is a statutory sentence of imprisonment possible that the accused has to be told of his right to be legally represented or to apply for legal aid, but I do hold that when a custodial sentence becomes probable or likely after conviction or on a plea of guilty ... the District Court Judge should inform the accused of his right to be legally represented or his right to apply for legal aid.

This rationale gave rise to a widespread practice in the District Court of the judge, when considering the issue of legal aid, at the outset of a case, enquiring of the prosecution as to the likelihood of the accused being 'at risk' (of custodial sentence) if convicted and where a risk of imprisonment was perceived, to grant legal aid where the means of the accused did not allow for payment of a lawyer. A person with previous convictions could be perceived to qualify for legal aid on this basis, where a person with no prior convictions may not.

However, in *Joyce v Brady & anor* [2011] IESC 36 the scope of the defendant's right to a legal aid in this regard was extended. Mr Joyce, who had no previous convictions, was charged with a theft offence. He did not have the means to pay for legal representation. The District Court judge refused an application for legal aid. Judicial Review proceedings brought in the High Court to quash the decision to refuse legal aid were unsuccessful and the defendant then appealed to the Supreme Court. The Supreme Court ruled that the District Court should in the circumstances of the case have granted legal aid, and that the failure to do so, violated Mr Joyce's constitutional right to a fair trial. The judgment states:

> It is apparent that the first named respondent took a simple if strict view both of the language of the Act of 1962 (as amended), and of the landmark decision in *State (Healy) v Donoghue*. It was, he considered, necessary to establish the gravity of the offence and that in turn was determined by the sole question as to whether or not the accused was adjudged to be 'at risk'.

It is quite true to say that a number of the more well known passages in the judgment in *State (Healy) v Donoghue* refer to the injustice created by a person whose liberty was at risk of facing a prosecution without the assistance of legal aid, and it is also clear that that case establishes the fact that not all criminal cases in the District Court require that legal aid. However, it is flawed logic to seek to conclude that because a person who was at risk of imprisonment must receive legal aid, it necessarily follows that absent a risk of imprisonment (the assessment of which is always somewhat speculative) that legal aid should not be provided. More importantly such a conclusion is in my view inconsistent with the reasoning of the Court in *State (Healy) v Donoghue*.

The full text of *Joyce v Brady & anor* [2011] IESC 36 should be read by any practitioner intending to practice criminal law as it sets out the rationale for the decision in detail and includes the following passages:

13.   It may well be that to a long serving District Judge, a busy practitioner or an experienced Garda, that this case could be considered a routine District Court matter. But for a person who has never appeared in court before and who faces the possibility of conviction for theft an offence of dishonesty with all that that entails for prospects of employment, I do not think it could be considered anything other than serious. Indeed it is of some significance that Garda Curtin could only observe that 'while not trivial the charge facing the Applicant is by no means at the more serious end of the scale'.

14.   It is worth considering what would be involved in a professional defence of the case. It would be necessary to know that the offence itself was indictable but could be tried in the District Court but only with the agreement of the accused. It would be necessary therefore to form some view as to which court would be the most desirable from this accused's point of view. If the matter was to proceed in the District Court it would be also necessary to know that an application could be made for disclosure which might inform the accused of the case which he had to meet. It might also be necessary to know the extensive law that has grown up in recent years about the significance of CCTV evidence, and more particularly, its absence. Careful consideration would have to be paid, to both the legal and factual basis upon which it could be said that the actions of the two women in the Spar shop could be attributed to the applicant. In addition to all of these steps a lawyer would have to consider what witnesses would be available for the defence. Leaving aside the statutory formula for one moment, if the sole question for a court was whether anyone would think this was the sort of case that could be fairly defended by a litigant on their own whilst suffering perhaps from that 'fumbling incompetence that may occur when an accused is precipitated into the public glare and alien complexity of courtroom procedures, and is confronted with the might of a prosecution backed by the State' (*State (Healy) v. Donoghue* [1976] IR 325, 354), then there could in my view, be only one correct answer.

8.4   The Practical Application *Inter Alia* of the Legal Aid Scheme

As all criminal proceedings (with exception of those in the Special Criminal Court) commence in the District Court, it is in the District Court where the issue of free legal aid will be determined. Note the provisions of s. 2 (2). A decision of the District Court in relation to an application under this section shall be final and shall not be appealable.

The general practice is where an accused is charged before the District Court on an indictable offence or a summary offence which carries a statutory penalty of imprisonment that the District Judge will enquire:

• into the means of the accused, in order to establish if the accused is in a financial position to afford legal representation; and

• the Judge will consider the gravity of the offence with which he is charged or...exceptional circumstances to determine if it is essential in the interests of justice that he should have legal aid in the preparation and conduct of his defence before it.

Where the judge decides to grant a legal aid certificate he will then ask the accused if he wishes to nominate a solicitor from the legal aid panel (established pursuant to s. 10 of the 1962 Act regulations) for the court area. If the solicitor is in attendance s/he may make the application on behalf of the client in the first instance. If an accused does not know the name of a solicitor then the judge may nominate one from the panel. Usually, the judge will nominate a solicitor who is present in court. Once a solicitor has been assigned it is usual for the case to be remanded for the purpose of taking instructions and giving legal advice. Occasionally, a judge may decide that a case appears relatively straightforward and put the case to 'second calling', to enable the solicitor to advise a client briefly in relation to the charge, and to then indicate to the court whether the accused is pleading guilty or seeking a date for the hearing of the case. Obviously the former practice is preferable to the latter. It can be difficult in a busy court scenario to adequately access the merits of even a relatively minor case and to properly advise a client, particularly a new client who one has just met when assigned by the judge.

Where an accused person is sent forward for trial on indictment to a court of higher jurisdiction (Circuit, Special or Central Court), the issue of legal aid is dealt with *de nova*. Where the accused was granted legal aid at the outset of proceedings, in the absence of a change of financial fortune, a legal aid certificate is granted for the purpose of the trial to include provision for a solicitor and up to two counsel, depending on the seriousness of the charge.

Where a person was in a position to discharge fees for the purpose of proceedings in the District Court, it is generally accepted that the cost of proceedings in the higher courts are such that most people will qualify for legal aid and an application can be made at the return for trial stage. The legal aid certificate will cover the cost of a solicitor and one counsel but more serious cases, and in particular cases returned to the Central Criminal Court, will usually certify for solicitor and two counsel (i.e. one senior barrister and one junior barrister).

A solicitor who wishes to be included on the legal aid panel notifies the County Registrar, in writing, of the courts in which s/he will be available for legal aid assignments and must provide up-to-date tax compliance certificates. Solicitors are paid in accordance with a fixed scale of fees per court appearance on completion of an LA1 claim form submitted to the Criminal Legal Aid Payment Section of the Department of Justice and Law Reform. (See Department of Justice website http://www.justice.ie for the latest version of all relevant legal aid application forms.) The legal aid scheme also makes provision for the payment of fees in respect of prison visits to a client who has been granted a legal aid certificate. Similarly, a solicitor should ensure that a client who is legally advised in a Garda station or attended during an ID parade and cannot afford to discharge fees should complete a form (GSAS 1). As outlined in **Chapter 5**, changes in practice as a resuly of the *Gormley and White* case has created a legal payment structure for solicitors who attend Garda stations during the Garda interrogation of a client. The scales of payment fees are published by way of Statutory Instrument (SI) and available on the Department of Justice and Law Reform webpages.

8.5   Adjournments and Remands

Adjournments and remands are procedures that populate daily criminal practice in the processing of all cases from the commencement of proceedings to final disposal of those cases. Such terminology permeates all jurisdictions of the criminal justice system, and are therefore universally applicable. Adjournment of cases is intrinsically linked with practice and procedure dealing with bail, which has been discussed in detail in this text at **Chapter 7**.

- An 'adjournment' is a court order postponing a case until a later time or date and a 'remand' is the court order that the court makes when adjourning a criminal case.

- Where the accused person is 'on bail' the order is a 'remand on continuing bail'.

- Where the accused is in custody the order is a 'remand in custody'.

- Where no bail is fixed or where bail is fixed but the accused is not in a position to 'take up bail' the order is a 'remand in custody with consent to bail', e.g. where the accused has not yet had an independent surety fixed or the bail is fixed at an amount that is outside the means of a surety and a High Court Appeal is anticipated.

In **Chapter 6** dealing with commencement of proceedings, the processes and procedures regarding how an individual is brought before a court to answer an allegation is addressed.

8.5.1 SUMMONS PROCESS

The summons process is discussed at **Chapter 6** where it is outlined that summons are issued under the Petty Sessions (Ireland) Act 1851. The person being prosecuted is described as the 'defendant'. If the summons is issued under the Courts (No. 3) Act 1986, the person being prosecuted is referred to as 'the accused'. Typically, a defendant who appears in answer to a summons will not be subject to a remand order during any period of adjournment of the case. Usually, such defendant is not subject to bail terms, although on a 'failure to appear', i.e. no return to court on a previously indicated date, a bench warrant may be issued for the defendant's arrest. Following the execution of the summons warrant there is a possibility of a subsequent 'remand in custody' or a 'remand on bail' of the defendant.

8.5.2 CHARGE SHEET PROCESS

The term 'defendant' is also used if the person before the court 'on a charge sheet' is charged with a summary offence. Where that person is charged with an indictable offence, the term 'the accused' is used. A practice has grown, however, where typically all those prosecuted are referred to as the accused.

The charge sheet process has also been previously outlined at **Chapter 6**, referencing the application of the District Court (Charge Sheet) Rules 1971. The arrested person is given a document called a 'charge sheet' setting out the allegation and making reference to the statute allegedly breached. This document also sets out the facts of the allegation. **Chapter 7** on bail discusses processes whereby the charged person may be released on 'station bail' subject to entering a bond that the accused will attend at the District Court at 'the next sitting' of that court or within 30 days of the next sitting.

On the first appearance before the court of the defendant/accused, a prosecutor on behalf of the Director of Public Prosecutions (DPP) presents evidence of the arrest, charge, and caution of the accused to the judge, indicating the 'reply after caution', if any, made by the accused person to the allegation. Typically, there will be a bail application if the accused is in custody and an application will be made for legal representation in circumstances where legal aid is applicable. The defendant/accused will then usually be remanded to appear in the same court on a later date. As previously indicated, this remand may be 'in custody' or 'on bail' or 'with consent to bail'. This first remand is often to facilitate discussions between a lawyer appointed under the legal aid scheme discussed earlier, and the defendant/accused who is now that lawyer's client. Typically such adjournment also suits the prosecution who will need to collate their evidence.

8.5.3 REASONS FOR ADJOURNMENTS

On occasion, some offences e.g. summonses for road traffic offences or public order offences, may be disposed of on their 'return date', i.e. the first date the case is before the court, particularly if the defendant/accused has retained a solicitor before the first day in court. In circumstances where a defendant/accused has not yet been in a position to employ the services of a solicitor, or secure free legal aid,, it is common practice for the judge to remand the case to facilitate the accused in receiving legal advice. The defence may also wish to apply for disclosure of evidence pursuant to *DPP v Gary Doyle* (1994) 2 IR 286 (SC) (a 'Gary Doyle' order). In circumstances where the prosecuting Garda is not present, and is not represented by a colleague or a solicitor from the Office of the DPP who can explain the Garda's absence, the summons or charge may be 'struck out', or dismissed 'for want of prosecution'.

It is good practice that the prosecutor or defendant/accused, or the representative lawyer gives prior notice to the other side if there is an intention to apply for an adjournment. In circumstances where a judge is concerned that there is undue delay in the prosecution of the matter at hand, the judge may determine that the remand is a 'peremptory' one by the judge as against the party applying for it, and it must then proceed or be struck out for want of prosecution on the adjourned date. The prosecution may seek a remand in a case because it is awaiting DPP directions. The case may then be disposed of summarily (see **Chapter 11**), in which circumstances the case will be remanded for the presentation of a plea of guilty or for a trial date referred to as a 'hearing date'. Alternatively, if the matter is for trial on indictment, detailed processes will occur, as discussed later in this manual at **Chapter 13**.

The prosecution of cases may be expedited in circumstances where an accused has been arrested on warrant and charged following the prior submission of a file to the DPP, with the consequence that the number of remands sought by the state (prosecution) will be minimised.

8.5.4 SICK WARRANTS AND BODY WARRANTS

Cases may be adjourned in the absence of an accused for medical reasons, which must be documented either at the time of the application or the next available opportunity. The court will remand the case for a period considered 'reasonable', but not exceeding 30 days, if the accused person is in custody, in which case the order is referred to as a 'sick warrant'. There is alternatively a discretionary procedure available to the judge who does not wish to grant an adjournment in the circumstances described above and may 'grant a stay' on the issuing of a bench warrant or recommend that the warrant be 'executed with discretion'.

If the reason that an accused is unable to appear in court on the due date is due to being in custody on another matter, the court may issue a 'body warrant'. This order, issued to the prison or detention centre that is detaining the accused, orders that prison or detention centre to produce the accused before the court on a particular date and time, usually within one week of the issuing of the order.

Post-conviction on either the processing of a 'plea of guilty' or a trial, where the prosecution proved the allegation 'beyond all reasonable doubt' there may be adjournments to facilitate the sentencing process outlined at **Chapter 14**. Adjournments may occur post-sentence where Probation Service supervision and monitoring recommendations have been ordered by the presiding judge or where the convicted person is required to pay compensation to the injured party.

8.5.5 TIME LIMITS IN REMANDING CASES

There are specific statutory provisions which determine the length of time that a defendant/accused can be remanded. Whether a person is:

- appearing on a first occasion on a charge;
- appearing on a subsequent occasion on a charge;
- being remanded on bail;
- being remanded in custody;
- being remanded in custody with consent to bail;

the length of the remand period is intrinsically linked to whichever of the above categories the accused finds himself or herself in. The relevant legislation is s. 24 of the Criminal Procedure Act 1967, as substituted by s. 4 of the Criminal Justice (Miscellaneous Provisions) Act 1997 (the 1997 Act) as follows:

- An accused remanded in custody on the occasion of first appearing before the court can be remanded for a maximum of longest eight days, inclusive of the day of the first appearance.
- An accused remanded on bail when the first appearing before the court, may be remanded on the occasion of the first remand and any subsequent remand 'on continuing bail' for more than eight days, if both the accused and the prosecutor consent to such an order.
- An accused who is granted bail, but is unable to take up bail there and then, will be remanded in custody 'with consent to bail' and the time limits will be the same as for a remand in custody.

On the second or subsequent appearance of an accused who was remanded in custody, the maximum time limit on a further remand in custody, without the consent of the accused, is 15 days; however, if the accused is in custody, and the prosecutor consents, a further remand in custody of up to 30 days is permissible.

Where an accused is pleading 'not guilty' to charges in the District Court, the hearing of the charges may not occur for some weeks, due to the logistical pressures on court diaries. Under the principle of presumption of innocence, this delay in getting to trial may present as problematical where the accused is in custody with no prospect of obtaining bail. Compliance with legislative requirements regarding time limits applicable to longer remand periods is achieved by remanding the accused at two-week intervals, especially in circumstances where the accused refuses to consent to longer periods. Remands at monthly intervals may occur where the accused who is in custody consents to such intervals.

Where an accused person is found guilty and a term of imprisonment is being imposed, the court may exercise its discretion, on an application from the defence solicitor, to backdate the sentence to take account of time spent in custody since the commencement of the proceedings.

CHAPTER 9

JUVENILE JUSTICE

9.1   Introduction

Throughout the twentieth century the primary legislation governing juvenile justice in Ireland was the Children Act 1908 (the 1908 Act). There had been a number of minor amendments to that Act but the main body of the Act remained unchanged and juvenile justice in Ireland had been governed primarily by legislation enacted at the beginning of that century.

9.2   The Children Act

On 8 July 2001 the Children Act 2001 (the 2001 Act), a piece of legislation containing some 271 sections, was signed into law. The repeal section provided for the repeal of the whole of the 1908 Act. However, it was not until April 2002 that the then Minister for Justice signed a commencement order implementing certain provisions of the new Act effective from 1 May 2002 and allowing for the repeal of certain sections of the old Act.

The implementation of certain sections of the 2001 Act and a repeal of certain sections of the 1908 Act continued sporadically up until September 2007 when the final sections of the 2001 Act as amended by Criminal Justice Act 2006 (CJA 2006) were commenced. Throughout this period practitioners sourced the law with a copy of the 1908 Act in one hand, a copy of the 2001 Act in the other hand, together with copies of the various commencement orders balanced between both Acts. As practitioners were coming to terms with these intermittent changes in legislation, the Criminal Justice Act 2006 Act was implemented. This Act in Parts 12 and 13 contained 37 sections introducing numerous amendments and substitutions to the 2001 Act and also inserted a new Part 12A into the 2001 Act dealing with 'Anti-Social Behaviour by Children'.

The Law Reform Commission published a revised consolidated version of the Children Act 2001 in January 2016 which is a lengthy piece of legislation and available at: http://www.lawreform.ie/_fileupload/RevisedActs/WithAnnotations/HTML/EN_ACT_2001_0024.HTM.

9.2.1   CRIMINAL RESPONSIBILITY

The interpretation section of the 2001 Act defines a 'child' as a person under the age of 18 years. The original s. 52 of the 2001 Act provided that a child under the age of 12 was presumed to be incapable of committing a criminal offence thereby establishing 12 as the age of criminal responsibility. Section 52 of the 2001 Act as published was, however, never commenced and CJA 2006 substituted a revised s. 52 and amended the title of Part 5 from 'Criminal Responsibility' to 'Restriction on Criminal Proceedings Against Certain Children'. Section 52 provides:

52.—(1) Subject to subsection (2), a child under 12 years of age shall not be charged with an offence.

(2)   Subsection (1) does not apply to a child aged 10 or 11 years who is charged with murder, manslaughter, rape, rape under section 4 of the Criminal Law (Rape) (Amendment) Act 1990 or aggravated sexual assault.

(3) *The rebuttable presumption under any rule of law, namely, that a child who is not less than 7 but under 14 years of age is incapable of committing an offence because the child did not have the capacity to know that the act or omission concerned was wrong, is abolished.*

(4) *Where a child under 14 years of age is charged with an offence, no further proceedings in the matter (other than any remand in custody or on bail) shall be taken except by or with the consent of the Director of Public Prosecutions.*

It is notable that the section now contains no age limit under which a child is presumed incapable of committing an offence and this is reflected in the change of title. Rather it states that 'a child under 12 shall not be charged with an offence' and exceptions are contained in s. 52(2). This legislation stands in contrast to the requirement of Article 40(3)(a) of the Convention on the Rights of the Child which requires that member states establish 'a minimum age below which children shall be presumed not to have the capacity to infringe the criminal law'.

One of the most important facts to be established by a practitioner dealing with a young person is the exact age of the client. It is certainly one of the first questions that will be asked by the judge when the case is brought to court. Section 76C of the 2001 Act states:

76C—When a child under 14 years of age is charged with an offence, the Court may, of its own motion or the application of any person, dismiss the case on its merits if, having had due regard to the child's age and level of maturity, it determines that the child did not have a full understanding of what was involved in the commission of the offence.

9.3   Arrest and Detention of Juveniles

Children are subject to the general legislative powers of arrest and detention (see detailed discussion at **Chapters 4 and 5**). They can be arrested for the purpose of being charged with a criminal offence and being brought before the court. They can also be arrested for the purposes of detention in a Garda station for questioning during the investigation of a crime. Depending on the legislation under which they are detained, they can be held for questioning in a Garda station for up to 24 hours (s. 4 Criminal Justice Act 1984 (as amended)) or in other instances for 72 hours (s. 30 Offences Against the State Act 1939 (as amended)) or under drug trafficking legislation for up to seven days (s. 2 Misuse of Drugs Act 1999 (as amended)).

Part 6 of the 2001 Act is headed 'Treatment of Child Suspects in Garda Síochána Stations'. This section obliges the member in charge of the Garda station to take certain precautionary measures when dealing with child detainees. These measures include *inter alia*:

• to keep detained children separate from adults being detained and to keep a child in a cell only in circumstances where there is no other secure accommodation available (s. 56);

• to notify the child of the reason for their arrest and his or her entitlement to consult a solicitor (s. 57);

• to notify the parent or guardian and to request their attendance at the Garda station (s. 58);

• to ensure that no questioning is commenced or statements taken in the absence of a parent or guardian (s. 61).

In the absence of a parent/guardian the member in charge may nominate 'another adult' to be present during the interviewing of a child.

A solicitor should enquire from the client as to the role played by the nominated adult in relation to the interview. Practitioners attending at a Garda station may often discover that proffered professional advice to a child client can directly conflict with the advice of a parent. One must be mindful of the detainee's right to legal advice and of the solicitor's professional obligation to the detained client.

Following a detention period, if charged with an offence, the child may be released on bail from the Garda station to appear in the Children Court on a specified date. Alternatively, the child is taken in custody to the Children Court where the presiding judge will decide whether to grant bail, having heard Garda objections during the bail application.

9.4   Diversion Programme

Prior to the implementation of the 2001 Act a non-statutory scheme existed, known as the Juvenile Liaison Officer (JLO) Scheme. The Gardaí, in implementing this scheme, sought to divert the child from entering the criminal justice system, by administering a series of cautions, rather than charging a child or young person who had admitted a minor offence.

Part 4 of the 2001 Act introduces a Diversion Programme which effectively placed the former JLO system on a statutory basis.

Section 19 states:

(1)   *The objective of the Programme is to divert from committing further offences any child who accepts responsibility for his or her criminal behaviour.*

(2)   *The objective shall be achieved primarily by administering a caution to such child and, where appropriate, by placing him or her under the supervision of a juvenile liaison officer and by convening a conference to be attended by the child, family members and other concerned persons.*

The Diversion Programme is managed by a member of An Garda Síochána not below the rank of Superintendent, who shall be assigned by the Commissioner, and referred to as the Director. The Director shall decide whether to admit a child who admits responsibility for criminal behaviour to the Programme and shall decide the category of caution that should be administered. Section 25 of the 2001 Act outlines the details of the categories of caution.

In general a formal caution will be administered to the young person in a Garda station by a member of the Garda Síochána not below the rank of Inspector, or a Juvenile Liaison Officer trained in mediation skills, in the presence of the parents or a guardian. An informal caution may be administered either in a Garda station or at the child's place of residence, by a Juvenile Liaison Officer in the presence of the parents or a guardian.

Where a child receives a formal caution, that child shall be placed under the supervision of a Juvenile Liaison Officer for a period of 12 months. Only in exceptional circumstances will an informal caution be followed by a supervisory period (s. 27, 2001 Act).

The Diversion Programme was commenced in May 2002 and research figures show very encouraging results relating to reaching the objectives stated in s. 19.

The introduction of the new Part 12A of the 2001 Act through s. 159 of the Criminal Justice Act 2006 gave power to An Garda Síochána to deal with children who may be involved in what is described as 'anti-social behaviour'. The Children Court may on application by a member of An Garda Síochána not below the rank of Superintendent make a 'behaviour order' prohibiting a child from doing anything the court specifies in the order. 'A child commits an offence' who 'without reasonable excuse does not comply with a behaviour order' punishable by a fine not exceeding €800 and/or a period of three months' detention (s. 257F of the 2001 Act).

These latter provisions have caused concern to many people working in the area of juvenile justice. The body of research from other jurisdictions relating to anti-social behaviour legislation indicates negative and counter-productive results of criminalising children in this manner bearing in mind that the child's original behaviour had not merited charging the child with a criminal offence. In fact in the UK, reports at one point indicated that the number of juveniles detained as a result of breach of anti-social behaviour orders (ASBOs) had risen by one third.

9.5   The Jurisdiction of the Children Court

Part 7 of the 2001 Act is titled 'Children Court' and sets out the provisions relating to jurisdiction and procedure. Section 71 states:

The District Court, when hearing charges against children or when hearing applications for orders relating to a child at which the attendance of the child is required . . . shall be known as the Children Court.

The Dublin Metropolitan Children Court is the only purpose-built courthouse for children in Ireland. In other Court Districts the normal District Court sits as a Children Court on specific days or times in an effort to comply with the aspiration of s. 71(2) that children should not be brought into contact with adult defendants when attending at court proceedings. A practice direction outlining steps to be employed in procedures in the Dublin Metropolitan Children Court, 'to ensure compliance' with Constitutional rights and international Convention standards for juvenile justice, was issued in January 2014 by the President of the District Court and is available on Courts Service website http://www.courts.ie.

The jurisdiction of the Children Court is set out in s.75(1) and provides that:

75–(1) … *subject to subsection (3), the Court may deal summarily with a child charged with any indictable offence, other than an offence which is required to be tried by the Central Criminal Court or manslaughter, unless the Court is of opinion that the offence does not constitute a minor offence fit to be tried summarily or, where the child wishes to plead guilty, to be dealt with summarily.*

(2) *In deciding whether to try or deal with a child summarily for an indictable offence, the Court shall also take account of—*

    (a) *the age and level of maturity of the child concerned, and*

    (b) *any other facts that it considers relevant.*

(3) *The Court shall not deal summarily with an indictable offence where the child, on being informed by the Court of his or her right to be tried by a jury, does not consent to the case being so dealt with.*

Section 75 of the 2001 Act therefore outlines the extremely broad jurisdiction of the Children Court in dealing summarily with any indictable offence other than that which is required to be tried at Central Criminal Court or in cases of manslaughter. The absence of the input or consent of the Director of Public Prosecutions (DPP) in relation to indictable offences is notable.

It is the Children Court that decides, subject to the consent of the child, whether the matter will be dealt with summarily. It would appear to be the practice that the DPP will in certain cases recommend to the Children Court whether the matter should be dealt with on indictment in the Circuit Court, but the 2001 Act is specific that the judge determines this issue.

It is not uncommon for a case in the Children Court to be remanded for a s. 75 hearing to allow the prosecution and defence to present argument to the judge before the issue of jurisdiction is decided. Section 75 is highly significant as it gives the court the discretion to deal with a broad range of indictable offences with the potential to avoid sending a child forward to be dealt with through the formal procedures of a jury trial (which may often be outside of the understanding of a child) and to limit the sentencing scope for the offence to the limit of the District Court jurisdiction.

Section 74 of the 2001 Act provides that, subject to the discretion of the Court, where a child is charged with summary offences jointly with adults, that the charge or charges against the child and adult shall be heard by the Children Court unless the Court considers that the charges should be heard by the District Court sitting otherwise than as the Children Court (s. 74 of the 2001 Act). Where a child is charged with indictable offences jointly with adults, s. 76 of the 2001 Act provides that s. 75 shall apply to the child while the adult or adults shall be dealt with 'in accordance with the enactments governing proceedings in the District Court against a person charged with an indictable offence'.

9.5.1   PERSONS ENTITLED TO BE PRESENT IN CHILDREN COURT

Section 94 specifies that only certain persons are entitled to be present at the hearing of proceedings in the Children Court including, *inter alia*, officers of the court, the parents/or guardian of the child concerned, an adult relative of the child, persons directly concerned in the proceedings, *bona fide* representatives of the press, and such other persons as the court may at its discretion permit to remain.

Attendance by the parents or guardian of a child is required at all stages of proceedings and failure to attend, without reasonable excuse, may result in an adjournment of the case and the issue of a bench warrant for the arrest of the parents or guardian, in order to ensure attendance at the resumption of the case (s. 91 of the 2001 Act).

9.5.2   RESTRICTIONS ON REPORTS OF PROCEEDINGS

There are restrictions on court reporting to protect the anonymity of a child concerned in proceedings.

> 93.—(1) In relation to proceedings before any court concerning a child—
>
>   (a) no report which reveals the name, address or school of any child concerned in the proceedings or includes any particulars likely to lead to the identification of any such child shall be published or included in a broadcast or any other form of communication, and
>
>   (b) no still or moving picture of or including any such child or which is likely to lead to his or her identification shall be so published or included.
>
> (2) A court may dispense, in whole or in part, with the requirements of this section in relation to a child if satisfied that to do so is necessary
>
>   (a) where the child is charged with an offence
>
>   (i)   to avoid injustice to the child,
>
>   (ii)   where the child is unlawfully at large, for the purpose of apprehending the child.

It is noteworthy that the restrictions apply to 'proceedings before any court concerning a child'. However, the section allows for the court to dispense with this restriction in a number of circumstances, including where it is deemed as in the public interest to do so or to ensure that a behaviour order will be complied with.

9.5.3   'SPECIAL DUTY' TO EXPEDITE PROSECUTIONS

A number of cases have led to increased pressure on the prosecution to expedite criminal proceedings involving children to ensure that undue delay does not result in a child offender being either charged with or convicted of an offence after his or her 18th birthday and as a consequence the loss of protections afforded by the Children Act 2001. In *BF v DPP* [2001] 1 IR 656, the Supreme Court stated that there was 'a special duty' on the state to ensure a speedy trial in the case of juveniles. In *Donoghue v DPP* [2014] IESC 56, the Supreme Court upheld a decision of the High Court to prohibit a criminal trial in circumstances where a 16-year-old youth had made admissions during a drugs investigation but was not charged with the offence until 17 months later and it was not for another two months that a 'substantive court hearing' took place. By virtue of this delay he was likely to be an adult by the time the proceedings were completed. Dunne J. in her judgment referring to the High Court decision noted:

> The learned trial judge in the course of his judgment outlined a number of features that would have applied to Mr. Donoghue had he been prosecuted expeditiously which were no longer applicable given that Mr. Donoghue would be tried as an adult as opposed to a child. They included the loss of anonymity, the fact that s. 96 of the Act (to the effect that a sentence of detention should only be used as a last resort) would no longer apply and the loss of the mandatory requirement to obtain a Probation Report in the circumstances set out in s. 99 of the Act. As the learned trial judge said, these are matters of real significance.

However, it is important to note that each case will turn on its own facts and prosecutorial delay *per se* may not, in every case, lead to a prohibition of a prosecution, as Dunne J noted:

> There is no doubt that once there is a finding that blameworthy prosecutorial delay has occurred, a balancing exercise must be conducted to establish if there is by reason of the delay something additional to the delay itself to outweigh the public interest in the prosecution of serious offences. In the case of a child there may well be adverse consequences caused by a blameworthy prosecutorial delay which flow from the fact that the person facing trial is no longer a child. However, the facts and circumstances of each case will have to be considered carefully. The nature of the case may be such that notwithstanding the fact that a person who was a child at the time of the commission of the alleged offence may face trial as an adult, the public interest in having the matter brought to trial may be such as to require the trial to proceed.

9.5.4   BAIL CONDITIONS

Section 90 sets out a number of conditions of bail which the court may make when releasing a child on bail:

(1)   (a)   *that the child resides with his or her parents or guardian or such other specified adult as the Court considers appropriate,*

(b)   *that the child receives education or undergoes training, as appropriate,*

(c)   *that the child reports to a specified Garda Síochána station at a specified time at such intervals as the Court considers appropriate,*

(d)   *that the child does not associate with a specified individual or individuals,*

(e)   *that the child stays away from a specified building, place or locality except in such circumstances and at such times as the Court may specify,*

(e)   *such other conditions as the Court considers appropriate.*

(2)   *Where a child who is released on bail does not comply with any condition to which the release was subject and is subsequently found guilty of an offence, the Court, in dealing with the child for the offence, may take into account the non-compliance in question and the circumstances in which it occurred.*

9.6   Sentencing

The sentencing function of the criminal justice process is discussed in detail elsewhere in this manual at **Chapter 14**. There are, however, specific statutory provisions and principles relating to dealing with children on a finding of guilt.

The principles relating to the exercise of the sentencing function of criminal jurisdiction over children are set out in s. 96 of the 2001 Act. This section provides that:

(1)   *Any court when dealing with children charged with offences shall have regard to—*

(a)   *the principle that children have rights and freedom before the law equal to those enjoyed by adults and, in particular, a right to be heard and to participate in any proceedings of the court that can affect them, and*

(b)   *the principle that criminal proceedings shall not be used solely to provide any assistance or service needed to care for or protect a child.*

(2)   *Because it is desirable wherever possible—*

(a)   *to allow the education, training or employment of children to proceed without interruption,*

(b)   *to preserve and strengthen the relationship between children and their parents and other family members,*

(c)   *to foster the ability of families to develop their own means of dealing with offending by their children, and,*

(d)   *to allow children to reside in their own homes,*

any penalty imposed on a child for an offence should cause as little interference as possible with the child's legitimate activities and pursuits, should take the form most likely to maintain and promote the development of the child and should take the least restrictive form that is appropriate in the circumstances; in particular, a period of detention should be imposed only as a measure of last resort.

(3)   *A court may take into consideration as mitigating factors a child's age and level of maturity in determining the nature of any penalty imposed, unless the penalty is fixed by law.*

(4)   *The penalty imposed on a child for an offence should be no greater than that which would be appropriate in the case of an adult who commits an offence of the same kind and may be less, where so provided for in this Part.*

(5)   *When dealing with a child charged with an offence, a court shall have due regard to the child's best interests, the interests of the victim of the offence and the protection of society.*

One of the very relevant aspects of s. 96 of the 2001 Act is that the period of detention imposed as a sanction, should be imposed *only as a measure of last resort*.

The sentencing options open to the court are outlined in s. 98:

> 98.— *Where a court is satisfied of the guilt of a child charged with an offence it may, without prejudice to its general powers and in accordance with this Part, reprimand the child or deal with the case by making one or more than one of the following orders:*
>
> (a)   *a conditional discharge order,*
>
> (b)   *an order that the child pay a fine or costs,*
>
> (c)   *an order that the parent or guardian be bound over,*
>
> (d)   *a compensation order,*
>
> (e)   *a parental supervision order,*
>
> (f)   *an order that the parent or guardian pay compensation,*
>
> (g)   *an order imposing a community sanction,*
>
> (h)   *an order (the making of which may be deferred pursuant to section 144) that the child be detained in a children detention school or children detention centre, including an order under section 155(1),*
>
> (i)   *a detention and supervision order.*

Section 98 is a very significant section as it lists the orders that the court may make on the finding of guilt. The community sanction orders referred to at (g) above are later listed at s. 115 of the 2001 Act and include probation order, restriction on movement order and community service order.

Under s. 99 there is a requirement that proceedings should be adjourned for the preparation of a probation orders report in certain circumstances.

Section 99 provides that:

> (1)   *Subject to subsections (2) and (3), where a court is satisfied of the guilt of a child, it—(a) may in any case, and (b) shall, where it is of opinion that the appropriate decision would be to impose a community sanction, detention (whether or not deferred under Section 144) or detention and supervision, adjourn the proceedings, remand the child and request a probation and welfare officer to prepare a report in writing (a 'probation officer's report') which—(i) would assist the court in determining a suitable community sanction (if any) or another way of dealing with the child, and (ii) would contain information on such matters as may be prescribed, including any information specifically requested by the court.*
>
> (2)   *The probation officer's report shall, at the request of the court, indicate whether, and if so how, in his or her opinion any lack of care or control by the parents or guardian of the child concerned contributed to the behaviour which resulted in the child being found guilty of an offence.*
>
> (3)   *The court may, in addition, request that a victim impact report be furnished to it in respect of any victim of the child where it considers that such a report would assist it in dealing with the case.*
>
> (4)   *The court may decide not to request a probation officer's report where—(a) the penalty for the offence of which the child is guilty is fixed by law, or (b) (i) the child was the subject of a probation officer's report prepared not more than 2 years previously, (ii) the attitude of the child to, and the circumstances of, the offence or offences to which that report relates are similar to his or her attitude to, and the circumstances of, the offence of which the child has been found guilty, and (iii) the previous report is available to the court and the court is satisfied that the material in it is sufficient to enable it to deal with the case.*

Section 78 of the 2001 Act, as amended, enables a court to make an order directing the Probation Service to convene a Family Conference, in order to formulate an action plan for a child who has admitted responsibility for his or her criminal behaviour where the child and the child's parent, guardian, or family member agree to participate in such conference. This is the first instance of legislation providing for family participation in seeking a solution to the circumstances that have led to a juvenile becoming involved in the criminal justice system.

Section 108 of the 2001 Act provides that any fine imposed on a child *'shall not exceed half the amount which the District Court could impose on a person of full age and capacity on summary conviction for such an offence'*. It is notable that in s. 110 the court is prohibited from imposing a custodial sanction where the child defaults on payment, rather the court may impose a community sanction in in lieu of that fine.

The court may make an order directing a parent or guardian to pay compensation where the court is satisfied that the 'wilful failure' to care for or control the child contributed to the child's criminal behaviour.

Section 142 of the 2001 Act as amended allows the court to impose a period of detention in a children detention school. Section 143 of the 2001 Act specifies that a detention order shall not be made unless the court is satisfied that detention is the only suitable way of dealing with the child. Section 156 of the 2001 Act states no court shall pass a sentence of imprisonment on a child or commit a child to prison. This effectively abolished the much abhorred 'unruly' provision of the 1908 Children Act. A point of particular importance in relation to sentencing is that minimum mandatory sentences prescribed by legislation, cannot be imposed on persons under the age of 18.

Despite being categorised as 'Miscellaneous' in Part 13 of the 2001 Act, s. 258 is a significant section. It provides for the non-disclosure of record of conviction or a 'clean slate', after a three-year period has elapsed, where a child was convicted of an offence and has not re-offended during the subsequent three-year period. This section does not apply to offences which must be tried in the Central Criminal Court.

> 258.—(1)*Where a person has been found guilty of an offence whether before or after the commencement of this section, and—*
>
> (a)   *the offence was committed before the person attained the age of 18 years,*
>
> (b)   *the offence is not an offence required to be tried by the Central Criminal Court,*
>
> (c)   *a period of not less than 3 years has elapsed since the finding of guilt, and*
>
> (d)   *the person has not been dealt with for an offence in that 3-year period, then after the end of the 3-year period or, where the period ended before the commencement of this section, after the commencement of this section, the provisions of subsection (4) shall apply to the finding of guilt.*

9.7   Conclusion

The full implementation and proper resourcing of the Children Act 2001 as amended has the potential to advance the delivery of juvenile justice in Ireland. The 2001 Act declares a preference for utilising non-custodial sanctions and offers the court a range of community-based options. It has established a Diversion Programme to divert children from crime without bringing them into the criminal court process. Provision has been made for Family Welfare Conferences, which may be convened at the direction of the court. Family involvement in this manner represents a radical departure from the previous norm in juvenile justice practice.

PART IV

APPLIED EVIDENCE AND SUMMARY TRIAL PROCEDURE

CHAPTER 10

APPLICATION OF EVIDENTIAL RULES

10.1 Introduction

This chapter is not a substitute for an academic textbook on the rules of evidence. There are many relevant texts which deal with this in-depth area of law, some of which are listed at **10.7**. At a minimum an advocate in criminal litigation practice must have a thorough understanding of a myriad of rules of evidence including rules and case law emanating from the following concepts:

- Standard of proof

- Evidentiary and legal burden of proof

- Tactical burden of proof

- Exceptions to burden of proof including certain defences such as statutory insanity, self-defence, provocation etc.

- Other exceptions including the 'peculiar knowledge' principle

- The Custody Regulations 1987 and the different rules applicable to children

- The Judges' Rules

- The Electronic Recording Regulations 1997

- Hearsay evidence

- *Res Gestae* statements

- Rebuttable presumptions of Law

- Rebuttable presumptions of fact

- Presumptions without facts

- Visual identification evidence

- Unconstitutionally obtained evidence and the distinction of illegally obtained evidence

- Corroboration of evidence

- Real evidence

- Opinion evidence and expert evidence

- Documentary evidence

- Accomplice evidence

- Competence and compellability of witnesses

- The rule in *Hollington v Hewthorn*

- Refreshing witness memory

- The Doctrine of Recent Complaint

- State Witness Protection Programme.

This chapter aims to do three things:

    (a)   Briefly set out the application of a variety of core rules of evidence;

    (b)   Categorise the types of evidence normally seen at a criminal trial; and

    (c)   Set out two case studies where those rules are applied to the evidence in those cases.

The aim of any criminal lawyer is to know the rules of evidence and to apply them to each criminal case. This is best achieved by identifying the various categories of evidence which can be tendered at a criminal trial and knowing the rules of evidence applicable to each of those categories. The practical case studies included in this chapter at **10.5** are good examples of this exercise of identifying categories and applying the relevant rules. After studying them one should then be in a position to follow this methodology when furnished with disclosure in a criminal matter. It is through that exercise that a defence lawyer will be able to fully advise one's client as to whether there is a legal reason to enter a guilty or not guilty plea. It is also through that exercise that a prosecution lawyer can identify weaknesses in his or her case and seek to address missing proofs prior to trial.

10.2   Core Concepts and Issues in Criminal Evidence

10.2.1   THE BURDEN AND STANDARD OF PROOF

The burden of proof remains on the prosecution throughout the entirety of the trial. That means that the prosecution must prove the case or allegation against the accused. To what standard must the prosecution prove that allegation?

It is common knowledge that the 'standard of proof' which is relevant in a criminal trial is that of 'beyond a reasonable doubt'. The prosecution bears the legal burden of proving the guilt of the accused person to that standard. Judges often explain to juries that this standard is not a mathematical standard or formula but a standard which would allow one to make a decision about a serious issue in their lives such as moving home, getting married or changing job. While one may have a reservation about making such a decision, such reservation would not stop one from making the decision. However, if perhaps the reservation or doubt was not inconsequential or not capable of being logically addressed then one could say that the doubt was a reasonable one.

Sometimes confusion arises when the 'evidential burden of proof' shifts to the defence.

This only happens when certain defences are raised. A well-known example of this is the issue of self-defence. The lawyer for the defence must prove that the accused person was acting in self-defence. The applicable standard of proof in such circumstances is different to the one which rests on the prosecution throughout the trial. The defence must prove that the accused acted in self-defence on the civil standard of proof, i.e. 'the balance of probabilities'. Once that defence is proved to that standard then the prosecution must disprove it, i.e. the legal burden of proof remains on the prosecution, even though the evidential burden of raising a defence shifted to the defence initially.

In some cases the prosecution are aided by what are referred to as evidential presumptions. These are statutory provisions which state that something is deemed as proven until the contrary is shown to be the case. Such evidential presumptions can obviate the necessity for the prosecution to call a number of witnesses to prove something, e.g. the prosecution of drink-driving offences where a certain printout from the Intoxilyzer machine will be deemed to be proof that the proper procedures have been followed until the contrary is shown. That presumption can be rebutted by a robust cross-examination where it is shown that the correct procedures were not followed or by the defence lawyers tendering evidence to prove the absence of acceptable procedures. Such rebuttal of a statutory presumption raises issues about ensuing legal consequences. Case law has held that the rebuttal of the presumption is not fatal to the prosecution case; however, it can significantly weaken the prosecution's case, depending on what the presumption related to in the first instance.

It is important to stress that individual statutory presumptions require individual study as the manner in which a statutory presumption can be rebutted, and the consequence of such rebuttal, is determined according to the case law relevant to that particular statutory provision.

In summary, it can be stated that the prosecution bears the legal burden of proof at all times but at times the defence may bear an evidential burden of proof.

10.2.2   WHAT IS ADMISSIBLE EVIDENCE?

In a nutshell, in order for evidence to be held to be admissible it must be relevant to the guilt or innocence of the defendant. In most instances that test is clearly met. However, in some instances evidence may be relevant but may also be prejudicial to the defendant and in such circumstances the prosecution is obliged to prove that the evidence is more probative than prejudicial.

The procedure which is followed in order to make this decision is usually a *voir dire*. An example of this procedure would arise in respect of a category of evidence referred to as 'misconduct evidence'. The prosecution may argue that the prior misconduct of the defendant establishes a strikingly similar system of behaviour that is probative, whereas the defence may argue that such evidence does not show such a system and is more prejudicial than probative.

Therefore, in most *voir dire* or legal arguments before a trial judge the following process is adhered to:

(a)   Before evidence can be admitted in either instance, it must be relevant to the guilt or innocence of the defendant.

(b)   The evidence must be relevant and probative before a court can begin to regard it as admissible.

(c)   It must be more probative than prejudicial.

(d)   Even if the evidence in question is relevant, probative and not unduly prejudicial it may still not be admissible by virtue of the fact that the evidence has been obtained in breach of the defendant's constitutional rights or contrary to a statutory provision.

These are the four tiers that have to be met before the evidence can be deemed to be admissible. It is a process that can best be understood on a case by case basis.

Interestingly the legislature had not seen the need to set down a statutory version of the above-mentioned common law rules until 2009. Section 13 of the Criminal Justice (Amendment) Act 2009 amended the Criminal Justice Act 2006 by inserting a new s. 74B into that 2006 Act. It allows the court to exclude admissible evidence where the prejudicial effect outweighs probative value. It is a very general provision which since its enactment has not added much in practice as to whether evidence is deemed admissible or not, as all it does is put one strand of the common law test on a statutory footing.

10.2.3   RELEVANT SOURCES OF LAW

Although the law of evidence is mainly case law based, since 2006 there have been a number of significant pieces of legislation passed, which have had a great impact on this area of law. The nuances of how these pieces of legislation should be interpreted are dealt with in judgments considering the applicability of the statute.

While a comprehensive list of cases considering evidential interpretation in a voluminous array of case law is outside the remit of this chapter, it is fair to say that a discreet list of statutes are relevant sources to commence learning about the procedural law of evidence. The main statutes are as follows:

- The Documentary Evidence Acts 1868–1925
- The Bankers' Books Evidence Acts 1879–1959
- The Criminal Evidence Act 1898
- The Criminal Justice (Evidence) Act 1924
- The Criminal Procedure Act 1967
- The Criminal Justice Act 1984
- The Criminal Justice (Forensic Evidence) Act 1990 (as amended by the Criminal Justice Acts 2006 and 2007)
- The Criminal Evidence Act 1992
- The Children Act 2001

- The Criminal Justice Acts 2006–2013

- The Criminal Justice (Forensic Evidence and DNA Database System) Act 2014.

10.2.4 DUTY OF GARDAÍ TO SEEK AND PRESERVE EVIDENCE

The Gardaí or investigating officers of an alleged crime owe a duty to the potential accused to seek out and preserve all relevant evidence. The main issue arises where the Gardaí have sought out and preserved what they believe to be all evidence relevant to them as investigators. It is often the case that the defence will argue that evidence relevant to an ability to defend the accused person has not been sought by the Gardaí or, having been sought out by them, has not been preserved.

The case law in this area is capacious and the case most often cited at the commencement of legal argument on the preservation of evidence is *Murphy v DPP* [1989] ILRM 71. The principle therein is often referred to in the courts as the 'principle in *Braddish and Dunne*', a reference emanating from the cases of *Braddish v DPP* [2001] 3 IR 127 and *Dunne v DPP* [2002] 2 IR 25. Cases of this nature are argued annually, mainly in the form of judicial review proceedings seeking an order of prohibition on the continued prosecution of the alleged offence (see general discussion in the chapter dealing with Judicial Review at **Chapter 16** of this text). The High Court and Supreme Court have been vocal in their criticism of cases being brought before them on this issue, in circumstances where applicants have not engaged with the facts of the case, e.g. Fennelly J. in the Supreme Court criticised the practice of seeking an order of prohibition on foot of 'the absent missing bullet – which can put a stop to any trial' without full consideration of the evidence which has been sought out and preserved (see *CD v DPP* [2009] IESC 70).

However such 'missing evidence cases', as they are colloquially referred to, have been instrumental in the significant evolution of the law referable to the duties of Gardaí to seek out and preserve evidence. In *English v DPP* [2009] IEHC 27 the High Court commented on the lack of facilities in Garda stations for the storage of video recordings in stating:

> It is incomprehensible that every Garda station does not have a facility for the secure storage of this kind of evidence. It is wholly unacceptable that evidence of this kind invariably ends up in the personal locker of investigating Gardaí.

The key test which must be met before an order for prohibition is granted is that the applicant shows a real risk of an unfair trial. The risk must be real and not a remote risk. The difference in those levels of risk was illustrated in the case of *Dunne v DPP* [2009] IESC 14. Quirke J. in the High Court had granted an order of prohibition saying that there was 'a risk, however remote, of a miscarriage of justice'. The Supreme Court overturned this High Court decision, saying that the test was that there be 'a real risk' in order for prohibition to be granted.

In *O'Sullivan, Herlihy and Moore v DPP* [2007] IEHC 137, Feeney J. said:

> A court should be circumspect in exercising the power to prohibit trials and should only do so in relation to evidence which was either not sought out or not preserved, and where the applicant has discharged the onus of showing a real risk of an unfair trial or prejudice or unfairness . . . All the applicant has done here is merely invoke the possibility that exculpatory evidence at one time existed, that there was something visible on the video despite the new evidence. He must do more than that.

In relation to CCTV footage the Gardaí must seek out and preserve footage from sources that may have relevant material. In *Keogh v DPP* [2009] IEHC 502 the fact that the CCTV could have shown what had happened before the alleged offence occurred was a key factor for the High Court in granting an order of prohibition. The facts of the case centred on a laneway at the back of a pub where a number of people were gathered and where, when the Gardaí arrived, the accused was found in possession of a firearm. The issue as to who was in possession of what and at what time was directly relevant to the accused's defence. The High Court held that there was a real risk of an unfair trial. The accused's case was greatly strengthened by the fact that his solicitor had written to the Gardaí eight days after his arrest asking them to preserve all relevant footage. As an order for prohibition is exercised from the High Court's equitable jurisdiction, it is important to note that the behaviour of the accused person and the defence solicitor in meeting the case will be taken into account in determining whether an order for prohibition is granted. In instances where a defence solicitor believes that there may be a possible issue arising with regard to how the Gardaí have investigated an alleged offence, it is good practice to write to the local Superintendent as soon as possible outlining those concerns and calling on the investigating team to take action.

10.2.5   EVIDENCE OBTAINED IN BREACH OF CONSTITUTIONAL RIGHTS OR ILLEGALLY OBTAINED EVIDENCE

Some of the matters focused on from an evidential perspective in this section are dealt with in considerable detail in **Chapter 4** and **Chapter 5** of this text.

There is a difference between evidence which has been obtained in breach of the constitutional rights of an accused and illegally obtained evidence. There can be significant overlap between the two categories. The clearest way of understanding the difference between the two categories is to look at evidence obtained during the course of a detention.

In order for a detention to be legal, all statutory provisions relevant to the manner in which it is conducted, must be followed rigorously. If the time limits for the detention provisions being evoked are exceeded, or the applicable extension periods are not authorised properly, then the detention can 'fall into illegality'. This may mean that the detention can be considered legal up and until the breach occurs, which would allow evidence obtained prior to the illegality to be admitted and evidence obtained thereafter to be excluded.

In contrast a scenario can exist where the detention was at all times unconstitutional, for example when an accused is arrested on foot of a warrant which lacks any jurisdiction. Evidence flowing from that detention will in all likelihood be excluded subject to the remarks below following the recent case of *DPP v JC* [2015] IESC 31, which is discussed briefly in **Chapter 4**.

The consequences of a finding that the evidence was obtained illegally are less serious than a finding by a judge that the evidence was obtained in breach of the accused's constitutional rights. A finding of illegality can nevertheless allow a judge discretion to admit the evidence if it is the interests of justice to do so. However, a finding that the evidence was obtained unconstitutionally did, up until the judgment in *DPP v JC* [2015] IESC 31, amount to automatic exclusion under the rule in *The People (DPP) v Kenny* [1990] 2 IR 110, unless there were extraordinary excusing circumstances as allowed for under the case law of *The People (AG) v O'Brien* [1965] IR 142. Although commentary in the judgment of *JC* indicates that *Kenny de facto* overruled *O'Brien*, there was in practice an allowance for the 'extraordinary excusing circumstances' line of reasoning and in that respect *Kenny* was said to be operating in tandem with regard to that line of authority in *O'Brien*.

The 'automatic exclusion' rule has been revisited by the Supreme Court in the six separate judgments of *DPP v JC* [2015] IESC 31 (hereinafter '*JC*'). As of 2016 it is difficult to see the anticipated fallout from this judgment in the day-to-day practice in Irish criminal trials. However, it can be expected that future legal arguments relating to whether or not certain evidence should or should not be admitted will be affected by the various judgments within that case.

While it is nearly impossible to distil the ratio of those judgments within a paragraph or two, it is worth noting that Clarke J. has said 'evidence obtained unconstitutionally will be admissible if the Prosecution can show that the breach was due to inadvertence" or "subsequent legal developments"'. This test of 'inadvertence' or 'subsequent legal developments' has been criticised by various commentators. The concern is that it may be interpreted as admitting evidence obtained in breach of an accused's constitutional rights on a wholesale basis, thereby allowing the Gardaí to act with impunity when it comes to applying for search warrants or affecting an arrest. The concern of Mr Justice Hardiman and the other two dissenting judgments was that it would not provide sufficient impetus for An Garda Síochána or other investigative agencies to abide by the rule of law to the highest possible standard. They said, if a Garda could simply escape the consequences of abiding by the law (i.e. having unconstitutionally obtained evidence ruled admissible at trial) due to an inadvertent mistake then where was the stick to ensure s/he acted with due regard for a citizen's constitutional rights?

However, to balance those concerns it is worth noting that the test as set out by Clarke J. is comprehensively difficult. He is at pains to remark that inadvertence does not equal excusing negligent behaviour on the part of the Gardaí.

In addition, it is important to recognise the remarkably limiting facts of *JC* which related to evidence obtained under a search warrant pursuant to s. 29 of the Offences Against the State Act 1939 at a time when it was a valid piece of legislation, with a presumption of constitutionality attaching thereto.

Furthermore, various judgments within the case explicitly limit the findings of the case to evidence arising out of circumstances which do not affect the integrity or probative value of the evidence itself. There is little likelihood of a similar situation to *JC* arising, i.e. that Gardaí act in accordance with the law, the law subsequently changes and is applied retrospectively. In addition, as noted, the case does not impact on instances whereby the integrity or probative value of the evidence is in question, for example in instances where it is alleged that a confession has been obtained under oppression.

Nevertheless, it remains to be seen if this particular case will significantly rebalance the competing rights of the accused versus the rights of the community to have crime prosecuted to such an extent as to reset the criminal law back to the *O'Brien* era where unconstitutionally obtained evidence was admitted with less restraint. Bearing in mind the fact that the rights of the accused have been so well protected in law since 1965, it is doubtful that it will significantly tip the balance of admitting evidence in favour of the state, as much as it was feared it would do when the judgment first issued.

10.2.5.1   Access to legal advice

Another example of where the difference between illegally obtained evidence and unconstitutionally obtained evidence has developed over the years is evidence obtained where access to legal advice has either been refused or the Gardaí have proceeded to interview despite such a request. Until 6 March 2014 a detention which could be deemed to be unlawful would be one where the suspect has been refused reasonable access to a solicitor (see detailed discussion of the criminal investigation process at **Chapter 5**). Irish law has long held that there is a constitutional right of reasonable access to a solicitor (see *Lavery v Member in Charge of Carrickmacross Garda Station* [1999] 2 IR 390). The concept of reasonable access includes access while a suspect is in detention. However, up until 6 March 2014 as per the cases of *DPP v Gormley* and *DPP v White* [2014] IESC 17, this jurisdiction, unlike other common law jurisdictions, did not recognise a right to have a solicitor present while a suspect is being interviewed. In the *Lavery* case O'Flaherty J. said:

> Without any doubt, if a person in custody is denied blanket access to legal advice then that would render his detention unlawful.

However, the court said in this case that Gardaí were under no obligation to give solicitors of persons in custody 'regular updates and running accounts of the progress of their investigations'.

The cases of *DPP v Gormley* and *DPP v White* went further than that. At paragraph 9.13 Clarke J. said:

> The right to a trial in due course of law encompasses a right to early access to a lawyer after arrest and the right not to be interrogated without having had an opportunity to obtain such advice. The conviction of a person wholly or significantly on the basis of evidence obtained contrary to those constitutional entitlements represents a conviction following an unfair trial process.

The distinction is now very clear. A lack of access to a solicitor prior to interrogation will no longer be regarded as merely rendering a detention unlawful, but rather in breach of his constitutional right to a fair trial as guaranteed by Article 38.1 of Bunreacht na hÉireann. It is a very clear example of how the judicial interpretation of a constitutional article has developed over time and in light of emerging jurisprudence from the European Court of Human Rights (ECtHR) and elsewhere. The cases of *Cadder v Her Majesty's Advocate* [2010] UKSC 43 and *Salduz v Turkey* [2008] ECtHR 1542 are relevant in this latter regard. In both of those cases the suspects were denied access to legal advice while in detention. In the case of *Salduz* the ECtHR noted:

> in the present case, the applicant was undoubtedly affected by the restrictions on his access to a lawyer in that his statement to the police was used for his conviction. Neither the assistance provided subsequently by a lawyer nor the adversarial nature of the ensuing proceedings could cure the defects which had occurred during police custody.

Under the present system defence solicitors are not entitled to prescribe the manner in which interviews may be conducted nor what notes should be taken. However, if there is an issue which causes concerns for a suspect, the solicitor advising that suspect should consider asking the Garda member in charge to note those concerns in the custody record. The rules regarding behaviour of a solicitor present during a Garda interview are evolving. An Garda Síochána issued a Code of Practice on Access to a Solicitor by Persons in Garda Custody in April 2015. The Code is available on http://www.garda.ie. The Law Society of Ireland has a search facility on its website for anyone looking for a solicitor to attend a Garda station in circumstances where someone in custody requires legal representation and cannot nominate their own solicitor.

As the various agencies within the criminal justice sphere engage with this development, they may add to these Codes or Guidelines. Attention should be paid to the Department of Justice, Garda Síochána and Law Society websites as this situation develops.

10.2.5.2   Some consequences when statutory powers of detention are not properly implemented

A detention can be deemed to be illegal where there is a failure to abide by any of the mandatory statutory provisions which proscribe how a detainee must be treated. For example, it may be deemed illegal if the procedures which were followed were not followed correctly, e.g. where a Garda member authorising a detention did not hold the necessary belief, to ground a statutory power of detention, or where a detention overran its time limit, and was not properly extended by Gardaí or the court as required by law. The detention must be legal in order for any evidence, e.g. a confession or a DNA sample, to be categorised as admissible.

Evidence obtained during the course of an illegal detention may fall foul of the exclusionary rule. As noted earlier, there is a distinction as to whether an illegality or a breach of constitutional rights has occurred. The former is a much less serious breach than the latter and the tests in excluding evidence reflect that.

However, it is important to note that a detention may be severable under Irish law, in that such detention may have started out as legal and may subsequently fall into illegality. Admissions of guilt made by an accused prior to that illegality occurring may therefore be admissible at trial (see *People (DPP) v O'Brien* [2005] 2 IR 206).

In *DPP v Glen Creed* (unreported, 31 July 2009, Court of Criminal Appeal), the court found that on the facts there was no deliberate and conscious breach of the constitutional rights of the accused, and the detention of the accused was not thereafter unlawful. It found that it was a matter of discretion for the trial judge to rule as to whether any particular evidence obtained should be admitted. The court found that hair samples provided by the accused at a later stage of his detention were admissible, as they could have been procured with or without consent. The accused did not request a solicitor at this stage of the detention and it would therefore have been reasonable to assume that the accused did not require a solicitor in connection with the giving of the samples. The reasoning in this case was echoed in the case of *DPP v White* [2014] IESC 17, which distinguished between forensic samples obtained prior to a solicitor visiting the accused and that of admissions made at interview without the benefit of same.

10.2.6   EVIDENTIAL ISSUES RELATING TO FORENSIC EVIDENCE

Forensic evidence has been discussed already at **5.5**, in the context of the rights of the suspect detained in custody.

This type of evidence is usually evidence that requires examination, interpretation and determination by a scientist or expert. Therefore, quite frequently, forensic evidence also encompasses rules relating to expert evidence.

In Ireland most of the analysis of forensic evidence is done by the Forensic Science Ireland (FSI), the Garda Technical Bureau, the Office of the State Pathologist or the State Laboratory. Each of these organisations is financed by the state, although they are independent in carrying out their functions. Sometimes defence solicitors will have items of evidence analysed by other experts. It is common practice, for example in murder cases, to have the body of the deceased independently examined by way of post mortem by another pathologist.

The forensic integrity of this evidence is paramount. Consequently, all of the organisations outlined above have exacting protocols which are aimed at preventing the contamination of such evidence. It is important to ensure that the forensic evidence in each case has been properly treated at the crime scene by appropriate packaging, photography, labelling and transmission. While the courts are keen to remind juries that the television representation of forensic evidence is not accurately portrayed, there is a growing tendency to demand a high level of regard for forensic evidence. When the expert is finished with the examination of the exhibit, a statement is prepared setting out what the findings are. The exhibit is stored as prescribed by best practice and any transmission of the exhibit is logged. The movement of the exhibit both to and from the laboratory or other place must be accounted for by way of what is referred to as 'a continuous chain of custody'. Statements from each person who touched or dealt with the exhibit must be obtained, especially in drugs cases (see *Francis Whelan v Judge McMahon & DPP* ex tempore O'Neill J., 2 February 2009).

10.2.7   CRIMINAL JUSTICE (FORENSIC EVIDENCE AND DNA DATABASE SYSTEM) ACT 2014

It must be noted that with the enactment of the Criminal Justice (Forensic Evidence and DNA Database System) Act 2014 in June 2014 that the statutory schemes for the taking, retention and destruction of forensic samples have been significantly altered. This significant legislation has been commenced incrementally, with s. 107 commencing on enactment on 22 June 2014, followed by the following statutory instruments: SI No. 317 of 2014; SI No. 508 of 2015; SI 526 of 2015; SI 527 of 2015; and SI No. 528 of 2015.

At the time of writing the following sections have yet to be enacted:

- section 67(3) which provides for the Director of FSI to make arrangements with other laboratories for the generation of DNA profiles;

- section 72(2)(f) which relates to oversight provisions regarding FSI practice and procedure;

- sections 110–121 inclusive at Chapters 1, 2, and 7 of Part 12, which deal with automated searching for and automated comparison of DNA profiles and police cooperation within the context of international cooperation.

In summary, this 2014 Act amends the law as follows. It:

- authorises the taking of bodily samples from persons suspected of certain criminal offences for forensic testing;

- provides for the taking of certain bodily samples from persons who volunteer to have such samples taken from them for the purpose of the investigation of offences or incidents that may have involved the commission of offences;

- provides for the establishment and operation by Forensic Science Ireland of the Department of Justice and Equality of a DNA Database System;

- provides for the taking of certain bodily samples from persons suspected or convicted of certain criminal offences for the purpose of generating DNA profiles in respect of those persons to be entered in the investigation division of the DNA Database System;

- provides for the taking of certain bodily samples from certain persons for elimination purposes and, where appropriate, the entry of their DNA profiles in the DNA Database System;

- provides for the taking of bodily samples from persons, or samples from things, for the purpose of generating DNA profiles in respect of those persons or missing persons to be entered in the identification division of the DNA Database System;

- provides for the purposes of that System, in certain circumstances, for the destruction of samples taken under the Act and the destruction, or removal from the DNA Database System, of any DNA profiles generated from those samples;

- repeals the Criminal Justice (Forensic Evidence) Act 1990 and it's secondary legislation i.e. SI No. 130 of 1992 and SI No. 154 of 2008;

- gives effect to Council Decision 2008/615/JHA of 23 June 2008 and Council Decision 2008/616/JHA of 23 June 2008, the Agreement between the European Union and Iceland and Norway on the application of those two Council Decisions and an agreement between the state and another state insofar as those Council Decisions or agreements concern cooperation in relation to automated searching for or automated comparison of DNA data or automated searching for dactyloscopic data, as the case may be, and the exchange of such data and the reference data relating to them, by or between authorities which are responsible for the prevention, detection and investigation of criminal offences in the state and those other states or that other state, as the case may be; for that purpose to make provision for data protection and, in that regard,

- gives effect to Council Framework Decision 2009/905/JHA of 30 November 2009 on accreditation of forensic service providers carrying out laboratory activities;

- amends the criminal law relating to the taking of fingerprints and palm prints from certain persons;

- amends the Criminal Justice Act 1984 and other enactments to provide for the destruction of fingerprints, palm prints and photographs taken from or of certain persons in certain circumstances.

The creation of this statutory basis for a DNA database moves forensic evidence of this type from being just an evidential tool, as it also becomes an investigative tool. It brings changes with respect to the rights of many individuals i.e. suspects, volunteers who wish to be eliminated from enquiries, and current and former offenders. Those convicted of 'relevant offences' under legislation including that mentioned at **10.2.7.1** can have samples taken without their consent (s. 31).

The District Court may compel those who have served sentences to give samples (s. 33 and s. 34, which relates to juvenile offenders).

Taking volunteer samples and mass screenings require consent (s. 27 and s. 29, respectively. Section 35 permits the taking of samples from a deceased suspect subject to a successful application to a District Court. Those detained in custody are detained under detention provisions as outlined at **5.1.1**.

Codes of practice for the taking of samples in accordance with s. 157 of this Act have been drafted by the following: An Garda Síochána, The Garda Síochána Ombudsman, Irish Youth Justice Service, Forensic Science Ireland and the Irish Prison Service.

10.2.7.1 Impact of 2014 Act on other legislation

The 2014 Act has consequences that practitioners will need to assimilate with respect to the following legislation: Offences Against the State Act 1939; Criminal Justice Act 1984; Criminal Justice (Drug Trafficking) Act 1996; Children Act 2001; Garda Síochána (Amendment) Act 2015; International Criminal Court Act 2006; Criminal Justice Act 2007; Criminal Justice (Mutual Assistance) Act 2008; and Data Protection Act 1988.

10.2.7.2 Categories of samples, database and other provisions

The Criminal Justice (Forensic Evidence and DNA Database System) Act 2014 runs to 172 sections divided into 13 Parts with 4 Schedules. Typically, Part 1 deals with preliminary and general matters; Part 2 with taking of samples from persons in custody in a Garda Station; Part 3 with taking of samples from volunteers to generate DNA profiles; Part 4 with taking of samples from other persons or bodies for the Reference Index of DNA Database System; Part 5 with taking samples for elimination purposes; Part 6 with taking samples from persons or bodies for purposes of the Identification Division of DNA Database System; Part 7 with taking certain samples under Parts 3 and 6 from protected persons and children; Part 8 with the DNA Database System; Part 9 with the DNA Database System Oversight Committee; Part 10 with the destruction of samples and destruction or removal from DNA Database System of DNA profiles; Part 11 with provisions relating to fingerprints, palm prints and photographs; Part 12 with International Cooperation; and Part 13 with miscellaneous matters at ss. 149 to 172 inclusive.

10.2.7.3 Index categories in the DNA Database

The DNA Database has various index categories.

The Crime Scene Index will have DNA profiles found at crime scenes, which will be generated from crime scene samples. The Reference Index will have DNA profiles emanating from samples taken from persons in custody (s. 11), intimate samples taken during such custody (s. 12), non-intimate samples in such custody (s. 13), samples from offenders (s. 31), samples from child offenders (s. 32), samples from former offenders (s. 34), and samples from deceased persons suspected of having offended (s. 35).

The Elimination Indexes aim to ensure that Garda personnel, forensic scientists, state pathologists, Garda Ombudsman and Garda Commissioner have their DNA eliminated from the scene of a crime being investigated and the subsequent forensic collection and analysis of DNA materials with the aim to eliminate any contamination by any of those parties.

10.2.8   TAKING SAMPLES

The power to take samples from persons in custody of An Garda Síochána is outlined in s. 9 of the Act:

9.*(1)   Where a person is detained under any of the following provisions, a sample under section 11, an intimate sample or a non-intimate sample or more than one sample may be taken from the person:*

  (a)   section 30 of the Act of 1939;

  (b)   section 4 of the Act of 1984;

  (c)   section 2 of the Act of 1996;

  (d)   section 42 of the Criminal Justice Act 1999 ;

  (e)   section 50 of the Act of 2007;

  (f)   section 16 or 17 of the Criminal Procedure Act 2010.

  (2)   For the avoidance of doubt it is hereby declared that a reference to any statutory provision specified in a paragraph of subsection (1) under which a person may be detained shall include a reference to any other statutory provision pursuant to which a person may be arrested again and detained and which applies the first-mentioned statutory provision or another of the statutory provisions specified in subsection (1) with or without modification in relation to such detention.

10.2.8.1   Taking intimate samples

Authorisation to take an intimate sample must emanate from a Garda not below the rank of Inspector, once 'reasonable grounds' exist for suspecting that the detainee is involved in the commission of an offence and that the taking and analysis of the sample will likely confirm or eliminate such involvement. The detainee is required to sign a form of consent having been informed as follows:

• The nature of the offence of which he or she is suspected.

• The fact of authorisation of the relevant Garda member has been obtained.

• That the sample may be transmitted to others.

• That the results of forensic testing may be used in evidence during subsequent criminal proceedings.

• That the sample will be used as a DNA profile on the Reference Index of the DNA Database System, where it may be compared with other DNA profiles.

• That the sample may be compared with evidence taken from a crime scene.

• That the Garda authorisation lasts for one hour, so that if the initial sample that was taken is deemed 'insufficient', another such sample may be taken. Once the hour has expired, a new Garda authorisation may be given under s. 25.

Withdrawal of consent will be interpreted under the act as refusal to give consent. Sections 16 and 17 permit application to court to take samples from protected persons and children in circumstances where all efforts have been exhausted in endeavouring to secure the presence and consent of a parent or guardian. In the circumstances of such an application to court, the child and, if possible, the parent or guardian, should receive prior notice of that application, which must be made by a Garda member not below the rank of Inspector.

10.2.8.2   Adverse inferences

Adverse inferences may be drawn under s. 19 in circumstances where consent is withdrawn or refused. The suspect in such circumstances must have been informed of the reason of the request and the consequences of refusal. The suspect must also be informed by the Gardaí of a right to consult a solicitor and must be given an opportunity to so consult a solicitor before the occurrence of each withdrawal of consent or refusal to consent. For the prosecution to rely on this drawing of inferences provision, requests for intimate samples must be electronically recorded.

10.2.8.3   Non-intimate samples

Non-intimate samples taken from a suspect in custody under s. 13 may be used for forensic testing or the generation of a DNA profile in the Reference Index of the DNA Database System. The appropriate authorisation must emanate from a Garda not below the rank of Inspector who has 'reasonable grounds' for suspecting the suspect's involvement in the crime or or the probability that taking and analysing the sample will serve to confirm or disprove the suspect's involvement.

Reasonable force can be exerted by Gardaí in taking non-intimate samples as outlined at s. 24.

10.2.8.4   Destruction of samples taken

Destruction of intimate samples and non-intimate samples in certain circumstances is provided for in section 76:

> 76. (1) Subject to section 77 , an intimate sample or a non-intimate sample taken from a person shall, if not previously destroyed, be destroyed in any of the following circumstances not later than the expiration of the period of 3 months from the date on which such circumstances first apply to the person:
>
> (a)   where proceedings for a relevant offence—
>
>   (i)   are not instituted against the person within the period of 12 months from the date of the taking of the sample concerned, and the failure to institute such proceedings within that period is not due to the fact that he or she has absconded or cannot be found, or
>
>   (ii)   have been instituted and—
>
>   (I)   the person is acquitted of the relevant offence,
>
>   (II)   the charge against the person in respect of the relevant offence is dismissed under section 4E of the Criminal Procedure Act 1967 , or
>
>   (III)   the proceedings for the relevant offence are discontinued;
>
> (b)   the person is the subject of an order under section 1(1) of the Probation of Offenders Act 1907 in respect of the relevant offence concerned in connection with which the sample concerned was taken and he or she has not been convicted of a relevant offence during the period of 3 years from the making of the order under that Act;
>
> (c)   subject to subsection (2), the person is the subject of an order under section 1(2) of the Probation of Offenders Act 1907 in respect of the relevant offence concerned in connection with which the sample concerned was taken and he or she has not been convicted of a relevant offence during the period of 3 years from the making of the order under that Act;
>
> (d)   the person's conviction for the relevant offence concerned in connection with which the sample concerned was taken is quashed;
>
> (e)   the person's conviction for the relevant offence concerned in connection with which the sample concerned was taken is declared to be a miscarriage of justice under section 2 of the Criminal Procedure Act 1993.
>
> (2)   Subsection (1)(c) shall not apply to an order under section 1(2) of the Probation of Offenders Act 1907 discharged on the appeal of a person against conviction for the relevant offence concerned if on appeal his or her conviction is affirmed.
>
> (3)   For the purposes of this section the 'retention period', in relation to an intimate sample or a non-intimate sample, means the period from the taking of the sample concerned from a person to the latest date for the destruction of that sample under subsection (1).

Extension of retention period under section 76 for intimate samples and non-intimate samples in certain circumstances

> 77. (1) An intimate sample or a non-intimate sample taken from a person shall not be destroyed under section 76 in any case in which the Commissioner determines that circumstances outlined in that section, apply.

Destruction of intimate samples and non-intimate samples where exceptional circumstances prevail is provided for in ss. 78 and 79.

Section 78(1) states that notwithstanding ss. 76 and 77, if the Commissioner is satisfied that exceptional circumstances exist that justify the destruction of an intimate sample or a non-intimate sample, the sample concerned shall be destroyed as soon as practicable after the application of those circumstances in relation to that sample becomes known. Those exceptional circumstances are outlined in detail at s. 2(a), (b), and (c).

Section 79 deals with the destruction of certain samples taken for the purposes of the DNA Database System. The removal of certain DNA profiles in the Reference Index of DNA Database System from that system in certain circumstances is outlined at s. 80 which states:

> 80. (1) Subject to sections 81, 85 and 93, a DNA profile of a person generated from a sample taken from him or her under section 11, 12, 13, 31 or 32 and entered in the reference index of the DNA Database System shall, if not previously removed, be removed from that System in any of the following circumstances not later than the expiration of a period of 3 months from the date on which such circumstances first apply to the person:

10.2.9   PHOTOGRAPHS, FINGERPRINTS AND PALM PRINTS

Provisions relating to fingerprints, palm prints and photographs are dealt with in Part 11 of the 2014 Act. The power of Garda Síochána to take fingerprints and palm prints of persons arrested for purpose of charge are outlined as follows at s. 100:

> 100. (1) Where a person is arrested for the purpose of being charged with a relevant offence, a member of the Garda Síochána may take, or cause to be taken, the fingerprints and palm prints of the person in a Garda Síochána station before he or she is charged with the relevant offence concerned.
>
> (2) The power conferred by subsection (1) shall not be exercised unless a member of the Garda Síochána not below the rank of sergeant authorises it.
>
> (3) The provisions of subsection (1A) of section 6 and section 6A of the Act of 1984 shall apply to fingerprints and palm prints taken pursuant to this section as they apply to fingerprints and palm prints taken pursuant to the said section 6.
>
> (4) A person who obstructs or attempts to obstruct a member of the Garda Síochána acting under the power conferred by subsection (1) shall be guilty of an offence and shall be liable on summary conviction to a class A fine or imprisonment for a term not exceeding 12 months or both.
>
> (5) The power conferred by this section is without prejudice to any other power exercisable by a member of the Garda Síochána to take, or cause to be taken, the fingerprints and palm prints of a person.
>
> (6) Sections 8 to 8I of the Act of 1984 shall, with the following and any other necessary modifications, apply to fingerprints and palm prints taken from a person pursuant to this section as they apply to fingerprints and palm prints taken from a person pursuant to section 6 or 6A of that Act:
>
>   (a) references to an offence to which section 4 of the Act of 1984 applies shall be construed as references to a relevant offence;
>
>   (b) references to section 6 or 6A of the Act of 1984 shall be construed as references to this section; and
>
>   (c) references to the detention of the person under section 4 of the Act of 1984 shall be construed as references to the person being arrested for the purposes of being charged with a relevant offence under this section.

Section 101 permits the use of reasonable force and s. 6A of the Criminal Justice Act 1984 is amended by s. 102 of the 2014 Act, whereby it is a Garda Inspector (rather than a Superintendent) who authorises reasonable force and providing for that authorisation to be electronically recorded. There are other amendments in Part 11 ss. 104–108 to ss. 9 and 28 of the Criminal Justice Act 1984, s. 5 of the Criminal Justice (Drug Trafficking) Act 1996, s. 212 of the Criminal Justice Act 2006 and s. 52 of the Criminal Justice Act 2007.

The Criminal Justice Act 1984 retention of these samples provisions have not been amended and retention provisions regarding photographs are at s. 12 of the Criminal Justice Act 2006,

10.3 Witness Statements

10.3.1 ADMISSIBILITY OF CERTAIN WITNESS STATEMENTS

In criminal trials there is a common law rule which states that evidence should be given *viva voce*, i.e. orally in court. Witness statements that are taken during the criminal investigation do not form part of the evidence at trial, as they would amount to documentary hearsay without the sworn testimony of the actual witness who made that statement.

However, there has always been an issue where witnesses in criminal investigations make a statement but then later, when asked to give evidence at trial, they suddenly refuse or claim to suffer from amnesia. Consequently, a trial may collapse if the witness's evidence was crucial to the prosecution case in meeting its legal burden of proof. There was a lot of commentary in the mid-2000s that such refusal by witnesses to give evidence was due to witness intimidation. In order to circumvent the consequences of intimidation, Part 3 of the Criminal Justice Act 2006 was enacted. Section 16 of the Criminal Justice Act 2006 deals with situations where a witness 'recants' a statement, i.e. the witness 'turns hostile'. Section 16(1) sets out the circumstances in which the written statements of that hostile witness can be admitted at trial. The trial must be one where a person has been sent forward for trial on indictment in relation to an 'arrestable' offence, i.e. an offence that carries a penalty of five years or more upon conviction. The Criminal Justice Act 2006 sets out that a statement can be admitted as evidence if certain conditions are satisfied as follows:

There must be confirmation by the witness that the statement was made.

The court must be satisfied that:

- direct oral evidence of the facts in the statement would have been admissible;
- the statement was given voluntarily, is reliable and was given on oath/affirmation, or contains a statutory declaration to the effect that the witness was saying the truth at the time the statement was made.

The court when making its decision can have regard to a number of factors i.e. whether:

- the statement was video-taped;
- there is sufficient evidence of reliability;
- there is an explanation from the witness who is now recanting.

The court must then consider all the circumstances, i.e. whether:

- its omission or exclusion would be unfair to the accused; and
- it is in the interests of justice to admit the statement.

Lastly, the witness must be available for cross-examination.

Once the statement is admitted, the court can then go on to consider the evidential weight it would attach to the statement. The process thus introduced by Part 3 of the Criminal Justice Act 2006 is a huge departure from the standard rules of evidence in relation to documentary hearsay.

10.4 Categories of Evidence

In broad terms the following are the categories of evidence most commonly present in a criminal trial:

- Oral evidence which must be taken on oath or affirmation e.g.:
  - admissions/confessions;
  - eyewitness identification;
  - accomplice evidence;
  - hearsay.

- Real evidence, usually something which has a physical presence e.g.:
  - cash;
  - clothes;
  - drugs;
  - weapons;
  - CCTV;
  - photographs.
- Forensic evidence e.g.:
  - fingerprints;
  - DNA samples;
  - footprints or palm prints;
  - glass fibres;
  - paint chippings.
- Documentary evidence e.g.:
  - prior consistent statements/prior inconsistent statements;
  - Garda notebook entries;
  - mobile phone records;
  - medical reports;
  - transcripts.
- Opinion evidence:
  - experts in fields of knowledge outside the knowledge of an average juror, e.g. psychiatrists on mental health issues;
  - Garda opinions as to membership of an illegal organisation/organised crime gang.
- Circumstantial evidence:
  - individual strands of information that collectively taken together make up a rope of evidence leading to the guilt or innocence of the accused.
- Corroborative evidence:
  - any of the above which independently backs up another piece of evidence.
- Misconduct evidence, i.e. similar fact evidence:
  - evidence which relates to improper conduct of the accused or other witnesses in a previous context.

Importantly, as pointed out earlier in **Chapter 4**, all of the above categories of evidence must be obtained lawfully and without infringement of the defendant's constitutional rights. Usually, the main area of dispute at trial is whether the evidence has met both of these two criteria.

As mentioned earlier, Ireland operates a mostly exclusionary rule (see previous commentary regarding the case of *DPP v JC* [2015] IESC 31 at **10.2.5**) therefore any evidence obtained in breach of the defendant's constitutional rights is excluded from the trial unless the court holds that extraordinary circumstances should be taken into consideration. Other international jurisdictions employ a balancing test of competing interests which are the interest of the community to have matters prosecuted versus the interest of the accused person to have rights vindicated in accordance with law.

As discussed earlier, there is a difference between evidence obtained in breach of constitutional rights and that obtained unlawfully. In practice the two areas are often confused at trial. In reality the most important difference between the two (from an accused's perspective) lies in the consequence. The unconstitutionally obtained evidence is automatically excluded. The illegally obtained evidence can be admitted at the discretion of the trial judge. The case of *Kennedy v The Law Society of Ireland* [2002] 2 IR 458 discusses the differences between these two categories of evidence.

10.5   Applying the Rules of Evidence to Practical Scenarios

As outlined in the introduction to this chapter, it is necessary for the practitioner to understand the application of evidential rules, to ensure that the client can be fully advised to an acceptable standard.

In the following sections, rules of evidence are applied to two practical case studies by identifying:

- the relevant categories of evidence;
- the issues deriving from those categories.

10.5.1   CASE STUDY A

Defendant X is arrested and charged with robbery, an offence pursuant to s. 14 Criminal Justice (Theft and Fraud Offences) Act 2001. The allegation is that he used force and threats of violence to rob a pharmacy. He threatened a pharmacy assistant who was working behind the counter. Both controlled drugs and money were taken. There was no one else in the shop other than the pharmacy assistant and the pharmacist, who was in the back room. The suspect was wearing a grey striped top and navy tracksuit bottoms. He had his face partially covered with a scarf. The security manager downloaded CCTV footage from the pharmacy's hard drive onto disc the next day. He gave it to the investigating Garda. The pharmacy is on a busy street. CCTV from neighbouring shops was not recovered. Gardaí carried out enquiries the next day and were told that the CCTV was not working in one shop. They were told to call back to the other. The investigating Garda failed to call back until the following week when she was informed by the shop assistant that the CCTV re-records every 24 hours. Therefore the only CCTV footage available is the CCTV from the pharmacy itself from both internal and external cameras. The CCTV was later viewed in the Garda station and one of the Community Gardaí present recognised the suspect as the defendant—Mr X.

The defendant was detained under s. 4 of the Criminal Justice Act 1984 as amended, and during questioning made admissions about clothes he was wearing on the day and that he was in the area. He denied the direct allegation of robbery. There was no fingerprint evidence available. An eye witness across the street said he noticed a man coming out of the shop matching the description of the accused hailing a taxi. The taxi driver was tracked down and confirmed the description of the man and his dress. He recalled dropping the man to an area very close to the address of the defendant.

10.5.1.1   What are the categories of evidence in this case?

Oral evidence

Oral evidence, primarily leading to identification, includes:

- the pharmacy assistant who can provide eye-witness evidence;
- the pharmacist watching the event unfold in the back office via CCTV;
- the eye witness who saw a man fitting a description matching the defendant's clothing across the street. This is corroborative evidence;
- the taxi driver who can corroborate the previous witnesses' description of the man and who also can place him in a proximate area to the defendant's house. This is further corroborative evidence of a circumstantial nature;
- the Community Garda who identified the suspect as the defendant.

Real evidence

- the CCTV from the pharmacy.

Forensic evidence

- no fingerprints or DNA samples found, so there will not be any forensic evidence in this case.

Documentary evidence

- memorandum of interview of the accused, containing limited admissions.

10.5.1.2   What are the issues in relation to the evidence?

Oral evidence

Firstly, all witnesses who give oral evidence must be legally capable of giving evidence. Normally that means that they are over 18 and have full mental capacity. People under 18 can give evidence and there are special provisions dealing with this area (see **Chapter 9** on Juvenile Justice). The oral evidence in this case needs to be enough to establish that the person who committed the offence and Defendant X is one and the same person.

The issues arising regarding identification are:

• Is the identification evidence reliable?

• Who are the types of people making the identification?

The pharmacy assistant in this instance is very close to the person who robbed the pharmacy. That evidence is of more importance than the other eye witnesses.

However, it is important to remember that this assistant's evidence will require a mandatory warning as to the inherent dangers of identification evidence (see *The People (DPP) v Casey (No. 2)* [1963] IR 33).

The evidence of the pharmacist who witnessed the incident through the CCTV is admissible, as the CCTV acts as a modern day window. See *AG v Taylor* [1986] 1 WLR 1479 and *John Stirling v District Judge Collins & DPP* (unreported, 25 February 2010, High Court).

• How much value should attach to the evidence of the other identification witnesses?

– The witness on the street corroborating the description of the accused

– The taxi driver and his journey with a man who was similar to the description of the suspect to an area close to that of the defendant

– Again, identification warnings will be required before this evidence goes to the jury.

• What issues arise regarding the identification evidence of the Community Garda?

– In identifying Defendant X from the CCTV the question must be asked as to how does the Community Garda know the defendant?

– Will this Garda's evidence be more prejudicial than probative?

– If he works in the area and can say he knows the defendant from the community, then his evidence will be admissible (see *DPP v John Foley* [2006] IECCA 72 and *People (DPP) v Maguire* [1995] 2 IR 286).

There is no indication in the facts as outlined that there was any identification parade carried out and therefore, the general rule is that witnesses will not be allowed to identify the accused when he is standing before the court, i.e. make 'a dock identification' (see *DPP v Cooney* [1998] 1 ILRM 321; see also *People (DPP) v Lee* (unreported, 20 July 2004, Court of Criminal Appeal)). There are exceptions to that rule such as when the witnesses recognise the defendant, where the defendant refuses to take part in an identification parade or where it was not possible to hold such a parade. If there was an identification parade there are certain procedures which have to be followed before that evidence will be held to be admissible at trial (see **Chapter 4** and *The People (DPP) v Marley* [1985] ILRM 17, *DPP v O'Reilly* [1990] 2 IR 415 and *The People (DPP) v Brazil* (unreported, 22 March 2002, Court of Criminal Appeal)).

Real evidence

The general rule is that real evidence proves itself, i.e. that a watch found at the scene of a crime is proved to be a watch without the need for a horologist to give evidence to that effect. However, where and when it was found, and by whom, will be of significant relevance if the prosecution are alleging that the watch was taken in the course of a robbery.

In Case Study A there are a few examples of real evidence which will require further explanation before they become relevant and admissible pieces of evidence:

• The clothes that the defendant was wearing, which have the potential to link him to the suspect who was seen wearing certain clothes:

– Were they the same clothes that the defendant was wearing when he was arrested?

- How did the Gardaí get these clothes?

- Were these clothes that he was wearing found in his home when he was arrested?

- If so did the defendant give the clothes willingly or was there a search warrant required?

- If the defendant gave them willingly then all that is required is oral evidence to that effect.

- If they were taken on foot of a search warrant, then it will be necessary to prove that the search warrant was legally obtained and executed.

• The CCTV from the pharmacy itself is also real evidence. There is authority to state that it is admissible in and of itself. However, in the majority of criminal trials the providence of the CCTV is proved so that the jury or judge can be satisfied that it has not been tampered with.

- Therefore, the prosecution will call the security manager to outline what type of CCTV is used, how it records, whether there is any known time difference between the recording and real time, the date and time the security manager downloaded this relevant CCTV, how he downloaded it, whether it was a true and accurate recording of what was on the hard drive, to whom he gave it and in what format.

- The fact that CCTV evidence from the two surrounding shops was not sought out and preserved may possibly lead to a defence argument that the Garda's failure to seek out and preserve that possible evidence will result in a real risk that the defendant will not have a fair trial. It is possible that judicial review proceedings would be appropriate but as previously discussed, the High Court is loath to halt a trial unless the defendant can engage with the facts of each individual case and actually show a real risk of an unfair trial.

There are many cases that deal with this issue, e.g. *Braddish v DPP* [2001] 3 IR 127; *Dunne v DPP* [2002] 2 ILRM 242; *McKeown v DPP* (unreported, 9 April 2003, Supreme Court); *O'Callaghan v DPP* (unreported, 20 May 2004, High Court); *Connors v DPP* (unreported, 28 February 2006, High Court); *Scully v DPP* [2005] 1 IR 242; *Savage v DPP* [2008] IESC 39; *Kennealy v DPP* (unreported, 18 May 2010, High Court). As there is other evidence which needs to be considered in this case study, it is unlikely that an order for prohibition would result on the facts outlined.

Forensic evidence

There does not appear to be any available forensic evidence in this case. It may be helpful, if one is acting as solicitor for the accused, to point out the lack of fingerprint evidence to the jury. The point is neither positive nor negative proof of anything; however, it may be enough for the jury to have a doubt that the accused was the person who robbed the pharmacy.

Documentary evidence

The defendant was interviewed while he was detained under s. 4 of the Criminal Justice Act 1984, as amended. Therefore it will be necessary for the prosecution to prove that the detention was legal as follows:

• Call as a witness the Garda who arrested the defendant and who asked the Member in Charge of the Garda station to detain the defendant.

• The Member in Charge is required to give evidence to prove having had reasonable grounds for believing that the detention of the defendant was necessary for the proper investigation of the offence.

• The memorandum of interview of the accused should be entered into evidence. The defendant did not admit to the robbery, however, he made limited admissions.

• The prosecution must prove the memo of interview was taken legally, i.e. that it was taken in accordance with r. 12(11) of the Criminal Justice Act 1984 (Treatment of Persons in Garda Síochána Stations) Regulations, 1987.

• In addition, video recording of the interview must be produced and evidence that the detained person received a notice confirming this recording, in compliance with the Criminal Justice Act 1984 (Electronic Recording of Interviews) Regulations, 1997. Unless extraordinary circumstances are present, an interview which is not recorded will probably be held by the court as inadmissible (see *The People (DPP) v Martin Connolly* (unreported, 7 May 2002, Court of Criminal Appeal)).

- Garda notes taken at interview. The Garda must have taken handwritten notes of the questions and answers put to the defendant. In *The People (DPP) v James O'Driscoll*, Court of Criminal Appeal, ex tempore, 19 July 1999, it was held that minor omissions or breaches of the custody regulations in relation to the taking of interviews will not render a memorandum of interview inadmissible. The test is whether the interview was conducted fairly or whether the breach was a material breach.

- The prosecution must prove that the interview was conducted fairly and in the absence of any coercion.

- They must also prove that the memo was read over to the defendant and that he was asked to sign it, and that the tapes recording the interview were sealed and stored correctly prior to trial (see *The People (DPP) v Michael Murphy* [2005] 4 IR 504).

The fact that the defendant signed the memo of interview is relevant as it means that it can be shown to the jury. In *The People (DPP) v POC* (unreported, 7 March 2003, Court of Criminal Appeal) it was held that unsigned memos should not be shown to the jury as exhibits.

If the defence allege that a breach of the regulations in relation to how the memo was taken occurred:

The Court must assess whether the breach is either significant or material or insignificant or immaterial. If it is the latter, then non-compliance with the regulations per se will not render the custody unlawful or the statement inadmissible (see *The People (DPP) v Philip Murphy* (unreported, 12 July 2001, Court of Criminal Appeal) and *DPP v Spratt* [1995] 1 IR 585).

It is also relevant for the court to ask whether the defendant has suffered prejudice as a result of the breach, in determining whether the breach is significant (see *DPP v John Diver* (unreported, 29 July 2005, Supreme Court) and *Kevin McCormack v Judge of the Circuit Court & DPP* (unreported, 17 April 2007, High Court).

10.5.2   CASE STUDY B

Defendant B is arrested after a search of his house.

Gardaí have obtained a warrant based on evidence, described as a 'sworn information', in the District Court based on confidential information. The house is empty when the Gardaí arrive. The front door is broken down and the search commenced. Cannabis resin is found in the defendant's bedroom together with weighing scales and what is commonly referred to as 'a tick list'. Three mobile phones are also found in the house.

The defendant's mother returns mid-search. The search warrant is shown to her. She phones her son asking him to return to the house. He returns and is arrested. The exhibits are numbered, bagged and returned to the Garda station by the investigating Garda. The defendant is escorted to the station and the custody record process is commenced.

He is detained under s. 2 of the Criminal Justice (Drug Trafficking) Act 1996 as amended for an initial period of six hours. He is questioned and his detention is extended for a further 18 hours as authorised by a Superintendent. He is further questioned but states that he does not wish to say anything for fear that he will be shot by some of his acquaintances. His fingerprints are taken as well as a buccal or saliva swab for DNA purposes. He is released at the end of the second period of detention and a file is sent to the DPP for directions as to the prosecution of the alleged offender. The drugs and other paraphernalia seized on foot of the search warrant are analysed by the Forensic Science Laboratory and it is confirmed that the drugs found in the course of that search are cannabis. There is a trace of cannabis found on the weighing scales and the detainee's fingerprints are found on the outside of the plastic bag that the cannabis was wrapped in. In addition, the mobile phones that were seized have all been examined and the text messages and phone calls on one phone in particular are indicative of drug dealing.

10.5.2.1   What are the categories of the evidence?

Oral evidence

- the defendant has not made any admissions;
- the Gardaí who conducted the search will give oral evidence about what they found.

Real evidence

- the drugs;
- tick list;
- weighing scales;
- mobile phones.

Forensic evidence

- the fingerprint on the plastic bag;
- documentary evidence;
- the sworn information and search warrant;
- the written Garda authorisation to extend the detention;
- phone records.

Opinion evidence

- the evidence from the fingerprint expert.

Oral evidence

The defendant made no admissions while he was in Garda custody. Therefore, on that point in isolation there is no need for the prosecution to call evidence to prove the detention was legal.

Real evidence

The drugs have a physical presence and are, therefore, real evidence. The chain of continuity of custody of the drugs needs to be proved by the prosecution (see *DPP v Francis Whelan* (unreported, 2 February 2009, High Court). It will be necessary to adduce the following evidence:

- Who discovered the drugs?
- To whom were the drugs passed?
- How were the drugs labelled?
- How were the drugs stored?
- Who delivered them to the Forensic Science Laboratory?
- Does the description of the drugs found at the scene match the description of the drugs analysed at the laboratory?
- How were the drugs handed back to the Gardaí before trial?
- The fact that the drugs are actually controlled drugs must be proven by way of handing in the relevant regulations to the court of trial (see *DPP v Daniel Cleary* [2005] 2 IR 189; *Wayne Lynch v District Judge Fitzpatrick* (unreported, 31 January 2007, High Court) and also s. 4 of the Documentary Evidence Act 1925).
- It must also be proved that the defendant was in possession of the drugs. The concept of what constitutes possession is discussed in many cases e.g. *People (DPP) v Michael Tanner* (unreported, 30 November 2006, Court of Criminal Appeal). In this case the fact that they were found in his bedroom is indicative of possession. There is also the tick list and weighing scales, which are real evidence and are corroborative of drug dealing.

Forensic evidence

A fingerprint was found on the plastic bag. It is therefore necessary to prove the detention as the fingerprints were taken during the course of detention (see *The People (DPP) v Pringle* (1981) 2 Frewen 57 and *The People (DPP) v Raymond Casey & another* (unreported, 14 December 2004, Court of Criminal Appeal).

- How were the fingerprints taken?

- Were they taken pursuant to a statutory authority or did the defendant consent to his finger-prints being taken?

  - If it is the former, then the prosecution must prove that the correct statutory formalities were followed, in order for the fingerprints to be held admissible at trial.

  - The statutory written authorisation must be tendered as an exhibit.

The Inspector or other Garda member who gave permission for the prints to be taken must be called to give that evidence. The Garda who lifted the print from the plastic bag will be required to give evidence.

- It will be required that he give evidence as to how the print was taken, from where and how the print lift card was stored.

- The fingerprint expert who matched the two fingerprints will be required to give evidence outlining the typical 12 characteristics which link the two fingerprints.

Usually the Garda practice is to put forward at least 12 identical points of similarity but there is no rule in law for this (see *R v Buisson* [1990] 2 NZLR 542).

The oral evidence in relation to the fingerprint can also be classified as opinion evidence, which is discussed later.

Documentary evidence

There are a number of documentary exhibits in this case.

- Firstly, there is the sworn information grounding the search warrant. The sworn informa-tion is an application to a court or Peace Commissioner for a search warrant. This applica-tion can be set out in writing and sworn orally to either of these two bodies. In most Misuse of Drugs prosecutions the application will be made in writing, and then sworn orally before either the Judge or the Peace Commissioner. In this case it will be necessary to call the Garda who swore the evidence, in order to get the search warrant to give evidence to that effect.

- There are a number of potential issues which should be looked at when examining whether the search warrant was legally obtained.

  - The defence may question the basis for the sworn information and its sufficiency. If the information grounding the sworn information is confidential information received from a Garda informant, then the potential to question that information is very limited as it is covered by informer privilege (see *AG v Briant* [1846] 15 MW 169; *Marks v Beyfus* [1890] 25 QBD 494; *DPP v Sweeney* [1996] 2 IR 313).

The issue of process regarding informants is discussed at http://www.garda.ie (see information on the Garda Covert Human Intelligence System (CHIS)). (See also *The Right to a Fair Trial v The Claim of Privilege* [2007] 17(1) ICLJ 17).

- In order to admit the search warrant into evidence, it must be shown to be sufficient and proper. In instances not covered by informer privilege, the Garda who swore the information may be asked to outline the reasonable suspicion which grounded the application (see *DPP v Philip O'Driscoll* (unreported, 1 July 2010, Supreme Court)—quoting *R v Silva* [2006] 4 All ER 900 stating that a very low threshold is all that is required, below that of a *prima facie* case). (See also *DPP v Tallant, ex tempore*, Court of Criminal Appeal [2003] 4 IR 343.)

- The next question to ask is who issued the warrant—was it a Judge, a Peace Commissioner or a Garda Superintendent?

  - If it was a Superintendent who issued the warrant, was the opinion that of the Superin-tendent or another Garda? In *DPP v Sweeney* [1996] 2 IR 313 it was held that it must be the Superintendent's opinion.

  - If a Peace Commissioner issued the warrant, it must have been on oath, and the Peace Commissioner must be personally satisfied about the information (see *DPP v Yamanoha* [1994] 1 IR 565).

- The legislation under which the search warrant was issued must be examined.

- What exactly does the search warrant allow the Gardaí to do or seize?

- Each piece of legislation which allows for a search warrant is different and empowers the Gardaí or other state agents to do specific things for a specific duration. Search warrants vary from Act to Act. There are many similar provisions and similar considerations regarding all search warrants, but it is important to stress that they are not universal in terms. Obviously one of the main reasons why the legislature insists on search warrants is to avoid the occurrence of a dwelling place being improperly violated.

- There is a constitutional protection afforded by Art. 40.5 of the Constitution (see *Simple Imports Ltd v The Revenue Commissioners* [2000] 2 IR 243). It was held in *DPP v Lynch* [2009] IECCA 31 that a squatter can enjoy this constitutional protection. That decision was based on the Irish language version of Art. 40.5 'ionad cónaithe' or living place, rather than the English language version of Art. 40.5 which refers to 'dwelling'. The Court of Criminal Appeal held that the question as to whether a particular place was someone's dwelling was a question of fact in each individual case. A crucial fact in the determination in this case was that the Gardaí had sought the search warrant for this address, in the belief that the accused was actually living there.

- It must be established whether there was a specific Garda named on the search warrant, as the Garda who was responsible for conducting the search. One must then satisfy oneself that the named Garda actually conducted the search (see *DPP v Ian Horgan* (unreported, 27 July 2009, Court of Criminal Appeal)).

- It is important to ascertain if the warrant contains any errors. This issue has been considered in many cases, e.g. *The People (AG) v O'Brien* [1965] IR 142; *The People (DPP) v Kenny* [1990] 2 IR 110; *The People (DPP) v Balfe*, Court of Criminal Appeal [1998] 4 IR 50; *DPP v Edgeworth* [2001] 2 IR 131.

- Most recently, as at the time of writing, errors on search warrants have been extensively considered in the judgment of *DPP v Gareth Mallon*, Court of Criminal Appeal, 3 March 2011. The sufficiency or otherwise of a search warrant is a matter for the trial court to decide upon. See *Fergal McNulty v DPP & His Honour Judge White* (unreported, 18 February 2009, Supreme Court).

The written authorisation which allowed the Gardaí in Case Study B to hold the defendant in custody after the initial six-hour period, is also a piece of documentary evidence which must be admitted at trial.

- In relation to this piece of evidence, the prosecution must prove that the Superintendent had reasonable grounds for believing that the continued extension of detention was necessary for the investigation of the offence, and that the investigation was being carried out expeditiously.

- The written extension of detention authorisation will be tendered as a prosecution documentary exhibit.

- There will also be a written Certificate of Analysis from the Forensic Science Laboratory, which will be tendered into evidence by the prosecution.

Section 10 of the Misuse of Drugs Act 1984 sets out a rebuttable presumption that the facts on the certificate are evidence of any fact contained therein until otherwise proven.

- Another category of documentary evidence is the phone records that will raise the following questions in establishing their evidential value:

  - Who downloaded the data?

  - How did s/he do that?

  - Is s/he an expert in such downloading software?

  - Is the phone from which the data was downloaded still available for independent examination?

Usually the phone records are tendered by way of s. 6 of the Criminal Evidence Act 1992. That provision allows the production of business records that have been generated in the ordinary course of business, to be tendered in evidence by way of certificate. This process obviates the need for the people who took part in compiling the information in question to give evidence. It is generally used in instances where documents have been generated automatically by computer, or where the author of the document is unidentifiable. Specific evidential rules apply when attempting to adduce telephone evidence and these rules were discussed thoroughly in the case of *DPP v Joseph O'Reilly*, Court of Criminal Appeal, 6 March 2009. It is a very technical and specialised area which requires close study.

Opinion evidence

The general rule is that witnesses are not allowed to give evidence in relation to their opinion, only evidence in relation to fact. However, there are exceptions to that rule. Where it is necessary to call an expert witness to give evidence such witnesses are allowed to give an opinion.

In Case Study B the fingerprint expert must be established as an expert through evidence (see *AG (Ruddy) v Kenny* (1960) 94 ILTR 185).

The onus of proving this witness as an expert is on the party who is calling that witness so, the prosecution in this instance will have to establish the expert witnesses' professional qualifications by asking a number of questions:

• How long did this witness study and in what institution?

• How much experience has this witness in this field?

• Has the witness ever known two fingerprints to be the same?

• What are the techniques for establishing a fingerprint match?

While experts can give evidence in relation to an opinion, they can never give evidence as to what is called the ultimate issue, i.e. whether the expert thinks the defendant is guilty or innocent. The court will also determine what weight is to be attached to this evidence.

As fingerprint study is an established field, evidence of this nature is usually treated with a high degree of reliability. The same may not be said for other emerging areas of expertise. The weight to be given to expert evidence is determined on a case-by-case basis, having regard to who the expert is and what is the focus of the testimony. The duty of the expert is to furnish the court with the necessary criteria, scientific or otherwise, in order to test the accuracy of the conclusions or opinions proffered.

The judge or jury is under no obligation to agree with the expert's conclusions (see *The People (AG) v Fennell (No. 1)* [1940] IR 445). Where the judge or jury is capable of forming an opinion without the aid of expert evidence, then that type of evidence will not be admissible.

10.6   Conclusion

As mentioned in the introduction to this chapter, it is not intended to replace the excellent academic texts in this area of law. The point of the chapter is to ensure that one can break down the evidence, as mentioned in disclosure, into some form of category. One may then be aware that different types of evidence have different issues attaching to them. Conversely, different types of evidence may have the same issue in common, e.g. the identification of the suspect in Case Study A is one which presents in eye-witness oral evidence and in the CCTV evidence. What is paramount to note is that one applies the appropriate principles of evidence to the categories of evidence available in each trial.

10.7   Further Reading

R. Cannon and N. Neligan, *Evidence* (Round Hall, Sweet and Maxwell, 2002)

C. Fennell, *The Law of Evidence in Ireland* (2nd edn., Lexis, Butterworths, 2003)

J. Healy, *Irish Laws of Evidence* (Thompson, Round Hall, 2004)

D. McGrath, *Evidence* (2nd edn., Thompson, Round Hall, 2015)

D. Walsh, *Criminal Procedure* (Thompson, Round Hall, 2002)

CHAPTER 11

CONDUCT OF SUMMARY TRIALS

11.1   Introduction

Some of the concepts discussed in this chapter have been referred to in the context of Process and Procedure in the Commencement of Crime at **Chapter 6** (**6.7** and **6.8**) and are discussed in greater depth in **Chapter 12** (**12.4.1.1**, **12.2**, and **12.3**). Nevertheless, it would not be possible to discuss the summary trial structure of the District Court without setting some context around the various types of offences that are disposed of in the District Court jurisdiction and the instruments used in the prosecution of those offences.

Article 38.2 of the Constitution of Ireland provides that minor offences may be tried by courts of summary jurisdiction. This relates to the District Court. Article 34.3.4 provides that courts shall include courts of local and limited jurisdiction whose right of appeal is determined by law. The Courts of Justice Act 1924 established District, Circuit, High, and Supreme Courts in this jurisdiction. Part 3 of the Courts of Justice Act 1924 set up the District Court. This provided for the appointment of judges in assigned District Court areas. This Act was later repealed by the Courts (Establishment and Constitution) Act 1961, but the basic framework remains intact. The current District Court in Ireland is made up of a president and 63 judges. Ireland is divided into 25 districts and the Dublin Metropolitan District.

With the exception of charges that are commenced by way of prosecution in the Special Criminal Court, all criminal proceedings commence in the District Court. The location of the venue will depend on where the offence was committed, or where the accused resides or was arrested.

In cases where the Director of Public Prosecutions (DPP) has directed trial on indictment or where an accused person has elected for trial on indictment, the District Court's function is to oversee that the legislative framework is followed in respect of the service of a document commonly referred to as the book of evidence (see s. 4 of the Criminal Procedure Act 1967 as amended). The book of evidence procedure is further discussed at **13.4**. Upon service of the book of evidence, the District Court sends the accused forward for trial to either the Circuit, Central or Special Criminal Court.

11.2   Summary Proceedings

Three types of offences may be dealt with by the District Court:

1. Summary-only offences

2. 'Hybrid' offences

3. Indictable offences that can be tried summarily

Offences that are 'indictable only', e.g. murder and rape, are commenced in the District Court but the jurisdiction for dealing with such matters passes to the Central Criminal Court once the accused has been sent forward for trial. That disposal on indictment process is discussed in detail in **Chapter 13**. Once the District Court sends such cases forward to the indictable courts, it becomes *functus officio* unless circumstances arise whereby clerical inadvertent errors or omissions occurring in the Return for Trial Order need to be fixed using what is known as 'the slip rule' (see Order 12 Rule 16 of the latest District Court Rules). In *DPP v Reilly and Moorehouse* [2008] IEHC 419, the order actually made was not reflected on the Order printed up. In *Doran v Reilly* [2011] 1 IR 544, the charge sheet was not attached in error. If errors are more fundamental they can be litigated as outlined later at **Chapter 16**.

11.2.1   SUMMARY-ONLY OFFENCES

For offences created by statute, where the penalty provided for relates to summary conviction only, such cases can only be dealt with in the District Court. Common examples of these summary-only matters are as follows:

- Road traffic offences such as driving without a licence or insurance
- Certain public order offences such as engaging in threatening, abusive or insulting behaviour in a public place (contrary to s. 6 of the Criminal Justice (Public Order) Act 1994), or intoxication in a public place (contrary to s. 4 of that Act)
- A minor assault contrary to s. 2 of the Non-Fatal Offences Against the Person Act 1997

The exception to summary-only offences being dealt with in the District Court arises in circumstances where indictable matters are sent forward for trial and one or more summary-only matters arising from the same set of facts are later 'added to the indictment' pursuant to s. 6 of the Criminal Justice Act 1951. Once this occurs, the summary-only matters are then struck out in the District Court because a higher court will be dealing with them. For this to occur, there must be evidence substantiating the summary-only charge(s) contained within the book of evidence (see *MS v DPP, Ireland and the Attorney General*, judgment delivered by the Court of Appeal on 22 December 2015).

11.2.2   'HYBRID' OFFENCES

Statutory provisions that provide for a penalty on summary disposal and also on indictment are known as 'hybrid' offences. They may be dealt with in either the District Court, providing certain conditions are met, or else in a higher court. The distinguishing factor for hybrid offences is that in such cases, an accused has no right of election, i.e. s/he cannot elect for trial by jury. Common examples of hybrid offences are as follows:

- Criminal damage contrary to s. 2 of the Criminal Damage Act 1991
- Assault contrary to s. 3 of the Non-Fatal Offences Against the Person Act 1997

11.2.3   INDICTABLE OFFENCES THAT CAN BE TRIED SUMMARILY

These are distinguishable from 'hybrid' offences because the accused has a 'right of election', i.e. s/he can 'elect' to have the case disposed of in the District Court or 'on indictment' in the Superior Courts. The First Schedule of the Criminal Justice Act 1951, sets out a range of offences in this category (known as 'scheduled offences'), as does s. 53 of the Criminal Justice (Theft and Fraud Offences) Act 2001. Common examples of this category of offences are as follows:

- Violent disorder (formerly referred to as the offence of riot) contrary to s. 15 of the Criminal Justice (Public Order) Act 1994
- Theft contrary to s. 4 of the Criminal Justice (Theft and Fraud Offences) Act 2001
- Sexual assault contrary to s. 2(2) of the Criminal Law (Rape) (Amendment) Act 1990

11.2.4   PRACTICAL CONSIDERATIONS

Directions from the DPP with respect to the appropriate venue for the disposal of certain cases (DPP directions) are always required for indictable matters and are discussed in detail in **Chapter 12**. In most cases, by the time the proceedings have arrived at the first court date, the prosecuting Garda will either have submitted a file to the DPP or be in the process of doing so. A case may be adjourned for a number of weeks or months for the DPP's directions to issue. If directions are not forthcoming because of a delay, there is a risk the case will be struck out for want of prosecution. Historically, all matters requiring the DPP's directions needed to be considered by that office. However, as outlined in **Chapter 6** at **6.2**, s. 8 of the Garda Síochána Act 2005 allows the DPP to issue a general consent to prosecute in respect of offences like theft of property under a certain value, and drug offences up to a certain value. The latest version of this general consent is available on the DPP's website, http://www.dppireland.ie/filestore/documents/General_Direction_No._3.pdf.

If the DPP directs that a matter be dealt with on indictment, then the charge(s) will be returned for trial in a higher court. If the DPP directs summary disposal, then the District Court Judge will hear an outline of the facts of the case from either the prosecuting Garda or the Court Presenter, who will be a sergeant who presents the case on behalf of the prosecuting Garda. This is known as 'considering jurisdiction'. As only minor offences can be tried by courts of summary jurisdiction under Art. 38(2) of the Constitution, the judge, having heard an outline of the facts, may refuse jurisdiction if s/he deems the matter not to be a minor offence. When that occurs, the case is then adjourned for the service of a book of evidence and trial on indictment. Before any case can be sent forward for trial, the consent of the DPP is required as per s. 4A(2) of the Criminal Procedure Act 1967 (as inserted by s. 9 of the Criminal Justice Act 1999).

Finally, it is also possible that there can be summary disposal of an indictable offence where the DPP specifically directs 'summary disposal on a plea of guilty' by way of s. 13(2)(a) of the Criminal Procedure Act 1967. Before such a case can be dealt with in the District Court, the accused must plead guilty and the judge must accept that it is a minor offence (commonly referred to as 'accepting jurisdiction'). If the accused pleads not guilty following such a direction from the DPP, then there would be no need for the District Court Judge to consider jurisdiction because the case could then only be dealt with in a higher court.

11.3   Commencement of Summary Proceedings

As a general rule, all summary-only proceedings must be commenced within six months from the date of the alleged offence, otherwise they will be statute barred as per s. 10(4) of the Petty Sessions (Ireland) Act 1851. This does not apply to indictable matters being dealt with summarily. In that regard, s. 177 of the Criminal Justice Act 2006 specifically provides that there is no time limit in respect of commencing indictable matters summarily. The six-month limit also does not apply in cases where an alternative time limit is provided for in legislation. For example, s. 104 of the Garda Síochána Act 2005 provides that the DPP can prosecute offences following an investigation by An Garda Síochána Ombudsman Commission within 12 months from the date of the offence.

If a case is statute-barred, there is nothing that the prosecution can do to rectify that situation so this should always be checked.

11.3.1   PROSECUTION BY WAY OF CHARGE SHEET

When proceedings are commenced by way of charge sheet, following arrest, an accused would be charged and bailed to appear within a period of 30 days to the local District Court (see s. 31 Criminal Procedure Act 1967 as amended and discussion about remands in **Chapter 8**). On that date, evidence is given of arrest, charge, and caution. This can be done in one of two ways:

1. by the Garda personally who would appear in court and give evidence in relation of arrest, charge and caution, or

2. by way of certificate under s. 6 of the Criminal Justice (Miscellaneous Provisions) Act 1997, which provides that evidence of arrest, charge and caution can be given by way of a certificate.

This certificate is presented to the District Judge usually by a Court Presenter who will also be a Garda Sergeant. Evidence of arrest, charge, and caution constitutes the making of the complaint and it is only at this point that jurisdiction is conferred on the District Court and the clock stops in terms of the six-month time limit. A copy of the charge sheet must be given to the accused 'as soon as may be' (Order 17, Rule 1(2) of the District Court Rules) and must be lodged with the appropriate District Court Clerk as soon as possible (Order 17, Rule 1(3) of the DCR). Following evidence of arrest, charge and caution, if the case is indictable, then it may be remanded for DPP directions if those directions are not already available. If the case is being dealt with summarily, the solicitor for the accused may seek a 'Gary Doyle Order' and there may be a remand pending the disclosure of relevant materials. Once this has been complied with, the accused would be expected to indicate on the next date whether s/he is pleading guilty or not guilty.

In the event of the accused pleading guilty, a short outline of the evidence along with details of any previous convictions is given to the District Judge by either the arresting Garda or the Court Presenter. After a plea in mitigation has been offered by the defence, the Judge may impose a penalty immediately or else remand the case for the purposes of a report (such as a probation report, a community service report, or a restorative justice report), or for issues like compensation to be addressed. In the event that the accused pleads not guilty, the case will be remanded to a hearing date.

11.3.2   PROSECUTION BY WAY OF SUMMONS

Summonses may issue under the Courts (No. 3) Act 1986 or under the Petty Sessions (Ireland) Act 1851. The main difference is that in the former circumstance, a Garda applies to the appropriate District Court office for a summons to be issued in what may be described as an administrative act, whereas for the latter, the Garda is required to swear an Information and go before a District Judge who will issue the summons in what may be described as a judicial act. It is noteworthy that when a Garda applies for a summons under the 1986 Act, a complaint is deemed to have been made on the date of doing so, and therefore, that is the relevant date applicable to the six-month time limit.

On the date that an accused has been summoned to appear in court ('the return date'), if the matter is a minor summary matter, e.g. a speeding summons, it might be dealt with without the accused being legally represented. More serious cases will be dealt with in the same way as outlined at **11.3.1** regarding the charge sheet procedure.

Once an accused makes an appearance in court, it is not particularly significant whether s/he was brought there by way of the charge sheet or the summons procedure. In the case of *DPP v Gill* [1980] 1 IR 263, Henchy J. stated that it is the complaint that gives jurisdiction and the summons is merely the process to compel attendance. He compared it to a vehicle which is 'left at the door of the court and is no longer required' once the accused appears in court.

Herbert J. stated in the case of *Stephen Heaney v Judge Brady and the DPP* (High Court decision from 3 November 2009) that:

> the charge sheet procedure, the summons procedure under the Act of 1851, and the summons procedure under the Act of 1986, are simply alternative methods of procuring the attendance of an accused person before the court.

This sentiment was endorsed by Keane J. in the Supreme Court case of *DPP v Angela Murphy* ([1999] 1 IR 98—Supreme Court judgment of 29 July 1998) where he stated that:

> So far as the exercise of the court's substantive jurisdiction is concerned, it is perfectly immaterial in what way his attendance is secured, so long as he is present before the district justice in court at the material time. Even if he is brought there by an illegal process, the court's jurisdiction is nonetheless effective.

11.4   The 'Gary Doyle Order'

The seminal case on District Court disclosure is the Supreme Court decision in *DPP v Gary Doyle* ([1994] 2 IR 286), which will be referred in various discussions in this text.

The *Doyle* case posed a question: 'Where an indictable charge is being disposed of by way of summary trial in the District Court, is there a general obligation on the prosecution to furnish on request, the statements of the proposed prosecution witnesses? The answer to that question was that there is no general obligation to furnish statements, but *in any such instance the District Court may direct, having regard to the interest of justice, as set out in this judgment, the furnishing of such statements'* (emphasis added). It follows that the test to be applied is whether disclosure is warranted in the interests of justice on the facts of the particular case.

The Supreme Court set out the following criteria to be considered when deciding whether to grant disclosure in a District Court context:

(a)   the seriousness of the charge

(b)   the importance of the statements or documents

(c)   the fact that the accused has been adequately informed of the nature and substance of the accusation

(d)   the likelihood that there is no risk of injustice in failing to furnish the statements or documents to the accused

This disclosure order has become known as a *'Gary Doyle* Order' and it entitles the defence to copies of all relevant materials such as a précis of evidence prepared by the arresting Garda, witness statements, memos of interview with the accused, sworn Information, search warrants, CCTV evidence, etc.

While the *Gary Doyle* decision related to indictable offences being dealt with summarily, the principles apply to all cases before the District Court. In practice, there will rarely be any requirement to persuade a court of the criteria set out in Denham J.'s judgment as most judges accept the general principle that an accused is entitled to know the case against him or her.

11.4.1   THE IMPACT OF *DOYLE*

The decision in *Doyle* and the subsequent elaborations on it have led to greater efficiency in the processing of criminal cases. The disclosure of prosecution evidence to the defence ensures greater transparency with regard to the case that the accused is facing, and as a result, more informed advice can be given to the accused. The impact of this information sharing is most obvious in cases where the disclosure reveals that the best course of action for the accused is to plead guilty, without the necessity of court time being taken up by a hearing.

It has also been argued that the application of *Doyle* minimises the danger of miscarriages of justice in the summary court system. By promoting full disclosure of all relevant material, it reduces the possibility of intentional or accidental suppression of evidence by a prosecutor.

11.5   The District Court Rules

As noted by Walsh (*Criminal Procedure* (Thompson, Round Hall, 2002), p. 637), 'In matters of pleading, practice and procedure generally, the jurisdiction of the District Court must be exercised in the manner provided by rules of court made under section 91 of the Courts of Justice Act 1924.' There is a District Court Rules Committee authorised to make and amend these rules with the consent of the Minister for Justice. Order 12, Rule 15 of the District Court Rules states that:

> Non-compliance with these Rules does not render any criminal proceedings void, but in case of non-compliance, the Court may direct that the proceedings be treated as void, or that they be set aside in part as irregular, or that they be amended or otherwise dealt with in such manner and on such terms consistent with statute as the Court thinks fit.

11.6   Signed Pleas

As will be elaborated in **Chapter 12**, s. 13(2)(b) of the Criminal Procedure Act 1967 provides that an accused can be sent forward from the District Court for trial in an indictable court on a signed plea of guilty in relation to certain indictable offences provided that the DPP consents to the order being made. If an accused wishes to be 'sent forward on signed pleas', the prosecution will draft the relevant papers (the plea of guilty form and the draft return for trial order itself) which the accused will then sign, usually on the next District Court remand date. An accused cannot plead guilty in the District Court to the following offences:

• Murder

• Attempted murder

• Conspiracy to murder

• Crimes against humanity and war crimes

• Treason

• Piracy

• Genocide

11.7   Conduct of a Criminal Hearing in the District Court

The conduct of a hearing in the District Court is identical in respect of summary offences and indictable offences that are dealt with summarily. The prosecution open the case, directly examine their witnesses that are then cross-examined by the defence, all adhering to the rules of evidence as outlined in **Chapter 10** and using the solicitor advocate skills profiled in **Chapter 19**.

11.7.1   FAILURE TO APPEAR IN COURT

When a prosecutor fails to appear on the set hearing date, the court may strike out the case, dismiss the case without prejudice or adjourn the matter (see Order 23, Rule 5 of the District Court Rules).

When an essential prosecution witness fails to appear on the set hearing date, the prosecution will either:

(a)   Seek an adjournment which may not be granted given that District Court Practice Directive DCO3 states that: 'No adjournment or remand will be granted where a case has been fixed for hearing. In exceptional circumstances only, application for adjournment or remand may be made to the Court at least 7 days prior to the hearing date on 48 hours' notice to the other party'

(b)   Apply for a bench warrant for their own witness

(c)   Apply to withdraw the charge in circumstances where, for example, an essential witness has permanently left the jurisdiction or an injured party does not wish to proceed with the case.

When both sides fail to appear, the District Judge may strike out the charge as per Order 38, Rule 1(4) of the District Court Rules. When an accused is in custody and is not produced before the court, s. 37 of the Criminal Procedure Act 2010 (as amended by ss. 4, 4B, and 24(5) of the Criminal Procedure Act 1967) provides that the court can further remand that accused in custody provided that there is a good and sufficient reason for doing so. It is a matter for the judge to determine what constitutes a good and sufficient reason.

In general, when an accused fails to appear, the District Judge can either (a) adjourn the case if there are good grounds for doing so; (b) issue a bench warrant for the arrest of that person; or (c) if an accused person is not present on a hearing date, the District Judge can proceed in his or her absence provided that they are satisfied that the accused person has been served with the summons(es). See Order 23, Rule 4 of the latest District Court Rules.

In the case of *Lawlor v Hogan* [1993] ILRM 606, Murphy J. held that while an accused person has a constitutional right to be present, if a judge is satisfied that the accused has consciously decided to absent himself or herself from the proceedings, the judge has the discretion on whether or not to continue with the trial. However, in *Brennan v Windle* [2003] 3 IR 494, the Supreme Court stated that where the sentencing judge has in mind to impose a prison sentence of some length, the failure to ascertain whether the accused has a *bona fide* reason for non-attendance and the failure to hear the accused prior to imposing a sentence constitutes a breach of fair procedures and constitutional justice. In that case, a four-month sentence was imposed on an accused for driving without insurance in circumstances where the accused had not received the summons.

More recently, in the case of *Jason O'Brien v District Judge Coughlan and the DPP* ([2011] IEHC 330 (High Court, Kearns P., 29 July 2011 and Supreme Court judgment of Charleton J. delivered on 11 February 2016)), President Kearns in the High Court held that a District Judge was entitled to proceed to convict the applicant of a traffic offence in his absence, but he should have adjourned the matter prior to the imposition of a sentence of five months' imprisonment. The Supreme Court upheld this judgment on appeal and endorsed the *Brennan* decision.

Finally, in *Quilligan v Kilrane and Anor* ([2014] IEHC 116, 10 March 2014, High Court), the High Court held that where a District Judge intends to impose a custodial sentence that is more than short-term (five months in this case), then the court should ascertain whether there is a *bona fide* reason for non-attendance, or make some effort to secure the attendance of the accused and hear from him or her before imposing sentence.

11.7.2 INITIAL APPLICATIONS

The defence may make a preliminary application to have a case dismissed prior to a hearing commencing. Examples prompting this type of initial submission are as follows:

- Proceedings are statute-barred
- Prosecutorial delay has prejudiced the case against the defendant
- The state has failed to comply with an Order for disclosure
- An accused is unfit to be tried because of a mental illness (see s. 4 of the Criminal Law (Insanity) Act 2006)
- Proceedings have been commenced in the wrong District Court Area
- The offence before the court is one that is not known to law

Matters such as these ought to be dealt with before the commencement of the hearing.

11.7.3 LEGAL PRINCIPLES

Three main evidential principals as discussed in detail in **Chapter 10** are always relevant when proving a criminal case and warrant contextual discussion in this chapter. They are:

- the burden of proof
- the standard of proof
- the benefit of the doubt

11.7.3.1 The burden of proof

The burden of proof in a criminal case can be distinguished between the legal burden and the evidential burden. The former relates to the main issues involved in the hearing and is determined by reference to the elements of the offence. The legal burden can also be described as the ultimate burden, and it rests on the prosecution at all times barring a few rare exceptions.

The evidential burden is less onerous and applies to secondary issues or facts and obliges a party to present sufficient evidence to justify a finding in its favour in relation to that issue or fact. More succinctly, the evidential burden of proof is the burden of proving that there is evidence of a fact in issue.

In order to raise a defence, an accused must discharge an evidential burden of proof i.e. s/he must satisfy the court that there is some evidence of the defence. If, for example, a defence of self-defence is raised, it is not the case that the accused is guilty unless he succeeds in proving his defence. Once there is some evidence of a defence, it becomes a fact in issue and there is a burden on the prosecution to disprove it.

11.7.3.2 The standard of proof

The standard of proof that the prosecution must reach is proof beyond a reasonable doubt irrespective of the gravity of the charge. Lord Denning elaborated on the criminal standard of proof in these terms that are often quoted in this jurisdiction:

It need not reach certainty, but it must carry a high degree of probability. Proof beyond a reasonable doubt does not mean proof beyond the shadow of a doubt. The law would fail to protect the community if it admitted fanciful possibilities to deflect the course of justice. If the evidence is so strong against a man as to leave only a remote possibility in his favour, which can be dismissed with the sentence 'of course it is possible but not in the least bit probable' the case is proved beyond reasonable doubt, but nothing short of that will suffice. (*Miller v Minister for Pensions* [1947] 2 All ER 372)

11.7.3.3   Benefit of the doubt

Where a doubt arises, the accused has to be given the benefit of the doubt. In *People (Attorney General) v Byrne* ([1974] IR 1, Kenny J.), the Court of Criminal Appeal held that:

> The accused is entitled to the benefit of the doubt, and when two views on any part of the case are possible on the evidence, they should adopt that which is favourable to the accused unless the state has established the other beyond reasonable doubt.

11.7.4   WITNESSES

As mentioned already, in all trials, the prosecution will call evidence first. This process is an application of the evidential principle that the legal burden of proof rests on the prosecution. Each witness must give their evidence in person by way of oral (*viva voce*) evidence, and are subject to cross-examination by the legal representative for the defence. There are exceptions to this rule such as where a statement of evidence has been served on the defence by a notice under s. 21 of the Criminal Justice Act 1984 and no objection has been raised by the defence. In such circumstances, the statement is read into the record and the author of that statement is not required to give evidence at the hearing. Also, s. 19 of the Road Traffic Act 2010 provides that the evidence of a witness may be presented to a court in the form of a pre-trial statement, i.e. it allows the prosecution to hand in the statement of the Garda in a drink-driving case rather than requesting that Garda to come to court.

Generally speaking, the prosecution may call whatever witnesses they choose to prove their case. The defence solicitor should not assume that the prosecution will call witnesses that the defence may wish to cross-examine as they are not bound to do so. A number of cases support that principle: *The People (at the suit of the DPP) v Gerard Anthony Tuite* (CCA, Judgment of McCarthy J. delivered on 2 May 1983); *Paul O'Regan v DPP* ([1999] 7 JIC 2005, [2000] 2 ILRM 68 at 74); *John Geaney v Judge Connellan* (High Court judgment of O' Sullivan J. delivered on 8 December 1999); *Sterling Manson v Judge O'Donnell, DPP and MBRS* (High Court judgment of Kinlen J. delivered on 27 January 2000).

11.7.5   EXHIBITS

Exhibits generally comprise of documentary and real evidence as discussed in **Chapter 10**. To be admissible in court, evidence must be relevant to an issue in dispute, and obviously, a court has a discretion to exclude evidence that may prejudice the fairness of the trial. If a dispute arises about whether evidence ought to be disclosed, then the case is likely to be adjourned for a relevancy hearing which will determine the issue.

The admission of documentary or real evidence is premised on accompanying testimony from a witness who can introduce the evidence and place it in its appropriate context for the court. In other words, there must be an unbroken chain of evidence.

11.7.6   EXPERT EVIDENCE

The general rule for witnesses is that s/he must limit their testimony to facts within his or her personal knowledge. They are not permitted to offer opinions or to draw inferences from facts stated because that is the function of the court. The exception to this is an expert witness such as a forensic scientist, a pathologist or a ballistics expert. When calling an expert, that witness should be asked during direct examination in the witness box about his or her qualifications in order to prove that s/he is indeed an expert in their field.

Section 34 of the Criminal Procedure Act 2010 requires an accused who intends to call an expert witness to seek the leave of the court. The section requires notice to be given to the prosecution at least 10 days before the start of the trial. This notice must be in writing and include the name and address of the expert witness and any report prepared by them or a summary of the findings. The court can grant leave to call the witness even where no report or summary has been provided to the prosecution if the court is satisfied that the accused took all reasonable steps to secure the report or summary.

11.7.7 CLOSE OF THE CASE

At the close of the prosecution case, it is open to the defence to make an application for 'a direction' that the state has not proved its case. This is a similar application to that made in the Circuit Court or Central Criminal Court, where an application is made to the trial judge to direct a jury to acquit on the basis that a properly directed jury could not convict on the evidence presented. See the UK case of *R v Galbraith* [1981] 2 All ER 1060. In the event that such an application is successful, the case against the accused will be dismissed and that will be the end of the matter. Where the District Judge holds that there is a case to answer, the defence can decide whether or not to 'go into evidence'. However, the legal burden of proof rests with the prosecution to prove the case beyond all reasonable doubt and there is no obligation on the defence to go into evidence. Nevertheless, it is often pragmatic for an accused to have evidence presented that would successfully challenge the prosecution case. Otherwise, the prosecution evidence may be regarded as being uncontradicted. In the case of *Michael Oates v Judge Browne and the DPP* (High Court judgment delivered on 11 November 2010), Charleton J. held that although the defence are entitled to remain mute throughout a trial, 'failure to give evidence on a relevant issue means that there may be no evidence to contradict the prosecution case on that issue. Questions may be asked in cross-examination of prosecution witnesses, but these questions, often containing assertions of fact on the basis of the instructions of the accused, are not evidence. If the assertions put to prosecution witnesses are not backed up by evidence, then that evidence is absent. A question is not evidence. It may be that cross-examination by the defence can be argued to have weakened the prosecution's case to a degree, but the failure to contradict it by evidence may lead, in the ordinary way, to a fact being challenged but being uncontradicted.'

Should the defence decide to 'go into evidence', witnesses that are in a position to support the defence case or to challenge the prosecution case may be called, including the accused person. Any witnesses called by the defence are likely to be cross-examined by either the prosecuting Garda or a representative of the DPP.

At the close of the defence case, further submissions may be made by the defence to have the case dismissed. At the close of the prosecution case, the prosecution need only have shown there to be a *prima facie* case in order to survive a defence application for a direction. In the case of *DPP v Gerry Buckley* [2007] IEHC 150 (2007) (High Court, 8 May 2007), Charleton J. held that it is not a function of the trial judge to weigh the strength of the evidence at directions stage. The court should simply consider whether sufficient proofs are present to establish a *prima facie* case. However, at the close of the defence case, the prosecution must have proved its case beyond a reasonable doubt before a judge will convict.

If a complicated legal argument arises where there may be a need to fully investigate the law surrounding it, the case may be adjourned mid-hearing for both sides to prepare written submissions addressing the argument.

11.7.8 FOLLOWING CONVICTION

In the event that a person is convicted, a sentence hearing may take place immediately. There is a full discussion of sentencing in this text at **Chapter 14**. The court will hear evidence from the prosecution of any previous convictions. The defence will then make a plea in mitigation before the court imposes the appropriate penalty. Maximum penalties in respect of specific offences are set out in the section creating that offence or in the penalties section of the relevant statute.

In the District Court, the maximum sentence is 12 months and/or an alternative specified fine in respect of any individual offence. The District Court has, however, a power to deal with a number of different offences up to a maximum term of imprisonment of 24 months. The District

Court also has jurisdiction to impose a sentence consecutive to a Circuit Court sentence or a Central Criminal Court sentence, and can add up to two years to the sentence imposed by those courts. It is noteworthy also that a sentence for an offence committed by an accused while serving another sentence must be consecutive (as per s. 13(1) of the Criminal Law Act 1976), unless the accused is already serving a life sentence (see s. 13(2) of that Act). Also, s. 11 of the Criminal Justice Act 1984 provides for mandatory consecutive sentences for offences committed while the accused was on bail for other offences.

If, following conviction, an accused person is unhappy with the conviction and/or the penalty that has been imposed by the District Court Judge, there is a statutory right of appeal to the Circuit Court in respect of all matters. Appeal processes are discussed at **Chapter 16**. That appeal must be served and lodged within 14 days from the date of conviction. The Notice of Appeal allows for the case to be heard *de novo* in the Circuit Court, so in theory an accused could plead guilty in the District Court and then plead not guilty for the appeal hearing. The penalty imposed by the District Court is not suspended, unless recognisances (bail pending an appeal) are entered into. Accordingly, at the conclusion of any District Court hearing, it is best practice for a defence solicitor to request that recognisances be fixed pending an appeal. A District Judge cannot refuse to fix recognisance when requested to do so. In the event that an accused person decides to appeal, s/he should enter into those recognisances within a period of 14 days, and recognisances along with the Notice of Appeal should be lodged with the District Court Office within that period also. The effect of entering into a recognisance is to place a stay on the Order being appealed as per Order 101, Rule 6 of the District Court Rules. The accused remains convicted until the case is dealt with in the Circuit Court and the conviction is either affirmed or set aside.

PART V

TRIAL VENUE CHOICE AND INDICTABLE OFFENCES

CHAPTER 12

REASONS INFLUENCING CHOICE OF VENUE IN THE UNDERTAKING OF CRIMINAL PROSECUTIONS

12.1   Introduction

There are a number of factors that influence the choice of venue for the undertaking of criminal prosecutions. These factors can be broadly categorised as reflecting:

- the jurisdiction of different criminal courts;
- the classification of criminal offences within the Irish criminal justice system by which criminal offences can in general be classified according to whether they may be prosecuted:
  - o   summarily in the District Court only ('summary only' offences),
  - o   summarily in the District Court or on indictment in the Circuit Court ('hybrid' offences),
  - o   in the Central Criminal Court only (murder and rape prosecutions, competition offences),
  - o   in the Special Criminal Court (offences scheduled under the Offences Against the State Act 1939 (as amended), offences contrary to the Explosive Substances 1883, offences contrary to the Firearms Acts 1925–1971),
- the capacity of different actors within the criminal justice system, in particular the Director of Public Prosecutions (DPP) and District Judges, to affect the venue of criminal prosecution.

This chapter will discuss these factors and the manner in which they influence the choice of venue for the undertaking of criminal prosecutions.

12.2   The Constitutional Context

Any discussion as to jurisdiction of the criminal courts in Ireland is framed by the terms of Articles 34 and 38 of Bunreacht na hÉireann (Constitution of Ireland).

- Article 34.1 of Bunreacht na hÉireann provides as follows:

  Justice shall be administered in courts established by law by judges appointed in the manner provided by this Constitution, and, save in such special and limited cases as may be prescribed by law, shall be administered in public.

- Article 34.3.4 of Bunreacht na hÉireann provides as follows:

  The Courts of First Instance shall also include courts of local and limited jurisdiction with a right of appeal as determined by law.

- Article 38, ss. 1 and 2 of Bunreacht na hÉireann provide that:

  38.1 No person shall be tried on any criminal charge save in due course of law [and]

  38.2 Minor offences may be tried by courts of summary jurisdiction.

- Article 38, s. 3 of Bunreacht na hÉireann provides for prosecutions to be undertaken in the Special Criminal Court in circumstances where it is determined:

that the ordinary courts are inadequate to secure the effective administration of justice, and the preservation of public peace and order.

- Article 38.3.2 of Bunreacht na hÉireann provides that:

  The constitution, powers, jurisdiction and procedure of such special courts shall be prescribed by law.

- Article 38, s. 4 of Bunreacht na hÉireann provides for the prosecution of offences against military law to be undertaken before military tribunals.

- Article 38, s. 5 of Bunreacht na hÉireann provides that:

  Save in the case of the trial of offences under s. 2, s. 3 or s. 4 of this Article no person shall be tried on any criminal charge without a jury.

It is therefore the case that Bunreacht na hÉireann requires that all criminal prosecutions within the Irish jurisdiction must be undertaken before Courts of First Instance with a local and limited jurisdiction and before a jury except in circumstances where:

- the prosecution is in respect of a minor offence, in which case the prosecution can be undertaken before the District Court consistent with its status as a court of summary jurisdiction; or

- the prosecution is undertaken in the Special Criminal Court on account of the ordinary courts being inadequate to secure the effective administration of justice and the preservation of public peace in order; or

- the prosecution is in respect of an offence against military law, in which case it will be undertaken before a military tribunal.

12.3   Jurisdiction of Criminal Courts

In Ireland the following courts have varying jurisdiction in respect of the undertaking of criminal prosecutions:

- The District Court
- The Circuit Court
- The Central Criminal Court
- The Special Criminal Court
- The Children Court

The jurisdiction of each of these fora will be discussed in the paragraphs that follow.

12.3.1   CRIMINAL PROSECUTIONS IN THE DISTRICT COURT

The District Court is a court of local and limited jurisdiction as provided by Article 34.3.4 of Bunreacht na hÉireann. It is a single court composed of a President and 63 District Court Judges. The country is divided into the Dublin Metropolitan District and 23 District Court districts, with one or more judges permanently assigned to each district. Each district is further divided up into District Court areas. The President of the District Court is permanently assigned to the Dublin Metropolitan District.

The territorial jurisdiction of a District Court Judge is limited to the district to which s/he is assigned. As a general rule, a District Court Judge has jurisdiction to deal with a criminal case in circumstances where:

- the crime has been committed within the relevant district;
- the accused has been arrested within the relevant district; or
- the accused resides within the relevant district (per s. 79 of the Courts of Justice Act 1924 as amended, Consolidated District Court Rules Order 13, rule 1).

As has been already noted, Article 38.2 of Bunreacht na hÉireann provides that minor offences may be tried before a District Judge sitting alone in the District Court, consistent with the status of the District Court as a court of 'summary jurisdiction', i.e. a court that can determine criminal charges without a jury.

There is a greater emphasis in the undertaking of summary prosecutions expeditiously than is the case in prosecutions before the Circuit Court, the Special Criminal Court and the Central Criminal Court. Consistent with this emphasis upon an expeditious hearing, the prosecution of offences that can be prosecuted summarily only ('summary only' offences as discussed at **12.4.1**), must be commenced within six months of the offence occurring (per s. 10(4) of the Petty Sessions (Ireland) Act 1851). Such procedures represent the bulk of prosecutions before the District Court. The six-month time limit is not applicable in respect of indictable offences or indictable offences that are triable summarily (per s. 177 of the Criminal Justice Act 2006).

The nature of summary prosecution was characterised by Gannon J. in the case of *Clune v DPP and Clifford* [1981] ILRM 17 as follows:

> A summary trial is a trial which could be undertaken with some degree of expedition and informality without departing from the principles of justice. The purpose of summary procedures for minor offences is to ensure that such offences are tried as soon as reasonably possible after their alleged commission so that the recollection of witnesses may still be reasonably clear, that the attendance of witnesses and presentation of evidence may be procured and presented without great difficulty or complexity, and that there should be minimal delay in the disposal of the work-load of minor offences.

The rationale for permitting the prosecution of minor offences by means of summary trial has been explained by Hogan and Whyte as follows:

> It would be a sufficient reason for summary trial to say that the multiple disruption of jurors' private affairs, the expense, the delay, and the general panoply of a jury trial render this form of justice completely impractical for the mass of minor offences with which the State has to deal, and that the defendant's interest, where only a minor punishment can be imposed, is insufficient to outweigh those public considerations.
>
> G. W. Hogan and G. F. Whyte, *JM Kelly: The Irish Constitution* (3rd edn., Butterworths, 1994), at p. 627.

The status of the District Court as a court of local and limited jurisdiction, and the relative lack of formality attaching to proceedings in the District Court, does not diminish the obligation to act in accordance with the Constitution, and the constitutional rights of those appearing before the District Court must be fully respected and vindicated in the course of proceedings (*Coughlan v Patwell* [1993] 1 IR 31).

The District Court has jurisdiction to deal with the following offences:

- summary offences;
- hybrid offences that may be tried summarily at the election of the DPP, subject to the right of the District Court Judge to refuse jurisdiction on the basis that the offence in question is not 'minor' as to permit summary trial consistent with Article 38.2 of Bunreacht na hÉireann;
- indictable offences triable summarily, as set out in the First Schedule to the Criminal Justice Act 1951, in the event that the accused and the DPP consent to summary disposal and the District Judge is of the opinion that the offence is a 'minor' one fit to be tried summarily;
- specific indictable statutory offences that can be tried summarily at the election of the accused in the event that the DPP consents and the District Judge is satisfied that the offence is 'minor', e.g. indictable offences in the Criminal Justice (Theft and Fraud Offences) Act 2001;
- indictable offences that can be disposed of summarily in the event of a plea of guilty per s. 13 of the Criminal Procedure Act 1967.

The character of the different categories of offences noted above is discussed in greater detail at **12.4** *et seq*.

Consistent with its jurisdiction to deal with 'minor' offences only, the District Court can impose a maximum term of imprisonment of 12 months upon conviction for a single offence. In circumstances of conviction by the District Court on two or more offences consecutive sentences up to an aggregate term of two years may be imposed (s. 5 of the Criminal Justice Act 1951 as amended, *Mallon v Minister for Agriculture* [1996] 1 IR 517).

12.3.2   CRIMINAL PROSECUTIONS IN THE CIRCUIT COURT

The Circuit Court was established in its current form by s. 4(1) of the Courts (Establishment and Constitution) Act 1961. The Circuit Court is also a court of local and limited jurisdiction within the terms provided by Article 34.3.4 of Bunreacht na hÉireann. It consists of the President and 37 ordinary judges. The President of the District Court is, by virtue of their office, an additional judge of the Circuit Court. The country is divided into eight circuits with one judge assigned to each circuit, except in Dublin where ten judges may be assigned, and Cork, where there is provision for three judges. The jurisdiction of the Circuit Court is exercisable in the area where the offence has been committed, or where the accused person has been arrested or resides. In Circuit Courts outside Dublin the trial judge may transfer a trial to the Dublin Circuit Criminal Court on application by the DPP or the lawyers for the defence if satisfied that it would be unjust not to do so (s. 32 of the Courts and Court Officers Act 1995).

The Circuit Court and the Central Criminal Court both have jurisdiction over indictable offences, however the jurisdiction of the Circuit Court to try indictable offences does not extend to a number of offences that are reserved to the Central Criminal Court by the terms of s. 25(2) of the Courts (Supplemental Provisions) Act 1961. The most significant of the offences reserved to the jurisdiction of the Central Criminal Court are the offences of murder, attempted murder, rape offences and aggravated sexual assault including the prosecution of accessories before or after the fact.

Consistent with the terms of Articles 38.2 and 38.5 of Bunreacht na hÉireann, all crimes, with the exception of offences tried before the Special Criminal Court and military tribunals, that are not 'minor' must be tried before a judge and jury. Accordingly the Circuit Criminal Court is comprised of a Circuit Court Judge, who acts as an arbiter upon issues of law, and a jury that determines and makes findings of fact.

The only circumstances in which the Circuit Criminal Court will hear a case in the absence of a jury is in dealing with appeals of conviction and/or sentence from the District Court.

12.3.3   CRIMINAL PROSECUTIONS IN THE CENTRAL CRIMINAL COURT

Article 34.3.1 of Bunreacht na hÉireann provides that the courts of first instance shall include a High Court invested with full original jurisdiction in and power to determine all matters and questions whether of law or fact, civil or criminal.

The Central Criminal Court is the name given to the High Court when exercising its criminal jurisdiction (s. 11 of the Courts (Supplemental) Provisions Act 1961). It consists of a judge or judges of the High Court. The court sits at such time and in such places as the President of the High Court may direct, and tries criminal cases falling within the exclusive jurisdiction of the Central Criminal Court. The Central Criminal Court will additionally have jurisdiction over any offence which is included in the same indictment over which it has exclusive jurisdiction by the terms of s. 25(2) of the Courts (Supplemental Provisions) Act 1961.

In the event an accused has been sent forward for trial to the Circuit Court for an indictable offence and is later returned for trial to the Central Criminal Court for another indictable offence, arising out of and connected to the offence returned to the Circuit Court, the Circuit Court may transfer the trial of that offence to the Central Criminal Court unless it considers that it would not be in the interests of justice to do so (s. 4P of the Criminal Procedure Act 1967 as inserted by s. 9 of the Criminal Justice Act 1999).

12.3.4   CRIMINAL PROSECUTIONS IN THE SPECIAL CRIMINAL COURT

As has already been noted, the Special Criminal Court is provided for by Article 38, s. 3 of Bunreacht na hÉireann for the undertaking of prosecutions in circumstances where it is determined 'that the ordinary courts are inadequate to secure the effective administration of justice, and the preservation of public peace and order.'

Article 38.6 of Bunreacht na hÉireann provides that Articles 34 and 35 do not apply to any court established pursuant to Article 38.3 with the effect that there is no right to jury trial before the Special Criminal Court.

The legislative basis for the Special Criminal Court is provided by Part V of the Offences Against the State Act 1939, whereby in circumstances where the Government makes and publishes a proclamation declaring that it is satisfied that the ordinary courts are inadequate to secure the effective administration of justice and the preservation of public peace and order and that it is therefore necessary that Part V of the 1939 Act should come into force (s. 35(2) of the Offences Against the State Act 1939). Such a proclamation having been made, it will remain in force until it is annulled by means of a resolution of the Dáil (s. 35(5) of the Offences Against the State Act 1939) or until the government issues a further proclamation declaring that it is no longer necessary for Part V to remain in force. The Special Criminal Court as it is presently constituted was established by way of a government proclamation made in 1972, the Special Criminal Court having previously been in existence over the period 1939 to 1946 and 1961 to 1962.

Section 39(1) of the Offences against the State Act 1939 provides that the Special Criminal Court must be composed of an uneven number of members numbering not less than three. Each member shall be appointed and be removable at will by the Government (s. 39(2) of the Offences Against the State Act 1939). Since its establishment in 1972 the Special Criminal Court as it is presently constituted has been made up of three judges drawn from the High, Circuit, and District Courts respectively.

The Special Criminal Court is a creature of statute and has no inherent jurisdiction. Section 43 of the Offences Against the State Act 1939 provides that the Special Criminal Court shall have jurisdiction to try and to convict or acquit any person lawfully brought before that Court for trial under that Act. Strict compliance with statutory procedures is therefore required in order for the jurisdiction of the Special Criminal Court to subsist in relation to a particular prosecution.

While the Special Criminal Court has a particular jurisdiction to try offences scheduled under Part V of the 1939 Act, it can also try non-scheduled offences, subject to the DPP certifying the ordinary courts being inadequate to secure the effective administration of justice and the preservation of public peace and order. If an accused is before the District Court charged with a non-scheduled indictable offence, the District Court Judge must return him for trial to the Special Criminal Court, if the DPP makes such an application supported by a certificate signed by the DPP (per s. 46(2) of the Offences Against the State Act 1939).

A prosecution can be brought before the Special Criminal Court by a number of different means:

- an accused can be charged directly before the Special Criminal Court;

- an accused can be returned for trial by the District Court to the Special Criminal Court; or

- the High Court can order that a case awaiting trial in either the Central Criminal Court or Circuit Court be transferred to the Special Criminal Court.

Indictable offences scheduled under the Offences Against the State Acts are by default returned for trial to the Special Criminal Court unless the DPP directs prosecution in the ordinary courts (s. 45(2) of the Offences Against the State Act 1939). By way of contrast, the prosecution of offences that are not scheduled under the Offences Against the State Acts will by default be undertaken in the ordinary courts unless the DPP specifically directs that they should be sent for trial to the Special Criminal Court on the basis that the ordinary courts are inadequate to secure the effective administration of justice and the preservation of public peace and order. In practical terms prosecution of the overwhelming majority of scheduled offences prosecuted in the state is undertaken in the ordinary courts.

A District Court Judge must send an accused forward for trial in the Special Criminal Court in respect of a scheduled offence, which can be disposed of summarily, if the DPP so directs. If the DPP fails to give such a direction, a District Court Judge will, however, have jurisdiction to try the matter in the absence of such a direction even though the offence is a scheduled offence. An accused will automatically be dealt with in the District Court, unless the DPP directs that the accused be sent for trial in the Special Criminal Court (s. 45(1) of the Offences Against the State Act 1939).

If an accused is before the District Court charged with a non-scheduled offence which can be disposed of summarily, the District Court Judge must return him for trial to the Special Criminal Court if the DPP makes an application to that effect. The application must, once again, be grounded upon a written certificate signed by the DPP, who certifies that the ordinary courts are, in her opinion, inadequate to secure the effective administration of justice and the preservation of public peace (s. 46(1) of the Offences Against the State Act 1939).

If an accused has already been returned for trial to the Central Criminal Court or the Circuit Court, the DPP can make an application to the High Court certifying that the ordinary courts are inadequate to secure the effective administration of justice and the preservation of public peace. Upon hearing such an application the High Court must make the order applied for (per s. 48(a) of the Offences Against the State Act 1939).

The prosecution of an accused in respect of scheduled offences and unscheduled offences can be commenced by way of charging before the Special Criminal Court, in contrast to the conventional means of commencing the prosecutorial process by way of charging before the District Court, upon the direction of the DPP (per s. 47(1) of the Offences Against the State Act 1939). The commencement of the prosecutorial process in the Special Criminal Court must also be accompanied by certification on the part of the DPP that the ordinary courts are inadequate to secure the effective administration of justice and the preservation of public peace and order (s. 47(2) of the Offences Against the State Act 1939).

An accused can be returned from the District Court to the Special Criminal Court for the purpose of sentencing in respect of both scheduled and non-scheduled indictable offences on foot of a signed guilty plea (*State (Littlejohn) v Governor of Mountjoy Prison*, unreported, 18 March 1976, Supreme Court).

12.3.5   CRIMINAL PROSECUTIONS IN THE CHILDREN COURT

Chapter 9 addresses the distinguishing features of juvenile justice and outlines that when hearing charges against children or dealing with certain other matters arising under the Children Act 2001, the District Court sits as the Children Court (s. 71 of the Children Act 2001) and that s. 3(1) of the Children Act 2001 defines a child as a person under the age of 18 years.

Other matters outlined include the following:

- A child under the age of 12 years shall not be charged with an offence save that a child of 10 or 11 years may be tried for murder, manslaughter, rape, rape under s. 4 of the Criminal Law (Rape)(Amendment) Act 1990 or aggravated sexual assault (s. 52 of the Children Act 2001 Act as substituted by s. 129 of the Criminal Justice Act 2006).

- Where a prosecution has been commenced in respect of a child under the age of 14, the DPP must consent to the continuation of the proceedings (s. 52(4) of the Children Act 2001).

- Where a child under 14 years is charged with an offence, the court may dismiss the case on its merits if the judge is satisfied that, having regard to the child's age and level of maturity, the child did not have a full understanding of what was involved in the commission of the crime (s. 76C of the Children Act 2001).

12.3.5.1   Criminal prosecutions of children for indictable offences

The Children Court may try any indictable offence with the exception of indictable offences which must be tried in the Central Criminal Court and the offence of manslaughter, unless the Court is of the opinion that the offence is not a minor offence fit to be tried summarily or, if the child wishes to enter a guilty plea, that it is not fit to be dealt with summarily (s. 75(1) of the Children Act 2001). The decision as to whether the Children Court should try a child summarily in respect of an indictable offence must be taken in light of the age and level of maturity of the child and any other relevant facts (s. 75(2) of the Children Act 2001).

The Children Court cannot try an indictable offence in circumstances where the child, on being informed by the Court of his or her right to trial by jury, does not consent to the case being dealt with summarily in the Children Court. A child is entitled to the assistance of a parent, guardian, spouse or other appropriate adult in connection with the decision to consent to summary trial (s. 75(3) and (4) of the Children Act 2001).

In the event that the DPP elects for trial on indictment in respect of what is known as a hybrid offence (the characteristics of which are discussed at **12.4.2**), the Children Court can try the matter, subject to the judge being satisfied it is a minor matter fit to be tried summarily and the consent of the child.

The Children Court can send a child forward to the Central Criminal Court, on a charge within the exclusive jurisdiction of that forum, or the Circuit Court, on a charge of manslaughter, on a signed plea of guilty subject to the consent of the DPP (s. 75(5) of the Children Act 2001).

12.4   Categories of Criminal Offences

As alluded to previously in **Chapter 11**, criminal offences can be categorised into six distinct groups as follows:

1. Summary offences.

2. Hybrid offences.

3. Indictable offences for which there are specific statutory provisions permitting them to be tried summarily in certain circumstances.

4. Indictable offences which may be disposed of in the District Court in the event of a plea of guilty pursuant to s. 13 of the Criminal Procedure Act 1967.

5. Offences which may only be tried in the Central Criminal Court.

6. Scheduled offences or offences in respect of which the DPP has certified that the ordinary courts are inadequate to secure the effective administration of justice and are tried in the Special Criminal Court.

The features of each of these categories of offences will be discussed in the paragraphs that follow.

12.4.1   SUMMARY OFFENCES

A summary offence is a criminal offence for which the law provides only one mode of trial—namely by way of summary prosecution in the District Court only. Summary offences are created by Acts of the Oireachtas which will set out the elements of the offence and prescribe a maximum penalty that can be imposed; the maximum penalty for a summary offence will never be greater than a term of imprisonment of 12 months.

In the vast majority of cases, proceedings for purely summary offences must be instituted within six months of the date of the incident (s. 10(4) of the Petty Sessions (Ireland) Act 1851). After that period proceedings are statute barred and accordingly the prosecution cannot proceed.

Section 6 of the Criminal Justice Act 1951 provides that where a person has been sent forward for trial for an indictable offence, the indictment may contain a count for a summary offence with which that person has been charged, and which arises out of the same set of facts. This is the only circumstance in which a purely summary offence can be tried on indictment. From a practical point of view, the following steps are taken in the District Court when an accused is charged with summary offences alongside offences which are to be tried on indictment arising from the same facts:

• the District Court Judge will send the accused forward for trial to the appropriate Court on the indictable offences only and adjourns the related summary offences that are before the District Court;

• once the summary charges are placed in the indictment, the jurisdiction of the District Court is at an end and the Circuit, Central or Special Criminal Court, as the case may be, will have sole jurisdiction to deal with all matters in the indictment;

• the District Court Judge can at this point make an order of 'strike out, no jurisdiction by reason of pending indictment' in relation to the summary charges which had been adjourned in the District Court.

12.4.1.1   The characteristics of a 'minor' offence

All summary only offences are of their nature 'minor' in character and therefore suitable for summary disposal before a District Judge sitting without a jury consistent with the terms of Article 38.2 of Bunreacht na hÉireann.

As has already been noted, the distinction between 'minor' offences and other offences that are not of a minor character is of considerable significance to the division of labour between the District Court and the higher courts, the District Courts having no jurisdiction in respect of an offence that is not 'minor' in character.

While the characteristics of a 'minor' offence are not elaborated in Bunreacht na hÉireann there have been a number of judgments identifying the parameters of what constitutes a 'minor' offence.

In the judgment of *Melling v O'Mathghamhna* [1962] IR 1 the Supreme Court identified the following factors as being relevant to the assessment of whether an offence was 'minor' in character:

- the severity of the punishment authorised by law, whether imprisonment or a fine;

- the moral quality of the acts required constituting the offence, i.e. offences such as murder or rape could never be regarded as minor offences;

- the state of the law when the Constitution was enacted in 1937; and

- public opinion at the time of that enactment.

In the case of *Conroy v Attorney General* [1965] IR 411 the Supreme Court further indicated that in assessing the moral quality of the offence one should examine the inherent nature of the act itself rather than its possible consequences in the particular circumstances. In the judgment in *Re Haughey* [1971] IR 217 it was further indicated that the primary consideration in the determining of whether an offence was a minor offence was 'the severity of the penalty which is authorised to be imposed for commission of the offence' (at 247). Being charged with several minor offences will not in itself be sufficient to any one of these offences of their 'minor' character.

The assessment of the severity of the authorised penalty that can be imposed is undertaken with reference to the 'primary' punishment, which will ordinarily involve a threat of deprivation of liberty or property. The issue of the severity of the penalty should be assessed without reference to secondary or ancillary punishments such as a driving disqualification, or the forfeiture or revocation of a licence (*Conroy v Attorney General* [1965] IR 411).

In practical terms a District Judge will assess whether a particular offence meets the criteria of being 'minor' by means of a précis of the facts of the case being opened. A District Judge can decline jurisdiction either at the outset of a case, or during the hearing of a case. If facts emerge during the hearing that demonstrate that the offence is not minor in character, the District Judge will be obliged to reverse an initial determination on jurisdiction and allow the case to go forward to the Circuit Court where a higher range of sentence may be imposed (*State (O'Hagan) v Delap* [1982] IR 213). This duty to keep the offence being tried under scrutiny to ensure that it is a minor offence continues up to the point of conviction. In *Byrne v McDonnell* [1997] 1 IR 392 the High Court held that a District Court judge may permit a change of plea at any stage before the case is finally disposed of by sentence, which supports the conclusion that conviction does not take effect until sentence is pronounced.

12.4.2   HYBRID OFFENCES

Hybrid offences can be tried either in the District Court summarily, or in the Circuit Court on indictment, at the election of the DPP (*State (McEvitt) v Delap* [1981] IR 125) and in respect of which an accused has no right of election. Many statutory provisions creating new criminal offences do that on a hybrid basis allowing for the offence to be tried either summarily or on indictment.

A significant example of such a hybrid offence is the offence of assault causing harm contrary to s. 3 of the Non-Fatal Offences Against the Person Act 1997, which provides that a person guilty of such an offence shall be liable:

- on summary conviction to imprisonment for a term not exceeding 12 months or to a fine not exceeding €1,904.61 [£1,500] or to both; or

- on conviction of indictment to a fine or to imprisonment for a term not exceeding five years or to both.

Being a hybrid the decision as to the appropriate venue for prosecution is for the DPP, subject to the overriding constitutional imperative that a District Judge cannot determine the matter unless they are satisfied that the circumstances are such that the offence is 'minor' in character.

12.4.3   INDICTABLE OFFENCES THAT CAN BE TRIED SUMMARILY

The first schedule of the Criminal Justice Act 1951 sets out a list of indictable offences which may be tried summarily, in the event that three conditions are fulfilled, namely:

- the court is of the opinion that the offence is a minor offence;

- the accused, upon being informed of his right to trial by judge and jury, personally consents to the charge being disposed of summarily in the District Court; and

- the DPP consents to the accused being tried summarily for the offence (s. 2(2) of the Criminal Justice Act 1951).

In the event that all three conditions are fulfilled the indictable offence can be dealt with in the District Court.

Other indictable offences that can be disposed of summarily subject to these three conditions being fulfilled are:

- indictable offences in the Criminal Justice (Theft and Fraud Offences) Act 2001 (per s. 53 of the Criminal Justice (Theft and Fraud Offences) Act 2001);

- the offence of sexual assault contrary to s. 2 of the Criminal Law (Rape)(Amendment) Act 1990 (per s. 12 of the Criminal Law (Rape) Act 1981 [as amended]);

- the offence of attempting to engage in a sexual act with a child who is under the age of 15 years contrary to s. 2 (2) of the Criminal Law (Sexual Offences) Act 2006 (per s. 4 Criminal Law (Sexual Offences) Act 2006);

- the offence of attempting to engage in a sexual act with a child who is under the age of 17 years contrary to s. 3 (2) of the Criminal Law (Sexual Offences) Act 2006; and

- the offence of assaulting a Peace Officer in the course of the duty contrary to s. 19(1) Criminal Justice (Public Order) Act 1994.

12.4.4 INDICTABLE OFFENCES DISPOSED OF IN THE DISTRICT COURT ON A PLEA OF GUILTY

Section 13 of the Criminal Procedure Act 1967, as amended by s. 10 of the Criminal Justice Act 1999, provides that an indictable offence can be disposed of summarily in the event of a plea of guilty in circumstances where:

- the accused wishes for the offence to be dealt with summarily;

- the District Judge is satisfied that the accused understands the nature of the offence and the facts alleged;

- the District Judge is satisfied that the matter is suitable to be disposed of summarily in the event of a plea of guilty; and

- the prosecutor consents.

In such circumstances the District Court can impose a period of imprisonment of up to 12 months. In the event that the District Judge is not satisfied that the matter is set for summary disposal, the accused can be sent forward for sentence on the basis of the signed plea entered; an accused having been sent forward on a signed plea will retain the right to subsequently withdraw this plea and to enter a plea of not guilty to the charge.

Section 13 of the Criminal Procedure Act 1967 is applicable to all indictable offences with the exception of:

- an offence under the Treason Act 1939;

- the offence of murder, attempted murder, conspiracy to murder, attempted murder, murder under s. 2 of the Criminal Justice (Safety of United Nations Workers) Act 2000 or an attempt or conspiracy to commit that offence, the offence of killing or attempted killing under paragraph (h) or (j) of s. 2(1) of the Maritime Security Act 2004, murder under ss. 6 or 11 of the Criminal Justice (Terrorist Offences) Act 2005 or an attempt to commit such offence;

- the offence of piracy;

- an offence under ss. 7 or 8 of the International Criminal Court Act 2006 (genocide, crimes against humanity, and war crimes);

- an offence under the Criminal Justice (United Nations Convention Against Torture) Act 2000;

- an offence under ss. 71, 71A, 72 or 73 of the Criminal Justice Act 2006 (organised crime offences);

- grave breaches of the Geneva Conventions Act;

- offences of rape, rape under s. 4 of the Criminal Law (Rape) (Amendment) Act 1990, aggravated sexual assault (per s. 20 Criminal Law (Rape) (Amendment) Act 1990); and

- offences under ss. 15A and 15B of the Misuse of Drugs Act 1977 (offences of possession of controlled drugs with a value in excess of €13,000 with intent to supply and importation of controlled drugs with a value in excess of €13,000 with intent to supply).

12.4.5   OFFENCES THAT CAN ONLY BE TRIED IN THE CENTRAL CRIMINAL COURT

The following category of offences can only be tried on indictment in the Central Criminal Court:

- murder, attempted murder, conspiracy to murder (per s. 25(2) of the Courts (Supplemental Provisions) Act 1961);

- rape offences; the offences of aggravated sexual assault and attempted aggravated sexual assault; aiding, abetting, counselling, or procuring the offence of aggravated sexual assault or attempted aggravated sexual assault; incitement to the offence of aggravated sexual assault; or conspiracy to commit any of the foregoing offences (per s. 10 of the Criminal Law (Rape) (Amendment) Act 1990);

- the offence of piracy;

- the offence of genocide (s. 2(4) of the Genocide Act 1973);

- the offence of treason, treason felony, conspiracy to commit treason; (s. 25(2) of the Courts (Supplemental Provisions) Act 1961);

- offences under the Criminal Justice (United Nations Convention Against Torture) Act 2000 (s. 5(4) Criminal Justice (United Nations Convention Against Torture) Act 2000);

- offences under s. 3 of the Geneva Conventions Act 1962 (s. 3(4) Geneva Conventions Act 1962);

- offences under ss. 6 and 7 of the Competition Act 2002 or the offence of attempting to commit such an offence or the offence of conspiracy to commit such an offence (per s. 11 of the Competition Act 2002); and

- offences under s. 2 of the Maritime Security Act 2004.

12.4.6   OFFENCES TRIED IN THE SPECIAL CRIMINAL COURT

The following offences have been scheduled for the purposes of Part V of the Offences Against the State Act 1939 (as amended) and will therefore be tried in the Special Criminal Court unless the DPP certifies that the ordinary courts are suitable to hear the prosecution:

- offences under the Explosive Substances Act 1883;

- offences under the Firearms Acts 1925–1971;

- offences under the Offences Against the State Act 1939;

- offences under ss. 6–9 and ss. 12 of the Offences Against the State (Amendment) Act 1998;

- an offence under s. 14(2) of the Offences Against the State (Amendment) Act 1998 (directing an unlawful organisation, possession of articles for particular purposes, unlawful collection and withholding of information, training persons in making and use of firearms);

- organised crime offences under ss. 71A, 72, 73 and 76 of the Criminal Justice Act 2006;

- offences under the Malicious Damage Act 1861 (most offences under this Act have been repealed and only minor offences remain); and

- an attempt, conspiracy, incitement or aiding or abetting the commission of any of the above offences (per s. 37 of the Offences Against the State Act 1939).

12.5 The Role of Office of the Director of Public Prosecutions in the Determination of Venue for Trial

The Office of the DPP was established by the Prosecution of Offences Act 1974. All prosecutions on indictment in the state are undertaken by the Office of the DPP. Most summary prosecutions are undertaken by the Gardaí in the name of the DPP in the exercise of a power to initiate and conduct prosecutions pursuant to s. 8 of the Garda Síochána Act 2005 and 'General Direction No. 3' issued by the DPP. Additionally, a wide range of other public bodies may initiate and conduct summary prosecutions in respect of specific offences, which are generally regulatory in nature (see **Chapter 6**).

The criteria employed by the DPP in deciding whether and how a prosecution should be undertaken in any given case are set out in the published Guidelines for Prosecutors (Office of the DPP, 2010). In order for a prosecution to be taken the circumstances must meet the 'evidential' and 'public interest' tests. The Guidelines for Prosecutors characterise the evidential test as follows (at paragraph 4.10):

> A prosecution should not be instituted unless there is a prima facie case against the suspect. By this is meant that there is admissible, substantial and reliable evidence that a criminal offence known to the law has been committed by the suspect. The evidence must be such that a jury, properly instructed on the relevant law, could conclude beyond a reasonable doubt that the accused was guilty of the offence charged.

The criterion as to the public interest encompasses a wide range of as set out at paragraphs 4.18–4.22 of the Guidelines for Prosecutors, including issues of public policy.

As has been discussed earlier, the Office of the DPP has a substantial influence upon the venue in which criminal prosecutions are undertaken. When considering the appropriate venue for the undertaking of a prosecution and whether to elect for summary disposal, the DPP will, *inter alia*, consider whether upon conviction the District Court would be in a position to impose a sentence commensurate with the gravity of the particular offence and the relevant personal circumstances of the person sentenced consistent with sentencing principles set out in sentencing authorities such as that of *The People (DPP) v C (W)* [1994] 1 ILRM 435.

The Office of the DPP has had a long-standing policy of reviewing decisions not to undertake a prosecution in the event that a review of the decision is requested by a person with a sufficient interest in the undertaking of a prosecution. Reviews are undertaken by senior lawyers in the Office of the DPP who were not involved in the original decision not to prosecute, taking into account all of the material submitted by An Garda Síochána and any representations made by the person requesting the review.

Since 2008 the Office of the DPP has also provided to persons with a sufficient interest reasons for a decision not to undertake a prosecution in connection with offences where a death has occurred (per 'Policy on the Giving of Reasons for Decisions Not to Prosecute', Office of the DPP, 2008).

These initiatives on the part of the Office of the DPP will be augmented by the implementation of European Directive 2012/29/EU as discussed in **Chapter 3**, which establishes 'minimum standards on the rights, support and protection of victims' and which must be transposed into Irish law by 16 November 2015. The objective of the Directive is to improve the rights, support, protection and participation of victims in criminal proceedings in order to ensure that victims will have the same basic level of rights whatever their nationality and wherever in the EU a crime takes place. The terms of the Directive encompass the provision of information and support to victims, the participation of victims in criminal proceedings and the protection of victims. Of particular significance to the Office of the DPP are Article 6 of the Directive which entitles victims to be provided with reasons or a brief summary of reasons for decisions not to prosecute, and Article 11 of the Directive which provides victims with a right of review in the event of a decision not to prosecute. The Office of the DPP has established a special unit tasked with making preparations for the operational implications of the Directive.

CHAPTER 13

PROCEEDINGS RELATED TO INDICTABLE OFFENCES

13.1   What Is An Indictable Offence?

As has been outlined in **Chapter 12**, criminal offences fall into three categories: summary offences, indictable offences and 'hybrid' offences, which are triable either summarily or on indictment.

The defining characteristic of an indictable offence is that it may be tried by a judge and jury, whereas there is no option for jury trial in respect of purely summary offences. Offences that can only be tried summarily have been deemed by the Oireachtas to be minor offences, whereas, broadly speaking, indictable offences are non-minor, and as such, are unsuited to summary disposal in the District Court.

However, to delineate between summary and indictable offences on the basis that the former are minor and the latter non-minor offences, is something of an oversimplification, given that the circumstances and consequences of an offence are often relevant to consideration of its seriousness, the venue in which the accused ought to be tried, and consequently the maximum penalty the offence potentially attracts.

Equally, indictable offences cannot be distinguished by simply stating that such offences are tried by jury—not all indictable offences are, with some being disposed of in the District Court by a judge sitting alone, and others being tried before a panel of judges in the Special Criminal Court.

13.2   The Characteristics of Trial on Indictment

By comparison with the swift pace of the voluminous business of the District Court, trial on indictment is a slower process, as befits proceedings in which the liberty of an accused person is at stake to a greater degree (i.e. considerable sentences of imprisonment often apply). While the District Court can, and does, impose sentences of imprisonment, the presence of the jury, the involvement of counsel (barristers), the comparative seriousness of the charges and the attendant exposure to significant penalties, lends greater formality to trials in the Circuit and Central Criminal Courts.

The accused will have a number of pre-trial appearances between the charge and the trial, punctuated by adjournments that are known as remands (as discussed in **Chapter 8**). Pre-trial appearances serve a number of purposes including the following:

- to determine whether the accused should be admitted to bail or remanded in custody;

- for the directions of the Director of Public Prosecutions (DPP) to be ascertained and conveyed to the court;

- to allow time for the accused to consult with his or her legal advisers and prepare a defence; and

- for service of the book of evidence.

The involvement of the jury is a defining characteristic of trial on indictment. In a summary trial, the judge rules on the admissibility of evidence as well as making findings of fact. Juries are shielded from exposure to potentially prejudicial evidence, which ought not to be properly admitted, and legal argument is therefore often heard in the absence of the jury on what is referred to as a *voir dire*. A *voir dire* is known as a 'trial within a trial' in which the judge is asked to rule on a legal point arising before or during the trial, often to determine the admissibility of a piece of evidence that the prosecution proposes to adduce. Any number of legal issues can arise, e.g. the validity of a search warrant grounding a search may be questioned or the voluntariness of an incriminating admission by the accused may be put in issue. If the evidence is deemed inadmissible, it will be omitted from the prosecution case and the trial will continue without reference to it; if it is deemed admissible, it will be introduced in the presence of the jury, as the trial proceeds after the *voir dire*.

There is no time limit for the commencement of proceedings in the prosecution of indictable offences. However, there are certain time limits that must be adhered to, once proceedings have commenced.

Whereas proceedings in summary offences often begin with a summons, the indictable process begins with a charge, which is an accusation of criminal conduct. The charge is generally recorded on a charge sheet which outlines the details of the offence alleged to have been committed (District Court Rules, Order 17), with the District Court not having jurisdiction until the person is charged before the Court.

In **Chapter 12** it was indicated that prosecutions for all offences (except where proceedings are initiated in the Special Criminal Court) begin in the District Court. When a person is before the District Court charged with an indictable offence, they are 'sent forward' or 'returned' for trial to the Circuit or Central Criminal Court once the book of evidence is served. This procedure would not occur where the accused is unfit to be tried, or the case is to be dealt with summarily by way of a plea of guilty under s. 13 of the Criminal Procedure Act 1967.

The DPP must consent to the person being sent forward for trial, as prosecutions on indictment may only be taken with the consent of the DPP (save for a small category of offences prosecuted by the Attorney General) (see Criminal Justice (Administration) Act 1924, s. 9 and Prosecution of Offences Act 1974, s. 3). Indictable offences are prosecuted in the name of the 'People' at the suit of the 'Director'. The consent of the Director (DPP) may be conveyed in writing signed by the DPP, or orally by a person prosecuting at the suit of the Director or appearing on her behalf (Criminal Procedure Act 1967, s. 20).

In terms of sequence, trial on indictment opens with the prosecution case outlining as follows:

- the facts alleged;
- the evidence it is intended to call on behalf of the prosecution; and
- the nature of the charges against the accused.

Prosecution witnesses are then called and questioned by prosecution counsel (examination-in-chief), and exhibits and documents are introduced and may be examined by the jurors. At the conclusion of the examination-in-chief of each witness, the witness will be cross-examined by defence counsel.

The case for the defence is then presented by opening the defence case and calling defence witnesses, who will be cross-examined by the prosecution. The accused is not obliged to give evidence in his defence.

Prosecution and defence counsel then make closing speeches, before the judge sums up the case for the jury, guiding them as to the law which ought to be applied before the jury retires to consider its verdict.

13.3   Jurisdiction

13.3.1   DISTRICT COURT

The District Court has jurisdiction to deal with summary offences, with the Constitution providing in Article 38.2 that 'minor offences may be tried by courts of summary jurisdiction'. The maximum term of imprisonment which the District Court can impose is 12 months, or an aggregate of two years where consecutive sentences are imposed (Criminal Justice Act 1951, s. 5, as amended by the Criminal Justice Act 1984, s. 12(1)).

Chapter 12 makes reference to circumstances where indictable offences can be dealt with in the District Court in certain circumstances including:

- if the offence is one that affords the prosecutor an option to elect for disposal of the offence either summarily or on indictment and the prosecutor opts for summary disposal;

- where the accused and the prosecutor consent to summary disposal of indictable offences where that is statutorily provided for;

- where the prosecutor consents to summary disposal of the offence on a plea of guilty pursuant to s. 13 of the Criminal Procedure Act 1967;

- where the District Court is sitting as the Children Court and dealing with indictable offences alleged to have been committed by children who are under 18 years of age pursuant to s. 75 of the Children Act 2001.

Where it is proposed to deal with indictable offences in the District Court, the court must also accept jurisdiction by agreeing that the offence is a minor one fit to be tried summarily.

13.3.1.1   Consent to summary disposal on a plea of guilty

Certain indictable offences may be dealt with in the District Court, with the sentencing powers of the District Court being applicable, if the following conditions are met:

- it is indicated to the court that the person wishes to plead guilty;

- the court is satisfied that the suspect understands the nature of the offence and the facts alleged; and

- the DPP consents to the offence being dealt with summarily.

It should be noted that even if it is indicated to the court that the accused wishes to plead guilty and that the DPP consents to the matter being dealt with summarily, it is open to the court to refuse jurisdiction and to send the person forward to be tried on indictment.

In cases involving purely indictable offences, there is no mechanism for disposing of the matter summarily on a plea of guilty.

13.3.1.2   Sending forward on a signed plea

It is possible for the District Court to send a person forward for sentence to a higher court if the accused wishes to plead guilty, and the court is satisfied that the accused understands the nature of the offence and the facts alleged.

The procedure is that the accused signs a plea of guilty and the case progresses to the court in which the accused would have been tried were it not for the entry of the plea (Criminal Procedure Act 1967, s. 13(2)(b)). The DPP must have consented to the accused being sent forward for sentence.

An accused is not precluded from withdrawing a written plea and subsequently pleading 'not guilty', in which case the criminal process is the same as it would have been had the accused been sent forward for trial in the ordinary way.

A person may not be sent forward on a signed plea if the charge before the court is murder, piracy, genocide, rape, rape under s. 4 of the Criminal Law (Rape) (Amendment) Act 1990 or aggravated sexual assault.

13.3.2   CIRCUIT COURT

The Circuit Court has full jurisdiction in criminal matters, save for those offences which may only be dealt with by the Central Criminal Court (Courts (Supplemental Provisions) Act 1961, s. 25). The main business of the court is the trial of indictable offences, which are sent to the Circuit Court from the District Court.

The Circuit Court also hears District Court appeals, with the case being reheard in the Circuit Court and the maximum available penalty being limited to the sentence that would have been imposed in the District Court. In dealing with indictable matters the Circuit Court's sentencing powers are outlined in common law and in statute. The Circuit Court has the capacity to impose the maximum penalty of life imprisonment where that penalty has been provided in statute.

13.3.3 CENTRAL CRIMINAL COURT

The Central Criminal Court has full original jurisdiction in all criminal matters. It enjoys exclusive jurisdiction in the following offences:

- Treason (Treason Act 1939, s. 1).

- Conspiracy to commit treason (Treason Act 1939, s. 2).

- Misprision of treason (Treason Act 1939, s. 3).

- Usurpation of the functions of the government (Offences Against the State Act 1939, s. 6).

- Obstruction of Government (Offences Against the State Act 1939, s. 7).

- Obstruction of the President (Offences Against the State Act 1939, s. 8).

- Murder.

- Attempt to murder.

- Conspiracy to murder.

- Piracy.

- Genocide (Genocide Act 1973, s. 2).

Section 10 of the Criminal Law (Rape) (Amendment) Act 1990 added the following offences to the list of those triable exclusively in the Central Criminal Court:

- Rape (both rape contrary to s. 2 of the Criminal Law (Rape) Act 1981 and under s. 4 of the Criminal Law (Rape) (Amendment) Act 1990).

- Aggravated sexual assault.

- Attempted aggravated sexual assault.

- Aiding, abetting, counselling or procuring the offence of aggravated sexual assault.

- Incitement to the offence of aggravated sexual assault.

- Conspiracy to commit a rape offence, aggravated sexual assault or any of the inchoate offences associated with it.

Certain competition offences were added by s. 11 of the Competition Act 2002, which provides that persons indicted either as principals or as accessories to competition offences are to be tried in the Central Criminal Court where they are accused of:

- offences concerning anti-competitive agreements, decisions and concerted practices (Competition Act 2002, s. 6);

- offences concerning abuse of a dominant position (Competition Act 2002, s. 7);

- attempts and conspiracy to commit competition offences contrary to ss. 6 and 7 of the Competition Act 2002.

If an accused person is charged with a number of offences, of which some are exclusively reserved to the Central Criminal Court and some are triable in the Circuit Court, the return for trial should be to the Central Criminal Court.

13.3.4 THE SPECIAL CRIMINAL COURT

The Special Criminal Court is a non-jury court, established under Part V of the Offences Against the State Act 1939. The Court, composed of a minimum of three judges sitting together, deals with a limited range of 'scheduled offences' as well as ordinary offences in certain circumstances. Drafted with the threat to the state from subversive activity in mind, Article 38.3.1° of the Constitution provides:

> Special Courts may be established by law for the trial of offences in cases where it may be determined in accordance with such law that the ordinary courts are inadequate to secure the effective administration of justice, and the preservation of public peace and order.

Article 38.5, and its statement that 'no person shall be tried on any criminal charge without a jury', is specifically precluded from application to the Special Courts referred to in Article 38.3.1°. There is, therefore, no absolute constitutional entitlement in Irish law to trial by jury.

13.3.4.1 Scheduled offences

Section 36 of the Offences Against the State Act 1939 permits the designation of 'scheduled offences' if the Government is satisfied that the ordinary courts are inadequate to secure the effective administration of justice and the preservation of public peace in respect of the specified offences. Offences may be scheduled only if there is a government proclamation in force bringing Part V of the Act into operation, declaring the need for extraordinary powers.

Offences that remain scheduled pursuant to the Offences Against the State Act 1939 (Scheduled Offences) Order, 1972, include:

- offences under the Explosive Substances Act 1883;

- offences under the Firearms Acts, 1925 to 1971; and

- offences under the Offences against the State Act 1939.

A number of offences were added to the list of scheduled offences by s. 14 of the Offences Against the State (Amendment) Act 1998, including:

- directing an unlawful organisation (Offences Against the State (Amendment) Act 1998, s. 6, as substituted by the Criminal Justice (Amendment) Act 2009, s. 25);

- possession of articles for purposes connected with certain offences (Offences Against the State (Amendment) Act 1998, s. 7);

- unlawful collection of information (Offences Against the State (Amendment) Act 1998, s. 8);

- withholding information (Offences Against the State (Amendment) Act 1998, s. 9); and

- training persons in the making or use of firearms (Offences Against the State (Amendment) Act 1998, s. 12).

While the Criminal Justice (Terrorist Offences) Act 2005 extends the concept of membership of an unlawful organisation to international terrorist groups, offences that have as their basis the Criminal Justice (Terrorist Offences) Act 2005, are not scheduled offences for the purposes of s. 30 of the Offences Against the State Act 1939.

The Criminal Justice (Amendment) Act 2009 further adds to the list of scheduled offences by scheduling a number of 'organised crime' offences in the Criminal Justice Act 2006:

- directing a criminal organisation (Criminal Justice Act 2006, s. 71A, as inserted by the Criminal Justice (Amendment) Act 2009, s. 5);

- participating or contributing to organised crime (Criminal Justice Act 2006, s. 72, as substituted by s. 6 of the Criminal Justice (Amendment) Act 2009); and

- commission of an offence for a criminal organisation (Criminal Justice Act 2006, s. 73, as amended by the Criminal Justice (Amendment) Act 2009, s. 10).

The District Court must send a person charged with an indictable scheduled offence forward for trial to the Special Criminal Court, unless the DPP directs otherwise. In circumstances where the scheduled offences in question can be dealt with summarily, the District Court must send the offence forward for trial to the Special Criminal Court if the DPP so requests.

Non-scheduled offences will be dealt with by the Special Criminal Court, if the DPP certifies that the ordinary courts are in her opinion 'inadequate to secure the effective administration of justice and the preservation of peace and order in relation to the trial of such a person on such a charge' (Offences Against the State Act 1939, s. 46). Section 47 of the Offences Against the State

Act 1939 provides that persons may be brought directly before the Special Criminal Court on the direction of the DPP, where scheduled offences are to be charged or where the ordinary courts are considered by her to be inadequate.

13.4 The Book of Evidence

13.4.1 CONTENT AND SERVICE

The book of evidence contains a statement of the charge or charges against the accused, a list of the witnesses the prosecution proposes to call at the trial, their statements, documentary evidence and a list of exhibits (such as certificates and reports from the forensic science laboratory concerning drugs, fingerprints, DNA analysis, ballistic reports, CCTV and so on).

After consent has been given by the DPP to send the accused forward for trial, the book of evidence must be served on the accused, and a copy furnished to the court (s. 4B(2) of the Criminal Procedure Act 1967).

There is a 42-day period for service of the book of evidence, which begins when it has been determined that the accused person will be sent forward for trial on indictment for one of the reasons described below, that is:

- a determination made by the accused person opting for trial by jury;
- the decision of the prosecutor for trial on indictment; or
- by the District Judge refusing jurisdiction in relation to the offence on the basis that it is non-minor and accordingly unsuited to summary disposal (s. 4B(1) of the Criminal Procedure Act 1967, as substituted by s. 37 of the Criminal Procedure Act 2010).

13.4.2 EXTENSION OF TIME FOR SERVICE

Frequently applications are made for the extension of time for service of the book of evidence. Additional time may be required for various reasons, for instance, in the event that a certificate of analysis is not available from the Forensic Science Laboratory, where the case involves analysis of CCTV, telephone or other records, or where there are a very large number of statements to be considered.

The 42-day time limit for service of the book of evidence may be extended by the court, on the application of the prosecutor, if the court is satisfied that there is a good reason for the extension and that it would be in the interests of justice to do so (Criminal Procedure Act 1967, s. 4B (3), as inserted by the Criminal Justice Act 1999, s. 9). In the event that an application for an extension is refused, the case may be struck out (Criminal Procedure Act 1967, s. 4B (5), as inserted by s. 9 of the Criminal Justice Act 1999), but the prosecution is not precluded from instituting proceedings against the accused subsequently (Criminal Procedure Act 1967, s. 4B (6), as inserted by s. 9 of the Criminal Justice Act 1999).

The practice of extending time for service of the book of evidence was examined in the case of *Dunne v The Governor of Cloverhill Prison* [2009] 3 IR 378, where it was found by the Supreme Court to be a routine and necessary fact of legal life. There it had been argued that evidence should be adduced as to the reasons for the delay in the preparation of the book of evidence, an argument rejected on the basis that doing so would clutter the courts with witnesses and

> lead to 'trials within trials' at a point in the criminal process which may more aptly be described as administrative and procedural rather than adjudicative.

However, the prosecution must provide a full explanation of any procedural difficulty arising which necessitates an application for an extension of time. The court in *Dunne v Governor of Cloverhill Prison* stressed that a greater onus lies on the prosecution where the accused is in custody, in which case a District Judge faced with an unsatisfactory explanation or an unreasonable delay, may quite properly demand that evidence be given regarding any procedural difficulty arising, and where the requisite evidence is not forthcoming, decline to grant a further application by the prosecution for a remand.

13.4.3   SERVICE OF ADDITIONAL EVIDENCE

Additional evidence may be served at any time up until the trial date. Like the book of evidence, the prosecutor must serve on the accused, or his solicitor, any additional evidence proposed to be adduced at the trial, with copies to be furnished to the court. Such additional evidence might comprise a list of further witnesses, their statements, additional statements from witnesses whose evidence is already contained in the book of evidence, documentary evidence (and the relevant notices and certificates in relation to that documentary evidence required under the Criminal Evidence Act 1992), depositions and a list of any further exhibits (s. 4C of the Criminal Procedure Act 1999 as inserted by s. 9 of the Criminal Justice Act 1999).

13.5   The Indictment

The indictment is a written statement of the charges against the accused. Section 4(1) of the Criminal Justice (Administration) Act 1924 specifies that:

> Every indictment shall contain, and shall be sufficient if it contains, a statement of the specific offence or offences with which the accused person is charged, together with such particulars as may be necessary for giving reasonable information as to the nature of the charge.

The detailed rules that apply to indictments are contained in the First Schedule of the Criminal Justice (Administration) Act 1924.

The indictment is prepared by prosecution counsel and will outline the offences on which the accused has been sent forward for trial. Other offences (including summary offences) may be added or substituted (Criminal Procedure Act 1967, ss. 4M and 4N, as inserted by Criminal Justice Act 1999, s. 9). It is also open to the trial court to correct a defect in a charge against the accused, unless the correction would result in injustice (Criminal Procedure Act 1967, s. 4O, as inserted by Criminal Justice Act 1999, s. 9).

13.6   Arraignment

The arraignment is the starting point of the trial, where the accused is called to appear before the court, the indictment is read to him and he is asked if he pleads guilty or not guilty.

If a plea of guilty is entered, the court may proceed to sentence the accused, though usually the court will adjourn the case for sentence at a later date, to allow for preparation of reports that will assist the court in sentencing, including, e.g. victim impact reports, probation reports, etc.

If the accused enters a plea of not guilty, a trial date will be set. It is open to the accused to change his plea to one of guilty at any time subsequently, just as it is possible for an accused person who has entered a plea of guilty to withdraw that plea and enter a plea of not guilty.

13.7   Fitness to Be Tried

Where a question arises as to the capacity of the accused person to understand and participate in the proceedings, the fitness to be tried procedures outlined in the Criminal Law (Insanity) Act 2006 come into play. If by reason of a mental disorder the accused person is unable to understand the nature or course of the proceedings, so as to:

- plead to the charge;
- instruct a legal representative;
- in the case of an indictable offence which may be tried summarily, elect for a trial by jury;
- make a proper defence;

- in the case of a trial by jury, challenge a juror to whom he or she might wish to object; or

- understand the evidence,

they will be deemed unfit to be tried (Criminal Law (Insanity) Act 2006, s. 4).

The accused's fitness may be put in issue by the prosecution, the defence or the court (Criminal Law (Insanity) Act 2006, s. 4(1)). The decision as to the accused's fitness will be made by the judge. The District Court makes the determination in respect of summary offences or indictable offences being tried summarily (Criminal Law (Insanity) Act 2006, s. 4(3)(a)). The court to which the person would have been sent forward, if the accused were fit for trial, makes the determination in cases involving offences to be tried on indictment (Criminal Law (Insanity) Act 2006, s. 4(4)(a)).

A person who is found to be fit to be tried is then deemed to be before the court, as though the District Court had returned the person for trial in the ordinary way, and the trial continues accordingly. If the person is found to be unfit to be tried, the proceedings are adjourned and the court may order in-patient or out-patient treatment for the person.

13.8   Juveniles Charged With Indictable Offences

As referenced in **Chapter 9**, every child accused of a criminal offence, irrespective of gravity, is entitled to be considered for admission to the Juvenile Diversion Programme operated by An Garda Síochána (Children Act 2001, s. 18).

The objective of the Diversion Programme (as previously discussed at **8.4**) is the diversion of 'any child who accepts responsibility for his or her criminal or anti-social behaviour from committing further offences or engaging in further anti-social behaviour' (Children Act 2001, s. 19(1), as substituted by s. 124 of the Criminal Justice Act 2006). Any child who takes responsibility for his or her behaviour and agrees to be cautioned, and (where appropriate) agrees to be supervised by a juvenile liaison officer, is eligible for participation in the programme, once the Director of the Juvenile Diversion Programme is satisfied that admission to the programme is appropriate, in the best interests of the child, and not inconsistent with the interests of society and the victim of the offence (Children Act 2001, s. 23).

As previously outlined, the age of criminal responsibility in Ireland is 12. Children under the age of 12 are incapable of committing a crime (except the limited offences for which children between 10 and 12 may be prosecuted, i.e. murder, manslaughter, rape, rape under s. 4 of the Criminal Law (Rape) (Amendment) Act 1990 or aggravated sexual assault). Accordingly (save for the exceptions outlined), children under 12 can neither be brought before the courts nor admitted to the Diversion Programme.

If a child is considered unsuitable for diversion they can be prosecuted in the Children Court, which is a special sitting of the District Court. Where children are accused of indictable offences, jurisdiction is a matter for the court. The Children Court may deal summarily with any indictable offence other than those exclusively reserved to the Central Criminal Court, unless the court is of the opinion that the offence is not a minor offence fit to be tried (or dealt with on a plea of guilty) summarily.

The court must inform the child of his or her right to be tried by jury, and may not deal summarily with a child who does not consent to having the matter tried summarily (Children Act 2001, s. 75(3)). In determining whether to deal with an indictable offence with which a child is charged, the court must take into account the age and level of maturity of the child and any other facts considered relevant (Children Act 2001, s. 75(2)).

Children charged with manslaughter, or offences which are reserved to the Central Criminal Court, may be sent forward for sentence on a signed plea if the child signs a plea of guilty and the court is satisfied that the child understands the nature of the offence and facts alleged (Children Act 2001, s. 75(5)). Children may only be sent forward on a signed plea with the consent of the DPP (Children Act 2001, s. 75(6)). As is the case with adults who are sent forward on a signed plea, the child may withdraw his or her plea subsequently, in which case, they are tried as though they had been sent forward for trial as distinct from sentence (Children Act 2001, s. 75(7)).

There is an onus on prosecuting authorities to deal with cases involving juvenile defendants expeditiously, a duty 'over and above' the normal duty to ensure a reasonably expeditious trial for accused persons (*G v DPP* [2014] IEHC 33).

13.8.1   CHILDREN CHARGED JOINTLY WITH ADULTS

Where children are charged jointly with adults the child is dealt with in the Children Court and the adult is dealt with in the court in which they would ordinarily appear.

13.9   Indictable Trials Involving Juvenile Complainants

Chapter 10 deals with the application of evidence in criminal proceedings, generally. In cases concerning violence, the threat of violence or sexual offences, evidence may be given by live television link, whether from within or outside the state, where the witness is under 18 years of age, unless the court sees good reason to the contrary (Criminal Evidence Act 1992, s. 14 as amended by the Children Act 2001, s. 257(3)). There is provision for the giving of evidence by television link in any other case with the leave of the court.

Where children are giving evidence by television link, it is specified in legislation that traditional court apparel (wigs and gowns) should not be worn by the judge, barrister or solicitor concerned in the examination of the witness (Criminal Evidence Act 1992, s. 13).

Intermediaries may be used in the examination of child witnesses through live television link, if the court is satisfied that the interests of justice require an intermediary to help convey the meaning of the questions asked to the child, having regard to the age or mental condition of the witness (Criminal Evidence Act 1992, s. 14).

Where complainants are under 14 years of age, their evidence is frequently video recorded by members of the Gardaí who are trained specialist child victim interviewers. A video recording of any statement made by a child under 14 during an interview with a member of the Garda Síochána is admissible at trial as evidence of any fact stated therein of which direct oral evidence would be admissible, provided that the child whose statement was video recorded is available for cross-examination (Criminal Evidence Act 1992, s. 16). The court has discretion to exclude a video recording or a part of a video recording if the court is of the opinion that in the interests of justice the recording or part of the recording ought not to be admitted (Criminal Evidence Act 1992, s 16(2)).

13.10   *Nolle Prosequi*

If the DPP wishes to discontinue a prosecution, a *nolle prosequi* is entered. The entry of a *nolle prosequi* does not equate with an acquittal and does not preclude the subsequent institution of proceedings for the same offence. The Criminal Justice (Administration) Act 1924 provides at s. 12 that a *nolle prosequi* may be entered at any time after the indictment is preferred to the jury and before a verdict is returned. In practice, a *nolle prosequi* is normally entered before the indictment is 'preferred' to the jury.

13.11   Verdict

The verdicts available to juries are 'guilty', 'not guilty' or 'cannot agree'. Juries may also find that the accused is not guilty of the offence alleged, but is guilty of another offence. This is known as an alternative verdict.

Jury verdicts do not have to be unanimous. There must be 11 jurors, of whom 10 must agree. A verdict can be given where there are 11 or 12 unanimous jurors, or where the jury is divided 11:1, 10:1, or 10:2 (Criminal Justice Act 1984, s. 25). Such majority decisions are accepted after the jury has deliberated for a period of time as specified in the applicable 1984 Act.

PART VI

SENTENCING, ROAD TRAFFIC OFFENCES, APPEALS, AND JUDICIAL REVIEW

CHAPTER 14

SENTENCING

14.1   Introduction

When a solicitor represents a client before the criminal courts s/he must be aware of the practice and procedures of sentencing. If the client is convicted or pleads guilty to the criminal charge or charges before the court, then the court may proceed to sentence. The purpose of this chapter is to provide guidance to a solicitor as to how best to represent a client at this juncture in the solicitor–client relationship.

14.2   The Sentence Hearing

The right to a fair trial as protected by Articles 38.1 and 40.4.1 of the Constitution of Ireland extends beyond the point of conviction and protects the right to be sentenced in a fair and proportionate manner.

14.2.1   THE ROLE OF THE JUDGE OR JUDGES

In both the District Court and Circuit Court, sentence will be passed by one judge of that court sitting alone. In the Court of Criminal Appeal (now the Court of Appeal) and Special Criminal Court there will be three judges sitting together. Their function is to pass a sentence that is lawful.

14.2.2   THE FACTS OF THE CASE

If the accused pleads guilty to the criminal offence or offences for which s/he appears before the court, then the court will hear an outline of the facts of the criminal behaviour. This outline of the facts is usually given in evidence by the prosecuting Garda. If the defendant has contested the case by pleading 'not guilty' and has been found guilty after the subsequent trial, the court will have heard the facts of the case through the evidence presented during trial.

14.2.3   PREVIOUS CONVICTIONS

Having perused the facts of the case, the court will then seek information on oath from the prosecuting Garda as to whether the convicted person has previous convictions. If the defence accepts the convictions that are disclosed to the court, the fact of those convictions does not need to be formally proven. If, however, the convicted person does not accept the Garda's record of previous convictions, then they are regarded by the sentencing court as a matter that needs evidential proof through the production of the relevant court orders by the prosecution legal team through the prosecuting Garda.

14.2.3.1 Spent convictions

The Criminal Justice (Spent Convictions and Certain Disclosures) Act 2016 has yet to be commenced at the time of writing. When it is signed into law and enacted, some minor convictions that are more than seven years old will become 'spent'. The effect of this will be that those convictions do not need to be declared by an offender. It is important that a solicitor in practice keeps abreast of this development and ensures that any convictions record presented regarding a client, reflects this proposed new law.

14.2.4 THE PROSECUTION SOLICITOR OR COUNSEL

There will be a solicitor from the Office of Director of Public Prosecutions (DPP) instructed to appear in all cases in courts of a higher jurisdiction than the District Court. In the District Court the vast majority of cases do not involve the DPP. However, some more complex or contentious matters may require the presence of a solicitor for the DPP or counsel instructed by the DPP with a member of the DPP solicitor team in attendance (as counsel are not permitted to attend court alone). The solicitor or attended counsel will lead the Garda through the evidence. This process will be a series of leading questions from the solicitor or counsel asking the Garda to confirm the facts of the case, usually each relevant element of the offence or offences.

Having declined to establish sentencing guidelines in *The People (DPP) v Tiernan* [1988] IR 250, the Court of Criminal Appeal (now the Court of Appeal) specifically addressed the role of the prosecution solicitor in the sentencing process in three recent judgments namely *The People (DPP) v Fitzgibbon* [2014] 2 ILRM 116, *The People (DPP) v Ryan* [2014] 2 ILRM 98, and *The People (DPP) v Z* [2014] IECCA 13, [2014] 2 ILRM 132, which together clarify what that prosecution role now is in assisting the court by providing guidance as to the range of sentences that might be appropriate in a particular case. In *Z* paragraph 2.7 of the judgment states:

> In this Court's view, there is now an obligation on the prosecution to draw to the attention of a sentencing judge any guidance, whether arising from an analysis carried out by this Court or from ISIS or otherwise, which touches on the ranges or bands of sentences which may be considered appropriate to any offence under consideration and the factors which are properly, at least in ordinary cases, to be taken into account. In many cases, this should not impose any significant burden on the prosecution for the sources ought to be easily recognised. In addition, it seems to this Court that it is incumbent on the prosecution to suggest, where such guidance is available, where the offence under consideration fits into the scheme of sentencing identified and why that is said to be the case. Finally, the prosecution should indicate the extent to which it is accepted that factors urged in mitigation by the defence are appropriate and give at least a broad indication of the adjustment, if any, in the overall sentence which it is accepted ought to be considered appropriate in the light of such mitigation.

It is important that both prosecution and defence solicitors acquaint themselves with these decisions, which provide guidance to a Court in what may reasonably be regarded as appropriate sentences for a variety of commonly prosecuted offences with an awareness that whilst the court can seek guidance from the prosecution solicitor the defence solicitor has a right to be heard on the matter also.

14.2.5 THE DEFENCE SOLICITOR

The defence solicitor's responsibility is to present his or her client to the court in the best possible manner. It is a job that requires some skill, given that the defendant has been convicted of breaching a criminal code of conduct. It is appropriate at this stage to discuss the steps that must be taken prior to this point in the trial by the defence solicitor.

14.3 Preparing a Plea in Mitigation

The first step is that the defence solicitor must take instructions from the client. A client should be advised that if s/he pleads guilty or is convicted, the court will seek to proceed to the sentence procedure. In preparation for this possibility or inevitability, depending on the client's instructions, the solicitor should seek clear instructions.

14.3.1   SEEK BASIC NON-CONTENTIOUS INSTRUCTIONS

The personal details of the defendant are highly relevant. The defence solicitor should confirm the client's age, marital status, occupation, and income and living arrangements. It should also be ascertained whether or not the client has previous convictions or any other criminal matters pending before the courts. It must be confirmed whether there are any suspended sentences outstanding.

14.3.2   CAUTION WHEN SEEKING CONTENTIOUS INSTRUCTIONS

A solicitor should address the reason for the criminal conduct that the defendant faces sentence upon. It may be that the defendant contested the original allegation but has been convicted at trial and, therefore, cannot provide the defence solicitor with a reason for the offending behaviour. However, in the vast majority of cases there will be a plea of guilty and, therefore, it is prudent to address the reasons for the offending behaviour. The defence solicitor should exercise caution in the taking of these instructions as it is not necessary to have more information than is necessary to address the issue.

Care should also be taken by the defence solicitor in seeking instructions regarding any personal challenging difficulties the client may have to manage or be subject to, such as a drug addiction. A solicitor should not ask a question of the client, in preparation of their sentence hearing, that is not relevant to the sentence hearing and that may provide information that is irrelevant to the sentencing process.

14.3.3   INTERACTION WITH THE PROSECUTION ON OR BEFORE A SENTENCE HEARING

It is important for a defence solicitor to be able to interact with the Gardaí and members of the prosecution legal team, be they solicitors from the Office of the DPP or counsel. The facts of the offence(s), the subject of the defendant's sentence hearing, must be ascertained by the defence solicitor from the prosecution team and then confirmed with the client. Whilst it is possible to plead guilty but not accept the facts as alleged by the Gardaí, it is not an advisable course of action and is rarely utilised in any court.

It is also important for the defence solicitor to confirm with the Gardaí whether they are willing to accept, if asked of them, certain questions about the accused. These questions will usually relate to the character of the defendant before and after the alleged criminal conduct. They may also relate to the client's conduct with the Garda during the detection and investigation of the criminal conduct in question.

The purpose of this interaction with the prosecution is to allow the defence solicitor to ascertain how the client can be best presented by him or her before the presiding sentencing judge, without fear of a damaging contradiction from the Gardaí and prosecution. This level of preparation will subsequently allow the defence solicitor to advise the client in advance of the sentence hearing process with as much accuracy as is possible and prepare the client to anticipate the likely outcome in terms of the sentence that will be handed down by the judge.

14.4   Advising the Client in Advance of the Sentence Hearing

It is important to advise the client in advance of the sentence hearing about the range of possible outcomes. It is not possible to advise regarding a certain outcome as, unlike other jurisdictions, e.g. the USA, we do not have a plea bargaining system. However, with experience and knowledge of the law, it is possible to advise the client with reasonable accuracy regarding what a given judge is likely to deem an appropriate sentence.

14.4.1   ADVOCACY AT THE SENTENCE HEARING

The purpose of the plea in mitigation is to present the convicted client to the sentencing judge in the best possible light. At the point where the defence solicitor begins the plea in mitigation, the client will have been presented in a negative manner by the prosecution; the court will have heard the facts of the offending behaviour and may have heard about previous convictions of the offender.

14.4.2   FIRSTLY ADDRESS THE OFFENDING BEHAVIOUR

The offending behaviour should be addressed by the defence advocate at the outset of the plea in mitigation. The reason for the offence and the circumstances in which the behaviour was committed ought to be explained to the court where possible. If it is not possible to say anything about the offending behaviour that improves the defendant's position then the court should be simply told that it is accepted that the behaviour was criminal and nothing helpful can be said beyond this.

14.4.3   THE ACCUSED PERSON'S INTERACTION WITH THE GARDAÍ AND THE PROSECUTION

The manner in which the accused interacted with the Gardaí and the prosecution advocate is highly relevant. If the accused was cooperative and expressed remorse, the defence advocate should ask the Garda giving evidence at the sentence hearing to confirm that behaviour and statement, so that the sentencing judge can take such matters into consideration in determining the sentence. If it is agreed by the prosecution that the defendant offered a plea of guilty at an early stage of the criminal prosecution process, this fact should be brought to the sentencing court's attention, as it can (save for exceptional cases) attract some reduction in the severity of the sentence.

14.5   Crimes Involving Identifiable Victims

Many crimes do not have an identifiable victim. This is regularly the case in the context of white collar, regulatory or corporate crime. However, for a crime that has a clearly defined victim the defence solicitor must take particular care in preparation for and at the sentence hearing to demonstrate an awareness of the impact of the crime on the injured party/victim. Instructions ought to be taken from the convicted client regarding willingness to offer an apology and/or compensation or both.

14.5.1   COMPENSATION

If compensation is not forthcoming on a voluntary basis then the court can order compensation payment under s. 6(1) of the Criminal Justice Act 1993 (the 1993 Act). The court can order compensation where an offender is given the benefit of the Probation of Offenders Act 1907 as amended. However, the court should not order such a level of compensation that exceeds the civil jurisdiction of that sentencing court. A defence solicitor for the offender ought to take instructions regarding the client's means in order to address the court regarding the ability of the client to comply with any compensation order that it may wish to make. The client can subsequently appeal the compensation order.

14.5.2   VICTIM IMPACT REPORT

A defendant ought to be advised that a victim impact report will be read to the court in certain cases. For a thorough discussion on the victim-focused justice policies and court accommodation of the victim, see **Chapter 3**. The legal basis for this type of report was amended by ss. 4–6 of the Criminal Procedure Act 2010:

4.— *The Act of 1993 is amended by the substitution of the following section for section 5: 'Effect of certain offences on persons in respect of whom offence committed.*

5.— (1) *This section applies to—*

    (a) *a sexual offence within the meaning of the Criminal Evidence Act 1992,*

    (b) *an offence involving violence or the threat of violence to a person,*

    (c) *an offence under the Non-Fatal Offences Against the Person Act 1997, and*

    (d) *an offence consisting of attempting or conspiring to commit, or aiding, abetting, counselling, procuring or inciting the commission of, an offence mentioned in paragraph (a), (b) or (c).*

(2) (a) *When imposing sentence on a person for an offence to which this section applies, a court shall take into account, and may, where necessary, receive evidence or submissions concerning, any effect (whether long-term or otherwise) of the offence on the person in respect of whom the offence was committed.*

    (b) *For the purposes of paragraph (a), a "person in respect of whom the offence was committed" includes, where, as a result of the offence, that person has died, is ill or is otherwise incapacitated, a family member of that person.*

(3) (a) *When imposing sentence on a person for an offence to which this section applies, a court shall, upon application by the person in respect of whom such offence was committed, hear the evidence of the person in respect of whom the offence was committed as to the effect of the offence on such person.*

    (b) *For the purpose of paragraph (a), where the person in respect of whom the offence was committed—*

        (i) *is a child under the age of 14 years, the child, or his or her parent or guardian, may give evidence as to the effect of the offence concerned on that child,*

        (ii) *is—*

            (I) *a person with a mental disorder (not resulting from the offence concerned), the person or a family member,*

            (II) *a person with a mental disorder (not resulting from the offence concerned), who is a child, the person or his or her parent or guardian,*

        may give evidence as to the effect of the offence concerned on that person,

        (iii) *is a person who is ill or is otherwise incapacitated as a result of the offence, a family member of the person may give evidence as to the effect of the offence concerned on that person and on his or her family members,*

        (iv) *has died as a result of the offence, a family member of the person may give evidence as to the effect of the offence concerned—*

            (I) *on the person between the commission of the offence and his or her death (where relevant), and*

            (II) *on the family members of the person who has died.*

    (c) *A person who has been convicted of an offence to which this section applies may not give evidence pursuant to paragraph (b) in respect of that offence.*

    (d) *Where more than one family member seeks to avail of paragraph (b), the court may direct the family members to nominate one or more family members for the purpose of that paragraph.*

    (e) *Where the court directs the family members to nominate one or more family members pursuant to paragraph (d) and the family members are unable to reach agreement, the court may, having regard to the degree of relationship between the family members and the person in respect of whom the offence was committed, nominate one or more family members as it considers appropriate.*

  (4) *Where no evidence is given pursuant to subsection (3), the court shall not draw an inference that the offence had little or no effect (whether long-term or otherwise) on the person in respect of whom the offence was committed or, where appropriate, on his or her family members.*

(5) (a)   The court may, in the interests of justice, order that information relating to the evidence given under subsection (3) or a part of it shall not be published or broadcast.

   (b)   If any matter is published or broadcast in contravention of paragraph (a), the following persons, namely—

        (i)   in the case of a publication in a newspaper or periodical, any proprietor, any editor and any publisher of the newspaper or periodical,

        (ii)   in the case of any other publication, the person who publishes it, and

        (iii) in the case of a broadcast, any person who transmits or provides the programme in which the broadcast is made and any person having functions in relation to the programme corresponding to those of the editor of a newspaper,

shall be guilty of an offence.

   (c)   A person guilty of an offence under paragraph (b) shall be liable—

        (i)   on summary conviction, to a fine not exceeding €5,000 or to imprisonment for a term not exceeding 12 months or to both, or

        (ii)   on conviction on indictment, to a fine not exceeding €50,000 or to imprisonment for a term not exceeding 3 years or to both.

   (d)   Where an offence under paragraph (b) is committed by a body corporate and is proved to have been so committed with the consent, connivance or approval of or to be attributable to any neglect on the part of a person being a director, manager, secretary or other officer of the body corporate or any other person who was acting or purporting to act in any such capacity, that person as well as the body corporate shall be guilty of an offence and be liable to be proceeded against and punished as if he or she were guilty of the first-mentioned offence.

   (e)   Where the affairs of a body corporate are managed by its members, paragraph (d) shall apply in relation to the acts and defaults of a member in connection with his or her functions of management as if he or she were a director or manager of the body corporate.

(6)   In this section and in sections 5A and 5B, unless the context otherwise requires—

   "broadcast" has the meaning it has in section 2 of the Broadcasting Act 2009;

   "child" means a person under the age of 18;

   "family member" means—

   (a)   a spouse or partner of the person,

   (b)   a child, grandchild, parent, grandparent, brother, sister, uncle, aunt, nephew or niece of the person,

   (c)   a person who is acting in loco parentis to the person,

   (d)   a dependant of the person, or

   (e)   any other person whom the court considers to have had a close connection with the person;

   "guardian", in relation to a child, has the meaning it has in the Children Act 2001;

   "mental disorder" includes a mental illness, mental disability, dementia or any disease of the mind;

   "publish" means publish, other than by way of broadcast, to the public or a portion of the public.'

The above 2010 amendments reflect the desire from society to properly represent the victims of crime in the court process and especially at the sentence hearing. A defence solicitor ought to apply great care and skill in the approach to the victim impact report. This duty of care is heightened where the victim is a child or has a mental disorder where there is provision for a procedure to hear the evidence of the victim via video-link and through an intermediary.

Some civil society advocates, e.g. rape crisis agencies, believe that the right of the victim to give evidence extends to a right to have legal assistance from solicitor and/or counsel to so do. It is, nonetheless, a matter for the court to pass sentence and the victim cannot ask for a specific sentence.

As outlined in **Chapter 3**, there is a new EU-level legislation known as the 'Victims Rights Directive' that protects victims of crime. It was adopted at European level on 15 November 2012 and must be implemented by all national governments of EU Member States by 16 November 2015 at the latest, although at the time of writing this Directive has yet to be transposed into domestic legislation in Ireland.

14.6 The Offender's Personal Circumstances and Proportionality in Sentencing

The personal circumstances of the offender ought to be well known by the defence solicitor. Advocating with respect to these circumstances ought to be done sparingly, as 'less is usually more' in a sentence hearing. The most pertinent and compelling of personal circumstances ought to be brought to the court's attention. If the court is likely to be considering a custodial penalty, the effect of such a penalty in relation to these personal circumstances ought to be addressed. The mere fact that the offender is in poor health or suffers from addiction difficulties does not mean that a reduction in sentence will be considered. The more serious the offence, the less likely it is that the ill-health of the defendant will be given much consideration at the sentencing stage of proceedings.

In *DPP v Kelly* [2005] 2 IR 321 Denham J, stated:

> sentences must also be proportionate to the personal circumstances of the appellant. The essence of the discretionary nature of sentencing is that the personal situation of the appellant must be taken into consideration by the court … Thus, having assessed what is the appropriate sentence for a particular crime it is the duty of the court to consider then the particular circumstances of the convicted person. It is within this ambit that mitigating factors fall to be considered.

This passage perfectly encapsulates the basic principles of a sentence hearing and the role of the defence advocate.

14.6.1 THE HEALTH OF THE OFFENDER AND SEEKING THIRD PARTY REPORTS

The health of the client ought to be known by the solicitor. If the offender has suffered from any addictions to drugs or alcohol, instructions ought to be taken regarding the possibility of the offender's rehabilitation. It is advisable, where possible, to seek reports in advance from any third party professionals, such as a doctor or rehabilitation centre, to confirm the client's instructions. Care should be taken when seeking such reports. The solicitor should be reasonably confident of the client's instructions as, if such reports contradict those instructions, it may limit the defence advocate's presentation of the client to the sentencing court. Any reports sought by the defence solicitor to assist the presentation of the plea in mitigation need not be disclosed to the court or prosecution unless they are likely to be helpful in the mitigation of the anticipated sentence.

14.6.2 A COURT-SANCTIONED REPORT

A solicitor for a defendant ought to consider whether it would be appropriate to ask the court to order a probation report. It may be the case that the court will order one to assist it in passing an appropriate sentence. The practicalities of such a report should be explained to the offender, who will be obliged to meet with a probation officer on at least one occasion in the intervening period. It is usually the case that such a postponement of sentence will not result in the offender being remanded in custody in the intervening period. However, it is lawful for the court to revoke the bail of the offender at this conviction stage. It may be the case that the offender will consent to having bail revoked. If they do not consent, then the court ought to be slow to revoke bail for this purpose and should only do so if there is a rational and legal basis for such a revocation, such as the likelihood of committing further offences whilst on bail or the real fear that the convicted person will abscond. The applicable principles are outlined by Denham J. in *Howard v District Judge Early and DPP* (unreported, 4 July 2000, Supreme Court) stated at paragraphs 12–13:

Whilst the District Court has powers of remand in custody they should not be used for *de facto* sentencing.

Where there are probation and other reports before the court so that adequate information is available and the maximum sentence is a fine and not custody, it is for the court to exercise its power to remand with constitutional due process. This might include a remand in custody but would require due consideration.

14.7   Minimum and Maximum Sentences and Sentencing Guidelines—The Jurisdiction of the Court and Proportionality in the Imposition of Such Sentences

As previously indicated, a defence solicitor must advise a client as to the possible outcomes at a sentence hearing. The maximum and minimum sentences allowable under law are part of the jurisdiction of the court. It is also necessary for a prosecution solicitor appearing, as the representative of the Chief Prosecution Solicitor or another state agency that prosecutes criminal offences, to be aware of the jurisdiction of the court. On occasion the court may seek guidance from such prosecutors.

Section 29 of the Criminal Justice Act 1999 allows a court at sentence to impose the maximum sentence allowed by law, even where the accused proffered a plea of guilty and where other mitigating factors prevail. As recently as March 2014 the Court of Criminal Appeal in *DPP v Z* [2014] 2 ILRM 132 upheld the legality of a maximum sentence even where there was a plea of guilty. In that case, due to the exceptional circumstances of the case it was regarded as being

> difficult to overestimate to the severity of the many cruel and depraved crimes committed by Mr. Z against his own children.

There are various statutes which impose a minimum mandatory sentence for an offence. The most obvious example is the minimum mandatory sentence of 10 years' imprisonment imposed by s. 5 of the Criminal Justice Act 1999 for the possession of €13,500 worth of a controlled drug which is an offence under s.15A of the Misuse of Drugs Act 1977.

As a consequence of prevailing case law and legislation, a defence solicitor ought to advise the client clearly as to the maximum and minimum sentence possible.

There has been a wealth of decisions from the Court of Criminal Appeal (now Court of Appeal) and the Supreme Court regarding the appropriate considerations at a sentence hearing in relation to maximum and minimum sentences. It is best summarised by Denham J. (sitting in the Court of Criminal Appeal) in the 2009 case of *DPP v Rory Lenihan* [2009] IECCA 54. This case was an appeal by the state against the apparent leniency of a sentence in the Circuit Court for an offence contrary to s. 15A of the Misuse of Drugs Act 1977:

> While bearing the statute and case law in mind, each case requires to be decided in light of the particular offence and the particular circumstances of the accused. The Court should first determine what the appropriate notional sentence is, bearing in mind the maximum sentence of life imprisonment, then consider the aggravating and mitigating circumstances, and then apply the mitigating factors. If the consequent sentence is more than 10 years then that is the sentence.

The Court of Appeal has recognised the need for sentence ranges. It is now the accepted role of the Court of Appeal to offer general sentencing guidelines. In an effort to ensure the Court of Appeal can formulate accurate and fair sentencing guidelines the Irish Sentencing Information System (ISIS) was established some years ago to assist the Court by providing data and empirical research. Its website at http://www.irishsentencing.ie states:

> ISIS aims to design and develop a computerised information system, on sentences and other penalties imposed for offences in criminal proceedings, which may inform judges when considering the sentence to be imposed in an individual case. The sentencing information system enables a judge, by entering relevant criteria, to access information on the range of sentences and other penalties which have been imposed for particular types of offence in previous cases. The project is overseen by a Steering Committee of judges, together with an expert on sentencing

law, appointed by the Courts Service Board. The Steering Committee conducted a survey of similar systems in other countries and found those in New South Wales and Scotland to be most relevant. A study was undertaken of the Scottish system. The ISIS database is intended to be descriptive. The information is to assist a judge by providing information on sentences which have been given in previous cases.

The Court of Appeal is an appropriate place for a student to see how sentencing guidelines and principles are given effect on a daily basis.

14.8 Concurrent and Consecutive Sentences and Proportionality

A defence solicitor may often have instructions from a client indicating a desire to plead guilty simultaneously to a number of individual offences which are unconnected, having occurred on various dates. This occurrence is especially common in the District Court. The defence solicitor ought to advise in such circumstances that the court may impose a series of concurrent sentences but that there is a considerable risk of the imposition of consecutive sentences. An offender may wish to instruct the defence solicitor in such a manner when a sentence is already being served for another offence, in the hope that outstanding anticipated sentences will not increase the custodial period being served. The client should be advised that the court is allowed to impose consecutive sentences to a maximum of two years at District Court level and to a longer period on indictable offences, depending on the applicable sentencing tariff for the offences in question. However, in imposing any sentence a court must act proportionally.

A defence solicitor ought to confirm whether any offences for which the client instructs that a plea of guilty applies were committed whilst the client was on bail on another charge. Section 11 of the Criminal Justice Act 1984 as amended by s. 22 of the Criminal Justice Act 2007 states:

> 22.— *Section 11 of the Act of 1984 is amended by the substitution of the following subsection for subsection (1):*
>
> (1) *Any sentence of imprisonment passed on a person for an offence—*
>
> > (a) *committed while on bail, whether committed before or after the commencement of section 22 of the Criminal Justice Act 2007, or*
> >
> > (b) *committed after such commencement while the person is unlawfully at large after the issue of a warrant for his or her arrest for non-compliance with a condition of the recognisance concerned, shall be consecutive on any sentence passed on him or her for a previous offence or, if he or she is sentenced in respect of two or more previous offences, on the sentence last due to expire, so however that, where two or more consecutive sentences as required by this section are passed by the District Court, the aggregate term of imprisonment in respect of those consecutive sentences shall not exceed 2 years.*

The court therefore must impose consecutive sentences for offences committed whilst the client was already on bail. However, these are not the only circumstances which attract consecutive sentences. It is lawful for a court to impose consecutive sentences where it is rational and proportional in respect of the gravity of the offences to do so.

The imposition of consecutive sentences requires the court to take care not to offend the 'totality principle', as stated by O'Donnell J. in the Court of Criminal Appeal in the case of *DPP v Michael Farrell* [2010] IECCA 68.

> In the field of sentencing, it is certainly the case that there is a principle of totality, which requires that when consecutive sentences are employed, a court must be careful to take account of the overall impact of the sentence, the moral blameworthiness of the accused and the prospect of rehabilitation, and therefore recognises that the total sentence in some cases should be less than the sum of the component parts.

A solicitor for the state should also be able to guide the court on the maximum and minimum sentences, and in relation to consecutive and concurrent sentences as outlined in **14.2.4**. However, it is not lawful for a solicitor for the state to ask the court to pass a sentence or recommend the terms of a sentence.

14.9   Offences Taken Into Consideration

Section 8 of the 1951 Criminal Justice Act was amended by s. 9 of the Criminal Justice (Miscellaneous Provisions) Act 1997. This section permits a court to take offences into consideration when an accused person pleads guilty to a number of offences at the same time and when the DPP consents to the disposal of those offences in that manner. A solicitor for either an accused or the state ought to be aware that the court can only 'take offences into consideration' if it is acting within the permitted limits of its jurisdiction. Therefore, for example, the District Court could not take into consideration the offence of s. 15A of the Misuse of Drugs Act 1977 (as amended) as that offence cannot be tried by that court.

14.10   Sentencing and the Possibility for the Granting of a Probation Order

A solicitor must be aware of the full range of options available in relation to probation at a sentence hearing. The Probation Service of Ireland is a state agency that tries to assist offenders to desist from committing criminal acts and, thereby assist the community at large that wants to live in a crime-free environment. The Probation Service may be asked to intervene before and/or after sentence by a court. The court may also impose a statutory provision under the Probation Act 1907 without calling upon the Probation Service to intervene in the rehabilitation of the offender.

The role of the Probation Service has evolved and was most recently the subject of amending legislation in the Criminal Justice Act 2006 in that it now has a statutory duty to work with child offenders and sex offenders. Further amendments in the operation of the Service are anticipated in the Criminal Justice (Community Sanctions) Bill 2014, but on foot of a parliamentary question on 25 March 2016 the Minister for Justice has indicated that this bill is with the state's legal advisers for further consideration.

As discussed in **Chapter 9** on Juvenile Justice, solicitors must be aware that a child cannot be placed in detention or ordered to complete a community-based sanction without the court ordering a report from the Probation Service of Ireland.

14.10.1   THE PROBATION OF OFFENDERS ACT 1907

The Probation of Offenders Act 1907 (Probation Act) allows a court in certain cases to mark the facts of the offence as proven but to fall short of recording a conviction under s. 1(1). A defence solicitor will rely on this subsection on a regular basis in the District Court but must be aware that there is legislation to which it is not applicable, e.g. an offence that is commonly known as 'drink-driving' and many revenue offences.

The Probation Act states:

> (1)   *Where any person is charged before a court of summary jurisdiction with an offence punishable by such court, and the court think that the charge is proved, but is of opinion that, having regard to the character, antecedents, age, health or mental condition of the person charged, or to the trivial nature of the offence, or to the extenuating circumstances under which the offence was committed, it is inexpedient to inflict any punishment or any other than a nominal punishment, or that it is expedient to release the offender on probation, the court may, without proceeding to a conviction, make an order either:-*
>
> > (i)   *Dismissing the information or charge, or*
> >
> > (ii)   *Discharging the offender conditionally on his entering into a recognisance, with or without sureties, to be of good behaviour and to appear for conviction and sentence when called on at any time during such period, not exceeding three years, as may be specified in the order.*

It would be reckless and negligent for a defence solicitor to advise a client who has no previous convictions that this section will automatically apply. The solicitor should draw to the court's attention those aspects of the Probation Act which apply to the accused person's character and to the facts of the case.

A record of the application of the Probation Act will occur, therefore a defendant may find it necessary to declare it at a later stage when seeking employment or on entering another country, or its existence may be referred to at a later date if the beneficiary of its application appears before a court on a subsequent alleged offence.

14.10.2 A CONDITIONAL DISCHARGE

The Probation Act may be applied on a conditional basis for an offender who is before the court for an indictable offence punishable by imprisonment. This discharge is subject to s. 1(2) of the Probation Act, which requires the defendant to enter into a recognisance. The application of this conditional discharge is classified as a recorded conviction and that fact must be stressed by the defence solicitor to the offender.

It is possible for a court to sentence an accused who has committed either a summary or indictable matter under s. 1(2) of the Probation Act. This sentence is a 'probation order'. It may require the offender to comply with certain conditions whilst under the guidance of the Probation Service. These conditions ought to be related to the defendant's reasons for offending, e.g. treatment for an alcohol addiction.

14.11 Suspended Sentences

The Criminal Justice Act 2006 legislated for the power of the courts to suspend or partially suspend custodial sentences. Solicitors appearing for either an accused person or the state should be acquainted with s. 99 of this Act as amended by s. 60 of the Criminal Justice Act and by s. 51 of the Criminal Justice (Miscellaneous Provisions) Act 2009.

However, concomitant with the date of writing, s. 99 (as amended) has been struck down as unconstitutional in the case of *Edward Moore and others v DPP and The AG* [2013 No. 54 JR]; [2013 No. 70 JR]; [2013 No. 120 JR]; [2013 No. 925 JR]; and [2013 No. 86 JR].

The most important aspects of this legislation were the provisions regarding the power to suspend a sentence and the power to activate a suspended sentence. Offenders were advised that if any offence is committed during the lifetime of the suspended sentence, that offender may be ordered by the court to serve some, or all, of the originally suspended sentence in prison. The court has discretion not to revoke the sentence; however, such discretion is used sparingly.

There have been a number of legal challenges to s. 99 which include the judgments of *Anthony Sharlott v Judge Collins & Ors and the DPP (Notice Party)* [2010] IEHC 482 (unreported), *DPP v Carter* [2014] IEHC 179, and *Damien McCabe v The Governor of Mountjoy Prison & Ors* [2014] IEHC 309 (2014). The effect of the *Sharlott* case was that where a person is convicted in the District Court and is in breach of a suspended sentence and wished to appeal the most recent sentence, they were allowed to do so before the court which imposed the suspended sentence which was asked to finalise that sentence. The effect of the more recent *McCabe* judgment was to prevent the Circuit Court, when sitting as an appeal court of the District Court, from activating a suspended sentence imposed pursuant to s. 99 until such time as the legislation was amended to offer a right of appeal.

A solicitor for an offender or the state in practice appeared before the court that was considering whether to re-activate a sentence it has previously suspended. The legal principles the court considered were statutory (within s. 99 of the Act) and from cases previously decided. In *The People (DPP) v Stewart*, which was a Court of Criminal Appeal judgment from Hardiman J. (unreported, 12 January 2004), it was said:

> There is power to activate the sentence but it is not mandatory to do so in that a judge may decline to do so if the court considers that the breach might be described as trivial or *de minimis*.

In addition to that legal reasoning there was the statutory guidance of s. 9 of the 2006 Act which allowed the court to decline to reactivate the suspended sentence, if it would be unjust in the circumstances to do so. However, the court had the power to re-activate part of the term of imprisonment. Section 10 of the 2006 Act allowed the court to remand the defendant in custody pending the decision of the court that originally gave the defendant the benefit of a suspended sentence.

In *Edward Moore and others v DPP and The AG* the judgment of Moriarty J. delivered on 19 April 2016, having cited s. 99 (as amended) and reviewed various difficulties and challenges associated with the implementation of that section, stated at the conclusion of his judgment, that he found the decision of Hogan J. (when in the High Court) in the case of *Damian McCabe v Ireland and the Attorney General* [2014] IEHC 435 of significant influence in the instant case.

> This decision, relating to circumstances effecting the plaintiff that were broadly comparable with those of the present applicant, was partly reversed by Finlay-Geoghegan J. in her judgment in the Court of Appeal within the past year, but I accept the argument advanced by Mr. McDonagh S.C. that this was in the context of finding a subsisting right of appeal in the individual facts of that case, and that the primary reasoning of Hogan J. in the High Court as to the predicament faced by the applicant, and by analogy with the present applicants, remains valid and highly persuasive. Among the observations made by Hogan J. in that case relate to the importance of their being a rational basis for any disparity of treatment affecting individuals in legislative provisions. Amongst these, he states at para. 15:

> > The equal treatment of similarly situated persons within the criminal justice system is at the heart of the concept of equality before the law which, as the language of that provision makes clear, is one of the fundamental objectives of Article 40.1.

> Hogan J. shortly thereafter proceeds:

> > This is especially so given that the fundamentally different treatment with regard to sentencing which would then obtain would so greatly impact on the core constitutional right to liberty under Article 40.4.1.

> Hogan J. then at para. 21 proceeds to state:

> > Given that in the present case the significantly differing treatment of otherwise similarly situated accused, so far as rights of appeal are concerned, is incapable of objective justification, and let it be recalled, no such justification has really been advanced, the conclusion that such a state of affairs plainly offends the guarantee of equality before the law and Article 40.1 is, accordingly, inescapable.

> Hogan J. in his conclusion proceeds to conclude that any such law as the provisions comprised in the Section presently under review must, by virtue of Article 34.3.4 comply with the principles articulated by Henchy J. in the celebrated case of *King v. Attorney General* [1981] I.R. 233, since the law must not ignore the fundamental norms of the legal order postulated by the Constitution. In that celebrated case, it was held by the Supreme Court that the inconsistency found in the relevant statutory provision resulted from incompatibility with the requirement in Article 38 of the Constitution that no person shall be tried on a criminal charge save in due course of law, with the guarantee in Article 40, s. 4 sub-s. 1, that no citizen shall be deprived of his liberty save in accordance with law, the principle of equality before the law declared in Article 40, s. 1, and with the guarantee in Article 40, s. 1, to defend and vindicate the personal rights of citizens.

> In all the circumstances of the case, and having given the matter much careful consideration as I can, I am persuaded that notwithstanding the presumption of constitutionality that exists in relation to enactments, and the regard and respect that Courts must show to enactments of the Oireachtais, the subsections under review of s. 99 fall to be viewed as unconstitutional in the context of the facts reviewed and the arguments made.

The consequences and implications of Moriarty J.'s judgment are, at the time of writing, under urgent examination in consultation with the Attorney General.

14.12   Bind Over

The power to bind a person over to the peace is legislated for within s. 54 of the Court (Supplemental Provisions) Act 1961 as amended by the Court of Appeal Act 2014. It allows the court to release someone either with or without recognisance, with a requirement that s/he will be of good behaviour and/or keep the peace. It is possible for a defendant to appeal such an order from the District Court to the Circuit Court, if such an original order is made by the District Court. A Bind Over Order can be made by a District Court, a Circuit Court, the High Court or the Supreme Court.

14.13   A Community Service Order

A court may order that a defendant be subject to a Community Service Order in lieu of an alternative penalty such as imprisonment or a fine. The terms of such an order can be imposed against any offender over the age of 16. The imposition of such an order is a recorded conviction and does not prevent the court from making any consequential or ancillary order, such as a disqualification from driving if the offence involved a motor car or the payment of compensation if there was an identifiable victim.

A solicitor advising a defendant ought to be aware that such an order will not be made unless recommended by a Probation Officer and unless the offender consents.

The Fines (Payment and Recovery) Act 2014 allows for a person who has been ordered to pay a fine and has not done so to carry out community service instead of imprisonment for non-payment of the fine. The Fines Act 2010, when enacted, will allow for a receiver appointed by the court to order that a person who does not pay all or some of a fine to carry out a specified term of community service instead.

14.13.1   THE DISCRETION TO STRIKE A CASE OUT

The District Court has the power in cases that do not involve a fixed penalty to find that the facts of a case have been proven by the prosecution and then proceed to 'strike out' that case. This action will result in the accused person before the court being without a criminal record despite that finding. This judicial discretion is used sparingly in practice with respect to offences of a less serious nature and is typically accompanied by a donation to the Court Poor Box. This form of 'donation' is a practice that pre-dates the foundation of the state that is engaged in usually by District Courts who direct that money is paid into a poor box in lieu of, or in conjunction with another penalty. It has been mooted that this form of donation will be abolished in the Criminal Justice Community Sanctions Bill, when enacted. The individual amounts 'donated' can vary substantially depending on factors like ability to pay, other penalties imposed and the nature of the offences committed.

The District Court is not allowed to use this discretion for offences which have fixed penalties or offences which specifically remove discretion from a District Judge, e.g. the offence of driving whilst intoxicated.

14.14   Fines

The main provisions of the Fines Act 2010 came into operation on 4 January 2011 by way of SI No. 662 of 2010, and the Fines Act (Payment and Recovery) Act 2014 will legislate for the manner in which the court can impose a fine. The 2010 Act classifies fines from Class A through to Class E. Consequently, it is important for a defence solicitor to take the client's instructions regarding their financial circumstances, i.e. their ability to pay a designated fine. Section 12 of the 2010 Act defines the meaning of financial circumstances as:

- the amount of the person's annual income;
- the aggregate value of real and personal property;
- the aggregate amount of the person's liabilities including their obligations to support their family or others;
- the aggregate of monies owing to the person and the dates upon which such monies are to be repaid to them;
- other matters the court thinks relevant.

If an accused person is convicted in the superior courts, the court can impose a fine using a multiplier system and reference should be had to s. 9 of the 2010 Act in that regard. Section 10(3) of the Criminal Law Act 1997 also allows for the superior courts to impose a fine at the courts' own discretion where there is no sentence fixed by law. Section 5 of the 2014 Act will require a judge to make an enquiry as to the financial capacity of a person before they impose a fine and the court may allow for the fine to be paid by instalments. It is important to note that the 2014 Act, whilst signed by the President, has at the time of writing not yet been the subject of a Ministerial Commencement Order.

14.14.1 NON-PAYMENT OF FINES

It is not strictly speaking a matter for a sentence hearing, but a defence solicitor should be in a position to advise a client that non-payment of a fine can result in imprisonment. The Courts Act (No. 2) 1986 has recently been amended by s. 20 of the Fines Act 2014 as it is enacted. This new legislation allows for convicted persons to be given every opportunity to avoid imprisonment for non-payment of fines through instalment payments procedures and community service options. The effect of this 2014 Act will be to allow for a person who does not pay a fine within the prescribed time to be offered alternatives to imprisonment, such as payment by instalments or community service. In order for the state to lawfully imprison fines defaulters they will have to bring that person before a court for the purpose of hearing from that person or his or her legal representative and the court must then determine that alternatives to imprisonment are not appropriate.

14.15   Deferral of Sentence

It is very common for a court to postpone the imposition of a final sentence to allow the convicted person to address issues that may be relevant to the offending behaviour. Section 100 of the Criminal Justice Act 2006 legislates for such a deferral. A solicitor for a defendant ought to take the client's instructions regarding any addiction problems which may relate to the offending. If the defendant wishes to engage in rehabilitation, it would be wise to seek a deferral of sentence for this purpose. It is common in such circumstances for the sentencing court to order a Probation Report and defer sentence for consideration of the report.

14.16   Orders Consequent on Conviction

It is important that a solicitor for either the state or an accused person is aware of the power of the court to make orders consequent to conviction. These orders are mandatory and the most common example is the obligation of the court to disqualify from driving a defendant who is convicted of drink driving. A defence solicitor ought to be able to advise the client of the existence and impact of these orders as it may be highly relevant to the approach the solicitor then employs in advocating the case.

14.17   Orders Ancillary to Conviction

It is arguably of even more importance that a defence solicitor is aware of the power of the court to make ancillary orders upon conviction. These are discretionary orders which the court may decide on a case-by-case basis. The most common example is the power of the court to exercise its discretion to disqualify a defendant from driving, upon conviction for their first offence of driving without insurance contrary to s. 56 of the Road Traffic Act 1964 (as amended). It is important to consider whether a court has the jurisdiction to make an ancillary order. The Supreme Court decided in *Gilligan v The Special Criminal Courts and Others* [2005] IESC 86 that the Special Criminal Court did not have the jurisdiction to make an ancillary confiscation order for monies allegedly connected to drug trafficking, under s. 4 of the Criminal Justice Act 1994.

14.18 Conclusion

Chapter 16 on Appeals and Judicial Review looks at the appeals process in general, but in the context of managing clients' expectations regarding likely sentencing, it is crucially important to advise them that an appeal court can increase the sentence which is being appealed. Also a power vests in the DPP to appeal sentences that she considers too lenient.

All practitioners should be continually aware of developments in sentencing of all crimes, both ordinary and regulatory, as increasingly restorative practice is being employed. The research that informs the Courts Service Irish Sentencing Information System (ISIS) aims to design and develop a computerised information system on sentences and other penalties. Also, cognisance must be taken of the emerging relevance of EU Law to sentencing in the context of a post-Lisbon Treaty EU which is an area of 'freedom, security and justice'.

CHAPTER 15

ROAD TRAFFIC OFFENCES

15.1 Introduction

The objective of this chapter is to familiarise the reader with the law on the more common road traffic offences. At the time of writing there are 15 Acts and hundreds of statutory instruments which form the basis of the law in this area of practice, and these are cumulatively known as the Road Traffic Acts 1961–2014. There are also numerous common law authorities that should be examined for further guidance and clarity. When the Road Traffic Act 2010 is fully implemented, it will probably be considered the most significant development in road traffic law since the original 1961 Act. The 2010 Act introduces a radical overhaul of the law in relation to intoxicant offences, reducing the various limits and allowing in certain circumstances the disposal of certain intoxicant offences by fixed penalty notices. The Act also introduces a new offence of careless driving causing death or serious harm, to be tried on indictment.

Road traffic can be a technical area of law. The successful prosecution consists of proving that all of the constituent elements of the alleged offence are present. Conversely, the successful defence of road traffic charges depends on the practitioner's knowledge of the required proofs and ability to isolate the missing elements.

This chapter intends to identify the various elements and proofs of the offences examined, in order to assist new practitioners when advising clients or appearing before the courts. There are many textbooks which cover the huge litany of road traffic offences. This chapter covers the more common offences which a solicitor will encounter. However, the approach applied in this chapter is to analyse each offence having regard to its constituent elements, and that approach is equally effective for all road traffic offences.

The offences examined here include:

    (a)   driving without a licence;

    (b)   driving without insurance;

    (c)   driving without reasonable consideration;

    (d)   careless driving;

    (e)   dangerous driving;

    (f)   intoxicant offences.

15.2 Driving Without a Licence

15.2.1 PROHIBITION

Section 38(1) of the Road Traffic Act 1961 (hereinafter called the 'Principal Act') states that a person cannot drive or allow another to drive his vehicle in a public place without the driver holding a valid driving licence. Section 38(2) provides a presumption in favour of the prosecution that 'it shall be presumed, until the contrary is shown by the defendant, that he did not, at the time he drove the vehicle, hold a driving licence then having effect and licensing him to drive the vehicle'.

The related offences of driving in a public place without being able to produce a licence there and then, and failing to produce a licence in a nominated Garda station within 10 days of driving in a public place, are dealt with by s. 40 of the Principal Act. A new s. 40 was inserted by s. 59 of the Road Traffic Act 2010.

'Drive' is statutorily defined in s. 3 of the Principal Act as including managing or controlling and driving. There is very little litigation in our jurisdiction regarding the s. 3 definition of driving. We can take it as our normal understanding of driving, managing or controlling a moving vehicle.

While normally proving the fact of driving is achieved through the evidence of an eye witness, it may also be proved by the admission of an accused. In *DPP v Cormack* [1999] 1 ILRM 398, a drink driving charge was dismissed because there was insufficient evidence that the vehicle had been driven in a public place within the relevant period of three hours. The prosecution evidence was the Gardaí had come across the scene of a one-vehicle accident. Mr Cormack was present. He admitted driving the vehicle and stated the accident had happened 10 minutes prior to the arrival of the Gardaí. O'Flaherty J. held; 'once the man had made a (voluntary) admission, then it is clear evidence and the Judge was bound to accept it'.

There is no definition of 'vehicle' in the Road Traffic Acts; however, s. 3(1) of the Principal Act defines a 'mechanically propelled vehicle' as a vehicle intended or adapted for propulsion by mechanical (including electrical or partly electrical) means, including a bicycle or tricycle with an attachment for propelling it by mechanical power, whether or not the attachment is being used.

Section 3(2) of the Principal Act exempted a vehicle substantially disabled (by accident, break-down, engine, or vital part removal), so that it is no longer capable of being mechanically pro-pelled, from being a mechanically propelled vehicle for the purpose of the Act. This point was examined in the *DPP v Regina Brehony* case, an unreported judgment of Egan J (2 March 1993, Supreme Court). A new s. 3(2) was substituted by s. 72 of the Road Traffic Act 2010. The new s. 3(2) provides that if the vehicle becomes disabled through collision then it will for the purpose of the Road Traffic Acts remain a mechanically propelled vehicle.

'Public place' is defined by s. 3 of the Principal Act as substituted by s. 49(1)(a)(iv) of the Road Traffic Act 1994, as:

(a)   any public road; and

(b)   any street, road or other place to which the public have access with vehicles whether as of right or by permission and whether subject to or free of charge.

There are a number of Irish authorities examining the definition of a public place. The grounds of a holiday home for senior citizens was found not to be a public place in *Stanbridge v Healy* [1985] ILRM 290, while Poppintree Park in Ballymun was found to be a public place in *Richards v MIB*, an unreported Supreme Court judgment from 12 June 1996. Grafton Street in Dublin City after it was pedestrianised was held to be a public place in the unreported Supreme Court judgment of *DPP v Molloy* (1 June 1995).

15.2.2   DEFENCES

Section 35(5)(a) of the Principal Act, as substituted by s. 11 of the Road Traffic Act 2006, states that it is a good defence to show that the driver had an effective learner's permit for the particular class of vehicle which he was driving.

Section 35(5)(b) of the Principal Act, as substituted by s. 11 of the Road Traffic Act 2006, states that it is a defence for an employer, who is prosecuted under s. 38 for employing a person with-out a licence, to show that the employee had an effective learner permit.

15.2.3   EXEMPTIONS

There are a number of exemptions to the requirement to hold a valid driving licence. Section 38(6) of the Principal Act exempts members of the Gardaí who drive 'in the course of their duty'. Section 38(7) exempts persons using pedestrian controlled vehicles which are specifically exempted by ministerial regulation. Regulation 7 of the Road Traffic (Licensing of Drivers) Regulations 1989 (SI No. 285 of 1989) defines such vehicles as those neither constructed or adapted for use for carrying a driver or passenger and which do not exceed 407 kg unladen weight. Section 113 of the Defence Act 1954 exempts members of the defence forces driving state-owned or controlled mechanically propelled vehicles during a period of duty or emergency.

15.2.4   PENALTIES

In the case of breach of s. 38 of the Principal Act, both the driver and owner of the vehicle can be liable on summary conviction for the following penalties under the provisions of s. 38(2)(a) of the Principal Act as substituted by s. 12(a)(i) of the Road Traffic Act 2006:

(i)   *Where at the time of the commission of the offence he or she had been the holder of a driving licence (other than a learner permit) which had expired beyond its period of validity for a period of not more than 12 months before the commission of the offence, to a fine not exceeding €1,000, and*

(ii)   *In any other case, to a fine not exceeding €2,000.*

The penalty point provisions in respect of s. 38 are not yet operative. When they become operative the first schedule of the Road Traffic Act 2002 provides for 2 points on the payment of a fixed charge and for 5 points in the event of a conviction in court.

15.2.5   DISQUALIFICATION

There are three types of disqualification from driving:

1.   Special disqualification: Under the provisions of s. 28 of the Road Traffic Act 1961 as amended by s. 49(1)(c) of the Road Traffic Act 1994, the court has the discretion to disqualify a driver as a consequence of an application to it by a member of the Gardaí or appropriate licensing authority submitting that a person is unfit to drive a motor vehicle by reason of a physical disease, or physical or mental disability or evidence of incompetence to drive any vehicle or any class of vehicle.

2.   Consequential disqualification: Under the provisions of s. 26 of the Road Traffic Act 1961 and the Second Schedule to the 1961 Act as inserted by s. 65 of the Road Traffic Act, the court is obliged to impose an order of consequential disqualification upon conviction for specified offences. A new s. 26 has a greater number of offences to which consequential disqualification orders apply. Examples of offences which have consequential disqualifications include drink driving and dangerous driving.

3.   Ancillary disqualification: Pursuant to s. 27(1)(a) of the Road Traffic Act 1961, a judge has the discretion to impose a period of disqualification for the commission of any offence under the 1961 Act not being an offence which attracts a consequential disqualification order.

A person who is disqualified from driving may not drive any motor vehicle during the disqualification period unless they lodge an appeal against their conviction within 14 days of the date of their conviction. If a person does not appeal their disqualification they will receive a notice from the Fines Office of the District Court in the area in which they were convicted, requiring the defendant to hand in their driving licence forthwith in addition to the Court Order. Disqualification from driving for any reason carries an automatic three-year endorsement on the defendant's licence, which commences when the disqualification period ends. The Motor Taxation Office in the area in which the defendant is resident will hold the licence for collection until the period of disqualification ends.

Section 8 of the Road Traffic Act 2002 provides for all conviction and disqualification orders to be recorded on the central licence record rather than on the licence itself. Section 8 has now been commenced in full by the following statutory instruments: SI No. 214 of 2003; SI No. 321 of 2003; SI No. 248 of 2004; SI No. 134 of 2006; SI No. 443 of 2006; SI No. 149 of 2009; SI No. 296 of 2012; and SI No. 12 of 2013. The effect of s. 8 of the 2002 Act being fully enacted is that all disqualification orders are recorded against the disqualified person's driving record and not their driving licence.

15.2.6   ENDORSEMENT

Section 36(1) and (2) of the Road Traffic Act 1961 established the law relating to the endorsement of a driving licence. An endorsement is a stamp placed on a licence by the Motor Taxation Office in the area in which the defendant lives. An endorsement will remain on a licence for three years. The endorsement period will begin on the date on which the licence is stamped.

Subject to the enactment of s. 25(2) of the Road Traffic Act 2002, s. 36 of the 1961 Act provides that the court may endorse a licence where a person is convicted of any offence under the 1961 Act where it does not make an ancillary or consequential disqualification order. The court shall endorse a licence where it has made an ancillary or consequential disqualification order. Second or subsequent endorsements very frequently result in mandatory disqualification from driving. It may also lead to an increase in insurance premium.

Section 25(2) of the Road Traffic Act 2002 repeals s. 36(1) and (2) of the Road Traffic Act. Section 25(2) has been enacted through statutory instruments. There are no longer endorsements physically imposed on licences. This has been replaced by a new system under the 2002 Act, as described under **15.2.5**.

15.2.7   POWER OF ARREST

Section 6 of the Road Traffic Act 2014 amended s. 38 of the 1961 Act to allow the Gardaí to arrest without warrant any person in their opinion who was driving without a licence and who had been disqualified from holding a licence.

15.3   Driving Without Insurance

15.3.1   PROHIBITION

Section 56 (1) of the Road Traffic Act 1961, as substituted by s. 34 of the Road Traffic Act 2004 (which came into effect on 24 January 2005) provides:

(1)   *A person (in this subsection referred to as the user) shall not use in a public place a mechanically propelled vehicle unless—*

(a)   *either a vehicle insurer or an exempted person would be liable for injury caused by the negligent use of the vehicle by him at that time or*

(b)   *there is in force at that time either an approved policy of insurance whereby the user or some other person who would be liable for injury caused by the negligent use of the vehicle at that time by the user, is insured against all sums, subject to subsection (2) of this section, without limit, which the user or his personal representative or such other person or his personal representative becomes liable to pay to any person (exclusive of the excepted persons) by way of damages or costs on account of injury to person or property caused by the negligent use of the vehicle at that time by the user.*

Section 56(3) of the 1961 Act provides that where a person who contravenes s. 56(1) is not the owner, then the owner is guilty of an offence.

Accordingly, pursuant to s. 56 of the Principal Act, an insurer's obligations in respect of motor insurance can be summarised as follows:

A (user of a mechanically propelled vehicle) shall ensure that a vehicle insurer or exempted person is liable for the negligent use of a vehicle by him or her, with the exception of a pedestrian controlled vehicle and/or a State owned or driven vehicle.

A person/user must ensure that an approved policy of insurance issued by a vehicle insurer or a certificate of exemption from an exempt person shall cover any negligence on the part of the user, which includes such agents, servants or personal representatives, for injury without limitation, subject to the EU and international limits.

The interpretation of 'public place' and 'mechanically propelled vehicle' have been considered in the preceding discussion regarding driving without a licence.

'Use' in relation to a mechanically propelled vehicle is defined by s. 3(1) of the Principal Act as including parking.

'Use' should not be confused with 'driving', which is defined by s. 3 of the Principal Act as including the managing and controlling of a motor vehicle.

An 'exempted' person is defined by s. 60 of the 1961 Act, as inserted by s. 54 of the Road Traffic Act 1968, as:

(a)   a board or other body established by or under an Act of the Oireachtas or an Act of the Oireachtas of Saorstát Éireann,

(b)   a company (hereinafter referred to as a State-sponsored company) within the meaning of subsection (1) of s. 2 of the Companies Act, 1963, in which the majority of the shares are held by or on behalf of a Minister of State, or

(c)   a company within the meaning of subsection (1) of s. 2 of the Companies Act, 1963, in which the majority of the ordinary shares are held by a State-sponsored company or a board or other body mentioned in paragraph (a) of this subsection, in respect of which the Minister has issued a certificate that such board, other body or company is for the time being an exempted person for the purposes of this Act.

Regulation 6 of SI No. 347 of 1992 substitutes s. 58 of the 1961 Act and defines a vehicle insurer as follows:

The following section is hereby substituted for s. 58 of the Act—

(1)   In this Act, 'vehicle insurer' means, subject to subsection (1) of section 78 of this Act,—

(a)   an undertaking within the meaning of Article 2 (1) of the EC (Non-Life Insurance) Regulations 1976 (SI No 115 of 1976) as amended by Article 4 of the European Communities (Non-Life Insurance) (Amendment) (No 2) Regulations 1991 (SI No 142 of 1991) which carries on a class 10 mechanically propelled vehicle insurance business in the State, or a syndicate, within the meaning of s. 3 of the Act of 1936, carrying on that business in the State, or

(b)   a syndicate, within the meaning of section 3 of the Act of 1936, carrying on that business in the state.

(2)   For the purpose of this section and s. 78 —

'class 10 mechanically propelled vehicle insurance business' means a mechanically propelled vehicle insurance business within the meaning of s. 3 of the Act of 1936 in relation to a risk classified under class 10 of Schedule 1 of the European Communities (Non-Life Insurance) Regulations 1976 (SI No 115 of 1976) but excluding Carrier's liability;

'the Act of 1936' means the Insurance Act 1936 (No 45 of 1936).

An 'approved policy of insurance' is one which complies with the provisions of s. 62 of the Insurance Act 1961, as amended by various statutory instruments (SI No. 178 of 1975; SI No. 322 of 1987, and SI No. 347 of 1992).

15.3.2   DEFENCES

Section 56(5) and (6) of the Principal Act provide:

(5)   Where a person charged with an offence under this section is the owner of the vehicle, it shall be a good defence to the charge for the person to show that the vehicle was being used without his consent and either that he had taken all reasonable precautions to prevent its being used or that it was being used by his servant acting in contravention of his orders.

(6)   Where a person charged with an offence under this section was the servant of the owner of the vehicle, it shall be a good defence to the charge for the person to show that he was using the vehicle in obedience to the express orders of the owner.

Under s. 69(1) it is a defence for the defendant to show (a) that he did not use the vehicle or (b) he was the servant of the owner of the vehicle and was using the vehicle in obedience of the express order of the owner.

It is a defence for an owner to show that the vehicle was used without his consent. In the words of Henchy J. in *Lyons v Cooney* [1978] IR 41 (at p. 50).

> It will be seen, therefore, that when an owner of a vehicle is charged with an offence contrary to s. 56 which is alleged to have been committed when someone else was the user, the offence is not necessarily one of strict liability. Section 56, Subsection 4, ensures that the owner will be acquitted if, notwithstanding an earlier failure by the user to provide the necessary certificate in response to a demand made under Subsection 1 of s. 69, the owner produces the certificate at the hearing of the charge. Even if he fails to do that, Subsection 5 of s. 56 will ensure his acquittal if he shows that the vehicle was used without his consent and that he has taken the steps specified to prevent its use.

It is an absolute defence if the defendant can show that there was insurance on the vehicle. It is also a defence if it can be proven that the owner or driver was an exempted person or that the vehicle was an excepted vehicle.

An 'exempted person' is defined under s. 65'(1) of the Principal Act as:

(a) *any person claiming in respect of injury to himself sustained while he was in or on a mechanically propelled vehicle (or a vehicle drawn thereby) to which the relevant document relates other than a mechanically propelled vehicle or vehicles forming a combination of vehicles of a class specified for the purposes of this paragraph by regulations made by the Minister provided that such regulation shall not extend compulsory insurance for civil liability to passengers to—*

  (i) *any part of a mechanically propelled vehicle, other than a large public service vehicle, unless that part of the vehicle is designed and constructed with seating accommodation for passengers,*

  (ii) *or a passenger seated in a caravan attached to a mechanically propelled vehicle while such a combination of vehicles is moving in a public place.*

Section 4(2) of the Principal Act also provides three other exceptions to the general application of s. 56. These are:

(a) state-owned vehicles used by a person in the course of employment;

(b) vehicles seized by a state employee in the course of his duty or a person using such vehicles in the course of his employment; and

(c) members of the Gardaí or ministerial officials using vehicles for the purpose of a test, its removal, or disposition under the Act or regulations thereunder.

These exceptions do not confer an exemption on the state which is liable under s. 59 of the Civil Liability Act 1961.

15.3.3   PENALTIES

Section 56(3) of the Principal Act, as amended by s. 3(1) of the Road Traffic (Amendment) Act 1984 and ss. 2 and 23 of the Road Traffic Act 2002, provides that the penalties for breach of a person's obligation to insure are a maximum fine of €5,000 and/or six months of imprisonment. The disqualification provisions also apply in respect of a breach of the obligation to insure. The consequential disqualification is for a period of two years. This arises by virtue of the provisions of s. 26 of the Principal Act as substituted by the Road Traffic Act 1994 (as amended by s. 6 of the 2006 Act), which gives the court jurisdiction to impose a consequential disqualification order. Under s. 26(5)(b), as inserted into the Principal Act by the Road Traffic Act 1994, the court may on a first offence under this section, where it is satisfied that a special reason exists, decline to make a consequential disqualification order or specify a period of disqualification of less than one year. The court must disqualify for not less than four years in the case of a second or any subsequent offence under the same section committed within the period of three years from the date of the commission of the previous offence or in the case of more than one such offence, the last such offence.

Section 65 of the Road Traffic Act 2010 substitutes a new s. 26 but the position in relation to insurance remains unchanged. There is still a consequential disqualification of two years which upon good reason the judge may decline to make or may make a disqualification for a period of less than one year.

A consequential disqualification still automatically follows a conviction under s. 56 for no insurance, unless the court exercises its discretion to decline to make that order. The disqualification is consequential, rather than ancillary. The relief from endorsement of penalty points where an ancillary order is made, provided by s. 2(8) of the Road Traffic Act 2002, does not apply. A conviction for no insurance carries 5 penalty points.

15.3.4   PENALTY POINTS

The Road Traffic Act 2002, as amended by the Road Traffic Acts 2004 and 2014, governs the legislative framework for the penalty point system in Ireland. Initially, motorists guilty of speeding, driving without insurance, careless driving, and seat belt offences were awarded penalty points. Under the Road Traffic Act 2002, any driver who receives 12 penalty points in any three-year period will incur a six-month disqualification from driving.

At the time of writing, there are 63 offences to which penalty points apply.

15.3.5   COMPENSATION ORDER

Section 6 of the Criminal Justice Act 1993 provides for compensation orders in respect of road traffic cases. Section 6 (4) provides:

> A compensation order shall not be made in respect of an injury or loss that results from the use of a mechanically propelled vehicle (within the meaning of the Road Traffic Act 1961) in a public place unless it appears to the court that:
>
> (a) It is in respect of an injury or loss as respects which the use of the vehicle by the convicted person was in breach of their obligation to insure, or
>
> (b) It is in respect of a loss, which is treated by subsection (3) as having resulted from the offence.

Section 6 (3) provides:

> Where the commission of the offence by the convicted person involved the taking of property out of the possession of the injured party and the property has been recovered, any loss occurring to the injured party by reason of the property being damaged while out of his possession shall be treated for the purposes of subsection (1) as having resulted from the offence, irrespective of how the damage was caused or who caused it.

Accordingly, a compensation order can only be made where:

> (a) there is no insurance cover as provided for under Section 56 of the Principal Act; or
>
> (b) the offence involved the taking of property which was later recovered, but loss arose to the injured party by reason of the property being stolen and subsequently damaged.

A compensation order may be made in addition to or instead of a prison sentence, but it cannot exceed the jurisdiction of the court hearing the matter.

15.3.6   BURDEN OF PROOF

In a prosecution under s. 56 of the Principal Act, a presumption of non-insurance against the defendant exists where a member of the Gardaí has demanded the production of a certificate of insurance in accordance with s. 69 of the Principal Act and the party failed, refused, or neglected to produce same, or alternatively did produce the certificate but refused to allow the Garda member to examine it.

The prosecution ordinarily have two methods of proving a charge of no insurance, neatly summarised by Henchy J. in *Lyons v Cooney* [1978] IR 41 as follows:

> The fact the vehicle was uninsured can be proved by the prosecution in either of two ways. They could adduce evidence of a positive nature probative of the fact that the vehicle was uninsured. For example, they could put in evidence a statement by the defendant admitting that the vehicle was uninsured. Alternatively, they could rely on the provisions of s. 56, subsection 4, which cast on the defendant the onus of showing that the vehicle was not used in contravention of the section when 'the person on whom the demand was made' (not, be it noted, 'the defendant') refused or failed to produce the necessary certificate.

15.4 Driving Without Reasonable Consideration

15.4.1 PROHIBITION

Section 51A(1) of the Principal Act as inserted by s. 4 of the Road Traffic (No. 2) Act 2011 provides:

a person shall not drive a vehicle in a public place without reasonable consideration for other persons using the place.

'Drive', 'vehicle', and 'public place' are defined in the preceding discussion regarding driving without a licence.

There is no statutory definition as to what constitutes reasonable consideration and there is little authority to rely upon. This is now a fixed charge offence. There is no fixed penalty. The general penalty applies. It is regarded as a lesser offence than careless driving simpliciter (discussed below). The offence does not necessarily involve bad driving in the sense that it could result in danger but merely that it inconveniences other road users. A typical example commonly used is when a motorist drives at speed into a puddle and splashes pedestrians on the public footpath.

'Other persons using the place'—in *Dilkes v Bowman Shaw* [1981] RTR 4, it was held that an actual road user must be inconvenienced before a person may be convicted of this offence.

15.4.2 DEFENCES

Once the prosecution prove the various ingredients of the offence then most defences to this charge will rest on the definition of reasonable and whether the act complained of satisfied the 'without reasonable consideration' element of the offence in the circumstances. The defences discussed at **15.5.2** in relation to careless driving are also relevant to this offence.

15.4.3 PENALTIES

The Road Traffic Acts 1961–2005 (Fixed Charge Offences) Regulations 2006 apply to this offence. There is a fixed charge fine of €80 if paid within 28 days (€120 if paid between the 28th and 56th day) and two penalty points endorsed on the driver's licence where s/he admits to the offence in accordance with the practice and procedure set forth in the 2006 Regulations. On conviction, the defendant shall be liable to the general penalty provisions in s. 102 and 4 penalty points endorsed on their licence. No consequential disqualification provisions apply to offences under this section. However, the court does have the discretion to impose an ancillary disqualification order pursuant to s. 27 of the Principal Act as amended.

15.5 Careless Driving

15.5.1 PROHIBITION

Section 52 of the Principal Act as inserted by s. 4 of the Road Traffic (No. 2) Act 2011 provides:

A person shall not drive a vehicle in a public place without due care and attention.

Section 52(2) provides that where the contravention causes death or serious harm to another person then the offence will be tried on indictment.

'Person', 'drive', 'vehicle', and 'public place' are defined in the preceding discussion regarding driving without a licence.

There is no statutory definition of due care and attention, and there is also little precedent in this jurisdiction to define this term. It is a more serious charge than driving without reasonable consideration discussed at **15.4**. Whether driving is regarded as careless driving or dangerous driving will depend on the facts of each particular case. Careless driving is generally regarded as poor quality driving, or heedless and imprudent driving. It is often the result of a momentary lapse. In *Wilson v McPhail* [1991] SCCR 170, the court asked whether the driver demonstrated 'the standard of care, skill and attention which a competent and reasonably prudent driver is expected to show in the circumstances.'

Careless driving is an alternative verdict to the more serious charge of dangerous driving. The fact that 'careless driving' results in serious injury or death does not change the nature of the offence. If it is careless driving then it remains careless regardless of any consequences which resulted from the driving.

15.5.2   DEFENCES

15.5.2.1   Automatism

The defence of automatism has succeeded in numerous English cases where certain personal conditions such as an epileptic fit, unconsciousness or a sudden illness have all provided defences to cases of careless and dangerous driving.

In *A-G's Reference* (*No 2 of 1992*), The Times, 31 May 1993, it was held by the Court of Appeal that the defence of automatism required the total destruction of voluntary control. Impaired or reduced control was not enough.

15.5.2.2   Duress

A defence of driving in terror when the defendant and his friends were being pursued by a mob was accepted in the case of *DPP v Bell* [1992] RTR 335.

15.5.2.3   Emergency

A public emergency is not a defence even for a member of the Gardaí or emergency services.

15.5.2.4   Mechanical defect

In *R v Spurge* [1961] 2 QB 205, a sudden mechanical defect, due to no fault of the driver, causing loss of control, was held to be a good defence.

15.5.3   PENALTIES

Section 65 of the 2010 Act inserts a new s. 26 and a new second schedule in to the 1961 Act. There is an apparent contradiction between the new s. 26 and the new 2nd Schedule of the 1961 Act.

Section 26(5)(a) provides for a consequential disqualification order of not less than two years for a first offence and four years in the case of a second or subsequent offence within three years.

Section 26(5)(b) provides than on a first offence the court may, where a special reason has been proved, decline to make a consequential order or make one for a period of less than one year.

The 2nd Schedule to the Act which lists the offences to which consequential disqualification orders apply describes under careless driving 'being an offence committed in a period of 3 years in which 2 or more offences were committed by the person'.

The contradiction between s. 26, which implies a mandatory disqualification for a first offence of careless driving, and the 2nd Schedule, which implies that there is only a mandatory disqualification if it is a third or more conviction for careless driving in a period of three years, is not easily resolved.

We can expect to see it clarified in the near future by way of legislation or case stated.

Careless driving simpliciter will no longer carry a possible prison sentence, but the fine increases to up to a maximum of €5,000. Section 54 of the 2010 Act amends the first schedule of the Road Traffic Act 2002 to provide that this offence tried summarily will carry 5 penalty points.

15.5.3.1   On indictment

There is a minimum four-year consequential disqualification where a person is convicted of careless driving tried on indictment (where the contravention caused death or serious bodily harm). There is no provision to mitigate this disqualification unlike careless driving simpliciter tried in the District Court.

There is provision for a prison sentence of up to two years and/or a fine not exceeding €10,000.

The new s. 52(3) provides that where a Garda is of an opinion that a person has committed an offence under s. 52 and that contravention has caused death or serious bodily harm to another, then the Gardaí will have a power of arrest.

15.6   Dangerous Driving

15.6.1   PROHIBITION

Section 53 (1) of the Principal Act as inserted by s. 4 of the Road Traffic (No.2) Act 2011 provides:

> *A person shall not drive a vehicle in a public place in a manner (including speed) which, having regard to all the circumstances of the case (including the condition of the vehicle, the nature, condition and use of the place and the amount of traffic which then actually is or might reasonably be expected then to be therein) is or is likely to be dangerous to the public.*

'Person', 'drive', 'vehicle', and 'public place' are defined in the preceding discussion regarding driving without a licence.

'Traffic' is not statutorily defined. As a general rule, pedestrians are regarded as traffic in the Road Traffic Acts unless specifically excluded.

'Manner' shall be examined in the context of 'in a manner which is dangerous', discussed below.

'Speed' is a consideration in determining whether the driving is dangerous in the context of this offence. Where speed is taken into account in a conviction for dangerous driving this shall be a bar to any subsequent conviction for speed arising from the same set of facts.

'Circumstance' is defined as including various factors which the court can consider; however, it is not necessary for the court to state the circumstances or factors it relied upon when making a conviction. These circumstances include 'condition of the vehicle', 'nature of the place', 'condition of the place', 'use of the place', 'amount of traffic', and other circumstances.

'Condition of vehicle': the physical condition of the vehicle is relevant as is whether the driver could have reasonably known of any defect in the vehicle (*R v Strong* [1995] Crim LR 428).

'Nature of place' includes the width of the road, where it is situated, and traffic signals in its vicinity.

'Condition of place' would include the state of the road due to weather and other factors such as its state of maintenance.

'Use of place' would include whether it was a busy town, street, country road, primary road, secondary road or a motorway.

'Amount of traffic' would include the volume of traffic which could have been reasonably expected.

'Other circumstances' which the court could take into consideration would include whether the defendant had consumed alcohol or drugs and how long s/he had driven without a rest.

'Dangerous to the public' is not statutorily defined; however, Pierse in *Road Traffic Law, Volume 1 Commentary* (First Law), p. 430, cites from the judgment of O'Briain J. in the case of *People v Quinlan* [1962] ILT & SJ 123. In defining this term, Pierse states:

> Judge Barra O'Briain's (then president of the Circuit Court) standard charge to a jury is a good guide on the nature or the kernel of the offence, i.e.:—'driving in a manner (including speed) which a reasonable prudent man having knowledge of all the circumstances proved in court would clearly recognise as involving unjustifiably definite risk of harm to the public'.

15.6.2   DEFENCES

The defences available in a dangerous driving charge are the same as those which apply to careless driving. It should be noted, however, that s. 53(3) of the Road Traffic Act 1961, as inserted by s. 4 of the Road Traffic (No. 2) Act 2011, expressly excludes as a defence evidence of the fact that the alleged offender was not in excess of the speed limit applying in relation to the vehicle or the road.

15.6.3   PENALTIES

15.6.3.1   Mode of trial

If death or serious bodily harm is the result of the dangerous driving, then the trial is by way of indictment.

If the charge does not allege death or serious bodily harm, the offence is a summary one wherein there is no right to a jury trial.

15.6.3.2   Fines

Summarily, the accused can be fined up to a maximum of €5,000. On indictment (i.e. in death or serious bodily harm cases), the accused can be fined up to €20,000. The topic of fines in the context of sentencing generally is discussed at **Chapter 14**.

15.6.3.3   Imprisonment

Summarily, the maximum term of imprisonment is six months. On indictment (i.e. in death or serious bodily harm cases), the maximum term is 10 years.

15.6.3.4   Endorsement

A summary or indictable conviction for dangerous driving carries a compulsory endorsement on the defendant's licence.

15.6.3.5   Disqualification

Where a person is convicted summarily under s. 53 the penalty that applies is a two-year disqualification in the case of a first offence, and not less than four years in the case of a second or subsequent offence within three years from the date of the previous (or last) offence. On indictment (i.e. in death or serious bodily harm cases), the period of disqualification is four years on the first offence and six years on a second offence or subsequent offence.

Prior to the Road Traffic Act 2006, the court had a discretion in relation to the imposition of a consequential disqualification in a summary case on a first offence, where it was satisfied that a special reason existed. This discretion was removed by s. 6(1)(d) of the Road Traffic Act 2006.

15.6.3.6   Certificate of competency

Section 26 (3) of the Principal Act, as re-enacted by s. 3(a) of the Road Traffic (Amendment) Act 1995, provides that where the dangerous driving charge is successfully prosecuted on indictment, the consequential disqualification order shall operate also to disqualify the guilty driver from holding a driving licence during a specified period. Further, until s/he has produced to the appropriate licensing authority (as may be specified in the order) a certificate of competency or both a certificate of competency and a certificate of fitness, he or she shall not be entitled to a licence. Section 65 of the Road Traffic Act 2010 substitutes a new s. 26 in the Principal Act. It expands the requirement regarding a certificate of competency to careless driving tried on indictment. Both the Road Traffic Act 1994 and Road Traffic (Amendment) Act 1995 refer to 'special reasons' in relation to a disqualification order. Under s. 26(5) of the Principal Act for a first offence in a summary trial for a charge of s. 56 (driving without insurance) of the Principal Act, a court may decline to make a consequential order, where it is satisfied a special reason has been proven to exist. Alternatively, for such special reason, on conviction under either of the aforementioned sections, the court may specify that disqualification for a period of less than one year may be imposed.

Further, a special reason similarly proven under s. 26(3) of the Principal Act, as substituted by s. 2 of the 1995 Act, can obviate the necessity of an otherwise automatic order requiring a certificate of competency and/or fitness being incorporated with the consequential disqualification order following convictions on ss. 53 and 106(1)(a) or (b) of the Principal Act. This is repeated in the new s. 26 inserted by s. 65 of the Road Traffic Act 2010, and as a result also applies to s. 52 tried as indictment. It should further be noted that s. 30 of the Principal Act allows for postponement of disqualification for a special reason.

Special reasons which have been accepted by the courts include mitigating or extenuating circumstances which the court should take into account when considering sentence. These include circumstances which relate to the nature of the offence, do not affect public safety and must not relate to the driver's personal circumstances. In *Reynolds v Roche* [1972] RTR 282, the fact that a disqualification would cause serious hardship to the defendant's family was not accepted as a special reason. It must be noted that in all instances where a special reason is accepted by the courts, this special reason must be specified in the court order of conviction and sentence.

15.6.3.7   Sentencing criteria

There are no formal criteria in respect of sentencing in dangerous driving cases; however, where such driving causes death or serious bodily harm, the courts have enunciated factors which should be taken into account. In *R v Boswell* [1984] RTR 315, the factors which will go to severity of sentence are listed as including intoxicants, excessive speed, racing, competitive driving, disregarding warnings by passengers and others, prolonged, persistent bad driving, several people killed or injured, or the offence being committed while on bail. Factors which will go to mitigate a long sentence or a custodial sentence at all are stated to include: one-off mistake, plea of guilty, good character, remorse, the deceased is a friend, monetary recompense regarding culpability, injury to the defendant themselves, stopping at scene, and driving due to an emergency.

15.7   Intoxicant Offences

15.7.1   PROHIBITION

The two most common intoxicant offences which appear before the courts are created by s. 4 (commonly known as drunken driving) and s. 5 (commonly known as drunk in charge) of the Road Traffic Act 2010.

Section 4 of the Road Traffic Act 2010 provides as follows:

> 4.— (1)   *A person shall not drive or attempt to drive a mechanically propelled vehicle in a public place while he or she is under the influence of an intoxicant to such an extent as to be incapable of having proper control of the vehicle.*
>
> (2)   *A person shall not drive or attempt to drive a mechanically propelled vehicle in a public place while there is present in his or her body a quantity of alcohol such that, within 3 hours after so driving or attempting to drive, the concentration of alcohol in his or her blood will exceed a concentration of—*
>
> (a)   *50 milligrammes of alcohol per 100 millilitres of blood, or*
>
> (b)   *in case the person is a specified person, 20 milligrammes of alcohol per 100 millilitres of blood.*
>
> (3)   *A person shall not drive or attempt to drive a mechanically propelled vehicle in a public place while there is present in his or her body a quantity of alcohol such that, within 3 hours after so driving or attempting to drive, the concentration of alcohol in his or her urine will exceed a concentration of—*
>
> (a)   *67 milligrammes of alcohol per 100 millilitres of urine, or*
>
> (b)   *in case the person is a specified person, 27 milligrammes of alcohol per 100 millilitres of urine.*

(4) *A person shall not drive or attempt to drive a mechanically propelled vehicle in a public place while there is present in his or her body a quantity of alcohol such that, within 3 hours after so driving or attempting to drive, the concentration of alcohol in his or her breath will exceed a concentration of—*

    (a) *22 microgrammes of alcohol per 100 millilitres of breath, or*

    (b) *in case the person is a specified person, 9 microgrammes of alcohol per 100 millilitres of breath.*

(5) *A person who contravenes this section commits an offence and is liable on summary conviction to a fine not exceeding €5,000 or to imprisonment for a term not exceeding 6 months or to both.*

(6) *A person charged with an offence under this section may, in lieu of being found guilty of that offence, be found guilty of an offence under section 5.*

(7) *Section 1 (1) of the Probation of Offenders Act 1907 does not apply to an offence under this section.*

(8) *A member of the Garda Síochána may arrest without warrant a person who in the member's opinion is committing or has committed an offence under this section.*

Section 5 of the Road Traffic Act 2010 provides as follows:

5.—(1) *A person commits an offence if, when in charge of a mechanically propelled vehicle in a public place with intent to drive or attempt to drive the vehicle (but not driving or attempting to drive it), he or she is under the influence of an intoxicant to such an extent as to be incapable of having proper control of the vehicle.*

(2) *A person commits an offence if, when in charge of a mechanically propelled vehicle in a public place with intent to drive or attempt to drive the vehicle (but not driving or attempting to drive it), there is present in his or her body a quantity of alcohol such that, within 3 hours after so being in charge, the concentration of alcohol in his or her blood will exceed a concentration of—*

    (a) *50 milligrammes of alcohol per 100 millilitres of blood, or*

    (b) *in case the person is a specified person, 20 milligrammes of alcohol per 100 millilitres of blood.*

(3) *A person commits an offence if, when in charge of a mechanically propelled vehicle in a public place with intent to drive or attempt to drive the vehicle (but not driving or attempting to drive it), there is present in his or her body a quantity of alcohol such that, within 3 hours after so being in charge, the concentration of alcohol in his or her urine will exceed a concentration of—*

    (a) *67 milligrammes of alcohol per 100 millilitres of urine, or*

    (b) *in case the person is a specified person, 27 milligrammes of alcohol per 100 millilitres of urine.*

(4) *A person commits an offence if, when in charge of a mechanically propelled vehicle in a public place with intent to drive or attempt to drive the vehicle (but not driving or attempting to drive it), there is present in his or her body a quantity of alcohol such that, within 3 hours after so being in charge, the concentration of alcohol in his or her breath will exceed a concentration of—*

    (a) *22 microgrammes of alcohol per 100 millilitres of breath, or*

    (b) *in case the person is a specified person, 9 microgrammes of alcohol per 100 millilitres of breath.*

(5) *A person guilty of an offence under this section is liable on summary conviction to a fine not exceeding €5,000 or to imprisonment for a term not exceeding 6 months or to both.*

(6) *A person charged with an offence under this section may, in lieu of being found guilty of that offence, be found guilty of an offence under section 4.*

(7) *Section 1 (1) of the Probation of Offenders Act, 1907 does not apply to an offence under this section.*

(8) *In a prosecution for an offence under this section it shall be presumed that the defendant intended to drive or attempt to drive the vehicle concerned until he or she shows the contrary.*

(9)   A person liable to be charged with an offence under this section shall not, by reference to the same occurrence, be liable to be charged under section 12 of the Licensing Act 1872 with the offence of being drunk while in charge, on a highway or other public place, of a carriage.

(10) A member of the Garda Síochána may arrest without warrant a person who in the member's opinion is committing or has committed an offence under this section.

15.7.2   SPECIFIED PERSON

The primary differences between the old regime and new drunken driving and drunk in charge provisions relate to the lowering of the specified limits of alcohol allowed for ordinary drivers and the introduction of even lower defined limits for specified persons.

A specified person is defined in s. 3 of the 2010 Act as follows:

'specified person' means a person who at the time of an alleged offence under section 4 and 5—

(a)   is the holder of a learner permit,

(b)   holds his or her first driving licence, for a period not exceeding 2 years from its date of issue,

(c)   is the holder of a driving licence licensing the holder to drive a vehicle in the category C, C1, D, D1, EB, EC, EC1, ED, ED1 and W while driving, attempting to drive or being in charge of such a vehicle,

(d)   is the holder of a licence to drive a small public service vehicle granted under section 34 of the Taxi Regulation Act 2003 or section 82 of the Principal Act or a person purporting to be such a holder while driving, attempting to drive or being in charge of such a vehicle, when the vehicle is being used in the course of business,

(e)   does not hold at the time or, at any time within the period of 5 years prior to the commission of the alleged offence, a driving licence for the time being having effect and licensing the person to drive a vehicle of the category concerned, or

(f)   is deemed under section 8 to be a specified person.

15.7.3   DISCLOSURE OF THE PROSECUTION CASE

As with all criminal trials it is good practice to seek from the prosecution whatever evidence is in their possession. The practice as to how this is achieved varies according to the District Court district. When your client consults you s/he will normally only be in possession of a summons/charge sheet and the document giving his or her alcohol reading. The practice in some areas is to write to the Gardaí at that stage and seek copies of Garda statements, the custody record, the doctor's certificate and any other relevant material in their possession. The practice in other areas is to wait until the return date and seek a *Gary Doyle* Order. If the case is in a district with which you are not familiar, then you should check with a colleague from that district as to which practice is favoured by the local judge.

The disclosure when received should be carefully reviewed. The times and other details should be cross checked against the Garda statements provided.

15.7.4   THE GARDA STATEMENTS

The statement of the arresting Garda usually gives the first insight into whether the prosecution proofs are in order. It is important to go through the statement thoroughly and examine it for the presence of each individual proof. A typical Garda statement is as follows:

Sample Garda Statement

Statement of Evidence of Garda Joseph Bloggs stationed at Pearse Street Garda Station Dublin 2

I hereby declare that this statement is true to the best of my knowledge and belief and that I make it knowing that if it is tendered in evidence I will be liable to prosecution if I state in it anything which I know to be false or do not believe to be true.

I am a member of An Garda Síochána stationed at Pearse Street Garda Station. I remember Thursday the 14th of August 2014. My colleague Garda Mike Smith was driving a patrol car on North Brunswick Street a public place and I was the observer seated in the passenger seat. At approximately 8.50 pm I noticed a Toyota Camry registration number 06 D 14474 driving unusually slowly and was continually crossing the white line. I activated the blue lights of the patrol car to signal the car to pull over in order that I could ensure that everything was alright. I approached the window of driver. I noticed that it was a man and that he was alone in the car. I asked him to let down the window. He did so and I got a strong smell of alcohol from his breath. I asked him his name and address. He gave me his name as John Jones of Palmers Hill Dublin 2. I noticed that when he spoke that his speech was slurred. I asked him to step out of the vehicle and when he did I noticed he was unsteady on his feet. At 8.55 pm at North Brunswick Street a public place I formed the opinion that John Jones was under the influence of an intoxicant to such an extent as to be incapable of having proper control of an MPV in a public place and had committed an offence under s. 4(1), (2), (3), or (4) of the Road Traffic Act 2010. I informed John Jones that I was arresting him under s. 4(8) of the Road Traffic Act 2010. I also explained to Mr Jones in plain language that I was arresting him for the offence commonly known as drink driving. I cautioned him that he was not obliged to say anything unless he wished to do so but anything that he did say would be taken down in writing and may be given in evidence. I placed Mr Jones in the back of the patrol car.

We drove to Pearse Street Garda station and arrived there 9.10pm. I introduced Mr Jones to the member in charge Garda Kenny Noonan. I informed Garda Noonan that I had arrested Mr Jones for the offence of drink driving at North Brunswick Street. I was present when Garda Noonan completed the custody record in respect of Mr Jones and when Garda Kenny informed Mr Jones of his rights in accordance with Criminal Justice Act 1984 and the Treatment of Persons in Custody regulations 1987/2006.

I informed Mr Jones that I was a trained operator of the evidenzer, which was an instrument for measuring the level of alcohol in the breath. I informed him that I would be carrying out a breath test. I informed him that I would have to observe him for twenty minutes to ensure that he did not eat drink or smoke for twenty minutes. I told him that this was in line with best international practice. I began the observation at 9.25 pm and completed the observation at 9.45 pm. From the beginning of the observation to the time the completed sample was provided Mr Jones did not eat, drink, smoke or regurgitate.

I brought Mr Jones to the evidenzer room. I activated the machine. I entered my details and the details of MR. Jones in to the machine. When instructed I attached a new mouthpiece from a sealed packet. At 9.50 pm I then made the following demand to Mr Jones 'I am requiring you to provide two specimens of your breath by exhaling into this apparatus designed for determining the concentration of alcohol in your breath. Failure or refusal to comply with this requirement is an offence under s. 12(2) of the Road Traffic Act 2010. Penalty on summary conviction is liable to a fine not exceeding €5,000 or to a term of imprisonment not exceeding 6 months or both.'

Mr Jones provided two samples, the first at 9.57 and the second at 10 pm. The evidenzer printed two identical statements showing that Mr Jones had a concentration of alcohol of 63 microgrammes of alcohol per 100 millilitres of breath.

I signed both statements in front of Mr Jones and then I placed both of them in front of him. I then said 'under s. 13(2) of the Road Traffic Act 2010 I am now requiring you to acknowledge receipt of these two statements by signing each of them on the space provided and return one of them to me.' I also informed him that failure or refusal to comply with the requirement would be a separate offence which on conviction incurred a penalty of up to €5,000 and or 3 months in prison.

Mr Jones signed both statements retained one and returned the other to me.

I brought Mr Jones back to the public area where he was released from custody.

15.7.5   EXAMINING THE PROSECUTION CASE

The proofs in any intoxicant prosecution will vary depending on the alleged charge (e.g. failure to give a sample, drunk in charge etc.) and the particulars circumstances alleged (e.g. stopped at a checkpoint, roadside breath test, blood or urine sample etc.). Using the statement above as a typical example we can examine the common proofs. We can then look at some of the proofs in more detail and how they can vary depending on the charge and the circumstances of the case. It is important to remember that while the statement is useful for examining the prosecution case, it is the actual evidence given which will determine whether the prosecution have proven their case. There may be proofs missing in the statements which will be given in oral evidence or proofs present in the statements which are not given in evidence.

15.7.5.1   The date

The date of the alleged driving must correspond with the charge sheet or summons.

15.7.5.2   Driving

This was discussed previously at **15.2.1** dealing with driving without a licence. To recap, 'drive' is statutorily defined in s. 3 of the Principal Act as including managing or controlling and driving. There is very little litigation in our jurisdiction regarding the s. 3 definition of driving. We can take it as our normal understanding of driving, managing, or controlling a moving vehicle.

While normally proving the fact of driving is achieved through the evidence of an eye witness, it may also be proved by the admission of an accused. In *DPP v Cormack* [1999] 1 ILRM 398, a drink driving charge was dismissed because there was insufficient evidence that the vehicle had been driven in a public place within the relevant period of three hours. The prosecution evidence was the Gardaí had come across the scene of a one-vehicle accident. Mr Cormack was present. He admitted driving the vehicle and stated the accident had happened 10 minutes prior to the arrival of the Gardaí. O'Flaherty J. held: 'once the man had made a (voluntary) admission, then it is clear evidence and the Judge was bound to accept it'.

15.7.5.3   Time of driving

Where there is a prosecution for exceeding the concentration of alcohol the prosecution must, as per s. 4(2), (3), and (4) of the 2010 Act quoted earlier, prove the sample was taken within three hours of driving.

15.7.5.4   Location

The prosecution are required to show that the alleged place of driving is the one and the same as that on the charge sheet/summons.

15.7.5.5   Public place

This was previously discussed under driving without a licence. To recap, 'public place' is defined by s. 3 of the Principal Act as substituted by s. 49(1)(a)(iv) of the Road Traffic Act 1994, as:

(a)   *any public road, and*

(b)   *any street, road or other place to which the public have access with vehicles whether as of right or by permission and whether subject to or free of charge.*

There are a number of Irish authorities examining the definition of a public place. The grounds of a holiday home for senior citizens was found not to be a public place in *Stanbridge v Healy* [1985] ILRM 290, while Poppintree Park in Ballymun was found to be a public place in *Richards v MIB*, an unreported Supreme Court judgment from 12 June 1996. Grafton Street after pedestrianisation was held to be a public place in the unreported Supreme Court judgment of *DPP v Molloy* (1 June 1995).

15.7.5.6   Mechanically propelled vehicle

This was also reviewed under driving without a licence. There is no definition of 'vehicle' in the Road Traffic Acts; however, s. 3(1) of the Principal Act defines a 'mechanically propelled vehicle' as a vehicle intended or adapted for propulsion by mechanical (including electrical or partly electrical) means, including a bicycle or tricycle with an attachment for propelling it by mechanical power, whether or not the attachment is being used.

Section 3(2) of the Principal Act exempted a vehicle substantially disabled (by accident, break-down, engine, or vital part removal), so that it is no longer capable of being mechanically pro-pelled, from being a mechanically propelled vehicle for the purpose of the Act. This point was examined in the *DPP v Regina Brehony* case, an unreported judgment of Egan J (2 March 1993, Supreme Court). A new s. 3(2) was substituted by s. 72 of the Road Traffic Act 2010. The new s. 3(2) provides that if the vehicle becomes disabled through collision then it will for the purpose of the Road Traffic Acts remain a mechanically propelled vehicle.

15.7.5.7   The stop

The Gardaí have a common law power to stop vehicles in order to detect or prevent crime once it is not exercised 'in a capricious manner but in a constant fashion and with due civility and courtesy' (*DPP (Stratford) v Fagan* [1994] 2 ILRM 349).

There also exist legislative powers to stop vehicles such as s. 109 of the Road Traffic Act 1961. The most commonly used legislative provision in the context of drink driving prosecution is s. 10 of the Road Traffic Act 2010, which allows for stopping of motor vehicles at a checkpoint in order to require the drivers to submit to a roadside breath test. This is discussed in more detail at **15.7.7**.

15.7.5.8   The driver

The prosecution are required to identify the driver as the accused named on the summons/charge sheet.

15.7.5.9   The Garda opinion and the indicators grounding it

Before a Garda can invoke the arrest provision in s. 4(8) or s. 5(8) of the 2010 Act, s/he must have an opinion that an offence has occurred. Evidence is required that they believed that they were of the opinion that the accused had consumed an intoxicant to such an extent that he/she was incapable of having proper control of an MPV in a public place. According to Costello J. in *Hobbs v Hurley*, High Court (unreported), 'The opinion arrived at must, of course, be a reasonable one and must be one which results from an honest belief come to after facts have been ascertained and considered.'

A prosecuting Garda would usually outline to the court the facts (indicators) which went to forming his opinion that an accused had consumed an intoxicant to such an extent as to be incapable of having proper control of a mechanically propelled vehicle in a public place. These indicators are the usual symptoms associated with the over consumption of an intoxicant, for example, glazed eyes, smell of alcohol from the breath, slurred speech and so on.

The Gardaí are required to administer roadside breath tests under ss. 9 and 10 of the 2010 Act where they have not yet reached the required opinion, both of which are discussed in more detail at **15.7.7**. The required opinion may simply arise from a failed breath test (see *DPP v Gilmore* [1981] ILRM 102) or from a combination of failed breath test and other indicators.

15.7.5.10   The arrest

The proving of a valid arrest is essential to the prosecution case, without which all subsequent evidence will fall. Once the opinion evidence is given there are two necessary ingredients to establish the lawful arrest. Simply put the accused must know that he is no longer at liberty and he must be informed of the reason for his arrest in plain language or know from the circum-stances why he is being arrested. While a Garda may give evidence of advising the defendant in technical language of the reason for his arrest, the court will be more concerned that the defend-ant was told in plain language the reason for his arrest. The primary case on this point is *DPP v Mooney* [1993] ILRM 214.

The accused should be cautioned after the arrest. Any admissions should be noted and the accused should be offered the opportunity to sign them in accordance with the Judges' Rules which are discussed in **Chapter 4**. Failure to do so by the Garda will allow the judge the discre-tion to rule them inadmissible.

15.7.5.11   Custody regulations

Once the arrest has taken place the driver is escorted to a Garda Station. If the Gardaí are going to require the driver to give a breath sample at the Garda Station as discussed in the next section, then a period of observation to ensure that the driver consumes nil by mouth prior to giving the sample takes place. This is a recommended practice by the Medical Bureau of Road Safety. The Gardaí are obliged to comply with the Criminal Justice Act 1984 (Treatment of Persons in Custody in Garda Stations) Regulations 1987 (SI No. 119 of 1987), discussed in detail at **Chapter 4** and **Chapter 5**, which provide that a detainee be informed of their rights under the said Regulations.

In *DPP v Spratt* [1995] 2 ILRM 117, the defendant was arrested pursuant to s. 49 of the Principal Act, as amended. In the District Court, it was not established that the Criminal Justice Act 1984 (Treatment of Persons in Custody in Garda Stations) Regulations 1987 had been adhered to. The District Court stated a case for the opinion of the High Court as to the effect, if any, resulting from the non-compliance with the Regulations. The High Court stated that while it must be proven that the 1987 Regulations have been complied with, it is a matter for the court of trial to adjudicate in every case as to the impact of the non-compliance. Failure to comply does not necessarily lead to a dismissal of the charge against the accused. The decisions in *DPP v Spratt* and in *DPP v Devlin* suggest that the effect of breach of the regulations is a matter for the judge's discretion to be exercised on the basis of the prejudicial effect of the breach. If there is no prejudice to the accused then the breach may be overlooked. There is also a provision in the Act that the breach of the regulations does not of itself affect the admissibility of the evidence.

In the case of *DPP v Paul McCrea* [2010] IESC 60 (2010), it was held that the accused had the right of access to a solicitor prior to providing a sample.

15.7.5.12   Obligation to provide specimen following arrest

Section 12 of the 2010 Act (as amended by s. 9(d) of the Road Traffic (No.2) Act 2011) provides as follows:

12.— (1)   Where a person is arrested under section 4(8), 5(10), 6(4), 9(4), 10(7) or 11(5) of this Act or section 52(3), 53(5), 106(3A) or 112(6) of the Principal Act, a member of the Garda Síochána may, at a Garda Síochána station or hospital, do either or both of the following—

(a)   require the person to provide, by exhaling into an apparatus for determining the concentration of alcohol in the breath, 2 specimens of his or her breath and may indicate the manner in which he or she is to comply with the requirement,

(b)   require the person either—

(i)   to permit a designated doctor or designated nurse to take from the person a specimen of his or her blood, or

(ii)   at the option of the person, to provide for the designated doctor or designated nurse a specimen of his or her urine,

and if the doctor or nurse states in writing—

(I)   that he or she is unwilling, on medical grounds, to take from the person or be provided by him or her with the specimen to which the requirement in either of the foregoing subparagraphs related, or

(II)   that the person is unable or unlikely within the period of time referred to in section 4 or 5, as the case may be, to comply with the requirement,

the member may make a requirement of the person under this paragraph in relation to the specimen other than that to which the first requirement related.

(2)   Subject to section 22, a person who refuses or fails to comply immediately with a requirement under subsection (1) (a) commits an offence.

(3)   Subject to section 22, a person who, following a requirement under subsection (1)(b)—

(a)   refuses or fails to comply with the requirement, or

(b)   refuses or fails to comply with a requirement of a designated doctor or designated nurse in relation to the taking under that subsection of a specimen of blood or the provision under that subsection of a specimen of urine, commits an offence.

(4)   A person who commits an offence under this section is liable on summary conviction to a fine not exceeding €5,000 or to imprisonment for a term not exceeding 6 months or to both.

(5)   In a prosecution for an offence under this Part it shall be presumed, until the contrary is shown, that an apparatus provided by a member of the Garda Síochána for the purpose of enabling a person to provide 2 specimens of breath under this section is an apparatus for determining the concentration of alcohol in the breath.

(6)   Section 1 (1) of the Probation of Offenders Act 1907 does not apply to an offence under this section.

Section 12 provides for three possible specimen types, breath, blood or urine. The requirement that is made is at the discretion of the Garda. In the sample statement made earlier, the Garda made a requirement for a breath sample. It is the Gardaí who have the discretion as to whether a breath or blood sample is required. If the Garda decides to seek a blood sample then the person must be given an option to provide a urine sample in the alternative.

Where the requirement is made for a breath specimen, then it is best international practice for the person to be observed for 20 minutes prior to giving the sample to ensure that he or she has nil by mouth. This helps to ensure that the machine will accept the given breath samples. Without the 20 minutes there is a possibility the machine will not produce a result/certificate as contaminants may remain. The reason for the 20-minute observation should be explained to the court by the Garda administering the breath test, the time it started, the time it concluded, and the fact there was nothing taken by mouth. The Garda should explain to the person what is required of them and make the requirement under s. 12, explaining that it is an offence not to comply and the penalties arising as a result. Strictly speaking, the requirement itself is not a proof for drink driving, but is obviously an essential proof where the person fails or refuses to comply with the requirement.

In the event that the Gardaí proceed by way of blood/urine they must contact the doctor to attend. They introduce the designated doctor to the person and the person to the designated doctor. The Garda makes the requirement under s. 12(1)(b) of the Road Traffic Act 2010 for the person to allow the doctor to take a specimen of his/her blood or at the person's option urine. Again it is important that there is evidence that the person was told that it was an offence not to comply and the penalties involved, in order that the person can be prosecuted if s/he fails or refuses to comply.

15.7.5.13   Section 13 certificate (breath)

There are three certificates upon which the prosecution may attempt to rely for a drink driving prosecution. These certificates carry with them statutory presumptions arising from s. 20 of the Road Traffic Act 2010, which is examined later at **15.7.13**.

In the example involving our typical Garda statement, the person gave a breath sample. The certificate produced and relied upon by the prosecution in a breath case is known as a s. 13 certificate named after the section of the 2010 Act which governs the procedure following the provisions of breath specimens under s. 12.

Under s. 13 the apparatus must produce two identical statements. The Garda should first sign both statements. He should then give both statements to the person and require him to sign both statements and return one statement to the Garda. The Garda should inform the person that it is an offence not to comply and the penalties involved. This is obviously important if the person refuses to comply and the Gardaí wish later to prosecute him for non-compliance with the requirement. A completed s. 13 certificate (or in some cases a copy) is an essential proof for the prosecution.

The evidence of the Garda who made the requirement under s. 12 can be provided by written statement subject to certain conditions as contained in s. 19 of the Road Traffic Act 2010 as amended by s. 12 of the Road Traffic Act 2010.

15.7.5.14   The doctors certificate (blood/urine)

Section 15 of the Road Traffic Act 2010 provides as follows:

15.— (1)   Where under this Chapter a designated doctor or designated nurse has taken a specimen of blood from a person or has been provided by the person with a specimen of his or her urine, the doctor or nurse, as the case may be, shall divide the specimen into 2 parts, place each part in a container which he or she shall immediately seal, and complete the form prescribed for the purposes of this section.

(2) *Where a specimen of blood or urine of a person has been divided into 2 parts under subsection (1), a member of the Garda Síochána shall offer to the person one of the sealed containers and inform the person that he or she may retain either of the containers.*

(3) *As soon as practicable after subsection (2) has been complied with, a member of the Garda Síochána shall cause to be forwarded to the Bureau the completed form referred to in subsection (1), together with the relevant sealed container or, where the person has declined to retain one of the sealed containers, both relevant sealed containers.*

(4) *In a prosecution for an offence under this Chapter or under section 4 or 5, it shall be presumed until the contrary is shown that subsections (1) to (3) have been complied with.*

Where a person provides a blood or urine specimen the prosecution will rely on a certificate from the doctor who took the samples and the medical bureau which analysed the samples.

The doctor's certificate describes the procedure carried out by the doctor under s. 15(1) and in effect allows the doctor's proofs to be given in evidence without the doctor having to attend. This is essentially describes taking the sample, dividing the specimen in two, placing the samples in two sealed containers and completing the certificate. The Garda should still give evidence of offering to allow the person to retain either of the sealed containers, whether the person did retain a sample, and when the Garda forwarded the sample to the Medical Bureau of Road Safety.

Both provisions give rise to a presumption that the Garda member and doctor/nurse have complied with its provisions unless the contrary can be proved. This in addition to the presumption accorded to the doctor/nurse's certificate under s. 21 of the Road Traffic Act 1994 as amended and under s. 20 of the Road Traffic Act 2010, which is discussed later, mean that the prosecution is required to call any evidence of the steps taken by the doctor/nurse. If the defence allege that the procedure was not properly followed by the doctor/nurse, it is up to the accused to prove it.

The handing in of the s. 15 certificate to the court is a necessary proof in a drink driving case involving a blood/urine sample.

15.7.5.15   MBRS certificate (blood/urine cases)

Section 17 of the Road Traffic Act 2010 provides:

17—(1) *As soon as practicable after it has received a specimen forwarded to it under section 15, the Bureau shall analyse the specimen and determine the concentration of alcohol or (as may be appropriate) the presence of a drug or drugs in the specimen.*

(2) *Where the Bureau receives 2 specimens of blood so forwarded together in relation to the same person or 2 specimens of urine so forwarded together in relation to the same person, it shall be sufficient compliance with subsection (1) for the Bureau to make an analysis of and determination in relation to one of the 2 specimens of blood or (as may be appropriate) one of the 2 specimens of urine.*

(3) *As soon as practicable after compliance with subsection (1), the Bureau shall subject to section 17A(3) forward to the Garda Síochána station from which the specimen analysed was forwarded a completed certificate in the form prescribed for the purpose of this section and shall forward a copy of the completed certificate to the person who is named on the relevant form under section 15 as the person from whom the specimen was taken or who provided it.*

(4) *In a prosecution for an offence under this Chapter or under section 4 or 5, it shall be presumed until the contrary is shown that subsections (1) to (3) have been complied with.*

The Bureau is a corporate body and therefore acts in the same manner as any corporate body through its authorised agents or analysts. Accordingly, the Bureau, and not the analyst, certifies the accuracy of a tested specimen.

The phrase 'as soon as practicable' gives rise to two very serious obligations on the part of the Bureau:

(a)   The Bureau must forward as soon as practicable a completed certificate in the prescribed form to the Garda station from whom the specimen was received.

(b)   The Bureau must forward a copy of the certificate to the person from whom the specimen was taken.

In *Hobbs v Hurley* (unreported, 10 June 1980, High Court), a specimen received by the Bureau on 21 September and issued by the Bureau on 11 October was deemed to comply with the 'as soon as practicable' obligations on the part of the Bureau; 'as soon as practicable' was distinguished from 'as soon as possible'. In *DPP v Corrigan* [1988] RTR 52, a certificate issued on 13 November for a sample taken on 24 October was held to be as soon as practicable. In *DPP v Flahive* [1988] ILRM 133, a typographical error on the Bureau's certificate did not affect the admissibility of the certificate.

'Analyse' is defined by s. 9 of the Road Traffic Act 1994 as including any operation used in determining the concentration of alcohol in a specimen of breath, blood, or urine, and any operation used in determining the presence (if any) of a drug or drugs in a specimen of blood or urine.

The certificate issued by the Bureau contains the result of how much alcohol was in the person's blood/urine. The s. 17 certificate is an essential proof in blood and urine cases and must be handed in to the court by the prosecution.

The case of *DPP v Tate Croom Carroll* [1999] 4 IR 126 established that a doctor is required to write the name of the person giving the specimen on the container. In the event that s/he does not, then the prosecution will not be able to rely on the presumptions and will be required to call the doctor/nurse. This is quite a common scenario, and it usually only occurs when the bureau certificate states that there was no name on the actual container.

Section 12 of the 2014 Act introduced s. 17A to the Road Traffic Act 2010. The section provides for the giving of permission by a driver to the Medical Bureau to allow the Medical Bureau to forward to the Gardaí a completed certificate of analysis where a sample was taken when the driver was unconscious. A refusal to provide such permission without a good and substantial reason is in itself deemed to be a criminal offence.

15.7.6   DRUNK IN CHARGE PROSECUTIONS

Section 5 cases differ from s. 4 in that the prosecution do not have to prove driving, only that the accused was in charge of the vehicle. The most common scenario is the accused sitting in the driver's seat with the keys visible or in the ignition. While there is no statutory definition of 'in charge', the matter has been the subject of litigation. Kearns J. in *DPP v Jamie Stewart* [2001] 3 IR 103 reviewed the case law including the helpful English case of *DPP v Watkins* [1989] 1 All ER 1126. Kearns J quoted Taylor L.J. with the words 'the meaning of the phrase "in charge" does necessitate a close connection between the defendant and the control of a motor vehicle in the way I have endeavoured to indicate in this Judgment. It does not necessitate proof of a likelihood of the Defendant driving the vehicle'.

A common scenario which arises in the Irish courts is when the accused is found in the driver's seat asleep, often with the keys in the ignition. If the prosecution can prove on the facts that the accused was in charge of the vehicle then it is for the accused to show that he did not intend to drive or intend to attempt to drive the vehicle.

In the case of *DPP v Byrne* [2002] 2 ILRM 68, the Supreme Court found a driver asleep in his car, in charge with intent to drive for the purposes of an offence contrary to s. 50(3) of the Road Traffic Act 1961.

15.7.7   OBLIGATION TO PROVIDE A MANDATORY BREATH TEST

Section 10 of the Road Traffic Act 2010 provides for mandatory, random breath testing. Under s. 10, a member of the Garda Síochána, not below the rank of Inspector, may for the purpose of s. 4 of the Road Traffic Act 2010, authorise the establishment of a checkpoint or checkpoints in a public place or places at which members of the Garda Síochána may exercise the powers conferred under s. 10(4).

Section 10(8) creates a rebuttable presumption that the apparatus used by the Garda for testing alcohol is suitable for this purpose. In addition s. 10(9) creates an additional rebuttable presumption that an authorisation or copy of an authorisation of an Inspector shall be sufficient proof that the checkpoints were authorised in accordance with this section. The High Court has held that in the absence of exceptional circumstances, the written authorisation to set up the checkpoint under s. 4 of the 2006 Act is a necessary proof *Mary Weir v DPP* [2008] IEHC 268.

Section 10, sub-ss. 4–10 of the Road Traffic Act 2010 as amended by s. 9(e) of the Road Traffic (No. 2) Act 2011 provides:

> (4) *A member of the Garda Síochána, who is on duty at a checkpoint, may stop any vehicle at the checkpoint and, without prejudice to any other powers (including the functions under section 9) conferred on him or her by statute or at common law, may require a person in charge of the vehicle—*
>
> > (a) *to—*
> >
> > > (i) *provide (by exhaling into an apparatus for indicating the presence of alcohol in the breath) a specimen of his or her breath, or*
> > >
> > > (ii) *accompany him or her or another member of the Garda Síochána to a place (including a vehicle) at or in the vicinity of the checkpoint and there to provide, by exhaling into such an apparatus, a specimen of his or her breath, or*
> >
> > (b) *to—*
> >
> > > (i) *leave the vehicle at the place where it has been stopped, or*
> > >
> > > (ii) *move it to a place in the vicinity of the checkpoint, and*
> >
> > *keep or leave it there until the person has complied with a requirement made of him or her under paragraph (a).*
>
> (6) *A person who—*
>
> > (a) *refuses or fails to comply immediately with a requirement under subsection (4) (a) or (b) (i) or such a requirement in a manner indicated by a member of the Garda Síochána under subsection (5), or*
> >
> > (b) *without reasonable excuse, refuses or fails to comply immediately with a requirement under subsection (4)(b)(ii) or such a requirement in a manner indicated by a member of the Garda Síochána under subsection (5),*
> >
> > *commits an offence and is liable on summary conviction to a fine not exceeding €5,000 or to imprisonment for a term not exceeding 6 months or to both.*
>
> (7) *A member of the Garda Síochána may arrest without warrant a person who in the member's opinion is committing or has committed an offence under this section.*
>
> (8) *In a prosecution for an offence under section 4, it shall be presumed, until the contrary is shown, that an apparatus provided by a member of the Garda Síochána for the purpose of enabling a person to provide a specimen of breath under this section is an apparatus for indicating the presence of alcohol in the breath.*
>
> (9) *An authorisation or a copy expressing itself to be such authorisation shall, until the contrary is shown, be sufficient evidence in any proceedings under the Road Traffic Acts 1961 to 2010 of the facts stated in it, without proof of any signature on it or that the signatory was a person entitled under subsection (2) to sign it.*

15.7.8   OBLIGATION TO PROVIDE PRELIMINARY BREATH SPECIMEN

Section 9 of the 2010 Act (as inserted by s. 7 of the Road Traffic (No. 2) Act 2011), provides:

> 9.— (1) *This section applies to a person in charge of a mechanically propelled vehicle in a public place who, in the opinion of a member of the Garda Síochána—*
>
> > (a) *has consumed intoxicating liquor,*
> >
> > (b) *is committing or has committed an offence under the Road Traffic Acts 1961 to 2011,*
> >
> > (c) *is or has been, with the vehicle, involved in a collision, or*

    (d)   is or has been, with the vehicle, involved in an event in which death occurs or injury appears or is claimed to have been caused to a person of such nature as to require medical assistance for the person at the scene of the event or that the person be brought to a hospital for medical assistance.

  (2)   A member of the Garda Síochána shall, unless he or she is of opinion that the person should be arrested and subject to subsections (6) and (7), require a person to whom paragraph (a) or (d) of subsection (1) applies, and may require a person to whom paragraph (b) or (c) of that subsection applies—

    (a)   to provide, by exhaling into an apparatus for indicating the presence of alcohol in the breath, a specimen of his or her breath in the manner indicated by the member,

    (b)   to accompany him or her to a place (including a vehicle) at or in the vicinity of the public place concerned and there to provide, by exhaling into such an apparatus, a specimen of his or her breath in the manner indicated by the member, or

    (c)   where the member does not have such an apparatus with him or her, to remain at that place in his or her presence or in the presence of another member of the Garda Síochána (for a period that does not exceed one hour) until such an apparatus becomes available to him or her and then to provide, by exhaling into such an apparatus, a specimen of his or her breath in the manner indicated by the member.

  (3)   A person who refuses or fails to comply immediately with a requirement of a member of the Garda Síochána under this section commits an offence and is liable on summary conviction to a class A fine or to imprisonment for a term not exceeding 6 months or to both.

  (4)   A member of the Garda Síochána may arrest without warrant a person who in the member's opinion is committing or has committed an offence under this section.

  (5)   In a prosecution for an offence under section 4, 5 or 6 of this Act it shall be presumed, until the contrary is shown, that an apparatus provided by a member of the Garda Síochána for the purpose of enabling a person to provide a specimen of breath under this section is an apparatus for indicating the presence of alcohol in the breath.

  (6)   A member of the Garda Síochána shall not make a requirement under subsection (2) of a person to whom paragraph (a) of subsection (1) applies if, in the opinion of the member, such requirement would be prejudicial to the health of the person.

  (7)   A member of the Garda Síochána shall not make a requirement under subsection (2) of a person to whom paragraph (d) of subsection (1) applies if, in the opinion of the member or on the advice of a doctor or other medical personnel attending the scene of the event, such requirement would be prejudicial to the health of the person.

  (8)   Section 1(1) of the Probation of Offenders Act 1907 does not apply to an offence under this section.

  (9)   Nothing in this section affects any power of arrest conferred by law apart from this section.

  (10)   It is not a defence in any proceedings, other than proceedings under subsection (3), to show that a member of the Garda Síochána did not make a requirement under this section.

Unless the Garda has formed an opinion that the person has committed an offence under the Road Traffic Acts, or his or her vehicle has been involved in a collision, or s/he is involved with his vehicle in an event in which death or injury appears or claims to have been caused so as to require medical assistance, then the Garda must form the opinion that the person has consumed an intoxicant before requiring a sample under s. 9. The difference between this and the requirement under s. 10 of the 2010 Act is that under the mandatory checkpoint provision, the Garda does not have to form an opinion of a consumed intoxicant once he is making the requirement at a checkpoint created for the purpose of random breath testing and authorised by a Garda not below the rank of Inspector.

In *DPP v Joyce* [1985] ILRM 206, the court held that in order to comply with the provisions of the equivalent of s. 9, a Garda member is obliged to request the specimen of breath from a person in charge of a mechanically propelled vehicle in a public place.

'Person', 'public place', and 'mechanically propelled vehicle' are defined in the preceding discussion regarding driving without a licence. 'In charge' is discussed earlier regarding s. 4 of the 2010 Act.

In *DPP v Gilmore* [1981] ILRM 102, the court held that a positive breathalyser result would be sufficient to ground the opinion of a Garda member that a s. 49(2) or a s. 49(3) offence had been committed.

15.7.9 FAILURE/REFUSAL TO PROVIDE SPECIMENS: PROSECUTIONS, CASE LAW, AND DEFENCES

Section 22 of the Road Traffic Act 2010 provides a legislative defence for a failure or a refusal to provide a sample as follows:

22.—(1) *In a prosecution of a person for an offence under section 12 for refusing or failing to comply with a requirement to provide 2 specimens of his or her breath, it shall be a defence for the defendant to satisfy the court that there was a special and substantial reason for his or her refusal or failure and that, as soon as practicable after the refusal or failure concerned, he or she complied (or offered, but was not called upon, to comply) with a requirement under the section concerned in relation to the taking of a specimen of blood or the provision of a specimen of urine.*

(2) *In a prosecution of a person for an offence under section 12 or 14 for refusing or failing to comply with a requirement to permit a designated doctor or designated nurse to take a specimen of blood or for refusing or failing to comply with a requirement of a designated doctor or designated nurse in relation to the taking of a specimen of blood, it shall be a defence for the defendant to satisfy the court that there was a special and substantial reason for his or her refusal or failure and that, as soon as practicable after the refusal or failure concerned, he or she complied (or offered, but was not called upon, to comply) with a requirement under the section concerned in relation to the provision of a specimen of urine.*

(3) *Notwithstanding subsections (1) and (2), evidence may be given at the hearing of a charge of an offence under section 4 or 5 that the defendant refused or failed to comply with a requirement to provide 2 specimens of his or her breath, or that the defendant refused or failed to comply with a requirement to permit the taking of a specimen of his or her blood or to comply with a requirement of a designated doctor in relation to the taking of a specimen of blood, as the case may be.*

(4) *In a prosecution for an offence under section 11(4) for refusing or failing to perform a test, it is a defence for the defendant to satisfy the court that there was a special and substantial reason for his or her refusal or failure and that, as soon as practicable after the refusal or failure concerned, he or she complied (or offered, but was not called upon, to comply) with a requirement under the provision concerned in relation to the performance of a test.*

(5) *Notwithstanding subsection (4), evidence may be given at the hearing of a charge of an offence under section 4, 5 or 6 of the Road Traffic Act 2010 that the defendant failed to comply with a requirement to perform a test.*

What constitutes a good and substantial reason is a matter of fact for the court to decide; what is usually put forward as a good and substantial reason is a medical condition. When such a defence is raised it is normal practice for the defence to bring a medical professional to testify to the accused's alleged medical condition.

In the case of the *DPP v Maresa Cagney* [2013] IESC 13, the defendant was prosecuted for failing to provide a breath sample at the Garda station. The judge hearing the case found as a matter of fact that she was unable to do so due to a 'transient medical condition'. Ms Cagney was not offered an alternative of giving a sample of blood or urine.

A similar case had been decided in 2004 in *DPP v Redmond Cabot* [2004] IEHC 79. Failure or refusal is a strict liability offence with a limited defence offered by s. 23 of the Road Traffic Act 1994 (the equivalent of s. 22 of the 2010 Act).

The law according to *Cabot* was that not only must a good and substantial reason be found to exist as per s. 23 for a person to fail or refuse to provide a sample, but that the suspect must also offer to provide an alternative sample, even if not asked to do so by the Gardaí. In *Cagney* the trial judge found as a matter of fact that Ms Cagney had a transient medical condition which prevented her from providing the samples. The trial judge, whose view was approved by the Supreme Court, found that this constituted a 'special and substantial' reason within the meaning of the first of the two-pronged test contained within s. 23.The Court went on to find that where a defendant has established a special and substantial reason for failure or refusal to provide a breath sample, they will be entitled to a dismissal where they were not warned by the Gardaí that a failure to offer a blood or urine sample will preclude them from being able to rely on a defence of having a special and substantial reason.

It has been the practice of Gardaí for some time to enquire whether a suspect has any medical conditions, when they are being told of their rights by the member in charge and by the intoxilysing Garda. The fact that a defendant does not mention any such medical condition will not necessarily prevent them from relying on that medical condition later.

In the case of *DPP v O'Connor* [1999] IESC 35, it was held that in order to escape the obligation to permit a blood specimen to be taken, the defendant must actually provide a specimen of urine and not merely agree to provide one within a reasonable time.

Time of driving is not a necessary proof for a charge of failing or refusing to comply with a requirement to provide a specimen (*DPP v Clinton* (1984) ILRM 127).

In the case of *DPP v Bernard Joyce* [2004] IEHC 132, it was held that although a valid arrest is required, a s. 13 charge will hold even if the opinion of the Garda grounding the arrest was inaccurate, so long as it was reasonably held. Therefore the fact that a person was not driving is defence to a refusal charge, it is not necessarily a defence to a refusal/failure charge. This was once again reaffirmed in the case of *DPP v Finnegan* [2008] IEHC 347, where Clarke J. held that where Gardaí had a reasonable suspicion for the arrest then claims by the accused that s/he was not driving would not be regarded as a good and substantial reason for refusing to provide a sample.

15.7.10 OBLIGATION TO PROVIDE BLOOD OR URINE SPECIMEN WHILE IN HOSPITAL

Section 14 of the 2010 Act as substituted by s. 8 of the Road Traffic (No.2) Act 2011, as amended by s. 12 of the Road Traffic Act 2014 regulates the taking of blood and urine samples where the person has been admitted to hospital and it provides as follows:

14.— (1)   *Where, in a public place, an event occurs in relation to a mechanically propelled vehicle in consequence of or following which a person is injured, or claims or appears to have been injured, and is admitted to, or attends at, a hospital and a member of the Garda Síochána is of opinion that, at the time of the event the person was driving or attempting to drive, or in charge of with intent to drive or attempt to drive (but not driving or attempting to drive), the mechanically propelled vehicle, then, subject to subsection (4) and unless the is of the opinion that the person should be arrested, the member shall, in the hospital, require the person either—*

(a)   *to permit a designated doctor or designated nurse to take from the person a specimen of his or her blood, or*

(b)   *at the option of the person, to provide for the designated doctor or designated nurse a specimen of his or her urine, and if the doctor or nurse states in writing—*

(i)   *that he or she is unwilling, on medical grounds, to take from the person or be provided by the person with the specimen to which the requirement in either of the foregoing paragraphs related, or*

(ii)   *that the person is unable or unlikely within the period of time referred to in section 4 or 5, as the case may be, to comply with the requirement,*

the member may make a requirement of the person under this subsection in relation to the specimen other than that to which the first requirement related.

(2)   *Subject to section 22, a person who, following a requirement under subsection (1)—*

(a)   *refuses or fails to comply with the requirement, or*

(b)   *refuses or fails to comply with a requirement of a designated doctor or designated nurse in relation to the taking under that subsection of a specimen of blood or the provision under that subsection of a specimen of urine, commits an offence and is liable on summary conviction to a class A fine or to imprisonment for a term not exceeding 6 months or to both.*

(3) *Notwithstanding subsection (2), it is not an offence for a person to refuse or fail to comply with a requirement under subsection (1) where, following his or her admission to, or attendance at, a hospital, the person comes under the care of a doctor or nurse and the doctor or nurse refuses, on medical grounds, to permit the taking or provision of the specimen concerned.*

(3A) *Where it appears to the member of the Garda Siochana concerned that, for medical reasons, a person referred to in subsection (1) cannot be the subject of, or is incapable of complying with, a requirement under that subsection the member shall direct a designated doctor or designated nurse to take from the person a specimen of his or her blood.*

(4) *Before making a requirement of a person under subsection (1) or a direction under subsection (3A) the member of the Garda Síochána concerned shall consult with a doctor treating the person, and if a doctor treating the person advises the member that such a requirement would be prejudicial to the health of the person the member shall not make such requirement or direction.*

(5) *A member of the Garda Síochána may, for the purpose of making a requirement of a person under subsection (1) or a direction under subsection (3A), enter without warrant any hospital where the person is or where the member, with reasonable cause, suspects the person to be.*

(6) *A designated doctor or designated nurse may, for the purpose of taking from a person a specimen of his or her blood or being provided by a person with a specimen of his or her urine under subsection (1) or of taking a specimen of his or her blood as directed under subsection (3A) enter any hospital where the person is or where the doctor or nurse is informed by a member of the Garda Síochána that the person is.*

(7) *Section 1(1) of the Probation of Offenders Act 1907 does not apply to an offence under this section.*

(8) *Nothing in this section affects any power of arrest conferred by law apart from this section.*

(9) *It is not a defence in any proceedings, other than proceedings under subsection (2), to show that a member of the Garda Síochána did not make a requirement under this section.*

(10) *It shall be lawful for a designated doctor or nurse to take from thje person a specimen of his or her blood as directed under subsection (3A).*

The original section created a new power on the part of Gardaí, in that it authorises a Garda member with a designated doctor to enter a hospital where an injured person, or a person who claims or appears to have been injured, is suspected of having consumed an intoxicant, to take a blood or urine sample from the injured person. This is repeated in the 2010 Act. It should be noted that the injured person's doctor may refuse to permit the taking of the said sample for medical reasons only. The amendments introduced by the 2014 Act provide for the taking of samples where a person is unconscious.

15.7.11 DETENTION OF INTOXICATED DRIVERS WHERE A DANGER TO SELVES OR OTHERS

Section 16 of the 2010 Act allows the Gardaí to detain someone for their own safety and that of others because of the person's intoxication where s/he has been arrested for a number of serious road traffic offences. It provides as follows:

16.— (1) *Where a person is at a Garda Síochána station having been arrested under section 4(8), 5(10), 6(4), 9(4), 10(7) or 11(5) of this Act or section 52(3), 53(5), 106(3A) or 112(6) of the Principal Act, he or she may, at the Garda Síochána station, if the member of the Garda Síochána for the time being in charge of the station is of opinion that the person is under the influence of an intoxicant to such an extent as to be a threat to the safety of himself or herself or others, be detained in custody for such period (not exceeding 6 hours from the time of his or her arrest or, as the case may be, from the time he or she was required to accompany a member to the station) as the member of the Garda Síochána so in charge considers necessary.*

(2) *Where a person is detained under subsection (1), the member of the Garda Síochána for the time being in charge of the Garda Síochána station shall—*

(a) *in case the person detained is or the said member is of opinion that he or she is 18 years of age or more, as soon as is practicable, if it is reasonably possible to do so, inform a relative of the person or such other person as the person so detained may specify of the detention, unless the person so detained does not wish any person to be so informed, and*

(b) *in case the person detained is or the said member is of opinion that he or she is under the age of 18 years, as soon as is practicable, if it is reasonably possible to do so, inform a relative of the person or such other person as the person so detained may specify of the detention.*

(3) *A person detained under subsection (1) shall—*

(a) *in case he or she is or the member of the Garda Síochána for the time being in charge of the Garda Síochána station is of opinion that he or she is 18 years of age or more, upon the attendance at the station of a person being either a relative of, or a person specified under subsection (2) by, the person so detained, be released by the said member into the custody of that person, unless—*

(i) *the latter person is or the member is of opinion that he or she is under the age of 18 years,*

(ii) *the person so detained does not wish to be released into the custody of the latter person, or*

(iii) *the member is of opinion that the person so detained continues to be under the influence of an intoxicant to such an extent that, if he or she is then released into the custody of the latter person, he or she will continue to be a threat to the safety of himself or herself or others,*

and shall, if not so released, be released at the expiration of the period of detention authorised by subsection (1), and

(b) *in case he or she is or the member of the Garda Síochána for the time being in charge of the Garda Síochána station is of opinion that he or she is under the age of 18 years, upon the attendance at the station of a person being either a relative of, or a person specified under subsection (2) by, the person so detained, be released by the said member into the custody of that person, unless the latter person is or the said member is of opinion that he or she is under the age of 18 years, and shall, if not so released, be released at the expiration of the period of detention authorised by subsection (1).*

The maximum period of detention under this section is six hours. The detainee is also entitled to have a relative or a person nominated by him or her informed of his detention as soon as practicable. It should be noted that the detainee is entitled to the same rights as any person in custody.

15.7.12 PROVISIONS REGARDING CERTAIN EVIDENCE IN PROSECUTIONS UNDER SECTIONS 4 AND 5 OF THE ROAD TRAFFIC ACT 2010—THE HIP FLASK DEFENCE

Section 18 in the 2010 Act relates to the hip flask defence and attempts to frustrate a prosecution. It provides as follows:

18.— (1) *On the hearing of a charge for an offence under section 4 or 5 it shall not be necessary to show that the defendant had not consumed intoxicating liquor after the time when the offence is alleged to have been committed but before the taking or provision of a specimen under section 12 or 14.*

(2) *Where, on the hearing of a charge for an offence under section 4 or 5 evidence is given by or on behalf of the defendant that, after the time when the offence is alleged to have been committed but before the taking or provision of a specimen under section 12 or 14, he or she had consumed intoxicating liquor, the court shall disregard the evidence unless satisfied by or on behalf of the defendant—*

(a) *that, but for that consumption, the concentration of alcohol in the defendant's blood (as specified in a certificate under section 17) would not have exceeded the concentration of alcohol for the time being standing specified in subsection (2) of section 4 or 5, as may be appropriate, whether generally or in respect of the class of person of which the defendant is a member,*

(b)   that, but for that consumption, the concentration of alcohol in the defendant's urine (as specified in a certificate under section 17) would not have exceeded the concentration of alcohol for the time being standing specified in subsection (3) of section 4 or 5, as may be appropriate, whether generally or in respect of the class of person of which the defendant is a member, or

(c)   that, but for that consumption, the concentration of alcohol in the defendant's breath (as specified in a statement under section 13) would not have exceeded the concentration of alcohol for the time being standing specified in subsection (4) of section 4 or 5, as may be appropriate, whether generally or in respect of the class of person of which the defendant is a member.

(3)   (a)   A person shall not take or attempt to take any action (including consumption of alcohol but excluding a refusal or failure to provide a specimen of his or her breath or urine or to permit the taking of a specimen of his or her blood) with the intention of frustrating a prosecution under section 4 or 5.

(b)   A person who contravenes this subsection commits an offence and is liable on summary conviction to a fine not exceeding €5,000 or to imprisonment for a term not exceeding 6 months or to both.

(4)   Where, on the hearing of a charge for an offence under section 4 or 5, the court is satisfied that any action taken by the defendant (including consumption of alcohol but excluding a refusal or failure to provide a specimen of his or her breath or urine or to permit the taking of a specimen of his or her blood) was so taken with the intention of frustrating a prosecution under any of those sections, the court may find that he or she has committed an offence under subsection (3).

The court will disregard evidence that alcohol was consumed after the time of the alleged offence but before the sample was taken unless the court believes that but for that consumption the accused would not have exceeded the prescribed limit. It also makes any action (which includes deliberately consuming alcohol), which has the intention of frustrating a prosecution, an offence.

It should be noted that offences committed under ss. 4(1) and 5(1), as amended, are dependent from an evidential perspective on the opinion evidence of a witness, who is usually a Garda member. This opinion is normally based upon observations of the defendant at the time of the commission of the offence, as opposed to evidence of a scientific nature. Offences committed in breach of ss. 4(2), (3), and (4), in contrast depend from an evidentiary perspective on proof of concentration of alcohol (s. 4(2) and (3) of the Act) and breath (s. 4(4) of the Act). A defendant may not be convicted of both classes of offence arising out of the same set of circumstances.

15.7.13 SECTION 20 OF THE ROAD TRAFFIC ACT 2010, EVIDENTIAL PRESUMPTIONS ATTACHING TO CERTIFICATES

Section 20 of the 2010 Act provides as follows:

20.— (1)   A duly completed statement purporting to have been supplied under section 13 shall, until the contrary is shown, be sufficient evidence in any proceedings under the Road Traffic Acts 1961 to 2010 of the facts stated in it, without proof of any signature on it or that the signatory was the proper person to sign it, and shall, until the contrary is shown, be sufficient evidence of compliance by the member of the Garda Síochána concerned with the requirements imposed on him or her by or under Chapter 4 prior to and in connection with the supply by him or her under section 13 of such statement.

(2)   A duly completed form under section 15 shall, until the contrary is shown, be sufficient evidence in any proceedings under the Road Traffic Acts 1961 to 2010 of the facts stated in it, without proof of any signature on it or that the signatory was the proper person to sign it, and shall, until the contrary is shown, be sufficient evidence of compliance by the designated doctor or designated nurse concerned with the requirements imposed on him or her by or under Chapter 4.

(3)   A certificate expressed to have been issued under section 17 shall, until the contrary is shown, be sufficient evidence in any proceedings under the Road Traffic Acts 1961 to 2010 of the facts stated in it, without proof of any signature on it or that the signatory was the proper person to sign it, and shall, until the contrary is shown, be sufficient evidence of compliance by the Bureau with the requirements imposed on it by or under Chapter 4.

(4) *In a prosecution for an offence under section 4, 5, 12 or 14 it shall be presumed until the contrary is shown that each of the following persons is a designated doctor or designated nurse—*

(a) *person who by virtue of powers conferred on him or her by Chapter 4 took from another person a specimen of that other person's blood or was provided by another person with a specimen of that other person's urine,*

(b) *person for whom, following a requirement under section 12 (1) or 14 (1) to permit the taking by him or her of a specimen of blood, there was a refusal or failure to give such permission or to comply with a requirement of his or hers in relation to the taking of such a specimen,*

(c) *person for whom, following a requirement under section 12(1) or 14(1) to provide for him or her of a specimen of urine, there was a refusal or failure to provide such a specimen or to comply with a requirement of his or hers in relation to the provision of such a specimen.*

(5) *Where, under section 12 or 14, a designated doctor or designated nurse states in writing that he or she is unwilling, on medical grounds, to take from a person a specimen of his or her blood or be provided by him or her with a specimen of his or her urine, the statement signed by the doctor shall, in any proceedings under the Road Traffic Acts 1961 to 2010, be sufficient evidence, until the contrary is shown, of the facts stated in it, without proof of any signature on it or that the signatory was the proper person to sign it.*

These sections create the presumptions that the certificate in respect of the Evidenzer and the certificate of the doctor or Medical Bureau certificates are presumed to be correct, until the defendant proves the contrary.

15.7.14 OFFENCES UNDER SECTIONS 4(1) AND 5(1) OF THE ROAD TRAFFIC ACT 2010

It should be noted that offences committed under s. 4(1) and 5(1) of the 2010 Act, as amended, are dependent from an evidential perspective on the opinion evidence of a witness, who is usually a Garda member. This opinion is normally based upon observations of the defendant at the time of the commission of the offence, as opposed to evidence of a scientific nature. Offences committed in breach of ss. 4(2), (3), and (4), in contrast depend from an evidentiary perspective on proof of concentration of alcohol (s. 4(2) and (3) of the Act) and breath (s. 4(4) of the Act). A defendant may not be convicted of both classes of offence arising out of the same set of circumstances.

Section 11 of the 2010 Act as substituted by the Road Traffic Act 2014 allows the Gardaí to require a person to perform preliminary impairment tests and a refusal to do so without reasonable excuse will be an offence.

Section 23 of the Road Traffic Act 2010 provides:

It is not a defence for a person charged with an offence under section 4(1), 5(1) or 6(1) to show that, in relation to the facts alleged to constitute the offence, an analysis or determination under this Part has not been carried out or that he or she has not been required under section 9 or 10 to provide a specimen of his or her breath.

Where a person is charged with driving while unfit on the basis of evidence of incapacity, the person is barred from relying upon the fact that the prosecution did not seek to obtain a breath, urine, or alcohol sample from him or her. This prohibition is recognised at common law in the case of *DPP v Lee* (unreported, 2 March 1988, High Court).

15.7.15 PENALTIES

(a) Disqualification.

(b) Fine and/or imprisonment.

(c) Penalty points.

(d) Costs.

Up until the 2010 Act, disqualification was mandatory in the event of a conviction for drunken driving. The period of disqualification was dependent upon the level of alcohol in the blood, breath, or urine and is more particularly set forth in the preceding paragraphs where the relevant offences are cited. The 2010 Act reduced the blood, urine, and breath alcohol levels allowed. The 2010 Act created a category of person known as specified person (see **15.7.2**).

The ranges of people who fit into this category or may be deemed to fit into this category are listed in s. 3 of the 2010 Act. They include holders of a learner permit, drivers who hold a full licence for less than two years and taxi drivers.

The disqualification appropriate for non-specified person is best described in the following table:

APPENDIX 1: Table of Penalties (Non-Specified Persons)

Concentration of alcohol	Penalty Points	Fine/ fixed charge	Prison (max)	Disqualification: 1st offence under S. 4 or 5	Disqualification: 2nd or any
a) 50–80 **blood** b) 67–107 **urine** c) 22–35 **breath**	3	€200 (fixed charge)	6 months if fixed charge not paid & goes to court	None if fine is paid (fixed charge notice). If not paid, summons issues – court – 6 months s. 29(1)(a) RTA 2010)	1 year
a) 80–100 **blood** b) 107–135 **urine** c) 35–44 **breath**		€400 (fixed charge)	6 months if fixed charge not paid & goes to court	6 months if fine is paid (fixed charge notice) – otherwise summons – court – 1 year (s. 29(1)(b) RTA 2010)	2 years
a) 100–150 **blood** b) 135–200 **urine** c) 44–66 **breath**		€5,000	6 months	2 years	4 years
a) Exceeding 150 **blood** b) Exceeding 200 **urine** c) Exceeding 66 **breath**		€5,000	6 months	3 years	6 years

The disqualification categories appropriate to specified drivers are as follows:

APPENDIX 2: Table of Penalties (Specified Persons)

Concentration of alcohol	Penalty Points	Fixed charge	Prison (max)	Disqualification: 1st offence under S. 4 or 5	Disqualification: 2nd or any
a) 20–80 **blood** b) 27–107 **urine** c) 9–35 **breath**	3	€200	6 months if it goes to court	3 months if fixed charge paid. If unpaid then summons issues and 6 months	1 year
a) 80–100 **blood** b) 107–135 **urine** c) 35–44 **breath**		€5,000	6 months	1 year	2 years
a) 100–150 **blood** b) 135–200 **urine** c) 44–66 **breath**		€5,000	6 months	2 years	4 years
a) Exceeding 150 **blood** b) Exceeding 200 **urine** c) Exceeding 66 **breath**		€5,000	6 months	3 years	6 years

A person may also be fined and/or imprisoned in accordance with the provisions of the relevant offence for which they have been convicted.

Section 82 of the Road Traffic Act 2010 provides that where a person is convicted of an offence under the Road Traffic Acts 1961 to 2010, the court can make the convicted person pay costs in respect of the detection and prosecution of the offence. Section 21 of the 2010 Act is a separate costs provision which allows the court to order the payment of a contribution to the costs of the Medical Bureau of Road Safety by a convicted person.

15.7.16 APPEAL

Appeals are discussed in general at **Chapter 16**. Penalties and disqualifications come into effect 14 days from the date of conviction. This allows the defendant 14 days in which to appeal the conviction. In the event of an appeal lodged within the 14 days, the conviction for motoring offences including drunken driving offences will be stayed pending the outcome of the appeal.

CHAPTER 16

APPEALS AND JUDICIAL REVIEW

16.1 Introduction

Should a defendant disagree with the verdict or sentence of a criminal court then the possibility of appeal is available.

However, an appeal by way of judicial review in the High Court may be the appropriate course of action, where it is contended that a court or prosecuting authority or detaining authority:

- has acted in excess or breach of its jurisdiction, or
- fails to observe constitutional or natural justice, or
- has failed to act according to its legal duty, or
- where the constitutionality of a legislative provision is challenged, or
- where there is an error on the face of the record, or
- where it is alleged that there is a breach of the European Convention on Human Rights.

The Rules of the Superior Courts 1986 to 2016 at Order 84 (as amended) state the remedies that may be sought and these rules outline the procedures for making such applications. Order 84 was extensively amended by SI No. 691 of the 2011 Rules of the Superior Courts (Judicial Review) 2011.

Since the enactment of the European Convention on Human Rights Act 2003, any alleged breaches of Convention rights should also be pleaded in judicial review cases.

16.2 The Judicial Review Remedies

The reliefs outlined below are not mutually exclusive and an application for judicial review would frequently seek more than one remedy, e.g. where it is argued that a judge has not allowed a party to the proceedings to be 'heard' before making a decision, an applicant may seek an order for certiorari quashing that judicial decision and also seek an order for prohibition, which would prevent that particular judge from hearing the matter any further.

16.2.1 *CERTIORARI*

An order of *certiorari* quashes the decision of a court. A circumstance where such an order may be applied for arises where a court has acted in excess of its jurisdiction by imposing a sentence for an offence which is greater than the sentence provided by statute. Another such circumstance arises where the court breaches constitutional rights by failing to grant an accused person of a right to legal aid, in circumstances where that accused is entitled to that right. It was established in *State (Healy) v Donoghue* [1976] IR 325 that legal representation funded by the state was a constitutional right in certain circumstances. Following this decision a practice developed in some District Courts that when a new criminal matter came before the court, the judge would enquire firstly as to whether the accused was of insufficient means to a pay for representation but secondly enquired as to whether the accused was 'at risk'. This latter question was enquiring as to whether the accused was likely to attract a custodial sentence, if convicted; if the answer was in the negative, legal aid was likely to be refused. In *David Joyce v Judge Patrick Brady and The DPP* [2011] IESC 36, the Supreme Court criticised this 'at risk' formula (O'Donnell J.):

> It is flawed logic to conclude that because a person who was at risk of imprisonment must receive legal aid, it necessarily follows that absent a risk of imprisonment (the assessment of which is always somewhat speculative) that legal aid should not be provided. More importantly such a conclusion is in my view inconsistent with the reasoning of the Court in *State (Healy) v Donoghue*.

The judgment in *Joyce* stated that what *State (Healy) v Donoghue* affirmed, was the right to a fair trial and that that right cannot be reduced to a right not to be deprived of liberty without legal aid. The Supreme Court allowed the appeal on behalf of Mr Joyce and quashed the order of the District Court refusing him legal aid.

16.2.2 PROHIBITION

An order of prohibition prevents a body from pursuing a certain course of action. Such orders are often sought against the Director of Public Prosecutions (DPP). A common application to prevent a prosecution from proceeding is where it is contended that there is such a delay in a prosecution that it has prejudiced an applicant's chance of a fair trial. Such a delay breaches the applicant's rights under Article 38.1 of the Constitution. Decisions of the court in such cases will be based on:

* the circumstances of each individual case;

* the complexity of the offence alleged;

* the cause of the delay; and

* the possibility of prejudice to the defence.

(See *PM v Malone* [IESC] 46 and *DPP v Byrne* [1994] 2I R 236.)

Offences involving the sexual abuse of children and young people constitute a special category in relation to the issue of delay, which was discussed in the context of the commencement of proceedings in **Chapter 6** (see *G v DPP* [1994] 1 IR 374).

In *B v DPP* [1997] 2 ILRM 118 it was decided that the factors that should be taken into account in determining delay in child sex abuse cases include:

* the interpersonal relationship between the parties;

* the extent of control exerted by the alleged abuser; and

* the availability of alibis and witnesses.

However, there has been developing jurisprudence in these types of cases, and as regards the issue of dominion or control, the Supreme Court in *H v DPP* [2006] IESC 55 held that there was no longer any need, except in exceptional circumstances, to establish reasons for a delay in making a complaint, and that the only issue is whether such a delay resulted in prejudice to the defendant, which would give rise to a real or serious risk of an unfair trial. Kearns J. in *CK v DPP* [2007] IESC 5 held:

> Either the accused's ability to defend proceedings has been fatally compromised to such a degree as to be incapable of being rectified by appropriate directions or warnings from the trial judge or it has not. The resolution of that issue will turn on the facts and circumstances of each individual case. It is therefore now essential in those applications for prohibition in old sexual delay cases to fully and actively engage with the facts of the particular case. This is the main consequence of the simplification brought about by the decision in *H v DPP*.

Prohibition is often sought to prevent a trial proceeding, where evidence has not been preserved as discussed in *Daniel Braddish v DPP and Mr Justice Haugh* (2002) 1 ILRM 151 where a failure to preserve a video of a robbery from which stills had been taken was fatal to the prosecution (see further discussion of this case in **Chapter 10**). In *DPP v D* (2009) IEHC 132 an order for prohibition was refused in circumstances where two cameras had been trained on an assault but the tape from one was missing. However, the second tape showed the entire incident and it was decided that the missing evidence would not prejudice a fair trial.

16.2.3   *MANDAMUS*

An order of *mandamus* compels a relevant body to perform a legal duty. A prisoner, for example, may take judicial review proceedings against prison authorities where it is contended that appropriate medical treatment has been requested and not provided. See *Edward Ryan v the Governor of Midlands Prison* [2014] IESC 54 at **16.11.1** for a discussion on when judicial review or *habeas corpus* is the appropriate application, in particular, in respect of sentenced prisoners who have complaints about their detention.

16.2.4   *QUO WARRANTO*

This remedy is directed to a person and directs that person to show by what authority any office or privilege of a public nature is claimed.

16.2.5   **DECLARATION AND INJUNCTION**

An application for declaration or injunction may be made by way of judicial review if the court considers it just and convenient, having regard to the nature of the matters in respect of which relief may be granted (see Order 84, Rule 18(2) of the Rules of the Superior Courts, 1986).

In *Patrick Donoghue v The DPP* [2014] IESC 56, the Supreme Court refused an appeal by the state against an injunction granted by the High Court prohibiting the applicant's trial, on the grounds that blameworthy prosecutorial delay (not in itself necessarily amounting to a delay sufficient to grant such an injunction) was aggravated by the special duty owed to a child or young person by state authorities, to ensure the processing of a speedy trial. While, in the particular case the court prevented the prosecution from proceeding, it indicated that the circumstances of each case involving children and young persons, where delay was alleged, would have to be considered carefully. The court in this case went on to say that a balancing exercise would have to be carried out and various factors put into the melting pot to include: the length of the delay itself; the age of the person at the time of the alleged offence; the seriousness of the charge; the complexity of the case; and any other relevant facts and circumstances.

16.2.6   **DAMAGES**

Damages may be awarded where the court is satisfied that if the applicant had proceeded by way of civil claim and if the claim had been included in the statement to ground the application, damages would have been awarded (see Order 84, Rule 25 of the Rules of the Superior Courts, as amended by substitution by SI No. 691 of 2011: Rules of the Superior Courts (Judicial Review) 2011).

16.3   Bail Pending Judicial Review

If the applicant is in custody by virtue of the order which is being reviewed, an application for bail can be made to the High Court Judge before whom the application for leave to apply is being made (see Bail generally at **Chapter 7**).

16.4   Time Limits

Order 84, Rule 21(2) (SI No. 691 of 2011) provides all applications for relief by way of judicial review must be made within three months from the date when the grounds for the application arose:

> Should the application be delayed, an application to extend the time to submit can be made to the court but the court will only accede to this request if there is 'good and sufficient reason for

doing so'. The court will have to be persuaded that the circumstances that resulted in the failure to bring the application within the applicable time limit was 'outside the control' or 'could not have been reasonably anticipated by the Applicant who is applying for the extension'.

An application for an extension of time to apply has to be grounded on an affidavit sworn by the applicant setting out the reasons for the failure to apply within time. Even if an extension of time is granted, it does not prevent delay being pleaded by the respondent in applications for relief by way of judicial review, wherein the court may dismiss the application for relief on that delay ground (this rationale applies even if the application is made within time—Rule 21(6)).

16.5   Procedures

16.5.1   LEAVE TO APPLY

The application is founded on two documents:

1.   a statement which states each relief and each legal ground on which the application is being sought; and

2.   an affidavit which verifies the facts in each relief and grounds in the statement.

Rule 20 of Order 84 (SI No. 691 of 2011) sets out the format that these statements and affidavits should take. The statement and affidavit are filed in the Central Office of the High Court beforehand and certified copies are handed in to the court when the application is actually being made.

The application is *ex parte* and the respondents are not present and not on notice. However, Rule 24(1) allows the court on hearing an application for leave to direct that the application should be heard on notice. At the leave stage, the High Court must just be satisfied that the applicant has an 'arguable case' on the documents before it, and the fact that leave is granted is no indication of the ultimate likely outcome of the case.

It is open to the High Court to grant leave to apply on some of the grounds stated and not on other grounds and also it can amend the grounds by the addition of other grounds. A refusal to grant leave to apply can be appealed. Traditionally, it would be appealed to the Supreme Court, but in the wake of the establishment of the Court of Appeal (replacing the Court of Criminal Appeal), it is assumed that most refusals to grant leave will be appealed to that court.

Generally procedure is dictated by:

* the Rules of the Superior Courts, 1986 to 2016 at Order 84;

* direction of the court in individual cases; and

* practice directions, which appear from time to time in the Legal Diary.

16.5.2   NOTICE OF MOTION/SERVICE ON THE RESPONDENTS

When the court grants leave to apply, it will direct that the respondents should be served with a notice of motion and copies of the statement grounding the application and the affidavit and a copy of the High Court order granting the leave. Unless the court directs otherwise, this service must take place within seven days (Rule 22(3)) after the perfection of the order granting leave or within another period which the court can direct.

There may be parties other than the actual respondents that must be served, e.g. a clerk or registrar of a court, and care should be taken to ensure service is both within time and to the correct parties.

Unless the court directs otherwise the motion shall be returnable for the first available motion day after the expiry of seven weeks. The notice of motion document is filed in the Central Office of the High Court. That office will require sight of a certified copy of the High Court order so that it can confirm that the notice of motion corresponds to it. Service must be in person or by registered post and an affidavit of service must be filed subsequently. If for some reason the notice of motion is not filed and/or all the documents are not served within time, then the order granting leave will lapse and a further application must be made to the High Court to grant an extension of time for service of relevant documentation.

16.5.3   NOTICE OF OPPOSITION AND REPLYING AFFIDAVITS

If the respondent intends to oppose the application, a statement of opposition outlining the grounds and a verifying affidavit, if required, must be filed and served not later than three weeks (Rule 22(4)) from the date of service of the notice of motion, or within a time specified by the court.

16.6   Fixing a Date

The parties to the proceedings should be in a position to brief the judge on the main issues in the case on the first motion date, and to give an indication of realistic time limits for the exchange of documents.

The case will then be adjourned from motion day to motion day to allow applicant and respondents to reply to each other's documents, and when the case is ready, it will be given a date for hearing by the court. In certain cases where delay in hearing the case would prejudice the parties in some way, an application may be made to give the case a date in priority over other cases.

16.7   Notice to Cross-Examine

Although the judicial review procedure is essentially based on the filed documents, either party may require any party who has sworn an affidavit in the proceeding to attend at the hearing of the case, in order to cross-examine them on the contents of their affidavit. Order 40, Rule 31 allows notices to be served at any time before the expiration of 14 days after the end of time allowed for the filing of affidavits in reply.

16.8   Preparing a Brief

A bound book of pleadings containing all the documentation previously referred to must be lodged with the Central Office prior to the hearing. They should be presented in the following order:

- Notice of motion.
- Order of the High Court.
- Statement to ground the application.
- Verifying affidavit and exhibits.
- Notice of opposition.
- Verifying affidavits.
- Replying affidavits.
- Notice to cross-examine.
- Affidavit of service.

One should also file and serve legal submissions that one proposes to make on the hearing date on the litigants on the other side of the case, before the hearing date.

16.9   The Hearing

On the hearing date there may be a few cases listed for hearing on the same day. A call over of the court list will ascertain which cases can actually proceed and which judges are available to hear them. The applicant opens the case to the judge and matters proceed from there. No other grounds apart from those set out in the statement to ground the application can be relied upon; however, the court may allow either party to amend the statement during the hearing if it thinks it is appropriate. Judgment may be given on the day or it can be reserved.

16.10   Costs and Legal Aid—Custody Issues Scheme

The award of costs is at the discretion of the court. Even if the applicant is unsuccessful the court may be prepared to make an order in the applicant's favour if the legal issues or point raised were deemed to be of importance. If the applicant is of insufficient means to fund the case the Legal Aid—Custody Issues Scheme for payment can be applied for in applications relating to criminal matters. Notification to the court that the applicant intends to apply for the Scheme must be made at the *ex parte* stage (a statement of means will be required from the applicant) and mentioned again at the end of the case. If the application has been made and not contested at the outset, then usually, the Scheme will still be paid, whether the applicant loses the case or not. It should be noted, however, that the final decision regarding payment rests with the Criminal Legal Aid Board.

As outlined in the Court of Appeal Act 2014, an appeal from decisions of the High Court are made to the new Court of Appeal, unless the Supreme Court decides they involve matters of exceptional public importance or the interest of justice demand it. The latter are known as 'leapfrog appeals'. Order 86A of the Rules of the Superior Courts (Court of Appeal Act 2014) 2014 SI No. 485 of 2014 governs the procedures for appeal to the Court of Appeal.

16.11   *Habeas Corpus*

16.11.1   INTRODUCTION

An application under Article 40.4.2 of the Constitution may be made in the High Court when it is alleged that a person is detained without lawful authority in a prison, Garda station, mental hospital, etc. Practitioners refer to this application, a remedy available in Ireland since the seventeenth century, as a '*habeas corpus*' application, meaning 'you have the body'.

The Constitution outlines the procedure, which takes the form of an *ex parte* application, usually by way of affidavit setting out the reasons why it is claimed that the person is illegally detained. The application is made before a High Court judge who, on having the affidavit opened to the court and on hearing any submissions deems that there is a case to answer, will order the production of the prisoner. The respondents will then be served with a copy of the affidavit and a copy of the order of the High Court and at the hearing of the matter they will respond to the claim and certify the grounds of detention. Because an unlawful detention is such a serious infringement of one's constitutional rights, the detained person will normally be produced in court on the day of the *ex parte* application or as soon as possible afterwards, and a full hearing will be commenced immediately.

Some of the more common examples encountered by the criminal practitioner where such an application may be considered are:

- when the warrant 'is illegal on its face', e.g. the warrant does not disclose any offence known to law. However, in a case where the warrant does not reflect the order of the court it is open to the authorities to substitute a correct warrant;

- when the person named on the warrant is not the person detained;

- where illegalities have been adopted in the person's committal, or procedures adopted while the person is in custody, make a previously legal detention illegal, e.g. refusing access to a solicitor during detention in a Garda station;

- where a young person is being held in a place not certified as being suitable for the detention of a person of that age;

- where there has been a breach of rights guaranteed under the European Convention on Human Rights, sufficient to render the detention unlawful.

In the summer vacation of 2014 the Supreme Court sat to consider an appeal by the state from an order of the High Court releasing a prisoner where the High Court had found that he was unlawfully detained, as he was entitled to enhanced remission of one-third and that two-thirds of his sentence had already expired. In *Edward Ryan v The Governor of Midlands Prison* [2014] IESC 54, the Supreme Court decided that *habeas corpus* was not the remedy that should have been employed to deal with Mr Ryan's case, saying:

> the general principle of law is that if the order of the court does not show an invalidity on its face, in particular if it is an order in relation to post conviction detention, then the route of the constitutional and immediate remedy of habeas corpus is not appropriate. An appropriate remedy may be an appeal or an application to seek leave for judicial review. In such circumstances the remedy of Article 40 arises only if there has been an absence of jurisdiction; a fundamental denial of justice, or a fundamental flaw.

The court identified a number of post-conviction cases where *habeas corpus* was the appropriate remedy, such as *Cirpaci v The Governor of Mountjoy Prison* [2014] IEHC 76 (2014). In that case, they said, there was a complete absence of jurisdiction in the District Court as he had pleaded guilty without being informed of his right to trial by jury. *In Sweeney v Governor of Loughan House Open Prison* [2014] IESC 42, there was also a complete absence of jurisdiction. In *Richardson v The Governor of Mountjoy Prison* [1980] ILRM 82, the issue was that the sentenced prisoner was suffering such ill treatment as a result of the conditions in which she was kept, so as to potentially undermine the lawfulness of her detention.

The Court in *Edward Ryan* did not mention the leading case of *McDonagh v Governor of Cloverhill Prison* [2005] 1 IR 394; *McDonagh* did not involve a sentenced prisoner but a refusal of bail and it is clear from the Supreme Court judgment in that case that the court found that the procedural and other deficiencies of the hearing before the District Court Judge were such as would invalidate essential steps in the proceedings leading to his detention (a test which had been formulated in *The State (Royle) v Kelly* [1974] IR 259). In *McDonagh*, among other alleged deficiencies in the hearing, the accused was not put on notice of the objections to bail, which were raised by the judge of his own volition, and comments were made about the travelling community of which the accused was a member.

16.11.2 COSTS

All applicants can apply for costs at the end of the case, or if it is a suitable case, the Legal Aid—Custody Issue Scheme mentioned earlier may be applied for at the *ex parte* stage. Where the point at issue was validly raised, even if the case is not won, the judge may feel that costs should be granted or the Legal Aid—Custody Issues Scheme recommended.

16.12 Appeals

16.12.1 APPEALS FROM THE DISTRICT COURT TO THE CIRCUIT COURT

A general right of appeal is contained in s. 18(1) of the Courts of Justice Act 1928. An appeal may be made against conviction and severity of punishment, or against severity alone, but an appeal cannot be made against conviction only. 'Leave to apply for appeal' is not necessary.

The appeal hearing in the Circuit Court is a hearing held in front of a Circuit Court judge sitting alone and evidence that had not been given at the District Court may be adduced. An accused person may change an original plea of guilty in this court. The Circuit Court may decrease, vary, affirm, or increase a sentence, but only within the jurisdiction of the District Court, e.g. s. 3 of the Non-Fatal Offences Against the Person Act 1997, assault causing harm, allows for a maximum sentence of imprisonment of 12 months when dealt with summarily and a maximum of five years when dealt with on indictment in the Circuit Court. In an appeal from the District Court to the Circuit Court for this offence, the latter court may only apply the lower tariff. There is no further right of appeal from the Circuit Court decision to a higher court; however, the decisions of the court are of course reviewable by way of judicial review, where such grounds present themselves.

16.12.1.1 Procedure

Procedures regarding the making of an appeal are listed at Rule 101 of the District Court Rules, 1997 and SI No. 93 of 1997 and the District Court (Appeals to the Circuit Court) Rules, 2003 SI No. 484 of 2003. Rule 4 states:

> where a person is desirous of appealing in criminal proceedings ... a recognisance for the purpose of appeal shall be fixed by the Court. The amount of the recognisance in which the appellant and the surety or sureties, if any, are to be bound shall be fixed by the Court and shall be of such reasonable amount as the Court shall see fit ... The recognizance ... shall be entered into within the fourteen days fixed by rule 1 of this order.

A notice of appeal must be served on the respondent, and a copy of it with a declaration of service and a copy of the recognisances must be filed with the District Court clerk within 14 days of the decision. Note that the 14 days includes the day of the decision and weekends; however, if the 14th day falls on a Saturday or Sunday or any other day when the District Court office is closed then that day will be excluded and the papers should be filed on the following day.

Once an appeal is in being, the original order of the District Court is suspended until the appeal is determined. Should the recognisances for appeal be set too high, the appellant can apply to the High Court bail list to have the monetary amount reduced. The Criminal Justice Act 2007 amended the Bail Act 1997 by the substitution of s. 15 for s. 9, and gives power to the District Court to fix conditions on the applicant, and allows for the prosecution to re-enter the matter before the District Court should it be alleged that those conditions have been breached. At that stage the court can revoke the recognisances and the appellant will be returned to jail to continue the sentence. The appeal will still be heard but the appellant may well have served a significant part of the sentence by the time the case is listed. A revocation of the recognisances can be appealed also to the High Court bail list. (See further discussion on Bail at **Chapter 7**.)

16.12.1.2 Extension of time to appeal

If the appeal is not lodged within 14 days, an application to extend time to appeal may be made. The appellant has no automatic right to an extension and will have to explain why the application was not filed on time. If the extension is granted, the appellant must serve and lodge papers in the time specified by the court, i.e. the time granted may be less than 14 days.

Road traffic offences are discussed in detail in **Chapter 15** and it should be noted that in the case of an appellant who is appealing a driving disqualification, such order will only be suspended pending the outcome of the appeal when the appeal has been lodged within 14 days. In other words, while an extension of time to appeal may be granted, it is not within the power of the court to suspend the operation of the disqualification. Consequently, given the delays experienced in certain court districts, in the listing of appeal hearings, the suspension may have already been served by the time the appeal has been heard.

16.12.1.3 Notification and reinstatement of appeals

The appeal is heard in the Circuit Court area in which the original case was determined, and the appellant will be notified personally of the date the appeal will be heard. It is the appellant's responsibility to notify the authorities of any change of address since the original conviction date in the lower court. Should the appeal be struck out due to the appellant's non-attendance, application can be made to reinstate the appeal in the Circuit Court, subject to the appellant showing to the court's satisfaction that there was a good reason for the non-attendance.

16.12.2 APPEALS TO THE COURT OF APPEAL AND TO THE SUPREME COURT

16.12.2.1 The Court of Appeal

In 2013 the people of Ireland voted in a referendum to amend the Constitution so as to permit the establishment of a Court of Appeal from all decisions of the High Court, and to transfer the work of the Court of Criminal Appeal to that new Court of Appeal. The Court of Appeal was established on 20 October 2014.

The Court of Appeal Act 2014 provides for the various functions of the court, the appoint-ment of permanent judges to the court and the transfer of powers from the Court of Criminal Appeal (CCA) to the Court of Appeal. Provision was made for the necessary amending clauses and repealing clauses in other legislation. Section 77 of the Court of Appeal Act provides that all references to the Court of Criminal Appeal in legislation are to be construed as the Court of Appeal unless otherwise indicated. Like the Court of Criminal Appeal previously, the new Court of Appeal hears appeals from the Circuit Criminal Court, the Special Criminal Court and the Central Criminal Court. The court consists of not less than three judges. Decisions of the District Court may not be appealed to this court.

Cases deemed to be dealing with matters of exceptional public importance, or if the interests of justice demand it, will still be heard in the Supreme Court.

16.12.2.2   Process, procedure and time limits

The rules for the Court of Appeal were established by the Rules of the Superior Courts (Court of Appeal Act 2014) 2014, SI No. 485 of 2014—Order 86C referring specifically to criminal mat-ters. If a defendant wishes to appeal against conviction, sentence or both, Order 86C, Rule 4(1) requires that the application be lodged with the Court of Appeal within 28 days from the date of sentence or conviction. Notice must be given as per Form 9 of the rules and appeals against con-viction must include the grounds of appeal in the notice. Should the appeal be out of time, Order 86C Rule 5(1) allows the defendant to apply to the Court of Appeal to 'enlarge the time'. In this case the defendant/appellant will have to specify the grounds for enlarging time and will have to include the grounds of appeal regardless of whether it is an appeal against sentence or conviction.

16.12.2.3   Bail

Bail pending an appeal to the Court of Appeal must be made to that court. Order 86C, Rule 13(2) specifies that it must be by way of Notice of Motion and Affidavit. The Affidavit must set out fully the grounds on which the application is made, the grounds of appeal and the grounds on which bail is sought. If the defendant/appellant was on bail pre-trial then the terms of that bail must be averred to in the affidavit.

It is unusual to be granted bail in the Court of Appeal as the court must be persuaded that there are substantial grounds for appeal and a strong chance that the appeal will succeed. (See *People (DPP) v Corbally* (2001) 1 IR 180 and *DPP v Dunne* [2009] IECCA 3.)

16.12.2.4   Appeals on a point of law or the conduct of the trial

The appellant can appeal against severity of sentence, sentence and conviction, and, in contrast to appeals from the District Court, against conviction only. The appeal to the Court of Appeal can be made:

- on a point of law, or
- a point concerning the conduct of the trial, or
- where there appears to the court to be any other sufficient ground of appeal.

If the appeal is against severity of sentence, then the appellant will have to persuade the court that the trial judge made a departure from the principles of sentencing such that the Court of Appeal should allow the appeal and substitute the sentence with one of its own. When appealing against conviction, the appellant will be grounding the appeal on errors made in law or in fact by the trial judge during the course of the trial. Such issues would normally have been raised with the judge during the course of the trial. If, for example, defence counsel believes that there has been some flaw in the judge's charge to the jury, this should have been raised by way of 'requisition' after the 'judge's charge' and before the jury began to deliberate. If this requisition had not been raised as outlined, the applicant may be stopped from relying on this ground for the purposes of an appeal.

The appeal itself is based on the transcript of the trial and it would therefore be unusual to have evidence heard by the appeal court.

Where costs have been granted to a defendant who has been acquitted, s. 24 of the Criminal Justice Act 2006, the DPP or Attorney General is allowed to appeal that order for costs to the Court of Appeal. As most defendants are represented under the Legal Aid Scheme, such an occurrence is unusual.

16.12.2.5 Powers of the Court of Appeal

The Court of Appeal can:

- quash sentences and substitute them with others including increasing the sentence appealed; and

- quash convictions and make no further order or remit the matter for retrial.

16.12.3 MISCARRIAGE OF JUSTICE

Where it is alleged that a new or newly discovered fact shows that there has been a miscarriage of justice in relation to a conviction, or that the sentence was excessive, recourse may be had to s. 2 of the Criminal Procedure Act 1993. This allows the court to revisit a case where the court has already refused an appeal. The court's powers include:

(a)   quashing of convictions,

(b)   affirming sentences,

(c)   varying sentences, or

(d)   substituting alternative verdicts,

(e)   substituting alternative sentences, and

(f)   remitting matters for re-trial, and

(g)   ordering the payment of compensation, where a miscarriage of justice is found.

There is no specified time limit applicable to the lodging of the application as the appeal is grounded on new or newly discovered facts since the time of conviction. Order 86C, Rule 3(2) specifies the notice of appeal (Form 10) must be supported by a statement of grounds (Form 11) which must be verified on affidavit.

16.12.3.1 Prosecution appeals to the Court of Appeal

DPP's right of appeal against leniency of sentence

Section 2 of the Criminal Justice Act 1993 as amended by s. 23 of the Criminal Justice Act 2006 allowed the DPP a right to appeal to the Court of Criminal Appeal, on the grounds of the leniency of any sentence pursuant to the trial on indictment of any offence. This right now applies in respect of the same type of application to the Court of Appeal. The DPP must lodge the appeal with the court within 28 days (Rule 6, Form 14) and can apply to the court to enlarge the time but only for a further 28 days.

Applications for retrials after acquittal

The Criminal Procedure Act 2010 (the 2010 Act) introduced new and as yet untested limits to the rule against double jeopardy. Applications for retrials can be sought by the DPP after acquittal by direction, by jury or after an appeal to the Court of Appeal as outlined at s. 8 and s. 9 of the 2010 Act. Section 8 provides for circumstances where the DPP believes there is new and compelling evidence not available at the time of the original trial and it is in the interest of justice to make the application. Section 9 provides for circumstances where the DPP believes that evidence leading to an acquittal was tainted, and a person was convicted of an offence against the administration of justice such as perjury, which related to the proceedings. In the latter circumstances the DPP must also believe that the evidence is compelling and that it is in the interests of justice to make the application.

In respect of s. 8 applications, the provisions apply to only certain offences tried on indictment, though it should be noted that that list is quite substantial and includes murder, manslaughter, rape, aggravated sexual assault, trafficking of persons, supply of drugs, directing a criminal organisation certain firearm offences, robbery and aggravated burglary. Section 9 applications refer to all offences tried on indictment.

In deciding to order a retrial the court shall have regard to s. 10 of the 2010 Act in considering:

(a)   the likelihood of a fair trial;

(b)   the amount of time that has passed since the original trial;

(c)   the interests of the victim; and

(d)   any other matters it considers relevant.

16.12.3.2   Appeals from the Court of Appeal to the Supreme Court

The convicted person may appeal the decision of the Court of Appeal once the court and the DPP or the Attorney General certify that the case involves a point of law of exceptional public importance, and that it is desirable in the public interest that such an appeal should be taken, as outlined in s. 29 of the Courts of Justice Act 1924 as substituted by s. 22 of the Criminal Justice Act 2006. In reality, such appeals are rare.

Section 31 of the Criminal Procedure Act 2010 amends s. 29 of the Courts of Justice Act 1924 by the insertion of s. 29A in that Act and allows for a defendant (having appealed and where a retrial is ordered by the court) to appeal without prejudice the decision of the appeal court to the Supreme Court in respect of a matter raised by them in the Court of Appeal about which the court did not make a determination or made a determination against them, e.g. a defendant appeals his or her conviction on three distinct grounds but the appeal is allowed on just two of the grounds and the matter is remitted for a retrial. That decision, on the issue of the omitted ground of appeal, is appealable to the Supreme Court, but only if the subject of the appeal is relevant to the re-trial and the court or the AG or the DPP certifies that the matter involves a point of law of exceptional public importance and that it is desirable in the public interest that the person should take an appeal to the Supreme Court.

Where the Court of Appeal has made a decision regarding an application under s. 8 and s. 9 of the 2010 Act, s. 14 of the Criminal Procedure Act 2010 also allows for an appeal on a point of law by the accused person or the DPP if the court, Attorney General or the DPP certifies the point of being of exceptional public importance and in the public interest.

16.12.3.3   Appeals by the prosecution directly from the trial courts to the Court of Appeal and the Supreme Court

Section 34(1) of the Criminal Procedure Act 1967, as amended by s. 21 of the Criminal Justice Act 2006, allowed the DPP or Attorney General, in a case where the accused is acquitted (by direction of the judge or otherwise), to refer a question of law arising during the trial to the Supreme Court, having consulted with the trial judge. This referral is without prejudice to the verdict and protects the identity of the acquitted person. The Court of Appeal Act 2014 substitutes s. 34(1) so that the reference on a question of law is made to the Court of Appeal except for offences dealt with in the Central Criminal Court where the referral can still be made to the Supreme Court under Article 34.5.4 of the Constitution.

In a radical departure from the rule against double jeopardy the Criminal Procedure Act 2010 at s. 23(1) (as amended by the substitution of s. 71(b)(i) of the Court of Appeal Act 2014) allows for an appeal against an acquittal by the DPP or Attorney General on a point of law to the Court of Appeal in respect of offences dealt with in the Circuit Court and Special Criminal Court. It also permits an appeal against acquittal to either the Court of Appeal or to Supreme Court under Article 34.5.4 of the Constitution in the case of offences dealt with in the Central Criminal Court, where it is contended that the acquittal was as a result of the erroneous exclusion of evidence, or it is contended that the jury were wrongly directed by the trial judge to acquit in circumstances where there was evidence on which they could have been convicted.

The DPP or AG has 28 days from the acquittal to appeal; an extension to 56 days can be sought. In other words this is a 'with prejudice' appeal and the Court of Appeal or the Supreme Court, as the case may be, has powers after hearing the appeal to order a retrial.

16.12.4   APPEAL BY WAY OF CASE STATED

A case stated under the Summary Jurisdiction Act 1857, s. 2 as extended by s. 51 of the Courts (Supplemental Provisions) Act 1961 is an appeal to the High Court from a decision of the District Court where the proceedings have concluded. The purpose of the appeal is to ask the opinion of the High Court on a point of law, or a mixture of law and fact, but not fact alone. All summary matters and indictable matters dealt with summarily are capable of being appealed by way of case stated.

Any party to the proceedings who is dissatisfied with the decision of the court can apply, within 14 days of the determination of proceedings, to the District Court judge to sign and state a case. The case stated will outline the facts of the case, the submissions made by parties to the case, and the grounds upon which the District Court judge reached his or her decision. The High Court is thereby asked for its opinion as to whether the District Court decision was correct. Drafts of the case stated may be circulated to the parties to it, before transmission to the High Court in order to confirm that they are in agreement as to the facts of the case. If the facts are in dispute then the facts 'shall be found' by the District Court judge. The signed case stated should be transmitted to the High Court within six months of the determination. The decision of the District Court is suspended pending the outcome of the case stated.

The High Court on hearing the case can:

(a)   reverse,

(b)   affirm, or

(c)   amend

the decision of the District Court and can:

(d)   award costs, although in criminal cases the defendant may be covered by the Criminal Legal Aid Scheme.

16.12.5   APPEAL BY WAY OF CONSULTATIVE CASE STATED

A consultative case stated lies before the determination of proceedings pursuant to s. 52 of the Courts (Supplemental Provisions) Act 1961. This procedure enables a District Court judge, at any time before s/he gives her or his decision in a case, to refer a question of law to the High Court. Any party to the proceedings may request that a consultative case be stated or the judge may refer such a case. The judge may refuse to state such a case and, unlike a case stated, the decision of the District Court judge is final.

The District Court case will be adjourned pending the outcome of the High Court case. The case is prepared in the same manner as the appeal by way of case stated outlined earlier, and should be transmitted within six months of the matter arising to the High Court. The High Court will answer the questions posed and the case is remitted to the District Court for a determination in accordance with those answers.

A defendant does not lose the normal right of appeal against the ultimate determination of the District Court to the Circuit Court.

The case stated procedure is available only from the District Court but a consultative case stated may be requested in both the Circuit Court and the High Court and where formally these were made to the Supreme Court, they will now be made to the Court of Appeal.

PART VII

EUROPEAN CONVENTION ON HUMAN RIGHTS AND EUROPEAN ARREST WARRANT

THE IMPACT OF THE EUROPEAN CONVENTION ON HUMAN RIGHTS ON IRISH CRIMINAL LITIGATION PRACTICE

17.1 Introduction

The European Convention on Human Rights (the Convention) was drafted as a charter of first generation, or civil and political rights. In over 55 years of jurisprudence, the European Court of Human Rights (ECtHR) in Strasbourg has broadened the interpretation of the Convention to provide protection for a wide range of individuals and groups in society. The Convention was indirectly incorporated into Irish law formally by the European Convention on Human Rights Act 2003 (ECHR Act). Strictly, the Convention is not part of domestic law but rather the rights contained in the Convention form part of Irish law by way of the ECHR Act. Prior to 2003, although the state had international obligations under the Convention and had to answer before the courts in Strasbourg for any breaches of Convention rights, it did not have to do so in any real, effective way before our domestic courts.

Lawyers might have anticipated that the impact of the Convention in Ireland and particularly in the area of criminal litigation would be less marked because of our pre-existing and often overlapping constitutional rights and protections. The purpose of this chapter is to consider the substantive effect which the Convention, via the ECHR Act, has had on criminal law and procedure. A second purpose is to highlight how the constitutional protections afforded to criminal defendants in Ireland can be enhanced by developing Convention jurisprudence.

17.2 Relationship between the Convention and Irish Criminal Law

17.2.1 THE INTERPRETATIVE OBLIGATION—SECTION 2 OF THE ECHR ACT

Section 2 of the ECHR Act requires that any legal statute or other form of law must be interpreted *'insofar as is possible'* in a manner which ensures that it is Convention-compliant.

17.2.2 PERFORMANCE OF FUNCTIONS IN A MANNER COMPATIBLE WITH THE CONVENTION—SECTION 3 OF THE ECHR ACT

Section 3 imposes a duty on 'organs of the State' to perform their functions in a manner compatible with the state's obligations under the Convention. The courts are themselves excluded from the definition of organs of the state in the ECHR Act but are nonetheless charged with the responsibility of ensuring that other organs of state, including the Gardaí and the prosecuting authorities, perform their functions in a Convention-compliant manner.

17.2.3   CONSISTENT INTERPRETATION—SECTION 4 OF THE ECHR ACT

Section 4 of the ECHR Act requires all courts here to 'take due account' of the judgments of the ECtHR when interpreting and applying Convention provisions. This creates the basis therefore for a litigant to rely on case law emanating from the ECtHR when making submissions to an Irish court. In Ireland, the main method of challenging administrative decisions in this jurisdiction is by way of an application for judicial review to the High Court. The courts here have taken a very restrictive view of their role in judicial review applications. The classic position is that judicial reviews are concerned with the procedure and manner in which decisions are taken rather than the merits of the decisions themselves. The ECtHR on the other hand tends to a more proactive approach when reviewing claims that Convention rights have been violated.

17.3   Section 5 Declaration of Incompatibility

Section 5(1) of the ECHR Act provides that the High Court and the Supreme Court may, on application to it by a party or of its own motion, and where no other legal remedy is adequate and available, make a 'declaration of incompatibility', that a statutory provision or rule of law is incompatible with the state's obligations under the Convention. An award of damages can be made against the organ of state responsible. A finding of incompatibility does not, without more, effect a change in the law but should prompt legislative reform. The Taoiseach is obliged to bring the incompatible provision before the Oireachtas within 21 days. It is not open to the District or Circuit Court to make declarations of incompatibility.

It has been observed that, in the same way that Acts of the Oireachtas are presumed to be compliant with the Constitution, there exists an effective presumption of compatibility with the Convention which any applicant must seek to dislodge.

It should be noted that many cases in which breaches of the Convention have been argued have ultimately been decided on another legal basis. It has been held by the Supreme Court that where an applicant challenges both the constitutionality of a legislative provision as well as its compatibility with the Convention, the constitutional claim must be disposed of first (see *Carmody v Minister for Justice Equality and Law Reform* [2010] IR 653 at **17.10.2**).

17.4   General Principles of Interpretation

The ECtHR has developed guiding principles of interpretation in order to ensure uniformity and consistency in its reasoning. The ECtHR has long acknowledged that human rights legislation calls for 'a broad and purposive approach to construction' owing to its transnational character and its status as a 'living instrument'.

17.4.1   MAINTENANCE OF DEMOCRATIC IDEALS

Among the general principles established by the ECtHR is the idea that the Convention is an instrument designed to maintain and promote the ideals and values of a democratic society. The ECtHR notes in *Dudgeon v UK* (1982) 4 EHRR 149 that the essential features of a democratic society include respect for the rule of law and the promotion of pluralism, tolerance, and broad-mindedness.

17.4.2   PROPORTIONALITY

In broad terms the principle of proportionality, which the court applies in assessing the validity of any restrictions on rights, essentially involves balancing the demands of the community and the protection of fundamental rights of individuals. This principle is routinely argued before both the ECtHR and domestic courts.

The ECtHR has characterised proportionality in a number of different ways. On occasion it has described its role as striking a 'fair balance' in determining whether a particular restriction on a right is permissible (*Bosphorus v Ireland* (App. No. 45036/98)). On other occasions it has applied proportionality somewhat differently, asking whether the state can justify an interference with Convention rights on the basis that the interference addresses 'a pressing social need' (*A, B and C v Ireland* (2011) 53 EHRR 13).

Therefore the ECtHR may inquire whether the legitimate aims sought by the state could have been achieved in a less intrusive manner.

17.4.3   MARGIN OF APPRECIATION

Article 18 of the Convention prohibits states from applying restrictions on rights and freedoms for purposes other than those prescribed in the Convention. The ECtHR has granted national authorities some space to manoeuvre in fulfilling their obligations under the Convention. This 'margin of appreciation' is allowed in terms of moral and social policy and amounts to an acknowledgement that each state may have different standards that will inform how it deals with particular issues of a human rights nature.

17.5   Substantive Convention Protections in the Criminal Justice and Prison Systems

17.5.1   ARTICLE 3 PROHIBITION ON TORTURE: PRISONERS' RIGHTS

Article 3 of the Convention provides a non-derogable protection against torture or other forms of inhuman or degrading treatment or punishment. The ECtHR has noted that any recourse to physical force that has not been made strictly necessary by the applicant's own conduct diminishes his or her human dignity and is in principle a breach of Article 3 (*Ribitsch v Austria* [1996] 21 EHRR 573). A state may not avoid liability under Article 3 by blaming the attitude and behaviour of a prisoner (*Testa v Croatia*, 12 July 2007, Application No. 20877/04).

The ECtHR has made a number of rulings in respect of specific aspects of prison regimes, including the duration of a prisoner's confinement to his or her cell (*Sikorski v Poland*, 22 July 2009, Application No. 17599/05), the appropriate minimum conditions and dimensions of multiple-occupancy cells (*Davydov v Ukraine*, 1 July 2010, Application No. 17674/02 39081/02 and *Ananyev v Russia*, 10 January 2012, Application No. 42525/07 60800/08), and the frequency of transfers of a prisoner from one prison to another (*Orchowski v Poland*, 15 July 2002, Application No. 47095/99).

Prisoners' rights cases at European level have influenced Irish jurisprudence in the area. Despite this, there is a lack of specific guidance as to what constitutes treatment in breach of Article 3 and the cases have turned on their individual facts. While there has been no specific definition of the terms 'inhuman and degrading' at a Convention level, MacMenamin J. in the High Court made it clear in the decision of *Mulligan v Governor of Portlaoise Prison* [2010] IEHC 269 that the treatment complained of must attain a minimum level of severity in order to fall into this category. In the *Mulligan* decision, the applicant claimed that his right to freedom from inhuman or degrading treatment under Article 3 of the Convention had been breached by the lack of in-cell sanitation in Portlaoise prison.

MacMenamin J. noted that under Article 3, the totality of the conditions and their cumulative effect must be examined. In the court's view, time allowed out of the cell and the other aspects of the prisoner's detention outweighed the effect of the conditions in the prison and the claim under Article 3 failed. Overall then, 'slopping out' without other factors did not constitute inhuman or degrading treatment for the purposes of the Convention.

Article 3 was also argued in *Gibbons v Governor of Wheatfield Prison* [2008] IEHC 206. In that case, the High Court refused to grant an order of *certiorari* quashing the order of the Governor of Wheatfield Prison in disciplinary proceedings for alleged misconduct, holding that this did not amount to 'inhuman and degrading treatment' for the purposes of the Convention.

17.6   Article 5 Right to Liberty and Security: Arrest, Detention, and Prosecutorial Delay

Article 5 of the Convention asserts the right of any person not to be deprived of their liberty in an arbitrary way. In *Bazorkina v Russia* (2008) 46 EHRR 15 the ECtHR outlined the importance of Article 5:

> The Court stresses the fundamental importance of the guarantees contained in Article 5 for securing the right of individuals in a democracy to be free from arbitrary detention at the hands of the authorities. It has stressed in that connection that any deprivation of liberty must not only have been effected in conformity with the substantive and procedural rules of national law but must equally be in keeping with the very purpose of Article 5, namely to protect the individual from arbitrary detention. In order to minimise the risks of arbitrary detention, Article 5 provides a corpus of substantive rights intended to ensure that the act of deprivation of liberty be amenable to independent judicial scrutiny and secures the accountability of the authorities for that measure.

Article 5(1) states that no one shall be deprived of his liberty 'save in accordance with a procedure prescribed by law'. The ECtHR made it clear in *Strock v Germany* (2006) 43 EHRR 96 that:

> Having regard to this, the Court considers that Article 5(1), first sentence, of the Convention must equally be construed as laying down a positive obligation on the State to protect the liberty of its citizens. Any conclusion to the effect that this was not the case would not only be inconsistent with the Court's case-law, notably under Articles 2, 3 and 8 of the Convention, it would also leave a sizeable gap in the protection from arbitrary detention, which would be inconsistent with the importance of personal liberty in a democratic society. The State is therefore obliged to take measures providing effective protection of vulnerable persons, including reasonable steps to prevent a deprivation of liberty of which the authorities have or ought to have knowledge.

Paragraphs (a)–(f) of Article 5(1) sets out the circumstances in which individuals may lawfully be deprived of their liberty, Those most relevant in the criminal court are as follows:

17.6.1   ARTICLE 5(1)(A) DETENTION AFTER CONVICTION

Detention following a conviction by a competent court, is lawful. The ECtHR has no power to consider the legality of the convictions before national courts (*Ilaşcu v Moldova and Russia* (2005) 40 EHRR 1040). (See at **17.7**: Article 6; while the ECtHR may not reopen cases, it can assess the fairness of the procedures employed.)

17.6.2   ARTICLE 5(1)(B) FAILURE TO COMPLY WITH AN OBLIGATION PRESCRIBED BY LAW

Article 5(1)(b) provides for the deprivation of liberty following 'the lawful arrest or detention of a person for non-compliance with the lawful order of a court or in order to secure the fulfilment of any obligation prescribed by law'.

The ECtHR has stated that such a detention must be proportionate to the aim pursued by the court order. In *Vasileva v Denmark* (2005) EHRR 681, the court found that the detention of the applicant in police custody for 24 hours for failing to provide her name and address having been arrested for non-payment of a bus fare was disproportionate to its object.

17.6.3   ARTICLE 5(1)(C) PRE-TRIAL DETENTION

Article 5(1)(c) allows for the arrest and detention of suspected criminals.

This detention must be based on a 'reasonable suspicion' of the detained person having committed an offence, or when it is reasonably considered necessary to prevent his committing an offence or fleeing after having done so.

The ECtHR has held that Article 5(1) prohibits the arrest of a person unless s/he is reasonably suspected of committing an offence. In *Fox, Campbell and Hartley v United Kingdom* (1991) EHRR 157, this 'reasonableness' standard was applied to the arrest and detention of three suspects under the Northern Ireland (Emergency Provisions) Act 1978. The ECtHR stated:

> The 'reasonableness' of the suspicion on which an arrest must be based forms an essential part of the safeguard against arbitrary arrest and detention which is laid down in Article 5(1)(c). The Court agrees with the Commission and the Government that having a 'reasonable suspicion' presupposes the existence of facts or information which would satisfy an objective observer that the person concerned may have committed the offence. What may be regarded as 'reasonable' will however depend upon all the circumstances.

In this respect, terrorist crime falls into a special category. Because of the attendant risk of loss of life and human suffering, the police are obliged to act with utmost urgency in following up all information, including information from secret sources. Further, the police may frequently have to arrest a suspected terrorist on the basis of information which is reliable but which cannot, without putting in jeopardy the source of the information, be revealed to the suspect or produced in court to support a charge. As the Government pointed out, in view of the difficulties inherent in the investigation and prosecution of terrorist-type offences in Northern Ireland, the 'reasonableness' of the suspicion justifying such arrests cannot always be judged according to the same standards as are applied in dealing with conventional crime. Nevertheless, the exigencies of dealing with terrorist crime cannot justify stretching the notion of 'reasonableness' to the point where the essence of the safeguard secured by Article 5(1)(c) is impaired.

17.6.4   ARTICLE 5(1)(F) LAWFULNESS OF ARREST FOR DEPORTATION

Article 5(1)(f) provides 'for the lawful arrest or detention of a person to prevent his or her effecting an unauthorised entry into the country or of a person against whom an action is being taken with a view to deportation or extradition'. In *Chahal v United Kingdom* (1997) EHRR 413, it was clarified that in respect of a detention for the purpose of extradition, there is no requirement on a state to show that the detention was considered reasonably necessary for the purpose of preventing a detainee from absconding or committing a crime. (See **17.14** and **Chapter 18** for a further consideration of the influence of the Convention on the operation of European arrest warrants in the Irish courts.)

17.6.5   ARTICLE 5(2) PROPERLY INFORMED OF REASONS FOR ARREST

Under Article 5(2), once arrested a person shall be informed promptly, in a language which s/he understands, of the reasons for such arrest and the charge against him.

Refusal of bail may be justified on various grounds including the risk of absconding; interference with justice; the prevention of crime; the preservation of public order; and the safety of the person. However, the individual should only be detained if a condition of bail could not mitigate the risk in question. The authorities must consider measures to counteract any risks, such as requiring security to be lodged or court supervision. They are obliged to give proper consideration to any offer of a financial guarantee to ensure the accused's presence at the hearing.

17.6.6   ARTICLE 5(3) PROMPT ACCESS TO A COURT

Article 5(3) obliges states to ensure that an arrested person be brought 'promptly' before an independent judge who has the power to order release. It is clear from the statements made by the court in both *Neumeister v Austria* (1968) and *IA v France* (1998) that Article 5(3) protects the right of any person deprived of their liberty to be put on trial within reasonable time or be released pending trial. The ECtHR has considered a number of cases regarding the length of detention following arrest. In *O'Hara v UK* [2001] ECHR 598, the court held that the United Kingdom was in breach of Article 5(3) in a case where an applicant was held for six days before being brought before a judge.

A further and ongoing obligation arises 'to review the continued detention of a person pending his trial with a view to ensuring his release when the circumstances do not justify the continued deprivation of liberty'.

17.6.7   ARTICLE 5(4) RIGHT TO REVIEW A DETENTION

Article 5(4) of the Convention notes that 'everyone who is deprived of his liberty by arrest or detention shall be entitled to take proceedings by which the lawfulness of his detention shall be decided speedily by a court and his release ordered if the detention is not lawful'.

In *De Wilde Ooms and Versyp v Belgium* (1979) 1 EHRR 373, the court held that certain sentences of 'preventive detention', imposed by magistrates in cases of vagrancy and begging, were in violation of Article 5(4). The court clarified the meaning of the term 'court' in Article 5(4) as being a concept more flexible than a judicial body in the full sense, but nonetheless requiring certain minimum characteristics of independence and decision-making.

Importantly, the court also made it clear that Article 5(4) would not normally apply to deprivation of liberty arising under a sentence of imprisonment for a criminal offence, as the 'review' required under Article 5(4) here would be incorporated into the original sentencing decision.

What Article 5(4) is therefore primarily concerned with is the review of deprivations of liberty imposed by an administrative body and in situations other than those involving a sentence of imprisonment following conviction.

The legality of the mandatory life sentence for murder has been discussed by the ECtHR. In *Wynne v United Kingdom* (1995) 19 EHRR 333, it was held that the administration of the mandatory life sentence for murder did not fall within the scope of Article 5(4) and was therefore outside the remit of the Convention. However, in the more recent case, *Stafford v United Kingdom* (2002) 35 EHRR 1121, the court decided that the mandatory life sentence, as then administered in the United Kingdom, did attract the protection of Article 5(4).

This question of the legality of mandatory life sentences was recently dealt with in an Irish context. In *Whelan and Lynch v Minister for Justice* [2012] 1 IR 27, the applicants challenged the imposition of mandatory life sentences by the courts for the offence of murder under s. 2 of the Criminal Justice Act 1990 on Convention and constitutional grounds.

The first argument made by the applicant was that the automatic imposition of a mandatory life sentence in Ireland was entirely punitive in rationale, and therefore lacked the review requirements of Article 5(4).

In respect of this argument, Murray C.J. applied a test outlined by the ECtHR in *Kafkaris v Cyprus* (2008) 49 EHRR 877 in order to illustrate that the sentence being served by the appellants was not 'arbitrary'. The *Kafkaris* analysis involved an examination of whether there exists:

> a clear and sufficient causal connection between the conviction and the applicant's continuing detention which is pursuant to his conviction and in accordance with the mandatory life sentence imposed on him by a competent court.

It was held by Murray C.J. that in the instant case, the prisoners were being 'detained in accordance with the punishment provided by law and ordered by the court of trial'. Murray C.J. further relied on *Kafkaris* in making a clear distinction between the imposition of a mandatory and punitive life sentence and the exercise of an executive discretion:

> mandatory life sentence as a punitive measures for a serious crime ... in accordance with national law does not as such offend against any provision of the Convention provided at least that national law affords the possibility of review with a view to its commutation or conditional release.

The applicants also sought to argue that the minister's involvement in decisions regarding the commutation of a life sentence and release on licence amounted to an unlawful determination of sentence. The argument was that Article 5(4) of the Convention requires that any review of detention for the purpose of relief must be carried out by a 'court' within the meaning of the Article and thus it was contended that the minister, in determining when a person was to be released, was exercising a judicial function.

The Supreme Court ultimately rejected this argument, holding that 'discretionary' compassionate or humanitarian release is part of an executive function, unlinked to the imposition of a criminal punishment.

In the later case of *Nascimento v Minister for Justice, Equality and Law Reform, Ireland and the Attorney General* [2011] 1 IR 1, the applicant sought a declaration that s. 2 of the Criminal Justice Act 1990 was unconstitutional and incompatible with Article 5(4) of the Convention.

Dunne J. in the High Court, following the previous decision in *Lynch and Whelan*, refused the declaratory relief sought, on the ground that the minister's function in determining when a life sentence prisoner should be released constituted 'giving effect' to a sentence of a court in accordance with the separation of powers, rather than a trespass into the sentencing area. Further, the court took the view that the Convention authorities were of little relevance, particularly given the absence of any 'preventive detention' component in the Irish life sentence.

17.6.8   ARTICLE 5(5) RIGHT TO COMPENSATION FOR ILLEGAL DETENTION

The right to compensation for illegal detention is provided for in Article 5(5) of the Convention. It follows that any breach of Article 5 found by either national courts or the ECtHR will give rise to a breach of Article 5(5) if there is no enforceable right to compensation in national law. In *Brogan v United Kingdom* (1989) 11 EHRR 117 and *Fox, Campbell and Hartley v United Kingdom* (1991) EHRR 157, the ECtHR found a breach of Article 5(5) as no provision existed in domestic law providing compensation in the cases of arrest and prolonged detention under terrorism legislation in the UK.

17.7   Article 6 The Right to a Fair Trial

Although the ECtHR has no jurisdiction to reopen cases that have previously been decided by the national courts, it possesses the power to determine whether the proceedings were fair and met the minimum requirements under the Convention. Article 6 and the specific guarantees contained in the various subsections have been interpreted broadly by the ECtHR. Article 6 is based on democratic accountability and the principle of the 'equality of arms', which is the idea that each party to a proceeding should have an equal opportunity to present their case and that, in criminal proceedings, the state should not enjoy any substantial advantage over any individual defendant.

17.7.1   ARTICLE 6(1) EVIDENCE AND FAIR TRIAL PROCEDURES

Article 6(1) entitles everyone to a fair and public hearing within a reasonable time by an independent and impartial tribunal established by law. As the court explained in its recent decision, *Pichugin v Russia* (Application No. 38623/03, 23 October 2012):

> The Court's primary concern under Article 6(1) is to evaluate the overall fairness of the criminal proceedings. In making this assessment the Court will look at the proceedings as a whole having regard to the rights of the defence but also to the interests of the public and the victims that crime is properly prosecuted.

17.7.1.1   Fair trial in a reasonable period of time

A significant number of cases have considered the impact of Article 6(1) of the Convention and the right to have a trial within a reasonable period of time, as also provided by Article 38.1 of the Constitution. The ECtHR has made a number of specific findings against Ireland for undue delay under Article 6(1) of the Convention. This in turn has shaped Constitutional jurisprudence in the area.

On the issue of whether damages would be an effective remedy for delay, the ECtHR, in *Barry v Ireland* [2005] ECHR 865, noted that there was significant uncertainty as to whether a damages claim under the Constitution would succeed and that damages would not provide an effective remedy for systemic delay in a case. It is important to note that nowhere in cases against Ireland has the ECtHR stated that delay in bringing a prosecution should result in the dismissal of criminal charges.

In *TH v DPP* [2006] 3 IR 520, the applicant sought to prohibit his trial on a charge of sexual assault by relying on the finding of the ECtHR in *Barry v Ireland*. Fennelly J. speaking for a unanimous Supreme Court addressed this in the following passage:

It is important to clear up any misunderstanding concerning the import of such decisions of the Court of Human Rights. The Court does not and did not, in that case, hold that the prosecution had to be stopped. It would be most surprising if a judgment of that Court holding that the prosecuting authorities were 'partially or completely responsible' for certain periods of delay had the automatic consequence that a prosecution had to be halted . . . the decision of the Court leads to a monetary award. It has no consequence for the pending prosecution.

In *McFarlane v Ireland* (2011) 52 EHRR 20, the ECtHR held that a 10 year and 6 month delay in bringing the applicant to trial (at which he was acquitted) was a violation of Article 6(1) of the Convention. In particular it noted:

its constant case law to the effect that the reasonableness of the length of proceedings must be assessed in the light of the circumstances of the case and with reference to the following criteria: the complexity of the case, the conduct of the applicant and of the relevant authorities and what was at stake for the applicant.

While accepting that certain actions of the applicant may have contributed to the delay, this was not such so as to justify the 10 year and six months delay given that the state had a duty to organise court systems and processes in order to deal with issues within 'a reasonable period of time'.

In *Kennedy v DPP* [2011] IEHC 311, the applicant sought to prevent his trial on charges of corruption on grounds of delay. Hedigan J. in the High Court noted that while an individual might be entitled to damages for breach of Article 6(1), it did not follow that the trial has to be prevented stating that:

It is possible that the State could be found to have acted in contravention of Article 6 due to the duration of the Tribunal and the consequent unavailability of the main witness. However, violation of Article 6 does not ipso facto result in a prohibition of the trial in question.

In the Supreme Court ([2012] 3 IR 744), the majority also refused to prevent Mr Kennedy's trial from proceeding. Clarke J. noted:

[I]t does not follow that every case in which the European Court of Human Rights finds a breach of the right to a reasonably expeditious trial also involves a finding by that court to the effect that the trial was unfair ... It does not, therefore, follow that the ECHR requires, for the avoidance of a breach of its provisions, that a trial be prohibited in every case where there has been a breach of the right to a reasonably expeditious trial.

Clarke J. expressed the view that the available remedies under the Constitution, namely a right to damages or to obtain a prohibition on the trial occurring, were more extensive than the remedies of damages available under the Convention or the ECHR Act. In any case, as the applicant had not pursued a claim of damages under the ECHR Act, the Supreme Court was unable to make a determination on this point.

17.7.2   GIVING REASONS FOR A DECISION

It is a basic requirement of a fair trial in criminal law that judges should give reasons for their decisions.

In *Vrabec and Others v Slovakia* (Application No. 31312/08), the ECtHR noted the requirements for a court to give reasons for its judgments but stated that this is not to be understood 'as requiring a detailed answer to every argument'. The court has also pointed out that the extent to which the duty to give reasons applies may vary according to the nature of the decision and must be determined in all the circumstances of the case (*Ruiz Torija v Spain*).

However, it was made clear in the earlier decision of *Hiro Bilani v Spain* (1995) 19 EHRR 566 that where a submission made to the court in the course of a trial would be determinative of the outcome of a case, it must be specifically addressed in the ruling of the court.

The Supreme Court in *Kenny v Judge Coughlan* [2014] IESC 15 considered the extent to which a District Court judge was obliged to give reasons in determining a summary road traffic matter. Denham C.J. in relying on the Convention jurisprudence, and in particular on the *Vrabec* decision, noted that the obligation to give reasons is dependent on context so that the extent to which a decision of the District Court must be explained and reasons given will depend on the nature and circumstances of the case.

Denham C.J. considered that there had been a clear discussion of the relevant issues in the case, with the District Judge deciding to accept the prosecution evidence. It was determined that this was sufficiently clear to the appellant, and that any further elaboration by the District Judge was not required.

17.7.3   EXCLUSIONARY RULES IN CRIMINAL TRIALS

The ECtHR has made it clear that while Article 6(1) guarantees the right to a fair hearing, it does not lay down any rules on the admissibility of evidence as such, this being primarily a matter for regulation under national law (*Schenk v Switzerland* (1991) 13 EHRR 242).

The ECtHR has determined that, where evidence is obtained unlawfully under domestic law, the question for the court is whether the proceedings as a whole, including the way in which the evidence was obtained, were fair.

In determining whether this is the case, regard must also be had to whether the rights of the defence have been respected. In cases such as *Bykov v Russia* (Application No. 4378/02) it is clear that the quality of the evidence must be taken into consideration, as must the circumstances in which it was obtained and whether these circumstances cast doubt on its reliability or accuracy.

The Irish Superior Courts have considered the influence of the Convention jurisprudence on the 'exclusionary rule'. In the case of *DPP (Walsh) v Cash* [2007] IEHC 108, after reviewing issues of criminal due process under the Constitution, Charleton J., relied on the decision of the ECtHR in *X and Y v Netherlands* (1986) 8 EHRR 235 in considering the impact of Article 6(1) of the European Convention on Irish Law:

> A domestic legal obligation arises by virtue of ss. 2 and 3 of the European Convention on Human Rights Act, 2003. I consider that a rule providing for the automatic exclusion of evidence obtained in consequence of any mistake that infringes any constitutional right of an accused, may be incompatible with Ireland's obligations to provide, for both the accused and the community, a fair disposal of criminal charges.

Charleton J. further notes that: 'is not a principle of Convention Law that unlawfully obtained evidence shall not be admissible'.

In the decision of *DPP v JC* [2015] IESC 31, a majority of the Supreme Court revised the 'exclusionary rule' on the admissibility of unlawfully and unconstitutionally obtained evidence. While the decision was mainly based on the re-evaluation of constitutional jurisprudence which had developed in the area, the impact of Convention rights was considered by Mc Menamin J. who, in writing for the majority, notes that:

> The reputation and integrity of the system of justice should not be adversely affected by properly and faithfully applied good faith exception to the rule, constitutionally applied here, as in other jurisdictions. The bar set by the majority judgments herein is significantly higher than that to be found elsewhere in the common law world. It is in no way inconsistent with the ECHR (*Schenk v Switzerland* (1991) 13 EHRR 242). It redresses the balance so as to encompass community interests, while ensuring that egregious breaches of a suspect's rights and police misconduct are checked. It restores meaning to the terms 'deliberate and conscious' which have caused a lack of clarity in the law.

In a strongly worded minority judgment, Hardiman J., who also referred to the Convention, rejected this new test of 'inadvertence':

> If the State have their way in this case, it will be possible to disregard breaches of the Constitution and of constitutional rights and to admit the fruits of them in evidence just as if the Constitution has not been breached at all. In my opinion, that state of affairs which is ardently desired by the State would amount to 'setting aside or circumventing' constitutional rights.

17.7.4   PREJUDICIAL PRE-TRIAL PUBLICITY

The ECtHR and the Irish courts have been asked to consider whether a trial should be prohibited on the basis that the pre-trial publicity has rendered it impossible for the accused to receive a fair trial.

In *X v Austria* 11 CD 31 [1963], it was held that 'a virulent press campaign against an accused' is capable of violating a right to a fair trial by jury. However, it was also held that a court is obliged to take account of the fact that press commentary is inevitable in a case of public interest and that there is a further obligation on a court to consider what steps have been taken by judge to counter such prejudice in the charge to the jury.

In *Kyprianou v Cyprus* (Application No. 73797/01), the applicant contended that the judges of the domestic court had failed to satisfy the requirement of impartiality under both an objective and subjective test on the basis of pre-trial publicity. The ECtHR examined a number of aspects of the judges' conduct. The court was referred to the specific language adopted by the judges and held:

> the emphatic language used by the judges throughout their decision conveyed a sense of indignation and shock, which runs counter to the detached approach expected of judicial pronouncements.

In the Irish case *O'Brien v DPP* [2014] IESC 39, the Irish Supreme Court held that a High Court judge's statement in separate civil proceedings that there was *prima facie* evidence of criminal activity by the applicant did not interfere with his right to a fair trial in the criminal court. The applicant sought a prohibition of his trial proceeding on the basis of adverse pre-trial publicity and argued the presumption of innocence protection in Article 6(2). Denham C.J. placed significant reliance on Convention cases on prejudicial pre-trial publicity but noted that there had been a sufficient period of time to allow public memory of the remarks to fade and that there was therefore no real risk of an unfair trial.

17.7.5   RIGHT TO SILENCE

The ECtHR has generally considered that the right to silence and the right not to incriminate oneself are at the heart of fair criminal procedure guaranteed under Article 6(1) of the Convention (*O'Halloran and Francis v UK* (2008) 46 EHRR 21).

In *Saunders v United Kingdom* (1997) 23 EHRR 313, the ECtHR held that the right to silence and the right not to incriminate oneself were generally recognised international standards. Specifically, it held that the powers of government-appointed inspectors to compel individuals to answer certain questions was not a breach of Article 6(1), but that the use of those answers in criminal proceedings violated the accused's right to silence.

The ECtHR has held that different standards apply to laws permitting the drawing of adverse inferences at trial from the silence of suspects during interrogation. In *John Murray v United Kingdom* (1996) 22 EHRR 29, the ECtHR considered whether adverse inferences were absolutely prohibited under Article 6(1) of the Convention. The court ruled that it would be incompatible with the right to silence if a conviction were based solely on the accused's failure or refusal to answer police questions. However, it held that adverse inferences could be permitted for several reasons, including the fact that the accused had been given the appropriate warnings as to the effect of remaining silent and that there was no evidence of his misunderstanding such warnings.

In *Quinn v Ireland* (2001) 33 EHRR 344 and *Heaney and McGuinness v Ireland* (2000) ECHR 684, the ECtHR, while acknowledging that the right to silence and the right not to incriminate oneself as laid out in Article 6 of the Convention were not absolute, ruled that s. 52 of the Offences Against the State Act 1939 went further than was necessary to meet the needs of state security.

The approach of the ECtHR seems to have informed the Irish courts when interpreting and restating the right to silence under the Constitution. In *Re National Irish Bank* [1999] 3 IR 145, the Supreme Court was asked to consider whether s. 18 of the Companies Act 1990 was constitutional. This section effectively compelled officers and agents to answer the questions of court-appointed inspectors and allowed the answers given to be used in evidence against them at trial.

Barrington J., citing a number of decisions from the ECtHR, including the *Saunders* decision, said the court could not authorise the introduction into evidence in a criminal trial of a non-voluntary confession by an accused.

However Noonan J. of the High Court recently applied Convention jurisprudence to opposite effect in *Donnelly v Judges of Dublin Metropolitan District Court* [2015] IEHC 125. Here the applicant was charged with an offence contrary to s. 9(5) and (6) of the Firearms and Offensive Weapons Act 1990 which reads as follows:

(5) *Where a person has with him in any public place any article intended by him unlawfully to cause injury to, incapacitate or intimidate any person either in a particular eventuality or otherwise, he shall be guilty of an offence.*

(6) *In a prosecution for an offence under subsection (5), it shall not be necessary for the prosecution to allege or prove that the intent to cause injury, incapacitate or intimidate was intent to cause injury to, incapacitate or intimidate a particular person; and if, having regard to all the circumstances (including the type of the article alleged to have been intended to cause injury, incapacitate or intimidate, the time of the day or night, and the place), the court (or the jury as the case may be) thinks it reasonable to do so, it may regard possession of the article as sufficient evidence of intent in the absence of any adequate explanation by the accused.*

The applicant's contention was that s. 9(6), in allowing a court to draw an adverse inference from the silence of an accused person and failing to require the administration of a caution, warning that such an inference may be drawn, amounted to an unlawful infringement of the accused's right to silence and was thus unconstitutional and incompatible with Article 6(1) of the Convention. Noonan J. noted that:

> The right to silence is an incident of the presumption of innocence and a cornerstone of our criminal justice system protected by constitutional guarantees. It is not an absolute right and may be circumscribed by legislation. Such legislation will be valid provided it is proportionate and does not represent an unnecessary incursion on the rights of the accused. It falls to be weighed and assessed by reference to a number of different factors.

Noonan J. held that s. 9(6) of the Firearms and Offensive Weapons Act 1990 was a proportionate measure, not incompatible with the Constitution or Convention as the section did not provide that failure to offer adequate explanation for possession of an item amounted of itself to proof of guilt.

17.7.6   DETERMINING WHETHER AN OFFENCE IS CRIMINAL OR CIVIL

In determining whether a provision is civil or criminal in nature the ECtHR has taken an 'autonomous' approach in that it is not bound by the categorisation of a respondent state. In making its inquiry the court will ask: 'whether or not the text defining the offence belongs to the criminal law, next the nature of the offence and finally the nature and degree of severity of the penalty that the person concerned risks occurring' (*Bendenoun v France* (1998) 18 EHRR 54).

Other determinants which the ECtHR has employed have included the severity of the sanction proposed and whether its objective is to impose a deterrent to address wrongs done in society; and the extent to which the crimes apply to the public at large as opposed to private or professional activity and whether the imposition of a penalty is dependent on a finding of culpability (*Oztiirk v Germany* (1984) 6 EHRR 409; *Engel v Netherlands* (1979) 1 EHRR 647).

17.8   Influence of the ECHR on Presumption of Innocence

As Charleton J. in *The People (DPP) v Smyth* [2010] 3 IR 688 stated:

> The fundamental principle of our criminal justice system is that an accused should not be convicted unless it is proven beyond reasonable doubt that the accused committed the offence. The legal presumption that the accused is innocent, until his guilt is proven to that standard, operates to ensure objectivity within the system. It is a matter for the Oireachtas to decide whether on a particular element of the offence an evidential burden of proof should be cast on an accused person. Of itself, this does not infringe the constitutional principle that the accused should be presumed to be innocent until found guilty.

Article 6(2) notes that 'everyone charged with a criminal offence shall be presumed innocent until proved guilty according to law'. The ECtHR and the Irish courts have considered the effect of the operation of Article 6(2) on shifting the burden of proof in criminal trials and on pre-trial publicity.

17.8.1 PRE-TRIAL PUBLICITY AND THE PRESUMPTION OF INNOCENCE

In *Allenet de Ribemount v France* (Application No. 15175/89), two high-ranking police officers referred at a press conference to de Ribemount being one of the instigators in a murder which they were directly involved in investigating. The ECtHR determined that that statement had breached his presumption of innocence.

In *Butkevicius v Lithuania* the ECtHR held that there was a breach of Article 6(2) of the Convention where the Chairman of the Lithuanian Parliament had stated in a public interview to the national press that he had no doubt that the applicant had taken a bribe.

In the decision of *O'Brien v DPP* [2014] IESC 39, mentioned at **17.7.4**, Denham C.J. analysed the decisions of the ECtHR in *Butkevicius* and *de Ribemount* and distinguished these cases from the applicant's case on its facts. Denham C.J. did this primarily on the basis that the judge's statements in the High Court civil case were not unequivocal statements of the accused's guilt.

17.8.2 THE PRESUMPTION OF INNOCENCE AND THE EVIDENTIAL SHIFTING THE BURDEN OF PROOF

In *Salabiaku v France* [1988] 13 EHRR 379, an accused was convicted of an offence contrary to the French Criminal Code for the possession of prohibited goods. The applicant argued that the provision contained a presumption of criminal liability which was incompatible with the operation of Article 6(2). The court held:

> Article 6(2) does not … regard presumptions of fact or of law provided for in the criminal law with indifference. It requires States to confine them within reasonable limits which take into account the importance of what is at stake and maintain the rights of the defence.

In *Telfner v Austria* (2002) 34 EHRR 207, the ECtHR found that a requirement that the accused provide an explanation for an alleged offence, notwithstanding that the prosecution had not established a convincing *prima facie* case, was a violation of the presumption of innocence under Article 6(2) of the Convention.

> Article 6(2) requires, inter alia, that when carrying out their duties, the members of the court should not start with the preconceived idea that the accused has committed the offence charged; the burden of proof is on the prosecution, and any doubt should benefit the accused … Thus, the presumption of innocence will be infringed where the burden of proof is shifted from the prosecution to the defence.

The Supreme Court in *McNulty v Ireland and the Attorney General* [2015] IESC 357 recently considered the impact of Article 6(2) of the Convention on the presumption of innocence in Irish law. The case concerned an applicant who was convicted of the offence of intimidating a witness with the intention of obstructing, perverting or interfering with an investigation or the course of justice contrary to s. 41 of the Criminal Justice Act 1999.

Section 41(3) provided that proof of the act shall be 'evidence' of the requisite intention to commit the offence. The applicant contended that this meant that proof of the act was sufficient to sustain a conviction without any further evidence and as such the section was in breach of Article 38 of the Constitution and Article 6(2) of the Convention.

The Supreme Court considered the decisions of the ECtHR in *Salabiaku* and *Telfner*. In upholding the order of Gilligan J. in the High Court refusing reliefs, Denham C.J. found that s. 41(3) of the 199 Act allows the court full discretion to assess all of the evidence and does not oblige the court to infer that an act was done with the required intention.

The influence of Article 6(2) of the Convention on the presumption of innocence in Irish criminal law was recently considered by Noonan J. of the High Court in *Donnelly v Judges of Dublin Metropolitan District Court* [2015] IEHC 125, which is considered in more detail at **17.7.5**. Noonan J., following the ECtHR in *Salabiaku*, noted that a *prima facie* statutory reversal of the legal onus of proof onto the accused will be incompatible with the presumption of innocence but distinguished this from a reversal of the evidential burden:

> Our law does not permit a presumption of guilt until proven innocent. Thus, a requirement to convict in the absence of evidence from the accused is constitutionally dubious. It always remains for the prosecution to prove the guilt of the accused beyond reasonable doubt. It is

however well settled that it is legitimate to shift the evidential as distinct from legal burden onto the accused where the test of proportionality is satisfied. That test recognises the inevitable tensions between protecting the rights of the accused and maintaining law and order in the interests of the common good.

17.9   Specific Guarantees Section 6(3)

Specific guarantees to ensure fairness in criminal trials are contained in Article 6(3) of the Convention. Most, if not all, of these protections are already contained in the Constitution provisions but may still be pleaded by an applicant.

17.9.1   ARTICLE 6(3)(A) RIGHT TO BE INFORMED PROMPTLY, IN A LANGUAGE WHICH THE ACCUSED UNDERSTANDS AND IN DETAIL, OF THE NATURE AND CAUSE OF THE ACCUSATION AGAINST HIM

Article 6(3)(a) is concerned with protecting a defendant at the time of charge by ensuring that they are provided with sufficient information at the time of a charge to challenge all accusations.

The basic principles attaching to the right to be informed of the charges were enunciated in *Brozicek v Italy* (1989) 12 EHRR 371. In *Brozicek* the applicant, who was of German origin, made clear to the domestic court that he had difficulties with the Italian language. The ECtHR noted that the Italian authorities had the obligation to get the information translated unless they had reasonable grounds to believe that he understood same.

In *Mattocia v Italy* (2000) 36 EHRR 825, the accused was given insufficient information about the charge against him, including the time and place of the offence he was alleged to have committed. The ECtHR ruled that as these details were 'material facts' which formed the basis of the allegation, the non-provision of this information breached the essential procedural guarantee under s. 6(3)(a). The provision of vague and informal information was held to be insufficient to satisfy the requirements of the Convention.

17.9.2   ARTICLE 6(3)(B) RIGHT TO HAVE ADEQUATE TIME AND THE FACILITIES FOR THE PREPARATION OF HIS DEFENCE

Similar to Article 6(3)(a), Article 6(3)(b) concerns the rights of a defendant to sufficient protection prior to the hearing of charges brought against them. In *Can v Austria* (1985) 8 EHRR 14, it was held that an accused must have:

> the opportunity to organise his defence in an appropriate way and without restriction to the possibility to put all relevant defence arguments before the trial court, and thus to influence the proceedings.

The case law from the ECtHR reveals that what will be deemed to constitute 'adequate time' will vary according to the circumstances. For example in *X and Y v Austria* [1978] 12 DR 160, a period of 17 days was considered adequate time to prepare for a misappropriation case, but two weeks to prepare in *Ocalan v Turkey* (2005) 41 EHRR 45 was held to be inadequate given the volume of correspondence in evidence.

As is made clear in the decision of *Jespers v Belgium* (1981) 27 DR 61, the requirement to afford adequate facilities for the preparation of a defence also obliges the state to adopt measures to place the defence on an equal footing with the prosecution. An issue which arises from this obligation is whether the defence is entitled to unrestricted disclosure by the prosecution or whether material may be withheld on grounds of public interest. In *Rowe and Davis v United Kingdom* (2000) 30 EHRR 1 and *Fitt v United Kingdom* (2000) EHRR 1, the ECtHR found compliance with Article 6(3)(b) as:

> The Court was satisfied that the defence were kept informed and were permitted to make submissions and participate in the decision-making process as far as possible and noted that the need for disclosure was at all times under the assessment of the trial judge, providing a further, important, safeguard.

In *Natunen v Finland* (Application No. 21022/04, 31 March 2009), the applicant was facing proceedings relating to the purchase and supply of drugs and requested the disclosure of recorded phone calls allegedly demonstrating his complicity in the offences. This request was not granted as the relevant evidence had been destroyed, as required by Finnish law at the time, as the evidence was not being relied upon at trial.

The applicant argued that the destroyed evidence would have enabled him to exonerate himself or have his sentence reduced and that the failure to afford him this disclosure would constitute a refusal of facilities necessary for the preparation of the defence and a breach of Article 6(3). The court noted that:

> the entitlement to disclosure of relevant evidence is not an absolute right. In any criminal proceedings there may be competing interests, such as national security or the need to protect witnesses at risk of reprisals or keep secret police methods of investigation of crime, which must be weighed against the rights of the accused ... the requirements of Article 6 presuppose that having given specific reasons for the request for disclosure of certain evidence which could enable the accused to exonerate himself, he should be entitled to have the validity of those reasons examined by a court.

In Ireland the constitutional duty on the prosecution to 'seek out and preserve evidence' as set out in *Braddish v DPP* [2001] 3 IR 127 should mean that Article 6(3)(b) need not be argued. However, it is still an interesting safeguard against any potential judicial retrenchment on this duty.

17.10   Article 6(3)(c) Right to Legal Representation and Access to a Solicitor

Article 6(3)(c) of the Convention provides an accused with the right to represent themselves in person or, should they wish, through legal assistance of their own choosing. The same Article requires that the state may provide free legal assistance to an applicant subject to them not having sufficient means and also in the interests of justice.

17.10.1   RIGHT TO SELECT ONE'S OWN LAWYER

The right to select one's own lawyer has been articulated in the High Court in an Irish criminal and constitutional context. In the case of the *Law Society v Competition Authority* (unreported, 21 December 2005, High Court), O'Neill J., in referring to s. 6(3)(c), noted that the Convention does not confer an unfettered right to select a lawyer under any free legal aid scheme. He quotes from *Croissant v Germany* (1993) 16 EHRR 135:

> It is true that Article 6(3)(c) entitles 'everyone charged with a criminal offence' to be defended by counsel of his own choosing. Nevertheless, and notwithstanding the importance of a relationship of confidence between lawyer and client, this right cannot be considered to be absolute. It is necessarily subject to certain limitations where free legal aid is concerned and also whereas in the present case, it is for the courts to decide whether the interests of justice require that the accused be defended by counsel appointed by them. When appointing defence counsel the national courts must certainly have regard to the defendant's wishes; indeed German law contemplates such a course. However, they can override those wishes when they are relevant and sufficient grounds for holding that is necessary in the interests of justice.

17.10.2   EQUALITY OF ARMS IN FREE LEGAL ASSISTANCE

Where it is found that the accused has the right to legal assistance, the ECtHR has determined that this must be practical and effective rather than an impractical or an illusory right (*Neumister v Austria* [1968] ECHR 1).

In *Carmody v Minister for Justice Equality and Law Reform* [2010] 1 IR 635, the applicant, who was charged with a number of criminal offences in the District Court, had been granted legal aid by the presiding judge pursuant to s. 2 of the Criminal Justice (Legal Aid) Act 1962. The only situation in which s. 2 of the 1962 Act permitted certification for counsel in the District Court was where the charge was one of murder. In Mr Carmody's case, the state was represented by both a solicitor and junior counsel in the District Court.

Mr Carmody argued that his constitutional rights and his right under Article 6(3)(c) of the Convention to criminal legal aid were violated due to the disparity between the legal representation afforded to him as a criminal defendant and that employed by the prosecution, who appeared to have total discretion as to whom they could instruct in the matter.

In the High Court, Laffoy J. reviewed case law from the ECtHR and found that there was no obligation under the Convention to provide Mr Carmody with both a solicitor and counsel and the fact that Mr Carmody had access to a solicitor only did not, in the court's opinion, result in any a violation of Article 6(3)(c).

As noted earlier, the Supreme Court judgment provides an important statement on the correct sequencing of constitutional and Convention arguments where both are advanced. Murray C.J. noted that, if it was accepted that the impugned provision was in fact incompatible with Irish obligations under the Convention, then the only remedy open to the court would be a declaration of incompatibility. Such a declaration, he held, could not resolve the issue before the court and it would ultimately be for the Oireachtas to determine how to remedy the alleged breach of the state's obligations under the Convention:

> [T]he remedies which are being afforded to the plaintiff in these proceedings are adequate to remedy the complaints which he has made with regard to his constitutional rights to legal aid, therefore, the question considering the compatibility of any provision of the Act of 1962 with the European Convention on Human Rights pursuant to Section 5 of the Act of 2003 does not arise.

The Supreme Court was satisfied that, although s. 2 of the 1962 Act was not unconstitutional, it would be a violation of Article 38.1, guaranteeing the right to fair trial, if Mr Carmody was denied the opportunity to apply for legal aid to include a solicitor and counsel.

17.10.3 DENIAL OF ACCESS TO A SOLICITOR DURING QUESTIONING

The protections afforded to an accused under Article 6(3)(c) have also been considered by the Irish Courts in considering the question of access to a solicitor during detention in a Garda Station. In *Lavery v Member in Charge Carrickmacross Garda Station* [1999] 2 IR 390, the High Court steadfastly rejected any attempt to interpret constitutional rights to a fair trial as including the right for questioning to be paused prior to an accused having access to a solicitor.

The ECtHR has taken a contrary view to the courts in *Lavery* and has strongly upheld the rights of an accused person under s. 6(3)(c) to access a lawyer prior to and during their detention for questioning. In *Dayanan v Turkey* (Application No. 7377/03 (Second Section), 13 October 2009) it was stated that:

> an accused person is entitled, as soon as he or she is taken into custody, to be assisted by a lawyer, and not only while being questioned... Indeed, the fairness of proceedings requires that an accused be able to obtain the whole range of services specifically associated with legal assistance. In this regard, counsel has to be able to secure without restriction the fundamental aspects of that person's defence: discussion of the case, organisation of the defence, collection of evidence favourable to the accused, preparation for questioning, support of an accused in distress and checking of the conditions of detention.

In *The People (DPP) v Gormley* [2014] 1 ILRM 377, the Supreme Court revisited the approach taken in *Lavery* in deciding whether statements made by an accused after he requested a solicitor but before the solicitor was available for a consultation, were admissible in evidence. Clarke J. paid particular attention to the cases of *Salduz v Turkey* (2009) 49 EHRR 19 and *Panovits v Cyprus* (Application No. 4268/04 (First Section), 11 December 2008), where the ECtHR held that Article 6 would normally require that the accused be allowed the assistance of a lawyer at the initial stages of an investigation. With reference to this approach, Clarke J. held, in the context of interpreting the relevant Constitutional guarantees that:

There would be little point in giving constitutional recognition to a right of access to a lawyer while in custody if one of the principal purposes of that custody in many cases, being the questioning of the relevant suspect, could continue prior to legal advice being obtained.

Although the Supreme Court ultimately decided the case on the basis of the Constitution, the influence of Convention jurisprudence is evident. Clarke J.'s judgment shows the court's receptiveness to this cross-fertilisation of Convention and constitutional protections:

If it be the case that the State has not, to date, organised itself in a manner sufficient to allow such questioning to take place in conformity with the Constitution but also with the well-established jurisprudence of the ECtHR, then it is those who are in charge of putting such provisions in place who must accept responsibility.

17.11   Article 6(3)(d) Prohibition on Hearsay

Article 6(3)(d) provides that an accused has a right to examine or have examined witnesses against him and to obtain the attendance and examination of witnesses on his behalf under the same conditions as witnesses against him. The Convention has thus been deemed to contain a broad presumption against the use of hearsay evidence against a defendant in criminal proceedings.

The inadmissibility of hearsay under Article 6(3)(d) was argued in the UK decisions, *Al-Khawaja and Tahery v United Kingdom* [2009] ECHR 26766/05 and *R v Horncastle and Others* [2009] UKSC 14 (9 December 2009).

In *Al-Khawaja and Tahery v United Kingdom*, both defendants had been convicted on a single piece of hearsay evidence. In respect of the first applicant, it was determined that a statement of the victim was admissible evidence and the applicant was duly convicted on the contents of this statement. The evidence was admitted under an exception to the hearsay rule contained in the Criminal Justice Act 1988, which provides for the admission of first-hand documentary hearsay in a criminal trial.

The second applicant was convicted of a stabbing on the statement of a single witness. At the trial the prosecution made an application to read this witness's statement rather than calling her to give oral evidence, on the grounds that she feared serious personal harm and the trial judge held that there would be unfairness if the statement was excluded.

The defendants appealed their convictions to the Court of Appeal on the ground that the statements breached Article 6(3)(d) of the Convention. The Court of Appeal dismissed the appeal, holding that, while evidence must normally be produced at a public hearing and as a general rule Article 6(3)(d) requires a defendant to be given a proper and adequate opportunity to challenge and question witnesses, it was not incompatible with Article 6(3)(d) for depositions to be read and this can be the case even where there has been no opportunity to question the witnesses at any stage of the proceedings.

In the ECtHR the Court of Appeal was criticised for failing to respect the rights of both defendants under Article 6(3)(d). The ECtHR held that this was because the decisive evidence against them had been statements from witnesses whom the defendants no opportunity to cross-examine.

The argument of the UK was that the right conferred by Article 6(3)(d) is instrumental, that is, that it exists to ensure that the defendants are not convicted on evidence that is unreliable and there may be in place other safeguards to secure the reliability of the evidence. The ECtHR held, however, that the right is absolute and cannot be fulfilled by other measures.

17.12   Article 7 Non-Retrospective Effect of Criminal Legislation

Article 7 prohibits the retrospective application of a criminal penalty. It seeks to avoid penalisation of conduct that was not criminal at the time the relevant act occurred. In *Scoppola v Italy (No. 2)* (Application No. 10249/03), the ECtHR considered whether a retrospective change in criminal procedure was permissible under the Convention. The Grand Chamber held that it was:

contrary to the principle of legal certainty and the protection of the legitimate trust of persons engaged in judicial proceedings for a State to be able to reduce unilaterally the advantages attached to the waiver of certain rights inherent in the concept of fair trial. As such a waiver is made in exchange for the advantages mentioned, it cannot be regarded as fair if, once the competent domestic authorities have agreed to adopt a simplified procedure, a crucial element of the agreement between the State and the defendant is altered to the latter's detriment without his consent.

As a result it found that the prohibition of retroactivity in Article 7 had been violated. Several of the protocols to the Convention have also been considered in cases concerning criminal practice and procedure and the deprivation of liberty.

17.13 Protocols

17.13.1 PROTOCOL 4 IMPRISONMENT FOR DEBT

Article 1 of Protocol 4 provides that:

> No one shall be deprived of his liberty merely on the ground of inability to fulfil a contractual obligation.

In *McCann v Judges of Monaghan District Court* [2010] ILRM 17, the plaintiff challenged the validity of an order for her arrest and imprisonment for failing to comply with a court instalment order under s. 6 of the Enforcement of Court Orders Act 1940. The applicant argued that this order was incompatible with the Constitution and Article 1 Protocol 4 of the Convention. Laffoy J. ultimately decided the case on Constitutional grounds and thus was not required to make a declaration of incompatibility.

17.13.2 PROTOCOL 7 DOUBLE JEOPARDY

The common law rule, in its purest form, is that a person, once acquitted at trial of criminal offences, can never be retried for the same offence. Article 4(2) of Protocol 7 of the Convention challenges the notion of the finality of an acquittal by permitting a re-trial:

> If there is evidence of new or newly discovered facts, or if there is a fundamental defect in the previous proceedings which would affect the outcome of a case.

The influence of Article 4(2) Protocol 7 was recently considered by Hardiman J. in his judgment in *DPP v JC* (see **17.7.3**). Hardiman J. quoted from the decision in *Zoltukhin v Russia* [2009] ECHR 252, which held that Article 4(2) Protocol 7 prohibits the retrial of a case except in cases of fresh evidence or error:

> The Convention must be interpreted and applied in a manner which rendered its rights practical and effective, and not theoretical or illusory. Accordingly, the Court takes the view that Article 4 of Protocol 7 must be understood as prohibiting the prosecution or trial of a second 'offence' in so far as it arises from identical facts or facts which are substantially the same.

17.14 European Arrest Warrants

As profiled in **Chapter 18**, a significant number of cases in our courts have considered the impact of the Convention on the operation of European arrest warrants. Section 37 of the European Arrest Warrant Act 2003 provides that a person shall not be surrendered to a requesting state where this would be incompatible with the state's obligations under the Convention. In opposing their extradition, applicants have relied on diverse Convention protections, raising arguments under Articles 3, 5, 6, and 8.

In *Minister for Justice, Equality and Law Reform v Rettinger* [2010] IESC 45, the applicant argued that he would be subjected to inhumane and overcrowded prison conditions if returned to Poland.

The Supreme Court held that if there is cogent evidence of a real risk of torture, inhuman or degrading treatment contrary to Article 3, then the onus is on the requesting state to rebut that evidence. In subsequent cases, the High Court refused to return respondents to Lithuania on the basis that they would be exposed to degrading conditions in prison pre- and post-trial (*Minister for Justice Equality and Law Reform v McGuigan* [2013] IEHC 216; *Minister for Justice and Equality v Holden* [2013] IEHC 62).

In *Minister for Justice and Equality v Nolan* [2013] IESC 54, the Supreme Court refused the surrender of the respondent to the UK on the basis that he would be exposed to a system of indeterminate sentencing which had been found to be in breach of Article 5(1) of the Convention.

In *Minister for Justice, Equality and Law Reform v Stapleton* [2006] 3 IR 26, the High Court heard arguments that to give effect to the European arrest warrant would be in breach of the respondent's right to a fair and timely trial under Article 6. The offences were alleged to have occurred almost 30 years previously. Peart J. noted that the concept of what is a reasonable time is an objective one, although subjective considerations may be borne in mind, including the extent to which a respondent has contributed to the delay. In *Minister for Justice v Corrigan* [2007] 2 IR 448, the court held that the relevant consideration under Article 6 is not the lapse of time between the alleged offences and the contemplated trial but whether criminal proceedings, once initiated, are prosecuted without undue delay.

In *Minister for Justice and Equality v Rostas*, the High Court refused to surrender the respondent, who was ethnic Roma, to Romania on the basis that this would be in breach of Article 6 and of the prohibition on discrimination contained in Article 14 of the Convention. The evidence was that the respondent had been convicted and sentenced almost 20 years previously. Independent reports supported her claim that there had been grave deficiencies at her trial and that her conviction was unfair. Edwards J. was a careful to note the very particular facts of the case and stated that his ruling was not a comment on contemporary standards in the requesting state.

In a number of cases, respondents have sought to argue that their surrender on a European arrest warrant will interfere with their rights to privacy and family life under Article 8 of the Convention. This argument has prevailed in only a minority of cases. In *Minister for Justice, Equality and Law Reform v Gheorghe* [2009] IESC 76, Fennelly J. stated:

> Persons sought for prosecution in another state will very often suffer disruption of their personal and family life. No authority has been produced to support the proposition that surrender is to be refused where a person will, as a consequence, suffer disruption, even severe disruption of family relationships.

The courts have applied a proportionality standard, acknowledging that the return of a respondent on a European arrest warrant is an interference with family life under Article 8 but that this can be done in a Convention-compliant way where it is carried out in accordance with law, in pursuit of a legitimate aim which is necessary in a democratic society (namely the prosecution of criminal offences), and in a way which is proportionate to that aim. In *Minister for Justice and Equality v TE* [2013] IEHC 323, Edwards J. in the High Court elaborated a list of 22 criteria to be applied where extradition is opposed on the basis of Article 8 arguments, noting in particular the weight to be given to the interests of children who may be affected.

17.15   Conclusion

The rights and liberties of suspects and defendants in criminal litigation have always enjoyed protection under the Irish Constitution. Increasingly, we see that these constitutional protections are enhanced by the Convention via the ECHR Act. Courts at all levels must interpret and apply criminal law and procedure in a manner compliant with the Convention. All organs of the state must discharge their functions in compliance with the Convention and can be held to account by our domestic courts if they fail to do so. Further, there is demonstrable readiness on the part of our superior courts to engage with developing ECtHR jurisprudence and to apply Convention standards and norms in a range of criminal law matters. Used creatively, the Convention has the potential to become an important tool for criminal practitioners.

CHAPTER 18

THE EUROPEAN ARREST WARRANT

18.1 Introduction

18.1.1 BACKGROUND TO THE EUROPEAN ARREST WARRANT

On 15 and 16 October 1999 the European Council held a special EU Summit meeting in Tampere, Finland on the creation of an area of freedom, security and justice in the European Union. The conclusion of the special meeting set out the 'Tampere Milestones'.

(a) A common EU asylum and migration policy.

(b) A genuine European area of justice.

(c) A Union-wide fight against crime.

(d) Stronger external action.

Clause 35 of the Summit conclusions specifically calls for:

> With respect to criminal matters . . . Member States to speedily ratify the 1995 and 1996 EU Conventions on extradition. It considers that the formal extradition procedure should be abolished among the Member States as far as persons are concerned who are fleeing from justice after having been finally sentenced, and replaced by a simple transfer of such persons, in compliance with Article 6 Treaty on European Union. Consideration should also be given to fast track extradition procedures, without prejudice to the principle of fair trial. The European Council invites the Commission to make proposals on this matter in the light of the Schengen Implementing Agreement.

In order to further this proposal the Summit also concluded that there was a need for mutual recognition of judicial decisions as well as judicial cooperation in both civil and criminal matters within the Union.

Following the Tampere Summit, the EU began preparation of a Framework Decision in respect of extradition. Progress was slow; however, the attacks on the USA in September 2001 provided the impetus needed to encourage the member states to reach agreement. The Framework Decision on the European arrest warrant and the surrender procedures between member states (an instrument of EU law) was adopted by the member states on 13 June 2002:

> *The objective set for the Union to become an area of freedom, security and justice leads to abolishing extradition between Member States and replacing it by a system of surrender between judicial authorities. Further, the introduction of a new simplified system of surrender of sentenced or suspected persons for the purposes of execution or prosecution of criminal sentences makes it possible to remove the complexity and potential for delay inherent in the present extradition procedures. Traditional cooperation relations which have prevailed up till now between Member States should be replaced by a system of free movement of judicial decisions in criminal matters, covering both pre-sentence and final decisions, within an area of freedom, security and justice...*

> *(6) The European arrest warrant provided for in this Framework Decision is the first concrete measure in the field of criminal law implementing the principle of mutual recognition which the European Council referred to as the cornerstone of judicial cooperation.*

18.1.2   THE NATURE OF EXTRADITION

Extradition is defined as the handing over of a person who either stands convicted or accused of a crime for the purpose of being tried or punished for it.

18.1.3   HISTORY—EXTRADITION IN IRELAND

Prior to 1964, extradition in Ireland was a 'backing of warrants' procedure, whereby suspected criminals were taken into custody and handed over to the requesting authorities. The Supreme Court denounced this procedure as unconstitutional in *The State (Quinn) v Ryan* [1965] IR 70 and as a result the Extradition Act 1965 was introduced. Part II of the Act dealt with extradition to all countries other than the UK; Part III dealt with extradition to the UK.

18.1.4   CURRENT LEGISLATION

Extradition law in Ireland is currently governed by the Extradition Act 1965, as amended, which is still the effective legislation for extradition applications from outside the European Union, and the European Arrest Warrant Act 2003, as amended, which applies to applications for surrender from designated EU member states, and to third countries when specific provisions are applied and are passed by a resolution of the Oireachtas.

The European Arrest Warrant Act 2003 was enacted to implement the provisions of the European Council Framework Decision of 13 June 2002. The Act of 2003 came into operation on 1 January 2004 and it has subsequently been amended by Part 8 of the Criminal Justice (Terrorist Offences) Act 2005, the Criminal Justice (Miscellaneous Provisions) Act 2009, and the European Arrest Warrant (Application to Third Countries and Amendment) and Extradition (Amendments) Act 2012. In *Minister for Justice, Equality and Law Reform v Alteravicius* [2006] 3 IR 148, Denham J. described the European arrest warrant as 'a new scheme introduced with the intent of simplifying the procedure of rendition between the Member States'.

The term rendition is preferred to extradition when referring to the European arrest warrant.

18.2   The European Arrest Warrant Act 2003

In this section the European Arrest Warrant Act 2003, as amended (hereinafter referred to as 'the Act') will be examined in some detail.

18.2.1   DEFINITION

Section 2 of the Act defines a European arrest warrant as:

> *a warrant, order or decision of a judicial authority of a Member State, issued under such laws as give effect to the Framework Decision in that Member State, for the arrest and surrender by the State to that Member State of a person in respect of an offence committed or alleged to have been committed by him or her under the law of that Member State.*

18.2.2   POWERS OF THE MINISTER

Section 3 of the Act provides for orders to be made by the Minister for Justice and Law Reform designating member states for the purpose of surrender procedures.

18.2.3   DESIGNATED STATES AND DATE OF DESIGNATION

The following list delineates the designation of member states of the EU for the purpose of surrender procedures and specifies the effective dates of such designation:

- Austria   5 May 2004
- Belgium   1 January 2004
- Bulgaria   13 February 2007
- Cyprus   5 May 2004
- Czech Republic   25 January 2005
- Denmark   1 January 2004
- Estonia   21 July 2004
- Finland   1 January 2004
- France   2 April 2004
- Germany   31 August 2004
- Greece   21 July 2004
- Hungary   5 May 2004
- Italy   15 May 2005
- Latvia   21 July 2004
- Lithuania   5 May 2004
- Luxembourg   2 April 2004
- Malta   24 June 2004
- Netherlands   24 June 2004
- Poland   5 May 2004
- Portugal   1 January 2004
- Republic of Croatia 12 February 2014
- Romania   13 February 2007
- Slovakia   31 August 2004
- Slovenia   5 May 2004
- Spain   1 January 2004
- Sweden   1 January 2004
- United Kingdom   1 January 2004.

18.2.4   PROCEDURE FOR ISSUING A EUROPEAN ARREST WARRANT

A 'judicial authority' of a designated European Member State may issue a European arrest warrant in the format specified in the Framework Decision. Relevant precedents are delineated in SI No. 23 of 2005—Rules of the Superior Courts (European Arrest Warrant Act 2003 and Extradition Acts 1965 to 2001), 2005 as amended by SI No. 117 of 2013 at http://www.irishstatutebook.ie and http://www.courts.ie). The European arrest warrant is transmitted to the Central Authority of the member state where it is believed the sought person is located.

A European arrest warrant must be issued by a judicial authority defined in s. 2 of the Act as: 'the judge, magistrate or other person authorized under the law of the Member State'.

In Ireland the Minister for Justice is the designated Central Authority for the purposes of receiving European arrest warrants (s. 6) and the High Court is the executing judicial authority (s. 9). In other member states the judicial authority can vary widely and it may surprise Irish practitioners that the prosecutor in a case can be the person authorised to issue a European arrest warrant, e.g. in The Netherlands. However, in the recent case of *The Minister for Justice and Equality v MV* [2015] IEHC 524, Donnelly J. refused the application for surrender to Lithuania in respect of a European arrest warrant issued by the Minister for Justice of the issuing state at the request of an executive agency (i.e. the Lithuanian prison service) on the ground that 'the person who issued the EAW cannot in the particular circumstances of this case . . . be considered a judicial authority' as there was no underlying judicial decision.

The applicant in proceedings before the High Court is the Minister for Justice; the person named in the European arrest warrant is the respondent to the proceedings.

18.2.5 OBLIGATION TO SURRENDER

Section 10 of the Act sets out the obligation to surrender as being when a European arrest warrant is issued in respect of a person:

- against whom the issuing state intends to bring a prosecution proceedings for the offence in the warrant, or
- who is the subject of proceedings for the offence in the warrant, or
- who has been convicted of but not yet sentenced in respect of the offence in the warrant, or
- is a person on whom a sentence of imprisonment has been imposed in respect of the offence in the warrant.

18.2.6 THE ARREST WARRANT

The European arrest warrant must be in a specific form (as per the SI referenced at **18.2.4**) containing specified information (s. 11):

- the name and the nationality of the person in respect of whom it is issued,
- the name of the judicial authority that issued the European arrest warrant, and the address of its principal office,
- the telephone number, fax number, and e-mail address (if any) of that judicial authority,
- the offence to which the European arrest warrant relates including the nature and classification under the law of the issuing state of the offence concerned,
- that a conviction, sentence, or detention order is immediately enforceable against the person, or that a warrant for his or her arrest or other order of a judicial authority in the issuing state having the same effect has been issued in respect of one of the offences to which the European arrest warrant relates,
- the circumstances in which the offence was committed or is alleged to have been committed, including the time and place of its commission or alleged commission, and the degree of involvement or alleged degree of involvement of the person in the commission of the offence, and
  - the penalties to which that person would, if convicted of the offence specified in the European arrest warrant, be liable,
  - where that person has been convicted of the offence specified in the European arrest warrant but has not yet been sentenced, the penalties to which he or she is liable in respect of the offence, or
  - where that person has been convicted of the offence specified in the European arrest warrant and a sentence has been imposed in respect thereof, the penalties of which that sentence consists.

A European arrest warrant transmitted to Ireland must be in Irish or English and if in another language must be accompanied by a translation into either Irish or English and must be delivered to the Central Authority or be transmitted by any means capable of producing a written record under conditions allowing the Central Authority to verify its authenticity.

18.2.7 PROCEDURE ON RECEIPT OF A WARRANT

Section 13 of the Act sets out the procedure to be followed by the state on receipt of a warrant from a member state.

On receipt and after verification by the Central Authority the European arrest warrant is forwarded to the Chief State Solicitor's Office, the state's legal department with responsibility for the court proceedings, which then makes an application to the High Court for the warrant to be endorsed for execution 'as soon as may be' (s. 13(1)). A European arrest warrant must be endorsed for execution for it to become effective in the state. The application to endorse is made *ex parte* before the High Court.

If the High Court is satisfied that the warrant complies with the provisions of the Act the court may make an order endorsing the warrant for execution (s. 13(2)).

Once endorsed for execution the warrant is transmitted to the Gardaí for the purpose of arresting the person named (s. 13(3)).

18.2.8 ARREST

Although there is a specialist Extradition Unit of An Garda Síochána based in Garda Headquarters, any member of An Garda Síochána may arrest the requested person in any part of the state.

An arrested person must be shown a copy of the European arrest warrant (within 24 hours if not immediately available on arrest) and once formally arrested shall be informed of certain rights as outlined in s. 13(4) and now listed as follows:

(a)   right to consent to surrender to the issuing state;

(b)   right to professional legal advice and representation;

(c)   right to an interpreter where appropriate.

Section 13(5) provides that the person arrested shall be brought to the High Court 'as soon as may be'.

There is no set time limit within which a European arrest warrant must be executed.

If a person sought on a European arrest warrant is in custody, he may be arrested on the warrant having been brought to the High Court for that purpose.

18.2.9 POST-ARREST—HIGH COURT PROCEEDINGS

Once arrested and before the High Court the representative of the applicant minister will outline the content of the European arrest warrant to the court, call the arresting Garda to give evidence of arrest and make any further application in respect of bail, custody or adjournment as considered necessary.

The arrested person either himself or through his legal adviser may cross-examine the arresting Garda, and make any application to the court considered necessary at that point.

The only issue at this stage of the proceedings for the High Court to adjudicate is whether the person arrested is the person in respect of whom the European arrest warrant was issued. If satisfied the person before the court is the person named in the warrant, the court will inform the person of the three rights (consent to surrender, obtain legal advice, interpreter) contained in s. 13(5)(c) which they had already been informed of at the time of arrest. Unless at this point the arrested person indicates a clear wish to consent to his surrender, the court will either remand him or her in custody or on bail to a notional hearing date which must be not more than 21 days from the date of arrest (s. 13(5)(b)). Such notional hearing date would rarely be the actual date on which the hearing of the application for surrender would take place.

The High Court has jurisdiction to admit an arrested person to bail (s. 13(5)(a)) subject to the overriding obligation under Article 12 of the Framework Decision to ensure that the respondent is ultimately made available for surrender. In practice an application for bail may be made on the first appearance in the High Court but if there is an objection to bail the court may require the application for bail to be brought by the respondent by way of affidavit and Notice of Motion on due notice to the applicant minister.

Should bail be granted to the respondent by the High Court the terms and conditions imposed will invariably include a condition to surrender passport and/or national identity card, an undertaking not to apply for a new one or to apply for any travel document capable of enabling travel out of the state, and an undertaking not to leave the jurisdiction, as well as more familiar terms such as signing on at a local Garda station and attending court on every occasion required.

There is an 'Extradition List' every Tuesday during the legal term in the High Court sitting in the Criminal Courts of Justice. All applications by either the applicant or the respondent, including notional hearing dates, bail, and adjournments, are dealt with in the Extradition Lists, on affidavit and by Notice of Motion if necessary. Hearing dates are allocated by the High Court judge dealing with European arrest warrant and extradition cases on any date available and the hearings take place in the High Court sitting in the Criminal Courts of Justice.

18.2.10 ARREST WITHOUT A WARRANT

Section 14 of the Act provides for emergency procedures allowing arrest without a warrant.

The Schengen Information System is a law enforcement database of participating countries holding information currently relating to 10 million persons and vehicles. It is constantly updated. The Criminal Justice (Miscellaneous Provisions) Act 2009 provides for active participation in the Schengen Information System by Gardaí and customs officers. Irish involvement is limited to the granting of a power of arrest to the Gardaí for the arrest of a person believed to be named in an 'alert . . . entered in the Schengen Information System for the arrest and surrender on foot of a European arrest warrant of a person named therein' (s. 2 definition).

A similar procedure on arrest applies to a person arrested under s. 14 as applies under s. 13. The person arrested is entitled to a copy of the 'alert' (as opposed to the warrant under s. 13), to professional legal advice and to the services of an interpreter (if required). A person arrested will be brought before the High Court and may be remanded in custody or on bail if the High Court is satisfied that the person before the court is the person named in the 'alert'. The court shall remand the person for a period not exceeding 14 days for production to the High Court of the European arrest warrant on foot of which the arrest was made (s. 14(3)(b)(ii)).

Once the European arrest warrant is received by the Central Authority the person arrested shall be brought to the High Court as soon as may be, and if the court is satisfied that the conditions of the Act have been complied with and the person before it is the person named in the warrant, the person will be informed of the right to consent to surrender, and if that right is not exercised at that time, shall be remanded either in custody or on bail to a notional hearing date within not less than 21 days. If the European arrest warrant is not produced on the date fixed by the court under s. 14(3)(b)(ii) the person shall be released from custody (s. 14(5)).

18.2.11 SURRENDER HEARING

Section 15 of the Act provides for a respondent to consent to surrender. The Framework Decision makes it clear that the responsibility for explaining the consequences of voluntary surrender to the respondent falls to legal counsel. Since the amendments to the Act introduced by the Criminal Justice (Miscellaneous Provisions) Act 2009, consent to surrender is effectively irrevocable and, therefore, it is imperative that the respondent's consent is fully informed.

Although the consent surrender hearing procedure is set out in s. 15, the hearing is not a mere formality. The court must be satisfied of a number of matters, including that the respondent is fully aware of the consequences of voluntary surrender and that legal advice has been received in that regard, and that the court is not precluded by ss. 21A, 22, 23, 24 or by Part 3 of the Act or the Framework Decision from making an order of surrender (see **18.2.21** and **18.3.1–18.3.8** for further discussion).

Section 16 of the Act provides that where a person does not consent to his or her surrender the court may make an order for surrender provided it is satisfied of a number of issues as set out in s. 16 and not precluded by the Act or the Framework Decision, as when making an order under s. 15 and as discussed later.

The procedure to be followed where a respondent does not consent to surrender is provided for by Order 98, Rule 5(1) of the Rules of the Superior Courts: 'where a person does not consent to his or her surrender to the issuing state . . . he shall be at liberty . . . to deliver to the solicitor for the Central Authority and file in the Central Office, Points of Objection to his or her surrender'.

Order 98, Rule 5(2) sets out in brief what Points of Objection should contain:

Points of Objection shall contain a statement in summary form of the grounds and of the material facts on which the person relies to resist the execution of the European arrest warrant but not the evidence by which such material facts are to be proved.

The evidence in a contested hearing under s. 16 is by way of affidavit (Order 98, Rule 7 of the Rules of the Superior Courts) and s. 20(3) allows the court to receive sworn documents in the form of declarations, affirmations or attestations in addition to affidavit evidence (precedents as per the SI referenced at **18.2.4**).

18.2.12 ORDERS FOR SURRENDER UNDER SECTIONS 15 AND 16

The High Court when making an order under s. 15 or s. 16 must be satisfied of a number of issues:

15.—(1) Where a person is brought before the High Court under section 13 , he or she may consent to his or her being surrendered to the issuing state and, where he or she does so consent, the High Court shall, if it is satisfied that—

(a) the European arrest warrant, or a facsimile or true copy thereof, has been endorsed in accordance with section 13 for execution of the warrant,

(b) the surrender of the person is not prohibited by section 22 , 23 or 24,

(c) the surrender of the person is not prohibited by Part 3 or the Framework Decision (including the recitals thereto),

(d) the person voluntarily consents to his or her being surrendered to the issuing state concerned and is aware of the consequences of his or her so consenting, and

(e) the person has obtained, or been given the opportunity of obtaining or being provided with, professional legal advice before consenting to his or her surrender,

make an order directing that the person be surrendered to such other person as is duly authorised by the issuing state to receive him or her.

(2) Where a person is brought before the High Court under section 14 , he or she may consent to his or her being surrendered to the issuing state and, where he or she does so consent, the High Court shall—

(a) upon production to it of the European arrest warrant and, where appropriate, a statement under section 11(3), or facsimile or true copies thereof, and

(b) if it is satisfied that—

(i) the surrender of the person is not prohibited by section 22 , 23 or 24,

(ii) the surrender of the person is not prohibited by Part 3 or the Framework Decision (including the recitals thereto),

(iii) the person voluntarily consents to his or her being surrendered to the issuing state and is aware of the consequences of his or her so consenting, and

(iv) the person has obtained, or been given the opportunity of obtaining or being provided with, professional legal advice and representation before consenting to his or her surrender,

make an order directing that the person be surrendered to such other person as is duly authorised by the issuing state to receive him or her.

(3) An order under this section shall not take effect until the expiration of a period of 10 days beginning on the date of the making of the order.

(4) Where the High Court makes an order under this section, it shall—

(a) inform the person to whom the order relates of his or her right to make a complaint under Article 40.4.2° of the Constitution at any time before his or her surrender to the issuing state,

(b) record in writing that the person concerned has consented to his or her being surrendered to the issuing state concerned, and

(c)   commit the person to a prison (or, if the person is not more than 21 years of age, to a remand institution) pending the carrying out of the terms of the order.

(5)   Subject to subsection (6) and section 18, a person to whom an order for the time being in force under this section applies shall be surrendered to the issuing state concerned not later than 10 days after—

(a)   the expiration of the period specified in subsection (3), or

(b)   such date (being a date that falls after the expiration of that period) as may be agreed by the Central Authority in the State and the issuing state.

(6)   Where a person makes a complaint under Article 40.4.2° of the Constitution, he or she shall not be surrendered to the issuing state while proceedings relating to the complaint are pending.

(7)   Subject to subsection (8), a person (to whom an order for the time being in force under this section applies) who is not surrendered to the issuing state in accordance with subsection (5), shall be released from custody immediately upon the expiration of the 10 days referred to in subsection (5), unless, upon such expiration, proceedings referred to in subsection (6) are pending.

(8)   Subsection (7) shall not apply if—

(a)   (i)   the person has been sentenced to a term of imprisonment for an offence of which he or she was convicted in the State,

(ii)   on the date on which he or she would, but for this subsection, be entitled to be released from custody under subsection (7), all or part of that term of imprisonment remains unexpired, and

(iii)   the person is required to serve all or part of the remainder of that term of imprisonment,

or

(b)   (i) the person has been charged with or convicted of an offence in the State, and

(ii)   on the date on which he or she would, but for this paragraph, be entitled to be released from custody under subsection (7), he or she is required to be in custody by virtue of having been remanded in custody pending his or her being tried, or the imposition of sentence, in respect of that offence.

(9)   A person who has consented under this section to his or her being surrendered may, at any time thereafter but before his or her surrender in accordance with an order under this section, withdraw his or her consent and, where he or she withdraws his or her consent—

(a)   the order made by the High Court under this section shall stand annulled, and

(b)   the period between the giving of such consent before the High Court and the withdrawal by him or her of such consent shall not be taken into account for the purposes of calculating the periods specified in subsections (10) and (11) of section 16.

16.—(1) Where a person does not consent to his or her surrender to the issuing state or has withdrawn his or her consent under section 15(9), the High Court may, upon such date as is fixed under section 13, make an order directing that the person be surrendered to such other person as is duly authorised by the issuing state to receive him or her provided that—

(a)   the High Court is satisfied that the person before it is the person in respect of whom the European arrest warrant was issued,

(b)   the European arrest warrant, or a facsimile or true copy thereof, has been endorsed in accordance with section 13 for execution of the warrant,

(c)   such undertakings as are required under this Act, or facsimile or true copies thereof, are provided to the court.

(d)   the surrender of the person is not prohibited by section 22 , 23 or 24, and

(e)   the surrender of the person is not prohibited by Part 3 or the Framework Decision (including the recitals thereto).

(2) Where a person does not consent to his or her surrender to the issuing state or has withdrawn his or her consent under section 15 (9), the High Court may, upon such date as is fixed under section 14, make an order directing that the person be surrendered to such other person as is duly authorised by the issuing state to receive him or her, provided that—

    (a) the European arrest warrant and, where appropriate, a statement under section 11(3), and such other undertakings as are required under this Act, or facsimile copies or true copies thereof are provided to the court,

    (b) the High Court is satisfied that the person before it is the person in respect of whom the European arrest warrant was issued,

    (c) the surrender of the person is not prohibited by section 22 , 23 or 24, and

    (d) the surrender of the person is not prohibited by Part 3 or the Framework Decision (including the recitals thereto).

(3) An order under this section shall not take effect until the expiration of 15 days beginning on the date of the making of the order.

(4) When making an order under this section the High Court shall also make an order committing the person to a prison (or if he or she is not more than 21 years of age, to a remand institution) there to remain pending his or her surrender in accordance with the order under this section, and shall inform the person—

    (a) that he or she will not, without his or her consent, be surrendered to the issuing state, before the expiration of the period of 15 days specified in subsection (3), and

    (b) of his or her right to make a complaint under Article 40.4.2° of the Constitution at any time before his or her surrender to the issuing state.

(5) Subject to subsection (6) and section 18, a person to whom an order for the time being in force under this section applies shall be surrendered to the issuing state not later than 10 days after—

    (a) the expiration of the period specified in subsection (3), or

    (b) such date (being a date that falls after the expiration of that period) as may be agreed by the Central Authority in the State and the issuing state.

(6) Where a person makes a complaint under Article 40.4.2° of the Constitution, he or she shall not be surrendered to the issuing state while proceedings relating to the complaint are pending.

(7) Subject to subsection (9), a person (to whom an order for the time being in force under this section applies) who is not surrendered to the issuing state in accordance with subsection (5), shall be released from custody immediately upon the expiration of the 10 days referred to in subsection (5), unless, upon such expiration, proceedings referred to in subsection (6) are pending.

(8) Where the High Court decides not to make an order under this section—

    (a) it shall give reasons for its decision, and

    (b) the person shall, subject to subsection (9), be released from custody.

(9) Subsection (8) shall not apply if—

    (a) (i) the person has been sentenced to a term of imprisonment for an offence of which he or she was convicted in the State,

        (ii) on the date on which he or she would, but for this subsection, be entitled to be released under subsection (8), all or part of the term of imprisonment remains unexpired, and

        (iii) the person is required to serve all or part of the remainder of that term of imprisonment,

    or

    (b) (i) the person has been charged with or convicted of an offence in the State, and

        (ii) on the date on which he or she would, but for this paragraph, be entitled to be released from custody under subsection (8), he or she is required to be in custody by virtue of having been remanded in custody pending his or her being tried, or the imposition of sentence, in respect of that offence.

(10) If the High Court has not, after the expiration of 60 days from the arrest of the person concerned under section 13 or 14, made an order under this section or section 15, or has decided not to make an order under this section, it shall direct the Central Authority in the State to inform the issuing judicial authority and, where appropriate, Eurojust in relation thereto and of the reasons therefor specified in the direction, and the Central Authority in the State shall comply with such direction.

(11) If the High Court has not, after the expiration of 90 days from the arrest of the person concerned under section 13 or 14, made an order under this section or section 15, or has decided not to make an order under this section, it shall direct the Central Authority in the State to inform the issuing judicial authority and, where appropriate, Eurojust in relation thereto and of the reason therefor specified in the direction, and the Central Authority in the State shall comply with such direction.

(12) An appeal against an order under this section or a decision not to make such an order may be brought in the Supreme Court on a point of law only.

The European arrest warrant states, where appropriate, the matters required by s. 45, i.e. that where the person arrested did not appear in person at the proceedings resulting in the sentence or detention order in respect of which the European arrest warrant was issued, certain criteria regarding notification are satisfied.

18.2.13   PROHIBITIONS UNDER SECTIONS 21A, 22, 23, 24

The court must also be satisfied that the surrender is not prohibited by s. 21A, 22, 23, or 24 of the Act, in that:

- there is an intention to prosecute (s. 21A);

- there is no intention to proceed against the person for offences other than those in the warrant (s. 22—rule of specialty); and

- there is no intention to surrender the person to another member state (s. 23) or to a third state (s. 24).

See **18.2.21** for further discussion.

18.2.14   REFUSAL OF SURRENDER

If surrender is refused by the High Court the respondent will be discharged from the proceedings. In the event that surrender is refused by the High Court because of a defect in proofs or a technical reason it is open for the issuing state to issue a subsequent warrant and for the Central Authority to make a further application under the Act.

In *MJELR v C McG* [2007] IEHC 47, where the issue of identity had not been proved to the satisfaction of the High Court in a previous application for surrender to the UK, the court on the subsequent application noted that the issue of identity had been resolved and there could be no abuse of process in that regard. In *MJELR v O Falluin* [2010] IESC 37, Finnegan J. rejected the argument that the issue of estoppel applied to a subsequent application for surrender stating 'I am satisfied that neither estoppel nor *res judicata* arise'. It is possible to resist a second application for surrender as in *MJELR v Aamond* [2006] IEHC 382, where given the exceptional circumstances of delay in that case the court held it would be oppressive to surrender.

18.2.15   SURRENDER ONCE AN ORDER IS MADE

Section 15(3) provides that an order made under s. 15 where a person consents to surrender shall not take effect for 10 days and s. 16(3) provides that the order made pursuant to that section shall not take effect for 15 days. Then, following the expiration of the 10- or 15-day time limits, surrender must be effected within 10 days. Sections 15(4)(d)(ii) and 16(4)(c)(ii) provide an exception to that rule in that they allow the Central Authority to apply to the High Court if it appears to the Central Authority that because of circumstances beyond the control of the state or the issuing state, the person will not be surrendered within the expiration of the time limit ordered. Upon such application the court, if satisfied of the circumstances of the application, will fix a new date for surrender and remand the person for a period not exceeding 10 days from the previous date fixed for surrender.

Following the decision of the Supreme Court in *Butenas v The Governor of Cloverhill Prison* [2008] 4 IR 189, a respondent is entitled to apply to the High Court for bail pending surrender and the court may grant bail where it deems it appropriate. Article 26 of the Framework Decision specifically provides for any time spent in custody on foot of the European arrest warrant to be deducted from any sentence to be served in the issuing state. The Central Authority should provide such information to the issuing state upon the surrender of the respondent.

18.2.16 PRACTICAL ARRANGEMENTS FOR SURRENDER

Once an order under s. 15 or s. 16 has been made by the court, arrangements will be made between the Central Authority and the issuing state for the person to be surrendered to representatives of the issuing state.

If remanded in custody pending surrender, the person will be brought from prison to the port (usually airport) by the Gardaí and there handed over to police from the issuing state. If that person is on bail pending surrender, the terms of bail will include an undertaking to attend at a time and place notified by the Gardaí for the purpose of surrender.

18.2.17 POSTPONEMENT OF ORDERS OF SURRENDER MADE UNDER SECTION 15 OR SECTION 16

Section 18 of the Act provides for the postponement of an order for surrender made pursuant to either s. 15 or s. 16. Postponement usually arises in circumstances where the respondent is subject to domestic proceedings and/or is serving a domestic sentence. Any order made by the High Court in such circumstances will reflect that surrender will only take place upon the conclusion of the domestic proceedings and/or any sentence imposed, and the court will make an order ending the postponement at the relevant time.

Postponement on humanitarian grounds is provided by s. 18(1)(a):

18.— (1) *The High Court may direct that the surrender of a person to whom an order under subsection (1) or (2) of section 15 or subsection (1) or (2) of section 16 applies be postponed in accordance with this section where—*

    (a) *the High Court is satisfied that circumstances exist that would warrant postponement on humanitarian grounds, including that a manifest danger to the life or health of the person concerned would likely be occasioned by his or her surrender to the issuing state.*

The humanitarian grounds must be exceptional to give rise to a postponement under s. 18, and any postponement is temporary and will be monitored by the court on an ongoing basis, and the High Court shall make an order ending the postponement of surrender when the court is satisfied that the circumstances referred to no longer exist.

18.2.18 CONDITIONAL SURRENDER

Section 19 of the Act provides for the High Court to direct a person whose surrender has been ordered under s. 15 or s. 16 who is serving a sentence in the state to be surrendered prior to the expiry of that sentence subject to conditions, and any term of imprisonment that the person is required to serve in the state shall be reduced by any period of time spent in custody or detention in the issuing state.

18.2.19 APPEAL

The unfettered right of appeal on a point of law available in the 2003 Act is now limited pursuant to s. 16(11), which provides that an appeal may only be brought to the Court of Appeal 'if, and only if, the High Court certifies that the order or decision involves a point of law of exceptional public importance and that it is desirable in the public interest that an appeal should be taken to the Court of Appeal'. Either the respondent or the applicant may make an application for a certificate of appeal following either the making of or refusal to make an order for surrender under s. 16.

An application for a certificate of appeal is made to the High Court at a hearing on a date allocated by the High Court, within a short time of the hearing of the substantive matter, where a point or a number of points of law are submitted to the court as being of exceptional public importance and also as being in the public interest for the Court of Appeal to determine.

A respondent may be remanded on bail or in custody, pending an application to the High Court for a certificate of appeal and pending appeal should a certificate be granted. The filing of a Notice of Appeal acts as a stay on the surrender.

18.2.20   ARTICLE 40 APPLICATIONS

Under both s. 15 and s. 16 of the European Arrest Warrant Act 2003, as amended, when making an order for surrender, the High Court is obliged to advise the respondent of his or her right to bring proceedings under Article 40.4.2 of the Constitution should he consider his or her detention is in any way unlawful. Following the decision of the Supreme Court in *McArdle v The Governor of Cloverhill Prison* [2005] 4 IR 249, it appears that there will be no distinction between Article 40 applications brought by those detained on foot of an order of the High Court for surrender pursuant to s. 15 or s. 16, and those brought by convicted prisoners.

18.2.21   PROHIBITIONS TO SURRENDER UNDER SECTIONS 21A, 22, 23, 24

18.2.21.1   Section 21A—refusal to surrender where no decision to prosecute

The difference between criminal justice systems in Europe has been a cause of many of the raised objections to surrender under s. 21A. In *MJELR v Olsson* [2011] IESC 1, it was argued that there had been no decision to prosecute by the issuing state (Sweden).

O'Donnell J. in his judgment stated:

> It is noteworthy, that on the evidence in this case, the position in relation to the appellant is not by any means unusual in the Swedish system, and indeed represents the norm in a number of European countries. It would be a surprising result if either the Framework Decision or the Act of 2003 were to be interpreted so as to prevent the execution of the European arrest warrant in respect of such countries and where (as here) the requesting authority had in the terms of the warrant, and in sworn evidence in the case, stated that the warrant was issued for the purposes of conducting a criminal prosecution. The High Court was entirely correct to conclude that there was here a clear intention to bring proceedings within the meaning of s10, and that the warrant could be said to be for the purposes of conducting a criminal prosecution within the meaning of the Framework Decision and that the only thing which stood in the way of commencement of such prosecution was the requirement of presence of the accused and the interview where he could respond to the investigation. In short, the intention of the Swedish prosecution authority to bring the appellant before the Swedish Court for the purpose of being charged is but a step in the prosecution process.

In *MJE v Jociene* [2013] IEHC 290, the High Court applied the test in *Olsson* and determined that the case was only at the pre-trial stage and the respondent a suspect. The strict requirements of s. 21A applied, and an intention to charge does not satisfy the conjunctive necessity to also try her. In *MJELR v Bailey* [2012] IESC 16, a document from the French state prosecutor specifically stated the case was at the investigation stage and the Supreme Court decided that the material provided by the issuing authority rebutted the presumption of a decision to charge in s. 21A(2).

18.2.21.2   Section 22—the Rule of Specialty

It was held in *Minister for Justice, Equality and Law Reform v Gotzlik* [2009] 3 IR 390, by Denham J. as follows:

The specialty rule, which has long been part of extradition law, arises to protect the person surrendered from being prosecuted or sentenced for another offence on which he has not been surrendered. Thus, a State could not request a person for one offence and then prosecute or sentence him for another offence on which he had not been surrendered. This protection is and was important to protect persons. It has arisen especially to protect persons from being prosecuted for political offences or for offences on which there was no double criminality.

Section 22 of the Act provides a general prohibition on surrender where there would result in a breach of the rule of specialty subject to certain exceptions such as where a surrendered person would receive a non-custodial sentence. There is also a provision in s. 22 which enables the issuing state to apply to the High Court, subsequent to surrender, for permission to either prosecute the surrendered person for other offences or to impose a sentence for other offences.

18.2.21.3 Surrender to another member state or third country

Section 23 of the Act allows the court to refuse to surrender where the issuing state 'does not provide' that a person surrendered to it will not be surrendered to another member state pursuant to a European arrest warrant. Section 24 of the Act allows the court to refuse to surrender in almost identical terms to s. 23 but to a 'third country'.

Section 30 of the Act provides that if two warrants are received by the state an extradition warrant shall have precedence over a European arrest warrant unless the minister requests otherwise.

18.3 Prohibition of Surrender—Part 3 of the European Arrest Warrant Act 2003

18.3.1 FUNDAMENTAL RIGHTS

Chapter 17 of this text gives detailed consideration to fundamental rights in the context of criminal proceedings. Section 37 of the Act prohibits surrender where it would contravene either the Constitution or the European Convention on Human Rights and there are reasonable grounds for believing that the warrant was issued for reasons based on the respondent's sex, race, religion, ethnic origin, nationality, language, political opinion or sexual orientation, or where the respondent would be subject to the death penalty or torture or other inhuman or degrading treatment.

Although many respondents have argued that surrender would be a breach of their constitutional rights or their rights under the European Convention, most arguments have been rejected by the High Court and/or the Supreme Court because of the overriding principle of mutual trust and confidence between member states.

18.3.1.1 Article 6 ECHR—Right to a fair trial

In *MJELR v Iordache* [2008] IEHC 186, arguments that the respondent's right to a fair trial and discrimination on grounds he was Roma were rejected. However, in the High Court decision of *MJE v Rostas* [2014] EHC 391, the s. 37(1)(a) objection was upheld and surrender was refused as the court believed the supporting evidence was sufficient to demonstrate consistency with commonplace ill treatment and discrimination by police and officials against Roma persons at the time of her trial and a denial of justice had been suffered in her Romanian trial. In *MJELR v Stapleton* [2008] 1 IR 669, the Supreme Court rejected the argument that delay and the right to an expeditious trial would be a breach of the respondent's rights. Fennelly J. stated in his judgment: 'It follows, in my view, that the courts of the executing member state, when deciding whether to make an order for surrender must proceed on the assumption that the courts of the issuing member state will, as is required by Article 6.1 of the Treaty on European Union, "respect … human rights and fundamental freedoms"'. It is therefore only rights affected by the actual surrender of the respondent (as opposed to trial or imprisonment) which the courts will consider under s. 37, on the basis that any such potential breach can be litigated in the requesting state. However, in the recent case of *The Minister for Justice and Equality v Savachenko* [2015] High Court (unreported), Edwards J. refused an application for surrender to Russia where there was 'strong evidence to suggest that in many Russian trials no more than lip service is paid to the presumption of innocence'.

18.3.1.2   Article 3 ECHR—Prohibition of torture

In *MJELR v Rettinger* [2010] IESC 45, a case where prison conditions in Poland were argued as being in breach of the right not to be subjected to inhuman or degrading treatment, the Supreme Court set out the approach to be taken when considering an objection to surrender on Article 3 grounds 'must be substantial grounds for believing there is a real risk of ill treatment if returned'.

In *MJELR v McGuigan* [2013] IEHC 216, evidence of prison conditions in Lithuania was such as to uphold the s. 37 objection, but the court emphasised its decision on prison conditions in this case was based on the strength of the evidence adduced and does not purport to propound any new principle of law and does not have precedent value; it represents a decision on the facts of the individual case.

18.3.1.3   Article 8 ECHR—Right to respect for private and family life

In *MJELR v Gorman* [2010] IEHC 210 it was argued, *inter alia*, that surrender to the UK would be a breach of Article 8 of the European Convention on Human Rights. The High Court considered in the exceptional circumstances of the case that: 'the obligation to surrender which this State is under by virtue of its international obligations must yield to the Article 8 rights of the respondent'.

In *MJE v TE* [2013] IEHC 323, the High Court sets out a 22-point test to be applied by the court in Article 8 cases. In *MJLR v ES* [2014] IEHC 376, as the Article 8 rights of the respondent and her daughter were supported by expert psychological evidence that separation would cause the daughter devastating and irreversible effects, it was held surrender would be injurious and harmful and disproportionate in the circumstances, and the s. 37(1) objection was upheld. However, many other cases where Article 8 rights have been raised as objections to surrender have not been successful, e.g. in *MJLR v JAT* [2014] IEHC 320, it was held the private interests of the respondent and family do not outweigh the substantial public interest in the extradition.

In view of the decisions of the High Court in cases where ECHR rights and constitutional rights are raised, it is incumbent on all practitioners to take comprehensive instructions from clients and seek expert reports in respect of issues such as prison conditions or medical or psychological issues.

18.3.2   CORRESPONDENCE AND MINIMUM GRAVITY

Section 38 of the Act states that the offence in the European arrest warrant must correspond to an offence in the state and minimum gravity criteria must apply.

18.3.2.1   Correspondence

Dual criminality or correspondence of offences has long been the cornerstone of extradition proceedings. Section 10 of the Extradition Act 1965 requires that the offence be one which is: 'punishable under the laws of the requesting country and the State'.

Article 2.2 of the Framework Decision lists the categories of offences to be set out in a European arrest warrant and to be ticked as appropriate to each case:

- participation in a criminal organisation;
- terrorism;
- trafficking in human beings;
- sexual exploitation of children and child pornography;
- illicit trafficking in narcotic drugs and psychotropic substances;
- illicit trafficking in weapons, munitions and explosives;
- corruption;

- fraud, including that affecting the financial interests of the European Communities within the meaning of the Convention of 26 July 1995 on the protection of the European Communities' financial interests;
- laundering of the proceeds of crime;
- counterfeiting currency, including of the euro;
- computer-related crime;
- environmental crime, including illicit trafficking in endangered animal species and in endangered plant species and varieties;
- facilitation of unauthorised entry and residence;
- murder, grievous bodily injury;
- illicit trade in human organs and tissue;
- kidnapping, illegal restraint and hostage-taking;
- racism and xenophobia;
- organised or armed robbery;
- illicit trafficking in cultural goods, including antiques and works of art;
- swindling;
- racketeering and extortion;
- counterfeiting and piracy of products;
- forgery of administrative documents and trafficking therein;
- forgery of means of payment;
- illicit trafficking in hormonal substances and other growth promoters;
- illicit trafficking in nuclear or radioactive materials;
- trafficking in stolen vehicles;
- rape;
- arson;
- crimes within the jurisdiction of the International Criminal Court;
- unlawful seizure of aircraft/ships;
- sabotage.

If a listed offence is ticked on the warrant there is no need for correspondence to be proved unless there is a manifest incongruity between the ticked offence and the offence described in the body of the warrant. In the event that there is no ticked offence on the warrant the court must be satisfied that the offence specified in the warrant does correspond to an offence in this state.

18.3.2.2   Minimum gravity

Not only must the offence correspond with an offence in this state but the minimum gravity requirement must also be satisfied.

Section 38 of the Act provides:

    (a)   ...

        (i)   under the law of the issuing state the offence is punishable by imprisonment or detention for a maximum period of not less than 12 months, or

        (ii)   a term of imprisonment or detention of not less than 4 months has been imposed on the person in respect of the offence in the issuing state, and the person is required under the law of the issuing state to serve all or part of that term of imprisonment, or

    (b)   the offence is an offence to which paragraph 2 of Article 2 of the Framework Decision applies and under the law of the issuing state the offence is punishable by imprisonment for a maximum period of not less than 3 years.

In cases where no sentence has been imposed and the respondent is wanted for prosecution, surrender may only be ordered where the maximum sentence for the offence is at least 12 months' imprisonment. Where the warrant cites an Article 2.2 offence, that is a ticked offence, s. 38 provides that the offence must be punishable by a maximum sentence of at least three years.

18.3.2.3   Pardon or amnesty

Section 39 of the Act provides that a person shall not be surrendered where he has been granted a pardon under Article 13.6 of the Constitution or a pardon or amnesty under the laws of the issuing state for the offence specified in the warrant, or where he has become immune from prosecution or punishment by virtue of an Act of the Oireachtas for the offence as specified in the warrant.

18.3.2.4   Double jeopardy

Section 41 of the Act seeks to prevent a person being tried within member states in relation to the same conduct. Section 42 of the Act provides for a court to refuse to surrender a person where: 'proceedings are pending in the State against the person for an offence consisting of an act or omission of which the offence specified in the European arrest warrant in respect of him or her consists in whole or in part'.

18.3.2.5   Age limits

Section 43 of the Act prohibits surrender where the offence specified in the European arrest warrant corresponds to an offence in the state but where a person of the same age as the person for which the warrant was issued could not be proceeded against in the state by virtue of age.

18.3.2.6   Extra territorial offences

Section 44 of the Act provides:

> *A person shall not be surrendered under this Act if the offence specified in the European arrest warrant issued in respect of him or her was committed or is alleged to have been committed in a place other than the issuing state and the act or omission of which the offence consists does not, by virtue of having been committed in a place other than the State, constitute an offence under the law of the State.*

Two cases in 2012, *MJELR v Bailey* [2012] IESC 16 and *MJE v Connolly* [2012] IEHC 575, were decided in favour of the respondents and surrender refused on issues relating to extraterritoriality, but both were decided on the specific circumstances and the facts of the case. However, there are a number of statutes which provide for extraterritorial jurisdiction, the offences covered being, *inter alia*, murder, manslaughter, conspiracy or soliciting murder, offences aboard Irish registered ships or aircraft, terrorism offences, certain sexual offences, offences relating to organised crime, treason, interference with witnesses or jurors, war crimes.

18.3.2.7   Trials in absentia

In summary, s. 45 of the Act provides:

> *A person shall not be surrendered under this Act if he or she did not appear in person at the proceedings resulting in the sentence or detention order in respect of which the EAW was issued unless the warrant indicates the matters required as set out in the table to this section.*

The table referred to in s. 45 is a questionnaire to be completed by the issuing state including information regarding the person's presence or not at trial, whether summoned or not, whether aware of a scheduled trial or not, whether served with the result of the trial or not, and if not so served, they will be served without delay after surrender and informed of their rights to a retrial or appeal, and is incorporated into the warrant. The recent Court of Appeal decision in *The Minister for Justice and Equality v Palonka* [2015] IECA 69 and the High Court decision in *The Minister for Justice and Equality v Lipinski* [2015] (unreported) provide detailed analyses of the provisions of s. 45.

18.4   The Legal Aid (Custody Issues) Scheme

The right of the respondent to be provided with professional legal representation is provided for by s. 13 of the Act. High Court European arrest warrant and extradition proceedings are not covered by legal aid legislation and therefore the discretionary Legal Aid (Custody Issues) Scheme applies to those eligible. A statement of means is required to be submitted to the court and to the Chief State Solicitor. An eligible respondent's legal representative may be paid their reasonable legal fees and disbursements on the granting of a recommendation by the High Court at the conclusion of the proceedings. The court should be informed at the earliest opportunity in the proceedings that it is intended an application will be made for a recommendation under the scheme. If it is intended to obtain expert reports on behalf of the respondent, the court should be asked to note that fact as soon as possible so that any final order can reflect that the scheme will cover experts' fees.

18.5   Proportionality

Throughout the proposals in the Tampere Milestones the issue of serious crime is the focus, specifically 'juvenile, urban and drug-related crime', 'trafficking in drugs and human beings as well as terrorism' and 'Special action against money laundering', i.e. serious criminal activity.

Although the intended purpose of the European arrest warrant was to combat serious criminal activity within member states, in practice the vast majority of warrants are issued for relatively minor offences, and it is the view of eminent practitioners in the field that this is causing unavoidable delay in the courts and imposing a considerable expense upon the state out of all proportion to the offence for which surrender is sought.

In an Interim Report on Best Evidence in EAW Cases prepared by Justice/The International Commission of Jurists/The European Criminal Bar Association, it has been observed:

> There have been arguments that European arrest warrants have been issued in cases which do not justify the costs of the surrender procedure. Because the Framework Decision does not include a proportionality test there is no need for the issuing Member State to consider the necessity and suitability of a European arrest warrant in a specific case … (It is recognized there is a) need for a test which balances the seriousness of the offence against the consequences of … (surrender).

The Council of the EU following a review of recommendations in the final report on the fourth round of mutual evaluations concerning the European arrest warrant and surrender procedures among member states of the EU has concluded that with a view to reaching a coherent solution at European Union level regarding the proportionality requirement for the issuing of any European arrest warrant, the competent authorities should, before deciding to issue a warrant, consider proportionality by assessing a number of important factors including the seriousness of the offence and the likely penalty but that a re-examination of this issue is required.

18.6   Conclusion

In practice the law in Ireland relating to extradition is a hybrid of criminal and civil law. Essentially criminal matters are dealt with through the High Court civil process of Notices of Motion and affidavits.

It has been stated that the European Arrest Warrant Act 2003, as originally passed, was unworkable due to the complexity of the system and the lack of engagement in the legislative process by the Oireachtas at the time the Act was passed. This position has been remedied to a large extent by the various amendments contained in the Criminal Justice (Terrorist Offences) Act 2005, the Criminal Justice (Miscellaneous Provisions) Act 2009, and the European Arrest Warrant (Application to Third Countries and Amendment) and Extradition (Amendment) Act 2012, and matters have improved considerably.

PART VIII

PRACTICE SKILLS AND MANAGEMENT

CHAPTER 19

THE SKILLS OF THE CRIMINAL ADVOCATE

19.1 Introduction

Advocacy is typically presented as both an art and a science. Consequently, it has been accorded an aura that can appear daunting to the trainee and the newly qualified practitioner. It is helpful therefore to demystify it and place this skill in context. Advocacy skills generically encompass interaction within all elements of society, presenting as sharing of ideas, opinions, and arguments.

Advocacy in a legal context, of necessity, builds on these generic advocacy skills within society. Coupled with an understanding of the principles of a given area of law and the manner in which it is procedurally applied, all solicitors have the potential to become advocates in any area of law.

Applied in legal practice, this general conceptualisation of advocacy would occur as a solicitor advises a client as to the various legal options available in relation to a specific problem or set of problems, between lawyers discussing a case over the phone, or between those engaged in the negotiation process.

19.2 Advocacy in the Criminal Practice

A solicitor has a right of audience in all courts in our criminal justice system. There is little room for negotiation in the Irish criminal justice process, although there are unofficial custom and practice overtures in existence with regard to plea bargaining. Other legal skills are also employed in criminal litigation practice, e.g. client interviewing and counselling, legal and factual investigation, and drafting skills.

19.2.1 THE DISTRICT COURT ENVIRONMENT

Solicitor advocacy exists throughout criminal defence and prosecution practice, in the context of the District Court system, including the attendance by the defence solicitor on the client who has been detained at the Garda station. The solicitor will interact as an advocate in the following situations:

- during the initial visit to the client in custody;
- during interviewing or questioning of the suspect by the Gardaí;
- when conversing with the member in charge of the Garda station;
- while presiding and representing the client's interests at an identification parade;
- when presenting the initial applications for legal aid and bail;
- when taking the client's instructions;
- when advising the client with regard to the plea options that are open to him or her;
- while remanding cases;

- when presenting pleas in mitigation;
- while running a trial;
- during the presentation of probation and community services reports.

The solicitor who represents the Director of Public Prosecutions (DPP) will have consultations with the prosecuting Gardaí, advise them on proofs, and assist in the presentation of the facts on behalf of the state when the accused pleads either 'guilty' or 'not guilty'.

19.2.2   THE SUPERIOR COURTS ENVIRONMENT

In the context of the superior courts, the solicitor typically employs a barrister but if s/he chooses to, s/he may assume the role of advocate in the following situations:

- High Court bail applications;
- appeals to the High Court against a District Court refusal to grant bail;
- appeals to the High Court against bail terms that were fixed by the District Court and that the accused believes are excessive;
- judicial reviews at a High Court level;
- the arraignment of the accused client sent forward for trial to the Circuit Criminal Court, Special Criminal Court, and the Central Criminal Court;
- the empanelling of juries (where seven challenges can be made 'without cause' and seven 'with cause shown');
- the application to the trial court for a dismissal where the defence is of the view that the prosecution has not established a *prima facie* case.

19.3   Collaboration Between the Solicitor and the Criminal Bar

Because a busy criminal practitioner cannot appear for every client on a given day, in practice, a lot of the pre-trial procedures are delegated to colleagues at the Criminal Bar, both at District Court and Superior Court levels. Invariably, those colleagues will also be instructed in relation to the trial itself and will collaborate with the instructing solicitor with regard to advice on proofs in preparation for trial.

It is crucial that best practice be followed with regard to the early introduction of the barrister to the client. Whilst the seminal relationship is between the solicitor and the client, an accused whose liberty is at stake must have a fiduciary relationship with instructed counsel.

Further guidance with regard to the correct management of a criminal practice can be gleaned from **Chapter 20**.

19.4   Sensitivity to Client Needs

19.4.1   THE DEFENCE SOLICITOR

As implied in **Chapter 20** on Managing a Criminal Litigation Practice, sometimes, one's clients may emanate from a less privileged background than that of the practitioner. By analogy, a dearth of literacy skills may prejudice the client's ability to comprehend the content of the charge sheet, witness statements, reports from expert witnesses retained, and the contents of the book of evidence, where applicable. It is important to be mindful of such impediments, and to incorporate a sensitive methodology to facilitate the reading of materials and the dictation by the client of relevant statements and instructions.

Some clients will be suffering the consequences of substance abuse due to their addiction to alcohol, drugs or other intoxicants. Others may present with psychological or psychiatric disabilities.

Clients who face criminal prosecution are usually tense and worried. Those who have knowledge of the criminal justice system may present as nonchalant, but nevertheless it is crucial to be acutely aware that their continued liberty may be at stake if the prosecution proves the allegation against them beyond reasonable doubt. Many clients are not familiar with the criminal justice system at any level and are therefore terrified to find themselves in what they consider an alien environment: e.g. juveniles, a first-time alleged offender, and those who are accused of road traffic offences or regulatory crime. Consequently, sensitivity to a client's needs is a prerequisite to put the client at ease, culminating in the solicitor's enhanced ability to obtain clear instructions and to render salient advice.

19.4.2   THE PROSECUTING SOLICITOR

As a prosecutor, similar client-focused skills are required to ensure that full and relevant instructions are received through the members of the Gardaí from the alleged victims of crime, witnesses to crime, and forensic experts.

The fact that the victim is 'just another prosecution witness', because the DPP prosecutes on behalf of the people of Ireland, can leave that victim with a sense of being marginalised. Our adversarial criminal justice system also tends to exacerbate the victim's anxiousness. Due to some lobbying by rape crisis centres, a level of access to legal advice has been given to victims of sexual offences to ensure that they are aware of court procedure. The victim's legal adviser does not, however, partake in the processes of the criminal trial. Victim impact reports apply to the sentencing of perpetrators of violent crime. This procedure is discussed in detail in **Chapter 14**, which deals with sentencing matters in general. The sensitivity of the prosecution team to the concerns of the victim will result in the improved composure of that witness at trial.

As outlined in **Chapter 3**, Irish criminal justice policy at government, DPP, and criminal justice agency level now embraces victim-centred justice processes. Directive 2012/29/EU establishing minimum standards on the rights, support, and protection of victims of crime, has brought victim-centred justice centre stage. As a Directive, it has direct effect in all EU member states but it has yet to be transposed into Irish domestic legislation. The prosecuting solicitor will have received the file through the Office of the DPP, who, in turn, has been briefed by the investigating Gardaí. Mindful of the burden of proof that applies to the prosecution of a criminal matter, as outlined in **Chapter 10**, the state must ensure that there is no break in the chain of evidence presented at trial. Consequently, the evidence must be scrutinised and extra statements of evidence must be obtained, where necessary and possible, to ensure that a *prima facie* case is presented in court.

19.5   The Preparation of a Criminal Case

19.5.1   DUTIES OF DEFENCE AND PROSECUTION SOLICITORS

Every advocate in court is only as good as the instructions obtained from the client and the legal research undertaken in preparing the case for trial. It is the defence solicitor's duty to ensure that:

- the instructions taken are detailed;
- all appropriate witnesses have been interviewed;
- subpoenas have been issued where necessary; and
- all necessary expert witnesses have been approached, have produced the necessary reports, and are available or 'on standby' for the trial date.

It is the prosecuting solicitor's duty to ensure that:

- all statements have been obtained legally as outlined in **Chapter 10**;
- statements have been accurately recorded;

- all witnesses are notified of the date on which they are required to attend at court, having received subpoenas where necessary; and

- the defence solicitor is notified of all relevant dates.

A prosecutor has a duty to ensure that all relevant facts and law are before the court.

19.5.2   RESEARCH

It is incumbent on both prosecution and defence criminal lawyers to ensure that they are up to date with all recent developments in criminal law. It is reckless and negligent in the extreme for a defence lawyer to consider appearing in a criminal case without diligent preparation through proper research of the applicable statute and case law. In criminal cases, the right to liberty of a citizen is at stake, or some other penalty (other than the loss of liberty) will apply on conviction. The risk of a conviction for any accused person can have serious consequences for his or her lifetime.

Similarly, the victim of the alleged crime has a right to expect best practice from the organs of the state. When the DPP, at the suit of a member of the Gardaí, is prosecuting on behalf of the people of Ireland through the chief prosecuting solicitor and his or her colleagues, the appointed state advocate must ensure that there has been meticulous preparation of the prosecution's case.

19.5.3   TAKING INSTRUCTIONS FROM A CLIENT

The same best-practice rules that apply to all areas of practice apply to the skill of taking instructions from the client. The matters averted to in **Chapter 20** are a minimum standard to ensure the provision of a good service to one's client, and taking initial instructions will require at least an hour to facilitate the interview of, and advice to, the client.

The defence solicitor will be on notice of the offence alleged and of the necessary research required in advance of the first consultation through attendance on the accused whilst in detention, the presence of the solicitor during the Garda interview, presence in the court when the client is brought there in custody, or on receipt of a certificate of legal aid. This level of preparation will assist the advice on proofs process, the ascertaining of gaps that appear in relation to those proofs on receipt of the client's instructions and decisions regarding the best strategy in court. The relationship between solicitor and client that is forged at this first consultation will permeate for the duration of the case. Care should be taken, before embarking on any case, that the solicitor is acting in compliance with the accepted applicable codes of ethical conductas outlined in **Chapters 1** and **20**.

19.5.3.1   Initial instructions and the use of a checklist method

Checklists are an invaluable aid in executing any process successfully. Having one for trial preparation will ensure that you get all relevant personal details from your client, including:

- name;
- address;
- contact numbers;
- nationality (where applicable);
- special needs and disabilities;
- substance addiction history (if any);
- medical history (where relevant, e.g. substance addiction);
- responsibilities to dependants (if any);
- educational achievements;
- practical training courses attended, e.g. FÁS or SOLAS courses;
- acquired skills;

- any history of involvement with the criminal justice system, particularly previous convictions (if any);

- any other pending charges, appeals or judicial review matters, or outstanding bench warrants for breach of bail conditions;

- any temporary release (parole) conditions that are in operation;

- the details of any potential bails persons (if necessary);

- the details of any medical condition during the detention period that warrants being attended on by a doctor.

The very personal nature of some of the questions that arise in these circumstances warrants that it is incumbent on the practitioner to explain to the client in advance that it is necessary to obtain such information for the following reasons, some of which will require diplomatic explanation.

- If the accused is in custody or in custody with consent to bail, it will be necessary to ascertain that a proposed bails person is acceptable to the courts under the terms of the Bail Act 1997, as outlined in **Chapter 7**.

- If the accused is a foreign national, it may be necessary to apply to the court for the services of an interpreter.

- It may sometimes be necessary to assess the possibility of psychological or psychiatric difficulties that could influence a client's 'fitness to plead', and the consequent presence of the *mens rea* necessary for the crime alleged and the ability to comprehend the difficulty that presents with the allegation.

- Particular skills and educational background, as well as the court's recognition of dependant responsibilities, could favour the imposition of non-custodial sentences of a community service nature, in the event of the court handing down a conviction.

- The risk of incarceration and other forms of sentencing, in the event of a conviction, warrants the advance preparation of pleas in mitigation.

- Previous convictions, applicable temporary release conditions, and the fact that there may be other pending litigation against the client have a direct bearing on the advice given by the solicitor on the risk of incarceration and sentencing generally.

- Addiction difficulties may require that the case be disposed of in what are colloquially referred to as 'the Drugs Courts', where the focus is on rehabilitation rather than retribution.

- The administering of any drugs by the duty medical practitioner during the detention period may adversely affect the admissibility of any statement of admission allegedly made.

- The attendance of a doctor on the detainee may occasionally corroborate an account of the accused alleging the statement was not voluntary and was acquired under duress.

- Attendance by a medical practitioner in the context of a charge of driving whilst intoxicated, for the purpose of obtaining a blood or urine sample, as outlined in **Chapter 15**.

19.5.3.2   Initial documentation requirements

The initial consultation may be at the solicitor's office if the accused is released on bail to the next remand date, as outlined in **Chapter 8**. Alternatively, the first consultation may occur in a place of detention or imprisonment, because the accused may be on bail on the instant charge, but in custody on another matter. It is also possible that bail was refused, resulting in a remand in custody, or that the status quo is one of a remand in custody with consent to bail. If either of the latter two situations prevails, the issue of having one's client released on bail will take precedence during the first consultation. For an in-depth discussion on bail go to **Chapter 7**.

The client will have been handed a charge sheet after being arrested, detained, and cautioned. Alternatively, the client may have received a summons some time after the Gardaí made their initial inquiries. The prosecution may have commenced the investigation as a result of confidential information that resulted in the issue of a search warrant. As discussed in **Chapter 5**, it is customary that the defence solicitor will have been in attendance at the Garda station when the accused was detained and had sight of the custody record and attended an identification parade. However, if the solicitor was for some reason not present s/he is obliged to become fully briefed on all that occurred in the Garda station as soon as possible, in which circumstances an application for a *Gary Doyle* order as discussed in **Chapter 11** arises. The accused may or may not have made a voluntary statement of admission to the police. The provisions of certain legislation, as discussed in **Chapter 4**, which limits the right of the detainee to remain silent during interrogation, may or may not apply (e.g. the Offences Against the State Act 1939 (as amended), the Criminal Justice Act 1984 (as amended), and the Criminal Justice (Drug Trafficking) Act 1996). It should be noted that Part 4 of the Criminal Justice Act 2007 makes inroads into the right to silence and inferences as discussed in **Chapters 5, 10**, and **17**.

It is usual that one is in receipt of the certificate of legal aid at the time of the first consultation. If an application for legal aid has yet to be made, the accused should complete one, or be facilitated in so doing if literacy difficulties prevail. The ramifications of false declarations by the accused with regard to his or her disposable income or employment circumstances should be carefully explained.

19.5.3.3　Initial documentation checklist

A checklist outlining all of the following permutations is a useful discipline to aid the recording of initial instructions:

- a statement of means;
- a legal aid certificate;
- a copy of the custody record (if relevant);
- the charge sheet or summons;
- the search warrant;
- a copy of sworn information grounding the warrant;
- the details of the identification parade;
- copies of all statements made by witnesses, including any voluntary statement made by the accused;
- the criminal record of any prosecution witness;
- if a client has been videotaped, one should also ask for a copy of the tape;
- copies of, or access to, any relevant exhibits.

Since the introduction of s. 56 of the Criminal Justice Act 2007, the production of the videotape of a client's questioning at the Garda station is now at the discretion of the court.

19.5.3.4　The '*Gary Doyle* Letter' procedure

As discussed in **Chapter 11**, the defence is entitled to a copy of any alleged voluntary statement of admission made by the accused and should always seek it from the prosecuting Garda. If the Garda does not comply with the request, the defence should apply to the judge for a direction of compliance with the request, followed by a letter of request to the Garda or the assigned state prosecutor.

The disclosure of documentation is governed by *DPP v Gary Doyle* [1994] 1 ILRM 529. Essentially, this case decided that a district judge may, at his or her discretion, order that statements be handed over to the defence, if this is deemed necessary in the interests of justice. The criteria that determine a judge's consideration of disclosure include:

- the seriousness of the charge;
- the importance of the statements or documents;
- the fact that the accused had been adequately informed of the nature and substance of the accusation; and
- the likelihood of risk of injustice in failing to furnish the statements or documents to the accused.

19.5.3.5　The penultimate preparatory steps

Prior to trial all charge sheets, statements, books of evidence, additional evidence, and depositions should be read by the solicitor to the client whilst recording the client's responses to their content. On completion of instructions from the client, the record of those instructions should also be read over and the client should be invited to sign that record. Occasionally, a manipulative client who wishes to delay the inevitable conclusion of a case that is likely to result in a conviction may endeavour to disagree with the manner in which the solicitor is handling a case. A signed record of instructions will militate against protracted discussions and/or argument on that issue. Instructions that have been methodically recorded in a logical sequence can be of enormous benefit when the instructed solicitor is involved in the examination, cross-examination, and re-examination of witnesses in the case.

The client should be given an initial indication with regard to the procedure that will apply at each stage of the proceedings in court. Lack of such clarification often results in confusion and uncertainty on the client's part, sometimes resulting in the irritation of the bench as the client tries to address the court in the presence of, and to the embarrassment of, the instructed solicitor.

A client should be advised that if he or she recalls any salient details that were omitted at the first consultation, another appointment should be arranged immediately. Similarly, the solicitor should contact the client for further consultation upon receipt of documentation pertinent to the trial.

It is always necessary to have a final consultation with the client on the day before the trial. Some time may have passed since the trial date was originally fixed. The client will need to be advised with regard to the application of the rules of the law of evidence during the trial, in a manner that is practically comprehensible and, in particular, what to expect from the examination, cross-examination, and re-examination process.

19.5.3.6   Consultations with other witnesses

One should ascertain whether or not it is necessary to secure expert evidence on behalf of the client. On engaging an expert witness for a client who is on legal aid, the Department of Justice and Equality will discharge the relevant fee on receipt of its completed form 'LA5' which is available on its website http://www.justice.ie. The client's instructions may reveal the necessity to interview and access the potential probative value of independent witnesses or alibi witnesses. Once notified that the accused has alibi witnesses in relation to matters being tried on indictment, the state prosecutor's office will interview these witnesses to determine the veracity of such statements and the consequent effect on the continued prosecution of the matter.

Witness summonses should be obtained where necessary to secure the presence of witnesses. Any witness who does not attend in answer to a summons is deemed to be in contempt of court and the trial judge has jurisdiction to issue a warrant for the arrest of that errant witness.

19.6   The Trial Date

Having researched the law, taken full instructions, obtained necessary reports, and arranged the presence of all necessary witnesses, including expert witnesses where appropriate, it is necessary thereafter to concentrate on the skills necessary for the prosecution and defence of the evidence presented. In the exercise of these skills, one must be prepared, have a goal, a clear strategy, have audible voice projection, and, finally, act confidently.

19.6.1   THE COMPETING GOALS OF ADVOCATES

In a criminal prosecution in an adversarial criminal justice system, the basic goal is to 'win'. This goal will obviously be linked to whether one is a prosecutor or defence solicitor. The prosecutor will be endeavouring beyond a reasonable doubt to establish the presence of all of the ingredients of the offence, whereas the defence solicitor will endeavour to create a 'reasonable doubt' as to the presence of one or more of those ingredients. Where a number of charges have been made against a particular accused, a defence goal may be an acquittal on one of the more serious charges, coupled with an acceptance of the likelihood of a conviction on one of the lesser charges.

19.6.2   THE ADVOCATES' RULES OF ENGAGEMENT

19.6.2.1   The skills armoury

The methodology engaged by both prosecutors and defence solicitors is to analyse the facts of the case through the media of:

- examination-in-chief (direct examination) of one's own witnesses;
- cross-examination of witnesses for the 'other side'; and
- re-examination, where permitted.

Rules exist that assist the advocate in:

- eliciting the relevant information from one's witness;
- achieving familiarity with the permissible use of leading questions;
- identifying the objectives of cross-examination;
- prioritising the sequence and types of questions (e.g. open questions and closed questions);
- knowing when one should press an advantage; and
- developing an intuition regarding when it is prudent not to question further.

It is necessary that an advocate, in direct examination, can guide the witness when giving salient evidence under oath and then, in cross-examination, discredit the opponent's witnesses' testimony, thereby supporting his or her own client's side of the story.

If an advocate has an intention to refer to case law or a textbook at District Court level, she or he should photocopy the relevant pages twice, thereby providing one's own copy and a copy for the opposing advocate, whilst giving the original to the presiding judge.

19.6.2.2   The strategy of opposing advocates

On completion of case preparation, a clear strategy is needed, which will be dependent on whether one is a prosecutor or a defence solicitor. A prosecutor will introduce the allegation to the court and will endeavour to establish a chain of evidence that links the accused to the wrong committed. If any single ingredient of an offence is not established, there will be a link missing in that chain and the case for the prosecution will fail.

If one is acting on the defence side, the strategy will be to look for that missing link in the prosecution chain of evidence. A chain is only as strong as its weakest link; therefore, in deciding strategy, the defence solicitor will seek the weakest link in the chain of evidence and capitalise on it, with the intention of establishing a reasonable doubt with regard to the reliability of the evidence against the accused. If submissions to this effect are successfully submitted, the presiding judge will be persuaded that the client is entitled to an acquittal.

19.6.2.3   Audible advocacy

It is essential that one can project one's voice sufficiently whereby the judge, witnesses, and opposing advocate can hear everything that is said. The witness who is being examined must hear questions asked and answers given, as must the judge and other participants. In particular, the accused must be aware of everything that occurs. He or she must be in a position to instruct his or her advocate to rebut any evidence given or allegations made against him or her by witnesses or, if s/he chooses to give sworn testimony, to rebut that evidence or those allegations in his or her direct evidence.

19.6.2.4   The confident profile

Confidence is an important element in good advocacy and has a positive effect on one's client, and an audible presence will serve to create and enhance the necessary confidence. The trainee advocate should build confidence during the in-office training period, by assisting senior colleagues in the advisory and preparatory stages of pre-trial procedure.

An appropriate example of the armoury available to advocates can be observed in bail applications, pleas in mitigation, trials, and sentencing procedures. Such observation will inform the nervous beginner.

With regard to appropriate advocacy skills, the competent examination of witnesses, the recognition of the duties of one's position as an officer of the court, and the proffering of courtesy towards the judiciary, all witnesses, and colleagues, one can initially acquire skills by advocating in simple adjournments. Such modest beginnings will yield dividends in the creation of an environment that is amenable to the advocate, culminating in a positive self-image.

The judge determines matters of law and fact in a court of summary trial. Maintaining eye contact with the District Court judge will variously strengthen the impact of one's advocacy or alert one to the necessity of not pursuing a line of argument that does not appear to gain favour.

It is stating the obvious to say that appropriate professional attire also serves to project a confident profile.

19.6.2.5   Witness management

One should never engage in arguments with witnesses; neither should one badger or ridicule them. The clever use of closed questions can control the most aggressive hostile witness. Having a flexible list of the logical sequence of the facts of the case can lead the advocate to his or her goal. Dexterity in the use of open questions may endear one's witness to the court, if one has deduced a capacity in that witness for brevity and the ability to be logical and succinct. The fatal attraction of becoming carried away with one's own exuberance can lead to asking one question too many. One must acquire the discipline to cease examination when the set goal has been achieved.

The prosecution gets to advocate its case first and the defence then cross-examines the state's witnesses. It is important for the defence advocate to remember to put the defence case to the witness for the other side during such cross-examination. Such evidence cannot be raised *de novo* in direct evidence by the defence, which may follow in rebuttal. It is not necessary for the accused person to present sworn evidence, because the burden of proof lies squarely with the prosecution. It may be strategically prudent to do so however, if there is available evidence to rebut the prosecution case. Some accused persons who have poor self-assessment skills should be advised not to give evidence. If they are truculent in insisting on presiding in the witness box, a full attendance of advice given and rejected should be recorded on file. It is always the province of an advocate to resign from a case in which the client insists on deciding trial strategy. The court is willing to discharge legal aid certificates in such circumstances.

19.6.2.6   Court etiquette

When the District Court clerk calls the case, the state and defence solicitors identify themselves to the judge. Usually, at District Court level, the expression 'I appear in this case, Judge, on behalf of the state/the Director' or 'I appear in this case, Judge, on behalf of the accused' will suffice. The prosecuting Garda member, rather than a prosecuting solicitor, may represent the state.

The prosecutor may briefly outline the case to the judge, although the defence advocate would prefer that this advantage does not fall to the prosecutor, who is the first to present his or her case. The prosecutor then calls his or her witnesses to give their evidence orally and under oath. The oath states as follows: 'I swear by Almighty God that my evidence to the court in this case shall be the truth, the whole truth and nothing but the truth.' Non-Christians who do not wish to swear an oath on the Bible can affirm that they will tell the truth. Any false evidence given on oath or on affirmation will result in charges of perjury.

19.6.2.7   Rules pertaining to the examination of witnesses

The examination of a witness can be divided into three categories as outlined earlier: examination-in-chief; cross-examination; and re-examination. The principles of the law of evidence outlined in **Chapter 10** are applied in the courtroom. In brief, it should be noted that hearsay evidence is not permitted, except as part of *res gestae* or if the evidence that the advocate seeks to admit was spoken in the presence of either party to the proceedings. No expressions of opinion will be tolerated, with the notable exception of evidence proffered by expert witnesses. Restrictions also apply to the admissibility and relevance of evidence, illegally obtained evidence, direct and circumstantial evidence, primary and secondary evidence, the shifting of the legal burden, formal admissions, competence and compellability, corroboration, identification evidence, evidence of character, similar fact evidence, DNA fingerprinting, confession evidence, public policy considerations, the application of the principles of the Judges' Rules, and the admissibility of documentary evidence, as outlined in that chapter.

19.7   Trial Advocacy Skills

19.7.1   THE CHARACTERISTICS OF EXAMINATION-IN-CHIEF

Examination-in-chief—sometimes referred to as 'direct examination'—by the party calling a witness must not include leading questions. A leading question is one that is effectively rhetorical in character. If the matter that is being elicited is not in dispute, however, opposing advocates can agree that a leading question may be permissible in the context of an examination-in-chief, e.g. the name, address, and occupation of the accused, or a statement that the accused was present at the scene of an assault when the defence is one of self-defence and therefore the accused is not contesting his or her own presence at the scene of the alleged crime. The witness should give the evidence; it is not for the advocate to proffer the evidence on the witness's behalf. Leading questions cannot be asked with regard to a matter in issue. Many practitioners have found it beneficial to prefix their questions in a direct examination context with words such as 'What ...?', 'Why ...?', 'When ...?', 'How ...?', 'Where ...?', and 'Who ...?'

It is important that all court advocates use simple, clear language and frame the questions asked in a chronologically logical fashion to ensure that the events applicable to the alleged crime unfold in the manner outlined in one's instructions. There is little disclosure of the evidence in advance of a summary trial and what disclosure does occur takes place through the '*Gary Doyle* procedure', as outlined previously. The judge is hearing this evidence for the first time and consequently a methodical, logical unfolding of the alleged events will greatly facilitate that judge's understanding of the case.

The position differs somewhat with regard to the trial on indictment, insofar as the facts of the case are disclosed to the judge through the medium of the book of evidence. At this level (with the exception of the Special Criminal Court), however, the decision of the discharge of the burden of proof on the facts as presented rests with the jury, who do not have any prior disclosure.

It is necessary to control one's witness during the examination-in-chief process. On occasion, it may prove useful to ask an open-ended question such as: 'What happened next?' If, however, the witness starts to wander, warbling irrelevancies, it may be necessary to bring the witness back to the issue at hand, e.g. by interjecting 'If I might stop you there for a moment' and then asking a closed question, by either referring to something previously stated by the witness or some fact already accepted by both sides of the case.

Evidence that has been satisfactorily established by a witness, in answer to a question in direct examination, should not be sought by repetition of the question as a matter of emphasis. It is unwise and unethical to coach a witness by preparing a list of questions for rehearsal before the commencement of the trial. The potential witness needs only a short, general summary of the matters on which one is likely to examine. The witness should be advised to maintain eye contact with the judge at summary trial, or judges in the Special Criminal Court, and with the jury in the Circuit and Central Criminal Courts.

19.7.2   THE CHARACTERISTICS OF CROSS-EXAMINATION

Leading questions are allowed, even advised, in the cross-examination process. One should not copper-fasten the opponent's case by giving his or her witness an opportunity to restate his or her version of the facts. A short cross-examination is much more effective than a long one. A comprehensive note of the evidence given in direct examination should be recorded, particularly any evidence that contradicts one's client's instructions.

It is imperative that one should not ask a question in cross-examination to which the answer is unknown, because exploratory questions are dangerous. It is necessary to be flexible in one's approach and be ready to change tactics—a process colloquially referred to as 'thinking on one's feet'.

It is generally unwise to accuse a witness of 'lying' or 'being economical with the truth' when a suggestion that the witness 'may be mistaken' will suffice without creating the same level of hostility. Experienced judges will be quick to notice inconsistencies and contradictions in the evidence. In a jury setting, the advocate will ensure, when summing up the evidence in the submission to the jury, to alert them to any such conflicts in the evidence proffered. Where a witness in cross-examination gives evidence that clearly contradicts evidence that one's client or the client's witness will give, one must, in cross-examination of that witness, put to that witness the evidence that such client or witness will give, to allow the testifying opposition witness the opportunity to rebut it.

One is bound by the answers given by a witness in cross-examination. It is important to know when to stop questioning the witness. If one gets an admission from a witness in cross-examination that benefits one's own client, it is not clever to press the advantage, because it may prompt an unhelpful elaboration or, indeed, a retraction.

19.7.3   THE CHARACTERISTICS OF RE-EXAMINATION

New evidence, which may have been elicited out of the cross-examination, may be re-examined for the purpose of clarification.

19.8   Objections

A solicitor acting for a party in court should object in the course of a trial to:

- any leading questions being put by the opposing advocate in the direct examination of a witness;

- any question that is irrelevant; and

- any attempt to adduce hearsay evidence.

One must state the grounds on which the objection is based. The objection should not be frivolous, and should be made clearly and distinctly. When making legal submissions at the conclusion of a trial, it is imperative that they are logically and coherently presented, and that one is cautious of not patronising the bench.

19.9   The Determination of Guilt or Innocence

When the prosecutor informs the court that there is no further evidence to be called on behalf of the state, at this point, the prosecution case is closed. At the conclusion of the prosecution's case, the defence may apply for a direction or an acquittal if the evidence adduced does not establish the facts alleged against the accused. If there is a material defect in the summons or charge sheet, and/or there has been a failure to adduce certain essential proofs, a similar application may be made. If appropriate, case law or other legal authority may be submitted to show that the prosecution has failed to discharge the burden imposed on it.

19.10   Pleas in Mitigation of Sentence

Once there has been a finding of 'guilty as charged', the defence advocate endeavours to minimise the impact of the punishment that the court is entitled to impose. **Chapter 14** addresses the issue of sentencing in detail. The persuasive powers of the advocate must be at their peak during this procedure. Particular attention should rest on professional conduct standards, which determine that the court must not be misled in one's zeal to minimise the punishment that is imminent.

One should check the facts of the case beforehand with the prosecution. Such facts should not be disputed if one's client is pleading 'guilty'. One can, of course, clarify any point and, in particular, elicit evidence from the prosecuting Garda that is advantageous to one's client. For example, in a theft case the facts of recovery of stolen goods, that the client has no previous convictions, was cooperative, and/or apologetic, that compensation has been proffered to the injured party, that the client has prospects of employment, and that the client supports his or her spouse/partner and young family, if applicable, can be mentioned in mitigation of a heavy sentence.

The defence lawyer decides whether or not it is appropriate to call the defendant to give sworn evidence on his or her own behalf where a 'guilty' plea has been entered. It is never appropriate to ask the judge if s/he would like to hear the client. One should never suggest, or propose, or even hint to the judge the order that s/he should make. Since 2014, in limited circumstances the prosecution may be asked to give the sentencing judge guidance, e.g. citing information from previous similar cases. During the sentencing process, the judge has a number of options open to include adjournment of the case for the purpose of ascertaining suitability for supervision of a probation officer, community service officer, or to determine whether a fine, compensation or incarceration are the appropriate options.

19.11   The Composition of the Courts

19.11.1   ESTABLISHMENT

The jurisdiction of the criminal courts derives from Art. 34.1 of the Constitution. The enabling legislation includes the Courts (Establishment and Constitutional) Act 1961, the Courts (Supplemental Provisions) Act 1961, the Offences Against the State Act 1939 (as amended), and the Defence Act 1954.

The latter two Acts refer respectively to the Special Criminal Court and courts martial. What are referred to as the ordinary courts with criminal jurisdiction include the District Court, the Circuit Court, the High Court, the Court of Appeal, and the Supreme Court.

19.11.2   THE COURTS SERVICE

The day-to-day central administration of all courts has been vested in the Courts Service—an independent body set up under the Courts Service Act 1998—more information about which can be found online at http://www.courts.ie. Its functions include the management of the courts, the provision, management, and maintenance of court buildings, the provision of support services to members of the judiciary, the dissemination of information on the courts system to the public, and the provision of facilities for those who use the courts.

19.11.3   THE DISTRICT COURT

The District Court system comprises the Dublin Metropolitan District and 23 District Court districts, which are presided over by the President of the District Court and 52 District Court judges. The Districts are divided into District Court Areas. The geographical jurisdiction of each area is limited to those before the court who are from its area and those who are accused of criminal matters arising within the court area.

19.11.3.1   The Jurisdiction of the District Court

The District Court is referred to as a 'court of summary jurisdiction'. It can deal with offences referred to as 'summary' or 'minor' offences. It can also deal with some 'hybrid offences', which are indictable offences of a minor nature, in relation to which the accused chooses to 'plead guilty as charged' with the consent of the DPP before the District Court.

The vast majority of criminal offences, both summary and indictable, commence procedurally in the District Court. In exceptional circumstances, the Special Criminal Court will be the accused's first port of call in the courts system.

The administration of the courts often permits specialisation, insofar as a particular court may deal exclusively with road traffic offences or where the District Court sits as the Children Court. A pilot 'Drug Court' project has been in existence since 2001.

The District Court can exercise a constitutional jurisdiction with regard to the exclusion of any illegally obtained evidence that confronts the constitutional rights of the accused. **Chapter 10** deals with instances that could give rise to the existence of such evidence. A District Court judge may refer a 'case stated' to the High Court should s/he need to seek clarification and direction with regard to the correct interpretation of the law as it arises in a case before the District Court. This type of procedure is discussed in **Chapter 16**. The exercise of the jurisdiction of district judges and circuit judges has been expanded by ss. 178 and 179 of the Criminal Justice Act 2006, in cases in which the exact location of offence is unknown or in which offence(s) occurred in a number of district areas or circuits. Section 180 of the same Act extends the judge's arrest and search warrant powers.

19.11.3.2 The Children Court

The Children Act 1908 was amended by the Children Act 2001. Those who appear before the District Court as juveniles are entitled to have their cases heard 'in camera' and to have their cases segregated from the usual District Court list for adults, if a separate building is not available. The juvenile justice system is dealt with in **Chapter 9**.

19.12   The Constitution Courts of Trial on Indictment and their Jurisdiction

When an accused is charged with an offence that is too serious a matter for disposal in the District Court, that accused is sent for trial to the higher courts—i.e. the Circuit Criminal Court, the Central Criminal Court or the Special Criminal Court. The Circuit Criminal Court and the Central Criminal Court are constituted to sit with a Circuit Court judge in the former venue and a High Court judge in the latter. A jury of 12 citizens sits in both venues. The Circuit Criminal Court deals with all indictable offences except murder, rape, and other offences scheduled in the Offences Against the State Act 1939, where the DPP has not intervened under s. 45(2) of that Act.

The Central Criminal Court has jurisdiction to deal with all indictable offences returnable to it, but specifically murder and rape, and some competition law offences. Theoretically, the Central Criminal Court may deal with any criminal allegation, even without any return, since it has full original jurisdiction under the Constitution.

The Special Criminal Court ('the Special') is a judge-only court, i.e. it sits without the assistance of a jury. Typically, there will be a sitting of three judges simultaneously: one District Court judge, one Circuit Court judge, and one High Court judge. The Special may deal with all offences, summary and indictable. There are specific areas of jurisdiction that are confined to the Special:

(a) scheduled offences (under the 1939 Act) that arrive before the Special:

    i. by valid return from District Court where the DPP has not intervened under s. 45(2) of the Act;

    ii. by reason of an accused having been charged before the Special bypassing the District Court and the DPP has so directed;

(b) non-scheduled offences (under s. 46 of the 1939 Act) that arrive before the Special:

    i. by virtue of an accused having been charged before the Special, on the DPP's direction coupled with a DPP's certificate that ordinary courts are inadequate to secure the effective administration of justice;

    ii. by transfer from ordinary courts by the DPP's direction and certificate;

    iii. by virtue of a valid return to the trial court, coupled with a certificate from the DPP that the ordinary courts are inadequate to secure the effective administration of justice.

19.13   The Functions of a Judge in the Indictable Courts

The judges in the Circuit Criminal Court and the Central Criminal Court have many functions, as follows:

(a) to preside over court and exercise his or her inherent jurisdiction to ensure that its process is not abused;

(b) to ensure a fair trial and the vindication of the rights of parties before it;

(c) to rule on procedure to be adopted in the court of trial;

(d) to rule on all questions of law, e.g. admissibility of evidence, publicity of trial;

(e) to rule on the adequacy of the prosecution case on receipt of an application from the defence for an acquittal on the basis that it has 'no case to answer' at the conclusion of the prosecution's evidence;

(f) to instruct the jury on the law that applies to the instant case;

(g) to review the evidence for the jury;

(h) to charge the jury;

(i) to instruct the jury on questions of fact for their consideration in deciding guilt or innocence;

(j) to instruct the jury on alternative verdicts or special verdicts;

(k) to consider evidence and/or submissions deemed relevant prior to sentence where there has been a finding of 'guilty' against the accused;

(l) to impose sentence.

19.14 The Jury

The function of a jury in the Circuit Criminal Court and the Central Criminal Court is to decide the issues of fact having being advised by the trial judge in relation to the legal burden of proof. Thereafter, they must, through their foreperson, announce their verdict of guilt or innocence to the trial court.

19.14.1 THE COMPOSITION OF THE JURY

A jury consists of 12 men and/or women selected at random from a jury panel. The jury may, in the course of the trial, fall to a minimum of 10 through excusal (e.g. sickness), or possibly through ineligibility or disqualification not discovered prior to commencement of the trial.

The jury are asked, in the first instance, to seek to arrive at a unanimous verdict. If a jury have not been able to reach such a unanimous verdict in such period as seems reasonable to the judge (and never less than two hours), a majority verdict of not less than 10:2 or 11:1 shall be accepted (Criminal Justice Act 1984, s. 25(1)).

A 'hung jury' is a jury that is unable to reach a verdict. In such circumstances, they are discharged and the accused is free to leave the court. There is the possibility that the state will charge the accused again and look for a retrial date.

19.14.2 JURY EMPANELMENT

Jury summonses are served on persons whose names appear on the electoral register for Dáil Éireann. They are delivered by post or served by hand. The entire panel is generally required to attend on the first day of a court sitting. In Dublin, the panel is subdivided and called on certain days (usually Mondays) in the course of the sittings as is thought appropriate.

If a summonsed jury panellist does not attend an empanelment, an offence has been committed, which is triable summarily. The registrar of the trial court calls out the names of those summonsed. As each potential juror answers, s/he is called towards the bench and asked:

• to affirm his/her identity;

• to outline any reason why s/he should not serve as a juror.

The judge will outline to the jurors circumstances that would deem them disqualified or ineligible and furthermore warn them with regard to the penalty applicable to participating as jurors in such circumstances. It is possible to object to a juror by reason of his/her disqualification or ineligibility.

19.14.2.1 Challenges under the Juries Act 1976

A list of the panel of available jurors is available for inspection by the defence and prosecution lawyers. This list outlines the names, addresses, and occupations of the potential jurors. The prosecution, defence, or the accused may challenge or object on seven occasions in the course of an empanelment 'without showing cause' (giving a reason). It is provided that any further challenge must be for cause shown, i.e. that 'cause must be demonstrated upon objection being made'. There is no right to question a potential juror in advance of showing challenge for cause, but having challenged for cause, questioning is permitted to demonstrate the cause. As the jury panel provided to advocates discloses little information apart from the name, address, and occupation of potential jurors, it is not usually possible to base an objection on it, unless the accused knows the person to whom s/he wishes to object or knows of some reason that might manifest as prejudice towards the accused. Objections without cause are usually on the basis of subjective assessment based on the visual inspection of jurors, their demeanour, and, occasionally, their occupations.

19.14.2.2 Eligibility to become juror

Eligibility for citizens to engage in jury service has been widened considerably since the original qualification of being a property owner was dispensed with (*De Búrca v AG* [1976] IR 38). Each county constitutes a jury district and juries are summonsed to sittings of the court within the jury district (Juries Act 1976, s. 5(4)). Otherwise, every citizen aged 18–70 years and whose name appears on the Dáil electoral register is eligible. Persons involved in the administration of justice—i.e. solicitors, barristers, court personnel, Gardaí, prison officers, defence forces, or the President of Ireland—are not eligible for jury service.

19.14.2.3 Circumstances that disqualify a potential juror

The following categories of person are disqualified from jury service:

- persons convicted of an offence in any part of Ireland and sentenced to five years' imprisonment/detention are disqualified for life;
- persons convicted of an offence in any part of Ireland and sentenced to three months' imprisonment or detention are disqualified for 10 years.

19.14.2.4 Circumstances that excuse a potential juror

The following categories of person are excused from service as of right, if exercised:

- members of the Oireachtas;
- religious ministers;
- doctors/nurses;
- chemists;
- persons who have served on a jury in the three years preceding;
- those excused for life by a court.

The following reasons may excuse a potential juror from service at the discretion of the registrar or court of trial:

- illness;
- any other reason that is acceptable.

CHAPTER 20

MANAGING A CRIMINAL LITIGATION PRACTICE

20.1 Introduction

As discussed in **Chapter 2**, criminal litigation has evolved from the traditionally presented 'ordinary crime on the streets' model to include a wide expanse of increasing and extensive application of sanctions for breach of what are referred to as regulatory or corporate or white collar crime. Increasingly, many legal practices that were hitherto focused on business and commercial work need to enter criminal practice to meet the needs of their private clients, in areas such as competition law, environmental protection, health and safety law, and consumer and corporate affairs, as society and our legislators at international, EU, and domestic level move towards using criminalisation as the last-resort strategy when compliance through negotiation and monitoring has failed.

Criminal practice structures vary. Of its nature criminal practice is divided into prosecution and defence practitioners. As demonstrated throughout this text, the main organ of prosecution is the Office of the Director of Public Prosecutions (DPP) which has a very comprehensive managerial structure which will not be the focus of this chapter. Large commercial legal firms who increasingly open White Collar Crime Departments similarly have invested heavily in robust practice management structures. There are 32 Local State Solicitors whose legal firms provide a solicitor service to the DPP and there is a large number of firms and sole practitioners that exclusively focus on criminal defence practice. It is this later cohort of defence solicitors that will be the predominant focus of this chapter. Many criminal defence clients, particularly those requiring advice or representation for regulatory crime matters, are privately funded. However, a large proportion of those who need professional services from criminal defence solicitors rely on the provisions of the free criminal legal aid schemes financed by the state, as profiled at **Chapter 8** and **Chapter 16**.

To a greater extent than perhaps any other area of legal practice, criminal litigation requires a commitment of time and emotional resources that borders on a vocation.

If a solicitor is to undertake criminal defence work seriously, then s/he must be prepared to be available for urgent calls at most hours of most days, often from panicky or distressed clients or their relatives, and often in circumstances of great pressure, for financial rewards that are, by the standards of the legal profession, relatively modest. Those legal practices in our larger cities that are substantial and successful have been developed and built over many years, by dint of long hours and hard work.

This is not to say that there are no attractions: virtually no two cases are alike, there is constant human contact, and the work is never dull or boring. The memoirs of a successful criminal solicitor would make endlessly fascinating reading. There are even times when it is possible to affect a client's entire life for the better. Substantial personal and professional satisfaction can accrue from an acquittal, or from using one's solicitor advocacy skills to persuade a court not to give a heavy sentence of imprisonment or detention to one's client who has either been convicted after a trial or pleaded 'guilty' and to instead apply a community sentence or other sanction as outlined in **Chapter 14**.

Equally, because the work undertaken will impact on the reputation and, frequently, liberty of citizens, it is of the utmost importance that an appropriate level of skill and commitment is devoted to it. It is, more than most fields of employment, an area in which one should not dabble. Balancing the demands of the clients, the prosecution, and the courts together with the daily demands of practice management requires constant vigilance and concentration. Ultimately, the greatest asset of a solicitor is one's professional reputation, and one needs to be aware of the practical and ethical pitfalls that can undermine it. That reputation must be without blemish so far as concerns judges, colleagues, the Gardaí, and clients.

It is ironic that criminal work, which was seen by many who are ill-informed as 'seedy' and untouchable over generations, should have acquired a superficial glamour and attractiveness in the last few years, mainly as a result of numerous novels and television series devoted to the subject, but the reality of the work is not well reflected through the mirror of fiction. For every high-profile case, there are a hundred mundane, but nonetheless important ones. Even those few major cases often carry enormous, very public, pressures. In all cases, the rights of the victims of crime are a paramount concern for society as outlined in **Chapter 3**. The constitutional and Convention rights of the accused person are similarly of paramount concern and for the most part, criminal work is conducted in challenging surroundings, often during anti-social hours during Garda station and prison representation and consultations.

It follows that embarking on a career in criminal litigation is not to be undertaken lightly. Those planning on setting up in practice should have a good working knowledge of the law of evidence, criminal law and procedure, some experience in advocacy skills, and a readiness to take on any case, no matter how unpleasant or apparently trivial, with a view to advocating rights whilst also establishing a client base. The reputations of the best solicitors tend to spread by word of mouth, and that takes time. Unfortunately, it seems accepted that one bad recommendation can undo many good ones and each solicitor advocate is only as good as his or her last case.

It is recommended that new entrants to criminal practice should undertake as many courses as possible in the relevant fields and, of course, commit themselves to a programme of continuing legal education. Developments in criminal law and procedure are relentlessly voluminous and will continue to be so as criminal justice policy at government level evolves.

The most important attributes to be brought to criminal defence practice are the willingness to act fearlessly and independently on behalf of all clients, in facilitating the proper administration of justice, and to respect without exception their dignity and human rights.

20.2   Ethics

Ethics has been dealt with more fully in **Chapter 1**. Reference to the ethics in this chapter is solely for the purpose of underlining the need to be constantly alert. No field of legal work is as likely to present ethical difficulties or conflicts of interest as criminal practice does and nowhere are so many 'grey areas' present. All practising solicitors need to exercise constant care to maintain the highest ethical standards and all need to be fully familiar with the Law Society of Ireland's *Guide to Good Professional Conduct*. There are also helpful codes of conduct developed and published by the International Bar Association and the Association of Criminal Lawyers and the 2014 Law Society review of Regulation 13 on ethics in advertising, to prevent unethical and unseemly touting by solicitors for clients. Solicitors must not shirk difficult ethical decisions. If such a decision means losing a client or a substantial, possibly lucrative, case, then so be it. The alternative is to gain a reputation for sharp practice and ultimately risk the loss of future clientele and thereby one's livelihood.

When ethical difficulties of any kind arise, they must be addressed at once. There is no obstacle to seeking independent advice outside the firm, if there are no colleagues of sufficient seniority within the firm. Senior peers, members of the appropriate Law Society committees, and even counsel will all be capable of offering relevant advice. An approach can be formal or informal, as the situation requires. When in doubt, one should always err on the side of caution.

20.3   Diary Management

Absolutely rigid diary maintenance is the only acceptable standard for the good management of one's legal practice. Technological developments have greatly enhanced access by all within legal practices to centrally stored information. As with every such system, engagement with central data input is only as good as the manifestation of the training and processes that the firm's management has put in place for all to apply. Missing a case in court is evidence of complete disregard for the welfare of one's client, is visible to all, discourteous to the judge, potentially negligent, appears unprofessional, and is generally bad for business. All members of staff of a solicitor's office should be inculcated with the idea that an appointment date or court date should go into a central diary and, as appropriate, each individual solicitor's diary as soon as that date becomes known to them.

The office diary commitments should be reviewed regularly to compare available resources with potential work commitments. Where necessary, counsel should be instructed, preferably in good time, and arrangements made to have a member of staff 'attend' counsel. It is strategically wise practice to avoid overextending the firm, by avoiding taking on work outside the usual geographical catchment area. Such cases invariably take on a life of their own and become a huge drain on the office's resources.

A regular review of the firm's diary commitments should operate in tandem with a watchful eye on one's duty to engage in having resources available for consultations with clients who are in custody in a Garda station or for prison visits. Clients who are in prison may wish to discuss an appeal, may be serving a sentence on one matter whilst another is proceeding, or be in custody without having the desired bail terms in place. Again, a full record must always be centrally available to all members of staff with regard to clients who are in custody. Failure to visit clients in custody, which is often the most time-consuming activity in a criminal practice, demonstrates a lack of client care and will rightly result in the disintegration of that practice. The reverse also holds true as there are some firms that have an exceptional reputation for advising prisoners and this tends to lead to a demand for their services.

20.4 Record Keeping and File Management

When it comes to record keeping and file management, although it may sound morbid, the ideal to which to work is to assume that you will die suddenly and a colleague will have to take over your entire workload with no knowledge of the cases except what is contained in your files, and recorded centrally on in the practice IT systems. In that scenario, the incoming solicitor will have the benefit of a note or copy of every attendance, meeting, consultation, letter, or telephone call undertaken in the matter. This desired best practice is a useful aspiration for a number of reasons, not least because it makes one's work as efficient as possible. In particular, in a practice with more than one fee-earner, it makes work practices considerably more flexible, transferable, and transparent in its processes.

By way of a cautionary note, an increasing number of solicitors have found themselves giving evidence in court over the last few years, in a variety of circumstances. As a consequence, having robust dated, timed attendances and notes of telephone calls are becoming increasingly important from a corroborative evidence perspective.

Many criminal cases are of relatively short duration and generate little paperwork. There is accordingly no excuse for sloppy file management. The District Court, as a court of first instance, is the venue where most criminal cases are processed. Of their nature, as explained throughout this text, such cases are usually of short duration and are minor and summary in nature, but they engage with the same high standard of evidential proofs as apply across the board in criminal litigation practice. Once closed, files should be kept securely for (it is suggested) seven years. It is probably acceptable to retain electronic versions of closed files and to shred the originals, with the concomitant savings of space and expense. Different considerations may prevail in major cases.

It may be worth considering an application for approval under a business management quality system. Certainly, the very high standard of professional practice and procedures required for, say, a 'Q' mark will give some idea of the target to be aimed for by way of delivery of an excellent service. Annually all solicitors are required to complete a defined number of continuing professional development (CPD) training courses in practice management, providing opportunities to augment one's management processes.

20.5   Office Personnel

Although major cities in Ireland now all have a number of small criminal practices operating, with uncomplicated management structures, desired best practice is obviously to aim for the operation of a proper and fully serviced office. The staffing level required will clearly depend on the workload. As the practice develops, extra staff will be recruited, justifying the creation of roles for a managing partner, a financial manager, an office manager, a franchise manager, etc. In the early years of a firm, however, an able, computer-literate legal assistant can perform a number of functions, including those of secretary and receptionist, and can attend court and consultations with counsel and do some legal research, etc. Sensible use of resources requires advance planning. Ideally, as a firm grows, the fee-earners can concentrate on the legal issues and backup and administrative staff can deal with all other business management tasks.

It must always be remembered, however, that no matter how able one's staff, the final responsibility for any case rests with the principal or partners of any legal firm. Accordingly, suitable levels of supervision must be maintained at all times. From the point of view of the client, the ideal engagement with the legal practice is to have a single contact person who will always be aware of the up-to-date situation in his or her case. In this context, it is imperative that each and every member of staff is imbued with the need for absolute client confidentiality. All clients of all solicitors are entitled to expect that their affairs will be dealt with in complete privacy and the clients of criminal practitioners are no exception to this general ethical standard. It is particularly important that staff joining or leaving one's legal firm are reminded of the confidentiality requirement. Again, a failure to adhere to this standard will ultimately be the responsibility of the principal or partners of the firm.

A particular problem for smaller firms is ensuring suitable staffing to cover for annual leave and major holidays. Larger firms can obviously deal more comfortably with staff absences. For small firms, including sole practitioners, holidays can mean no effective emergency cover of services for a period. Some sort of contingency arrangement should be made to advise potential clients of the position and referring them to a reputable local firm. The unpalatable alternative may be unhappy clients who have been arrested and unable to contact their trusted adviser in circumstances where they do not know why s/he was not available, and who have therefore decided to take their business elsewhere as a consequence.

20.6   Garda Stations

There is nothing more likely to throw a carefully planned day into chaos than the frequent scenario of the sudden arrest and detention of a person for questioning at the Garda station requiring the solicitor's attendance. The duties of solicitors to their clients in such circumstances are discussed at length at **Chapter 5**. Furthermore, there is often a high degree of stress attaching to attending by the solicitor and advising at the station.

A telephone call received from, or on behalf of, a detained client should be dealt with urgently. If it cannot be attended to rapidly and competently, a decision should be made as to whether the client should be referred to a colleague who will provide the necessary legal service.

All practising criminal defence solicitors should familiarise themselves with the powers of detention of the Gardaí and the investigative entitlements as outlined in this text. Although some emergency situations can be dealt with by telephone, the most desirable course is to visit the client in custody. The decision in *Gormley and White* discussed in detail at **Chapter 5** now requires more extensive services from a solicitor at the station. If the client wants a visit for advice and that cannot be undertaken promptly, both client and Gardaí should be so advised, so that the client can choose another solicitor if necessary. Under no circumstances should the client or Gardaí be advised of a time for a visit that is not, in the context of existing commitments, likely to be met.

Expertise as to the procedures at Garda stations is crucial to the criminal litigation practice. Solicitors should attend courses, read articles, statutes, and judgments, and otherwise develop their skills and knowledge in this area. Many cases are won or lost at this criminal investigation stage and experience is the only teacher. It is ironic that one's best work, if it prevents one's client being charged, will cost one the fees for a case, but such an outcome can only enhance one's reputation.

Recent developments in the wake of *Gormley and White*, as outlined in **Chapter 4**, must now be incorporated within the ethics and time management of all solicitors who undertake criminal defence work.

20.7   Relationships with the Client

As indicated earlier, clients should be treated with absolute respect, regardless of the allegations against them or the difficulties that they may pose for the solicitor. All office personnel should treat clients politely and courteously. It is axiomatic that staff will follow the example of the solicitor. Telephone calls should be returned promptly and correspondence answered without delay. Client care policies demand that no reputable practice should countenance the denigration of client behaviour or alleged behaviour because this will only lessen the respect with which they should be treated by those working in that practice.

Many clients will be reasonably familiar with the criminal justice system, but for those who are not, special consideration is required. In many ways, the most important cases will be those accused who are new to the system. All clients should be made aware of the respective roles of the solicitor and client, and the limitations on the function of the solicitor. Some clients, particularly those new to the system, assume that the solicitor will make all key decisions for them. This misapprehension must be cleared up from the start.

A course in interviewing skills is recommended. In terms of cost-effectiveness in the business of running a practice, for every veteran whose demands on one's time are modest, there will be a client who will need careful, and sometimes repeated, advice.

The manner in which a solicitor deals with a client is a personal matter. It seems obvious that the better the client and solicitor communicate, the more they are likely to understand one another. The reality is probably subtler. The solicitor must be careful to maintain a distance from the client, because a perception that one is too close to the client will dilute necessary objectivity in giving advice and may threaten one's reputation. So a careful balance is required, enabling a good solicitor/client relationship to flourish, without impinging on one's perceived independence. Experience is the key.

At a minimum, the client must always understand the advice that is being given. Without that, s/he is unable to make any informed choices. Lawyers have long been criticised for using pompous and verbose language. Criminal clients allegedly involved in 'ordinary crime' are statistically likely to be poorly educated. It is entirely the responsibility of the solicitor to ensure that there is appropriate communication, in good time, to enable the client to make appropriate decisions. The client should be kept informed, in straightforward language, of all material developments in the case.

Solicitors should not shrink from spelling out certain hard realities to clients. Clients may not appreciate bad news when they first hear it, but it is better that they should understand the position they are in before they go to court than, for example, to receive a sentence of imprisonment or detention when they are not expecting it. Again, experience will gradually enhance both the quality of the advice and the manner of its delivery.

20.8   The Use of, and Relationships with, Counsel

Judicious use of counsel is an invaluable aid to a criminal practice. Counsel will be asked to assist in various sets of circumstances, but some ground rules remain constant. Firstly, the solicitor will always be responsible for the fees of the counsel who is instructed in a case. It follows that the firm should secure the payment of adequate fees for the case, or be in receipt of free legal Aaid payments. Secondly, counsel should be appropriately and fully instructed. The job, whatever it is, cannot be properly done unless counsel is apprised of all of the facts. Thirdly, instructing counsel at the last minute should be avoided. This is sometimes unavoidable, such as when there is a late handover of the case file from another barrister, but in general, astute practice management should enable papers to go to counsel well in advance.

Most, if not all, of the advocacy in the higher courts will be done by counsel. It is essential that a responsible member of staff of the firm attend that barrister both for last-minute consultations and so that a good record of the proceedings is taken. The solicitor must also ensure the attendance of any witnesses whom it is proposed to call and must deal with any other preparation as advised by counsel.

Counsel can also be briefed for the District Court, but solicitors who defend regularly in that arena would expect to be well capable of dealing with most matters in the lower court. Very occasionally, a client will have business of such a nature as to justify retaining counsel for a District Court matter, usually when privately retained. This retention may occur in a drink driving prosecution, for example, in relation to which the technical proofs are constantly becoming more refined and complex. Again, for the same reasons as above, it is vital to attend counsel. Occasionally, workloads demand the use of counsel for routine District Court work, because solicitors are unable to appear. Ideally, counsel should also be attended by a member of the firm's staff on these occasions.

Finally, solicitors may ask counsel to advise in consultation at an early stage of proceedings or if an unusual problem has arisen. It is worth developing good relationships with a number of junior and senior counsel, so that informal discussions can establish whether there is a ready solution to the problem, perhaps obviating the need for formal instructions.

20.9   Fees/Legal Aid

Most criminal defence work that is not white collar in nature is dealt with by way of legal aid and hence standard fees. That, in turn, presents a temptation to cut corners and to try to maximise profits—a temptation that must be resisted. In the worst-case scenario, the Law Society of Ireland or the Irish courts—or even a hostile team of lawyers in the event of an action for professional negligence—may, at some point, seek to scrutinise your file. It must not be forgotten that a failure to maintain a reasonable standard of work amounts to professional misconduct, for which solicitors can be sued or disciplined.

In the event that one is privately retained, a proper basis for fees should be agreed with the client, committed to writing in accordance with the statutory requirements, and retained on file. If an hourly rate is agreed, then proper time recording is essential, both to enable a full and proper account to be rendered to the client and to set out your record in the event of dispute.

Always remember that when counsel is retained in the District Court, whether in a legal aid case or if the firm is privately retained, the obligation for the payment of fees rests directly with the solicitor. By contrast, with trials on indictment in which, once legal aid is granted, counsel's fees are paid directly by the Department of Justice, there is no such system for payment of counsel through the legal aid system in the District Court. There is therefore a private retainer in existence as between the solicitor and counsel.

20.10   The Use of Information Technology (IT)

There is no doubt now that firms of solicitors that have not yet grasped the nettle of IT are living in the Stone Age. IT packages, from the simplest to the most complex, are readily, easily, and relatively inexpensively available. The efficiency savings generated by a good and suitable IT package are very considerable. These range from case management systems, standard letters, and time recording (not usually necessary in criminal litigation practices, but occasionally helpful), to digital dictation and research facilities by way of access to online resources from the desktop. As many members of the Bar are discovering, digital dictation enables a completely remote and inexpensive relationship with a secretarial service, as part of which all of the overheads are the responsibility of the secretary and the only expense to the user of the service is that of the work actually done.

An inevitable trend is the 'outsourcing' of secretarial services altogether. It is now relatively unusual for a trainee solicitor not to have quite advanced IT skills and, as a consequence, future generations of criminal litigation firms are likely to see significant changes in the solicitor/secretary ratio.

Even the most Luddite solicitor should, at this stage, be able to, at a minimum, work via email and be capable of basic online research. There are many free legal research sites and, for example, all statutes, statutory instruments, and reported cases are now available free online. It follows that the speed and ease of research has facilitated greatly the quality of advice giving to clients, and solicitors owe it both to themselves and to their clients to be able to make use of contemporary developments in IT.

20.11 Interpreters in Criminal Proceedings

20.11.1 THE LAW

Article 6 of the European Convention on Human Rights and Fundamental Freedom stipulates that everyone charged with a criminal offence has minimum rights 'to be informed promptly, in a language that he understands and in detail, of the nature and cause of the accusation against him' and 'to have the free assistance of an interpreter if he cannot understand or speak the language used in court'.

The legal position that has prevailed in Ireland is that common law discretion of the presiding judge must be relied upon by the accused.

Directive 2010/64/EU of the European Parliament and of the Council of 20 October 2010 on the right to interpretation and translation in criminal proceedings was adopted. It includes the right to interpretation assistance for people with hearing or speech impediments. This Directive aims to implement common minimum standards on the right to interpretation and translation in criminal cases in the EU, which will also apply to the execution of a European arrest warrant (discussed at **Chapter 18**), and are set out in a proposed EU directive to improve the rights of suspects or accused persons who do not speak or understand the language of the proceedings. The new rights are intended to apply from the time the person is made aware that s/he is suspected or accused of having committed a criminal offence until the conclusion of the proceedings, including sentencing and the resolution of any appeal.

Best practice in the provision of interpretation and translation services are that the accused has access to his native language or any other language that is understood and that allows the exercise of full rights to defend the proceedings. All essential documents, including decisions depriving a person of his liberty, the charge/indictment, and any judgment, should also be translated. Technology such as video-conferencing or communication by telephone or internet could be employed, unless the physical presence of the interpreter is required in order to safeguard the fairness of the proceedings.

The accused would have the right to challenge a decision by the court that there is no need for interpretation and, where interpretation or translation has been provided, the accused has the right to complain that the quality is not sufficient to ensure the fairness of the proceedings.

Accordingly, member states 'shall endeavour to establish a register or registers of independent translators and interpreters' who are appropriately qualified. Once established, it is required that such a register or registers should be made available to legal counsel and relevant authorities. The Directive also sets out provisions on the quality of interpretation and translation and on training of judges, prosecutors and judicial staff.

The Directive is regarded as the first concrete measure of the 'Roadmap' for strengthening procedural rights of suspected and accused persons in criminal proceedings, which was adopted by the Council in November 2009. The Council unanimously agreed on this wider package of legislative and non-legislative initiatives in October 2009 ((14552/1/09) at 1 OJ C 295, 4 December 2009, p. 1. 14414/10 3). The roadmap identifies six main areas on which legislative or other initiatives are desirable:

- translation and interpretation;

- information on rights and information about charges;

- legal advice and legal aid;

- communication with relatives, employers, and consular authorities;

- special safeguards for suspected or accused persons who are vulnerable; and

- a green paper on pre-trial detention.

20.11.2   THE SOLICITOR'S ROLE WITH THE INTERPRETER

The Irish Translators' and Interpreters' Association/Cumann Aistritheoirí agus Teangairí na hÉireann (ITIA) is the only professional association in Ireland representing the interests of practising translators and interpreters (see http://www.translatorsassociation.ie/). It has a Code of Ethics that references best practice in communicating with all actors in the criminal justice process. They indicate that the interpreter should not act as a cultural expert and to preserve the register and style of the original utterances.

As the solicitor for the client who is in need of interpreter services, it is incumbent to ensure that the foreign national's rights are preserved and to keep in mind the following:

- The initial decision as to whether or not a client needs the services of an interpreter. One would not wish to either prejudice the client or find oneself as negligent in one's client care and professional obligations.

- Care and time must be allocated during case preparation to become familiar with how any cultural difference may prove problematic for the interpreter or the court and its personnel.

- Ensure that the role of the interpreter is clearly explained to the client.

- In jury cases, the judge should be requested to explain the interpreter's role to the jury, including that cultural differences in style of speech and difficulties with literal translation and dialect may impede communication, and must not be interpreted by the jury as indicative of a person who is not cooperating with the process e.g. where there is hesitation in speech.

- If briefing the interpreter in advance regarding the facts of the case, great care must be taken not to breach any professional ethics that prohibit the coaching of a trial participant.

- The client should be addressed directly and not through the interpreter.

- The use of dictionaries, where required should be clarified with the court prior to the advocate's commencement of representation.

20.12   Clients who Wish to have Cases Processed through the Irish Language 'An Ghaeilge'

Article 8 of the Constitution provides that the Irish language, as the national language, is the first official language of the state and recognises English as the second official language. Where a divergence occurs between both texts of the Constitution, the text in the Irish language will prevail. Consequently, where an accused person indicates a desire to have the case heard through the Irish language, there is a constitutional imperative on the criminal justice system to facilitate that right. A flavour of the case law in this aspect of practice is available on the Courts Service website http://www.courts.ie once one enters the site through its Gaeilge version.

A growing number of criminal lawyers are acquiring an expertise in legal practice Irish and there is a Register of such practitioners maintained by the Law Society of Ireland and the Honorable Society of Kings Inns.

20.13   Compliance

Without wishing to exaggerate, there is a real risk that busy lawyers, managing a busy practice, can find themselves caught out by the many compliance issues thrust upon them by regulatory provisions of all kinds.

Revenue issues are perhaps the most obvious. Any firm, no matter of what size, should retain a competent accountant and act strictly upon his or her direction in relation to declarations and due payments of VAT, other taxes, and social welfare payments deducted from the wages of employees. The prospect of a Revenue Commissioners audit is always a slightly disquieting prospect, but a well-organised and managed firm has nothing whatsoever to fear. Occasionally, the Law Society will conduct its own audit of files, to ensure compliance with the Solicitors' Accounts Regulations 2014 (SI No. 516 of 2014). If there is any comfort in a visit from either Revenue Commissioners or the Law Society, it is that, in most cases, some notice is given of a forthcoming visit. (Needless to say, in cases in which serious wrongdoing is suspected, the firm is likely to be visited without notice.)

In relation to financial matters, solicitors should also familiarise themselves with the anti-money laundering provisions and guidance available from the Law Society of Ireland website and other international websites. Many firms of solicitors have, over the years, received visits from the Criminal Assets Bureau (CAB), but in only a tiny minority of cases is it suspected that the solicitors themselves are responsible for any wrongdoing and, almost invariably, a client has misled a solicitor in respect of financial transactions. Notwithstanding that fact, any solicitor who does receive a visit from CAB should seek advice either formally or informally from another, appropriately expert, solicitor.

Issues relating to health and safety are also the responsibility of the firm. All employers owe both statutory and common law obligations to employees to provide both a safe workplace and safe systems of work, and employers should ensure that appropriate steps are taken to safeguard the working environment and also to ensure that appropriate insurance is in place in the event of accidents. It must be noted that the obligations here are two-fold: firstly, directly to the employees; secondly, obligations owed to the state on foot of statute.

In relation to CPD, every solicitor is responsible for his or her own CPD. Needless to say, any failures to maintain CPD hours at the required levels can, ultimately, result in the loss of a practising certificate. Neither a principal in a firm nor an assistant can afford to be without a current practising certificate and while, as aforementioned, the obligation is upon the individual solicitor to maintain his or her CPD, the damage to the firm by the loss of a practising certificate will impact on the entire practice.

INDEX